Logical Form and Language

LOGICAL FORM
AND
LANGUAGE

Edited by

Gerhard Preyer
and
Georg Peter

CLARENDON PRESS · OXFORD

OXFORD

UNIVERSITY PRESS

Great Clarendon Street, Oxford OX2 6DP

Oxford University Press is a department of the University of Oxford.
It furthers the University's objective of excellence in research, scholarship,
and education by publishing worldwide in

Oxford New York

Auckland Bangkok Buenos Aires Cape Town Chennai
Dar es Salaam Delhi Hong Kong Istanbul Karachi Kolkata
Kuala Lumpur Madrid Melbourne Mexico City Mumbai Nairobi
São Paulo Shanghai Singapore Taipei Tokyo Toronto
with an associated company in Berlin

Oxford is a registered trade mark of Oxford University Press
in the UK and in certain other countries

Published in the United States
By Oxford University Press Inc., New York

British Library Cataloguing in Publication Data

Data available

Library of Congress Cataloging in Publication Data

Data available
Logical form and language/edited by Gerhard Preyer and Georg Peter.
    p. cm.
    Includes bibliographical references and index.
    1. Language and logic. 2. Form (Logic) I. Preyer, Gerhard. II. Peter, Georg.
    P39 .L5965 2002   146'.42–dc21   2001039752
ISBN 0–19–924460–X
ISBN 0–19–924555–X (Pbk.)
1 3 5 7 9 10 8 6 4 2

Typeset in 11/13.5 pt AGaramond
by Kolam Information Services Pvt. Ltd, Pondicherry, India
Printed in Great Britain by
T. J. International Ltd
Padstow, Cornwall

To Donald Davidson

Contents

Part I *The Nature of Logical Form*

Part II *Intensionality, Events, and Semantic Content*

Part III *Logical Form, Belief Ascription, and Proper Names*

Contributors

Professor Lenny Clapp, Department of Philosophy, Carleton University, Ottawa, Canada.

Professor Reinaldo Elugardo, Department of Philosophy, University of Oklahoma, USA.

Professor R. F. Fiengo, Linguistics, University of California-Irvine, USA.

Professor James Higginbotham, Linguistics, University of Southern California, USA.

Professor Norbert Hornstein, Linguistics, University of Maryland, College Park, Md., USA.

Professor Jeffrey King, Department of philosophy, University of California, Davis, Calif., USA.

Professor Richard Larson, Linguistics, State University of New York at Stony Brook, USA.

Professor Ernie Lepore, Rutgers University, Center for Cognitive Studies, Psychology (Annex), Busch Campus, New Brunswick, NJ, USA.

Professor Bernard Linsky, Department of Philosophy, University of Alberta, Edmonton, Canada.

Professor Peter Ludlow, Department of Philosophy, State University of New York at Stony Brook, USA.

Professor Kirk Ludwig, Department of Philosophy, University of Florida, Gainesville, USA.

Professor Robert Matthews, Department of Philosophy, Rutgers University, New Brunswick, NJ, USA.

Professor Robert May, Linguistics, University of California-Irvine, USA.

Professor Stephen Neale, Department of Philosophy, University of California, Berkeley, Calif., USA.

DR GEORG PETER, J. W. Goethe-Universität, *Protosociology: An International Journal of Interdiscplinary Research*, 60054 Frankfurt am Main, Germany.

PROFESSOR PAUL M. PIETROSKI, Department of Philosophy, Skinner Building, College Park, Md., USA.

DR HABIL. GERHARD PREYER, Privatdozent, J. W. Goethe-Universität, *Protosociology: An International Journal of Interdiscplinary Research*, 60054 Frankfurt am Main, Germany.

PROFESSOR MARGA REIMER, Department of Philosophy, University of Arizona, Tucson, Ariz., USA.

PROFESSOR BARRY SCHEIN, Linguistics, MC-16, University of Southern California, Los Angeles, USA.

PROFESSOR ROBERT STAINTON, Department of Philosophy, Carleton University, Ottawa, Canada.

PROFESSOR JASON STANLEY, Department of Philosophy, University of Michigan, Ann Arbor, MJ, USA.

I

Introduction: On Contemporary Philosophy of Language

GERHARD PREYER AND GEORG PETER

I propose to consider whether anything, and if so, what can be inferred from the structure of language as to the structure of world.

(Bernard Russell)

Logical form has been a central concern of the analytic tradition in philosophy from Frege and Russell to the present. The logical form of a sentence is thought to reveal both the structure of the thoughts we are expressing, and the structure of the world we think about if our thoughts are true. Thus, investigation into logical forms has played a central methodological role in investigations into the nature of the mind and into the nature of reality. However, the concept of logical form has not received as much attention as might have been expected from the central role it has played in philosophy in the analytic tradition. This book aims to help redress this by bringing together essays on logical form written from a variety of different theoretical perspectives in linguistics and philosophy. The book is divided into three thematically unified parts. The first part is concerned with issues to do with the nature of logical form. The second part is concerned with issues to do with logical form, intensionality, events, and semantic content. The third part is concerned with issues to do with logical form, belief ascription, and proper names. These parts are all in one way or another concerned with logical form. A brief synopsis of the essays in each part follows.

Part I brings together essays by Stephen Neale, Ernie Lepore and Kirk Ludwig, Paul M. Pietroski, Jeffrey King, Peter Ludlow, Robert May, and R. F. Fiengo.

In his essay, Stephen Neale elaborates a proposal of a semantic theory such as for English in a particular way. In the first step he reconstructs and prepares a formal instrument—formalism and notations—given in Whitehead's and Russell's *Principia*, assuming a more 'rudimentary' Tarskian truth definition for L. From this account it is no dramatic step from the Theory of Description in the *Principia* to a systematic theory of quantification in natural languages. Neale shows in a second step that the use of a formal language which contains advices of restricted quantifications for the analysis of descriptions is not in any conflict with the general assumption that descriptions are incomplete symbols. Therefore Neale argues we can capture Russell's result of analysis 'descriptions are not singular terms' and 'sentences containing definite descriptions have quantificational truth conditions' and it is not conclusive to eliminate descriptions or define such expressions in a contextual way. The so-called gap between surface syntax and logical form has—following this theory—nothing to do with descriptions itself. Implementing restricted quantifiers shows that the syntactical and semantical similarities of expression such as "every", "some", "a", "the", etc. are obvious in the scope of a description of formal notation. Yet Neale discusses also some common interpretative errors of understanding Russell's theory, in particular the criticism that the logical form analysis cannot give us an adequate contribution to the semantics of natural languages. In their essay, Ernie Lepore and Kirk Ludwig argue that one conception of logical form that has played a central role in the analytic tradition that stretches back to Russell is best understood a conception of semantic form as it is revealed in an interpretive truth theory for a language. The logical form of a sentence on this conception is determined by the semantic types of its primitive elements and their mode of combination as it relates to determining the conditions under which the sentence is true. The logical form of a sentence is revealed by its "canonical proof" in an interpretive truth theory for a language and two sentences in the same or a different language are said to be the same in logical form just in case there are interpretive truth theories for the languages of the sentences in which there are proofs of T-sentences for them which have the same structure. On this approach, logical forms are not reified, and the notion of sameness of logical form is treated as conceptually basic. Lepore and Ludwig discuss also the relation of this conception of logical form to the project of identifying logical constants, reviewing two approaches, one of which takes topic neutrality as central, the other recursion, and argue that the aim of identifying logical constants for the purposes of classifying valid arguments is largely independent of that of identifying the logical form of sentences. They urge an ecumenical approach to extending talk of logical constants beyond where it is currently well-grounded.

The logical form of a (natural language) sentence depends in part on the semantic contribution of relevant syntax, and this contribution is not exhausted by the ordering that syntax imposes on lexical items. According to one view, syntax makes a minimal—or "contentless"—contribution to truth-conditions: each phrase combines (1) an expression semantically associated with some function, and (2) an expression semantically associated with some element in the domain of that function; so the semantic correlate of syntactic combination is simply function-application, as in standard formal languages. But recent work suggests that phrases are concatenations of predicates, satisfied by those things that satisfy both constituents. In his essay, Paul M. Pietroski argues that, on this view, which is motivated by certain eventish hypotheses about the logical forms of natural sentences, the semantic correlate of syntactic combination is predicate-conjunction. If this is correct, and syntax makes a substantive semantic contribution, then the meanings of sentences are not determined by the meanings of words, in the way that the sum of two numbers is determined by those numbers and the addition function. Given eventish hypotheses about logical forms, one might think that natural language syntax makes a further semantic contribution via the relation between argument structure and thematic roles. In so far as these aspects of meaning are covert, sentences of natural language do not manifest their logical forms. But one can still maintain that syntactic structure determines logical form—or at least those aspects of logical form that we are currently in a position to study. Pietroski shows that it could be useful to make a terminological turn to speak of semantic forms as properties of natural sentences, and this we can also conclude from Davidson's event analysis. In his essay, Jeffrey King sketches a framework within which claims about the logical form of some class of sentences, or the analysis of some notion, can be taken in two importantly different ways. He notes that in making claims about logical form (or in offering analyses) philosophers have not been careful to distinguish the two ways their claims can be taken. He provides examples of claims about logical form (or correct analyses) made by philosophers, and he shows how these may be understood in the two ways he distinguishes. King's aim in distinguishing two sorts of claims about logical form is to achieve conceptual clarity and, more importantly, to make clear that the different sorts of claims have different implications, are subject to different sorts of objections and have to be defended differently. Thus, King claims that the resolution of a variety of debates in different areas of philosophy would be facilitated by philosophers making clear which sort of claim about logical form they are making in a given case.

Current theories of logical form within linguistic theory are typically taken to provide structures that are the input to the semantical component of the grammar. So, for example, logical forms are supposed to be the structures over which we give recursive characterizations of truth when we attempt to provide T-theories for natural languages, or (alternatively) logical forms are taken to be the input to some form of model-theoretic semantics. It is only rarely suggested, however, that one can also define logical inferences directly off of the kinds of logical forms that are proposed within linguistic theory. Inferences, it is widely assumed, must be handled semantically—typically via a model-theoretic semantics. In his essay, Peter Ludlow argues that an extremely broad class of inferences can be defined over logical form representations in natural language and that it can be done by syntactically specifying environments that are upward entailing and downward entailing. The key idea, borrowed from the work of medieval logicians on the "dictum de omni e nullo" is that most of the classical inference paradigms can be reduced to two inference rules, one corresponding to upward entailing environments and the other corresponding to downward entailing environments. Ludlow first shows that for certain formal languages upward and downward entailing environments can be syntactically defined—even formal languages with the full expressive power of generalized quantifier theory. He then argues that there is good reason to suppose that all the relevant properties of those formal languages can be argued to hold in natural language and to be reflected in the LF representations that are posited within current versions of generative grammar. The conclusion is that a program of 'natural logic'—giving a syntactic characterization of natural language inferences—is not only feasible but very promising. In their essay, Robert May and R. F. Fiengo present a new analysis of the logical form of 'identity statements' which builds on Frege's intuition, which remains clearly enough in mind, but they consistently distinguish themselves from him in the analytical resources they employ in order to analyze these statements. For this purpose they introduce the logical form, including 'The Assignment Principle' of a speaker's belief in the redescription and the translation of identity statements. A communicative value condition follows from the given account, because an interpretation of such statements has to share the prior belief expressed in a translation sentence. This is only possible if both speaker and interpreter share a language with a given analyzable structure, and in this situation reference is not a semantic feature of names but of syntactic expressions. Just such requirements lead us to an introduction of an assignment relation, and therefore May and Fiengo also give us objections to the rigid designation such as Kripke has used in his analysis.

Part II brings together essays by James Higginbotham, Richard K. Larson, Barry Schein, Norbert Hornstein, and Jason Stanley. For an understanding of the logical and semantic features of reported speech, it is necessary to analyze the tense construction in natural language. Yet significant questions emerge such as "Is tense anaphoric?", "Does tense express relations between implicit arguments?" In his essay, James Higginbotham defends the proposal, within an explicitly quantificational theory of tense, that the principles governing sequence of tense are a special case of anaphora between open positions in predicates. The tenses themselves express binary relations between events or times; thus simple sentences such as "John ran", are construed as placing some event of John's running prior to the speaker's utterance. Events themselves are taken up as proposed originally by Davidson. Anaphoric relations can in general be optional or obligatory, depending upon the linguistic forms involved. The phenomena for which Hans Reichenbach created the notion of "reference time" are, Higginbotham believes, a special case of anaphora; and, following Michela Ippolito, he assumes that the imperfect tenses are essentially anaphoric. What we observe in the case of sequence of tense, however (as first discussed in contemporary terms by William Ladusaw) is that anaphoric tense is in general optional for embedded relative clauses, but obligatory for embedded complement clauses. The obligatoriness is not therefore a matter of tense form, but of containing context; here Higginbotham examines the question why this should be so. After reviewing proposals that he has advanced elsewhere, and their relation to the recent account of Toshi Ogihara, he argues that the obligatoriness of tense anaphora cannot after all be explained by metaphysical conditions such as he and Ogihara have earlier proposed, but instead should receive a syntactic treatment in the spirit of suggestions of Tim Stowell, on the one hand, and Alessandra Giorgi and Fabio Pianesi on the other. He applies his proposal to the peculiar properties of present-tense complements to past-tense superordinate predicates, the so-called "double-access" cases illustrated by examples such as "John said that Mary is pregnant" in English (and similar cases in Italian). He proposes that, because of the special complementizer structure of embedded clauses, the present tense of the complement clause is interpreted twice over, once as asserting that the time of John's speech overlaps the time of the (purported) pregnancy, and once as asserting that it overlaps the time of the speaker's report of what John said. For this syntactic suggestion Higginbotham supplies also an explicit semantics.

Phenomena of intensionality were first discussed by Frege (1893) in the context of sentential complement constructions, and indeed effects of intensionality are not generally observed with non-clausal complements. These results raise a simple question, namely, is intensionality connected with a particular grammatical environment, or is the semantic phenomenon a more general one? In his essay, Richard K. Larson discusses the following two opposing views. Sententialism holds to a grammatically conditioned view of intensionality and intensionalism holds that intensionality is quite general in occurrence and is to be found in a wide range of constructions. More exactly, he examines three putative cases of intensionality effects in non-clausal complement structures: (i) so-called intensional transitives, (ii) adverbial modifiers, and (iii) adjectival modifiers. Larson argues that, in each case, recent work in syntax and semantics casts doubt upon the claim that these structures provide evidence for intensionality divorced from clausal complementation. Intensional transitives can be argued to be a form of concealed clausal structure, and hence simply a case of clausal complementation after all. By contrast, adverbial and adjectival modifiers can be shown to be non-intensional in the crucial range of cases. Larson's conclusion is that the more restricted, sententialist picture appears sustainable.

Analyses descending from Davidson's (1967) logical form for action sentences appeal to thematic relations such as Agent, Patient, Theme, Goal, Location and Instrument, to relate events to their participants. In his essay, Barry Schein notes speakers' partial understanding of nonsense (*The blog looked the clob out of the droom, You keated the marbles onto the board when you keated the board with the marbles*) and argues that their content is invariant under lexical innovation and across the verbal lexicon. Alongside their robust grasp of thematic relations, speakers' judgements and verbal behaviour also demonstrate that there can be alternative descriptions of the same event. Sometimes, at least, the Carnegie Deli sitting opposite Carnegie Hall is the same event as Carnegie Hall sitting opposite the Carnegie Deli, Herb's body vibrating is the same event as his body's parts vibrating, and sometimes drinking some beers in an hour is the same event as drinking a beer for an hour. These modest observations lead to the unexpected result that logical form distinguishes scenes and the events they are scenes of and that temporal adverbials, *In an hour* ('In(e, 1 hr)') apply to a concealed, plural definite description of events. If speakers' recognition of robust events and thematic relations was not enough to justify this last refinement to logical form, the telicity conditions that such temporal adverbials impose are shown to derive from the conditions under which the definite description successfully refers to some events. Until the

1990s, Chomsky's theory of logical form and Davidson's interpretive truth theory were not overlapping paradigms. But do our minimalistic proposals show a "Davidsonian shadow"? In his essay, Norbert Hornstein provides a syntactic argument for a Neo-Davidsonian analysis of the clause in terms of thematic roles. The claim is that treating thematic roles as features fits well with the Davidsonian analysis of the clause in terms of events and participants of events while the Fregean analysis of the clause fits nicely with the analysis of thematic roles as relational/positional properties of arguments. Hornstein presents some arguments concerning scope and binding in favor of the featural analysis of theta roles and this in turn supports the Davidsonian view of the proposition as an event-centered set of conjuncts whose arguments are related to the proposition via its thematic structure.

Extra-linguistic context appears to have a profound and varied effect on semantic content. If we adhere to relatively straightforward linguistic intuition about semantic content, we seem to be leading to the conclusion that facts about the non-linguistic context play many different roles in determining it. That so many different constructions betray this sort of sensitivity to extra-linguistic context understandably leads to pessimism about rescuing the straightforward intuitions while preserving any sort of systematicity in the theory of meaning. One central strategy in defending the systematicity of semantics against the threat posed by context-dependence is to reject the semantic significance of ordinary intuitions. In his essay, Jason Stanley explores a different line of defense, by arguing that what appear to be very different effects of extra-linguistic context on semantic content can in fact be due to the same source. As a case-study, Stanley considers the effects of context on three apparently very different kinds of constructions, quantified noun phrases, comparative adjectives, and mass terms. Stanley argues that all three apparently very different effects are due to the same fact about the logical form of nominal expressions. Stanley concludes by drawing some consequences of his analysis for the theory of reference for natural kind terms.

Part III brings together essays by Bernard Linsky, Lenny Clapp and Robert Stainton, Robert Matthews, Marga Reimer, and Reinaldo Elugardo. In his essay, Bernard Linsky contrasts Russell's notion of logical form which underlies his famous theory of descriptions, with two different contemporary accounts. Russell's views on logical form were influenced by his logicist aim of reducing mathematics to logic, and by his ontological views on propositions and the ultimate constituents of the world. Linsky points out that Russell's distinction between apparent and real logical form should be distinguished from producing a recursive account of truth conditions for natural language, which is the basis for the Davidsonian interpretive truth theory described by Lepore and Ludwig. Russell's notion of the structure of propositions should, according to Linsky, also be distinguished from the syntactically motivated structure called "*LF*" by the other contemporary approach to logical form. Linsky particularly discusses Stephen Neale's view in his book *Descriptions* (1990). *LF* structures are intended to capture syntactic regularities, and they are less directly motivated by the semantic or ontological considerations which drive other accounts. A comparison with Russell's own notions of scope and incomplete symbols illustrates these aspects of the *LF* account of logical form. Linsky argues also that metaphysical views on the constituents of propositions were integral to Russell's notion of logical form, and that they override some of the linguistic considerations that inform more recent accounts. Moreover, Russell's notion was particularly involved with his theory of logical types. In their essay, Lenny Clapp and Robert J. Stainton begin by exploring Russell's rejection of propositions. In his 'Philosophy of Logical Atomism' and elsewhere, Russell maintains that propositions are 'obviously nothing'. Why he asserts this is not entirely clear. One may assume, however, that Russell reasoned as follows: If propositions "are", then they must be facts, but if propositions are facts, they cannot be false (or true, for that matter). Hence, seemingly Russell concludes, propositions are not facts, and hence "are not". Given this, they cannot be a constituent in a belief-relation. Therefore, Russell concludes, belief reports cannot state a relation between an agent and a proposition. While keeping an eye on exegesis, Clapp and Stainton's central concern is as follows: do Russell's arguments threaten the contemporary consensus about the logical form of belief reports which maintains that they do state a relation between an agent and something such a proposition? Their conclusion is that Russell's arguments do indeed rule out certain non-linguistic accounts of propositions, hence these cannot be the objects of belief. Nevertheless, despite what Russell himself probably believed, Clapp and Stainton show that his arguments leave Higginbotham-style Interpreted Logical Forms quite untouched; these can both "be" and not be facts. The ILF account of belief reports is therefore supported on metaphysical grounds.

Most philosophers embrace a relational conception of belief according to which belief is a relation which relates a believer to a semantically evaluable, causally efficacious particular that is the 'object' of belief, that is, the belief. It is difficult to find even the most cursory defense of this conception. Relationalists, as they might be called, presume that the relational nature of belief, and indeed the relational nature of all propositional attitudes, can simply be read off the relational logical form of the sentences by which we ascribe them. In his essay Robert J. Matthews argues that the case for the relational conception is not so easily made. It is difficult to find any plausible candidate that can be at once the semantical and psychological 'object' of belief. The logical form of belief ascriptions is indeed relational, but it does not follow that belief itself is a relation. Belief could, consistent with the relational logical form of belief ascriptions, turn out to be a monadic property of believers. Matthews sketches a measurement-theoretic account of belief ascriptions that has just this consequence. The belief predicate ascribes a certain belief state to a subject by relating that subject to a semantic object that indexes that belief state, in very much the way that a numerical measure predicate ascribes a physical magnitude to an object by relating that object to a number that indexes that magnitude.

What is the logical form of a sentence containing an ordinary proper name in the subject position? What, in other words, is the structure of the proposition expressed by such a sentence? According to one currently popular view (Millianism), the proposition expressed in such cases is a singular one, one containing the name's bearer as a constituent. On such a view, the semantic value (or propositional contribution) of a name is simply its bearer. According to another somewhat less popular view (Descriptivism), the proposition expressed is a "general" one, one containing "concepts" (rather than objects) as constituents. On the Russellian version of such a view, ordinary proper names are semantically equivalent to definite descriptions, of which the latter are to be analysed in accordance with Russell's theory of descriptions. In her essay, Marga Reimer claims that both accounts of names are flawed, as neither can provide a plausible rendering of the proposition expressed in "all" of the relevant sorts of cases. Thus, for instance, while a Millian account has trouble handling identity sentences involving co-referring names, a Russellian account has trouble handling cases of the sort made famous by Kripke. Reimer accordingly proposes an alternative account, one according to which the proposition expressed by a sentence of the kind in question varies with the (contextually constrained) communicative intentions of the speaker. For instance, in the case of sentences of the form "a=b", a name typically functions in accordance with a (roughly) Russellian account. In contrast, when a name occurs in a sentence used to describe a counterfactual scenario involving the name's bearer, the name typically functions in accordance with a Millian account of names. In this way, Reimer argues, semantic function mirrors communicative intent. The orthodox view of proper names is that they are unstructured, single-valued, referring terms. Tyler Burge once defended a very unorthodox view of names: at the level of logical form, proper names are predicates, that is, general terms, in their own right. Reinaldo Elugardo defends Burge's view by arguing that predicative uses of proper names are not parasitic on their referential roles, as some philosophers have said in response to Burge's arguments. He examines two general strategies—a descriptivist approach and a causal-theoretic approach—to explain away their apparent predicative uses and argue that both strategies fail. His aim is to show that the Predicate View has a lot to recommend it and that it deserves another look.

Our contributions show a new open-minded view of co-operation between theorists of language. Following a broader philosophical perspective on logical form, the book contains new essays in the philosophy of language which bridge grammar and semantics. The collection brings together contributions by philosophers from diverse points of view, and as such, it illuminates the lively and ongoing debate which the concept of logical form still arouses within contemporary philosophy, and shows us a way to the future. The project was first initiated by the periodical *Protosociology: An International Journal of Interdisciplinary Research*, J. W. Goethe-University, Frankfurt am Main (www.rz.uni-frankfurt.de/protosociology). We wish to express our thanks to all contributors who have made their results available. Without their encouragement and support the work would not have been possible. In particular we thank Peter Momtchiloff and Ernie Lepore who encouraged us to undertake the project.

Part I

THE NATURE OF
LOGICAL FORM

2

Abbreviation, Scope, and Ontology

STEPHEN NEALE

I Abbreviation

Consider a language L containing several one-place predicates, an unending supply of variables $x_1 \ldots x_n$, left and right parentheses as devices of punctuation, and the following logical vocabulary: $\forall$, $\vee$, $\sim$, $=$. Assume a rudimentary Tarskian truth definition for L, where s ranges over infinite sequences of objects in the domain, k ranges over the natural numbers, s_k is the object in the kth position of s, and ϕ and ψ range over formulae of L:

(1) $\forall s \forall k$ (with respect to s, the referent of $x_k = s_k$);
(2) $\forall s \forall k \forall \phi$ ($\forall x_k \phi$ is satisfied by s iff ϕ is satisfied by every sequence differing from s at most in the kth position);
(3) $\forall s \forall \phi$ ($\sim \phi$ is satisfied by s iff ϕ is not satisfied by s);
(4) $\forall s \forall \phi \forall \psi$ (($\phi \vee \psi$) is satisfied by s iff ϕ is satisfied by s or ψ is satisfied by s).

(I do not bother with quotation marks around symbols as it is obvious where I am talking *about* than rather than using them. No confusion should arise.) Now suppose we were to find ourselves using a great number of formulae involving negation and disjunction (because we wanted to express conjunction) and wanted to save ink. Within a broad range of options, we can distinguish (i) introducing some metalinguistic shorthand and (ii) adding new symbols to L.

(i) An attractive way of introducing metalinguistic shorthand would be to use "quasi-formulae" to represent genuine formulae of L. For example, we could use (ϕ • ψ) as a convenient shorthand for $\sim (\sim \phi \vee \sim \psi)$ without actually adding • to L.

(ii) *a*. One way of adding to L itself would be to introduce a two-place connective • by way of an appropriate syntactical rule and a new semantical axiom involving the connectives $\vee$ and $\sim$:

(5) $\forall s \forall \phi \forall \psi \,(($$\phi$ • ψ) is satisfied by s iff $\sim (\sim \phi \vee \sim \psi)$ is satisfied by s).

(ii) *b*. Alternatively, we might add • to L more directly, i.e. by way of an appropriate syntactical rule and a new semantical axiom that does not involve any other expressions of L:

(6) $\forall s \forall \phi \forall \psi \,(($$\phi$ • ψ) is satisfied by s iff ϕ is satisfied by s and ψ is satisfied by s).

Similarly, any of methods (i), (ii*a*), or (ii*b*) could be used in connection with other symbols we might consider, for example $\supset$, $\equiv$, $\neq$, and $\exists$.

Consider now a language L', just like L but containing the following logical vocabulary: $\forall, \exists, \sim , \bullet , \vee , \supset , \equiv , = , \neq$. There is nothing that can be said in L' that cannot be said in L; but many things can be said with fewer symbols in L' and in ways that are more readily understandable.

Within a middle range, there is a trade-off between economy of symbols and ease of interpretation. Obviously economy of symbols is not the only criterion we invoke in designing formal languages with which we work. If we are doing the metatheory of first-order logic, we are naturally drawn to the economy afforded by a language with fewer symbols; when we come to *use* (rather than discuss) first-order logical formulae, we are naturally drawn to the economy of length and simplicity afforded by a language with a greater number of symbols. Imagine how difficult it would be to train ourselves readily to understand sentences whose logical vocabulary contains just $\exists$, $=$, and | (Scheffer's two-place stroke, expressing incompatibility). Whitehead and Russell were sufficiently impressed by | to say, in the Introduction to the second edition of *Principia*, that the whole work should be understood as rewritten with just that one sentence connective. At the same time, Russell was confident that negation is more primitive *psychologically* than stroke.)

Finally, consider a language L'', just like L' but containing three individual constants a, b, c, understood as primitive singular terms (names if you like). Suppose we were to find ourselves wanting to talk about things in the domain not named a, b, or c, or about things satisfying certain descriptive conditions and not known by us to be named by a, b, or c. We could render the statement that the unique thing satisfying the predicate F also satisfies the predicate G (i.e. the statement that the F is G) as follows:[1]

(7) $\exists x (\forall y (Fy \equiv y = x) \bullet Gx)$.

(In place of x_1, x_2, etc., occasionally I use x, y, etc.) Again, there are things we could do to save ink and present ourselves with more readily interpretable formulae. We could introduce some shorthand. In particular, we could follow Russell, who viewed (7) as rendering the logical form of the English sentence 'the F is G'. Adapting Peano's *iota* notation, Russell represents a definite description 'the F' by an expression of the form $\imath x F x$, read as 'the unique x such that Fx'. The *iota*-operator *looks like* a variable-binding operator for creating a term $\imath x \phi$ from a formula ϕ. But there is an important feature of Russell's theory that makes this characterization a little misleading. True, a simple one-place predicate symbol G may be prefixed to a description $\imath x \phi$ to form a something of the form $G\imath x \phi$. But this is not a formula of Russell's formal language; it is a quasi-formula, an abbreviation, a piece of shorthand for a genuine formula of the form of (8) (where $\phi(y)$ is the result of replacing all free occurrences of x in ϕ by y):

(8) $\exists x (\forall y (\phi(y) \equiv y = xr) \bullet Gx)$.

For Russell, a phrase of the form '$\imath x \phi$' is *not* a genuine singular term; it is an *abbreviatory device* that permits (provably legitimate) shortcuts in the course of proofs, and the use of quasi-formulae that are usually easier to grasp than the genuine formulae for which they go proxy. The important point for present concerns is that *the iota-operator has not been added to L'' itself.* A quasi-formula of the form $G\imath x \phi$ is just shorthand for a genuine formula of the form of (8).[2]

At this point, then, the following contextual definition of definite descriptions might be considered, where $\Sigma(\imath x \phi)$ is a sentence containing $\imath x \phi$, $\Sigma(x)$ is the result of replacing an occurrence of $\imath x \phi$ in $\Sigma(\imath x \phi)$ by x, and $\phi(y)$ is the result of replacing an occurrence of x in ϕ by y:

(9) $\Sigma(\imath x \phi) =_{df} \exists x (\forall y (\phi(y) \equiv y = x) \bullet \Sigma(x))$.

But this will not suffice once more complex examples are examined. Whitehead and Russell bring this out with the quasi-formula (10):

(10) $G\imath x \phi \supset \psi$.

---

[1] See Russell (1905) and Whitehead and Russell (1925), *14.

[2] On Russell's official account, even expressions of the form of (8) are quasi-formulae as '$\bullet$', '$\equiv$', and '$=$' are not primitive but defined symbols.

Depending upon how definition (9) is applied, (10) could be viewed as shorthand for either (11) or (12), which are not equivalent in respect of truth-conditions:

(11) $(\exists x(\forall y(\phi(y) \equiv y = x) \bullet Gx) \supset \psi)$
(12) $\exists x(\forall y(\phi(y) \equiv y = x) \bullet (Gx \supset \psi))$.

So unlike any genuine formula of L'' (or the language of *Principia*), a quasi-formula of the form of (10) is, at the moment, ambiguous. Consequently, some sort of modification of or supplement to the system of abbreviation is required if it is to be of service.

The point is worth stressing in connection with another sort of example of more immediate interest. Depending upon how (9) is applied, the quasi-formula $\sim G\iota x\phi$ could be viewed as shorthand for either (13) or (14), which are not equivalent in respect of truth-conditions:

(13) $\sim \exists x(\forall y(\phi(y) \equiv y = x) \bullet Gx)$
(14) $\exists x(\forall y(\phi(y) \equiv y = x) \bullet \sim Gx)$.

(The former, unlike the latter, can be true if nothing uniquely satisfies ϕ.) Whitehead and Russell adopt a rather cumbersome supplementation of their shorthand in order to eradicate ambiguity in their quasi-formulae: they place a copy of the description inside square brackets at the front of the formula that constitutes the scope of the relevant existential quantifier. Thus (13) and (14) are abbreviated as (13′) and (14′) respectively:

(13′) $\sim [\iota x\phi] G\iota x\phi$
(14′) $[\iota x\phi] \sim G\iota x\phi$.

Since they are concerned mostly with formulae in which descriptions have minimal scope, Whitehead and Russell allow themselves to omit the square-bracketed copy of the description whenever the scope of the description is understood to be minimal. Thus (13′), but not (14′), can be simplified to $\sim G\iota x\phi$, now understood as unambiguous—after all, this is just an abbreviatory notation that has no effect on the primitive language.

Using these scope conventions, the Theory of Descriptions can be summarized in two succinct propositions. The central proposition is the following contextual definition:

*14.01 $[\iota x\phi]\Sigma(\iota x\phi) =_{df} \exists x(\forall y(\phi(y) \equiv y = x) \bullet \Sigma(x))$.[3]

---

[3] Throughout, I shall use $\iota x\phi$ where Russell uses $(\iota x)(\phi x)$. This policy will be applied in all contexts, even when I quote from *Principia*.

The second proposition is relevant only to statements that seem to involve talk of existence. For Russell, a genuine singular term cannot fail to refer, so no predicate letter in the language of *Principia* stands for 'exists'. But a statement of the form 'the *F* exists' is meaningful and Russell introduces an abbreviatory symbol E! that may be combined with a description $\iota x\phi$ to create a second type of quasi-formula E!$\iota x\phi$, which is also to be understood in terms of a contextual definition:

*14.02 $E!\iota x\phi =_{df} \exists x \forall y(\phi(y) \equiv y = x)$.

The Theory of Descriptions claims that any well-formed formula containing a definite description (regardless of the complexity of $\Sigma(\iota x\phi)$ in *14.01) can be replaced by an equivalent formula that is description-free.[4] It is clear that using Russell's abbreviatory convention does not add to the expressive power of L''.

Once certain derived rules of inference have been proved for truth-functional contexts, most importantly,

*14.15 $(\iota x\phi = \alpha) \supset \{\Sigma(\iota x\phi) \equiv \Sigma(\alpha)\}$
*14.16 $(\iota x\phi = \iota x\psi) \supset \{\Sigma(\iota x\phi) \equiv \Sigma(\iota x\psi)\}$

it is useful for certain purposes of proof to be able to regard the definite descriptions '*s* (*x*)', '$\sqrt{x}$', 'log *x*', 'sin *x*', '*x* + *y*' and so on *as if* they were singular terms.[5]

Another useful theorem for truth-functional contexts is *14.18:

*14.18 $E!\iota x\phi \supset \{\forall x \Sigma(x) \supset \Sigma(\iota x\phi)\}$.

---

[4] In unpublished work, Saul Kripke has produced examples of what he calls 'hydras' which cast doubt on the systematicity of unpacking using solely *14.01 and *14.02. That there might be interesting issues in this area is hinted by Mates (1973), who informs me that he became convinced by problem cases concocted by Tarski.

[5] The *iota*-notation is rarely used in *Principia* after *14, 'being chiefly required to lead up to another notation' (1925: 67), namely the inverted comma *of*-notation:

(i) $R'z$

is used as shorthand for 'the object that bears R to z' and is introduced by a further contextual definition:

(ii) $R'z =_{df} \iota x Rxz$.

Russell calls both (ii) and *14.01 'contextual definitions', and he also says that '$\iota x\phi$' and '$R'z$' are both 'defined in use'. Notice that in *14.01 we get whole formulae on both the right and left of '$=_{df}$', whereas in (ii) we do not. On Russell's account, then, technically it is not in the nature of a contextual definition that it involve whole formulae (Quine's shift from terms to sentences is not mandatory). Of course, (ii) can easily be recast in terms of formulae—just attach a one-place predicate to either side—but this would buy Russell nothing. According to (ii), (iii) is analysed as (iv) which, according to *14.01 is, in turn, analysed as (v):

This says that if there exists exactly one thing satisfying ϕ, then that thing 'has any property which belongs to everything' (p. 174). The description $\iota x\phi$ 'has (speaking formally) all the logical properties of symbols which directly represent objects . . . the fact that it is an incomplete symbol becomes irrelevant to the truth-values of logical propositions in which it occurs' (p. 180).

The fact that Whitehead and Russell prove some interesting theorems about contextually defined definite descriptions occurring in truth-functional contexts should not obscure the quantificational character of the Theory of Descriptions, which comes through clearly not only in *14.01 and *14.02 themselves but also in Russell's talk of *general* propositions and *general* facts. By the time of *Principia*, having more or less given up on the notion of propositions as non-linguistic entities of theoretical utility, Russell takes a true sentence to stand for a fact. But in order to avoid unnecessary distractions that emerge in connection with false sentences, it will be convenient, for a moment, to go back a few years, to when Russell was first presenting the Theory of Descriptions, to a period when he took propositions more seriously as non-linguistic entities.

For Russell, a singular term α may be combined with a one-place predicate phrase '— is G' to express a proposition that simply could not be entertained or expressed if the entity referred to by α did not exist. Russell often puts this by saying that the referent of α is a *constituent* of such a proposition, a so-called *singular* proposition whose existence is contingent upon the existence of the referent of α.

A sentence of the form 'the F is G' does *not* express a singular proposition; it expresses a *general* (or *quantificational*) proposition, a proposition that is not *about* a specific entity (described by 'the F'), and whose existence is not contingent upon the existence of the entity which in fact satisfies the predicate F (if anything does).[6] If one does not see that on Russell's account 'the F is G' expresses a *general* proposition, that 'the F' *never* refers, one simply does not understand the theory.

(iii) $G(R\dot{z})$
(iv) $G(\iota x Rxz)$
(v) $\exists x(\forall y(Ryz \equiv y = x) \bullet Gx)$.
*14.01 differs from (ii) in that it involves a *logical reparsing*. It is only in the context of a whole formula that the analysis of '$\iota x\phi$' can be stated. Of course, *ultimately* this is true of '$R\dot{z}$' too.

[6] For Russell, all of this is intimately tied up with his epistemology and psychology. Just as one can grasp the proposition expressed by an utterance of a sentence of the form 'every F is G' or 'no F is G' without knowing who or what satisfies the matrix Fx, indeed independently of

To say that the proposition expressed by a sentence *S* is singular is really just to say that the grammatical subject of *S stands for* an object and *contributes* that object to the proposition expressed by an utterance of *S* (or, if you prefer, contributes that object to the truth-conditions of an utterance of *S*). To say that a sentence *S* expresses a *general* proposition is just to say that the grammatical subject of *S* is not the sort of expression that stands for an object or contributes an object to the proposition expressed by (or the truth-conditions of) an utterance of *S*. This is the heart of Russell's position that English phrases of the form 'the *F*', as well as those of the form 'every *F*', 'some *F*', and so on— i.e. all "denoting phrases"—are *incomplete* symbols: they are incomplete because they do not "stand for" or "directly represent" objects in the way proper names and predicates do.[7] Which is not to say, of course, that one could not construct theories according to which 'the *F*', 'every *F*' and so on stand for entities—higher-order functions, for example, as in numerous theories that use generalized quantifiers—theories which also deliver the same Russellian truth-conditions.

The literature on Russell's Theory of Descriptions contains a number of common complaints about its formal properties, complaints that seem to do serious injustice to the theory or its place in a semantic theory for natural language. Some recurrent claims of this nature are the following. (i) If ϕ is a formula containing a singular term that refers to *A* and if ϕ itself is uniquely satisfied by *A*, then the definite description $\iota x \phi$ is not really Russellian: it is a singular term that refers to *A*. (ii) Russell's theory artificially deprives languages of definite descriptions. (iii) It gives rise to problems of scope. (iv) Russell's notion of the scope of a description has no formal analogue in natural language; furthermore, any theory of logical form that contains the resources necessary to represent descriptions as taking various scopes will have an *ad hoc* character. (v) Russell's theory cannot constitute a serious contribution to the

whether or not anything does satisfy it, so one can perfectly well grasp the proposition expressed by an utterance of a sentence of the form 'the *F* is *G*' without knowing who or what satisfies *Fx* and independently of whether or not anything does satisfy it. As it is sometimes put, one can perfectly well grasp the proposition expressed without knowing who or what is "denoted" by 'the *F*', indeed independently of whether or not anything actually is "denoted" by it. To this extent, it makes no sense to say that the existence of the proposition depends upon the identity of the "denotation" of 'the *F*'; so the proposition expressed is not singular.

[7] There is an unfortunate tendency in the literature on Russell to construe the notion of an incomplete symbol as driven by largely notational considerations and to see Russell's Theory of Descriptions as requiring the use of a privileged formula in rendering the logical form of 'the *F* is *G*'. See e.g. Evans (1977, 1982) and esp. Linsky (1992, 2000). For discussion, see Section IV.

semantics of natural language because the "logical forms" it delivers bear so little relation to surface syntax or to what we now know about syntactical structure in the light of advances in theoretical linguistics. (vi) Attempts to provide theories that deliver improved "logical forms" conflict with Russell's theory, which uses a privileged sentence of a fixed primitive notation to capture the logical form of any particular sentence containing 'the F'. (vii) Attempts to render sentences containing descriptions in terms of formal sentences that make use of restricted quantifiers must involve fundamental departures from Russell's theory, because descriptions have "no meaning in isolation", being "incomplete symbols" that "disappear on analysis". (viii) The existence of complex definite descriptions that contain as proper parts quantified noun phrases upon which subsequent ("donkey") pronouns are anaphoric—as in, for example, 'the farmer who bought a donkey vaccinated it'—demonstrates conclusively that descriptions in natural language cannot be treated as logical or semantical units.

There is little substance in these charges, which seem to stem from mis-understandings concerning the inherently quantificational character of Russell's theory, the distinction between the theory itself and the notation used in its formal implementation, and the concepts of scope, incompleteness, analysis, contextual definition, and variable-binding. In passing, I made an attempt to straighten some of this out some years ago; I want to do a more thorough job here, taking into account various misunderstandings I have recently encountered and raising several formal and philosophical issues that seem to me to be hampering some work in the philosophy of language and logic.

II Scope

A truth-function, according to Whitehead and Russell, is 'a function whose truth or falsehood depends only upon the truth or falsity of its arguments. This covers all the cases with which we are ever concerned' (p. 184). The restriction of the theorems of *Principia* to formulae containing descriptions in truth-functional contexts comes out clearly in *14.3 below, which is meant to state that when ϕ is uniquely satisfied, the scope of $\iota x\phi$ does not matter to the truth-value of any truth-functional sentence in which it occurs:

$$*14.3 \quad \forall f[\{\forall p \forall q((p \equiv q) \supset f(p) \equiv f(q)) \bullet E!\iota x\phi)\} \supset$$
$$\{f([\iota x\phi]G\iota x\phi) \equiv [\iota x\phi]f(G\iota x\phi)\}].$$

The variable f is meant to range over functions of propositions (I have added the quantifier $\forall f$ which is not present in *Principia*, but retained the authors' desire to keep the theorem short by ignoring issues of use and mention that will not lead to confusion).[8] Whitehead and Russell conclude their discussion of this topic with the observation that 'the proposition in which $\iota x\phi$ has larger scope always implies the corresponding one in which it has the smaller scope, but the converse implication holds only if either (*a*) we have E!$\iota x\phi$ or (*b*) the proposition in which $\iota x\phi$ has the smaller scope implies E!$\iota x\phi$' (p. 186).

The restriction of scope permutation to truth-functional contexts expressed (or meant to be expressed) by *14.3 is something Quine overlooked in his 1953 and 1961 responses to Smullyan's (1948) postulation of truth-conditional ambiguity in sentences containing descriptions and modal operators. Mirroring Russell's postulation of an ambiguity of scope in sentences containing descriptions and psychological verbs—an ambiguity Russell milked to tackle puzzles about substitutivity—Smullyan sought to characterize in terms of scope what he saw as an example of the same type of ambiguity in modal contexts. Using Px for 'x numbers the planets in our solar system', the surface sentences (15) and (16) can be given their respective (*a*) and (*b*) readings below:

(15) George wondered whether the number of planets in our solar system > 7
   a. George wondered whether $\exists x(\forall y(Py \equiv y = x) \bullet (x > 7))$
   b. $\exists x(\forall y(Py \equiv y = x) \bullet$ George IV wondered whether $(x > 7))$

(16) Necessarily the number of planets in our solar system > 7
   a. necessarily $\exists x(\forall y(Py \equiv y = x) \bullet (x > 7))$
   b. $\exists x(\forall y(Py \equiv y = x) \bullet$ necessarily $(x > 7))$.

Notoriously, Quine has expressed the view that the interpretation of (15*b*) and (16*b*) pose great philosophical difficulties. For present purposes, it will suffice to make a minor point on behalf of Smullyan (1947, 1948), who mistakenly thought he had defused Quine's worries.[9] As Quine later

---

[8] Whitehead and Russell do not appeal to *14.3 in subsequent proofs because of its use of propositions as values of variables 'an apparatus not required elsewhere' (1925: 185.) They proceed by individual cases, as they arise. Notice that *14.3 does not entail that the scope of a *relativized* description—i.e. a description containing a free variable such as $\iota x Wxy$ (representing, say, 'the woman sitting opposite him' as it occurs in 'every man talked to the woman sitting opposite him')—is irrelevant in truth-functional contexts. In order for E!$\iota x\phi$ to be true, $\iota x\phi$ cannot contain a free variable.

[9] This claim is defended by Neale (2000) in the face of the (bad) arguments and scholarship of Neale (1990) on this matter. A more thorough defence will appear in forthcoming work.

recognized, he erred in *From a Logical Point of View* in 1953 and again in a revised 1961 edition when he accused Smullyan of 'propounding, in modal contexts, an alteration of Russell's familiar logic of descriptions' by 'allow[ing] difference of scope to affect truth value even in cases where the description concerned succeeds in naming [*sic*]' (1961: 154). By the time of the 1980 reprinting of the book, the charge against Smullyan on p. 154 has been excised. In a new foreword, Quine points out that the page in question originally 'contained mistaken criticisms of Church and Smullyan' (p. vii), and the relevant part of the page now reads as follows:

Then, taking a leaf from Russell ['On Denoting'], he [Smullyan] explains the failure of substitutivity [in modal contexts] by differences in the structure of the contexts, in respect of what Russell called the scopes of the descriptions. [*Footnote*: Unless a descriptions fails to name [*sic*], its scope is indifferent to extensional contexts. But it can still matter to intensional ones.] (1980: 154)

I mention this because it highlights a lingering misunderstanding in discussions of Smullyan's position on the failure of substitutivity in modal contexts: Smullyan does *not* claim that substitutivity is restored by appealing to the scopes of descriptions; his position is that on Russell's account (i) descriptions are not singular terms and so do not appear in primitive notation, and (ii) the false reading of (15), namely (15*b*), cannot be derived from 'necessarily 9 > 7' and '9 = the number of planets'.[10] The putative existence and truth (cf. Smullyan) or unintelligibility (cf. Quine) of (16*a*) is irrelevant to *this* point—which is *not* to say that Smullyan's observation defuses Quine's objections to quantified modal logic, which it does not.

Quine's initial interpretive error about applications of Russell's Theory of Descriptions in modal contexts has been repeated by others, and in some cases this has led to further error.[11] The fact that the error is so widespread naturally leads one to speculate why, especially as Russell is explicit as early as 1905 in 'On Denoting' that altering the scope of a description—even one whose matrix is uniquely satisfied—*can* alter truth-value in non-extensional constructions: that is how he deals with the puzzle involving 'George IV wondered whether Scott was the author of *Waverley*'. (The point is made again in *Principia*.) I suspect the answer lies in the contrast between, on the one hand, the

---

[10]   This misunderstanding infects the last sections of two articles by Linsky (1992, 2000).

[11]   See (e.g.) Carnap (1947), Føllesdal (1966), Hintikka (1968, 1989), Hintikka and Kulas (1985), Hintikka and Sandu (1991), Kalish *et al.* (1980), Lambert (1991), B. Linsky (1966), L. Linsky (1992, 2000), Scott (1967), Thomason (1969), Wallace (1969), Wedberg (1984), and Wilson (1959).

discussion of descriptions in the Introduction to *Principia* and in the informal remarks at the end of *14 and, on the other, the formal presentation of the theory and the relevant theorems. For example, in the introduction, Whitehead and Russell say that 'when E!ɩ*x*φ, we may enlarge or diminish the scope of ɩ*x*φ as much as we please without altering the truth-value of any proposition in which it occurs' (p. 70); and at the end of *14 they say 'when E!ɩ*x*φ, the scope of ɩ*x*φ does not matter to the truth-value of any proposition in which ɩ*x*φ occurs. This proposition cannot be proved generally, but it can be proved in each particular case' (p. 184). But then they go on to add that 'The proposition can be proved generally when ɩ*x*φ occurs in the form χɩ*x*φ and χɩ*x*φ occurs in what we may call a "truth function", i.e. a function whose truth or falsehood depends only upon the truth or falsehood of its argument or arguments' (p. 184). This, of course, is what theorem *14.3 says.

In this terrain, errors readily compound. Consider what Hintikka (1968: 5) has to say:

> ... when the Russellian theory [of descriptions] is put to work in modal and other complicated contexts, much of its success depends on a clever choice of scope conventions and on similar adjustments. With a clever choice of these, a suitable modification of the theory gives us a certain amount of mileage (cf. e.g. Smullyan [1948], Montague and Kalish [1959], Linsky [1966]), but the deeper reasons for the choice remain unaccounted for, and cry out for further analysis.

Thus far, Hintikka is amplifying Quine's original error. But from here he goes straight on to say,

> Donnellan [1966*a*, 1966*b*] has even argued that definite descriptions are used in two essentially different ways in ordinary language. No matter whether these can be caught by juggling the scope conventions, the reasons for doing so will remain in the dark. (...) Thus it also seems to me that the theoretical significance (or lack thereof) of the ingenious use of the theory of descriptions to simplify one's 'canonical notation' by Quine [1960: ch. 5] and others is too incompletely understood to be evaluated here.

This passage betrays a confusion. It has seemed attractive to some philosophers to explicate the *de re* readings of sentences containing descriptions and non-extensional devices in terms of something like Donnellan's (1966*a*) 'referential' (rather than 'attributive' ≅ Russellian) interpretation of the relevant description. For example, Rundle (1965) makes this suggestion for descriptions in modal contexts; and Hintikka (1968), Stalnaker (1972), and others suggest that a referential interpretation can be used in characterizing the *de re* readings of descriptions in non-extensional contexts more generally. But this will not do. Cartwright (1968) and Kripke (1971, 1977) have pointed out that attempts to provide accounts of either the large scope–small scope distinction or the *de re–de dicto* distinction in terms of a referential/attributive distinction are misguided. A speaker may make a *de re* use of (16), or the variant (17), without using the definite description 'the number of planets' referentially:

(17) The number of planets, whatever it is, is necessarily odd.

The following passage from Kripke makes the point very clearly:

Suppose I have no idea how many planets there are, but (for some reason) astronomical theory dictates that that number must be odd. If I say, 'The number of planets (whatever it may be) is odd,' my description is used attributively. If I am an essentialist, I will also say, 'The number of planets (whatever it may be) is necessarily odd,' on the grounds that all odd numbers are necessarily odd; and my use is just as attributive as the first case. (1977: 9)[12]

The point, quite simply, is that the proposition expressed by an utterance of (17) is not *singular*, even if the description is understood *de re*. The Russellian account is quite consistent with this fact. The proposition expressed is general; the *de re* reading is obtained by giving the description large scope over the modal operator as in (16*b*) above. As Kripke goes on to point out, we find exactly the same situation with definite descriptions in attitude contexts. Suppose Smith has an object-dependent wonder concerning the man who lives upstairs: he wonders whether the man is Greek. I may correctly report this state of affairs by saying

(18) Smith wonders whether the man who lives upstairs is Greek

with the definite description 'the man who lives upstairs' understood *de re*. But this does not mean that I have used the description referentially. I may have no relevant singular thought about the man who lives upstairs and no intention of communicating such a thought. Russell captures this *de re* reading by giving the definite description maximal scope:

(18′) $\exists x(\forall y(My \equiv y = x)$ • Smith wonders whether x is Greek).

It is also stressed by Kripke that no binary semantical distinction can *replace* Russell's notion of scope. A sentence like (19) is *three* ways ambiguous according as the description is given maximal, intermediate, or minimal scope:

---

[12] See also Cartwright (1968: 618).

(19) Smith hopes that Jones believes that the man upstairs is Greek
    a. $\exists x(\forall y(My \equiv y = x) \bullet$ (Smith hopes that (Jones believes that x is Greek))
    b. Smith hopes that $\exists x(\forall y(My \equiv y = x) \bullet$ (Jones believes that x is Greek))
    c. Smith hopes that (Jones believes that $\exists x(\forall y(My \equiv y = x) \bullet x$ is Greek)).

The reading given by (19*b*) is neither *de re* nor fully *de dicto*.[13]

These facts demonstrate quite conclusively that descriptions understood *de re* cannot, in general, be identified with descriptions understood referentially, and that a semantical ambiguity between Russellian and referential interpretations of descriptions cannot *replace* either the *de re–de dicto* distinction or the large scope–small scope distinction as it shows up in non-extensional contexts. So even if one could provide good arguments for the existence of referential interpretations of the definite and indefinite descriptions in some of the examples we have been considering, *the large scope readings would still be needed.*

If it were not for the particular aims of *Principia*, Whitehead and Russell could have pushed their abbreviatory conventions to their logical resting place. The square-bracketed occurrence of a description that is used to indicate scope is effectively marking the scope of an existential quantifier, and to that extent it is actually functioning rather like a quantifier itself. So why not replace the *original occurrence* of the description in the formula to which the square-bracketed occurrence is attached by a *variable* bound by the square-bracketed occurrence? After all, this is just an abbreviatory notation. On this simplification, (13′) and (14′) are reduced to (13″) and (14″) respectively, effectively yielding the notation of restricted quantification (see below):

(13′) $\sim [\imath x \phi]\, G \imath x \phi$ (13″) $\sim [\imath x \phi]\, Gx$
(14′) $[\imath x \phi] \sim G \imath x \phi$ (14″) $[\imath x \phi] \sim Gx.$

If this notational suggestion had been adopted, *14.01 and *14.02 would have looked like this:

*14.01′ $[\imath x \phi]\, Gx =_{df} \exists x(\forall y(\phi(y) \equiv y = x) \bullet Gx)$
*14.02′ $[\imath x \phi]E!x =_{df} \exists x \forall y(\phi(y) \equiv y = x).$

---

[13] Again, the situation is the same with indefinite descriptions. As Kripke (1972) observes, the following example is three ways ambiguous according as 'a high American official' is given large, intermediate, or narrow scope: '(i) Hoover charged that the Berrigans plotted to kidnap a high American official.' Similar examples can be constructed using iterated modalities.

This would be real progress, but it is not what Whitehead and Russell do, for reasons to which I have already alluded.

If we were so disposed, we could add the *iota*-operator directly to L'' by way of other symbols of L''. There would be some work involved if *iota*-compounds were to continue to occupy singular term positions yet not be subject to reference axioms.[14] It would be much easier to use the more transparently quantificational notation above, according to which expressions of the form $\iota x \phi$ are one-place variable-binding operators:

(20) If ϕ and ψ are formulae and x_k is a variable, then $[\iota x_k \phi]\psi$ is a formula;

(21) $\forall k \forall j \forall \phi \forall \psi \forall s$ $\{[\iota x_k \phi]\psi$ is satisfied by s iff $\exists x_k (\forall x_j (\phi(y) \equiv x_j = x_k) \bullet \psi)$ is satisfied by $s\}$.

Alternatively, we could add the *iota*-operator to L'' by way of the same syntactic rule and a semantic axiom that does not involve any other primitive symbols of L'':

(22) $\forall k \forall \phi \forall \psi \forall s$ $\{[\iota x_k \phi]\psi$ is satisfied by s iff ϕ is satisfied by exactly one sequence differing from s at most in the kth position and ψ is satisfied by every such sequence$\}$.

The right-hand side of (22) simply encodes Russell's truth-conditions. It is a very short step from here to understanding how the Theory of Descriptions fits into a systematic account of quantification in natural language, quantified noun phrases functioning as restricted quantifiers.[15]

---

[14] In fact, there is even work to be done if *iota*-compounds are to occupy singular term positions and be subject to reference axioms, as in non-Russellian theories that treat descriptions as singular terms. The work is caused by the fact that descriptions contain formulae (sometimes quantified formulae) but at the same time occupy term positions in formulae; this makes it impossible to first define the class of terms, and then the class of formulae, as one does standardly; the classes must be defined together. It is surprising how often this fact is overlooked by those proposing referential theories of descriptions (or of class and functional abstracts for that matter).

[15] Philosophers often appeal to Russell's Theory of Descriptions when attempting to shed light on the logical forms of certain statements, perhaps the premises or the conclusions of certain philosophical arguments, particularly when issues of scope arise. Curiously, it is less common for such philosophers to construe Russell's theory as a component of a systematic and compositional semantics for natural language. Now I would have thought that it is only *because* the Theory of Descriptions can be construed as a component of a systematic semantical theory that philosophers are entitled to appeal to it in the ways they do. Consequently, I would maintain that there is an onus on anyone who wishes to appeal to the theory in explicating the logical forms of statements of English to be explicit about its place within a systematic semantics for English.

III Restricted Quantification

Unlike the official, unabbreviated language of *Principia*, English contains definite descriptions. From the perspective of constructing a semantic theory for English, one would like to find a way of capturing Russell's semantic insights—that descriptions are not singular terms, that sentences containing definite descriptions have quantificational truth-conditions—without any sort of special machinery that eliminates them. Russell's own formal implementation of the Theory of Descriptions suggests a significant gap between surface syntax and "logical form". But upon reflection it is clear the gap has little to do with descriptions *per se*. In order to characterize the logical forms of quantified sentences 'every *F* is *G*' or 'some *F* is *G*' in standard first-order logic we have to use formulae containing sentence connectives, no counterparts of which occur in the surface forms of the sentences. And when we turn to a sentence like 'just two *F*s are *G*', we have to use many more expressions that do not have counterparts in surface syntax, as well as repetitions of a number that do:

(23) $\exists x \exists y ((x \neq y \bullet Fx \bullet Fy \bullet Gx \bullet Gy) \bullet \forall z ((Fz \bullet Gz) \supset (z = x \lor z = y)))$.

The case involving descriptions is a symptom of—and also helps us to see the severity of—a larger problem involving the use of standard first-order logic to characterize the logical forms of sentences of natural language. Similarly, if Russell's theory predicts that ambiguities of scope arise where there actually *is* ambiguity in natural language, this is a virtue rather than a vice; and if there is any 'problem', it concerns only the fact that the use of Russell's abbreviatory conventions may, on occasion, require the insertion of scope indicators in order to make it clear which of two (or more) unambiguous formulae in primitive notation is being abbreviated by a particular pseudo-formula. It is nonsense to claim that Russell's Theory of Descriptions suffers from complications concerning scope.

For the purposes of providing a systematic semantics for natural language we can capture Russell's insights about the logic and semantics of descriptions without using Russell's own notation or even the notation of standard first-order logic. Indeed, a more perspicuous notation is not hard to construct and is already widely used. Suppose we were to modify our simple quantificational language L'' by throwing out the two unrestricted quantifiers $\forall$ and $\exists$ (and associated rules of syntax and semantics) and bringing in two quantificational determiners '*every*' and '*some*', devices which are used to create *restricted* quantifiers. A determiner D_k combines with a formula ϕ to form a restricted quantifier $[D_k: \phi]$ such as (24) or (25):

(24) $[every_1: man\ x_1]$
(25) $[some_1: man\ x_1]$.

And a restricted quantifier $[D_k: \phi]$ combines with a formula ψ to form a formula $[D_k: \phi]\psi$, such as (26) or (27):

(26) $[every_1: man\ x_1]\ snores\ x_1$
(27) $[some_1: man\ x_1]\ snores\ x_1$.

Adding axioms such as the following will suffice for defining truth:

(28) $\forall_s \forall k \forall \phi \forall \psi ([every_k: \phi]\psi$ is satisfied by s iff ψ is satisfied by every sequence satisfying ϕ and differing from s at most in the kth position)
(29) $\forall s \forall k \forall \phi \forall \psi ([some_k: \phi]\psi$ is satisfied by s iff ψ is satisfied by some sequence satisfying ϕ and differing from s at most in the kth position).

In this system, we could represent 'no man snores' as (30) or (31) (henceforth I shall often make use of the convention I adopted in earlier work of dropping the variable inside the quantifier and attaching its subscript directly to the predicate[16]):

(30) $\sim [some_1: man_1]\ snores\ x_1$
(31) $[every_1: man_1] \sim snores\ x_1$.

But of course we could make for a more direct mapping between sentences of English and our new formalism by adding to the latter a new quantificational determiner '*no*' and an appropriate axiom. The formula in (32) would be subject to the axiom in (33):

(32) $[no_1: man_1]\ snores\ x_1$
(33) $\forall s \forall k \forall \phi \forall \psi ([no_k: \phi]\psi$ is satisfied by s iff ψ is satisfied by no sequence satisfying ϕ and differing from s at most in the kth position satisfies).

This might be particularly useful if we are interested in constructing a systematic semantic theory for English that respects facts about syntactic structure uncovered by theoretical linguistics.

---

[16] As Graff (forthcoming) notes, this allows us to get a little closer to English not just in a superficial sense but ultimately in allowing us to see determiners as attaching to predicates in a logical sense. Of course, this presupposes tailoring axioms of satisfaction for predicates accordingly.

Now what about definite descriptions? The particular formalism and notation of *Principia* are not essential to the Theory of Descriptions itself, except in so far as one has orthogonal philosophical aims, as Russell did. Indeed, the theory was presented in 'On Denoting' without this particular formalism and notation; but in *Principia* the theory was presented much more clearly *with* it. It would be a mistake to equate the theory with that particular formal implementation itself, despite the fact that the consequences of the theory, in that notation, are exhausted by the consequences of *14.01 and *14.02. If we want, we can use the formal language containing restricted quantifiers, *i.e.* we can use the following formula to represent 'the king snores':

(34) $[some_1: king_1]$ $[every_2: king_2]$ $(x_1 = x_2 \bullet x_1$ *snores).*

To do this would *not* be to present a serious *alternative* to the Theory of Descriptions; it would be to choose a language other than that of *Principia* in which to state it.

However, there is no need for anything as indirect as (34). In English, the word 'the' is a one-place determiner just like 'every', 'some', 'no', 'most', and so on; so we could add to our new formalism yet another quantificational determiner *the* and an appropriate axiom. The formula in (35) would be subject to the axiom in (36), which captures Russell's insights perfectly:

(35) $[the_1: king_1]$ *snores* x_1
(36) $\forall s \forall k \forall \phi \forall \psi ([the$ $x_k: \phi] \psi$ is satisfied by s iff ψ is satisfied by the sequence satisfying ϕ and differing from s at most in the kth position also satisfies).

I have used an English determiner 'the' in the metalanguage so as to make (36) congruent with the axioms for the other determiners in (28), (29), and (33) above. The right-hand side of (36) is to be understood as equivalent to "ϕ is satisfied by exactly one sequence differing from s at most in the kth position and ψ is satisfied by every such sequence".[17] The viability of a formal language containing restricted quantifiers shows that the language of *Principia* is not an essential ingredient of a theory of quantification and logical form; in particular, it is not an essential ingredient of the Theory of Descriptions construed as a component of a systematic semantics for natural language.

---

[17] See Neale (1992). The axiom can be simplified; however, questions about the syntax, semantics, and systematicity of the axioms (and the metalanguage in which they are stated), as well as questions about the distinction between semantics and analysis have a considerable bearing on the proper form of any truth definition that is to play a serious role in a semantical theory for natural language and also on the characterization of that role itself.

The restricted quantifier implementation of the theory I have outlined has a great deal to recommend it. For one thing, it draws out the syntactical and semantical similarities between 'every', 'some', 'a', 'the', and so on; for another, it makes the scope of a description utterly transparent in the formal notation. For example, Russell's (37) and (38) will be rendered as (37′) and (38′) respectively:

(37) $\sim [\imath x Fx]\, G\imath x Fx$
(38) $[\imath x Fx]\sim G\imath x Fx$

(37′) $\sim [the\ x\colon Fx]\, Gx$
(38′) $[the\ x\colon Fx]\sim Gx.$

To use a restricted quantifier notation in connection with descriptions is to make a move that Russell failed to make when he did not simplify his abbreviatory notation in the way I mentioned earlier, according to which (37) reduces to (37″) and (38) to (38″):

(37″) $\sim [\imath x Fx]\, Gx$
(38″) $[\imath x Fx]\sim Gx.$

Russell's failure to make this elementary simplification has already been explained.

Many English sentences containing two or more quantified noun phrases admit of distinct readings, i.e. readings with distinct truth-conditions; and in many cases the readings can be captured in terms of relative scope; thus 'every man likes some woman' can be read as either (39′) and (39″):

(39′) $[every_1\colon man_1][some_2\colon woman_2]x_1\ likes\ x_2$
(39″) $[some_2\colon woman_2][every_1\colon man_1]x_1\ likes\ x_2.$

Permuting quantifiers does not always result in a difference in truth-conditions. For example, the truth-conditions of 'every man likes every woman' are unaffected by relative scope (reflecting the fact that $\forall x_1 \forall x_2\, Rx_1x_2$ and $\forall x_2 \forall x_1\, Rx_1x_2$ are equivalent):

(40′) $[every_1\colon man_1][every_2\colon woman_2]x_1\ likes\ x_2$
(40″) $[every_2\colon woman_2][every_1\colon man_1]x_1\ likes\ x_2.$

None the less, (40′) and (40″) are distinct formulae (just as $\forall x_1 \forall x_2\, Rx_1x_2$ and $\forall x_2 \forall x_1\, Rx_1x_2$ are), and to the extent that quantifiers in natural language need to be assigned scope for interpretation, we can say that 'every man likes every woman' is structurally ambiguous without being truth-conditionally ambiguous. Sameness of quantificational determiner is neither necessary nor sufficient for a scope ambiguity to engender a truth-conditional ambiguity. 'Most men like most women' is truth-conditionally ambiguous; 'every man likes the queen' is not (as noted by Whitehead and Russell). Although the original motivation in logic for positing ambiguities of scope involved ambiguity of truth-conditions, clearly the right strategy for thinking about these matters *now*, within the context of a general theory of quantifier scope, is to treat structural ambiguity seriously whether or not it is of truth-conditional import.[18]

Analogues of (37′) and (38′) can be used to represent the notorious ambiguities that arise in natural language when non-extensional connectives or verbs of propositional attitude occur with definite descriptions. For example, it should be possible to characterize the so-called *de dicto* and *de re* readings of (41) and (42):[19]

(41) George wonders whether Scott is the author of *Waverley*
    a. *George wonders whether* [the_1: x_1 *authored* Waverley] *Scott* = x_1
    b. [the_1: x_1 *authored* Waverley] *George wonders whether Scott* = x_1

(42) Necessarily, nine is the number of planets
    a. $\Box$ [the_1: x_1 *numbers the planets*] $9 = x_1$
    b. [the_1: x_1 *numbers the planets*] $\Box 9 = x_1$.

The claim that (41) and (42) are ambiguous in this way has gained the status of something of an orthodoxy and has gone largely unchallenged for decades, as has the claim that the ambiguities multiply in the obvious way when (41) and (42) are further embedded, as in, say "Mary doubts that George wonders whether Scott is the author of *Waverley*."[20] In interesting recent work, Delia Graff (forthcoming) has challenged the orthodoxy, claiming that a sentence in which a description combines with the copula to form a verb phrase is *always* equivalent to the reading the Russellian obtains by giving the description small scope. Among other things, this entails the rejection of both (41b) and (42b) as genuine readings of (41) and (42), which might strike some as a disastrous result.

---

[18] This is a matter on which Linsky (1992, 2000) seems confused.

[19] Adding an appropriate axiom even for œ is not straightforward; difficult choices have to be made which have repercussions for the rest of the axiomatization and the philosophical status of the axioms themselves.

[20] I say largely because Quine (1947, 1953e, 1961, 1980) has attempted to show that (48b) is unintelligible, at least when $\Box$ is read as expressing logical or analytic necessity.

Graff's proposal appears to have been designed, at least in part, with the aim of treating instances of the negated form "*a* is not the *F*" as unambiguous, the description always understood as taking small scope.[21] The issues here are not always in the sharpest of relief, but ultimately they do not seem to support this stringent proposal. Consider the following:

(43) Cicero is Tully
(44) Cicero is the winner
(45) The winner is Cicero.

It is commonly—but not universally—held that the copula in (43) expresses identity, the whole sentence understood as the relational:

(43′) Cicero = Tully.[22]

This raises a question as to its syntax. (43′) is usually assumed to have a symmetrical structure; but linguistic theory is more likely to favour an asymmetric structure in which "is Tully" is a constituent verb phrase:

(43″) [$_S$ [$_{NP}$ Cicero] [$_{VP}$ is [$_{NP}$ Tully]]].

There is nothing in this structure, of course, that prohibits its being *interpreted* as true if and only if (49′) is true.

It has been common practice for some time to see the copula as behaving in the same way in (44) and (45), to see these sentences as differing from (43) only in the presence of quantification induced by the descriptions.[23] On such an account, (44) and (45) will be read as (44′) and (45′) respectively:

(44′) [*the*$_1$: *winner* x_1] *Cicero* = x_1
(45′) [*the*$_1$: *winner* x_1] x_1 = *Cicero*.

---

[21] It is often said that the indefinite counterpart, "*a* is not an *F*", is unambiguous, that if "an *F*" is a quantified noun phrase then it is one that insists on small scope when it combines with the copula in this way. One way of accounting for this would be to take the seemingly unreflective practice in logic and philosophy of treating indefinite descriptions in this position as ordinary predicates as basically correct. Graff's article is (roughly) an attempt to extend such a predicational analysis of indefinities to definites.

[22] See e.g. Russell (1905), Smullyan (1947, 1948), and especially Kripke's (1971) discussions of (49), "Saul Kripke is Saul Kripke", "Hesperus is Phosphorous", and other examples.

[23] Again, see Russell (1905), Smullyan (1948), and Kripke (1971). I followed suit in *Descriptions*. In particular, I treated sentences of the forms "*a* is the *F*" and "the *F* is *a*" occurring in psychological and modal statements such as (41) and (42) in this traditional way. Given my long—and glaringly misguided—discussion of (42) and similar modal sentences, it is odd that Graff claims I did not discuss descriptions combining with the copula (which, following tradition, I viewed as expressing identity in such contexts, wrongly if Graff is right).

If one were to give up the idea that the copula expresses identity in (44) and (45), certainly one would be strongly inclined to give it up for (43) too, and vice versa. Graff provides an interesting argument for giving it up in (44) based on an alleged asymmetry between (46) and (47) (the negation of (44)), which, on a rote Russellian account, should be ambiguous according as the description or the negation takes larger scope:

(46) Cicero did not meet the winner
      a. $\sim [\mathit{the_1}\colon \mathit{winner}\ x_1]\ \mathit{Cicero\ met\ x_1}$
      b. $[\mathit{the_1}\colon \mathit{winner}\ x_1]\ \sim \mathit{Cicero\ met\ x_1}$

(47) Cicero is not the winner
      a. $\sim [\mathit{the_1}\colon \mathit{winner}\ x_1]\ \mathit{Cicero} = x_1$
      b. $[\mathit{the_1}\colon \mathit{winner}\ x_1]\ \sim \mathit{Cicero} = x_1.$

Graff feels that although (46) is ambiguous in this way, (47) has to be read as (47*a*); the feeling that (47*b*) is a genuine reading is the product of illusion and explained in terms of conversational implicature.[24] She proposes to obtain what she regards as the right result by treating "is the F", as it occurs in structures like (44) and (47) as a complex predicate (Y*x*: *Fx*) contextually defined as follows:

$$\Sigma[(Yx\colon Fx)\alpha] =_{\mathrm{df}} \Sigma[F\alpha \bullet \forall x(Fx \supset x = \alpha)].$$

Assuming existential generalization, obviously Graff's analysis of (50) is equivalent to the Russellian (44′) for it says that Cicero wins (Cicero is a winner) and every winner is Cicero. It is in connection with (47) that the analyses diverge, the Russellian analysis serving up (47a) and (47b) to Graff's solitary reading, equivalent to (47a).

Similarly, where the Russellian quantificational analysis delivers (41a) and (41b) as readings of (41), and (42a) and (42b) as readings of (42), Graff's delivers only (readings equivalent to) the (a) readings. There is a hefty tradition in modal logic of taking both (a) and (b) readings seriously; but perhaps the tradition is wrong. If Graff's Gricean explanation of the "illusion" of (47b) could be transposed to explain the "illusions" cf (41b) and (42b), then her position might look more attractive.

But there is also the matter of (43) and (45). Graff's analysis of sentences containing "the F" after the copula is not meant to be ad hoc; it is meant to flow directly from a comprehensive account of "the F". To this extent, it

---

[24] See Grice (1989), who has a variety of interesting things to say about implicatures involving negation and descriptions in the chapter 'Presupposition and Conversational Implicature'.

should declare (44) and (45) equivalent, but it should declare (48) and (49), in which the descriptions occur in subject position, ambiguous (unless some sort of implicature defence is to be mounted again):

    (48) the winner is not Cicero
    (49) necessarily, the number of planets is nine.[25]

In the absence of strong evidence to the contrary, I shall continue with the traditional policy of seeing the descriptions as capable of taking large in the examples just examined.

IV   Incomplete Symbols and Contextual Definition

Some authors have questioned whether a restricted quantifier analysis of definite descriptions is 'truly Russellian', i.e. whether it is compatible with Russell's idea that descriptions are *incomplete symbols*. The matter is of some historical importance, and enough of the literature evinces confusion about the relevant philosophical and technical issues for it to warrant some attention.[26]

---

[25] Note also that if 'is' is to be treated identically in (43)–(45) and (47)–(49) one of the advantages Graff sees her proposal as having over a straightforward Russellian proposal is that it avoids multiplying the meanings of the copula in verb phrases—the semantics of, say, 'is Cicero' ought to be deducible by the theorist from the semantics of 'Cicero' and Graff's semantics for 'is the *F*', and it should, on one of 'necessarily', declare (i) and (ii) equivalent: (i) necessarily, Cicero is Tully; (ii) necessarily, Tully is Cicero. It is unclear how the proposal as it stands can succeed in doing this. Although Graff's paper is now in press, she informs me that her position should be viewed as tentative and that a more detailed or modified version may appear in future work.

[26] The problems seem to have begun with Evans's (1977, 1982) confused claim that the use of a *binary* quantification $[the_i]$ $(Fx_i; Gx_i)$ to represent 'the *F* is *G*' is compatible with Russell's claim that descriptions are incomplete symbols whereas the use of a unary restricted quantification $[the_i: Fx_i] Gx_i$ is not. (Evans argues (fallaciously) that certain facts about anaphora that can be captured using binary quantifiers cannot be captured using unary restricted quantifiers. For discussion, see Neale (1992).) A variety of related mistakes about incomplete symbols can be found in recent work by Linsky (1992, 2000), including the false claim that because it allows descriptions to contain demonstrative elements, 'Neale's distinction between descriptions and "purely referential expressions" is not an exclusive one' (1992: 683 n. 1). Apparently, Linsky has failed to appreciate the distinction between *being* a referential expression and *containing* a referential expression as a constituent: 'the table over *there*', 'the car behind *this one*' and 'the king of *France*' all contain referential expressions (italicized) but that does not alter the fact that the Russellian is treating them as quantificational noun phrases.

Are Russell's definitions *14.01 and *14.02 meant to have ontological import, to be reductive? Or are they intended merely to set out the truth-conditional contributions of descriptions? Or does the truth lie somewhere in between? The matter is complicated by Russell's prose, which includes the claims (i) that descriptions are 'incomplete symbols', (ii) that they 'disappear on analysis', and (iii) that they 'have no meaning in isolation'. Upon examination, it seems that requiring a contextual definition, being incomplete, and disappearing on analysis are quite distinct concepts. An important range of expressions (including quantifiers and connectives) are incomplete symbols and at least some require contextual definitions (on at least one construal) yet do not disappear on analysis. Furthermore, descriptions are incomplete symbols even in systems of restricted quantification.

At the time Russell was arguing for the Theory of Descriptions, he espoused what is often called a 'realist' theory of meaning, according to which the meaning of an expression is some entity or other, the entity for which it *stands*.[27] Other things being equal, singular terms stand for particulars; predicates (common nouns, verbs, adjectives) stand for universals; and true sentences stand for facts. But what about quantified noun phases ('denoting phrases', as Russell calls them) and also logical connectives?

Quantified noun phrases do not have meanings in Russell's sense: they do not *stand for* things in the way names and predicates do. This is made abundantly clear as early as 'On Denoting':

Everything, nothing, and *something* are not assumed to have any meaning in isolation, but a meaning is assigned to *every* proposition in which they occur. This is the principle of the theory of denoting I wish to advocate: that denoting phrases never have any meaning in themselves, but that every proposition in whose verbal expression they occur has a meaning. (1905: 42)

It requires no great effort to construct semantic theories according to which denoting phrases *do* stand for things, for example, higher-order functions as in some versions of the theory of generalized quantification stand for higher-order functions. Given the intimate connection between his theory of meaning and his theory of knowledge—in particular, the link expressed by his Principle of Acquaintance, which states that every proposition which we can understand must be composed wholly of constituents with which we are acquainted—when wearing his epistemological rather than his mathematical hat Russell seems to have thought that no symbol should stand for a function, and he

---

[27] See e.g. Sainsbury (1979, 1993). My interpretation of Russell in this section is influenced by Sainsbury.

consequently accepted that there are 'meaningful' expressions that do not mean, i.e. do not stand for anything—namely, the logical constants and quantificational noun phrases.[28] Definite descriptions belong to the latter class.

Here are three apparently different things we might say about a symbol x: (i) x is incomplete (or has no 'meaning in isolation'); (ii) x's semantic power is given by a 'definition in use' (a 'contextual definition'); (iii) x disappears on analysis. Many commentators view (i)–(iii) as three ways of expressing the same point, but this is surely incorrect. Let us begin with certain key passages from pp. 66–7 of *Principia* (Whitehead and Russell, 1925):

By an 'incomplete' symbol we mean a symbol which is not supposed to have any meaning in isolation but is only defined in certain contexts.

Such symbols have what may be called a 'definition in use.'

. . . we define the *use* of [such a symbol], but [the symbol] itself remains without meaning.

This distinguishes such symbols from what (in a generalized sense) we may call *proper names*: 'Socrates,' for example, stands for a certain man, and therefore has a meaning by itself, without the need of any context. If we supply a context, as in 'Socrates is mortal,' these words express a fact of which Socrates himself is a constituent: there is a certain object, namely Socrates, which does have the property of mortality, and this object is a constituent of the complex fact which we assert when we say 'Socrates is mortal.'

Where there is talk of descriptions, we must be careful to distinguish those occurring in sentences of English ('the king of France', etc.) from those occurring in Russell's abbreviations of formulae of the language of *Principia* ('$\imath x F x$' etc.). It is surely clear in Russell's remarks that what makes a symbol *incomplete* is the fact that it is not the sort of expression that stands for something. Now certainly there are grammatical, notational, and analytical repercussions of a symbol's being incomplete, for example where noun phrases—the sorts of expressions that may occupy the grammatical subject position of a sentence—are concerned:

Whenever the grammatical subject of a proposition can be supposed not to exist without rendering the proposition meaningless, it is plain that the grammatical

---

[28] The Principle of Acquaintance is stated in more or less the same way by Russell (1905: 56; 1911: 159; 1912: 32). Russell does, on occasion, say that quantifiers and connectives 'involve' logical notions and that in order to use these expressions intelligibly we must grasp the notions involved. This does not, of course, entail that the expressions stand for objects.

subject is not a proper name, *i.e.* not a name directly representing an object. Thus in all such cases, the proposition must be capable of being so analysed that what was the grammatical subject shall have disappeared.

Russell is here using 'proposition' in the sense of 'sentence', and the passage is fraught with characteristic use-mention sloppiness: When he says that 'Whenever the grammatical subject of a proposition can be supposed not to exist' Russell is trying to avoid saying: 'Whenever the grammatical subject of a proposition can be supposed to *stand for something* that does not exist', which is obviously problematic. What Russell means is: 'Whenever the grammatical subject of a proposition can be supposed not to *stand for something*'. On this account the grammatical subjects in each of the following sentences are not proper names: 'the round square does not exist', 'it is raining', 'there is a fly in my soup'. And two things follow from this: (*a*) they are incomplete symbols, and (*b*) if the sentences are to have truth-values, they must be 'capable of being so analysed that what was the grammatical subject shall have disappeared'. It is important to distinguish these claims. Here is what I think we can extract from Russell's discussions: (i) There are three types of expression that stand for things, namely, proper names, predicates, and sentences (standing for particulars, universals, and facts, respectively); any other symbol is incomplete. (ii) An expression that does not stand for something is an incomplete symbol. (iii) A definite description is neither a predicate nor a sentence; so if a description stands for something it must be a proper name. (iv) If the grammatical subject of a sentence can be supposed not to stand for something without rendering the sentence incapable of standing for a fact, the grammatical subject is not a proper name. (v) A definite description can be supposed not to stand for something without rendering the sentence incapable of standing for a fact; so a definite description is not a proper name. (vi) So a description is an incomplete symbol. (vii) If the grammatical subject of a sentence can be supposed not to stand for something without rendering the sentence incapable of standing for a fact, then the sentence must be 'capable of being so analysed that what was the grammatical subject shall have disappeared'. (viii) So a sentence with a definite description as grammatical subject must be 'capable of being so analysed that what was the grammatical subject shall have disappeared'.

So (*a*) if *x* disappears on analysis, then *x* is an incomplete symbol; but (*b*) it is not the case that if *x* is an incomplete symbol, then *x* disappears on analysis. In particular, quantifiers and connectives are incomplete symbols, but they do not disappear on analysis. Indeed, some of them appear in the analyses of sentences whose grammatical subjects *do* disappear on analysis; for example, in the analysis of sentences whose grammatical subjects are definite descriptions. In abbreviatory notation, (50) is represented as (50′), which is shorthand for (50″):

(50)   the F does not exist

(50′) $\sim E! \imath x Fx$

(50″) $\sim \exists x (\forall y (Fy \equiv y = x)$.

'Here,' says Russell, 'the apparent grammatical subject ['$\imath x Fx$'] has disappeared; thus in [(50′)] ['$\imath x Fx$'] is an incomplete symbol' (Whitehead and Russell, 1925: 66). The point here is that an incomplete symbol cannot appear as a 'logical subject', i.e. it cannot appear *logically* as a subject expression—i.e. more generally, it cannot appear as the argument of a predicate in any genuine formula of the language of analysis. (This cannot be definitional because *predicates* also do not show up in such positions but are not incomplete symbols.) Says Russell: ' . . . all phrases (other than propositions) containing the word *the* (in the singular) are incomplete symbols: they have a meaning in use, but not in isolation' (p. 67).

A contextual definition does not seem to be exactly a stipulative or an explicative definition.[29] If we look back at *14.01 and *14.02, there is a stipulative element to them, but this is really because they look as though they are stipulating a certain type of abbreviation, as far as the formal language of *Principia* is concerned. There is also an explicative element because Russell takes his contextual definitions to embody his analysis of definite descriptions in ordinary language, or at least a part (or form) of ordinary language precise or constrained enough to use in philosophical discussion. And I take it when Russell says descriptions are 'defined in use' he means that his contextual definitions explicate their semantic powers. So these contextual definitions are real hybrids. Notice also that they involve something 'disappearing on analysis', namely, expressions of the form $\imath x \phi$.

The question we need to ask now is whether contextual definitions of this ilk are characteristic of expressions 'defined in use'. Russell says that his definition of • in terms of v and $\sim$ is a contextual definition. A symbol is introduced as an abbreviation, the semantic power of that symbol is explicated, and the symbol disappears on analysis. If we were so inclined, we could provide contextual definitions for *all* of our logical vocabulary (to deal with negation straightforwardly, add the Scheffer stroke to our set of connectives). But of course this would be unsatisfactory as far as the explication of semantic powers is con-

---

[29] As noted by Kaplan (1972), who discusses the notion fruitfully.

cerned: we would have an explicative circle with no way in. It is here that notions like analysis and reduction begin to loom large. For Russell, *14.01 and *14.02 are useful contextual definitions because they define new symbols in terms of primitive symbols of his formal language. Similarly, for '•', '≡' and '=', which are not primitive but defined symbols in *Principia Mathematica*. But of course what is primitive for one purpose may not be for another. Rewriting the whole of *Principia* using the Scheffer stroke would certainly *reduce* the number of symbol types in play and so, in one way, simplify the execution the project. But of course doing this would add insurmountably to comprehension: as Russell himself stressed, negation, conjunction, and alternation are more primitive *psychologically*; and to that extent they are more primitive *semantically* in the sense of semantics that most interests people working on the theory of meaning for natural language.

What are we to make, then, of Russell's talk of quantifiers and connectives being 'defined in use'? We must, I think, either regard contextual definitions and definitions in use as rather different notions or else accept (more plausibly) that Russell had two closely related notions in mind when he talked ambiguously of contextual definitions, notions he had not cleanly separated. We might think of the truth-tables for ~ and v (or axioms based on those tables) as showing us the semantic powers of these symbols; and since they do this by invoking whole sentences—i.e. fuller expressions in which the symbols are *used*—we might think of these as definitions in use; but these are not what people have standardly understood as 'contextual definitions'.[30] We must conclude I think, that when Russell talks of 'definitions in use' he has at least two things in mind, and to the extent that there is a common core it is that contextual definitions are for symbols that are *incomplete*; they are ways of explaining the semantic powers of symbols that do not stand for things, i.e. symbols that do not stand for particulars or universals (or facts).

The proposition expressed by 'the *F* is *G*' is the general proposition that there is one and only one *F* and everything that is *F* is also *G*. That is, the truth-conditions of 'the *F* is *G*' can be given by a quantificational formula, which contains quantifiers and predicates but no singular term corresponding to the grammatical subject 'the *F*'. And this is what Russell means by saying that the *proposition* has no *logical subject*, even though the *sentence* has a *grammatical subject*; and what he means by saying that the sentence's *grammatical form* is

---

[30] The so-called contextual definition that Russell provides for the inverted-comma *of*-notation (see n. 2 above) does not use whole formulae at all: it looks a lot like a very straightforward abbreviation technique.

not a good indication of its *logical form* (or the logical form of the proposition the sentence expresses). The proposition is not about an object at all; it is about the relationship between two properties, F and G: exactly one thing has F, and nothing has F while lacking G. As we might put it today—but in a way not at all consonant with Russell's aims—'some F is G' is true if and only if the SOME relation holds between F and G; and 'the F is G' is true if and only if the THE relation holds between them (this idea has more bite once the Theory of Descriptions is properly located with a theory of quantification in natural language, such as the theory of restricted quantification outlined above).

The claim that treatments of descriptions in terms of restricted quantification involve abandoning Russell's view that descriptions are incomplete symbols is confused.[31] Certainly one is at liberty to interpret restricted quantifiers using the resources of generalized quantifier theory so that restricted quantifiers *stand for* things (typically, higher-order functions). But such an interpretation is not forced upon the theorist who uses the notation of restricted quantification any more than a Tarskian or a Fregean or a substitutional interpretation is forced upon a theorist who uses a standard notation for the unrestricted quantifiers $\exists$ and $\forall$.[32] Indeed there are recent traditions that provide either Tarskian or Fregean analyses of restricted and binary quantifiers.[33] Although Russell's Theory of Descriptions is often put forward as the paradigm case of a theory that invokes a distinction between *grammatical form* and *logical form*, ironically there is a sense in which it preserves symmetry: 'the F', 'every F', 'some F', 'no F', etc. are alike syntactically in that they are noun phrases that may occupy grammatically subject positions in surface grammar; but they are also *semantically* alike in that they are all incomplete symbols and, as their definitions in use make clear, induce quantification. On neither the account of quantification assumed by Russell nor the Tarskian account I have borrowed here do quantificational noun phrases *stand for* things. And neither the move from unrestricted to restricted quantification nor the use of a systematic *notation* for restricted quantification magically makes quantificational noun phrases start standing for things. In fact, the syntax and semantics of the particular notation I have used to represent restricted quantification

[31] The claim is made by Evans (1977, 1982) and Linsky (1992, 2000).

[32] Systems that mix restricted and unrestricted quantifiers are perfectly respectable—indeed, they may be desirable to capture all aspects of the semantics of natural language, especially where quantification over events, times, and places is involved.

[33] See (e.g.) Evans (1977, 1982), Wiggins (1980), Davies (1981), Sainsbury (1994, forthcoming), Higginbotham and May (1981), Neale (1992). I here use 'binary' in the sense of Evans and Wiggins (see n. 21).

might be thought to *highlight* the fact that I am treating quantified noun phrases as incomplete symbols. In the cases that are of any interest to us, the formula ψ with which a description $[the_i: \phi]$ combines to form a formula will contain a variable x_i that the quantifier binds:

(51) $[the_i: king_i]x_i$ *likes Cicero.*

The variable x_i occupies the 'logical subject position' of the formula x_i *likes Cicero* and, so to speak, marks the position upon which the quantifier has an impact, the position that, in effect, represents the spot the quantified noun phrase occupies in surface syntax. Since *Cicero* stands for an object (the same object, whatever the sequence) it is a complete symbol:

(52) $\forall s(\text{Ref}(Cicero, s) = \text{Cicero})$.

This axiom just says that the referent of *Cicero*, relative to any sequence s, is Cicero. Now perhaps there is a sense in which the *variable* in (51) might be construed as *complete-with-respect-to-a-sequence* by virtue of standing for an object in its own relativized way:

(53) $\forall s \forall k(\text{Ref}(x_i, s) = s_i)$.

But however you look at it, the way I have set things up neither the English definite description 'the king' nor the restricted quantifier $[the_i: king\ x_i]$ that binds the variable in (51) is a complete symbol. Given the axioms I have used, the quantifier does not even *purport* to stand for an object, not even when relativized to sequences. There is no interesting sense, then, in which the restricted quantifier treatment of descriptions conflicts with Russell's conception of descriptions as incomplete symbols. It is the element of quantification in 'the F is G', 'every F is G', and 'some F is G' that creates a gap between grammatical form and so-called "logical form".[34] And quantification, whether

---

[34] In recent work, which incorporates part of his 1992 review, Linsky (2000) seems to glimpse this in places, but his overall discussion is still marred by a misunderstanding about Russell's notion of an incomplete symbol. It is probably impossible to fully untangle Linsky's discussion as it is replete with intersecting confusions about truth conditions, the logical forms of sentences, the logical forms of arguments, and the relation between constituents of sentences and components of the facts that make them true, as well as strange talk of the logical forms of names and descriptions. Much of the trouble seems to stem from confusing properties of 'the' with properties of 'the F', confusing properties 'the F' with properties of '$[the_i F]$' (which, unlike 'the F', must be connected to an overt variable to do its job), a use-mention confusion that manifests itself in a pervasive equivocation about the meanings of the words 'proposition' and 'constituent' (on some occurrences 'sentence' and 'phrase' seem better; on others non-linguistic interpretations seem to be called for; on still others *neither* seems correct), and an

unrestricted, restricted, or binary, can be handled perfectly well while taking denoting phrases to be incomplete symbols.

V Ontological versus Semantic Elimination

The idea that certain words are syncategorematic, defined in linguistic context rather than in isolation, is an old one, much favoured by those with ontological angst. Nominalistic strands of mediaeval thought exploited this idea; so did a later nominalist, Jeremy Bentham, who called it 'definition by paraphrase' and deployed it in connection with seemingly categorematic expressions that he

equivocation about the meaning of 'logical form' (e.g., Linsky says that 'Neale argues that Russell's analysis is not the correct logical form' (p. 13); if by 'the correct logical form' Linsky means the assignation of a quantificational structure with Russell's truth conditions, then the claim is obviously false; if he means by it the particular representation of that quantificational structure, with Russell's truth conditions, within a system of restricted quantification, his claim is trivially true; either way it is uninteresting). Linsky seems to place too much emphasis on Russell's particular notation rather than the logical and philosophical ideas behind them, and this seems to blind him to the fact that even the expressions '$\bullet$' '$\equiv$' and '$=$' occurring in Russell's $\exists x (\forall y (\phi(y) \equiv y = x) \bullet \psi(x))$ are to be analysed away at some point for certain of Russell's purposes, perhaps using '$|$' if we are to take seriously comments in the Introduction to the 2nd edn. of *Principia*.

Linsky argues, correctly, that 'that Russell's project is committed to his account of definite descriptions as incomplete symbols' (2000: 13). He is quite wrong, however, when he claims that in *Descriptions* I hold that Russell's descriptions are incomplete symbols 'simply from the want of a more sophisticated logic' (ibid.). Not only do I not make this claim, I am committed to its negation. Apparently, Linsky still does not grasp what Russell means by 'incomplete symbol', the notation of restricted quantification that I and many others use, and the relationship between the notation of restricted quantification and the particular semantics of generalized quantifiers. The fact that Russell views descriptions as incomplete symbols has nothing to do with the fact that he does not have restricted quantifiers in his system, for the simple reason that a restricted quantifier '$[the_i : F_i]$' is just as much an incomplete symbol as Russell's '$\iota x F x$' in systems in which quantifiers do not stand for things, such as in the Tarskian systems I have been using. Linsky seems to think that because the restricted quantifier '$[the_i : F_i]$' is a syntactic constituent of '$[the_i : F_i] \psi$' (in the same way in which the unrestricted '$\exists x$' is a constituent of '$\exists x \psi$'), a semantic theory is somehow *required* to treat it as standing for something. But this is simply not so. It all depends on the overall semantic theory within which an account of restricted quantification is located. Some semanticists view such quantifiers as standing for things, others—notoriously, those of a Davidsonian persuasion—will not. One can only suppose that Linksy has something very different in mind from Russell when he uses the phrase 'incomplete symbol'. As far as I can ascertain, my interpretation of Russell squares with Kaplan's (1972) on matters pertaining to incomplete symbols, logical form, and contextual definition, Why Linsky sees Kaplan and me as taking opposing sides in a fruitless controversy is a mystery.

felt referred to 'fictions', amongst which he included qualities, relations, classes, and indeed all of the entities of mathematics. Bentham's strategy was to provide a systematic method for converting any sentence containing a dubious term X into a certain type of sentence that is X-free, thereby revealing X to be syncategorematic, despite grammatical appearances. And his point was to avoid embarrassing ontological commitments whilst still getting some basic grammatical work out of terms of dubious denotation.

These days, the method of paraphrasis is commonly called the method of *contextual definition*, and it impinged upon recent philosophy largely through the work of Frege and then Russell, most famously through the latter's Theory of Descriptions. We are apt to take this for granted today, but occasionally someone like Quine reminds us of what has happened:

Contextual definition precipitated a revolution in semantics: less sudden perhaps than the Copernican revolution in astronomy, but like it in being a shift of center. The primary vehicle of meaning is seen no longer as the word, but as the sentence. Terms, like grammatical particles, mean by contributing to the meaning of the sentences that contain them. The heliocentrism propounded by Copernicus was not obvious and neither is this . . . the meanings of words are abstractions from the truth conditions of sentences that contain them.

It was the recognition of this semantic primacy of sentences that gave us contextual definition, and vice versa. I attributed this to Bentham. Generations later we find Frege celebrating the primacy of sentences, and Russell giving contextual definition its fullest exploitation in technical logic. (1981: 69)

According to Quine, ordinary (constant) singular terms are ultimately redundant: any sentence containing an ordinary singular term is replaceable (without loss and in a manner suggested by the Theory of Descriptions) by a sentence that is term-free. Ordinary singular terms, names, for example, are no more than 'frills' (1970: 25) or practical 'conventions of abbreviation' (1941: 41); contextual definition is our 'reward', as Quine sees it, for 'for recognising that the unit of communication is the sentence not the word' (1981: 75).

Eliminating certain linguistic expressions or forms can certainly facilitate attempts to dispense with entities of one form or another, or with specific entities belonging to an otherwise acceptable category. But the tight connection between semantics and ontology does not justify equating linguistic and ontological elimination. In connection with Russell's Theory of Descriptions, Gödel (1944), Quine (1966), and no doubt others, have evinced a tendency to run the two together. The difference is most clearly seen in connection with Russell's views about classes, on the one hand, and descriptions, on the other. By contextually defining class *expressions*, Russell defined away *classes* themselves (so to speak). In contrast, by contextually defining descriptions, he defined away entities (so to speak) purporting to belong to the category of objects (for example, the king of France and the round square); but he did not define away the relevant *category*. In the form Russell presents it—which is constrained by notation and the choice of primitive symbols—the Theory of Descriptions eliminates a class of apparent singular terms, sentences containing them being replaced by sentences containing variables, unrestricted quantifiers, connectives, and the identity sign. (Using devices of restricted quantification, the same class of apparent singular terms is eliminated, sentences containing them being replaced by sentences containing variables and restricted quantifiers.) There is no direct ontological elimination because the entities the variables range over are not eliminated.

Russell certainly deployed his Theory of Descriptions to ontological benefit, but it was not an integral feature of the theory that certain types of entities could be defined away contextually. The chief ontological benefit for Russell was that it allowed him to treat certain sentences as true or false without seeing their grammatical subjects (or grammatical direct objects, for that matter) as standing for things that don't exist, an idea he rightly came to regard with repugnance. This gave him a basic ontology of particulars, universals, and facts.

Russell's semantics for descriptive phrases requires the postulation of no new entities, avoids problematic existence assumptions and truth-value gaps, provides a treatment of descriptions within first-order quantification theory with identity, and captures a range of inferences involving descriptions as a matter of first-order logic (for example, the inferences flowing from the fact that "the F is G" entails "there is at least one F", "there is at most one F", "there is at least one G", "some F is G", and "every F is G". As Gödel (1944) puts it, by defining the meaning of sentences involving descriptions in accordance with *14.01 and *14.02, Russell 'avoids in his logical system any axioms about the particle "the," i.e., the analyticity of the theorems about "the" is made explicit; they can be shown to follow from the explicit definition of the meaning of sentences involving "the"' (p. 130).

These evident virtues have led to numerous examinations of its potential application to noun phrases other than those of the form "the F", for example possessives ("Socrates' wife", "Socrates' death"), ordinary proper names ("Socrates"), *that*-clauses ("that Socrates died in prison"), demonstratives ("that", "this vase"), indexical pronouns ("I", "you"), anaphoric pronouns ("it" as it occurs in, e.g., "John gave Mary a vase; he had purchased it at Sotheby's").[35]

There are two reasons for this. The first stems from a somewhat a priori desire to eliminate singular terms, a desire that appears to be a reflex of the linguistic counterpart of a principle of ontological parsimony. The second is more empirical in nature. In the course of providing an adequate semantics of natural language and an account of many logical features of natural language, the possibility of analysing problematic noun phrases in terms of Russellian descriptions has promised instant solutions to nagging logical and ontological problems.

Quine has interesting ideas about the elimination of singular terms in connection with Russell's Theory of Descriptions. As an account of descriptive phrases, he sees only logical and philosophical good coming from it. Part of the appeal for Quine is that on this account descriptions are analysed in terms of the well-understood devices of first-order extensional logic. Secondly, he is happy with the idea that ordinary proper names can be 'trivially' reconstrued as descriptions—and thereby analysed in accordance with Russell's theory. Names are 'frills', he says, and can be omitted, 'a convenient redundancy' (1970: 25). Following Wittgenstein in the *Tractatus* (5.441, 5.47), he says that Fa is "equivalent" to $\exists x (Fx \bullet a = x)$. So the name a need never occur in a formula except in the context $a =$; but $a =$ can be rendered as a simple one-place predicate, uniquely true of the object picked out by a; so Fa can, in fact, be rendered as $\exists x (Fx \bullet Ax)$, which contains no occurrence of a; indeed all occurrences of a—or any other name—are everywhere replaceable by combinations of quantifiers, variables, connectives, and predicates.

Two minor issues arise here. The first concerns the nature of the predicate A. It must hold uniquely of the referent of a, and it is not entirely clear whether such a predicate can be drummed up without reintroducing a or implicitly appealing to some principle of linguistic, metaphysical or ostensive essentialism (for example, ostension under conditions understood as securing uniqueness). Like Church and Carnap, Quine balks at the idea that coreferring names are synonymous; now suppose $a = b$ is true; a and b should be intersubstitutable *salva veritate* (*s.v.*), at the very least in truth-functional contexts; thus A must be uniquely true of the referent of b (that is, the referent of a). But what if

---

[35] Russell (1905) treated possessive noun phrases as subject to the Theory of Descriptions. He also argued that from certain perspectives, ordinary proper names should be analysed in terms of definite descriptions (a handful of logically proper names (basically, 'this' and 'that', and in some moods 'I') resisting analysis). The precise content of this claim and its relevance to semantics, as opposed to pragmatics, are matters of debate.

a drops out of use leaving only *b* as a name of this entity? And what if *a* had never come into being in the first place, *b* being the only name of the entity in question? Unless the existence of *A* is ontologically dependent upon the existence of *a* (rather than the entity *a* refers to), in both scenarios *A* would still be true of that entity. Thus Quine's claim that (2) is equivalent to *Fa* seems to commit him to some form of essentialism, but this may turn out to be harmless if grounded in ostension.

Secondly, the Quinean "paraphrase" of *Fa* might be questioned on the following grounds: it is in the nature of an occurrence of a name that it is understood as applying to a single object; but it is not in the nature of an occurrence of a predicate that it is understood as satisfied by a single object; so the 'paraphrase deprives us of an assurance of uniqueness that the name afforded' (1970: 25). Quine's response to this point is straightforward: if we are worried about uniqueness we can import it explicitly in the way Russell does in his analyses of sentences containing definite descriptions. That is, $\exists x(Fx \bullet Ax)$ can give way to the following,

$$\exists x(\forall y(Ay \equiv x = y) \bullet Fx)$$

which is the Russellian spelling out of $F\imath x Ax$ (i.e. $F\imath x(x = a)$). So anything that can be said using names, Quine assures us, can be said using quantificational formulae because the objects that names name are the values of variables. Moreover: 'names can even be restored at pleasure, as a convenient redundancy, by a convention of abbreviation. This convention would be simply the converse of the procedure by which we just now eliminated names' (1970: 25–6). A predication such as *Fa* is an abbreviation. 'In effect,' Quine adds, 'this is somewhat the idea behind Russell's theory of singular descriptions' (p. 26).

So Quine envisions a language in which the devices of quantification, variation, identity, truth-functional connection, and predication do the work that we normally associate with names. Rightly or wrongly, he sees this idea as essentially a refinement of, or a twist on, Russell's idea that ordinary proper names can be analysed in terms of definite descriptions. The 'theoretical advantages' of analysing names as descriptions are 'overwhelming' says Quine. The whole category of singular terms is thereby swept away, so far as theory is concerned; for we know how to eliminate descriptions. Quine's quantificational analysis of names is an attempt to push Russell's Theory of Descriptions to its limit, to eliminate *all* constant singular terms. Russell resisted this extreme for epistemological reasons that were alien to Quine: he wanted to anchor singular thoughts about particulars in sense data, and to provide a means of capturing such thoughts in language using the simplest of demonstrative expressions. The Quinean extreme is out of favour today, but so is Russell's half-way house at which ordinary names are analysed descriptively. In the light of Kripke's (1971, 1980) work, it is now widely held that it is not possible to provide an adequate semantical analysis of ordinary proper names by treating them either as *synonymous* with definite descriptions or as having their *references fixed* by description.

The Theory of Descriptions intersects with Russell's theory of facts in interesting ways. For a start, since definite descriptions are treated quantificationally, the sentence 'the king is mortal' stands for a *general* fact, one whose conditions of individuation make no reference to any particular individual. A Russellian account of facts is meant to be committed neither to the view that every true sentence stands for a *distinct* fact nor to the view that they all stand for the *same* fact. As Davidson (1984) has stressed, the challenge for any friend of facts is to come up with something between these poles: if all true sentences stand for the *same* fact, the notion is useless; if every true sentence stands for a *distinct* fact, then facts can shed no light on truth as they are individuated in terms of true sentences (or statements). It is within the spirit of a Russellian account of facts that a true sentence might be reorganized or converted into a related sentence that stands for the same fact (in order, say, to highlight a particular expression for some purpose). For example, the following stand for the same fact on Russell's account:

(54) Cicero denounced Catiline
(55) Catiline was denounced by Cicero
(56) It was *Cicero* who denounced Catiline.

A more interesting case involves coreferring singular terms. If the fact for which a true sentence stands is determined by, and only by, its syntax and what its parts stand for, then two true sentences $\Sigma[\alpha]$ and $\Sigma[\beta]$ will stand for the same fact if they differ in just the following way: the position occupied by a singular term α in $\Sigma[\alpha]$ is occupied by a coreferring singular term β in $\Sigma[\beta]$. For example, taking 'Cicero' and 'Tully' to be coreferring singular terms, (57) stands for the same fact as (56)–(58):

(57) Tully denounced Catiline.[36]

---

[36] It is usually held that Russell's final semantics treats ordinary proper names like 'Cicero' and 'Tully' as disguised definite descriptions to which his Theory of Descriptions applies. (For a somewhat dissenting view, see Sainsbury (1992).) I shall treat ordinary proper names as singular terms.

By contrast, although Cicero is the author of *De Fato*, on Russell's account

(58) The author of *De Fato* denounced Catiline

stands for a quite different fact, the *general* fact that (i) exactly one individual authored *De Fato* and (ii) every individual who authored *De Fato* also denounced Catiline. Cicero is no more a component of that fact than I am. If Russell had treated 'the author of *De Fato*' as a singular term that referred to Cicero, then (60) would stand for the same fact as (54)–(57). According to Gödel (1944), this would have had a surprising and devastating consequence because there is an important connection between theories of facts and theories of descriptions: if a true sentence stands for a fact, then in order to avoid the collapse of all facts into one, the friend of facts must give up either (*a*) an intuitive and straightforward Fregean Principle of Composition or (*b*) the idea that definite descriptions are expressions that purport to stand for things. Russell, as Gödel sees it, is able to avoid the troublesome conclusion that all true sentences stand for the same fact by denying that descriptions stand for things, i.e. by treating them as incomplete symbols.[37] But Gödel was not entirely convinced that Russell was off the hook: 'I cannot help feeling that the problem raised . . . has only been evaded by Russell's theory of descriptions and that there is something behind it which is not yet completely understood' (1944: 130).

Gödel is silent on the nature of his worry, but I hazard he was responding to a superficial feature of Russell's theory that the use of, for example, restricted quantifiers has shown to be dispensable. Russell's own implementation of his theory involved defining descriptions contextually in such a way that they 'disappear on analysis' in primitive notation; and Gödel must have thought that excluding descriptions from the primitive notation was a formal manœuvre that created only an illusion of a solution by masking the real philosophical issue. This seems to be borne out by Gödel's next (and final) paragraph on the topic:

There seems to be one purely formal respect in which one may give preference to Russell's theory of descriptions. By defining the meaning of sentences involving descriptions in the above manner, he avoids in his logical system any axioms about the particle "the," *i.e.*, the analyticity of the theorems about "the" is made explicit; they can be shown to follow from the explicit definition of the meaning of sentences involving "the." Frege, on the contrary, has to assume an axiom about "the," which of course is also analytic, but only in the implicit sense that it follows from the meaning of

---

[37] For discussion of Gödel's argument, see Neale (1995, forthcoming) and Neale and Dever (1997).

the undefined terms. Closer examination, however, shows that this advantage of Russell's theory over Frege's subsists only as long as one interprets definitions as mere typographical abbreviations, not as introducing names for objects described by the definitions, a feature which is common to Frege and Russell. (1944: 130–1)

The final sentence of this passage is instructive. First, it is important to realize that it is *essential* to Russell's Theory of Descriptions that *14.01 and *14.02 *are* typographical abbreviations and that descriptive phrases are *not* introduced as names for the objects described by the definitions.[38] Secondly, Gödel thought some of the central difficulties of *Principia* arose precisely because Russell refused to admit classes and concepts as real objects. I suspect Gödel's worries about defining away classes by contextually defining the expressions that purport to refer to them may have clouded his thinking about contextually defining descriptions. There is an important ontological difference: contextually defining class expressions gave Russell a way of defining away *classes* themselves (so to speak); contextually defining descriptions gave him a way of defining away the king of France and the round square (so to speak) but it did not give him a way of defining away *objects*. Thirdly, in 1943/4 it was not obvious how descriptions, if analysed in such a way that sentences containing them are given the quantificational truth-conditions assigned by Russell's theory, should fit into general account of quantification. As Gödel's final sentence reveals, the possibilities that presented themselves to him at that time were just two in number: (i) descriptions are mere typographical abbreviations that disappear on analysis, or (ii) they are terms that have their references fixed quantificationally (for example, by overlapping satisfactions). But subsequent work on quantification and on the syntax and semantics of natural language has revealed a superior possibility: (iii) a description 'the *F*' is a quantified noun phrase on an equal footing with 'every *F*', 'some *F*', 'no *F*', etc. The fact that Russell's theory can be implemented within a theory of restricted quantification ought to dispel worries about the artificial banishment of descriptions as well as confusions about "incomplete symbols".

Using a formal language containing devices of restricted quantification to render a sentence containing a description does not conflict with Russell's claim that a description is an "incomplete symbol". A description no more *stands for something* if restricted quantifiers are used than it does if unrestricted quantifiers are used. Although Russell did not have the resources of restricted quantifier theory at his disposal, and although he had philosophical aims that went

---

[38] For reasons given by Kripke (1972), the abbreviations would be *rigid* if this were the case, and (typically) descriptions are not.

beyond the semantics of natural language, the restricted quantifier analysis of descriptions given above just *is* Russell's theory, semantically speaking, but stated in a way that allows us to see the relationship between surface syntax and logical form more clearly. By virtue of being Russellians about descriptions, we are not committed to the view that the only way to represent the "logical form" of a sentence *S* containing a description is to translate *S* into a formula of the language of *Principia* (or a similar language). As far as explicating the logical structure of sentences containing descriptions is concerned, treating them in terms of restricted quantifiers results not in a departure from, or a falling out with, Russell but in the beginnings of an elegant explanation of where his theory fits into a more general theory of quantification, a theory in which determiners like 'every', 'some', 'all', 'most', 'a', 'the', and so on are treated as members of a unified syntactical and semantical category.[39] The fact that Russell's theory can be so easily implemented in this way shows the hollowness of claims to the effect Russell's theory has difficulties that arise because of matters of scope, logical form, fidelity to surface syntax, and so on. Importantly, when augmented with an account of the semantics of purportedly non-extensional sentence connectives like 'necessarily', 'possibly', 'before', and 'because', Russell's theory will predict and explain ambiguities of scope involving descriptions and such expressions. Any rival theory of descriptions must explain the same data.

[39] Perhaps 'that' might be added, when it functions as a determiner. For it might be suggested that the characteristic feature of a noun phrase of the form 'that *F*' to be understood as equivalent to a descriptions, perhaps an indefinite description, understood in terms of an additional conjunct *that* = *x* containing a simple demonstrative *that*. An utterance of 'that *F* is *G*', it might be suggested, is understood as (i) [an_x: *that* = *x* • *Fx*] *Gx*. (Since uniqueness is secured by '*that* = *x*', in respect of truth conditions this analysis appears to be equivalent to one proposed by Lepore and Ludwig (2000) which uses the definite determiner *the* rather than the indefinite *an*. It was Tyler Burge who convinced me that our intuitions about 'that' and its connection to other determiners are better served if the indefinite is used.) This might seem to capture both the demonstrative and descriptive features of a demonstrative description. One might then go all the way and roll (i) up into a formula making use of a new determiner *that* within the language of restricted quantification: (ii) [$that_x$: *Fx*] *Gx*. An axiom for the determiner *that* might then invoke whatever axiom is to be used for the simple demonstrative *that*, as in the following: (iii) $\forall s \forall k \forall \phi \forall \psi$ ([$that_k$: ϕ]ψ is satisfied by *s* iff ψ is satisfied by at least one sequence satisfying '*that* = *x* • ϕ' and differing from *s* at most in the *k*th position). Presumably the axiom for the demonstrative 'that' would introduce parameters not yet given by (iii). (On this matter see e.g. Weinstein (1974), Larson and Segal (1995), and Lepore and Ludwig (2000).)

   Of course ϕ itself might be *another* identity statement, which suggests a treatment of 'that David Kaplan'. An utterance of 'that NAME is *G*' would be understood as (iv) [an_x: *that* = *x* • *name* = *x*] *Gx*. (Alternative treatment of 'that *F*' and 'that NAME' can be provided within a multiple proposition semantics of the sort I sketched in 'Coloring and Composition' but no longer find quite as conducive as I once did.)

REFERENCES

Carnap, R. (1947). *Meaning and Necessity, a Study in Meaning and Modal Logic* (Chicago: University of Chicago Press; 2nd edn., with additions, 1956).

Cartwright, R. (1968). 'Some Remarks on Essentialism', *Journal of Philosophy*, 65: 615–26.

Davidson, D. (1984). *Inquiries into Truth and Interpretation* (Oxford: Clarendon Press).

Evans, G. (1977). 'Pronouns, Quantifiers and Relative Clauses (I)', *Canadian Journal of Philosophy*, 7: 467–536.

——— (1982). *The Varieties of Reference* (Oxford: Clarendon Press).

Føllesdal, D. (1966). 'Referential Opacity and Modal Logic', *Filosofiske Problemer*, xxxii (Oslo: Universitetforslaget).

Frege, G. (1892). 'Über Sinn und Bedeutung', *Zeitschrift für Philosophie und Philosophische Kritik*, 100: 25–50. Translated as 'On Sense and Reference', in P. Geach and M. Black (eds.), *Translations from the Philosophical Writings of Gottlob Frege* (Oxford: Blackwell, 1952), 56–78.

Gödel, K. (1944). 'Russell's Mathematical Logic', in P. A. Schilpp (ed.), *The Philosophy of Bertrand Russell* (Evanston, Ill., and Chicago: Northwestern University Press), 125–53. Reprinted in S. Feferman *et al.* (eds.), *Kurt Gödel, Collected Works*, ii. 1938–1974 (Oxford: Oxford University Press, 1990), 119–41.

Graff, D. (forthcoming). 'Descriptions as Predicates', *Philosophical Studies*.

Grice, P. (1989). *Studies in the Way of Words* (Cambridge, Mass.: Harvard University Press).

Higginbotham, J., and May, R. (1981). 'Questions, Quantifiers, and Crossing', *Linguistic Review*, 1: 41–80.

Hintikka, J. (1968). 'Logic and Philosophy', in R. Klibansky (ed.), *Contemporary Philosophy* (Florence: La Nuova Italia Editrice), 3–30.

—— (1989). 'Logical Form and Linguistic Theory', in A. George (ed.), *Reflections on Chomsky* (Oxford: Blackwell), 41–57.

—— and Kulas, J. (1985). *Anaphora and Definite Descriptions* (Dordrecht: Reidel).

—— and Sandu, G. (1991). *The Methodology of Linguistics* (Oxford: Blackwell).

Kalish, D., Montague, R., and Mar, D. (1980). *Logic: Techniques of Formal Reasoning*, 2nd edn. (New York: Harcourt, Brace, Jovanovich).

Kaplan, D. (1972). 'What is Russell's Theory of Descriptions?', in D. F. Pears (ed.), *Bertrand Russell: A Collection of Critical Essays* (Garden City, NY: Doubleday Anchor), 227–44.

Kripke, S. (1972). 'Naming and Necessity', in D. Davidson and G. Harman (eds.), *Semantics of Natural Language* (Dordrecht: Reidel), 253–355, and 763–9.

Lambert, K. (1991). 'A Theory of Definite Descriptions', in K. Lambert (ed.), *Philosophical Applications of Free Logic* (Oxford: Clarendon Press), 17–27.

Linsky, L. (1966). 'Substitutivity and Descriptions', *Journal of Philosophy*, 63: 673–83.

Neale, S. R. A. (1990). *Descriptions* (Cambridge, Mass.: MIT Press).

—— (1993). 'Grammatical Form, Logical Form, and Incomplete Symbols', in A. D. Irvine and G. A. Wedeking (eds.), *Russell and Analytic Philosophy* (Toronto: University of Toronto Press), 97–139. Reprinted in G. Ostertag (ed.), *Definite Descriptions: A Reader* (Cambridge, Mass.: MIT Press, 1999).

—— (1995). 'The Philosophical Significance of Gödel's Slingshot', *Mind*, 104: 761–825.

—— (2000). 'On a Milestone of Empiricism', in P. Kotatko and A. Orenstein (eds.), *Knowledge, Language and Logic: Questions for Quine* (Dordrecht: Kluwer, 2000), 237–346.

—— (forthcoming). *Facing Facts* (Oxford: Oxford University Press).

—— and Dever, J. (1997). 'Slingshots and Boomerangs', *Mind*, 106: 143–68.

Quine, W. V. (1947). 'On the Problem of Interpreting Modal Logic', *Journal of Symbolic Logic*, 12: 43–8.

—— (1953). 'Reference and Modality', in *From a Logical Point of View* (Cambridge, Mass.: Harvard University Press), 139–59.

—— (1961). 'Reference and Modality' (revised version) in *From a Logical Point of View* (2nd edn. Cambridge, Mass.: Harvard University Press), 139–59.

—— (1980). 'Reference and Modality' (2nd revised version) in *From a Logical Point of View* (2nd edn., rev. printing, New York: Harper & Row), 139–59.

Rundle, B. (1965). 'Modality and Quantification', in R. J. Butler (ed.), *Analytical Philosophy, Second Series* (Oxford: Blackwell), 27–39.

Russell, B. (1905). 'On Denoting', *Mind*, 14: 479–93.

—— (1911). 'Knowledge by Acquaintance and Knowledge by Description', in *Mysticism and Logic* (London: George Allen & Unwin, 1917), 152–67.

—— (1912). *The Problems of Philosophy* (Oxford: Oxford University Press).

Sainsbury, M. (1979). *Russell* (London: Routledge).

—— (1991). *Logical Forms: An Introduction to Philosophical Logic* (Oxford: Blackwell).

—— (1993). 'Russell on Names and Communication', in A. D. Irvine and G. A. Wedeking (eds.), *Russell and Analytic Philosophy* (Toronto: University of Toronto Press), 3–21.

Scott, D. (1967). 'Existence and Description in Formal Logic', in R. Schoenman (ed.), *Bertrand Russell, Philosopher of the Century* (London: Allen & Unwin), 181–200.

Smullyan, A. F. (1947). Review of Quine's 'The Problem of Interpreting Modal Logic', *Journal of Symbolic Logic*, 12: 139–41.

—— (1948). 'Modality and Description', *Journal of Symbolic Logic*, 13: 31–7.

Stalnaker, R. (1972). 'Pragmatics', in D. Davidson and G. Harman (eds.), *Semantics of Natural Language* (Dordrecht: Reidel), 380–97.

Thomason, R. (1969). 'Modal Logic and Metaphysics', in K. Lambert (ed.), *The Logical Way of Doing Things* (New Haven: Yale University Press), 119–46.

Wallace, J. (1969). 'Propositional Attitudes and Identity', *Journal of Philosophy*, 66: 145–52.

Wedberg, A. (1984). *A History of Philosophy*, iii. *From Bolzano to Wittgenstein* (Oxford: Clarendon Press).

Whitehead, A. N., and Russell, B. (1925). *Principia Mathematica*, vol. i, (2nd edn. Cambridge: Cambridge University Press).

Wiggins, D. (1980). ' "Most" and "All": Some Comments on a Familiar Programme, and on the Logical Form of Quantified Sentences', in M. Platts (ed.), *Reference, Truth, and Reality* (London: Routledge & Kegan Paul), 318–46.

Wilson, N. (1959). *The Concept of Language* (Toronto: University of Toronto Press).

3

What is Logical Form?

Ernie Lepore and Kirk Ludwig

> Philosophy, as we use the word, is a fight against the fascination which
> forms of expression exert upon us.
>
> (Wittgenstein)

I

Bertrand Russell, in the second of his 1914 Lowell lectures, *Our Knowledge of the External World*, asserted famously that 'every philosophical problem, when it is subjected to the necessary analysis and purification, is found either to be not really philosophical at all, or else to be, in the sense in which we are using the word, logical' (Russell, 1993: 42). He went on to characterize that portion of logic that concerned the study of *forms* of propositions, or, as he called them, 'logical forms'. This portion of logic he called 'philosophical logic'. Russell asserted that 'some kind of knowledge of logical forms, though with most people it is not explicit, is involved in all understanding of discourse. It is the business of philosophical logic to extract this knowledge from its concrete integuments, and to render it explicit and pure' (1993: 53). Perhaps no one still endorses quite this grand a view of the role of logic and the investigation of logical form in philosophy. But *talk* of logical form retains a central role in analytic philosophy. Given its widespread use in philosophy and linguistics, it is rather surprising that the concept of logical form has not received more attention by philosophers than it has.

The concern of this chapter is to say something about what talk of logical form comes to, in a tradition that stretches back to (and arguably beyond) Russell's use of that expression. This will not be exactly Russell's conception.

For we do not endorse Russell's view that propositions are the bearers of logical form, or that appeal to propositions adds anything to our understanding of what talk of logical form comes to. But we will be concerned to provide an account responsive to the interests expressed by Russell in the above quotations, though one clarified of extraneous elements and expressed precisely. For this purpose, it is important to note that the concern expressed by Russell in the above passages, as the surrounding text makes clear, is a concern not just with logic conceived narrowly as the study of logical *terms*, but with propositional form more generally, which includes, for example, such features as those that correspond to the number of argument places in a propositional function, and the categories of objects which propositional functions can take as arguments. This very general concern with form is expressed above in the claim that *all* understanding of discourse involves some knowledge of logical forms. It is logical form in this very general sense, which is connected with an interest in getting clear about the nature of reality through getting clear about the forms of our thoughts or talk about it, with which we will be concerned.[1]

The conception we will champion dispenses with talk of propositions, reified sentence meanings, as a useless excrescence, and treats logical form as

---

[1] Russell expressed these views in numerous places. For example, in 'On Scientific Method in Philosophy', the Herbert Spencer lecture at Oxford in 1914, he says, 'Philosophy, if what has been said is correct, becomes indistinguishable from logic as that word has now come to be used' (Russell, 1959: 84–5). He distinguishes within logic two portions ('not very sharply distinguished'), one dealing with 'those general statements which can be made concerning everything without mentioning any one thing or predicate or relation'—roughly the topic neutral conception of logic—and one dealing with 'the analysis and enumeration of logical forms, i.e., with the kinds of propositions that may occur, with the various types of facts, and the classification of the constituents of facts'. 'In this way,' Russell says, 'logic provides an inventory of possibilities, a repertory of abstractly tenable hypotheses'. Likewise Wittgenstein's concern with logical form in the *Tractatus Logico-Philosophicus*, a concern that grew out of his work with Russell from 1911 to the outbreak of the first World War, was clearly a general concern for the form of representations, not a concern more narrowly with a restricted set of terms to be called 'logical'. See e.g. 3.32–3.325, *Tractatus*. Wittgenstein uses the notion of logical form throughout very broadly for the form of a representation, including the forms of elementary propositions. These conceptions of the primary task of philosophy and the correlative role of the notion of logical form in articulating it have had an enormous, though somewhat inchoate, influence on the philosophical tradition in English-speaking countries. Wittgenstein's greatest immediate influence was on the members of the Vienna Circle. Some sense of the impression created can be gleaned from Moritz Schlick's 'The Turning Point in Philosophy' (1959, the lead article in the first volume of *Erkenntnis*). The influence of the Vienna Circle and its sympathizers in turn has had a central role in shaping contemporary philosophy. This broad notion of logical form stretches back into the tradition. Kant's conception of the logical form of a judgement is in the same spirit, a concern with very general common features of judgements which yield a basic taxonomy of their

a feature of sentences. Consonant with Russell's general interest in the form of propositions, we will treat talk about the logical form of a *sentence* in a language L to be essentially about *semantic* form as revealed in a *compositional meaning theory for L*. We do not, however, treat logical form itself as a sentence, or anything else. On our account, it is a mistake to think that logical forms are *entities*, or to think of logical form as revealed by what symbols occur in a sentence, either in its surface syntax, or in the syntax of its translation into an 'ideal' language. Rather, we will take the relation of *sameness of logical form* as basic. We will give a precise account of the notion of sameness of logical form between any two sentences in any two languages, first for declarative sentences, then for sentences in any sentential mood. Our account is inspired by remarks of Davidson, and we develop the account for declaratives in the context of a Davidsonian truth-theoretic semantics. We develop the account for non-declaratives in terms of a generalization of the notion of an interpretive truth theory, namely, that of an interpretive fulfilment theory.

We will also be concerned to say something about the relation of this characterization of logical form to logic more narrowly conceived, that is, a study of the semantics of logical terms or structures. We will urge that these are distinct and, to some degree, independent concerns. We will also suggest a criterion (essentially due to Davidson) for picking out logical terms or structures that is particularly salient from the standpoint on logical form we advance, though we make no claim for its being the only way of extending in a principled way the use of the notion beyond where it is currently well-grounded. (This discussion will show, incidentally, that no good basis exists, contrary to what has been relatively recently alleged (Etchemendy, 1983, 1988, 1990; Lycan, 1989), for denying that a principled distinction between the logical and non-logical *terms* of a language can be drawn.)

The program of our chapter is as follows. In section II, we consider the origins of the notion of logical form in reflection on argument form, and criticize two traditional conceptions, one of which remains dominant. In section III, we introduce the notion of logical form we wish to develop, logical form as semantic form, and describe our conception of how to use a truth theory to give a compositional semantic theory for declarative sentences in a language as background for our development of this conception. In section IV, we give a precise characterization of sameness of logical form of sentences

kinds, abstracting from their particular matter. And a concern with logical form in broadly Russell's sense, as Russell himself has said, is clearly something philosophers from ancient times have been concerned with in thinking about how our forms of speech and thought relate us to reality.

applicable across languages in terms of the notion of corresponding proofs of the T-sentences for them in *interpretive truth theories* for the languages. This allows us to clarify what could be meant by the expression '*x* is the logical form of *y*'. In section V, we employ examples from natural language semantics in illustration of the usefulness of the present approach. In section VI, we show how the basic approach can be extended to non-declarative sentences. (This extension is based on some work by one of the authors (Ludwig) which the other (Lepore) has some reservations about, so it is put forward here as a *suggestion* about how this desirable extension might be effected.) In section VII, we discuss the relation of the conception of logical form we advance to the project of identifying logical terms or structures, and contrast it with an alternative conception articulated in terms of an invariance condition traceable back to Tarski (1986) and Lindstrom (1966). Section VIII is a brief summary and conclusion.

II

The origin of interest in logical form lies in the recognition that many intuitively valid natural language arguments can be classified together on the basis of common features, a form which guarantees their validity apart from their different content. We group together arguments which exemplify a pattern, and say that they share a form. Forms of arguments are represented by replacing (certain) of the expressions in their premises and conclusions with schematic letters—thereby abstracting away from what the arguments are about. This gives rise to a common characterization of the logical form of a sentence, namely, that structure of a sentence that determines from which sentences it can be validly deduced, and which sentences can be validly deduced from it and other premises, where these sentences are in turn characterized in terms of their logical structures.

This loose characterization is far from satisfactory because it leaves unexplicated how 'structure of a sentence' is being used. Logical form cannot be just any schema that results from replacing one or more expressions within a sentence. There are too many, and not every such schema will be taken to reveal logical form. In addition, for sentences with more than one reading, such as (1), we associate more than one logical form, but they will generate the same schemas.

(1) Everyone loves someone.

Similarly, sentences we are intuitively inclined to assign distinct logical forms, such as the pairs (1)–(2), (3)–(4), and (5)–(6), yield the same schemas. Likewise, sentences, as might be urged for the pair (6)–(7), to which we wish to assign the same logical form (in the same or different languages) may yield distinct schemas. Examples can be multiplied endlessly.

(2) John loves Mary.
(3) Dogs bark.
(4) Unicorns exist.
(5) The President is a scoundrel.
(6) The whale is a mammal.
(7) Everything which is a whale is a mammal.

Russell's response, of course, was to bypass sentences and to take logical form to be a property of the *propositions* that sentences express (as above). This renders intelligible talk of similar sentences having distinct logical forms, and of different sentences, in the same or different languages, having the same logical form. Sentences on this view can be said in a derivative sense to have logical form: sentences have the same logical form when they express propositions with the same logical form.

An alternative approach, more usual today, is to identify the logical form of a natural language sentence as the form of a sentence in a specially regimented, 'ideal', perhaps formal, language that translates it (or, in the case of an ambiguous sentence, the logical forms it can have are associated with the sentences that translate the various readings of it).[2] A regimented language must contain no ambiguities and syntactically encode all differences in the logical (or semantical) roles of terms. A common variant of this view, marking out a narrower conception of logical form, is to identify the logical form of the natural language sentence as the form determined by the pattern of logical constants in its regimented translation. Natural language sentences then can be said to share logical form if they translate into sentences the same in form in the regimented language of choice, and to have different logical forms if they

[2] This can almost be called the official view. It has made its way into the *Cambridge Dictionary of Philosophy* as the canonical account: logical form is 'the form of a proposition in a logically perfect language, determined by the grammatical form of the ideal sentence expressing that proposition (or statement, in one use of the latter term)'. (Note that this *mixes up* the two conceptions distinguished in the text.) The author goes on to characterize sameness of logical form as sameness of grammatical form in an ideal language, but in a way that resists characterization across languages of sameness of grammatical form or, hence, logical form.

translate into sentences different in form. (Cf. Frege in the *Begriffsschrift*, 'In my formalized language there is nothing that corresponds [to changes in word ordering that do not affect the inferential relations a sentence enters into]; only that part of judgments which affects the possible inferences is taken into consideration' (Black and Geach, 1960, p. 3).)

Neither of these approaches is satisfactory. On the one hand, any grasp we have on talk of the structure of propositions derives from our grasp on sentence structure in a regimented language which aims to express more clearly than ordinary language the structure of the proposition. On the other, the trouble with identifying the logical form of a natural language sentence with a sentence structure expressible in a regimented language is that we wish to be able to speak informatively about the logical form of sentences in our regimented language as well. It is no more plausible that it is simply the *pattern* of expressions in the sentence in the regimented language than in natural language. There can be more than one ideal language a natural language can be translated into, whose translations into each other take sentences into sentences with different patterns of expressions. Appeal to the pattern of logical expressions is of no help. First, we have not said when a term (or structure) counts as logical. Second, the pattern alluded to cannot consist of the actual arrangement of the logical terms in the regimented language, for the same reason that appeal to patterns of expressions more generally is futile: there are clearly different regimentations possible which would be said to exhibit the same form but differ in syntax (Polish notation and standard logical notation, for example).

Some philosophers have concluded that all talk about *the* logical form of a sentence is confused. Quine has claimed that the purpose of providing a paraphrase in a regimented language of a sentence, which is treated as its logical form, is 'to put the sentence into a form that admits most efficiently of logical calculation, or shows its implications and conceptual affinities most perspicuously, obviating fallacy and paradox' (Quine, 1971: 452). He argues there will be different ways of doing this, and consequently there can be no demand for *the* logical form of a natural language sentence.[3] Davidson follows Quine in seeing logical form as relative to the logic of one's theory for a

---

[3] Quine also uses this argument to urge that the grammarian's deep structure need not be identified with what is usually taken by logicians to be logical form. He gives as an instance of two ways of regimenting the same sentences, for purposes of keeping track of their implication relations, a language which eliminates proper names in favor of predicates by treating the name 'a' as equivalent to '$x = a$', and introducing a predicate letter for it, and then regimenting 'Fa' as '$(\exists x)(\mathrm{F}x.x = a)$', and a language which retains individual constants.

language (see 'Reply to Cargile', in Davidson (1984*b*: 140)).[4] More recently, Lycan (1989) and Etchemendy (1988) have suggested that there can be no principled distinction between logical and non-logical terms, which, if correct, would undercut the possibility of an objective account of logical form by appeal to patterns relating to logical terms. These skeptical reactions are unwarranted, as the sequel will show.

III

The account of logical form we advocate generalizes and refines a view Davidson urged in some early papers. A clear statement of this conception occurs in 'On Saying That':

> What should we ask of an adequate account of the logical form of a sentence? Above all, I would say, such an account must lead us to see the semantic character of the sentence—its truth or falsity—as owed to how it is composed, by a finite number of applications of some of a finite number of devices that suffice for the language as a whole, out of elements drawn from a finite stock (the vocabulary) that suffices for the language as a whole. To see a sentence in this light is to see it in the light of a theory for its language. A way to provide such a theory is by recursively characterizing a truth predicate, along the lines suggested by Tarski. (Davidson, 1968; 1984*c*: 94)

His suggestion is not precise enough (or, as will emerge, general enough) for our purposes. Not every true Tarski-style truth theory for a language issues in an account of the semantic features of the language, only an *interpretive truth theory*. In order to explain this, we must first explain our conception of how a truth theory for a natural language L may be employed in giving a compositional meaning theory for L.

> A compositional meaning theory for L should provide, from a specification of the meanings of finitely many primitive expressions and rules, a specification of the meaning of an utterance of any of the infinitely many sentences of L.

Confining our attention to declaratives for the moment, a compositional meaning theory for a context-*in*sensitive language L, i.e. a language without

---

[4] It is with some irony that we report this, since our own approach, which shows how to explicate the notion of sameness of logical form without relativizing to the logic of any particular theory, is, as we've said, based on the suggestion of Davidson's quoted below at the beginning of section III.

elements whose semantic contribution depends on context of use, would issue in theorems of the form,

(M) ϕ in L means that p,

where 'ϕ' is replaced by a structural description of a sentence of L and 'p' by a metalanguage sentence that translates it.

For context-insensitive languages, the connection between a theory meeting Tarski's famous Convention T and a compositional meaning theory meeting (R) is straightforward: a truth theory meets that convention only if it entails every instance of (T),

(T) ϕ is true in L iff p,

in which a structural description of a sentence of L replaces 'ϕ', and a synonymous metalanguage sentence replaces 'p'. We shall call such instances of (T) *T-sentences*. The relation between a structural description that replaces 'ϕ' and a metalanguage sentence that replaces 'p' in a T-sentence is the same as that between suitable substitution pairs in (M). Therefore, every instance of (S) is true when what replaces 'p' translates the sentence denoted by what replaces 'ϕ'.

(S) If ϕ is true in L iff p, then ϕ in L means that p.

Given a T-sentence for a sentence *s*, the appropriate instance of (S) enables us to specify its meaning. One advantage of a truth-theoretic approach (over trying to generate instances of (M) more directly) is its ability to provide recursions needed to generate meaning specifications for object language sentences from a finite base with no more ontological or logical resources than are required for a theory of reference. This turns out to be central also to its role in revealing something that deserves the label 'logical form'.

In natural languages, many (arguably all) sentences lack truth-values independently of use. 'I am tired' is true or false only as used. This requires discarding our simple accounts of the forms of theories of meaning and truth. In modifying a compositional meaning theory to accommodate context sensitivity, and a truth theory that serves as its recursive engine, a theorist must choose between two options. The first retains the basic form of the meaning specification, '*x* means in language *y* that p', and correspondingly retains within the truth theory a two-place predicate relating a truth bearer and a language. This requires conditionalizing on utterances of sentences in specifying truth-conditions. The second adds an argument place to each semantic predicate in the theory for every contextual parameter required to fix a context-sensitive element's contribution when used. For concreteness, we will suppose that the fundamental contextual parameters are utterer and utterance time.[5] Either approach is acceptable. We adopt the second because it simplifies the form of the theories. This approach yields theorems of the forms (M2) and (T2).

> (M2) For any speaker s, time t, sentence ϕ of L, ϕ means$_{(s,\,t)}$ in L that p.
> (T2) For any speaker s, time t, sentence ϕ of L, ϕ is true$_{(s,\,t)}$ in L iff p.

As a first gloss, we might try to treat 'means$_{(s,\,t)}$ in L' and 'is true$_{(s,\,t)}$ in L' as equivalent to 'means as potentially spoken by s at t in L' and 'is true as potentially spoken by s at t in L'. However, as Evans (1985: 359–60) points out, we cannot read these as, ⌜if ϕ were used by s at t in L, then, as spoken by s at t, ϕ would be true iff/mean that⌝, since, aside from worries about how to evaluate counterfactuals, these interpretations would assign sentences such as 'I am silent' false T-theorems. What we need are the readings, ⌜if ϕ were used by s at t in L, as things actually stand, ϕ would be true iff/mean that⌝, or, alternatively, ⌜ϕ understood as if spoken by s at t is in L true iff/means that⌝; *mutatis mutandis* for other semantic predicates.

We replace adequacy criterion (R) with (R′):

> (R′) A compositional meaning theory for a language L should entail, from a specification of the meanings of primitive expressions of L, all true sentences of form (M2)

The analog of Tarski's Convention T for recursive truth theories for natural languages we shall call *Davidson's Convention T,* given in (D).

> (D) An adequate truth theory for a language L must entail every instance of (T2) for which corresponding instances of (M2) are true.

A Tarski-style truth theory for L meeting (D) with axioms that *interpret* primitive expressions of L provides the resources to meet (R′). We will call any such theory an *interpretive truth theory.*

There are two parts of this requirement that deserve further comment. First, we have in mind a Tarski-style theory in the sense of a theory which employs a *satisfaction predicate* relating sequences or functions to expressions of the language and contextual parameters, supplemented by a similarly relativized reference function for assigning referents to singular terms. Second, the require-

---

[5] Though we will not argue for it here, we believe these are the only contextual parameters we need in order to devise an adequate semantics for tense. Throughout quantifiers over times will range over time intervals, and 'is a time' will be true of time intervals. We will include as a limiting case of a time interval a temporal instant.

ment that the axioms of the theory *interpret* primitive expressions of L is of great importance in understanding the present approach. We will therefore elaborate on this aspect of the requirement. For an axiom to be interpretive, it must treat the object language term for which it is an axiom as being of the right semantic category. Thus, predicates should receive satisfaction clauses that represent them as predicates, referring terms should receive reference axioms, recursive terms (or structures) should receive recursive axioms. For a context-insensitive language, a base axiom interprets an object language expression just in case its satisfaction conditions (or referent) are given using a term in the metalanguage that translates it. Thus, for example, to give an axiom for 'x is red' in English, taking the metalanguage to be English as well, we would write (ignoring tense and suppressing relativization to language when dealing with English):

for all functions f, f satisfies 'x is red' iff $f('x')$ is red.

This is an interpretive axiom for 'x is red', for the predicate used to give the satisfaction conditions translates the object language predicate for which satisfaction conditions are given. In contrast,

for all functions f, f satisfies 'x is red' iff $f('x')$ is red and the earth moves,

is not interpretive since 'is red and the earth moves' does not translate 'is red'. A recursive term, such as 'and', will receive a recursive axiom. To be interpretive, the recursive structure used in the metalanguage must translate that of the object language sentence on which the recursion is run. Thus, for 'and' in English, using English as the metalanguage, we would give the following recursive axiom:

for all functions f, sentences ϕ, ψ, f satisfies $\phi \frown$ 'and' $\frown \psi$ iff f satisfies ϕ and f satisfies ψ.

In contrast,

for all functions f, sentences ϕ, ψ, f satisfies $\phi \frown$ 'and' $\frown \psi$ iff it is not the case that if f satisfies ϕ, then it is not the case that f satisfies ψ,

is not interpretive, because the recursive structure used to give satisfaction conditions does not translate that for which satisfaction conditions are given. (See Appendix A for an important contrast with the development of a truth-theoretic semantics in Larson and Segal (1995).) These remarks apply directly to context-insensitive languages. For context-sensitive languages, when we have a verb which is context-sensitive, for example, tensed, we will have a metalanguage verb which has argument places expressing that relativization which, because it is not itself context-sensitive, will not be a strict translation of the object language verb. For example, consider the axiom for 'is red' when we take into account tense:

For all functions f, f satisfies$_{(s,\,t)}$ 'x is red' iff red(f('x'), t).

The metalanguage verb 'red(x, y)' is not tensed, but rather expresses a relation between an object and a time, the relation the object has to the time iff it is red at that time. What is it for such an axiom to be interpretive? Intuitively, the idea is clear: we want the metalanguage verb to express, relative to appropriate arguments, exactly the relation the object language verb expresses in use. We can make this precise as follows. Consider what we would say a predicate which is tensed *means* relative to use with respect to an object at a time. For example, we would say that a use of 'is red' relative to x and t means that red(x, t). Drawing on a generalization of this notion, we will say that an axiom for a predicate, with free variables 'x_1', 'x_2', ... 'x_n', denoted by '$Z(x_1, x_2, \ldots x_n)$', which is context-sensitive relative to parameters, p_1, p_2, ... p_m,

For all f, f satisfies$_{(p1,\,p2,\,\ldots,\,pm)}$ $Z(x_1, x_2, \ldots x_n)$ iff $\zeta(f('x_1'), \ldots, f('x_n'), p_1,$ $p_2, \ldots, p_m)$,

is interpretive just in case the *corresponding relativized meaning statement* is true:

For all f, $Z(x_1, x_2, \ldots x_n)$ means$_{(f,\,p1,\,p2,\,\ldots,\,pm)}$ that $\zeta(f('x_1'), \ldots, f('x_n'),$ p_1, p_2, \ldots, $p_m)$.

For a context-sensitive singular term, the term must be assigned the right referent relative to the context of use by the rule giving its referent relative to contextual parameters.

With this conception of how a truth theory can serve as a component of a compositional meaning theory (at least for declarative sentences) in place, we can return to the question how such a truth theory helps to give content to the notion of logical form.

IV

An interest in the logical form of a sentence[6] is an interest in those semantic properties it may share with distinct sentences relevant to the conditions under

---

[6]   We restrict our attention for the time being to declarative sentences.

which it is true, and the relations between the conditions under which it and other sentences are true. This interest is motivated by the traditional concern not to be misled by the surface form of sentences into assimilating one sort of claim to another quite different. The conception we are advocating is well-suited to meet this interest, since it identifies logical form with semantic form, insight into which is exactly what a compositional meaning theory provides. This can be made precise in terms of an interpretive truth theory for a language.

In addition to sentences, the notion of semantic form applies to significant subsentential expressions, complex and primitive. In this way, a notion of logical form associated with semantic form extends to include subsentential expressions, enabling us to talk of the logical form of a lexical item. The logical form of a sentence is determined by the logical forms of its lexical items and how their combination contributes to determining its interpretive truth-conditions. The logical form of a lexical item is that semantic feature it shares (at least potentially) with other lexical items that determines how it interacts with other vocabulary items likewise characterized in terms of features shared with other expressions. For example, one-place predicates will interact system-atically differently with quantifiers than will two-place predicates. This reveals itself in the base axioms of the truth theory, since all the axioms for one-place predicates will share a common form, and all the axioms for two-place predicates will share a different common form. The semantic type of a primitive term is given by the semantic type of the axiom it receives in the truth theory: its logical form is determined by its semantic type, i.e. sameness and difference of logical form for primitive terms is sameness and difference of semantic type.

There will be a variety of different levels of classification on the basis of semantic features that expressions share in common. Deictic elements can be classified together on the basis of their contributions to interpretive truth-conditions being relativized to contextual parameters (speaker and time, if our assumptions are correct). Among deictic elements we may press a further semantic division based on whether contextual parameters alone determine the contribution of a deictic element to the interpretive truth-conditions of an utterance of a sentence, or whether additional information is required, such as knowledge of a speaker's demonstrative intentions.

In general, features of the axioms for primitive expressions in the language which capture the way the expression contributes to the truth-conditions of sentences can be used to classify them by semantic type. The semantic theory for the language will contain all the information traditionally sought under the heading of logical form, but much more. In that sense this conception of logical form is a generalization as well as development of one strand in the traditional conception.

We said that the logical form of a sentence *s* is determined by the logical forms of the lexical items *s* contains and how they combine to determine the interpretive truth conditions of *s*. This needs to be made more precise. A compositional meaning theory for a language L can be cast as a formal theory. When it is, it must include enough logic to prove from its axioms every T-sentence. Its logic may be so circumscribed that it enables one to prove all *and only* T-sentences, or it may be more powerful. Intuitively, the contribution elements of a sentence *s* make to its interpretive truth-conditions (or the contribution of the elements of *s* to the truth-conditions of an utterance of *s*) will be revealed by a proof of its T-sentence which draws only upon the content of axioms. We shall call any such proof a *canonical* proof of the T-sentence (following Davidson). If the logic of the theory is so restricted that, for any object language sentence *s*, a T-sentence for *s* can be proved only by drawing solely upon the content of the axioms for terms in *s*, then every proof of a T-sentence will be canonical. If the logic is stronger, the characterization of a canonical proof will involve restrictions on the resources allowed in proofs and perhaps how these resources are deployed. (Of course, if one description of a proof procedure meets the intuitive condition for describing a canonical proof, many will.) Clearly, a canonical proof of a T-sentence for an object language sentence *shows* what its semantic structure is, for it *shows* how the semantic categories to which its constituent terms belong, determined by the type of axiom provided for each, contribute to determining its interpretive truth-conditions. We can say that a canonical proof of a T-sentence for a sentence *reveals* its logical form. However, to identity logical form with canonical proof would be a mistake on the order of identifying logical form with a sentence in an ideal language.

A canonical proof is relative to a metalanguage and its accompanying logic, while logical form is not. The canonical proof, together with our understanding of the metalanguage, reveals logical form, i.e. semantic form. The logical form of a sentence *s* is determined by the *semantic category of each primitive in s* and *how these combine* to determine *s*'s interpretive truth-conditions and so meaning. Thus, the logical form of *s* is a property of *s* revealed by the structure of the proof and by the axioms for the primitives in *s*. This property is determined once we can characterize when two sentences, in the same or different languages, share logical form. That characterization should not depend on any particular formal theory with respect to which a canonical proof procedure is formulated. We want something which all canonical proofs of T-sentences for a sentence *s* in interpretive truth theories for its language share in common. Intuitively, we want to say that two sentences share logical form when the same canonical proof *can* be given for them, *adjusting* for differences due to *differences in the object language*, and *differences between the axioms employed which are not based on the semantic category to which a term belongs*. For then all the proofs for either will share in common what reveals their semantic structure articulated in terms of the categories of their semantic primitives and how they combine to determine interpretive truth-conditions. With this intuitive characterization as a guide, we offer a more precise characterization. First, we define the notion of *corresponding proofs* in (8).

(8)   A proof P_1 of a T-sentence for s_1 in T_1 *corresponds* to a proof P_2 for a T-sentence for s_2 in T_2 iff$_{df}$
   a. P_1 and P_2 are sentence sequences identical in length;
   b.   at each stage of each proof identical rules are used;
   c.   the base axioms employed at each stage are of the same semantic type, and the recursive axioms employed at each stage interpret identically object language terms for which they specify satisfaction conditions (with respect to contributions to truth-conditions).

Using (8), we define *sameness of logical form* as a four-place relation among sentences and languages as in (9).

(9)   For any sentences s_1, s_2, languages L_1, L_2, s_1 in L_1 has the same logical form as s_2 in L_2 iff$_{df}$ there are interpretive truth theories T_1 for L_1 and T_2 for L_2 such that
   a.   they share the same logic;
   b.   there is a canonical proof P_1 of the T-sentence for s_1 in T_1;
   c.   there is a canonical proof P_2 of the T-sentence for s_2 in T_2, such that:
   d. P_1 *corresponds* to P_2.

(9) requires the contributions of the recursive elements and the way in which they combine with non-recursive elements in each sentence, relative to their languages, to be the same. Note that we have required sameness of interpretation up to contribution to truth-conditions in (8*c*). This qualification aims to exclude as irrelevant differences in meaning that make no difference to the way in which a recursive term determines how expressions it combines with contribute to fixing the conditions under which the sentence is true. For example, 'and' and 'but' arguably differ in meaning, but this difference is

irrelevant to how each determines the contribution of the sentences they conjoin to the truth of the sentences in which they occur.

The remaining free parameter is sameness of semantic type between base axioms in (8c). There may be room for different classifications, but in general it looks as if we will wish to classify axioms together on the basis of features neutral with respect to the extensions of predicates, though not with respect to the structure of the extensions (i.e. we will treat the number of argument places as relevant for the purposes of classification). (This captures one feature of the idea that logical form is a topic neutral feature of a sentence.) Reference axioms we can treat as of the same type iff they provide the same rule for determining the referent of the referring expression (proper names are a limiting case in which no rule is employed and the referent is given directly). In general, we wish to identify semantic categories with those such that a new base term falls into the category determines how it fits into the semantic pattern of sentences in the language independently of its extension or referent. (Note that we are not supposing that any terms except predicates and singular terms have extensions or referents.)

On our conception logical forms are not reified. The logical form of a sentence is not another sentence, a structure, or anything else. Talk of logical form is a *façon de parler*, proxy for talk of a complex feature of a sentence *s* of a language L determined by what all canonical proofs of T-sentences for *s* in various interpretive truth theories for L share. The relation *sameness of logical form* is conceptually basic. We want to urge that the expression '*x* is the logical form of *y*' should be retired from serious discussion. The basic expression is '*x* in L is the same in logical form as *y* in L'', where '... in ... is the same in logical form as ... in ...' is explicated as a unit as above. One can derivatively make sense of '*x* in L gives the logical form of *y* in L''. The practice of 'giving the logical form' of a sentence by exhibiting its paraphrase in a regimented language is a matter of replacing a sentence about whose semantic structure we are unclear with one whose semantic structure is clearer because it is formulated in a language for which the rules attaching to its various constituents and its structure have been clearly laid out. Thus, the relation expressed by '*x* in L gives the logical form of *y* in L'' is true of a 4-tuple $< x, L, y, L' >$ just in case *x* in L is the same in logical form as *y* in L', and *x*'s syntax understood relative to L makes perspicuous the semantic structure of *y* in L'. A paraphrase of a natural language sentence in a regimented language may capture the semantic structure of the original more or less well, and it may be that the language does not contain resources needed to yield a sentence with the same logical form as the original. That this occurs when a formal language is chosen as the translation target accounts for our intuition that sometimes indeterminacy about the logical form of a natural language sentence arises when we are forced to try to represent its semantic form in the absence of a worked out semantic theory for the language. It is no wonder the fit is sometimes awkward when we attempt to lay the semantic form of a sentence into the Procrustean bed of familiar logics. We toss and turn, settling on one tentative translation and then another, but none leaves us feeling comfortable.

We have so far ignored awkward facts about natural languages for the purposes of keeping the discussion relatively uncluttered. No formal truth theory can be applied directly to a natural language to reveal logical form because of ambiguity. Structurally ambiguous natural language sentences lack unique logical forms. In these cases, we must first disambiguate the language before we apply a truth theory to it. This makes regimentation, at least whatever is required to remove such ambiguity, necessary for a useful discussion of logical form for natural languages. Additional regimentation, perhaps motivated by considerations about syntactic decomposition, may recommend applying additional transformations before applying a truth theory, but these should not be necessary, as long as some description of the sentence is possible which accommodates all the features required for applying axioms for primitive expressions to generate a T-sentence for it. In an account of the logical form of a sentence, of course, we would want to track syntactic transformations, but, in a sense, its semantic structure would be revealed by a canonical proof of the T-sentence for its spruced up cousin, plus the fact that it means the same.

V

Treating logical form as we have above can help free us from overly simple models of the logical form of natural language sentences.[7] Too often we reach for the tools of elementary logic when trying to understand how natural languages work. The idea that logical form is to be determined by the translation of a sentence into an ideal language encourages this practice. By thinking about how to integrate an expression or construction into a interpretive truth theory, we free ourselves from those constraints, and from misconceptions

---

[7] 'Language disguises thought. So much so, that from the outward form of the clothing it is impossible to infer the form of the thought beneath it, because the outward form of the clothing is not designed to reveal the form of the body, but for entirely different purposes' (*Tractatus Logico-Philosophicus*, 4.002).

which may arise from trying to fit natural language constructions to a familiar pattern, in a well-understood artificial language.

An example of the difficulty philosophers have been led into by thinking of translation into a formal language as the proper approach to exhibiting logical form is the traditional treatment of natural language quantifiers in philosophy. Until recently, it was common to translate quantified noun phrases in natural languages like English into a paraphrase suitable for representation in a simple first order logic (the practice is still common). 'All men are mortal' goes into 'For all x, if x is a man, then x is mortal'. 'The king of France is bald' goes into 'There is an x such that x is king of France and for all y, if y is king of France then $x = y$, and x is bald'. 'Some men run for office' goes into 'There is an x such that x is a man and x runs for office'. Prima facie, all these paraphrases are of different forms than the originals, even though necessarily equivalent. That these paraphrases do not capture the semantic form of the originals is shown when we consider quantifiers such as 'few men' and 'most philosophers', for which the kinds of paraphrases given above fail. While most philosophers are not rich, most x are such that if they are philosophers, they are rich—since most things are not philosophers. The solution in a interpretive truth theory is to employ a semantic structure in the metalanguage which functions in the same way as that for the object language sentence (indeed, this is required to meet the condition that the axioms be interpretive). Thus, the satisfaction clause for a restricted quantifier (regimenting the object language sentence to introduce explicit variables) would have the following form (when the meta-language embeds the object language),

For any function f, speaker s, time t, f satisfies$_{(s,\,t)}$ '[Qx: x is F] (x are G)' iff Q 'x is F'/'x'-variants f' of f satisfy$_{(s,\,t)}$ 'x are G'.

We define 'ϕ/"x"-variant f' of f' in two stages as follows:

(Def.) For any functions f, f', f' is a ϕ/'x'-variant of f iff f' is an 'x'-variant of f and f' satisfies$_{(s,\,t)}\phi$.

(Def.) For any functions f, f', f' is a 'x'-variant of f iff f' differs from f at most in what it assigns to 'x'.

The virtues of this approach to logical form also emerge from its application to the puzzling case of complex demonstratives. Complex demonstratives are the concatenation of a demonstrative with a nominal, as in 'That man playing the piano is drunk'. What is the logical form of this sentence? Such constructions pull us in different directions. On the one hand, 'that' seems clearly to be a context-sensitive singular term, and 'man playing the piano' appears to be modifying it. This suggests giving 'That man playing the piano' a recursive reference clause in the truth theory, and treating the sentence as of subject-predicate form. On the other hand, the nominal in a complex demonstrative appears to play the same role as the nominal in quantified noun phrases. 'That man playing the piano is drunk' implies 'Someone is drunk', 'Someone is playing the piano', 'That man is playing something' and 'That man playing something is drunk' (fixing contextual parameters). These implications require the nominal be truth-conditionally relevant, and the last in particular requires that we be able to quantify into the nominal, and so relativize it to a universe of discourse, and so relativize to a universe of discourse the contribution of complex demonstratives to truth conditions, which makes no sense if they are singular terms. Such considerations suggest complex demonstratives are quantified noun phrases. Yet 'that' is no quantifier word, since there can be vacuous uses of it in both simple and complex demonstratives.

The proper course is to write into the satisfaction conditions for such a sentence the requirements these facts reveal. 'That man playing a piano is drunk' will be true on an occasion of use provided that the object the speaker demonstrates (i.e. *that*) which is a man playing a piano is drunk. That is, 'That man playing a piano is drunk' will have the same logical form as '[The x: $x =$ that and x is playing a piano] (x is drunk)'. This captures both features of the sentence noted above, the similarities in behavior between the complex demonstrative and quantified noun phrases, and the fact that 'that' functions as a genuine demonstrative. By refusing to look for a translation into a familiar idiom, but first asking how the parts contribute to the truth-conditions of the whole, we are led to a novel suggestion for the logical form of complex demonstratives and sentences containing complex demonstratives which reconciles what appeared to be irreconcilable features of the construction (see Lepore and Ludwig, n.d.). With complex demonstratives, the concatenation of a demonstrative with a nominal must be treated as introducing a quantifier.[8] This illustrates how grammatical categories such as that of determiner (which

---

[8] It turns out that there is considerable leeway in which quantifier we use in our paraphrase: 'some', 'the', and 'all' would work equally well, since the predicate restriction requires the variable to take on a value identical to the referent of the demonstrative as used by the speaker on that occasion. Here, perhaps, is a case where we can say there is indeterminacy of logical form: each captures as well as any other the semantic behavior of complex demonstratives. This is generated by forcing the object language structure to be interpreted in a language which requires one or another of these quantifier words to be used. It would be possible, however, to introduce into the metalanguage a structure which mimics exactly that of the object language, for example: for all f, f satisfies $_{(s, t)}$ '[That x: x is F] (x is G)' iff f' such that f' is a 'Fx and $x =$ that'/'x'-variant of f is such that f' satisfies$_{(s, t)}$ 'x is G'.

subsumes 'this', 'that', 'these', 'those', 'all', 'some', 'the', 'few', 'most', etc.) can provide a poor guide to semantic role.

We find in complex noun phrases an interesting example of how surface grammatical form[9] (we drop the qualifier for brevity) and semantic (or logical) form can come apart. Another example of this sort is provided by the contrast between attributive adjectives such as 'slow' and 'large', and those such as 'red' and 'bald'.[10] 'John is a bald man' and 'John is a large man' share grammatical form. But while the former will be treated by the truth theory as appealing to axioms for simple one-place predicates, 'is bald' and 'is a man', we propose the latter be treated as appealing to a quantifier and a relational predicate 'is larger than' as well as to the monadic predicate 'is a man'. Satisfaction clauses are given for the respective predicates in (10)–(11).[11]

(10) For all functions f, f satisfies$_{(s, t)}$ 'x is a bald man' iff f satisfies$_{(s, t)}$ 'x is bald' and f satisfies$_{(s, t)}$ 'x is a man'.

[9] We use 'surface grammatical form' advisedly, since one can characterize grammatical form so that the form of a sentence is exhibited only in a notation in which every semantic feature of the sentence is syntactically represented. This would not be, however, something to be read off from the words and their order in the sentence we write down or speak, and so characterizing grammatical form makes any current grammatical categories we use, like that of 'determiner', hostage to a correct semantic theory. It is perhaps worth noting, to avoid any misunderstandings, that when we use 'sentence' we mean the string of symbols we write out or the sequence of symbols we utter in speech, not a string of symbols which represents its analyzed structure.

[10] The treatment given below for attributives such as 'slow' and 'large' does not extend to all adjectives which do not interact purely extensionally with the nouns they modify. These form a semantically heterogeneous class since there is not a single mode of interaction. The treatment given here works well for attributive adjectives which have a related non-evaluative comparative, as 'slow' and 'large' do in 'slower' and 'larger'. The same treatment does not work, for example, for 'good', since to be a good knife or a good actor is not merely to be better than most knives or actors. Even a bad actor could be first among a very bad lot. In the case of evaluative attributives, it looks as if what is selected in the interaction for comparison is something like an ideal of the type modified. Likewise, other attributives can interact in distinct ways with nouns they modify. For example, adjectives which are formed from nouns for substances, such as 'iron', 'brass', or 'wooden', interact non-extensionally with some (though not all) nouns. While a brass railing is both brass and railing, a brass monkey is not both brass and a monkey, but monkey-shaped brass. This only helps to reinforce the point that surface grammatical form is a poor guide to semantic form.

[11] A general treatment will require a device for introducing variables not already present in a predicate. We elide this in (11) in the interests of keeping the presentation relatively perspicuous. A generalization is: For all functions f, f satisfies$_{(s, t)}$ 'x is a F G' iff most fresh('x is a F G')⌐'is a man'/fresh('x is a F G')-variants f' of f satisfy$_{(s, t)}$ 'x is larger than'⌐fresh('x is a F G') and f satisfies$_{(s, t)}$ 'x is a man'. The function fresh(ϕ) yields as value the first variable in some standard ordering not in ϕ.

(11) For all functions f, f satisfies$_{(s,\,t)}$ 'x is a large man' iff most 'y is a man'/ 'y'-variants f' of f satisfy$_{(s,\,t)}$ 'x is larger than y' and f satisfies$_{(s,\,t)}$ 'x is a man'.[12]

Once we consider how to provide recursive satisfaction conditions for our two intuitively different structures, vastly different logical forms are revealed— that is to say, we can see that the kinds of proofs of T-sentences for each and their starting-points are different: they will appeal to different kinds of axioms, classified according to semantic type, and hence yield proofs with different structures, exhibiting the components which play a similar grammatical role as playing quite different semantic roles. The concatenation of an attributive adjective such as 'large' or 'slow' with a noun is revealed to be a kind of restricted quantification.[13] This case helps to make clear the importance for a semantic theory of sorting lexical items into categories on the basis of their semantical roles.[14] The adjectives 'red' and 'large' look to share grammatical role, but play different semantic roles. No sorting of terms into grammatical

---

[12] A caveat: often ambiguities will need to be resolved before an appropriate satisfaction clause can be assigned. 'Jean Paul is a subtle French philosopher' can be read either as 'Jean Paul is a subtle philosopher and Jean Paul is a French philosopher' or as 'Jean Paul is a subtle (French philosopher)'. Similarly, 'Paul Bunyan is a large quick man' may be read as conjunctive, or 'large' may be read as modifying 'quick man'. Once ambiguities are resolved, the recursive clause provided in the text will yield the right satisfaction conditions.

[13] Gareth Evans (1976) tries to provide a satisfaction clause for attributive adjectives which makes no appeal to explicit quantifiers. Adapting it to our notation, his proposal for 'x is a large man' would be: 'For any function f, f satisfies$_{(s,\,t)}$ $\ulcorner x$ is a large man$\urcorner$ iff $f('x)$ is a large satisfier$_{(s,\,t)}$ of 'x is a man'.' (Two different satisfaction relations are introduced on this account.) The attempt fails, however, because Evans's clauses are not recursive, but adjectival phrases can be of arbitrary complexity. Given that attributive adjectives can interact, as in 'x is a large slow man', so that we cannot represent this as 'x is a large man' and 'x is a slow man', on at least one of its readings, we must introduce a new axiom for each additional iteration. Since there is no end to the iterations, there will be no end to the axioms required, which would represent the language as unlearnable.

[14] The point is not novel. In 'The average man is no better than he ought to be' we do not suppose 'average' is contributing a predicate with a variable bound by the definite article, or that in 'I had a quick cup of coffee' the adjective 'quick' contributes a predicate or a comparative with places bound by a restricted quantifier whose restricting predicate is 'x is a cup'. In the first, 'average' modifies the sentence, and in the second 'quick' modifies the verb, despite their displacement. These cases may well count as idioms, however. Clearly the case involving attributive adjectives is not. Adjectives such as 'fake' and 'phoney' present interesting cases. Such adjectives create an intensional context, which suggests they should receive a treatment as a part of a general account of opaque contexts. Such an account is presented in (Ludwig and Ray, 1998). But it would take us too far afield to show how to apply that account to the present case.

categories by tests not sensitive to their semantic roles, such as the traditional test of invariance of judgements of grammaticality under substitution, will provide a grammatical classification of terms that we will have reason to think a certain guide to semantic structure. For the purposes of regimenting sentences for input into a formal semantic theory, it is the semantical roles of the words that should be our guide. Our aim will be to assign different syntactical categories where there are differences in semantic structure.

VI

Non-declarative sentences, such as 'Open the door', and 'What time is it?', present an especially interesting challenge to any conception of logical form grounded in truth-theoretic semantics, since uses of them are neither true nor false. They have semantic form, and so, on a conception of logical form as semantic form, should have logical form. But how can it make sense to talk about their logical form on the model we have been using up to this point, and to try to characterize it in terms of a truth theory?

A generalization of the truth-theoretic approach may show the way to an answer. To keep the discussion simple, we will concentrate here on impera-tives, though we will indicate how the account might make room for interroga-tives. Intuitively, uses of imperatives admit of a bivalent evaluation, though they are not truth-valued. Rather, they are complied with or not. To generalize the truth-theoretic approach, we might try introducing a notion of fulfilment conditions which subsumes both compliance conditions for imperatives and truth-conditions for declaratives. Since it seems evident that our basic under-standing of predicates and referring terms in imperatives should be provided by an interpretive truth theory, we might try to exhibit compliance conditions as recursively specifiable in terms of truth-conditions. Imperative sentences would then be obtained from declaratives by a small number of transform-ations, from which the original declarative is easily recoverable. 'Open the door' might be obtained from 'You will open the door' by dropping its second person pronoun and modal auxiliary 'will'. Letting 'Core(ϕ)' represent the declarative core of an imperative sentence, Core('Tell me the time') = 'You will tell me the time'. The compliance conditions for imperatives will then be exhibited as given in terms of the truth-conditions for their declarative cores. Intuitively, an utterance of an imperative is complied with iff the addressee(s) makes it the case that the declarative core of the imperative is true as a result of the intention to comply with the directive issued with the imperative. Introducing a satisfaction predicate relating functions to sentences and formulas in imperative mood, we can exhibit satisfaction conditions for 'Open the door' as in (12):

(12) For any function f, f satisfies$^I_{(s, t)}$ 'Open the door' iff ref$_{(s, t)}$ ('you') makes it the case that f satisfies$_{(s, t)}$ Core('Open the door') with the intention of obeying the directive s issues at t.[15]

The satisfaction relation employed on the right-hand side of the quantified biconditional is that employed in the truth theory. So the satisfaction and so compliance conditions for imperatives are characterized recursively by the satisfaction conditions of their declarative cores. Note also that the forward-looking character of directives issued using imperatives is captured by the fact that the declarative core of an imperative is itself in future tense. A general satisfaction predicate, which we capitalize to distinguish it, can be defined in terms of the satisfaction predicates for imperatives and declaratives. For atomic sentences, we define 'Satisfies$_{(s, t)}$' as follows.

For any atomic sentence ϕ, function f, f Satisfies$_{(s, t)}\phi$ iff
if ϕ is declarative, f satisfies$_{(s, t)}\phi$;
if ϕ is imperative, f satisfies$^I_{(s, t)}\phi$.

For molecular sentences, 'Satisfies$_{(s, t)}$' will be defined recursively in the usual way, with the caveat that for mixed mood sentences the recursion selects the satisfaction relation appropriate for the mood of the component sentences. Satisfaction of open sentences in the imperative mood or in mixed moods is a straightforward generalization of the above. (A similar approach can be employed with respect to interrogatives. See Ludwig (1997) for a fuller working out of this approach, and its extension to interrogatives, which present additional complexities.) The connection between a fulfillment theory for natural languages and a compositional meaning theory is given by a general-ization of our earlier characterization. For an imperative (under which category we included molecular sentences which mixed imperatives and declaratives), we wish a compositional meaning theory to entail all true instances of schema (I),

For all speakers s, times t, ϕ commands$_{(s, t)}$ that p,

---

[15] A full treatment will introduce some additional complications, though none that affect the approach outlined here. Thus, for example, since more than one directive can be issued at a time, even using the same words (directed at different audiences), satisfaction and truth conditions ultimately need to be relativized to speech acts.

where φ is replaced by a structural description of an object language sentence. For an interrogative (under which we include mixed interrogative and declarative mood molecular sentences), we wish a compositional meaning theory to entail all true instances of the schema (Q),

(Q)   For all speakers s, times t, φ requests$_{(s, t)}$ that p,

where φ is replaced by a structural description of an object language sentence. The condition on an interpretive fulfillment condition theory for a language L is that

if ⌜φ is fulfilled$_{(s, t)}$ in L iff p⌝ is canonically provable from it,
then if φ is assertoric, then φ means$_{(s, t)}$ in L that p;
if φ is imperative, then φ commands$_{(s, t)}$ in L that p;
if φ is interrogative, then φ requests$_{(s, t)}$ in L that p.

This puts us in a position to extend the notion of logical form to non-declaratives, and to generalize the notion of logical form as semantic form. Letting 'F-sentence' stand for an interpretive sentence of the form ⌜φ is fulfilled$_{(s, t)}$ in L iff p⌝, we generalize the earlier characterization:

For sentences s_1, s_2, languages L_1, L_2, s_1 in L_1 has the same logical form as s_2 in L_2 iff there is an interpretive fulfillment condition theory F_1 for L_1 and an interpretive fulfillment condition theory F_2 for L_2 such that
   a. F_1 and F_2 share the same logic;
   b.   there is a canonical proof P_1 of the F-sentence for s_1 in F_1;
   c.   there is a canonical proof P_2 of the F-sentence for s_2 in F_2, such that:
   d. P_1 corresponds to P_2.

The notion of a corresponding proof similarly generalizes. Likewise, the notions of logical consequence, truth, etc., can be generalized in a straightforward way to include non-declaratives.

VII

The above sections present our basic approach to explicating logical form. It will be useful, however, to consider the relation of this characterization to the notion of a logical constant, or a slight generalization of this notion, the topic of this section.

Logical constants are a subset of primitive terms of a language thought to be especially useful for identifying classes of arguments the same in form. The notion of a logical constant, however, conceived of as subsuming only terms, is too narrow to do the work needed for regimenting valid natural language arguments. The inference from (13) to (14) is intuitively valid in virtue of form.

(13) Brutus is an honorable man.

(14) Brutus is a man.

(13), however, has no logical constant. The term 'honorable' functions semantically to contribute a predicate to the sentence, as is shown by the fact that (13) also implies in virtue of its form 'Brutus is honorable' (that is, 'A is an F G $\supset$ A is F' is a valid schema). The effect of modifying 'man' with 'honorable' is to add to the truth-conditions the requirement that Brutus be honorable as well as a man. It is not the use of 'honorable' that signals this, but rather that it is an adjective modifying the noun from which the predicate 'is a man' is formed. Thus, we need to identify here the structure,

noun phrase + 'is a' + adjective + nominal,

as itself semantically significant to the semantic compositional structure of the sentence. Intuitively, modifying the nominal with an adjective does the same semantic work as adding a conjunct to the sentence—in the case of (13), of adding 'and Brutus is honorable'. These are different ways of 'encoding' the same semantic information. To recognize this is to recognize that we need to talk not just about logical terms, but logical structures. A logical structure will in general be characterized in terms of a pattern of types of terms in a grammatical expression. What are traditionally thought of as logical constants may or may not appear in the pattern of terms. When they do, they count as part of the pattern that constitutes the logical structure. Indeed, the idea that an argument is valid in virtue of its logical terms is a mistake. It is rather patterns which include the constants which render an argument valid. Logical constants are useful because they help form patterns which provide information about how to understand the contribution of component expressions in which they occur to a sentence's truth-conditions. To express this notion of a logical structure, we will press into service the term 'logical syntax'.[16]

The aim of identifying logical syntax is to identify *syntactical* constants in sentences which help regiment natural language arguments into classes with shared forms that account for their validity. There will be in the nature of the case a variety of different levels of abstraction at which we can identify forms which

[16] It should be clear that here syntax is not thought of as a purely orthographical feature of an expression, but includes information about the semantic category of terms or places in a sentence structure.

help to regiment natural language arguments. We would like to find a way of isolating out for special consideration a class of structures salient from the point of view of a semantic theory for the language, and which seem to have something specially to do intuitively with the structures of the sentences of the language.

The notion of logical form we have articulated is neutral about what structures count as logical. Any of the competing criteria in the literature could simply be adjoined to our account. This points up an important fact about the relation between talk about logical form, if we are correct in holding that our explication tracks use of the term back to interests expressed by Russell in the quotation at the beginning of this chapter, and talk about logical syntax and the related notions of logical consequence and truth. The identification of *logical* syntax is not itself either central to or sufficient for understanding what talk of logical form comes to. Rather, it has been thought to be central because many of the kinds of terms identified as logical constants have been particularly important for understanding the semantic structure of sentences in which they appear. But identifying a particular class of terms as logical, for the purposes of identifying a class of logically valid sentences or argument forms, is not necessary to understand the semantic structure of such sentences. The interpretive truth theory contains all the information necessary whether or not we go on to select out a particular class of terms (or structures) for attention for more specialized interests. And, of course, the notion of the semantic structure of a sentence applies to sentences in which no logical constants as traditionally conceived appear.

Despite this independence, there are differences among primitive terms (and primitive terms and structures which carry important semantic information) which are particularly salient from the standpoint of an interpretive truth theory, namely, that between terms which can receive base clauses and *terms or structures which require a recursive treatment.* It is natural to seize on this difference and to urge that 'the logical constants may be identified as those iterative features of the language that require a recursive clause in the characterization of truth or satisfaction' (Davidson, 1984a: 71).[17] We must generalize

---

[17]   See 'Truth and Meaning', 33, 'In Defense of Convention T', 71, 'On Saying That', 94 in Davidson (1984). (Interestingly, Dummett (1973) gives a similar, if somewhat less precise, criterion and includes, in a footnote, an anticipation of the generality conception we discuss below, in discussing the logical status of the identity sign, which is otherwise excluded.) The requirement that a term must receive a recursive clause to be a logical constant is important in this characterization, and rules out what would otherwise be counterexamples. Adjective modifiers can be given a recursive clause *if* we ignore the use of connectives in adjectives and focus only on extensional adjectives that don't interact with other adjectives, as in the following

this a bit in the light of our discussion above. We will suggest that the recursive syntactical structures of the language be treated as its logical syntax. The recursive syntax of sentences gives them structure beyond that already expressed in the number of argument places in primitive predicates. It is natural to think of arguments made valid in virtue of the presence of recursive syntax in the premises and conclusion as valid in virtue of their *structure*. This gives one clear sense to the idea that in identifying the logical *terms* we identify those terms that we do not replace with schematic letters in identifying the structures or forms of sentences relevant to determining what other sentences similarly identified in terms of their structures they bear deductive relations to. The proposal rounds up many of the usual suspects, the so-called truth-functional connectives, and the quantifiers, as well as other iterative syntactical patterns that do similar work. As we have seen, truth-functionality is not always achieved lexically, as in 'Brutus is an honorable man'. Likewise, quantification need not be signaled by an explicit quantifier word, as in 'Whales are mammals'. Verb inflection for tense, too, is arguably best thought of as a quantificational device (Lepore and Ludwig, 2002).

We have indicated that both terms and structures may be treated recursively. One cannot identify a recursive term or structure by a syntactic test of iterability. We may concatenate 'Time is short and' with any sentence, and concatenate it with the result, and so on indefinitely. This does not mean that 'Time is short and' is a logical constant or a recursive structure. For we need a recursive clause for the concatenation of a sentence with 'and' with another sentence. The rule attaches to that structure, not to particular instances of it. Similarly, though 'honorable' may be added any number of times before 'man' in 'Brutus is an honorable man', we do not suppose 'honorable' is a logical constant or itself receives a recursive clause. Again, the rule attaches to a pattern exemplified by the sentence, not to the particular terms instantiating that pattern.

example. 'For all functions f, speakers s, times t, and nouns ϕ, f satisfies$_{(s,\,t)}$ $\ulcorner x$ is a red $\phi\urcorner$ iff f satisfies$_{(s,\,t)}$ $\ulcorner x$ is a $\phi\urcorner$ and $f('x)$ is red.' However, clearly this is unnecessary. The only feature of such constructions which requires recursive treatment is the concatenation of an adjective with a noun. The contribution of the adjective can, and in fact should, be cashed out in terms of the axiom for the corresponding predicate, as in the following. 'For all functions f, speakers s, times t, and noun ϕ, f satisfies$_{(s,\,t)}$ $\ulcorner x$ is a red $\phi\urcorner$ iff f satisfies$_{(s,\,t)}$ $\ulcorner x$ is a $\phi\urcorner$ and f satisfies$_{(s,\,t)}$ $'x$ is red'.' We note also that the approach represented by the first clause requires an axiom for each adjective in addition to axioms for their occurrences in predicates formed using the copula, though it seems clear that our understanding of the use of adjectives is of a piece with our understanding of the predicates formed from them. We show in no. 12, incidentally, that a similar recursive treatment of attributive adjectives such as 'large' and 'slow' is not viable.

These terms and structures by and large are intuitively topic neutral, as expected, since, with few exceptions, they determine only how the primitive predicates of the language contribute to the truth-conditions of complex sentences. Exceptions in natural languages are primitive restricted quantifiers, such as 'someone' and 'anytime'. Artificial examples may be constructed as well. It seems appropriate to divide recursive terms into the logical and what we can call the *purely logical*. In the case of 'Someone is in hiding', the satisfaction clause would be:

> For all f, f satisfies$_{(s, t)}$ 'Someone is in hiding' iff some 'x is a person'/'x'-variant f' of f satisfies$_{(s, t)}$ 'x is in hiding'.

Alternatively:

> For all f, f satisfies$_{(s, t)}$ 'Someone is in hiding' iff some 'x'-variant f' of f such that f' ('x') is a person satisfies$_{(s, t)}$ 'x is in hiding'.

These suggest the following condition on a purely logical term or structure: a term or structure is purely logical iff its satisfaction clause does not (*a*) introduce terms requiring appeal to base clauses other than those required for the terms to which the logical term is applied, or (*b*) introduce non-logical metalanguage terms not introduced by base clauses for the terms to which the logical term is applied.[18] If (*a*) or (*b*) is violated, the extra non-logical material is contributed by the logical term or structure itself.

This conception of logical syntax does omit, however, terms often included, such as the identity sign. On this conception, the identity sign is treated as having the logical form of a two-place relational predicate and, consequently, is not singled out for special attention. Likewise, the second-order relation 'is an element of', and such relational terms as 'is a subset of', 'is the union of', will not be counted as logical on this conception; and so on. (See Appendix B for a discussion of an alternative proposal which employs an epistemic criterion.) These sorts of terms would be counted on a conception introduced independently by Tarski (1986) and Lindstrom (1966), and motivated by the idea that the 'logical notions' or terms have greatest generality (see Sher (1996) for a

---

[18] Modal operators may be counterexamples as well if they must receive recursive clauses, for their contributions to determining the truth-conditions of sentences in which they occur are not intuitively independent of features of objects picked out by the predicates in sentences to which they apply. The exclusion criterion just given would not exclude modal operators, so they would have to be excluded independently. If they are (implausibly) treated as quantifiers over possible worlds, then, as lexically primitive restricted quantifiers, the exclusion rule given in the text would exclude them as well.

recent exposition of this line, though with differences from the way we develop it below). This is connected with the idea we have already invoked that logical syntax is topic neutral. But it is spelt out in a way that yields different results.

The basic idea is that terms express more general notions the more stable their extensions under transformations of the universe, and those terms that express the most general notions will be those whose extensions are invariant under all permutations of the universe, i.e. under all one–one mappings of the universe of discourse onto itself. For this to be applicable to all terms, of course, will require us to think of all terms as having extensions, and of truth-conditions of sentences as being given in terms of their extensions. Thus, this approach is most natural on a Fregean conception of semantics on which sentential connectives like 'and' and 'or' are thought of as functions, and the quantifiers as second-order functions. It is not difficult to see the upshot of this approach. Terms associated with sets invariant under all permutations of the universe will be counted as logical terms.[19] Thus, for example, proper names will not be logical terms because their referents (which we will treat as their extension) will not always be mapped onto themselves. Likewise, most n-place first-order relational terms will not be logical terms. Some will, however, for example, those one-place predicates whose extensions are the universal set ('exists' or 'is an object') and the empty set ('is nonexistent', 'is non-self-identical'), and those two-place predicates whose extensions are the set of ordered pairs consisting of an object and itself, and the set of ordered pairs of objects and some distinct object ('is identical with' and 'is nonidentical with'). There will be similar terms for any number of argument places. Likewise, there will be second-order relations (which take extensions of first-order relations as arguments) that will count as logical. If the universal quantifier has as its extension the set of the universal set, and the existential quantifier all subsets of the universal set except the empty set, these will count also as logical terms. 'Everything is F' will be true just in case ext('F') $\in$ ext('everything'). Binary quantifiers can be treated as appropriate sets of ordered pairs of sets. 'All', for example, can be assigned as its extension the set of all ordered pairs of sets such that the first is a subset of the second. 'All A are B' will be true provided that $<$ext('A'),ext('B')$>\in$ ext('All'). The result of systematically extending this idea is that all the so-called cardinality quantifiers will count as logical terms, as well as the standard set-theoretic relations. With contortions, truth-functional connectives can be treated as logical terms as

[19] We will be assuming that there are an infinite number of objects, e.g. all the real numbers, as well as spatio-temporal objects, so that concerns about the size of the universe need not affect this criterion.

well.[20] The approach could be extended straightforwardly to our broader notion of logical syntax.

We do not think there is an answer to the question which of these conceptions of logical syntax (or any of the others in the literature) is correct. Each is a projection for our intuitive starting-point in thinking about argument form and what sorts of constant structures we can identify to help us classify together arguments which are valid (or invalid) in virtue of those structures. Against the invariance conception, it might be said that it counts some terms as logical which do not seem helpful in this regard, such as, for example, 'is an object' and 'is nonexistent', and 'is nonidentical with'. Likewise, it might be said that, if our aim is to identify intuitively topic neutral syntax, the set-theoretic relations should not count as logical terms. Likewise, one may object that in order to count many terms as logical on this approach we must resort to a representation of the semantics of expressions which seems both gratuitous and misguided. On the other hand, there is no point to denying that classifying terms together as logical in this way may for some purposes be useful. We are inclined to say then that there is no substantive, as opposed to terminological, issue here. It may well be that in the place of the term 'logical syntax' what we need is a number of different terms with overlapping extensions. (See Appendix C for a discussion of extensions of the usual notions of logical truth, consequences and equivalence in terms of logical syntax which accommodates context sensitivity). This fact in itself could not be a reason to conclude no objective division is possible. Rather, it signifies that *many* objective divisions of 'logical' from 'non-logical' terms are possible, answering to different interests.

VIII

In this chapter, we have shown how to capture and generalize a notion of logical form used in the tradition in philosophy stretching back (at least) to Russell's enormously influential discussion of logical form in the first few decades of the twentieth century. To this end, we employed the notion of an

---

[20] We need to assign the logical constants extensions invariant under all permutations of the universe. Frege treated them as functions from truth-values to truth-values. If we associate The True with the universal set and The False with the empty set, the invariance criterion will classify the usual truth-functional connectives as logical terms. Rather than force fit truth-functional connectives to this criterion Sher (1996) gives a separate criterion for them. This admits, however, that no one notion of generality applies to every term we deem as logical.

interpretive truth theory for a natural language. The notion of logical form on this account is shown to be basically the notion of semantic form as it relates to the truth-conditions of sentences. The basic notion is *not* the logical form of a sentence, but rather sameness of logical form as between sentences interpreted relative to languages. Derivatively, we can make sense of the notion of 'giving the logical form' of a sentence in terms of offering a translation in a language which marks more explicitly in syntax the semantic features of the original and for which we have a better worked out semantics. There is, however, strictly speaking, no such *thing* as the logical form of any sentence. We have characterized the notion of sameness of logical form in terms of T-sentences for sentences with corresponding proofs in interpretive truth theories for their languages. The proofs encode the semantic structure of the sentence, abstracting away from differences in base axioms irrelevant to understanding how they combine with other kinds of expressions, and from differences in recursive axioms that make no difference to truth-conditions. Sameness of logical form of primitive terms is sameness of semantic type, characterized in terms of the way in which the terms systematically interact with other kinds of terms. The notion of logical form can be extended to non-declaratives, by way of a generalization of the truth-theoretic approach to giving a semantic theory for declaratives. The notion of sameness of logical form has been characterized independently of the notion of a logical constant or more broadly of logical syntax. The notion of logical form, i.e. semantic form, is more general. The interest in identifying logical syntax lies in its utility for classing together natural language arguments in terms of interesting broadly structural features they share which provide a common explanation for their validity. There is little reason to believe, so far as we can see, that the interest dictates a unique choice. However, we have urged a criterion for logical syntax particularly salient from the point of view of an interpretive truth theory, namely, logical syntax is that syntax which must be treated recursively in an interpretive truth theory. This provides one good reason for thinking of logical syntax as especially concerned with revealing the validity of arguments in virtue of the structures of the contained sentences, as well as respecting the requirement that logical syntax be topic neutral.[21]

[21] We wish to thank commentators on an earlier version of this paper presented at a symposium on logical form at the 1998 Central Division Meeting of the American Philosophical Association, Peter Ludlow, Robert May, and Robert Stainton, as well the audience at a departmental seminar at the University of Florida in February 1998. Particular thanks goes to Greg Ray.

APPENDIX A

In this appendix we draw attention to some important differences in the approach to truth-theoretic semantics outlined in section III and that pursued in Larson and Segal (1995). We wish to draw attention specifically to the failure of the semantics they introduce to adhere to our requirement of interpretiveness. To see how and why their account fails to meet this requirement, we need consider only their axioms for 'and' and 'or' represented in their PC′, and sentences formed using them (pp. 111–12).

(i) $Val(<z, z'>, \text{'and'})$ iff $z = t$ and $z' = t$

(ii) $Val(<z, z'>, \text{'or'})$ iff $z = t$ or $z' = t$

(iii) For any S, ConjP, $Val(t, (_sS\ ConjP))$ iff for some z, $Val(z, S)$ and $Val(z, ConjP)$

(iv) For any Conj, S, $Val(z, (_{conjP}\ Conj\ S))$ iff for some z', $Val(<z, z'>, Conj)$ and $Val(z', S)$

(v) For all conjunctions α, $Val(<z, z'>, (_{conj}\alpha))$ iff $Val(<z, z'>, \alpha)$

(vi) For any elementary sentence ζ, $Val(t, (_s\ \zeta))$ iff $Val(t, \zeta)$

'$Val(x,y)$' is read as 'x is a value of y'. '$(_sS\ ConjP)$' structurally describes a sentence formed from a sentence S and a conjunction ('and' or 'or') concatenated with a sentence P, the latter treated as a unit for purposes of decomposition. This is a device like the use of parentheses to disambiguate the order of evaluation of parts of complex sentences. Likewise '$(_{conjP}\ Conj\ S)$' is a structural description of a conjunction concatenated with a sentence S. It should be obvious that this is not, in our usage, an interpretive truth theory (or a fragment thereof), for a number of reasons. First, as we have said, we have in mind a Tarski-style theory in the sense of theory which uses a satisfaction predicate to relate sequences or functions to expressions of the language (and a reference function for singular referring terms). On our conception of an interpretive truth theory, no entities are assigned to any expressions in the language except referring terms; no terms (excepting singular terms) are said to have 'values' in the sense intended by Larson and Segal. The axioms above therefore fail to be axioms in an interpretive truth theory in our sense because they are not axioms in a Tarski-style theory in our sense. This point applies not just to PC′, but to all of the theories Larson and Segal discuss. (The motives which prompt Larson and Segal to introduce 'semantic values' for all expressions of natural languages are not shared by us, and are not part of any project of giving compositional semantics for natural languages which concerns us.) This is not unconnected with another way in which the above theory fails to be interpretive in our sense. The appeal to the assignments of ordered pairs as values to conjunctions allows the formulation of axioms (iii) and (iv) above as part of the recursion to generate T-sentences. The result of this, however, has a quantified sentence (or quantified open sentence) representing the recursive structure of an object language sentence that is not quantified. An interpretive axiom for a sentence with a recursive structure must not introduce recursive structures not present in the target sentence. But, of course, the introduction of this quantifier is directly connected with the decision to assign entities to sentential connectives, which represents the most fundamental departure from the style of theory with which we are concerned. These points are relevant to the semantic categories of axioms in an interpretive truth theory which are relevant for our characterization of sameness of logical form through the notion of corresponding proofs, explained in section IV. Questions about the relation of our approach to that of Larson and Segal, which prompted this note, were raised by Peter Ludlow in his comment on an earlier version of this paper presented at a symposium on logical form at the 1998 Central Division Meetings of the American Philosophical Association.

APPENDIX B

In this appendix we discuss an alternative to the proposal in Section VII of the chapter for how to use a truth theory to identify logical terms that has been proposed by Peacocke (1976), which also draws on the resources of a Tarski-style truth theory, and employs an epistemic criterion. Peacocke's proposal is that a term α is logical iff, with respect to a truth theory for a language containing α, from knowledge of (*a*) which sequences (or functions) satisfy formulas $\theta_1, \theta_2, \ldots \theta_n$ to which α can be applied and (*b*) knowledge of the satisfaction clause for α, one can infer a priori which sequences (or functions) satisfy $\alpha(\theta_1, \theta_2, \ldots \theta_n)$. The main idea behind his proposal is that it identifies *as* logical those terms knowledge of whose contributions to satisfaction conditions requires no knowledge of the properties of, or relations into which, objects enter. This is a way of trying to cash out the idea that the logical terms are topic neutral. (We can extend the proposal to terms that apply not just to formulae but to variables and singular terms: α is a logical term just in case, with respect to a truth theory for a language containing α, from knowledge of (*a*) which sequences (or functions) satisfy formulae $\theta_1, \theta_2, \ldots \theta_n$ and which objects sequences assign to terms $\tau_1, \tau_2, \ldots \tau_m$ to which α can be applied and (*b*) knowledge of the satisfaction clause for α, one can infer a priori which sequences (or functions) satisfy $\alpha(\theta_1, \theta_2, \ldots \theta_n, \tau_1, \tau_2, \ldots \tau_m)$, or if it is a singular term, what object each sequence (or function) assigns to it.)

What terms count as logical constants on this view depends on what knowledge we suppose we have about the sequences (or functions) that satisfy formulae or apply to terms. For example, knowing that sequences σ_1, σ_2, satisfy 'x is F' is not in itself sufficient to know that every sequence satisfies 'x is F', even if these are all the sequences, unless we also know that they are all the sequences, which is an additional bit of knowledge. Likewise, application of the criterion to numerical quantifiers and terms like the identity sign depends on whether we are supposed to know facts about the numbers of sequences that satisfy a formula and facts about the identity and diversity of objects in sequences.

The same idea may be approached non-epistemically by appeal to entailment relations as follows: α is a logical term iff, with respect to a truth theory for a language containing α, which sequences (or functions) satisfy formulae $\theta_1, \theta_2, \ldots \theta_n$ and which objects sequences assign to terms $\tau_1, \tau_2, \ldots \tau_m$ to which α can be applied and the proposition expressed by the satisfaction clause for α entail which sequences (or functions) satisfy $\alpha(\theta_1, \theta_2, \ldots \theta_n, \tau_1, \tau_2, \ldots \tau_m)$, or if it is a singular term, what object each sequence (or function) assigns to it. Here too what terms are counted as logical will depend on what propositions about the sequences (or functions) that satisfy a formula we are including. For the universal quantifier to be a logical constant, we have to include propositions about all 'x'-variants of a given function or sequence.

Both these ways of spelling out the idea suffer from an obvious difficulty noted by McCarthy (1981), namely, there are a priori inferences (entailments) not obviously grounded in the meanings of what have been traditionally taken to be logical constants. To see the difficulty, consider an arbitrary formula Ω, and a operator on it Σ, with satisfaction conditions as given in,

For any function f, f satisfies $\Sigma^\frown \Omega$ iff f satisfies Ω or A,

where 'A' is replaced by any a priori truth, e.g. '$1 < 2$'. Peacocke's criterion will count Σ as a logical constant, though intuitively it is not. Similarly, as McCarthy points out, if *de re* knowledge of which objects sequences or functions assign to terms includes whether they are numbers, many function signs denoting functions that take numbers as arguments, such as 'the successor of —', or '. . . + —' will be treated as logical constants, though intuitively these are not topic neutral terms. Peacocke intends to exclude from consideration number-theoretic terms, but this seems *ad hoc,* and in any case other a priori truths will do as well. An interesting example McCarthy mentions is the concatenation sign, '...⌢—'. Knowledge of what objects sequences assign to terms which can appear in the argument places for this functor and knowledge of the satisfaction clause for it suffices for knowledge of which objects sequences assign to the expression formed from those terms and the concatenation sign. Few will wish to treat '⌢' as a logical term, however. The feature that Peacocke identifies seems at best a necessary condition on a term's being a logical term, but not a sufficient one.

McCarthy's own suggestion is a version of the invariance approach which we discuss in the text. McCarthy's proposal identifies a narrower class of terms than the invariance approach we consider below, and, in particular, fails to count cardinality quantifiers as logical terms. We will not discuss it further here. But it helps to illustrate the variety of notions of logical constants one can identify, and to suggest that there is a family of related notions, to a greater or lesser extent topic neutral, which can be classified on the basis of a number of overlapping features, and that there is little point to insisting that one is the objectively correct way of extending the practice of using the term 'logical constant' beyond the territory in which it is currently well-grounded.

APPENDIX C

In this appendix, we discuss how to extend the notions of logical truth, consequence, and equivalence once we have a characterization of the notion of logical syntax we discuss in section VII of the chapter, with adjustments to accommodate for natural language sentences not being true or false independently of context. To do so, we relativize the notions to sets of contextual parameters. A sentence true under all interpretations of its non-logical terms for a given set of values for contextual parameters C is a logical truth relative to C; a sentence ϕ is a logical consequence of a set of sentences $\{\psi_1, \psi_2 \ldots \psi_n\}$ relative to a given set of contextual parameters C iff there is no interpretation of non-logical terms under which every sentence of $\{\psi_1, \psi_2 \ldots \psi_n\}$ is true relative to C and ϕ is false relative to C; sentences ϕ and ψ are logically equivalent relative to contextual parameters C iff each is a logical consequence of the other relative to C. (Stronger notions can be defined by universally quantifying over contextual parameters, though complications emerge for demonstratives.) Essentially, this picks out those consequences as logical (relative to contextual parameters) which are due to the meanings of the syntactical features of the language identified as logical.

We can also identify a notion of pragmatic consequence and necessity. ϕ is a pragmatic consequence of ψ iff ϕ is true in all contexts in which ψ is true; ϕ is pragmatically necessary if true in all contexts. 'I am here now' is pragmatically necessary (well, almost—for one can use 'here' to designate a place one is not e.g. by pointing to a map). But it is best to keep these notions distinct from those of logical consequence and necessity.

Evans (1976) has suggested distinguishing a notion of structural consequence from logical consequence. However, his proposal would identify structural consequences with a subset of what we are already committed to treating as logical consequences, on the basis of a feature of them which does not seem to mark them out as an interestingly distinct class. Evans treats logical consequences as hinging on the presence of logical *terms* in a sentence. Structural consequences hinge not on logical terms but on patterns in the construction of sentences. Thus, we recognize the validity of the argument from (i) to (ii) by recognizing forms (iii) and (iv):

   (i) Brutus is an honorable man;
  (ii) Brutus is honorable;
 (iii) noun phrase + 'is a' + adjective + noun;
 (iv) noun phrase + 'is a' + noun.

Understanding the semantic contribution of the adjective in a sentence of the first form is sufficient to know that the corresponding sentence of the second form is true if the first is. We have already, though, subsumed the sort of structure exhibited in (iii) under the heading 'logical'. It counts as logical because it, not the terms which instantiate it, receives a recursive treatment (the terms all get their own base clauses, or terms they are derived from do). Evans does not treat the entailment from (i) to (ii) as logical. But from our perspective, this is misguided. From the point of view of an interpretive truth theory, the difference between 'Brutus is an honorable man' and 'Brutus is honorable and Brutus is a man' is merely what syntactic features of a sentence are subserving a certain semantic role. Rather than distinguish a new notion of consequence, as Evans does, it is more reasonable to extend the notion of logicality from terms to structures.

REFERENCES

Audi, Robert (ed.) (1995). *The Cambridge Dictionary of Philosophy* (Cambridge: Cambridge University Press).

Black, Max, and Geach, Peter (eds.) (1960). *Translations from the Philosophical Writings of Gottlob Frege* (Oxford: Oxford University Press).

Davidson, Donald. (1968). 'On Saying That', *Synthese*, 19: 130–46.

—— (1984*a*). 'Defense of Convention', in *Inquiries into Truth and Interpretation* (New York: Clarendon Press).

—— (1984*b*). *Inquiries into Truth and Interpretation* (New York: Clarendon Press).

—— (1984*c*). 'On Saying That', in *Inquiries into Truth and Interpretation* (New York: Clarendon Press).

Dummett, Michael A. E. (1973). *Frege: Philosophy of Language* (London: Duckworth).

Etchemendy, John. (1983). 'The Doctrine of Logic As Form', *Linguistic and Philosophy* 6: 319–34.

—— (1988). 'Tarski on Truth and Logical Consequence', *Journal of Symbolic Logic* 53: 51–79.

—— (1990). *The Concept of Logical Consequence* (Cambridge Mass.: Harvard).

Evans, Gareth (1976). 'Semantic Structure and Logical Form', in J. McDowell and G. Evans (eds.), *Truth and Meaning* (London: Oxford University Press).

—— (1985). 'Does Tense Logic Rest on a Mistake?', in *Collected Papers* (Oxford: Clarendon Press).

Larson, Richard, and Segal, Gabriel (1995). *Knowledge of Meaning: An Introduction to Semantic Theory* (Cambridge, Mass.: MIT Press).

Lepore, Ernest, and Ludwig, Kirk (2002). 'Outline of a Truth Conditional Semantics for Tense', in Q. Smith (ed.), *Tense, Time and Reference* (Cambridge, Mass.: MIT Press).

—— —— (n.d.) 'Complex Demonstratives', TS.

Lindstrom, P. (1966). 'First Order Predicate Logic with Generalized Quantifiers', *Theoria*, 32: 186–95.

Ludwig, Kirk (1997). 'The Truth about Moods', *Protosociology*. Cognitive Semantics I—Conceptions of Meaning, 10: 19–66.

—— and Ray, Greg (1998). 'Semantics for Opaque Contexts', *Philosophical Perspectives*, 12: 141–66.

Lycan, William G. (1989). 'Logical Constants and the Glory of Truth-Conditional Semantics', *Notre Dame Journal of Symbolic Logic* 30(03): 390–400.

McCarthy, T. (1981). 'The Idea of a Logical Constant', *Journal of Philosophy*, 78: 499–523.

Peacocke, Christopher (1976). 'What is a Logical Constant?', *Journal of Philosophy*, 73(9): 221–40.

Quine, Willard Van Orman (1971). 'Methodological Reflections on Current Linguistic Theory', in D. Davidson and G. Harman (eds.), *Semantics of Natural Language*
(Boston, Mass.: D. Reidel Publishing Co.)

Russell, Bertrand (1959). *Mysticism and Logic, and Other Essays* (London: Allen &
Unwin).

—— (1993). *Our Knowledge of the External World: As a Field for Scientific Method in
Philosophy* (New York: Routledge).

Schlick, Mortiz (1959). 'The Turning Point in Philosophy', in A. J. Ayer (ed.), *Logical
Positivism* (New York: The Free Press).

Sher, Gila (1996). 'Semantics and Logic', in S. Lappin (ed.), *The Handbook of
Contemporary Semantic Theory* (Oxford: Blackwell).

Tarski, Alfred (1986). 'What are Logical Notions?', *History and Philosophy of Logic*,
7: 143–54.

Wittgenstein, Ludwig (1961). *Tractatus Logico-Philosophicus*, ed. D. F. Pears and
B. F. McGuinness (London: Routledge & Kegan Paul).

4

Function and Concatenation

Paul M. Pietroski

For any sentence of a natural language, we can ask the following questions: what is its meaning; what is its syntactic structure; and how is its meaning related to its syntactic structure? Attending to these questions, as they apply to sentences that provide evidence for Davidsonian event analyses, suggests that we reconsider some traditional views about how the syntax of a natural sentence is related to its meaning.

Many theorists have held, at least as an idealization, that every phrase—and in particular, every verb phrase—consists of (i) an expression semantically associated with some function, and (ii) an expression semantically associated with some element in the domain of that function. On this view, which makes it comfortable to speak of both verbs and functions as taking arguments, each phrase is semantically associated with the *value* of the relevant function given the relevant argument(s); the semantic contribution of natural language syntax is function-application, as in a Fregean *Begriffsschrift*; and the meaning of a sentence Σ is determined by the meanings of Σ's constituents, in the way that the sum of two numbers is determined by those numbers and the addition function. I want to urge a different conception of natural language semantics.

Some recent work suggests that phrases are concatenations of predicates, where a complex predicate of the form $\Phi \wedge \Psi$ is satisfied by those things that satisfy both Φ and Ψ. On this view, which is motivated by certain eventish hypotheses about the logical forms of natural sentences, the semantic contribution of syntactic branching is predicate-conjunction *and not* function-application. There is a corresponding sense in which sentences of natural language do not manifest their logical forms. But syntactic structure may still determine logical form; although opportunities for confusion abound, especially if 'logical form' is understood in terms of notions like 'good inference'.

1 Background

Let's assume that (1) has the syntactic structure indicated in (1S):

(1) Brutus stabbed Caesar

(1S) $\{(_\alpha\text{Brutus})[_\Phi(_\varphi\text{stabbed})(_\alpha\text{Caesar})]\}$

where the subscripted labels indicate that 'Brutus' and 'Caesar' are syntactic arguments, while 'stabbed' and 'stabbed Caesar' are predicates. The verb 'stabbed' is a binary predicate; and so the verb phrase 'stabbed Caesar' is a monadic predicate, whose phrasal status could be highlighted with the label 'ΦP'. While (1S) may be an incomplete representation of syntactic structure, it is presumably correct as far as it goes. Matters are less clear, however, with regard to meaning.

1.1

In order to formulate a proposal about how the meaning of (1) is related to its syntactic structure, we need a theoretically perspicuous representation of that meaning. A traditional suggestion is

(1*a*) $[\text{Stabbed}_2(\text{Caesar}_i)](\text{Brutus}_i)$

construed as a sentence of a formal language in which a subscripted numeral indicates a predicate which takes that many (ordered) argument-terms; predicates express functions; and a subscripted 'i' indicates a label for some individual in a canonical domain. Let 'Stabbed$_2$' express the function $\lambda y.\{\lambda x.\ true$ if x stabbed y and *false* otherwise$\}$; or more briefly, assuming exactly two truth-values, $\lambda y.\{\lambda x.\ true$ iff x stabbed y$\}$. Let 'Brutus$_i$' and 'Caesar$_i$' be labels for Brutus and Caesar, respectively. Then (1*a*), a variant of 'Stabbed$_2$(Brutus$_i$, Caesar$_i$)', is true by stipulation iff $[\lambda y.\{\lambda x.\ true$ iff x stabbed y$\}(\text{Caesar})](\text{Brutus})$. This highlights the asymmetry of semantic arguments in a way that parallels the asymmetry between internal and external syntactic arguments, as indicated in (1S).[1]

---

[1] But one idealizes by associating expressions of natural language with *functions* (whose extensions are not vague), or language-independent *entities* (with determinate properties). And

Having introduced talk of meanings and representations of them, a few clarifications are in order. (Those who dislike *any* talk of meanings may employ favored paraphrases.) I will follow tradition and take meanings to be compositionally structured abstract entities, leaving it open whether meanings ever have concrete constituents. But I do not assume that our best theories will quantify over such abstractions, or that semantics is happily characterized as an investigation of them. On the contrary, my own view is that meanings are of interest mainly as projections of certain intrinsic properties of sentences; it can be useful to model these properties, which are among the factors we gesture at when we say what sentences mean, with Fregean senses or Russellian propositions. That said, I am prepared to discover that a sentence has its meaning, wholly or in part, by virtue of bearing some interesting relation to that meaning. Perhaps there is even a theoretically frutiful sense in which natural sentences like (1) represent meanings; though I'm not betting on it.

There are nice questions about whether any formal expression like (1*a*), with stipulated *truth-conditions*, can adequately represent the *meaning* of a natural sentence. But let us set aside such questions, in order to focus on the semantic structure of (1). I assume that putative representations of meanings reflect hypotheses about the compositional structures of those meanings. According to (1*a*), the meaning of (1) has a function-argument architecture that involves a binary function expressed by 'Stabbed$_2$,' and a unary function expressed by 'Stabbed$_2$(Caesar$_i$)'. Given the disclaimers above, this is a fairly innocuous claim; the meaning of (1) has parts corresponding to Brutus, Caesar, and a certain function that maps these individuals (as ordered) to the truth-conditions of (1). But (1*a*) at least suggests a more tendentious hypothesis—namely, a semantics for English should associate the verb 'stabbed' with the binary function $\lambda y.\{\lambda x.$ *true* iff x stabbed y$\}$.

One can grant that '[Stabbed$_2$( )]( )' represents the meaning of (1), minus the parts corresponding to Brutus and Caesar, without granting that 'Stabbed$_2$,' represents the meaning of 'stabbed'. For '[Stabbed$_2$( )]( )' may represent *more* than just the semantic contribution of the verb (plus function-application). That is, the meaning of (1) may not be wholly determined by the meanings of 'stabbed', 'Brutus' and 'Caesar'. I will return to this point,

the fact that a sentence Σ has certain *truth*-conditions may well be an interaction effect, involving contextual factors not amenable to Kaplan-style relativization, with the meaning of Σ being one *contributing factor*; see Chomsky (1975, 2000*a*), Pietroski (forthcoming *b*). In which case, semanticists do not specify *truth*-conditions; they specify something that *constrains and contributes to* truth-conditions. But set these complications aside.

in the context of Frege's concept/object distinction. But for now, let me simply contrast (1a) with

(1b) $\exists e < \{[Stabbed_3(Caesar_i)](Brutus_i)\}(e) >$

(1c) $\exists e < \{[Agent_2(Brutus_i)](e) \ \& \ [Stabbed_1(e) \ \& \ [Theme_2(Caesar_i)]$
       $(e)]\} >$.

By stipulation, 'Stabbed$_3$' expresses $\lambda y.\{\lambda x.\{\lambda e. \ true$ iff e was a stabbing by x of y\}\}, and 'Stabbed$_1$' expresses $\lambda e. \ true$ iff e was a stabbing. The ampersands, existential quantifiers, and variables are to be understood in the usual way. Characterizing thematic relations raises questions not germane to this discussion. So I hope that the quasi-technical notions 'Agent' and 'Theme' are understood well enough to make homophonic stipulations comprehensible: 'Agent$_2$' expresses $\lambda x.\{\lambda e. \ true$ iff x is Agent of e\}; 'Theme$_2$' expresses $\lambda x.\{\lambda e.$ $true$ iff x is Theme of e\}.[2]

According to (1b), the meaning of (1) has a function-argument architecture that involves a ternary function expressed by 'Stabbed$_3$', a binary function expressed by 'Stabbed$_3$(Caesar$_i$)', and a unary function expressed by '[Stabbed$_3$(Caesar$_i$)](Brutus$_i$)'. According to (1c), the meaning of (1) involves a unary function expressed by 'Stabbed$_1$'; two binary functions expressed by 'Agent$_2$' and 'Theme$_2$'; two unary functions expressed by 'Agent$_2$(Brutus$_i$)' and 'Theme$_2$(Caesar$_i$)'; a binary conjunction function; and two conjunctive unary functions expressed by 'Stabbed$_1$(e) & [Theme$_2$(Caesar$_i$)](e)' and '[Agent$_2$(Brutus$_i$)](e) & [Stabbed$_1$(e) & [Theme$_2$(Caesar$_i$)](e)]'.

One can view (1b) and (1c), qua representations of meanings, as proposed elaborations of (1a). Perhaps '[Stabbed$_2$( )]( )' represents a subsentential meaning that has further structure as indicated in '$\exists e < \{[Stabbed_3( )]( )$ (e)>', and perhaps still further structure as indicated in '$\exists e < \{[Agent_2( )]$ (e) & [Stabbed$_1$(e) & [Theme$_2$( )](e)]\} >'. In this sense, the three proposals are compatible, while differing in the amount of semantic structure explicitly posited.[3] But the proposals are incompatible, if they incorporate the obvious suggestions about how the parts of (1) are related to the meaning of (1). For (1b) at least suggests that the semantic contribution of the verb 'stabbed' is the

---

[2] For an introduction to thematic roles that bears on the present discussion, see Larson and Segal (1995). Davidson (1967) and Castañeda (1967) used variants of (1b) and (1c), '$\exists e[Stabbed(e,$ Brutus, Caesar)]' and '$\exists e[Agent(e, Brutus) \ \& \ Stabbed(e) \ \& \ Theme(e, Caesar)$' that I will also use occasionally.

[3] Perhaps $\{<x,y>: x \text{ stabbed } y\} = \{<x,y>: \exists e[e \text{ was a stabbing by } x \text{ of } y]\} = \{<x,y>: \exists e[x \text{ was Agent of } e \ \& \ e \text{ was a stabbing } \& \ y \text{ was Theme of } e]\}$, and speakers of English know this; see Parsons (1990).

ternary function expressed by 'Stabbed$_3$', while (1c) at least suggests that the semantic contribution of 'stabbed' is the unary function λe. *true* iff e was a stabbing. Correspondingly, (1c) suggests that the syntactic arguments are *not* associated with relevant entities in the domain of the (unary) function associated with 'stabbed'; rather, 'Brutus' and 'Caesar' are associated with 'thematically separated' conjuncts of a complex event description.

Perhaps such suggestions should not be incorporated into hypotheses about meanings, which will prove interesting independently of how sentences are related to them. But however one defines 'hypothesis about meaning', we can ask which (if any) of the suggestions is best supported by available evidence. And if we settle on (1b) or (1c), as our hypothesis about how the parts of (1) are related to the meaning of (1), this raises (fruitful) questions about why the meaning of (1) has components that do not correspond to overt parts of (1). Of course, we must stay alive to the possibility that distinct formal sentences are equally good—and equally misleading—representations of the semantic facts (whatever they are). But in my view, there is ample evidence to support adoption of some eventish proposal as opposed to (1a), and there is sufficient evidence to tentatively adopt (1c) over (1b).

1.2

Arguments for adopting an event analysis should be familiar. So let me offer just a brief review. Davidson (1967) famously noted patterns of entailment like those exhibited in (1)–(5):

(1) Brutus stabbed Caesar
(2) Brutus stabbed Caesar with a knife
(3) Brutus stabbed Caesar on the Ides of March
(4) Brutus stabbed Caesar with a knife on the Ides of March
(5) Brutus stabbed Caesar on the Ides of March with a knife.

If (5) is true, so is (4); and *vice versa*. If (4) is true, so are (1)–(3); and if either (2) or (3) is true, so is (1). Speakers of English recognize these implications; and they usually treat 'prepositional-phrase detachment' as an impeccable form of inference. These facts are at least partly explained, if prepositional phrases are interpreted as conjuncts of complex event predicates as in

$$\text{Stabbed(e, Brutus, Caesar) \& With-a-knife(e).}$$

But evidence for this kind of view is not limited to entailment patterns; see Taylor (1985), Parsons (1990).

A compound sentence like

(6)   Booth fled after he shot Lincoln

is true iff the events described by the sentential clauses are suitably related; (6) is true iff ∃e∃f[Fled(e, Brutus) & After(e, f) & Shot(f, he, Lincoln)]. Similarly,

(7)   Booth pulled the trigger before Lincoln died

is true iff ∃e∃f[Pulled(e, Booth, the trigger) & Before(e, f) & Died(f, Lincoln)]. One can paraphrase (7) by replacing 'Lincoln died' with an overt event nominal, as in

(8)   Booth pulled the trigger before Lincoln's death.

Likewise, (9) and (10) are nearly synonymous:

(9)   Vesuvius erupted just before Pompeii was destroyed
(10) An eruption of Vesuvius occurred just before the destruction of Pompeii.

This suggests that (9) covertly involves the kind of quantification over events that is overt in (10).

As Gareth Evans observed, pairs of sentences like

(11) Shem hit Shaun sharply with a red stick
(12) Shem hit Shaun softly with a blue stick

can be true at the same time. But in such a case, the sentences have different 'truth-makers'. One hitting is sharp while a simultaneous hitting is soft. Moreover, (11)–(12) can be true while

(13) Shem hit Shaun softly with a red stick
(14) Shem hit Shaun sharply with a blue stick

are false. This makes sense, if (11)–(14) involve quantification over events as in,

∃e[Hit(e, Shem, Shaun) & Sharp/Soft(e) & With-a-red/blue-stick(e).[4]

Higginbotham (1983) and Vlach (1983) note that a perceptual report like

---

[4] If one tries to account for (1)–(5) by saying that adverbs express functions from functions to functions, without appeal to events, (11)–(14) present a stumbling block; see Taylor (1985). If (11)–(12) are true, each adverb must express a function F, such that [F(λx. *true* iff x hit Shaun)](Shem) = *true*; and similarly for the complex adverbs 'sharply with a red stick' and 'softly with a blue stick'. But if (13)–(14) are false, 'softly with a red stick' and 'sharply with a blue stick' must not express any such function F.

(15) Nora heard Fido bark

differs from the corresponding propositional attitude report

(16) Nora heard that Fido barked.

In (15), 'bark' is untensed, and substituting coreferential expressions for 'Fido' preserves truth. So one might analyze (15) as 'there was a hearing by Nora of a barking by Fido', which is true iff $\exists e \exists f [\text{Heard}(e, \text{Nora}, f) \& \text{Bark}(f, \text{Fido})]$. This would also explain the ambiguity of

(17) Nora heard Fido bark in her apartment.

The adjunct phrase can be a predicate of the e-position event (the hearing) or the f-position event (the barking). Moreover, these considerations interact, as shown by

(18) Nora saw Fido run in the park after seeing Pat poke Pete gently with a pen and also poke Pete less gently with a pencil at noon.

Those who wish to avoid appeal to events should try to deal with sentences like (18).

1.3

Finding evidence that supports thematically separated event analyses is harder. As the notation used in Section 1.2 suggests, many facts that suggest an eventish semantics can be accommodated without associating each syntactic argument (via some thematic role) with its own conjunct of an event description.[5] But Schein (1993) argues that plural expressions like

(19) Three linguists taught four students five theories

have readings that can only be represented by associating the syntactic arguments of the verb with (scopally independent) conjuncts of complex event predicates.

Prima facie, (19) has a reading on which three linguists (together) managed to teach each of four students five theories: the subject is collective, while 'four

---

[5] As in Davidson (1967); though cf. Davidson (1985). Moreover, one might say that 'Stabbed$_3$' gives the meaning of 'stabbed', *because* the English verb is satisfied by ordered triples $<e, x, y>$ such that: $[\text{Agent}_2(x)](e) \& [\text{Stabbed}_1(e) \& [\text{Theme}_2(y)](e)$; see n. 3. But this is not thematic *separation*, since the syntactic arguments still make their semantic contributions via (the function expressed by) the verb.

students' has scope over 'five theories' but not 'three linguists'. From an eventish perspective, this suggests twenty episodes of theory-teaching (all done by three linguists), with each student learning five theories. This in turn suggests a big teaching-event with subparts, much like a banquet is a big eating-event with subparts. So as a first pass, we might try to capture the meaning of (19) with

> (20) ∃e{Agent(e, three linguists) & Taught(e) &
>   for four students x, ∃f:f<e[Recipient(f, x) & Theme(f, five theories)]}

where 'f<e' means that f is a part of e. We can go on to say that 'Theme(f, five theories)' abbreviates 'for five theories y, ∃g:g<f[Theme(g, y)]', while 'Agent (e, three linguists)' abbreviates 'for three linguists x, ∃d:d<e[Agent(d, x)]'. The idea is that an event with multiple participants is an event with parts; see Carlson (1984). Eventually, one wants to hear more about the relevant mereology.[6] But for present purposes, the important point is that there seems to be no viable alternative to a thematically separated eventish treatment of (19). For example,

> (21) for four students x, ∃e[Taught(e, three linguists, x, five theories)]

fails to capture the Schein-reading, since it presumably implies that each of the linguists was involved in teaching each student; whereas (19) can be true, on the relevant reading, if the teaching labor was divided so that no linguist taught more than two students. (See Herburger (2000) for related arguments.[7])

The verb 'explain' provides another argument for thematic separation. Consider

> (22) Nora explained the fact that Fido barked
> (23) Nora explained that Fido barked.

While (22) is roughly synonymous with 'Nora explained why Fido barked', (23) is true (roughly) iff Nora *said* that Fido barked and thereby explained

---

[6] And (20) doesn't yet capture the meaning of (19), which implies that three linguists were *the* Agents of the relevant teaching—not just participants in some mass-teaching. Schein, following Boolos (1985), adopts second-order representations of plurality. The resulting modification of (20) is: '∃e< ∃S:{|S| = 3 & ∀x∈S[Linguist(x)]}∀x[Agent(e, x) ↔ x ∈ S] & Taught(e) & for 4 students x, ∃f:f<e[Recipient(f, x) & ∃S:{|S| = 5 & ∀x∈S[Theory(x)]}∀x[Theme(f, x) ↔ x ∈ S]]>', where an event e (with 5 subparts) can have multiple Agents/Themes.

[7] Schein also argues that if we treat 'three linguists' as a label for some (plural) entity in the domain of the function associated with 'taught', the resulting semantics will either lead to paradox or fail to account for certain entailments that speakers recognize—e.g. that every linguist sang iff every one of the linguists sang.

something else. If Nick asked why the cat ran away, and Nora replied 'Because Fido barked', then (23) is true but (22) is not. Similarly, if Nick asked why Fido barked, and Nora replied 'Because Fido saw the cat', then (22) is true but (23) is not. These facts are hard to account for if 'explained' expresses a ternary function, especially if the fact that Fido barked is not an entity distinct from (the proposition) that Fido barked. Given sentences like (22), one would be led to say that 'explained' expresses the function $\lambda y.\{\lambda x.\{\lambda e.$ *true* iff e is an explaining by x of y}}; where e is an explaining by x of y, only if y is the explanandum—the thing x explained. But this conflicts with (23), which is true (roughly) iff Nora's *explanans* is that Fido barked. This suggests that the meanings of (22)–(23) should be represented with (24)–(25), respectively:

(24) $\exists e[Agent(e, Nora) \& Explained(e) \& Theme(e, the fact Fido barked)]$

(25) $\exists e[Agent(e, Nora) \& Explained(e) \& Content(e, that Fido barked)]$

where the Theme of an explaining is the thing explained (the explanandum), and the Content of an explaining is the thing said in giving the explanation.[8]

Causative constructions can also be used to argue for thematic separation. As many theorists have discussed, sentences like

(26) Pat boiled the soup

have meanings that seem to be structured along lines indicated by

(27) $\exists e \exists x\{Agent(e, Pat) \& R(e, x) \& Boiled(x) \& Theme(x, the soup)\};$

where 'R' stands for some relation that an event e (done by the Agent) bears to the boiling of the soup, and 'Boiled' captures the meaning of the intransitive verb in

(28) The soup boiled.

---

[8] For more details, see Pietroski (2000*b*, forthcoming *c*). With many English verbs, the difference between 'that P' and 'the fact/claim/belief that P' is not apparent. For example, if you doubt the claim that P, you doubt that P. But the Japanese translation of 'doubted the claim that Kenji killed Mariko' involves marking the sentential complement of 'utagatta' with the accusative case morpheme 'o': '[Kenji-ga Mariko-o koroshita-koto]-o utagatta', where 'ga' is a nominative case morpheme, and 'koto' is some kind of complementizer or nominalizer. A different construction involves the morpheme 'to', which is used in the translation of 'explains that . . .' and generally seems to be correlated with the role of Content: '[Kenji-ga Mariko-o koroshita]-to utagatta'. The meaning, which parallels 'explained that P', is roughly: doubted *something* (e.g. that Mariko committed suicide) *by thinking* that Kenji killed Mariko. Similar remarks apply to 'hiteishita' ('denied') and 'koukaishita' ('regretted'). My thanks to Mitsue Motomura for this data.

I assume that the meaning of (28) is correctly represented with

(29) $\exists e$[Boiled(e) & Theme(e, the soup)}.

If (27) is true, so is (29); and arguably, this explains why (28) is true if (26) is. Following Chomsky's (1995) development of Baker's (1988) version of a much older idea, I think the *syntax* of (26) involves a hidden verbal element—like the overt causative element in many languages—with which the intransitive verb 'boiled' combines. And if the syntactic structure of (26) is

(26S) $\{(_\alpha \text{Pat})[(_\Phi v\text{--boiled}_j)[_\Phi t_j(_\alpha \text{ the soup})]]\}$

where intranstive 'boiled' raises to combine with the covert v, then we cannot explain the entailment in terms of facts about the lexical meaning of a transitive verb 'boiled$_T$'. For (26) does not contain any lexical item with the meaning of the transitive verb.[9]

Were it not for well-known objections to causative analyses—see Fodor (1970), Fodor and Lepore (2000)—I would leave matters here. But since replies are needed, let me sketch a proposal defended elsewhere; see Pietroski (1998, 2000a, forthcoming *a*, *c*). Suppose the meaning of (26) is given by

(30) $\exists e${Agent(e, Pat) & $\exists x$[Terminater(e, x) & Boil(x)] & Theme(e, the soup)}

where a Terminater of event e is itself an event that is a *final part* of e. It is a common thought that causatives are somehow related to 'accordion-style' events that begin with actions but end with certain effects of those actions. And we can gloss 'Agent(e, x)', ignoring plural subjects for simplicity, as 'x performed an action that is an Initiater of e'; where an Initiater of e is the *first part* of e. On this view, (26) is true iff: Pat performed an action that *started* an accordion-style event, whose Theme is the soup, that *ended with* an event of boiling. The boiling in question has to be the boiling of the soup, given that the Theme of an accordion-style event is the thing affected at the end of that event; see Tenny (1994). Thus, (28) is true if (26) is. But (26) is not synonymous with

(31) Pat caused the soup to boil.

For the truth of (31) does not ensure that there is an event that meets the requirements imposed by (30).

---

[9] The transitive verb in (22) has the intransitive 'boil' as a part; *cf.* Hale and Keyser (1993). Positing two lexical items, 'boil$_T$' and 'boil$_I$', is unparsimonius. And while the inference from (26) to (28) seems analytic, I am suspicious of analytic connections between lexical items; see Pietroski (forthcoming *a*, *c*).

Suppose that Pat set fire to a house that contains a pot of cold soup. Then (31) might well be true, while (26) is false. But (30) can also be false, since not every effect of an action will be the final part of some accordion-style event that begins with the action. The truth of (26) requires a *single* event that starts with Pat's action and ends with a boiling of the soup.[10] Thus, (26) is not synonymous with

(32) Pat caused$^+$ the soup to boil

where 'caused$^+$' means caused *via some normal method.* We can also represent the meaning of (33) with (34), which differs from both (35) and (36), neither of which capture the meaning of (33):

(33) Pat boiled the soup on Monday

(34) $\exists e\{Agent(e, Pat)\ \&\ \exists x[Terminater(e, x)\ \&\ Boil(x)]\ \&\ Theme(e, the soup)\ \&\ OM(e)\}$.

(35) $\exists e \exists x\{Agent(e, Pat)\ \&\ Cause^+(e, x)\ \&\ Boil(x)\ \&\ Theme(x, the soup)\ \&\ OM(e)$.

(36) $\exists e \exists x\{Agent(e, Pat)\ \&\ Cause^+(e, x)\ \&\ Boil(x)\ \&\ Theme(x, the soup)\ \&\ OM(x)$.

It is a fair question why (33) cannot have the meaning indicated in

(37) $\exists e\{Agent(e, Pat)\ \&\ \exists x[Terminater(e, x)\ \&\ Boil(x)\ \&\ OM(x)]\ \&\ Theme(e, the soup)\}$.

But I think the answer lies with syntactic details, motivated in part by cross-linguistic data, concerning the covert causative element in (33) and how it can be combined with overt elements; see Baker (1988), Pietroski (forthcoming *c*). Verbal compounding often eliminates ambiguity, as even English illustrates:

(38) He likes to hunt elephants with a gun

(39) He likes to elephant-hunt with a gun.

Only (38) can be used to report a desire to give the elephants a sporting chance. And (33) is arguably subject to a similar constraint. In any case, given the motivations for causative analyses of sentences like (26) and the availability of a reply to standard objections, we have reason to adopt such analyses; and such

---

[10] Cf. Parsons (1990). I return to the notion of unification below in the context of serial verbs. But the idea of 'breaking a causal chain' is familiar and entrenched in law; see Hart and Honoré (1959). In any case, one can reply to Fodor and Lepore by saying that there is no event (or at least no event relevant to semantics) that both starts with the arsonist's action and ends with the soup boiling.

analyses, in so far as they avoid the objections, evidently require thematic separation as in (30).

2 Natural Syntax and Fregean Concepts

Let us return now to (1), its syntactic structure, and the three hypotheses about its meaning:

(1) Brutus stabbed Caesar   (1S) $\{(_\alpha\text{Brutus})\ [_\Phi(_\phi\text{stabbed})\ (_\alpha\text{Caesar})]\}$

(1a) $[\text{Stabbed}_2(\text{Caesar}_i)](\text{Brutus}_i)$

(1b) $\exists e < \{[\text{Stabbed}_3(\text{Caesar}_i)](\text{Brutus}_i)\}(e) >$

(1c) $\exists e < \{[\text{Agent}_2(\text{Brutus}_i)]\ (e)\ \&\ [\text{Stabbed}_1\ (e)\ \&\ [\text{Theme}_2(\text{Caesar}_i)]$
      $(e)]\} >$

If (1c) represents the meaning of (1), the relation of natural language syntax to this meaning may differ from the relation of predicate calculus syntax to the stipulated meanings of (1a–c). This is worth noting.

2.1

If one takes the syntax and meaning of (1) to be as indicated in (1S) and (1a), with no further elaboration of (1a), the obvious hypothesis is that the constituents of (1a) represent the meanings of the corresponding constituents of (1). Given this, the contribution of natural syntax to the meaning of (1) is presumably the same as the contribution of formal syntax to the stipulated meaning of (1a): the semantic correlate (or *Bedeutung*) of each phrase is the value of the function expressed by the constituent predicate Φ given the entity labelled by the argument-term α; or abbreviating, $\|\Phi \wedge \alpha\| = \|\Phi\|(\|\alpha\|)$, where '$\|\dots\|$' stands for 'the semantic correlate of...'. This is not to say that syntax is semantically inert, since applying a function to an argument differs from simply listing a function and some element in its domain. But the idea is that the contribution of syntax is minimal, in that no specific content is added. By contrast, consider the following grossly implausible theses: $\|\Phi \wedge \alpha\| = \|\Phi\|$(the person closest to $\|\alpha\|$); $\|\Phi \wedge \alpha\| = true$ iff $\|\Phi\|(\|\alpha\|) = true$ or $\|\alpha\|$ is blue.

One can emphasize semantic minimality by identifying functions with sets of ordered pairs. For if $\|\Phi\|$ is such a set, S, one can claim that $\|\Phi \wedge \alpha\|$ just *is* the second element of the ordered pair in S with $\|\alpha\|$ as its first element. The syntax of a Fregean *Begriffsschrift* is semantically minimal in this sense, since this keeps all aspects of meaning manifest. But following Frege (1891), one can distinguish sets (or 'value-ranges') from the essentially *unsaturated* mappings (from arguments to truth-values) for which he introduced the technical term 'concept'. No set, not even a set of ordered pairs whose second elements are truth-values, is a Fregean concept. Speaking loosely, we might say that concepts are the semantic contributions of sentences-minus-argument-terms. And one can grant that the English verb-plus-sentential-frame '_[stabbed]_' is associated with a Fregean concept, from ordered pairs of individuals to truth-values, while doubting that the contribution of the verb 'stabbed' is a function from such ordered pairs to truth-values. Given a natural language, one can ask how the semantic role of Fregean concepts is divided between verbs and syntax. It is an empirical question whether natural languages respect the Functionist thesis, $\|\Phi \wedge \alpha\| = \|\Phi\|(\|\alpha\|)$, and are—in this respect—like a *Begriffsschrift* whose syntax makes the minimal semantic contribution. *Natural* syntax may bear a semantic load. (In particular, natural syntax may contribute the specific content of conjunction.)

Finding evidence that bears on this question is a nontrivial task. Setting aside (for the moment) the existential quantifier in (1*b*) and the variable it binds, (1*b*) does not challenge the Functionist thesis. One can say that $\|[_\Phi(_\Phi \text{ stabbed}) (_\alpha\text{Caesar})]\| = \|\text{stabbed}\|(\|\text{Caesar}\|) = \lambda x.\{\lambda e. \; true$ iff e is a stabbing by x of Caesar}. And one can say that $\|\{(_\alpha\text{Brutus}) [_\Phi(_\Phi \text{ stabbed})$ $(_\alpha\text{Caesar})]\}\| = \lambda e. \; true$ iff e is a stabbing by Brutus of Caesar, while still maintaining that the semantic correlate of sentence (1) is a truth-value. Perhaps (1) includes a syntactic argument that (1S) fails to represent, as in

(1S′) $\{[_\Delta(_\Delta some)(_\Phi event)]\{_\Phi (_\alpha\text{Brutus}) [_\Phi(_\Phi\text{stabbed}) (_\alpha\text{Caesar})]\}\}$

where covert elements are italicized, and the subscript 'Δ' indicates that the determiner 'some' combines with a predicate to form a structured syntactic argument.[11] Alternatively, perhaps (1) has only two syntactic arguments, but *sentences* (as opposed to mere syntactic structures) are *truth*-evaluable analogs of structures like the one indicated by (1S); where existential closure is the default way of turning an event predicate into something truth-evaluable. It would be nice to consider this possibility in light of Chomsky's (2000*b*) suggestion that expressions with multiple arguments are interpreted in *phases*, especially since his phase-markers include covert causative verbs (which are

---

[11] For discussion of generalized quantifiers and their semantics, see Barwise and Cooper (1981), Higginbotham and May (1981), Larson and Segal (1995). Perhaps all arguments have the syntactic form $[_\Delta(_\Delta \ldots)(_\Phi \ldots)]$. Names like 'Brutus' might contain a covert determiner akin to Kaplan's (1989) 'dthat'.

associated with existential closure on the view urged above); see also Uriagereka (1999), Pietroski (forthcoming c). But let us set aside questions about
where the existential quantifier in eventish logical forms comes from, and
focus on combinations of overt elements that clearly are syntactic constituents.

Consider (2) and its syntactic structure:

(2) Brutus stabbed Caesar with a knife
(2S) $\{(_\alpha\text{Brutus}) [_\Phi[_\Phi(_\Phi\text{stabbed}) (_\alpha\text{Caesar})][_\Phi \text{ with a knife}]]\}$.

I assume that 'with a knife' is a syntactic predicate, if only because of constructions like

(40) Caesar saw Brutus with a knife.

One might say that 'with a knife' *as it occurs in (2)* expresses a function $\mathbf{W}_1$,
from functions to functions; while 'with a knife' *as it occurs in (40)* expresses a
function from individuals to truth-values. Thus, following Montague (1970),
one might represent the meaning of (2) with

(2*a*) $\mathbf{W}_1\{[\text{Stabbed}_2(\text{Caesar}_i)]\}(\text{Brutus}_i)$.

In my view, this leads to an unsatisfactory semantics.[12] But more important
for present purposes is that the Functionist thesis $\|\Phi\wedge\alpha\| = \|\Phi\|(\|\alpha\|)$,
understood as a claim about how the syntax of a sentence is related to the
meaning of that sentence, has to be modified *however* we deal with (2).
Whether or not an expression counts as Φ-ish depends on the *syntax* of that
expression. One can hypothesize that the meaning of 'stabbed Caesar with a
knife' has two major constituents: a function from individuals to truth-values;
and a function from functions to functions. But even if this is true, which
I doubt, it does not preserve the Functionist thesis motivated by the straightforward mapping from (1S) to (1*a*). Appeals to type-shifting effectively concede this point.

One can claim that the Functionist thesis is an idealization—and that
adjunction is a deviation from the ideal manifested by (1). But I find this
implausible, since adjunction is a syntactically recursive and semantically
compositional aspect of natural language. If we set aside sentential connectives
(which are of limited interest) and sentential complements (which require
special treatment on any view), adjunction is where the recursivity of natural

---

[12] It is notoriously difficult to see how this *explains* the relevant facts concerning (speakers'
recognition of) entailments; see n. 4. And one wants motivation for the claim that 'stabbed
Caesar' is the semantic argument in (2) but the semantic predicate in (1); cf. Frege's (1892) appeal
to *Bedeutung*-shifting.

language lives. Verbs take a very finite number of arguments, but they can combine with endlessly many adjuncts. So it strikes me as perverse to treat adjunction as a 'nonideal' feature of natural language, just because it does not fit a Functionist mold.

2.2

Suppose we represent the meaning of (2), ignoring the existential quantifer, with

(2b) $\{[\text{Stabbed}_3(\text{Caesar}_i)](\text{Brutus}_j)\}(e)$ & With-a-knife(e).

Treating adjuncts like 'with a knife' as conjuncts in complex event predicates nicely accounts for the semantic contributions of such adjuncts. But where does the *conjunction* come from? One might conjecture, heroically, that (2) includes a covert conjoiner as in

(2S*) $\{(_\alpha\text{Brutus}) [_\Phi[_\Phi[_\Phi\text{stabbed}) (_\alpha\text{Caesar})] \textit{ and } [_\Phi\text{with a knife}]]\}$.

A simpler—and less clearly false—hypothesis is that the syntax itself contributes the conjunctive aspect of meaning. The formal details are easier to present, once one abandons the idea that 'stabbed' expresses a ternary function. But the basic idea is simple: 'Brutus stabbed Caesar' and 'with a knife' correspond to unary predicates of events; and the natural syntax of adjunction, which makes it possible to combine these predicates, corresponds to a kind of function-*conjunction* (as opposed to function-*application*). This is the radical aspect of Davidson's (1967) proposal. Positing a hidden argument was a minor variation on a traditional semantic theme; but the conjunctive treatment of adjuncts was an innovation.[13]

Especially if one is impressed by the fact that adjunction is the source of subsentential recursivity (and open-ended compositionality), one might wonder if *all* syntax makes the same kind of semantic contribution. Functionists will try to preserve the 'semantic uniformity' of syntax, by assimilating adjunction (via type-shifting) to argumentation; on this view, all syntax makes the same *minimal* contribution. But eventish theorists can try to assimilate argumentation to adjunction, treating all syntax as making the same conjunctive contribution. Initially, it is hard to see how 'stabbed Caesar' could be a

---

[13] Similarly, if the meaning of 'doctor from Seattle' is given by 'Doctor(x) & From-Seattle(x)', the contribution of syntax is function-conjunction; and insisting that 'from Seattle' expresses a function from functions to functions leads to complications. See Heim and Kratzer (1998) for formal discussion.

conjunctive predicate. But a thematically separated event analysis represents the meaning of the verb phrase with 'Stabbed$_1$(e) & [Theme$_2$(Caesar$_i$)](e)'. While this raises the question of where the conjunction comes from, a possible answer is that natural language syntax bears this semantic load; concatenation itself contributes an aspect of meaning.

Of course, one wants to know where the thematic functions come from, since they play the crucial role of mapping an individual like Caesar to a function. *If* one can maintain that in 'stabbed Caesar', $\|(_\alpha \text{Caesar})\| = \lambda e.\ true$ iff Caesar was Theme of e, then a Conjunctivist hypothesis about the contribution of syntax is tempting. For one can say that $\|(_\Phi \text{stabbed})\| = \lambda e.\ true$ iff e was a stabbing; $\|[_\Phi(_\Phi \text{stabbed})\ (_\alpha \text{Caesar})]\| = \lambda e.true$ iff e was a stabbing & Caesar was Theme of e; $\|(_\Phi \text{ with a knife})\| = \lambda e.true$ iff e was (done) with a knife; and $\|[_\Phi[_\Phi(_\Phi \text{ stabbed})\ (_\alpha \text{Caesar})][_\Phi \text{ with a knife}]]\| = \lambda e.true$ iff e is a stabbing & Caesar was Theme of e & e was with a knife. The obvious generalization, which might have be to modified in light of further data, is:

$$\|\Phi \wedge \Psi\| = \lambda e.\ true \text{ iff } \|\Phi\|(e) = true\ \&\ \|\Psi\|(e) = true$$

where 'Ψ' ranges over both adjoined predicates and syntactic arguments.[14] At this point, one might kick away the ladder of function-talk entirely, and simply speak of predicates satisfied by events. But regardless of terminology, one wants to know how a name like 'Caesar' can be semantically associated with a class of events, as suggested by (1c) and the Conjunctivist conception of how natural syntax contributes to meaning.

A simple answer is that sentences have hidden thematic constituents, as indicated below:

$$\{<_\Phi \textit{Agent}(_\alpha \text{Brutus}) > [_\Phi(_\Phi \text{stabbed}) <_\Phi \textit{Theme}(_\alpha \text{Caesar}) >]\}.$$

I do not rule out discovery of such sentential components, perhaps in the form of thematic features that verbs assign to their arguments; see Hornstein (forthcoming). But 'thematic separationists' need not assume a thematically elaborated syntax. Syntactic position is at least correlated with thematic role. And investigation suggests that within any sentence, a lower argument is never associated with the role of Agent, while a higher argument is never associated with the role of Theme; see Pesetsky (1995). Indeed, Baker (1988, 1997) argues

---

[14] There are many cases to consider, including (so-called) nonconjunctive adjectives. But even if $\|\text{first big dog}\| \neq \lambda x.true$ iff $\|\text{first}\|(x) = true\ \&\ \|\text{big}\|(x) = true\ \&\ \|\text{dog}\|(x) = true$—because of various context-sensitivities, failures of the idealization mentioned in n. 1, or something else—there is *some* conjunctive aspect to the meaning of 'his first big dog'. And syntax may well be the source.

that syntactic position *determines* thematic role; see Pietroski (forthcoming *c*) for discussion and defense. If this is correct, but not because sentences have thematic constituents (that are associated with certain syntactic positions), then the *interpretation* of syntactic arguments is constrained by a Baker-style mapping from syntactic position to thematic role; that is, the (source of) the Baker-style mapping is itself a determinant of meaning.

One way or another, separationists must say that syntactic arguments are always interpreted 'through a thematic lens'. But this makes sense from an eventish perspective. Each syntactic argument has to be associated with some *way of participating in* an event of the sort described by the verb. More formally, we can relativize the semantic correlates of argument terms to syntactic positions, in the following innocent sense: while the name 'Caesar' is always associated with Caesar, the specific semantic contribution of the *name as syntactic argument* depends on the relevant syntactic position; the semantic contribution can be $\lambda e.$ *true* iff Caesar was Theme of e, or $\lambda e.$ *true* iff Caesar was Agent of e, depending on whether 'Caesar' is the internal or external argument. It is part of the hypothesis encoded by (1*c*) that a name makes its semantic contribution *via* some thematic relation. So thematic separationists should embrace this idea. Let '$\|\text{Caesar}\|_\Theta$' stand for the semantic correlate of 'Caesar' *relative to* any syntactic position associated with the thematic function Θ; and assume, following Baker, that each syntactic position (in which 'Caesar' can appear) determines such a function. Then we can say:

$$\|\text{Caesar}\|_\Theta = \lambda e. \textit{ true } \text{iff } \exists x[x = \text{Caesar} \ \& \ \Theta(e, x) = \textit{true}].$$

Notational variations, including phrase markers in which the labels of argument terms are associated with unary thematic features, are possible. But the idea is that for purposes of interpretation, syntactic arguments are associated with functions from events to truth-values. While this is a kind of type-shifting, it is fairly innocuous and *very* limited. Relativized semantic axioms, like the one above, can capture the shifted contributions of argument terms in a uniform way; and this (single) kind of shift, from an individual x to functions from events (in which x is a certain kind of participant) to truth-values, is empirically motivated by the evidence for thematic separation. Given the Functionist tradition, it can seem strange to say that argumentation—not adjunction—is what calls for special treatment. But from an eventish perspective, this is unsurprising. How *could* one interpret the concatenation of an event predicate with a name for person, except by invoking thematic roles? If the contribution of syntax to meaning is Conjunctivist, the point is obvious; 'stabbed & Caesar' makes no sense. In short, 'thematic shifting' may be what lets us employ labels for things in truth-evaluable claims governed by an eventish (but not Functionist) semantics.[15]

2.3

Still, thematic shifting can seem like just a trick—a way of encoding certain facts, in a manner congenial to one's theory, without explaining them. Even if this is preferable to type-shifting treatments of adjunction, why not eschew both tricks and just say that the syntax of adjunction makes a Conjunctivist contribution to meaning, while the syntax of argumentation makes a Functionist contribution? But absent an account of what it would be for natural language to have different kinds of syntax, this is just another way of encoding the facts without explaining them. While natural language lets us combine various kinds of expressions, subject to certain constraints, this hardly shows that there are various modes of combination. To be sure, adjuncts differ from arguments in ways that matter for syntactic transformations. Correspondingly, we have reasons for labelling adjunct phrases differently than arguments; though syntacticians would (very much) like to know which facts the difference in labels labels. But semantics is not supposed to care about labels. The spirit of recent developments in syntactic theory also suggests that we should, as far as possible, try to understand syntactic structure as emerging from a single operation of Merge that simply concatenates items; see Chomsky (1995). And we won't find unifications we don't look for. That is mainly rhetoric, however. So let me end this section with a little case study, by way of suggesting that a Conjunctivist conception of how syntax contributes to meaning can have empirical payoffs in unexpected places.

Baker and Stewart (n.d.)—henceforth B&S—discuss the African language Edo, which allows serial verb constructions like

(41) Ozo will cook food eat.   [Òzó ghá lé èvbàré ré]

The meaning is that Ozo will cook some food and eat it, but with a further restriction along the following lines: the cooking and eating must be part of a unified process in which Ozo cooks the food with the plan of eating it. One

---

[15] From this perspective, functional aspects of meaning are covert. But what about connectives and determiners? Perhaps 'P or Q' is true iff $\exists x\{\text{External}(x, P)\ \&\ [\text{Or}(x)\ \&\ \text{Internal}(x, Q)]\}$. An ordered pair of *truth-values* can have P as its external argument, satisfy 'or', and have Q as its internal argument. And perhaps 'Every Φ is Ψ' is true iff some ordered pair of sets that satisfies 'every' has the relevant *extensions* as internal and external arguments. See Larson and Segal (1995), Pietroski (forthcoming *c*).

cannot use the serial verb construction, which contains a single overt object, to describe a scenario in which Ozo was planning to feed someone else—but then ate the food when his guest failed to arrive. Similarly, if Ozo buys a book and then reads it (as planned) when he gets home, one can say 'Ozo buy the book read'. But if he comes across a book in the store, reads it *and then* decides to buy it, one cannot say 'Ozo read the book buy'.[16]

B&S argue for the following syntactic structure, abstracting away from details not germane here:

(41S) $\{(_\alpha Ozo)[_\Phi[_\Phi(_\Phi cook-v)[_\Phi(_\alpha food_k)e]][_\Phi(_\Phi eat-v)[_\Phi(_\alpha pro_k)e]]]\}$

where 'cook' and 'eat' each raise, from the nearby position indicated with '*e*', to a higher position in which they can incorporate with a covert 'small verb' indicated by '*v*'. An underlying assumption is that 'food' and (the covert object) '*pro*' are, by virtue of their syntactic relation to (the original positions of) 'cook' and 'eat', still associated with the role of Theme.

From a semantic perspective, it is striking that the complex verb phrase is analyzed as a concatenation of predicates, each of which is a concatenation of predicates; in Edo, there is evidently no covert connective between 'cook food' and 'eat *pro*'. From a syntactic perspective, the most striking feature of (41S) concerns the unpronounced object of the second verb, whatever one takes that covert element to be. As the coindexing indicates, (41) requires that the food cooked be the food eaten, as if 'food$_k$' were the object of both 'eat' and 'cook'; but as the phrase marker indicates, 'food' does not c-command the position occupied by '*pro*'. So unless B&S have the syntax wrong, or current syntactic theory is badly mistaken, it cannot be that 'food' syntactically binds '*pro*'. Indeed, part of the puzzle these constructions present is that they seem to exhibit mandatory cointerpretation without c-command. B&S thus suggest, without offering a specific proposal, that the right eventish semantics will ensure that 'food' specifies the Theme of *both* the cooking *and* the eating. I think this promissory note can be cashed, given the view urged here.

[16] I am indebted to Mark Baker for conversation and data. A different Edo construction, with an overt pronoun following the second verb, does not imply any plan that connects the events in question. And appeals to unified events are not *ad hoc* if they can be correlated with independent syntactic phenomena. Added in press: B&S have recently revised their view (in a way that does not affect the present discussion). In place of the literally double-headed structure indicated in (41S) below, they now posit an asymmetry between 'code food' and 'eat pro'. But the key point remains: 'food' does not c-command 'pro', and the vPs are evidently not connected by a covert coordinator.

Suppose that each small verb treats its sister—i.e. the verb with which it incorporates—as a kind of internal argument, and that this argument is interpreted 'through a thematic lens' in the sense described above. And suppose that the first small verb is associated with an 'Initiater' lens, while the second small verb is associated with a 'Terminater' lens, in conscious imitation of the earlier discussion of causatives. This effectively posits two small verbs, v and v^*. So lens metaphors aside, suppose that 'v–cook' is true of events that start with a cooking, while 'v^*–eat' is true of events that end with an eating. Or more formally, and paralleling the earlier thematic relativization of arguments like 'Caesar': $\|v\text{–cook}\| = \lambda$e. *true* iff $\exists$x[Cooking(x) & Initiater(e, x)]; $\|v^*\text{–eat}\| = \lambda$e. *true* iff $\exists$x[Eating(x) & Terminater(e, x)]. The idea is that *any* first part of an accordion-event, an event that starts with an action and ends with some later (causally related) event, is an Initiater of e; basic actions may not be the only Initiaters of the accordion-events they Initiate. In particular, Ozo's cooking of the food can Initiate an event that starts with Ozo turning on the stove and ends with Ozo eating the last mouthful of food. (Compare an event of going to the airport, which has lots of subparts, but starts with getting in the car.) Similarly, any last part of an accordion-event e is a Terminater of e; so the event of Ozo's eating the food can Terminate a complex accordion-event that the cooking Initiates.

If branching predicates are conjunctive predicates, we get the desired results:

$\|[_{\Phi}(_{\Phi}\text{cook}–v)\ [_{\Phi}(_{\alpha}\text{food}_k)\ e]\| = \lambda$e. *true* iff $\exists$x[Cooking(x) & Initiater(e, x)] & Theme(e, food$_k$); and

$\|[_{\Phi}(_{\Phi}\text{eat}–v)\ [_{\Phi}(_{\alpha}\text{pro}_k)\ e]\ ]\| = \lambda$e. *true* iff $\exists$x[Eating(x) & Terminater(e, x)] & Theme(e, *pro*$_k$).

So the semantic correlate of the whole serial-verb phrase is

λe. *true* iff $\exists$x[Cooking(x) & Initiater(e, x)] & Theme(e, food$_k$) &
$\exists$x[Eating(x) & Terminater(e, x)] & Theme(e, *pro*$_k$).

The complex serial-verb phrase is true of events that start with a cooking, have the food as Theme, end with an eating, and have *pro* as Theme. On the assumption that each event has a single Theme, '*pro*' must be interpreted as the food, since '*pro*' represents the Theme of an event that has the food as its Theme. So the complex serial-verb event must start with a cooking of the food and end with an eating of that very food. And (41) is true iff Ozo is the Agent of some such event.

Initially, one might wonder how 'food' could specify the *Theme* of the serial-verb event, given that 'food' is the syntactic object of a verb that specifies how that event *begins*. But this is a point at which thematic separation (together with a Conjunctivist account of syntactic branching) pays off. By virtue of its syntactic position, 'food' is associated with the role of Theme; so it is interpreted as a Theme-specifier, regardless of what happens in the rest of the sentence. Similar remarks apply to '*pro*'. And branching is interpreted as function-conjunction, regardless of the functions conjoined. This allows for a kind of 'nonlocal' semantic relation, since each (nonplural) event can have only one Theme. Languages that do not allow for the double-headed structures indicated in (41S) may not manifest this kind of mandatory cointerpretation without c-command. But the Edo facts suggest that a semantics for natural language should treat syntactic arguments of verbs as separate conjuncts in an event description, with natural syntax itself as the source of the conjunction.

3 Logical Form as Eventish Semantic Form

If the syntax and meaning of (1) are as shown in (1S) and (1c)

(1) Brutus stabbed Caesar

(1S) $\{(_\alpha \text{Brutus})[_\Phi(_\Phi \text{stabbed})(_\alpha \text{Caesar})]\}$

(1c) $\exists e < \{[\text{Agent}_2(\text{Brutus}_i)](e) \ \& \ [\text{Stabbed}_1(e) \ \& \ [\text{Theme}_2(\text{Caesar}_i)]$
(e)]$\} >$

then we can say that the syntactic and semantic *forms* of (1) are as shown in

(42) $\{(_\alpha \ldots)[_\Phi(_\Phi \ldots)(_\alpha \ldots)]\}$

(43) $\exists e < \{[\text{Agent}_2(\ldots)](e) \ \& \ [S_1(e) \ \& \ [\text{Theme}_2(\ldots)](e)]\} >$

which abstract away from idiosyncratic features of (1) and its lexical items. For example, 'Shem poked Shaun' presumably has the same syntactic and semantic forms. If conjunction is the semantic correlate of concatenation, and syntactic position determines thematic role, then the syntactic form of (1) determines its semantic form—modulo the existential quantifier (briefly discusssed above).[17] There is a tradition of taking the logical form of a sentence Σ to be the form of Σ's meaning. So one might well say that (43) represents the logical form of (1),

---

[17] Poverty of stimulus considerations might suggest that these aspects of meaning reflect innate aspects of universal grammar. Other aspects of meaning are so reflected; see Crane and Pietroski (2001) for a review. If branching syntax means AND, as opposed to (say) OR, one would like to know *why*; and mere appeals to communicative efficiency are unsatisfying. So perhaps we should think about how conjunction is related to the mereology of 'banquet-style' and/or 'accordion-style' events.

and that the logical form of Σ is determined by the syntactic form of Σ—at least for sentences of this type, and perhaps for all sentences.

I am inclined to endorse this view and stop here. But there is also a tradition of doubting that sentences of a natural language like English really *have* logical forms—or meanings—as opposed to being associated with things that have logical forms. (Compare the Cartesian view that people are minds who 'have' heads only by virtue of bearing some relation to bodies that have heads.) In my view, this negative claim about natural language is either unmotivated or a product of stipulation; although natural sentences may in fact be associated with things that have semantic structures of their own. And this, alas, requires some comment.

At least for present purposes, let us say that Propositions are those things (whatever they are) that stand in *logical* relations. Propositions are potential premises/conclusions, each of which has a certain 'logical position'; each Proposition *follows from* certain others. Let us assume that Propositions have compositional structure, and that—modulo indeterminacy and certain referential failures—each use of a natural sentence is associated with a Proposition. But let us leave open the following possibilities: a natural sentence may not be isomorphic with the Proposition it is used to 'express'; and the relevant notion of association, which awaits characterization, may be use-sensitive in a way that precludes association of each natural sentence with a single Proposition—or even a single function from Kaplan-style contexts to Propositions. (Though if these possibilities are actual, one might wonder if there is a determinate mapping from natural sentences to Propositions.)

Propositions are effectively defined as bearers of logical form. So let us grant that *if* the semantic form of sentence Σ differs from the form(s) of the associated Proposition(s), then the logical form 'of Σ as used' is really the logical form of something else; in which case, Σ's semantic form should not be identified with Σ's logical form. But *pace* Frege–Russell–Wittgenstein, it is *not* obvious that syntactic/semantic form diverges importantly from logical form. The most famous examples of the alleged divergence—namely, quantificational constructions—evaporated upon further investigation. For example, if (42) is also the syntactic form of

(44) Brutus stabbed the emperor

while the associated logical form is '$\exists x\{E(x) \ \& \ \forall y[E(y) \rightarrow y = x] \ \& \ S(b, x)\}$', there appears to be a significant mismatch. But a more plausible syntactic representation is

(45) $\{[_\Delta(_\Delta \text{the})(_\Phi \text{emperor})]\{(_\alpha \text{Brutus})[_\Phi(_\Phi \text{stabbed})t]\}\}$

with 'the emperor' treated as a determiner phrase that raises, leaving a trace. And we can rewrite the Russellian hypothesis about logical form using restricted quantifiers (but ignoring events), as

(46) $\text{the}(x){:}E(x)\{S(b, x)\}$

where 'the' is satisfied by certain ordered pairs of extensions; see Neale (1990, 1993). Still, whatever one says about particular cases, analytic philosophy—born of modern logic, and long suspicious of transformational grammar—has bequeathed to us the idea that Propositional structures may not align with the syntactic structures of natural sentences. And this fits with an associated conception of logic.

If logic is the study of nonpsychologistic principles of Good Inference—or laws concerning The True, or The World at the most abstract level of generality—then the facts about what follows from what are independent of which inferences we *find* compelling; and these facts are, at least in principle, independent of the psychological states that underlie our ability to recognize the good arguments we do recognize. Correspondingly, 'P follows from Q' seems to be normative in a way that 'speakers find the inference from Σ to Σ^* impeccable' is not.[18] So perhaps claims about the logical forms of sentences are normative in a way that claims about the semantic forms of natural sentences are not. Maybe facts about Good Inference are uncovered by a process of reflective equilibrium that *begins* with judgements heavily influenced by grammar, but leads (via the development of formal languages with various virtues) to judgements about which inferences we *ought* to treat as impeccable. And logic-influenced judgements, which are arguably better justified than our original judgements, may suggest that propositions are structured differently than sentences. On this view, Propositional structure reflects ideal reasoning—i.e. the use of sentences with certain structures in accordance with certain rules of inference; and claims about the logical form of a natural sentence Σ are claims about which logical position one *ought* to associate with (a given use of) Σ.

Maybe there is an interesting project here, grounded by determinate facts, which will suggest that natural language sentences have structures that

---

[18] But note that facts about grammaticality, which are independent of what speakers find *acceptable*, are not independent of the psychological states that underlie speakers' linguistic abilities; and while one can define normative notions of grammaticality, the linguist's notion remains descriptive.

render them nonideal for purposes of conducting inferences. But if so, the moral would seem to be that logic and semantics are fundamentally different enterprises. Natural sentences *do not* have logical forms, in any interesting sense, if claims about logical forms are normative claims about how sentence-users should reason. And there is no reason to assume that semantic facts, at least some of which are reflected in the semantic forms of sentences, are facts (revealed in reflective equilibrium) about how we ought to reason. If we reject psychologistic conceptions of logic, we should be ready to reject logicist conceptions of semantics according to which sentential meanings are (functions from uses of sentences to) Propositions. The facts in virtue of which natural sentences have their semantic forms may well be psychological facts of the sort that logic is alleged to be independent of.[19]

There is, however, yet another wrinkle. Assume there is a language of thought, and that each use of a natural sentence—now using 'natural' to mean 'natural and public'—is associated with a sentence of mentalese, while leaving open the following possibilities: the compositional structure of a mentalese sentence may not match that of an associated natural sentence, even if the latter can be used to 'signal' the former; and the relevant notion of association, which awaits characterization (perhaps in the form of some brutely causal mechanism akin to transduction), may be use-sensitive in a way that precludes association of each natural sentence with a single mentalese sentence—or even a single function from Kaplan-style contexts to mentalese sentences. One might say that the *mental form* of a natural sentence, as used in a context, is (the semantic form of) the associated mentalese sentence. If the semantic forms of natural sentences differ from their mental forms, but we have reason for thinking that mental forms

---

[19] This skims over many issues that deserve attention, like why linguistic competence seems to involve a capacity to recognize *some* impeccable inferences as such; and why we should view certain sets of formal sentences as formalizations of the inferences we naturally make. But in so far as one takes 'logical form' to be a nonpsychologistic/normative notion (cf. n. 18), one cannot just assume that facts about logical forms (whatever they are) bear interestingly on facts about the meanings of sentences. Nor can one assume that natural sentences have meanings only by virtue of being translatable/regimentable into sentences of a *Begriffsschrift*. One can stipulate that the Meaning of Σ is a function from potential uses of Σ to the Propositions associated with those uses. But any facts about which Meanings natural sentences have may consist largely in facts concerning semantic forms. See n. 1; and see McGilvray (1999) for further discussion, in the context of Chomsky's (2000*a*) views, which I have been echoing.

reflect aspects of natural sentence meanings, there will be little point in identifying logical form with either notion of 'underlying' form.[20]

Given these complications, perhaps we should just drop the term 'logical form'. It might be better to speak of: semantic forms, understood as properties of natural sentences (independent of their relation to Good Inferences and any language of thought); logical positions, understood as 'addresses in an inferential space' modelled by Propositions that reflect which inferences we *ought* to treat as impeccable; and sentences of mentalese, whose semantic structures may (or may not) diverge from their public counterparts. But however we choose to speak, the phrase 'logical form' has been historically used to gesture at a neighborhood of facts that at least include some descriptive facts concerning sentences and their (intrinsic) grammatical properties. I have suggested that at least some of these facts concern the thematically separated semantic forms of natural sentences. I have also noted related senses in which natural languages differ from a *Begriffsschrift*, whose compositional semantics is Functionist, while still suggesting that the semantic forms of sentences (or least those aspects of semantic form discussed here) are determined by their syntactic forms. Perhaps a theory of logical position and/or mentalese will reveal interesting aspects of meaning not grammatically determined; but such speculations, while not implausible, still await defense. On the other hand, while there is no a priori guarantee that natural sentences have semantic forms that capture (interesting aspects of) their meanings, available evidence suggests that a certain development of Davidson's event analysis is on the right track as a proposal concerning the semantic forms of sentences. So if we want to study the facts in the 'logical form neighborhood', pursuing thematically elaborated event analyses—along with a Conjunctivist conception of how natural syntax contributes to meaning—looks like a good bet.[21]

[20] Especially if mentalese sentences align better with Propositions, and/or talk of a *truth-conditional* semantics involves less of an idealization for mentalese than it does for spoken languages; see n. 1. Fodor suggests the more radical possibility that spoken sentences do not have semantic forms (or meanings) of their own: their semantic properties are due entirely to their (heavily context-sensitive) association with mentalese sentences, which are the primary bearers of meaning. But as it stands, this is speculation in need of defense, especially given the apparent successes of natural language semantics.

[21] For helpful comments and discussion, I would like to thank: Mark Baker, Susan Dwyer, Norbert Hornstein, Richard Larson, Ernie Lepore and the 'Metropolitan' Semantics Group, Barry Schein, Juan Uriagareka, and audiences at Johns Hopkins and Maryland.

REFERENCES

Baker, M. (1988). *Incorporation* (Chicago: University of Chicago).

—— (1997). 'Thematic Roles and Grammatical Categories', in L. Haegeman (ed.), *Elements of Grammar* (Dordrecht: Kluwer), 73–137.

Baker, M., and Stewart, O. T. (n.d.). 'Verbal Serialization and the Anatomy of the Clause' (MS, Rutgers University).

Barwise, J., and Cooper, R. (1981). 'Generalized Quantifiers and Natural Language', *Linguistics and Philosophy*, 4: 159–219.

Boolos, G. (1985). 'Nominalist Platonism'. Reprinted in *Logic, Logic, and Logic* (Cambridge, Mass.: Harvard University Press, 1998).

Carlson, G. (1984). 'Thematic Roles and their Role in Semantic Interpretation', *Linguistics*, 22: 259–79.

Castañeda, H. (1967). 'Comments', in Rescher (1967).

Chomsky, N. (1975). 'Questions of Form and Interpretation', *Linguistic Analysis*, 1: 75–109.

—— (1995). *The Minimalist Program* (Cambridge, Mass.: MIT Press).

—— (2000*a*). *New Horizons in the Study of Language and Mind* (New York: Cambridge University Press).

—— (2000*b*). 'Minimalist Inquiries', in R. Martin, D.Michaels, and J.Uriagereka (eds.), *Step by Step* (Cambridge, Mass.: MIT Press).

Crane, S., and Pietroski, P. M. (2001). 'Nature, Nurture, and Universal Grammar', *Linguistics and Philosophy*, 24: 139–86.

Davidson, D. (1967). 'The Logical Form of Action Sentences', in Rescher (1967).

—— (1985). 'Adverbs of Action', in B. Vermazen and M. Hintikka (eds.), *Essays on Davidson: Actions and Events* (Oxford: Clarendon Press).

Fodor, J. (1970). 'Three Reasons for Not Deriving "Kill" from "Cause to Die"', *Linguistic Inquiry*, 1: 429–38.

—— and Lepore, E. (2000). 'Morphemes Matter', *Rutgers Center for Cognitive Science Technical Reports*, TR-34.

Frege, G. (1891). 'Function and Concept', in Geach and Black (1980).

—— (1892). 'Sense and Reference', in Geach and Black (1980).

Geach, P., and Black, M., trans. (1980). *Translations from the Philosophical Writings of Gottlob Frege* (Oxford: Blackwell).

Hale, K., and Keyser, J. (1993). 'On Argument Structure and the Lexical Expression of Syntactic Relations', in Hale and Keyser (eds.), *The View from Building 20* (Cambridge, Mass.: MIT Press).

Hart, H., and Honoré, A. (1959). *Causation and the Law* (Oxford: Oxford University Press).

Heim, I., and Kratzer, A. (1998). *Semantics in Generative Grammar* (Oxford: Blackwell).

Herburger, E. (2000). *What Counts* (Cambridge, Mass.: MIT Press).

Hornstein, N. (forthcoming). *Move! A Minimalist Theory of Construal* (Cambridge: Blackwell).

Higginbotham, J. (1983). 'The Logical Form of Perceptual Reports', *Journal of Philosophy*, 80: 100–27.

—— and May, R. (1981). 'Questions, Quantifiers, and Crossing', *Linguistic Review*, 1: 47–79.

Kaplan, D. (1989). 'Demonstratives', in J. Almog, J. Perry, and H. Wettstein (eds.), *Themes from Kaplan* (New York: Oxford University Press).

Larson, R., and Segal, G. (1995). *Knowledge of Meaning* (Cambridge, Mass.: MIT Press).

McGilvray, J. (1999). *Chomsky: Language, Mind and Politics* (Cambridge: Polity Press and Blackwell).

Montague, R. (1970). 'English as a Formal Language', reprinted in *Formal Philosophy* (New Haven: Yale University Press).

Neale, S. (1990). *Descriptions* (Cambridge, Mass.: MIT Press).

—— (1993). 'Grammatical Form, Logical Form, and Incomplete Symbols', in A. Irvine and G. Wedeking (eds.), *Russell and Analytic Philosophy* (Toronto: University of Toronto).

Parsons, T. (1990). *Events in the Semantics of English* (Cambridge, Mass.: MIT Press).

Pesetsky, D. (1995). *Zero Syntax* (Cambridge, Mass.: MIT Press).

Pietroski, P. (1998). 'Actions, Adjuncts, Agency', *Mind*, 107: 73–111.

—— (2000*a*). *Causing Actions* (Oxford: Oxford University Press).

—— (2000*b*). 'On Explaining That', *Journal of Philosophy*, 97: 655–62.

—— (forthcoming *a*). 'Small Verbs, Complex Events', in L. Anthony and N. Hornstein (eds.), *Chomsky and his Critics* (Oxford: Blackwell).

—— (forthcoming *b*). 'Function and Concatenation', in A. Barber (ed.), *Epistemology of Language* (Oxford: Oxford University Press).

—— (forthcoming *c*). *Events and Semantic Architecture* (Oxford: Oxford University Press).

Rescher, N., ed. (1967). *The Logic of Decision and Action* (Pittsburgh: University of Pittsburgh Press).

Schein, B. (1993). *Plurals* (Cambridge, Mass.: MIT Press).

Taylor, B. (1985). *Modes of Occurrence* (Oxford: Blackwell).

Tenny, C. (1994). *Aspectual Roles and the Syntax–Semantics Interface* (Dordrecht: Kluwer).

Uriagereka, J. (1999). 'Multiple Spell-Out', in S. Epstein and N. Hornstein (eds.), *Working Minimalism* (Cambridge, Mass.: MIT Press).

Vlach, F. (1983). 'On Situation Semantics for Perception', *Synthese*, 54: 129–52.

5

Two Sorts of Claim about "Logical Form"

JEFFREY C. KING

The notion of *logical form* broadly construed has been central to the enterprise of analytic philosophy. Indeed, much of what we call analytic philosophy can be understood as something like the attempt to "characterize the logical forms" of various classes of sentences. Thus metaethical investigations into the nature of moral goodness can be thought of as attempts to "characterize the logical form" of sentences such as 'x is morally good'; epistemological investigations into the nature of knowledge can be thought of as attempts to "characterize the logical forms" of sentences such as 'A knows that P', and so on.

However, at least when viewed from a certain perspective, there are two quite different sorts of philosophical claims that one might intend in attempting to "characterize the logical form" of a given class of sentences. Unfortunately, these two sorts of claims have not always been carefully distinguished. And they *should* be carefully distinguished, not only for the sake of conceptual clarity, but because a given philosophical claim will have different implications depending on which of the two sorts of claims it is taken to be. Hence, when taken one way a given philosophical claim will be subject to objections that it is not subject to when taken the other way; and when taken one way a given philosophical claim will be able to do work in a larger philosophical theory that it could not do when taken the other way.

Though I have focused thus far on claims about logical form, similar remarks apply to claims to the effect that one is providing a philosophical

Kent Bach, William Demopoulos, Patrick Findler, and George Wilson made helpful comments on an earlier draft of this chapter.

"analysis" or "account" of, for example, knowledge or moral goodness. Here too, such claims can be interpreted in two importantly different ways.

In order to make these points clear, I shall begin by sketching a perspective from which we can clearly distinguish these two sorts of claims about logical form. This perspective amounts to some minimal and quite plausible assumptions about propositions and their constituents. Once we have characterized the two different sorts of claims that one might intend when one makes a claim about "logical form", by way of illustration, we will consider Russell's (1905) theory of descriptions and note that the theory can be taken in two different ways, corresponding to the two different sorts of claims. Next, again by way of illustration, we shall consider a recent debate between Michael Smith and Geoffrey Sayre-McCord concerning Smith's (1994) account of the concept of having a reason. We shall see that clarifying which of our two sorts of claims is being made at a crucial point would facilitate resolution of the debate.

I wish to stress the point just mentioned: the discussions of Russell's theory of descriptions and the debate between Smith and Sayre-McCord are simply for illustrative purposes. The moral of the present chapter is quite general. In (implicitly or explicitly) making claims about "logical form" or in providing "analyses", philosophers need to be more explicit about which of the two sorts of claims discussed herein they are making.

Before turning to the two sorts of claims about logical form that shall occupy us for the rest of this piece, it is worth mentioning a third sort of claim about logical form so that we may set it aside. Much thinking in current syntax is predicated on the idea that the syntactic representations that are the inputs to semantic interpretation are not surface structure representations of sentences. Within the Chomskyan tradition in syntax, the level of syntactic representation whose representations are the inputs to semantics is usually called *LF* (for *logical form*). Linguistically minded philosophers sometimes put forward proposals about the structure and nature of LF representations (for example, that they contain event variables, time indices, etc.). Since LF is a level of syntactic representation, these are *syntactical* proposals, even though they are proposals about a level of syntax that is intimately connected to semantics. Such claims about LF representations, or "logical form", are not our concern here. We shall be concerned with sorts of claims about logical form that are "more semantic" in nature.

First, then, let us discuss propositions. I shall assume that propositions are structured entities that have individuals, properties, and relations as constituents. In saying that propositions are *structured*, I mean to say that they are complex entities with constituents, where something binds together the constituents of propositions in certain ways and thereby imposes structure on the propositions. I shall represent this thing that binds together the constituents of a proposition by means of brackets or tree diagrams. Thus the proposition expressed by

Jason loves Michelle

might be represented in either of the following two ways:

(1*a*) [Jason*[loves* Michelle*]]

(1*b*)

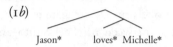

where for any expression e, e* is its propositional contribution—thus Jason* is Jason, loves* is the relation of loving, etc. The *constituents* of a structured proposition, as I use that term, are the entities inside the embedded brackets/at the terminal nodes of the proposition. In (1*a*/*b*), they are, of course, Jason*, loves*, and Michelle*.

Turning now to the treatment of quantification, I shall assume that *determiners* ('some', 'every', 'few', etc.) contribute to propositions relations between properties. Thus 'some' contributes the relation that obtains between properties A and B iff they are coinstantiated; 'few' contributes the relation that obtains between properties A and B iff few things that instantiate A instantiate B; and so on. Thus a quantified sentence like

(2) Few men are happy

expresses the proposition

(2*a*) [[Few*: x [men* x]]happy* x]

where Few* is the relation expressed by 'few'; men* is the property of being a man; etc. This proposition is true iff the properties men* and happy* stand in the relation Few* (i.e. iff few things that possess men* possess happy*).

Though I have assumed that individuals, properties, and relations are constituents of propositions, nothing I am going to say requires this. For present purposes it suffices to hold that propositions have constituents of *whatever* sort that can have some sort of "nature" or "internal structure"; and that these constituents are bound together in some way, resulting in a proposition that is structured in something like the way just described. Thus structured propositions with Fregean senses or "concepts" as constituents would do just as well. As promised, then, the framework that suffices for distinguishing between our two sorts of claims about logical form is plausible and minimal. We require that propositions are complex entities with constituents "bound together" in a certain way, and that these constituents have some sort of "nature" or "internal structure". I suspect that even more minimal assumptions would suffice for making our distinction or some analogue of it. But I leave this as an open question.

Against the background of this account of propositions, how are we to understand a claim to the effect that a certain sentence or class of sentences has such and such logical form? Clearly, we will understand such a claim to be a claim about the proposition(s) expressed by the sentence(s) in question. However, there are at least two different things that one might be claiming about the proposition(s) in question. One might be either:

(PSC) making a claim about the *structure* and *constituents* of the *proposition(s)* expressed by the sentence (class of sentences).

or

(NPC) making a claim about the 'natures' or 'internal structures' of one or more *constituents of the proposition(s)* expressed by the sentence (class of sentences).

I call the first sort of claim a *PSC claim*, since it is a claim about a proposition's *structure* and *constituents*. I call the second sort of claim an *NPC claim*, since it is a claim about the *nature* of (one or more) *propositional constituents*. As we shall see, these two sorts of claims are quite different, and very often a given philosophical proposal can be taken as either sort of claim. To see this, let us consider Russell's (1905) theory of descriptions.

In fact, it is misleading to say that I am discussing *Russell's* theory of descriptions. For I am not concerned with the question of how Russell is to be interpreted. Rather, I am supposing that all parties accept the minimal assumptions about propositions sketched at the outset and I am imagining a philosopher claiming that the logical form of a sentence like

(3) The F is G

is given by

(3*a*) $[\exists x][[y][Fy \leftrightarrow y=x] \& Gx]$[1]

---

[1] Though I am not claiming Russell ever said this himself, many philosophers have taken Russell's theory to specify the logical form of sentences containing definite descriptions. E.g. Neale (1990: 44) suggests that he takes Russell's theory this way, when, in noting that Russell's

My concern is with the two sorts of claims such a philosopher might be making about the proposition expressed by (3).

Taking the philosopher's assertion as a PSC claim, we would take (3*a*) to specify the structure and constituents of the proposition expressed by (3). If we represent this proposition in tree form for perspicuity, we get something like (3*b*).

(3*b*)

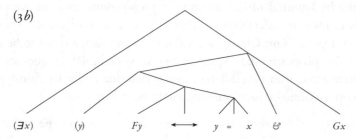

(∃*x*)   (*y*)   *Fy*   ⟷   *y* = *x*   &   *Gx*

This should make clear how (3*a*), taken as a PSC claim, specifies the structure and constituents of the proposition expressed by (3). It displays the *constituents* of the proposition at the terminal nodes of the tree; and it displays the *structure* of the proposition by means of the branching tree showing exactly how those constituents are bound together in the proposition.[2] Note that taken as a PSC claim, the claim that (3*a*) gives the logical form of sentences like (3) says nothing about the "*natures*" or "*internal structures*" of any of the *constituents* of the proposition expressed by (3). It simply tells us *what* the constituents of that proposition are and *how* they are bound together, and thus structured, in the proposition.

Suppose now that we take the claim that (3*a*) specifies the logical form of (3) as an NPC claim. So understood, this claim must be a claim about the nature or internal structure of a constituent or constituents of the proposition expressed by (3). And since presumably the primary concern of someone making this claim is the propositional contribution of the word 'the' (and not that of 'F' or 'G'), we ought to understand the claim as a claim about the nature or internal structure of the propositional contribution of the word 'the'.

theory of descriptions need not be wedded to the formalism of *Principia Mathematica*, he writes 'There is indeed a measure of inelegance involved in spelling out the logical form of a sentence of the form 'The F is G' as (∃x)((y)(Fy ↔ y=x) & Gx)'.

[2] Since the entities at the terminal nodes of (3*a*) are propositional constituents, e.g. (∃x) and & must be taken as the usual *propositional contributions* of 'some' and 'and' (even though 'some' and 'and' do not appear in (3)). This is why I have italicized them. If I had not, it would appear that e.g. 'G' occurs in both the *sentence* (3) and the *proposition* (3*b*). In (3*b*) 'G' represents the propositional contributions of 'G' in (3).

Assuming that in making this claim, our philosopher, like Russell himself, is in part claiming that definite descriptions function semantically like the quantifier phrases 'Some F', 'Every F' (and not like "genuine singular terms"), we should take our philosopher to be claiming in part that 'the' makes the same sort of contribution to propositions as 'every', 'some', etc. How can we understand the claim that (3a) gives the logical form of (3) in this way? Since, in the framework we have adopted, 'every', 'some' and so on contribute relations between properties to propositions, we must understand the claim that (3a) gives the logical form of (3) as a claim about the nature of the relation between properties contributed to propositions by 'the'. And now that we have put it this way, that is easy to do. Simply remove from (3a) features that are due to 'F' and 'G' in (3): namely, the occurrences of 'F' and 'G' in (3a). Next, let us put variables in their places to hold these places, and bind those variables by prefixing lamda operators so:

(3c) $\lambda H \lambda J([\exists x][[y][Hy \leftrightarrow y=x] \& Jx])$

Here we have the specification of a relation between arbitrary properties H and J. Thus we may understand the claim that (3a) gives the logical form of (3) as claiming that 'the' contributes a relation between properties to propositions expressed by sentences like (3), and that (3c) tells us what the "nature" or "internal structure" of that relation is. Further, since we are not understanding the claim that (3a) gives the logical form of (3) as a PSC claim, we should not take the claim to say *anything* about the structure of the proposition expressed by (3). Thus, we should assume as a default position that one making this claim takes the structure of the proposition expressed by (3) to be very much like the syntactic structure of (3) (if he/she didn't think this, he she would make a PSC claim!). Hence, taken as an NPC claim, the claim that (3a) gives the logical form of (3) (given the default assumption about propositional structure), amounts to the claim that the proposition expressed by (3) is something like

(3d)

The*   F*   G*

where The* is the relation expressed by 'the', F* is the property expressed by 'F' and so on. (3c), in turn, specifies the "nature" or "internal structure" of The*.

But precisely what is (3c) saying about the "nature" of The*? I think that this question raises an important point. In making an NPC claim, a philosopher needs to be quite explicit about what *precisely* he/she is claiming about the propositional constituent in question. Simply writing down something like (3c) is not enough. (3c) could be merely a way of specifying necessary and sufficient conditions for The* holding. Or it could be a way of saying something far more substantial about The*. For example, some philosophers hold that some properties and relations are complex, and have other properties and relations as component parts. It might be held, for example, that the property of being a bachelor is complex and has the properties of being unmarried, being adult, and being male as component parts, so that the property of being a bachelor is literally built out of these other properties. A philosopher who holds such a view might use (3c) as a way of specifying the component parts of The* and how they are combined to form it. Taken this way, (3c) commits one to the view that the identity relation, the relation between properties $\exists x$, and so on, are components of the complex relation expressed by 'the'.[3] Clearly, this is a much stronger claim than the claim that (3c) simply specifies necessary and sufficient conditions for The* to obtain! To repeat, a philosopher making an NPC claim ought to be explicit as to precisely what she is saying about the nature of the propositional constituent(s) in question. In many cases, this will require addressing substantial questions in metaphysics (for example, as in the last case, addressing the metaphysical nature of properties and relations). It is worth noting that the philosopher making a PSC claim incurs no such burden. For a fortiori she is making no claim about the *nature* of the constituents of a proposition, but simply specifying its structure and which its constituents *are*.

Suppose we take NPC claims in the "substantial" way just discussed. Thus we take them to be claims about the *component parts* of various complex properties and relations that are constituents of propositions. Then the distinction between NPC and PSC claims is a distinction between: (i) claims about the component parts of a propositional constituent and how they are combined to form that constituent; and (ii) claims about what the constituents of a proposition are and how they are bound together to form the proposition. Now someone might object to our distinction, saying that an NPC claim taken in this substantial way *is* just a claim about propositional structure and so a

---

[3] I shall use the term 'constituent', as already indicated, for entities at the terminal nodes of a proposition (though see n. 5), and the term 'component' for parts of complex entities like properties (or later concepts).

PSC claim. For a constituent of a proposition is part of that proposition. So an NPC claim about the component parts of a propositional constituent and how they are combined to form it is ultimately a claim about the structure and composition of a part of a proposition. But a claim about the structure and composition of a part of a proposition is ultimately a claim about the structure of the proposition. Thus it is a PSC claim, and our distinction collapses (when, at least, NPC claims are understood in the "substantial" way mentioned).

This objection really amounts to suggesting that we use the term 'propositional structure' differently from the way we have been using it, and fails to show that there is no distinction between PSC and NPC claims. Our theory of propositions holds that something binds together the constituents of a proposition, whether those constituents are themselves simple or complex, and imposes structure on those constituents (I have represented this thing by means of brackets or trees). For purposes of illustration, think of this thing as a relation whose relata are the (simple or complex) constituents of the proposition. It is one thing to make a (PSC) claim about the structure of *that relation* and what things stand in it. It is quite another thing to make a claim about the *component parts* (and how they are put together) of one or more *relata* of that relation. The objector is suggesting that we call both sorts of claims 'claims about propositional structure'. But whether we do so or not, there are clearly two different sorts of claims here.

I hope that what has been said so far is sufficient to show *both* the very great difference between PSC claims and NPC claims *and* how a given assertion about logical form could be taken as a claim of either sort. In order to reinforce these points, I shall illustrate how an objection may apply to a given position when taken as a PSC claim, but not apply to that position when taken as an NPC claim. Given the great difference between the two sorts of claims, this is not in itself surprising. Still, illustrating this in a concrete case will prove instructive.

So suppose again that a philosopher tells us that the logical form of (3) is given by (3*a*) (and let us suppress for a moment the question of whether she is making a PSC claim or an NPC claim). Now consider the following objection to this proposal.[4] Whatever its other virtues, the proposal that (3*a*) gives the logical form of (3) is unacceptable as part of a compositional semantics for

---

[4] This hypothetical objection is based loosely on objections Barwise and Cooper (1981: 165) make to the standard representations of sentences such as 'Every man sneezed' in the predicate calculus. But I do not mean to attribute *this* objection to them.

English because of the radical mismatch between sentential constituents in (3) and propositional constituents in (3*a*). The proposition (3*a*), after all, contains no constituent corresponding to the noun phrase 'the F' in (3)! Further, and worse yet, the proposition (3*a*) contains propositional constituents corresponding to sentential connectives ($\leftrightarrow$, &) and quantifiers (($\exists$x), (y)) that don't appear in (3) at all. Thus though (3*a*) may serve as an *ad hoc* specification of the truth-conditions of (3), a serious compositional semantics for English will not map (3) to the proposition (3*a*).

I am not concerned with the merits of this objection. Perhaps it is cogent, perhaps it is not. The important point for present purposes is that the objection applies to the proposal in question only if the proposal is taken as a PSC claim. For in claiming that *the proposition* (3*a*) has *no constituent* corresponding to the noun phrase 'The F' in (3) and that it *has constituents* corresponding to connectives and quantifiers that do not occur in (3), the objection clearly presupposes that (3*a*) is intended to specify the structure and constituents of the proposition expressed by (3).

Indeed, if we understand the proposal as an NPC claim of the sort sketched earlier, the objection loses its force entirely. For understood in that way (and given the default assumption about propositional structure mentioned earlier), the proposition expressed by (3), (3*d*), *does* have a constituent corresponding to the noun phrase 'The F' in (3), namely:[5]

The*   F*

And the proposition contains no constituents corresponding to sentential connectives or quantifiers that don't occur in (3). Its only constituents are The*, F*, and G*![6] So here we see quite graphically that an objection to a proposal about "logical form" may apply to the proposal when taken as a PSC

---

[5] This is actually a slight departure from the way in which I have used the term 'constituent' thus far. When a proposition is represented in tree form, I have called the entities at the terminal nodes 'constituents'. Obviously, the entity displayed below does not occur at a terminal node in (3*d*). Thus perhaps I should call the things at terminal nodes 'minimal constituents', and call subtrees of a proposition 'constituents'.

[6] Though, as I have remarked, I want to steer clear of interpretative questions regarding Russell (1905), the fact that Russell asserts that definite descriptions (and "denoting phrases" generally) are not to be regarded as 'standing for genuine constituents of the propositions in whose verbal expressions they occur' suggests to me that within our framework Russell ought to be interpreted as making a PSC claim. However, my own view is that Russell's proposal is more plausible (which is not to say I endorse it) when taken as an NPC claim.

claim and have no force at all against that proposal when taken as an NPC claim.[7]

Having considered a hypothetical example, let us now turn to an actual debate in which the distinction between PSC and NPC claims is relevant. One caveat before proceeding. The participants couch their discussion in terms of *concepts*. Though they talk of propositions too, it is difficult to see what they take the relation between concepts and propositions to be.[8] Much of their discussion suggests that they take concepts to be constituents of propositions, just as I have taken properties to be constituents of propositions.[9] I will assume in what follows that concepts instead of properties are constituents of propositions in the debate between Smith and Sayre-McCord. Even if I am wrong in interpreting them in this way, given present purposes it will be instructive to consider their debate from this perspective.

Michael Smith (1997: 88) provides the following 'analysis', as he calls it, of normative reasons (or desirability):

when we say of an agent A that she has a normative reason to, say, keep a promise in certain circumstances C, what we are saying is that, in nearby possible worlds in which A has a set of desires that are completely beyond reproach, from the point of view of reasoned criticism, A desires that, in those possible worlds in which she finds herself in circumstances C, she keeps her promise . . .

Smith goes on to say (1997: 103–4): 'my belief that it is desirable to ϕ in C has, as its content, the proposition that ϕing in C is what I would want myself to do if I had a maximally informed and coherent and unified desire set'. Thus Smith claims that the proposition that A has a normative reason to ϕ in C *is* the

---

[7] Of course, I did not show that the hypothetical objection *does* apply to the proposal that (3*a*) gives the logical form of (3) when it is taken as a PSC claim. But the point is that if it does not, it is ruled out on quite different grounds from those that rule it out as an objection to that proposal when taken as an NPC claim.

[8] It is at least possible that Michael Smith and Geoffrey Sayre-McCord accept a framework within which the distinction that I shall be urging them to make cannot be made. In other work I have tried to emphasize the virtues of a particular account of propositions that satisfies the sufficient conditions mentioned earlier in the text for making the distinction I want to make (see King, 1994, 1995, 1996, 1998).

[9] e.g. Smith (1997: 102–3) seems to say that, in showing that the *concepts* of being desirable and being something I would desire if I were fully rational are the same, he has thereby shown that the *proposition* believed when I believe something is desirable *is* the proposition that that thing is something I would desire if I were fully rational. That Smith takes the claim of conceptual identity to show that the two propositions in question are the same suggests to me that Smith takes concepts to be constituents of propositions.

proposition that φing in C is what A would desire if she had a maximally informed, coherent, unified set of desires.

Geoffrey Sayre-McCord (1997) objects to Smith's identifying the proposition that A has reason to φ in C with the proposition that φing in C is what A would desire if she had a maximally informed, coherent, unified set of desires. Sayre-McCord, as interpreted by Smith, claims that since one can be competent with the concept of a reason without being competent with, or even possessing, the concept of what a fully rational person would want, it cannot be that believing that A has a reason to φ *just is* believing that if A were fully rational, A would desire to φ. For if I have the concept of having a reason but not the concept of what a fully rational person would want, I could believe that A has reason to φ without believing that if A were fully rational, A would desire to φ. After all, how could I believe a proposition containing concepts I do not possess?

In responding to Sayre-McCord, Smith must defend the view that all those who believe the proposition that A has reason to φ believe the proposition that φing is what A would do if A had a maximally informed, coherent, unified set of desires, since these are the same proposition according to Smith. However, this proposition will be quite different depending on whether we take Smith's claim (that the proposition that A has a normative reason to φ in C *is* the proposition that φing in C is what A would desire if she had a maximally informed, coherent, unified set of desires) to be a PSC or an NPC claim.

Understood as an NPC claim, Smith is making a claim about *the internal structure and components of a propositional constituent*: the complex concept of having a reason. He is claiming that this concept has as components the concepts of desire, being fully rational, etc. Taken this way, Smith would apparently hold that the proposition expressed by 'A has a reason to φ' has a structure similar to that of the sentence itself (remember, he is not making a PSC claim!) and has as constituents A (or a concept of A), the (complex) concept of having a reason (whose components he has described), and the concept of φing. Thus the proposition in question looks something like this:

(4)

A*   has-a-reason*   to–φ*

where A* is the propositional constituent contributed by 'A', has-a-reason* is the propositional contribution of 'has a reason', etc. Hence when he says that the proposition that A has a normative reason to φ in C *is* the proposition that φing in C is what A would desire if she had a maximally informed, coherent, unified set of desires, Smith is just describing the components and internal structure of the complex concept has-a-reason*, which occurs as a single (but complex) constituent of the proposition that A has a reason to φ (i.e. (4)). So if Smith is making an NPC claim, to respond to Sayre-McCord he must argue that all those who believe that A has a reason to φ believe the proposition (4).

By contrast, if Smith is making a PSC claim, it turns out that the proposition expressed by 'A has reason to φ' has many more constituents than (4) has and more than it might have appeared to have. For on this way of interpreting Smith, the claim that the proposition that A has a normative reason to φ in C *is* the proposition that φing in C is what A would desire if she had a maximally informed, coherent, unified set of desires is an attempt to specify the *structure and constituents of the proposition* expressed by 'A has reason to φ'. Thus it turns out to have as constituents the concepts of desiring to φ, of being maximally informed, of being coherent, etc. These are no longer claimed to be *components* of the complex concept of having a reason which *itself* is a propositional constituent. Rather, they are *constituents* of the proposition taken individually *by themselves*. Thus, the proposition can no longer be taken to have only three constituents and to have a structure similar to that of the sentence 'A has reason to φ'. It has many *more* constituents and has a structure similar to that of the sentence 'φing in C is what A would desire if she had a maximally informed, coherent, unified set of desires'. Simplifying for ease of exposition, the proposition would look something like (5).

(5)

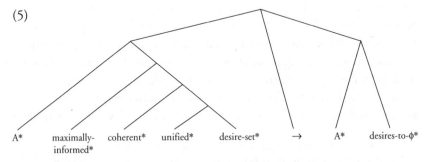

| A* | maximally-informed* | coherent* | unified* | desire-set* | → | A* | desires-to-φ* |

where A* is the propositional contribution of 'A', maximally informed* is the concept of being maximally informed, coherent* is the concept of being coherent, etc. Thus if Smith is making a PSC claim, in responding to Sayre-McCord he must argue that all those who believe that A has reason to φ believe the proposition (5).

To repeat, if Smith is making an NPC claim, in order to respond to Sayre-McCord's objection he must defend the view that all those who believe that A has reason to φ believe the proposition (4); whereas if he is making a PSC claim, he must defend the view that all those who believe that A has reason to φ believe the quite different proposition (5). Certainly, these views are quite distinct. And in fact, one of them has an unpalatable consequence that the other lacks.

In our ordinary practice of ascribing beliefs, we do not ascribe to someone belief in a proposition that has as a constituent something that he/she does not have a sufficiently robust cognitive grip on. For example, we would not ascribe to someone who accepts the law of excluded middle but has never heard of radioactivity belief in the proposition that the Hope diamond is either radioactive or it is not. Presumably, this is because the person has an insufficiently robust cognitive connection to the property of being radioactive. In holding that people who believe that A has a reason to φ but have never heard of or thought of being maximally informed, having unified desires, etc., none the less believe the proposition (5), one must hold that people may believe propositions that have as constituents entities that they have merely the weakest cognitive connection to.[10] Thus, it seems to me that one will end up with a view about the correctness of belief ascriptions that conflicts significantly and in very general ways with our practice of ascribing belief.[11]

On the other hand, claiming that all those who believe that A has reason to φ believe the proposition (4) has no such consequence. Those who believe that A has a reason to φ certainly do have a robust cognitive grip on the constituents of (4), including the complex concept of having a reason. True, we may be forced to say that some who have a cognitive grip on this complex concept have only the weakest grip on some of the components of this concept. But this does not seem problematic or surprising. Indeed, if concepts are complex in the way being suggested, it will quite often be the case that one has a firm cognitive grip on a given concept, but little or no cognitive grip on its components. In any case, whether I am right about the unpalatable consequences of the one claim as compared with the other or not, it is clear that Smith's claim interpreted as

[10] In fact, Smith tries to argue that, despite initial appearances, people of the sort just described do possess the concepts of being maximally informed, etc. He claims that their ability to wield the concept of a normative reason correctly shows that they are "sensitive to" things like being maximally informed, etc. But this just brings up the point I am making. If we hold that being "sensitive to" concepts in this way is all that is required to believe propositions containing them as constituents (even though one has never heard of or explicitly thought about the concept), we will end up making belief ascriptions that conflict violently with ordinary usage.

[11] This point is closely related to Sayre-McCord's objection (and thus in this sense I think his objection has more bite against Smith when Smith is taken as making a PSC claim).

an NPC claim is quite different from his claim interpreted as a PSC claim; and that, depending on which of these he intends, he must argue different things in response to Sayre-McCord's objection.

In conclusion, I have tried to show that (implicit or explicit) claims about logical form, or claims to the effect that one is providing an "analysis" or "account" of a certain notion, can often be taken in two different ways. As we have seen, whether a claim is taken in one way or the other can be crucial. Views may be subject to objections when taken one way and not when taken another. An objection to a view taken one way may involve a very different sort of response from what would be required if the view were taken another way. Further, though limitations of space have prevented me from discussing this point here, a view may gain unwarranted plausibility from trading on these two ways of being taken. A given argument may go through if a claim is taken one way; another argument may go through if that claim is taken another way. And even though both arguments are required for some larger philosophical purpose, it is not the case that *both* arguments would go through on any *one* way of taking the claim. For these and other reasons, philosophers need to be much more explicit about which sort of claim they are making in making a claim about logical form.

REFERENCES

Barwise, John, and Cooper, Robin (1981). 'Generalized Quantifiers and Natural Language', *Linguistics and Philosophy*, 4, 159–219.

King, Jeffrey C. (1994). 'Can Propositions be Naturalistically Acceptable?', *Midwest Studies in Philosophy*, 19: 53–75.

—— (1995). 'Structured Propositions and Complex Predicates', *Nous*, 29: 4516–35.

—— (1996). 'Structured Propositions and Sentence Structure', *Journal of Philosophical Logic*, 25: 495–521.

—— (1998). 'What is a Philosophical Analysis?', *Philosophical Studies*, 90: 155–79.

Neale, Stephen (1990). *Descriptions* (Cambridge, Mass.: The MIT Press).

Russell, Bertrand (1905). 'On Denoting', *Mind*, 14: 479–93.

Sayre-McCord, Geoffrey (1997). 'The Metaethical Problem', *Ethics*, 108 (Oct. 1997): 55–83.

Smith, Michael (1994). *The Moral Problem* (Oxford: Blackwell).

—— (1997). 'In Defense of *The Moral Problem*: A Reply to Brink, Copp and Sayre-McCord', *Ethics*, 108 (Oct. 1997): 84–119.

6

LF and Natural Logic

PETER LUDLOW

During the twentieth century, the focus of work in logic was principally on the development of logical calculi that bear little apparent relation to the structure of natural language. That is, the syntactic forms postulated for purposes of logical reasoning (for example, the logical forms of the propositional and predicate calculi) do not obviously resemble the forms postulated within current grammatical theory. This apparent mismatch between logical form and grammatical form is ordinarily taken as an unsurprising consequence of the fact that, since Frege and Russell, one of the central goals of logic has been to help clarify (if not establish) the foundations of mathematics. Mathematics aside, however, it has also been held that natural language is a rather poor medium in which to couch logical reasoning, since natural language is ambiguous, vague, etc.

Yet if we step back a bit and view the development of logic over the last two millennia, we find a rather different picture. Up until the beginning of the twentieth century, logic was very much concerned with representing

Many thanks are due to Victor Sánchez for encouraging me to pursue this project. His remarkable (1991) dissertation obviously has been very influential in my exposition of the historical and other parts of this paper. Portions of this paper were written while I held the Fulbright Chair in the Philosophy of Language at the University of Venice, during academic year 1997–8. Thanks are due to John Bailyn, Anna Cardinaletti, Guglielmo Cinque, Dan Finer, Richard Kayne, Richard Larson, Fabio Pianese and Michal Starke for discussion of ways to execute the syntax of this proposal in current linguistic theory. As my ideas have shifted radically with my education in this area, some of the above will not recognize the final proposal (which is just sketched here in any case) but their contributions in steering me in the right direction have been profound. An earlier version of this paper was presented to the Dept. of Linguistics at MIT. Thanks are due to that audience and to Richard Larson, Stuart Shieber and an anonymous reviewer for comments and suggestions on the penultimate draft.

the inferences that are made in natural language. So, as everyone knows, classical Aristotelian logic attempted to characterize the valid syllogistic arguments, the canonical example being the following:

(1) All men are animals
   <u>All animals are mortals</u>
   All men are mortals

And the strategy was to elucidate the natural language *forms* that underwrite valid inferences. Thus the argument above was valid because it instantiated the following form.

(2) All As are Bs
   <u>All Bs are Cs</u>
   All As are Cs

As everyone also knows, the syllogistic logic of Aristotle (sometimes called 'term logic') applied only to a very small fragment of natural language—basically only propositions of the form [Determiner Noun copula (negation) Noun], and even for this limited fragment, the inference rules were *ad hoc*—there are 256 possible forms of the Aristotelian syllogism, and the handful of valid forms share no obvious syntactic properties.[1]

It is less well known that in the 2000+ years after Aristotle a number of successful efforts were made to expand the scope of classical logic as well as to find ways of generalizing and simplifying the rules of inference to a few core cases.[2] Let us use the phrase 'natural logic' to cover this broad research program. As we will see, the two millennia of work in natural logic successfully unearthed a number of deep insights about the nature of inferences in natural language, but was hampered by a lack of understanding of the structure of natural language as well as by a lack of proper technical resources for describing such structure. In this chapter I am going to argue that recent work in generative linguistics and formal logic, when combined, can help us to preserve the insights of the traditional natural logic program as well as to expand it in a number of fruitful ways.

In a sense, the first step in updating the natural logic project was already undertaken by the development of modeltheoretic semantics for natural languages, principally following the work of Montague (1974). That work allowed us to give a *semantical* account of natural language entailment

---

[1] But see Sommers (1982) and Englebretsen (1987) for samples of efforts at extending the coverage of traditional term logic.

[2] See Sánchez (1994) and Kneale and Kneale (1962) for discussion.

relations. But can we take the second step and also give a *syntactic* account of entailment relations? If natural language was no more complex than first order logic, this would be a trivial problem, but as Rescher (1962) has shown, a number of natural language quantifiers are non-first-orderizable. More recent work by Hintikka (1974), Barwise (1979), and Boolos (1998: chs. 4 and 5) has stressed this point as well. Refining the question, we might ask whether we can give syntactic accounts of natural language inferences, given the non-first-order nature of natural language.

There are, of course, proof theories for the lambda calculus that was utilized in Montague (1974), but in this chapter I hope to show that that the technical resources for describing linguistic structure within the 'minimalist program' of Chomsky (1995) may make it possible to define entailment relations in a way that respects the insights from the investigation of naturalized logic prior to the twentieth century, and also may allow us to generalize those insights even further.

There will be a crucial intermediate step, however. After detailing the semantical approaches to inference in natural language, I will describe a formal language L* from Law and Ludlow (1985) in which the crucial model-theoretic properties governing entailment relations have *syntactic* reflexes. I will then argue that the LF representations in the minimalist program can easily reflect all the relevant syntactic properties of L*, and I will show how the LF representations might be derived within the minimalist framework.

My plan is therefore as follows. In part (I) I describe some of the insights acquired in natural logic over the last two millennia, and in (II) I survey some recent attempts to incorporate these insights into contemporary generative grammar. In (III) I show how these insights can be cashed out semantically, given current model-theoretic semantics. Then in (IV) I will show that the same insights can also be cashed out syntactically (and generalized) within the formal language L*. In (V) I argue that LF representations in the minimalist program can reflect the L* representations (or at least the crucial features of them), but will leave open the question of how they can be derived within minimalist syntax. Finally, in (VI), I offer some speculative remarks about possible avenues for future research in generative linguistics and natural logic.

I   Natural Logic and its Holy Grail

As the medieval logicians observed, the problem with classical Aristotelian logic is that it is both too constrained and too *ad hoc*. The theory is *ad hoc* because the class of valid argument forms is simply stipulated, with no apparent underlying principle or insight. It is too *constrained* because (as noted above) it covers only an extremely narrow class of natural language constructions. Inferences like the following simply do not fit the paradigm.

(3) Every man is mortal
<u>Socrates is a man</u>
Socrates is mortal

(4) No man flies
<u>Some bird flies</u>
Some bird is not a man

It is of course a standard exercise of undergraduate logic texts to force other natural language sentences into this format. Thus we have the following translations:

(5) Socrates is a man = Every Socrates is a man
(6) No man flies = No man is a thing that flies

But these paraphrases are unmotivated to say the least. The medievals saw this, and over a period of centuries pursued a research program that attempted to reduce the number of rules of inference and at the same time expand their coverage. Although the research program involved a lot of groping in the dark, one key idea appeared to be driving the best and most interesting research: one can reduce the Aristotelian inferences to two basic paradigms, and these paradigms can cover a broad class of natural language argument forms—certainly much broader than the original Aristotelian paradigm would have allowed.

The idea—the Holy Grail of natural logic—was that there are two distinct environments and that the class of inferences could be reduced to two rules, one corresponding to each of the two environments. The two basic paradigms, the *dictum de omni* and the *dictum de nullo*, are the inference paradigms which today we would think of as monotone increasing (or upward entailing) and monotone decreasing (or downward entailing) environments.[3] As 'de nullo' suggests, the *dictum de nullo* paradigm applied to environments that were intuitively negative, and the *dictum de omni* paradigm applied to environments that were intuitively positive. The basic idea can be summed up in the following way, where 'A < B' is a general way of indicating that all As are Bs, or

---

[3] This connection has been observed in Hoeksma (1986), van Benthem (1991), and Sánchez (1991), but see Sánchez (1994) for an observation that the parallelism between downward entailingness and the *dictum de nullo* is not perfect. Perhaps a bit carelessly, I am going to use the notions interchangeably in this chapter.

that every A is (a) B, or that all A is B (I'm avoiding set-theoretic terminology here, which would say that A is a subset of B).

(7) An environment α in a sentence φ is a *dictum de omni* environment iff,
$[_\phi \ldots [_\alpha \ldots A \ldots] \ldots]$ entails $[_\phi \ldots [_\alpha \ldots B \ldots] \ldots]$ iff A < B
An environment α in a sentence φ is a *dictum de nullo* environment iff,
$[_\phi \ldots [_\alpha \ldots A \ldots] \ldots]$ entails $[_\phi \ldots [_\alpha \ldots B \ldots] \ldots]$ iff B < A

To see that this works in the most obvious cases, simply consider some of the classical inferences discussed above. If we assume that the second (B) position in 'Every A is a B' is a *dictum de omni* environment, then we can simply swap 'mortal' for 'animal' in the argument below, since, following the second premise, animal < mortal.

(8) Every man is an animal
 Every animal is mortal
 Every man is mortal

But if we add a negation, as in the following argument, then we have to use the *de nullo* rule. Notice that here we can substitute 'animal' for 'mortal' (following the *de nullo* paradigm).

(9) Some man is not mortal
 Every animal is mortal
 Some man is not (an) animal

Not only can these two paradigms cover the Aristotelian syllogisms,[4] but they cover a number of other apparently valid inferences that fall outside of the Aristotelian paradigm as well. Consider the two cases discussed above. The first is simply a case of the *dictum de omni* paradigm.

---

[4] In most cases the actual formal derivation of the valid syllogisms is trivial, but in several cases the derivation requires the following equivalence rules.
 (i) No S is P = All S is not P
 (ii) Some S is P = Some P is S
  No S is P = No P is S
So, to take the most complicated case, the syllogism EIO in the fourth figure requires the following sort of derivation.
 (1) No P is M
 (2) Some M is S
 (3) No M is P (from 1, by (ii))
 (4) All M is not P (from 3, by (i))
 (5) Some S is M (from 2, by (ii))
 (6) Some S is not P (from 4, 5, by *dictum de omni*)

(10) Every man is mortal
      <u>Socrates is a man</u>
      Socrates is mortal

Since 'is a man' is in a *de omni* environment, the first premise licenses the substitution. Had the second premise been 'Socrates is not a mortal' then the de nullo paradigm would have applied and we would have been entitled to conclude 'Socrates is not a man'. Similar reasoning applies to the following:

(11) No man flies
      <u>Every bird flies</u>
      No man (is a) bird

Here, since 'flies' is in a *de nullo* environment we can substitute 'bird' for 'flies'.

Even the rules *modus ponens* and *modus tollens* of contemporary propositional logic fall within this paradigm if we extend A < B to include 'If A then B'. Then *modus ponens* is simply a specific instance of the *dictum de omni* rule (one where α contains only A),

(12) If Smith is tall then Jones is short
      <u>Smith is tall</u>
      Jones is short

and *modus tollens* is simply an instance of the *dictum de nullo* rule (again, the instance where α contains only A).

(13) If Smith is tall then Jones is short
      <u>Jones is not short</u>
      Smith is not tall

Notice what a radical departure this is from our contemporary way of thinking about the proper way of characterizing inferences. Typically, we suppose that various kinds of inferences should be handled in different ways. But the headline idea of the natural logic program incorporating the *dictum de omni et nullo* was that perhaps all that passes as logic could be treated in this manner—from the basic inferences discussed above to the logic of relations.

Despite the promise of the *dictum de omni et dictum de nullo* paradigm, certain questions arise already in the simple cases. Apparently the first position

---

The disputed syllogisms can also be derived, but (as one would expect) only given the following additional rule.
(iii) <u>All S are P</u>
       Some S are P

of 'every' (i.e. the noun) must be a downward entailing environment, but why?—especially given that there are no apparent negations. To get a hint of the range of phenomena consider the following facts, where we define the *first position* of a determiner as that in which the nominal occurs (what linguists call the 'restriction' of the determiner), and the *second position* as that in which the predicate occurs (what linguists call the 'nuclear scope' of the determiner).

'Some': *dictum de omni* applies in both first and second position.

(14) Some men run

(15) *a.* => Some things run
      b. ≠> Some tall men run

(16) *a.* => Some men move
      b. ≠> Some men run fast

'No': *dictum de nullo* applies in both first and second position.

(17) No man runs

(18) *a.* ≠> No things run
      b. => No tall men run

(19) *a.* ≠> No men move
      b. => No men run fast

'Every': *dictum de nullo* applies in the first position, but *dictum de omni* applies in the second position.

(20) Every man runs

(21) *a.* ≠> Every thing runs
      b. => Every tall man runs

(22) *a.* => Every man moves
      b. ≠> Every man runs fast

'Most': neither *dictum de omni* nor *dictum de nullo* applies in the first position. *Dictum de omni* applies in the second position.

(23) Most men run

(24) *a.* ≠> Most things run
      b. ≠> Most tall men run

(25) *a.* => Most men move
      b. ≠> Most men run fast

Also perplexing, however, is the fact that the behavior of these elements within relative clauses gives rise to even more diverse behavior. Consider the following inference:

(26)   No man who knows every dog in town runs a butcher shop
       <u>Every collie is a dog</u>
       No man who knows every collie in town runs a butcher shop

The above inference is valid if we take 'every dog in town' to have wide scope over 'no man', but it is not valid if we take the quantifiers to have their surface scope orderings ('No man' over 'every dog'), but what accounts for this? It appears that 'dog' should be in a downward entailing environment in the latter case, but it is not. Simply talking about being in the first (A) position of 'Every/No A is B' is not sufficient. Is there some principled way to characterize 'dog' in the first premise as being in a *dictum de omni* environment?

Questions like these led to some interesting investigations into the nature of 'relative terms' by the medieval logicians. Ockham (1951) developed a very subtle and sophisticated theory that detoured through the medieval doctrine of the *supposito*.[5] It is safe to say that the strategy was never successfully carried out, and to the extent it was carried out the theory had a distinctly *ad hoc* character.[6] In effect, the complexity of natural language stalled the natural logic program; the Holy Grail eluded the grasp of the natural logicians.

II Directional Entailingness in Generative Grammar

One way of thinking about these medieval efforts at defining the *dicta de omni et nullo* is that they were attempts at defining directional entailingness (monotonicity) in a syntactic way. Clearly, success in this endeavor would have important consequences. If all of natural logic can be reduced to cases of the *dicta de omni et nullo* and if those paradigms can in turn be identified as features of clearly identifiable syntactic forms, then the natural logic project becomes a chapter in the syntax of natural language. And who knows? Given the advances that have been made in generative linguistics, perhaps the natural

---

[5] See Sánchez (1991: 36 ff.) for discussion, and see Kneale and Kneale (1962: 246 ff.) for a discussion of the medieval arguments surrounding the nature of *supposito* theory.

[6] See Sánchez (1991: ch. 2) for discussion.

logic project can be successfully executed—perhaps its Holy Grail is within *our* grasp.

It is unusual to suppose that natural language syntax should have anything to do with logical entailment. Ordinarily, we take entailment relations to be the province of semantics. But there is no reason for this supposition. Pre-theoretically there is no reason to suppose that either syntax or semantics has exclusive claim on entailment relations, and a handful of linguists have pursued the idea that syntax has a good deal to say about them.

For example, Lakoff (1972) and McCawley (1972) both attempted to incorporate the natural logic program within generative semantics, and Suppes (1979) offered a number of inference rules that are defined off of forms generated by context-free phrase structure grammars. The Suppes project is particularly interesting in that the rules he defined effectively tracked the *dicta de omni et nullo*, albeit in a brute strength manner. For example, consider the following two rules which identify particular instances of the *dictum de omni* and *dictum de nullo* respectively.

Examples:

Some N'' + TV + All + $N2'$	Some dogs bite all animals
<u>All $N1'$ are $N2'$</u>	<u>All cats are animals</u>
Some N'' + TV + All + $N1'$	Some dogs bite all cats
All N'' + Aux + Neg + TV + All + $N1'$	All dogs do not love all cats
<u>All $N1'$ are $N2'$</u>	<u>All cats are animals</u>
All N'' + Aux + Neg + TV + All + $N2'$	All dogs do not love all animals

Instead of identifying two syntactic environments and providing two basic rules, Suppes offered seventy-five separate rules of inference, which, as a group, fleshed out the *dicta de omni et nullo* for a fragment of English. Of course, one would like to identify these environments with fewer rules (two in the ideal case) and one wonders how the project scales when we consider larger fragments of English and other languages. Just how many rules would be necessary in the end?

More recent attempts have sought to identify the relevant syntactic environments through the introduction of monotonicity marking. In particular, Sánchez (1991, 1995) and Dowty (1994) have offered theories in which one can define inferences off of linguistic representations (both utilize categorial grammar frameworks—the Lambek calculus in the former case—for describing linguistic forms) and at the same time incorporate the insights of traditional work on upward and downward entailing environments.

The Sánchez (1991) proposal, for example, involves a three-step process that begins with monotonicity marking of lexical items. The idea is that the primitive assignments give the category plus the internal monotonicity marking. So, whereas a determiner would ordinarily belong to the category $((e,t),((e,t),t))$ in a categorial grammar, in Sánchez's system we have the following additional primitive assignments.

(27) Every: $(e,t)^-, ((e,t)^+,t)$
     Some/a: $(e,t)^+, ((e,t)^+,t)$
     No: $(e,t)^-, ((e,t)^-,t)$

Notice that these markings are of purely syntactic significance and reflect but do not replace the semantic properties of the determiners (which would be specified by generalized quantifier theory). The second step in the monotonicity logic is external monotonicity marking, which governs how the markings on the lexical items affect the marking on the phrasal categories. The following three rules are applicable.

Positive monotone marking:

$$\frac{(\alpha^+, \beta)\ \alpha}{\beta} \rightarrow \quad \frac{(\alpha, \beta)\quad \alpha}{\beta}\ \ \frac{+\quad\quad +}{}$$

Negative monotone marking:

$$\frac{(\alpha^-, \beta)\ \alpha}{\beta} \rightarrow \quad \frac{(\alpha, \beta)\quad \alpha}{\beta}\ \ \frac{+\quad\quad -}{}$$

Neither positive nor negative monotone marking:

$$\frac{(\alpha, \beta)\ \alpha}{\beta} \rightarrow \quad \frac{(\alpha, \beta)\quad \alpha}{\beta}\ \ \frac{+}{}$$

Given these three rules and the primitive assignments introduced in step 1, we can generate trees with positive and negative markings at each node, as in the following structure generated for 'Abelard didn't catch every unicorn'.[7]

---

[7] This particular illustration is from Dowty (1994).

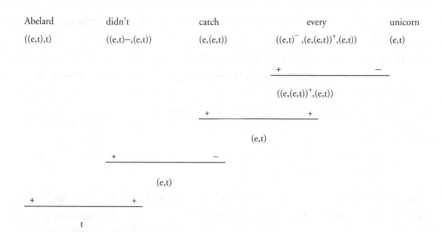

The final step is to determine the polarity of each constituent using the following rules.[8]

If T is a syntactic tree with root S, then

A node N has polarity in T iff all the nodes in the path from N to S are marked.

A node N is *positive* iff T has polarity and the number of nodes in the path marked "−" is even.

A node N is *negative* iff T has polarity and the number of nodes in the path marked "−" is odd.

For example, in the tree introduced above, the path to 'unicorn' has an even number of negative markings so 'unicorn' has positive polarity (is in a *dictum de omni* environment). The path to 'catch' has an odd number of negative markings, so 'catch' has negative polarity (is in a *dictum de nullo* environment).

The interest of this research should be obvious. The monotonicity marking in the syntax allows us to identify the upward and downward entailing environments simply by inspection of the syntactic forms. In addition, since the strategy can correctly assign monotonicity to elements that are embedded within negations and can also reflect relative operator scopes, the strategy can readily handle the kinds of relative clause constructions that exercised Ockham and subsequent natural logicians for centuries. In effect, we are very close to possessing the Holy Grail that eluded the natural logicians.

Close, but not quite there. Formally, once the monotonicity markings and rules are established, the system is quite elegant. The problem is that the monotonicity markings are not independently motivated; they are, in effect,

---

[8] See Dowty (1994) for a simplification of this proposal.

otherwise semantically inert. That is to say, the negative markings do not contribute in any way to the truth-conditions of the resulting grammatical form. This is troubling since they constitute syntactic elements that are all-important for defining entailment relations, but that make no apparent contribution to the truth-conditions of the form. At best a wedge has been driven between entailment relations and truth-conditions. At worst, this could be taken as evidence that the monotonicity marking strategy remains *ad hoc* (even if a much superior *ad hoc* strategy).

This objection may be a little bit abstract, so in the next section I want to show a case where the account of directional entailingness is not *ad hoc* at all, but is integrated into independently motivated accounts of determiner meaning. This will be a semantical account of determiners, and of course we are ultimately looking for a syntactic account of directional entailingness, but this detour through the semantics˙ should give us an example of a motivated account of directional entailingness, and perhaps also some insights into what a well-grounded syntactic account will ultimately look like.

III Directional Entailingness in Model-Theoretic Semantics

If the proper *formal* characterization of the valid inferences has escaped our grasp since the age of Aristotle, *semantical* characterizations have long been at hand. We know, for example, that the valid syllogisms of Aristotelian logic can be readily characterized using Venn diagrams. Recent work in model-theoretic semantics, however, suggests that not only can we give semantical (model-theoretic) accounts of the valid inferences, but that we can do so in a way that illuminates the nature of *dictum de omni* and *dictum de nullo* environments.

The key resource that allows us to make sense of the *dictum de omni/nullo* environments is the development of the generalized quantifier theory of Mostowski (1957) and its application to the semantics of natural language in Barwise and Cooper (1981), Higginbotham and May (1982), Keenan and Stavi (1986), and others. Very simply, the idea is that determiners ('all', 'some', 'no', 'most', etc.) denote relations between sets. To illustrate, following the notation of Larson and Segal (1995),[9] we would have the following set-theoretic denotations

___

[9] The 'Val' predicate is to be read as: 'The ordered pair consisting of the sets X and Y is a semantic value of . . . iff . . .'. There are some differences between their execution and this one, however.

for the basic determiners (here the term 'determiner' is being used very broadly—we may want to narrow that usage a bit later).

(28) Val($<X, Y>$, 'every') iff $|X - Y| = 0$
  Val($<X, Y>$, 'some') iff $|X \cap Y| > 0$
  Val($<X, Y>$, 'no') iff $|X \cap Y| = 0$
  Val($<X, Y>$, 'two') iff $|X \cap Y| = 2$
  Val($<X, Y>$, 'most') iff $|X \cap Y| > |X - Y|$

One of the interesting features of these set-theoretic accounts of the determiners—and one which, so far as I know, has not been highlighted in the semantics literature[10]—is that directional entailing environments can be semantically identified directly from the set-theoretic definitions of the determiners. For example, returning to the definition of 'some' above, we know simply from the properties of set theory that if $|X \cap Y| > 0$ is true, then the substitution of X and Y with supersets X' and Y' respectively will result in a true formula. Likewise 'no' will allow the substitution of subsets for X and Y, and 'every' will allow the substitution of a subset for X and a superset for Y.

The exciting insight to be gleaned from this work, in my opinion (as I noted earlier the point has largely passed unnoticed), is that we can now give a good *semantical* account of the *dictum de omni* and *dictum de nullo* environments; we now have some grasp on why the first position of 'every' should be downward entailing (*dictum de nullo*) and the second position should be upward entailing (*dictum de omni*). We also have a grasp on the upward and downward entailing properties of relative terms. Semantically, these two will be reflexes of the set-theoretic properties of generalized quantifier theory, and more generally of the model-theoretic semantics.

Notice that the features of the set-theoretic accounts of the determiners which we appealed to in identifying the *dicta de omni et nullo* environments are independently motivated. The determiners are defined solely so as to get the meanings right. We would like to see a similar result in our syntactic accounts of directional entailingness. That is, we would like to be able to identify directional entailing environments by pointing to features of natural language syntax that are motivated solely by getting the meanings (truth-conditions) right.

---

[10] The only place I know of where the observation is made in print is in Larson and Segal (1995: 284) who in turn attribute the point to discussion with me, but the point seems so obvious and important that it is hard to imagine that it has not been made elsewhere.

Of course some might argue that this is too much to ask for. The mono-tonicity accounts offered by Sánchez and Dowty are as close as we are ever going to come to the Holy Grail. Or worse, some might argue that we do not need syntactic accounts of these inferences, and more, that syntactic accounts are simply unavailable when we begin talking about non-elementary quantifiers. But this sort of pessimism strikes me as unmotivated. It is certainly the case that we cannot successfully give *first order* logical forms for sentences like 'most men are mortal'[11] but this does not close the door on non-first-order syntactic accounts. If we want to pursue the natural logic project we need to study logics which allow formal (i.e. syntactic) accounts of the non-elementary quantifiers, and which do so in a way that allows us to cash the notion of directional entailingness in a syntactic way.[12] Indeed, as we will see in the next section, we can identify formal languages in which directional entailing environments can be identified by independently motivated features of the syntax of the languages.

IV L* and the Syntax of Directional Entailing Environments

So far we have seen that the *dictum de omni* and *dictum de nullo* environments can be cashed out *semantically* as a reflex of basic set-theoretic properties. The question remains, however, as to whether there is any way to give a formal (syntactic) account of these same environments. In this section I will argue that the environments can be syntactically characterized within a particular formal language developed in Law and Ludlow (1985) and discussed in Ludlow (1995). In section V I will take up the issue of whether this formal language can be taken seriously as a way of giving the form of natural language expressions.

---

[11] See Rescher (1962).

[12] Does the non-first-order nature of such logics tell against them? Should it trouble us that they are not complete? As Sánchez (1991) observes we need to proceed with caution here. While higher order logics are incomplete with respect to standard models they may be complete with respect to generalized models such as those in Henkin (1950). As Kreisel (1952) puts the point, we should not talk about completeness simpliciter, but rather about completeness with respect to an interpretation of the system. Is there some reason why general models à la Henkin are inappropriate for the interpretation of natural language inferences? So far as I know, no argument exists which shows that general models are inappropriate for these purposes. Finally there is the question of whether completeness of any stripe is an important desideratum for natural logic. This too needs to be argued.

The basic idea underlying L* is that cardinality and cardinality relations can be expressed as features of the syntax of certain languages. So, for example, the set-theoretic relation $|\{x: Ax\}| \geq n$ will correspond to the L* expression $(\exists \geq_n x)Ax$. The basic structure of L* is as follows. To first order logic, we add subscripted objectual quantifiers: $(\exists \geq_2 x)$, $(\exists \geq_3 x)$, etc., which are understood as 'there are greater than or equal two xs such that...', 'there are greater than or equal three xs such that...', etc.[13] We also introduce substitutional quantifiers (Π a universal substitutional quantifier over numbers, and Σ the corresponding existential quantifier) which can quantify into the numerical subscript positions. For example:

(29) infinitely many: $\Pi n \exists \geq_n x(A(x) \ \& \ B(x))$
(30) at least finitely many: $\Sigma n \exists \geq_n x(A(x) \ \& \ B(x))$
(31) most: $\Pi n((\exists \geq_n x)A(x) \rightarrow (\exists \geq_{f(n)} x)(A(x) \ \& \ B(x))$

In (31), f is a primitive recursive operation on inscriptions that, in the case of the quantifier 'most', will yield $\frac{1}{2}n$ (less fractional remainder) plus 1.

Other examples include the following (obviously there are numerous ways to define each of these determiners, including ways that simply utilize the first order subset of L*).

(32) More As than Bs are Cs: $\Sigma n(\exists \geq_n x)(A(x) \ \& \ C(x))$
       $\& \sim (\exists \geq_n x(B(x) \ \& \ C(x)))$
(33) An A is B: $\exists \geq_1 x(A(x) \ \& \ B(x))$
(34) No A is B: $\sim \exists \geq_1 x(A(x) \ \& \ B(x))$ or $\forall \geq_1 x(A(x) \rightarrow \sim B(x))$
(35) All As are Bs: $\forall \geq_1 x(A(x) \rightarrow B(x))$
(36) The A is B: $\forall \geq_1 x(A(x) \rightarrow B(x)) \ \& \ \exists_{=1} x(A(x))$

In a bit we will see that it is useful to have a notion of L* canonical form. In particular, I will be adopting the following definition of canonical form.

(37) *L* canonical form.* A formula of L* is in L* canonical form iff it is built up from elementary formulae using only the symbols $\Pi, \Sigma, \exists, \forall$, n, $\geq$, f, (,), v, &, $\sim$, and the numerals, and the formula is in *disjunctive normal form* and *prenex normal form*.

Disjunctive normal form means of course that there can be disjunctions of conjunctions and negations, but there cannot be conjunctions or negations of

---

[13] These in turn can be interpreted as conjunctions of first order formulae. We can treat $\exists \geq_n xAx$ as the conjunction $\exists v_1, \ldots, \exists v_n[(\&_{i \neq j}, v_i \neq v_j) \ \& \ (\&_{1 \leq i \leq n} A(v_i))]$, where $v_1, \ldots, v_n$ are the first n L-variables which do not occur in A, and $A(v_i)$ is the result of substituting vi for x in A.

disjunctions. Prenex normal form means of course that the quantifiers must be fronted. It will also be useful for us to employ the following definitions.

(38) A. A *positive occurrence* is an occurrence within the scope of an even number of negations
      B. A *negative occurrence* is an occurrence within the scope of an odd number of negations
      C. $\forall_{\geq n} n =_{df} \sim \exists_{\geq n} n \sim$
      D. $\forall_{\geq n} xA =_{df} \sim \exists_{\geq n} x \sim A$

Given these definitions, it turns out that L* has a very interesting formal property: directional entailingness is a direct reflex of whether an element has all positive or all negative occurrences when it occurs in a formula in L* canonical form. More formally, as proved in Ludlow (1995), the following property holds in L*.

(39) For S, a sentence in L* canonical form, and α an elementary formula in S: If α has all positive occurrences in S, then α is in an upward entailing environment in S. If α has all negative occurrences in S then α is in a downward entailing environment in S.[14]

To illustrate, consider the examples from above but in their L* canonical form.

(33′) An A is B: $\exists_{\geq 1} x(A(x) \& B(x))$
(34′) No A is B: $\forall_{\geq 1} x(\sim A(x) v \sim B(x))$
(35′) All As are Bs: $\forall_{\geq 1} x(\sim A(x) v B(x))$

Notice that in each of the above cases, we can simply inspect the formula to see if there is going to be a downward entailing environment or an upward entailing environment. If the element is in the scope of an odd number of negations, it is a downward entailing (*dictum de nullo*) environment. If it is in the scope of an even number of negations it is in an upward entailing (*dictum de omni*) environment. So, for example, (35′) tells us that 'all' is downward entailing in the first position and upward entailing in the second. (34′) tells us that 'no' is downward entailing in each position.

---

[14] As I suggested in Ludlow (1995) I think it is also possible to prove the other direction as well (i.e. to show that that downward entailing environments are just the environments with all negative occurrences) if we say that a formula α in S has all negative occurrences iff all occurrences of α in S are in the scope of negation and S is constrained in certain ways (e.g. contains no tautologies like 'p v $\sim$ p').

These results also apply to non-elementary quantifiers like the following. In each case, the elements that occur exclusively in the scope of negation turn out to be the elements that are in downward entailing environments.

(29) Infinitely many As are Bs: $\Pi n \exists \geq_n x(A(x) \ \& \ B(x))$

(30′) At least finitely many As are Bs: $\Sigma n \forall \geq_n x(\sim A(x) v \sim B(x))$

(31′) Most As are Bs: $\Pi n \ (\forall \geq_n x)(\exists \geq_{f(n)} y)(\sim A(x) \ v \ (A(y) \ \& \ B(y)))$

More importantly, the analysis for 'most' in (31′) shows why the first (A) position of 'most As are Bs' is neither upward not downward entailing (since 'A' has both a positive and negative occurrence), but it also illuminates certain overlooked logical inferences that are a feature of directional entailingness in L*. For example, while the predicate 'A' has both a positive and a negative occurrence (and so is neither an upward nor downward entailing environment), in the structure revealed by the L* analysis the open formula 'A(x)' has all negative occurrences and 'A(y)' has all positive occurrences. It follows that if we are careful to keep track of which open formula is in the scope of negation and which is not we can substitute accordingly following the *dicta de omni et nullo*. And indeed, as (31*e) shows, there does appear to be a hidden *dictum de omni* environment, and as (31*d) shows, there also appears to be a hidden *dictum de nullo* environment.

(31*) *a.* Most people sing
      b. $\neq>$ Most women sing
      c. $\neq>$ Most animals sing

but

      d. $=>$ If there are n women then at least $\frac{1}{2}(n)$ people sing
      e. $=>$ If there are n people then at least $\frac{1}{2}(n)$ animals sing

One of the other nice properties of L* is that the upward and downward entailing environments are well defined for formulae of arbitrary complexity—including complex scope interactions between multiple quantifiers. For example, 'Every man loves some woman' would have the following two possible canonical L* representations corresponding to the two scope readings.

(40) $(\forall \geq_1 x)(\exists \geq_1 y)(\sim man(x) \ v \ (loves(x,y) \ \& \ woman \ (y)))$

(41) $(\exists \geq_1 y)(\forall \geq_1 x)(\sim man(x) \ v \ (loves(x,y) \ \& \ woman(y)))$

Interactions are a bit more interesting when we consider cases like 'Every man loves no woman'. Here the case where 'Every man' takes wide scope has the L* canonical form in (42), and the case where 'no woman' takes wide scope has the

L* canonical form in (43). (To see where (43) comes from think of the negation in the definition of 'no' being passed down through '($\forall \geq_1 x$)'.)

(42) $(\forall \geq_1 x)(\forall \geq_1 y)(\sim man(x) v \sim woman(y) v \sim loves(x,y))$

(43) $(\forall \geq_1 y)(\exists \geq_1 x)(\sim woman(y) v (man(x) \& \sim loves(x,y)))$

This correctly predicts that 'man' will be in a downward entailing environment when 'every' has wide scope, but in an upward entailing environment when it has narrow scope.

Turning to the case of determiners which are embedded in relative clauses, consider the sentence 'No man who knows every dog is a vet', where we would have the following two canonical L* representations.

(44) $(\forall \geq_1 x)(\forall \geq_1 y)(\sim man(x) \& dog(y) \& \sim knows(x,y)) v \sim vet(x))$

(45) $(\forall \geq_1 y)(\forall \geq_1 x)(\sim dog(y) v (\sim man(x) \& \sim knows(x,y)) v \sim vet(x)))$

Notice that this correctly predicts that the predicate 'dog' will be in an upward entailing environment when 'every dog' has narrow scope, and in a downward entailing environment when 'every dog' has wide scope. Thus L* gives us a handle on the problem that relative clauses posed for medieval accounts of *dictum de omni* and *dictum de nullo* environments. This property is also gratifying since dealing with multiple quantifiers and scope has been a subtle problem for montonicity marking logics.[15]

Most importantly, notice that as in generalized quantifier theory, the elements appealed to in defining directional entailing environments are independently motivated. The negations are not otherwise semantically inert. Indeed, if a negation is added to the B position of 'All', the result is a determiner with the meaning 'No'. Thus L* shows that, at least for certain formal languages, it is possible to have a syntactic account of directional entailingness that does not require otherwise unmotivated and inert monotonicity markings.

It might be argued at this point that, while directional entailing environments can be syntactically characterized in L*, and while this might allow for a very exciting way of characterizing the valid inferences within L*—indeed a way that exploits the classical insights about the *dictum de omni* and *dictum de nullo* argument paradigms—L* is as distant from the syntax of natural language as one could possibly imagine. Thus, L*, for all its intriguing properties, does nothing for the natural logic program; it simply fails to illuminate inferences in natural language. As we will see in the next section, however,

---

[15] See Sánchez (1991: ch. 6) for discussion.

this observation is without foundation; L* canonical forms *can* be reflected in the syntax of natural language.

V L*, LF, and the Minimalist Program

There are certainly ways in which the crucial syntactic properties of L* formulae can be encoded in LF syntax. It has long been recognized that scope relations can be encoded via a c-command relation, which can be defined off of phrase structure geometry. Here I adopt the definition of Aoun, Hornstein, and Sportiche (1981) in which α c-commands β if and only if the first maximal projection dominating α dominates β.[16] In addition, the role of logical connectives can be represented by use of the familiar linguistic strategy of introducing *functional heads*.[17] To illustrate a very simple example from the propositional calculus, a formula like '(p & q) v r' might be represented as in the diagram, where ConjP = conjunction phrase:[18]

(46)

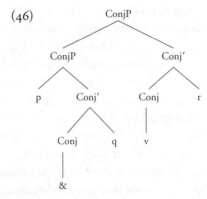

To save space we can linearize representations like (46) in notation like the following:

(46') $[_{ConjP}[_{ConjP} P[_{Conj'}[_{Conj} \&] q]][_{Conj'}[_{Conj} v]r]]$

---

[16] Where the maximal projection of X is XP. So e.g. the maximal projection of Conj is ConjP. Other authors, including Reinhart (1976) and May (1985), have offered alternative definitions of c-command, but the Aoun, Hornstein, and Sportiche definition allows us to avoid certain complications here.

[17] See Larson and Segal (1995) for a number of relevant examples. For a general discussion of abstract functional heads see Pollock (1989).

[18] To illustrate, the first maximal projection dominating '&' is the ConjP that dominates only 'p' and 'q', hence it has scope only over those elements. The first maximal projection dominating 'v' is the topmost ConjP, hence 'v' has scope over the entire structure.

Turning to a more complex L* representation like '$\forall \geq_1 x(\sim A(x) \vee B(x))$', it would be represented in LF notation as follows, where I suppose that the polarity markers and the logical connectives are functional heads (with PolP for polarity phrase):

(47) $[_{QP}-[_{Qj'} \forall \geq_1 x[_{ConjP}[_{PolP}-[_{Pol\text{æ}}[_{Pol} \sim][_{NP}A(x)]]][_{Conj'}[_{Conj}\vee][_{PolP}-[_{Pol'}[_{Pol}-][_{VP}B(x)]]]]]]$

While pretty clearly L* representations can be encoded in LF notation, it is quite another matter to show that they make sense as LF representations in current grammatical theory (obviously, not everything that is notationally possible is consistent with the mechanics of the theory). But I think it is possible to show not only how such representations make sense, but also how they can be generated given the mechanics of current theory. Space does not permit a complete exposition of this strategy but in the remainder of this section I will give a brief sketch of the strategy abstracting away from details that are not philosophically relevant.

Let us begin by simplifying the structures. The first thing we can see is that the quantificational operators themselves can be eliminated if we make certain basic assumptions about the interpretation of free variables. They are as follows:

(B1) If x is a free variable with one or more occurrences within a sentence S (for example, as in $[_S \ldots Ax \ldots Bx \ldots]$), and all occurrences of x are in the scope of an even number of abstract negations in S, then x is interpreted as being bound by an implicit existential quantifier with scope just wide enough to bind all occurrences of x (i.e. as $[_S \ldots (\exists x)[Ax \ldots Bx] \ldots]$).

(B2) If x is a free variable with one or more occurrences within a sentence S and one or more occurrences of x is within the scope of an odd number of abstract negations in S (for example, as in $[_S \& \sim Ax \ldots \& Bx \ldots]$), then x is interpreted as being bound by an implicit universal quantifier with scope just wide enough to bind all occurrences of x (i.e. as $[_S \& (\forall x)[\sim Ax \ldots Bx] \ldots]$).[19]

---

[19] Notice that these rules give rise to a choice with simple open formulae like '$\sim A(x)$'. We can either apply (B1), yielding '$\sim(\exists x)Ax$', or (B2), yielding the logically equivalent $(\forall x)\sim Ax$. (B2) can be eliminated if we make certain assumptions about the scope of negation and the scope of the implicit operator binding the variables. That is, if we suppose that the scope of negation is limited to Ax and that the operator $\exists x$ can bind anything to its right in the sentence, then the

If we assume that these rules also apply to the two substitutional quantifiers over numbers then we can eliminate all the operators from the above structures (and thus also eliminate the functional head Q and its projection).[20] The result is that the formidable-looking L* representation in (35′) has the more tame-looking LF representation within generative grammar.

(47′) $[_{ConjP} [_{PolP} - [_{Polj'} [_{Pol} \sim] [_{NP} n(x),$
$A(x)]]] [_{Conj'} [_{Conj} v] [_{PolP} - [_{Polj'} [_{Pol} +] [_{VP} B(x)]]]]]$[21]

In effect the resulting structure is equivalent to $[\sim A(x) \lor B(x)]$ and given our rules for interpreting free variables (in this case rule B2 applies) this is equivalent in meaning to 'Every A is B'. This holds for all of the determiners that are definable in L*. For example, consider the following structures as they would be interpreted with the help of rules (B1) and (B2):

All As are Bs: $[\sim A(x) \lor B(x)]$
No As are Bs: $[\sim A(x) \lor \sim B(x)]$
Some As are Bs: $[A(x) \& B(x)]$
Most As are Bs: $\sim [n(x) \& A(x)] \lor f(n)y[A(y) \& B(y)]$

Notice what is happening. On this picture determiners in and of themselves have no meanings—there is a shared rule for the interpretation of free variables, and everything else is structure. Among other things, this allows us to generalize the idea of Heim (1982) and Kamp (1984) that indefinite descriptions like 'a man' are really NPs with free variables that are unselectively bound.

In effect, one can think of determiners as principally having a structural bookkeeping function—determiners check the polarity of the noun phrase and the verb phrase, check to see if the right conjunction is in place, and then

structure $(\forall x) [_s \& \sim Ax \ldots Bx \ldots]$ turns out to be equivalent to $[_s \& \sim (\exists x)Ax \ldots Bx \ldots]$. I avoid that option here because of the issues it raises for the compositionality of the semantics.

[20] There are some vague similarities between where this is going and a proposal due to Slater (1987). Slater's idea is that you can simplify traditional term logic through the introduction of free variables. The result is a kind of cross between term logic and contemporary logic. Notice, however, that if one relies upon indices on the predicates then even the variables can be eliminated. It is enough to have the indexed predicates, polarity features, and relative scope assignments.

[21] Note that the 'x' variables are also eliminable if we assume a mechanism such as 'theta-marking' by which a predicate can mark its argument. Suppose, for example, that theta-marking was indicated by coindexing the VP predicate and its argument so that the result is as in (47″). The semantics could then regard coindexed terms as though they were predicates with a shared variable.

(47″) $[_{ConjP} [_{PolP} - [_{Polj'} [_{Pol} \sim] [_{NP} n_i, A_i]]] [_{Conj'} [_{Conj} v] [_{PolP} - [_{Polj'} [_{Pol} +] [_{VP} B_i]]]]]$

dissolve away. Put another way, determiners control structure-building and have no interpretation of their own. In this sense, the monotonicity-marking logics of Sánchez (1991, 1995) and Dowty (1994) when conjoined with a traditional generalized quantifier theory constitute a kind of overkill. If you have the monotonicity marking, you do not need a robust semantics for determiners. Indeed, I hypothesize that the semantics of determiners can be reduced to the interpretation of free variables following the rules (B1) and (B2).

This is a philosophy paper and I promised not to go into too much linguistic detail here, but it *is* an important part of the project to show that this is a genuine story about the structure of natural language. Accordingly I want to devote the remainder of this section to some speculation on how the appropriate structures are derived. Specifically, I will be developing a proposal that is broadly within the framework of Chomsky's (1995) *minimalist program*. The key technical ideas within this program are the following.

First, there are two levels of linguistic representation, PF and LF, and a well-formed sentence (or linguistic *structure*) must be an ordered pair $<\pi, \lambda>$ of these representations. PF is taken to be the level of representation that is the input to the performance system (for example, speech generation) and LF is, in Chomsky's terminology, the input to the conceptual/intensional system (I would prefer to think of it as the level of representation which is visible to the semantics).

It is assumed that each sentence (or better, *structure* Σ) is constructed out of an *array* or *enumeration* N of lexical items. Some of the items in the numeration will be part of the pronounced (written) sentence, and others will be part of a universal inventory of lexical items that are freely inserted into all numerations. Given the numeration N, the computational system (C_{HL}) attempts to derive (compute) well-formed PF and LF representations, converging on the pair $<\pi, \lambda>$. The derivation is said to *converge* at a certain level if it yields a representation that is well-formed at that level. If it fails to yield a well-formed representation the derivation *crashes*.

Not all converging derivations yield structures that belong to a given language L. Derivations must also meet certain economy conditions—they must be *optimal*. In effect, more economical derivations (following certain articulated economy principles) take precedence over less economical derivations. (Or perhaps only the most economical derivation is possible—all others are ruled out.[22]) Two basic operations govern the derivation of phrase markers and hence all LF representations: *merge* and *move* α. (I'll come back to

[22] See Chomsky (1995).

move α in a bit.) Merge governs the combination of smaller grammatical elements into larger ones. When two elements merge, the category of one of the elements is projected to the new higher node. This would be an example of a more general process of *feature projection*. The process of feature projection determines the *label* of the new object. We can represent this idea in the following way. The result of applying merge to α and β is $\{\alpha, \beta\}$. The independent process of feature projection determines the label, δ, of this new object. δ is in turn a set of features that is constructed from features of the two constituents α and β. Hence the product of merge and project is a complex object $\gamma = \{\delta, \{\alpha, \beta\}\}$.

I assume that the structures resulting from the merge operation will reflect basic X-bar theory principles. Each head X will project to a maximal projection XP, yielding a structure like that in the diagram (48), where Spec is the *specifier* of XP1 and XP2 is the *complement* of XP1. All structures below will conform to this basic pattern.[23]

(48)

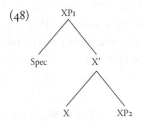

The features of a lexical item will obviously play an important role in this theory. Following Chomsky (1995) we can take a lexical item l to be $\{\alpha, \{F_1, F_2, \ldots, F_n\}\}$, where α is a morphological complex and $F_1, \ldots, F_n$ are inflectional features plus all the relevant semantic, syntactic, and phonological properties of l.

The move operation is driven by feature-checking operations. A number of the features of l are interpretable features (and hence will remain in the final LF representation) but a number of other features are not interpretable and rather are features that need to be checked and subsequently erased. A grammatical element may move in order to satisfy certain feature checking operations. So, to take a standard example, an element may have a case feature which needs to be checked, and the element must then move to a case-checking position.

---

[23] There is currently some question about the status of the X′ projection. I pass over that controversy here. Following Kayne (1984, 1994) and much recent work in generative linguistics I will assume that all phrase makers are binary branching and (initially) branch exclusively downward and to the right (movement will allow us to derive more complex structures).

I will remain neutral on whether movement depends entirely upon the features of the moved element or whether it involves the possibility of elements that *attract* the moved element. I will also be assuming that feature-checking takes place only in certain local relations (i.e. the Spec-head relation, the head–head relation, but not in the head–complement relation.[24])

Here, finally, is the proposal. The lexicon will contain a number of phonologically empty elements that can be entered into the numeration if doing so will prevent the derivation from crashing. Among these are the following logical elements with their corresponding features indicated in brackets.

(L1)

$\sim$ $\{-_{\text{restric}}\}$
$\sim$ $\{-_{\text{scope}}\}$
v $\{v\}$
& $\{\&\}$

In effect, there are two negations; one, intuitively associated with the NP, has the $-_{\text{restric}}$ feature, and the other, intuitively associated with the IP, has the $-_{\text{scope}}$ feature. The lexical entries for the determiners are constituted by bundles of features which include not just standard features like number and (in some languages) gender, but also polarity features. Assuming a very constrained set of possible features we will be able to generate a class of LF representations whose members mirror all the desirable properties of the formal language L*.

Beginning with the basic determiners, we introduce the following lexical entries (here I ignore phonological features and basic category information).[25]

(L2)

Some: $\{\&\}$
All: $\{-_{\text{scope}}, v\}$
Only: $\{-_{\text{restric}}, v\}$[26]
No: $\{-_{\text{scope}}, -_{\text{restric}}, v\}$

[24] On this last score I part company with Bobaljik (1995), Bobaljik and Thrainsson (1997), who argue for checking in the head–complement relation. There are compelling reasons for allowing such checking relations, and it may even help the proposal above to work more smoothly, but for the current discussion I avoid that option.

[25] Naturally one would want to use the basic template here to help delimit a class of basic determiners.

[26] Arguably 'only' is not a determiner. I pass over that dispute here.

So-called numerical quantifiers like 'seven' and 'three' are probably best construed as plural predicates rather than determiners (which is what linguists suppose anyway; note that you can say 'the seven men', just as you can say 'the tall men', but you can't say 'seven the men', 'seven all men', etc.).[27]

Following an assumption that has been prevalent in generative grammar since Abney (1987) I assume that there is a kind of structural parallelism between sentential structure and noun phrase structure. At a minimum (and only for starters), I assume the following parallelism:

(49) $[_{IP-}[_{I'} \text{Infl VP}]]$ $[_{DP-}[_{I'} \text{Det NP}]]$

Along with much recent work in generative grammar, we can suppose that both IP and DP form 'templates' into which various functional heads can 'slotted'. This has the effect of controlling the initial ordering of functional heads within both IP and DP.[28] Let us consider first the fine structure of the DP. On the view being sketched here, it is not the determiner that is the highest functional projection, but rather the DP will be contained within a polarity phrase (Pol$_r$P). Intervening between the DP and Pol$_r$P projections will be a projection that I will call PropP, for 'proportion phrase' (phrases like 'half', 'all', as in 'not all the men'). Intervening between the DP projection and the NP projection we can also hypothesize the presence of a projection, NumP,[29] for number (as in 'the seven men'), which might be filled by a substitutional variable 'n' if no explicit number is present. The resulting template is the following:[30]

(50) $[_{PolrP-}[_{PropP-}[_{DP-}[_{NumP-}[_{NP-}]]]]]$

Apparently each projection can be filled by an explicit element (as in 'not all the seven men'). There may well be a parallel structure in the sentential context (say with adverbs of numerical frequency like 'seven times' and proportional adverbs of quantification like 'usually') but I pass over that fine structure now (as well as any other structure that might appear in the Infl projection). The key thing will be that the sentential Pol$_s$P will itself

---

[27] There are some options about the treatment of plurals. In order to avoid plural objects, I would opt for a treament of plurals along the lines in Schein (1993). One way of thinking about the treatment of of a numerical plural n on that theory is that the following sort of equivilence holds: $(\exists y)[n(y) \& A(y)] =_{df} [\exists \geq_n y \, A(y)]$.

[28] For good examples of this general strategy see Pollock (1989) and in particular Cinque (1998).

[29] See Valois (1991) for the NumP proposal.

[30] It would be equally acceptable to me if the number phrase were in fact an NP adjunct, as in the following: $[_{NP}[_{NumP-}][_{NP-}]]$.

be located within another functional projection—our ConjP from example (47). The resulting sentential structure is as follows: $[_{ConjP}-[_{PolsP}-[_{IP}-[_{VP}-]]]]$.[31]

So, what happens? Consider the sentence 'No men are mortal'. The determiner 'no' needs to check its features. It has the following relevant features: $\{-_{scope}, -_{restric}, v\}$. Since there are no overt (pronounced) negations or disjunctions in the sentence, these will have to be entered into the numeration of the sentence or else the derivation will crash. Accordingly, we know that if the derivation for 'No men are mortal' is to converge there will have to be negations in the heads of the PolPs associated with the IP and the DP of the sentence, and we also know that there will have to be an implicit disjunction in the head of ConjP.

Looking first at the DP, we have the the initial structure in (51) before feature-checking. (Here ignoring the intervening PropP projection between DP and PolP.)

(51)

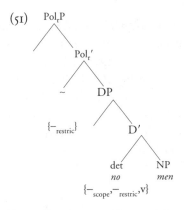

The polarity of the restriction cannot be checked directly, as the DP will not be in a checking relation with the polarity phrase, hence the determiner will have to move and adjoin to the head of PolP where it will check and erase the $-_{restric}$ feature in a head–head checking relation (Ω).[32]

---

[31] The introduction of ConjP seems to break the parallelism between VP and NP, but it can be restored if we suppose that there is also a ConjP projection for the NP. This makes sense, given the obvious acceptability of conjoined $[_{PolP}-[_{PropP}-[_{DP}-[_{NumP}-[_{NP}-]]]]]$ structures like 'not all the boys or half the girls arrived'.

[32] This is a fairly typical example of head movement. It is also possible that the noun moves first and adjoins to the determiner and then that pair moves on and adjoins to Pol. Such movement appears to occur explicitly in languages like Selayarese. See Finer (forthcoming) for details.

(52)

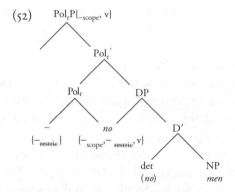

In other words, the feature bundle of the determiner will move to Pol, and check for the presence of negation. If a negation is present, the feature for the polarity of the restriction of the determiner is erased and the remaining features project to Pol$_r$P. If a negation is not present the derivation crashes.[33]

If this story is right we now have a polarity phrase with several features that need to be checked—all of them inherited from the determiner. There are the usual case features, plus a disjunction feature and a negation feature. After standard syntactic movement for case-checking, the Pol$_r$P will move out of the VP into the spec of IP. It then moves into the Spec of the higher PolP (Pol$_s$P) where it checks (in the Spec–head relation) the polarity of the nuclear scope, and into the Spec of ConjP where it checks (again in the Spec–head relation) for the presence of a disjunction feature. The resulting structure is shown in (53).

___

[33] As noted earlier, I assume that the unpronounced negation element is part of the universal inventory that may be entered into the numeration. If the element is inserted and there is no appropriate determiner to check for it, the derivation will crash. Obviously the negation element itself has to have a neg feature which will be checked and erased. It is possible to speculate that negative concord exists for precisely this purpose—the concord element has no semantic content, but is simply a feature that can license the negation. In a sense, talk about licensing negative polarity items has things upside-down—perhaps NPIs are rather items that license the presence of negation in certain cases. It would also seem plausible to speculate that the true negation in the French 'ne . . . pas' construction is 'ne', contrary to standard assumptions. If 'pas' can stand on its own, it is because it is an element that can license the unpronounced neg element. This raises questions about what the negation checks against in sentences like 'Bill didn't sleep well', which have no apparent concord elements. One possibility is that 'not' is not the true negation, but is a negation licenser that can license either unpronounced or pronounced negative elements (as in 'No he didn't sleep well'). An idea very much like this is proposed in Ladusaw (1992).

(53)

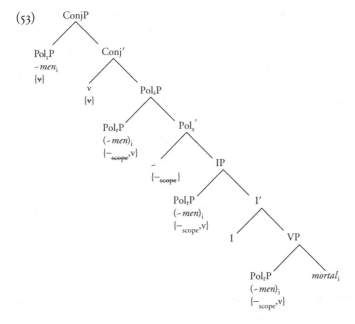

In this example a chain is formed from the successive copying of the Pol$_r$P. If we assume that only the final copy in the chain is interpreted, then we effectively end up with a representation that is equivalent to [~man(x) v mortal(x)]. Following (B2) the structure will be interpreted as though the variables are bound by an implicit universal quantifier, so the structure ends up with the same truth-conditions as ($\forall$ x)[~man(x) v mortal(x)] would in a standard first order semantics.

Relative quantifier scope can be generated in a similar way, but before we consider full-fledged LF representations, it might be useful to consider some stripped-down L*/LF representations. The idea is that a sentence like 'Every man loves some woman' has the following two representations,

(54) [~man(x) v [woman(y) & loves(x,y)]]
(55) [woman(y) & [~man(x) v loves(x,y)]]

which, given rules (B1) and (B2), would have the truth-conditions of (54') and (55') respectively.

(54') ($\forall$x)[~man(x) v ($\exists$y)[woman(y) & loves(x,y)]]
(55') ($\exists$y)[woman(y) & ($\forall$x)[~man(x) v loves(x,y)]]

What this shows, in effect, is that relative quantifer scope is a mis-nomer. What we actually have in this case is the relative scope of disjunction and conjunction. The two possible structures are generated from the two possible ways in which the features of the determiners can be satisfied ('every' will be looking for negative polarity in its restriction but not its scope and 'some' will be looking for positive polarity in both positions).

Of particular interest are cases where there is a kind of 'polarity-flipping' intuitively associated with different scope possibilities. One excellent example of this is the sentence 'Every man loves no woman', which, abstracting from detail, would have the following two LF representations.

(56) $[\sim man(x) \vee [\sim woman(y) \vee \sim loves(x,y)]]$
(57) $[\sim woman(y) \vee \sim [\sim man(x) \vee \sim loves(x,y)]]$

Given our rules (B1) and (B2), these structures will be logically equivalent to the following:

(56′) [every x: man(x)] [no y: woman(y)] loves(x,y)
(57′) [no y: woman(y)] [every x: man(x)] loves(x,y)

Once again, 'relative quantifier scope' is actually a feature of structure-building that is supervised by the feature inventory of the determiners.

One might object that the generation of a representation like (57′) is not exactly minimalistically legitimate, given that it requires some long-distance movement and could, on some conceptions of minimalism, violate the minimal link constraint. How can the DP containing 'woman' travel so far? One tantalizing possibility is that we adopt a suggestion due to Poole (1996), that if movement and chain formation are separate operations (as in Chomsky, 1995) one could allow movement so long as a chain is not formed. Put another way, movement could be allowed if the original and the copy are not taken to share an index or variable.

So far we have been supposing that movement consists in a copying operation in which a chain is formed and in which only one copy in the chain will be interpreted. Alternatively, we might propose that these elements are moved, that no chain is formed, and that both the original and the copy are interpreted. To see what I have in mind here, consider the following simplified initial structure for 'Some man is mortal'.

(58) $[_{ConjP} \& [_{IP}[_{VP}[_{DP} man(x)], mortal(x)]]]]$

We have been supposing that the DP (or PolP containing it) will be copied into the Spec of ConjP and that only the copy will be interpreted:

(59) $[_{ConjP} [_{DP} man(x)] \& [_{IP} [_{VP} [_{DP} (man(x))], mortal(x)]]]]$

But why not suppose that there is no chain formed by this operation and that both the original and the copy are interpreted? In other words, why not suppose that the result is something like the following?

(60) [$_{ConjP}$ [$_{DP}$ man(y)] & [$_{IP}$ [$_{VP}$ [$_{DP}$ man(x)], mortal(x)]]]]

This trades on the truth-conditional equivalence of 'Some man is mortal' and 'There is a man and he's a mortal man'. Indeed, it has been observed since Barwise and Cooper (1981) that the determiners are 'conservative' in the following sense: that 'Det[As are Bs]' is true iff Det[As are As that are Bs]. Notice also that if this picture is right then it explains how a number of intuitively natural inferences fall under the *dicta de omni et nullo* paradigms. For example:

(61) All men are animals
Some man is mortal
Some animal is a mortal man

If this story about interpreting both the original and the copy is correct, then it provides us with some interesting insights into the derivation of the LF/L* structures for the nonelementary quantifiers like 'most'. If the DP moves and no chain is formed and if the original and the copy are both interpreted, the resulting structure is essentially as follows, where f is a primitive recursive operation on inscriptions as it is in L*.[34]

(62) [$_{ConjP}$ [$_{PolP}$ −[$_{Pol'}$ [$_{Pol}$ ∼][$_{DP}$ −[$_{det'}$ det [$_{NP}$ n(x), A(x)]]]]][$_{Conj'}$ [$_{Conj}$ v] [$_{PolP}$ [$_{Pol'}$ [$_{Pol}$ −] [$_{VP}$ f(n)(y), A(y), B(y)]]]]]]

Because the n variable occurs in the scope of negation in the disjunctive structure (. . . ∼n(x) . . . v f(n) . . .) it is bound by an implicit universal substitutional quantifier over numbers. The individual variable 'x' is in negation-free environments so it is existentially bound.[35] The 'y' variable can be bound by either the tacit universal or existential operator, depending on whether the operator is inserted inside or outside the scope of negation. I represent adjoining structures with a comma, as in 'A(y), B(y)', and I assume that the

[34] There is, however, a technical problem to be solved if one goes this route. If the full NegP is generated and then copied, there is the question of how the negation is eliminated from the original position (or at least why the original neg is ignored by the semantics). Similarly, there is a question about why the feature f is either not copied or the copied feature is uninterpreted. These remain open technical questions within the minimalist program.

[35] The issue of why there are separate variables here turns on issues about the form chain operation in the minimalist program. Space does not permit the discussion of this issue here.

semantics will interpret such structures as though they are conjunctions. One tricky element to 'most' is determining the structural position of the operator f and the substitutional variable n. If we suppose that the variable n always sits in the NumP functional projection if no explicit numerical adjective is present, then we merely have to introduce the recursive operator f (with something close to the meaning of 'half'), which would appear to have its natural home in the PropP postulated earlier. Head movement of the determiner will bring the feature f into the head of NumP where it is brought into proximity with the free variable n (and then that cluster of features will move into the head of the PolP). Accordingly, it seems that the relevant features of 'most' will be the following (where, in this case, $\frac{1}{2}+1$ is an *interpreted* feature).

(63) Most: $\{\frac{1}{2}+1(n), -_{\text{restric}}, v\}$

The crucial thing to see about these polarity features is that they are not motivated by getting monotonicity facts right (i.e. they are not set as they are to get the proper upward and downward entailing environments). To the contrary, the polarity settings are crucial to getting the meanings of the determiners right—i.e. to getting their truth-conditions right. If the polarity features are changed, the result is a determiner with another meaning altogether. For example, if the feature $-_{\text{scope}}$ is added to the feature inventory for 'all', the result is the determiner meaning for 'no'. In effect, the only difference in the meaning of those two determiners is the presence of that single feature. It seems like something of a miracle that this single feature could also be the element that signals a downward entailing environment, but perhaps we should not find it so surprising. Philosophers have long suspected an interesting connection between truth-conditions and logical inference. Perhaps we should expect a proper analysis of both to unify these two phenomena.

VI Consequences

I have only briefly sketched the details of this proposal, but it is already possible to see a number of intriguing consequences for both the natural logic program and for contemporary linguistic theory. While space does not permit a full discussion of the possible consequences, we can briefly take up a few issues.

First, while we can always follow the Suppes (1979) strategy of writing numerous inference rules for linguistic phrase structures, the hard work undertaken above helps us to simplify that project a great deal. Now, for starters at least, we need only two basic rules governing a broad class of linguistic structures, where the + and − represent positive and negative occurrences respectively. *Dictum de Omni* for LFs:

$$\alpha < \beta$$
$$[_{XP} \ldots + \alpha \ldots]$$
$$[_{XP} \ldots + \beta \ldots]$$

Dictum de Nullo for LFs:

$$\alpha < \beta$$
$$[_{XP} \ldots - \beta \ldots]$$
$$[_{XP} \ldots - \alpha \ldots]$$

This is not the end of the road of course. The coverage of these two simple rules, while extensive, is not complete. The above proposal merely gives us new tools for integrating some classical ideas in current linguistic theory, and hopefully also opens the door to the discover of new and more far-reaching generalizations.

On the linguistic end, one area of particular interest is the analysis of *negative polarity items*. According to Ladusaw (1980) negative polarity items (expressions such as 'any', 'ever', 'budge an inch', 'give a damn', etc.) are licensed (or triggered) by downward entailing environments. Thus, we have the following range of facts.

(64) *a.* *John saw anything/anyone
     b. John didn't see anything/anyone
(65) *a.* *I believe that she will budge an inch
     b. I don't believe she will budge an inch
(66) *a.* *Max said that he had ever been there
     b. Max never said he had ever been there
(67) *a.* *Frankly Scarlet, I give a damn
     b. Frankly Scarlet, I don't give a damn
(68) *a.* Every [person who has ever been to NY] [has returned to it]
     b. *Every [person who has been to NY] [has ever returned to it]
(69) *a.* *Some [person who has ever been to NY] [has returned to it]
     b. *Some [person who has been to NY] [has ever returned to it]
(70) *a.* No [person who has ever been to NY] [has returned to it]
     b. No [person who has been to NY] [has ever returned to it]

For Ladusaw (and most subsequent writers in this area) there is a semantical explanation for this phenomenon; the directional entailing property of the environment determines if a negative polarity item is licensed. Indeed Ladusaw seems to argue that there can *only* be a semantical explanation for these facts:

We have seen that the property of [unacceptable sentences with NPIs] which renders them unacceptable is to be defined in terms of the entailments licensed by certain lexical items, rather than by simply marking certain morphemes with a semantic feature. It seems to follow directly that no grammar can in principle distinguish [between acceptable and unacceptable sentences with NPIs] unless its semantic component aims higher than at simply disambiguating sentences by deriving 'logical forms' for them to the goal of providing a theory of entailment for the language it generates. (1980; pp. 14–15)

Yet, from the point of view of syntactic theory a semantical explanation raises more questions than it answers here. Why should the syntactic well-formedness of the above examples depend upon a semantical fact? How does the syntactic process governing this well-formedness condition have access to this semantic information—how does the syntax know that the environment is semantically downward entailing?

The proposal given in section (V) provides us an alternative explanation—one that avoids the detour through the semantics. The syntax does not know that the environment is downward entailing, but it does know if these environments are in the scope of an odd number of local negations.[36] It is a simple matter of inspecting the phrase marker to determine whether a negative polarity item is licensed.[37] Ladusaw was basically right in the above passage, however, when he saw the importance of the link between NPIs and directional entailingness. What he did not foresee was the possibility of a syntactic account of directional entailingness like one finds in L*, and, as I have argued, in natural language LF representations.

This proposal also has some empirical advantages over the straight contention that downward entailing environments license negative polarity items. For example, there are the following counterexamples to Ladusaw's generalization:

---

[36] The proviso that the negations be local was brought to my attention by an audience at MIT (and initially, if memory serves, by Kai von Fintel).

[37] Something also needs to be said about questions and intuitively negative predicates like 'fail' which also license negative polarity items. In Ludlow (1995) I argued that in these cases there is good reason to suppose that there are implicit negative elements built into these predicates (as well as in the logical form of questions).

(71) Most [people who know anything about politics] [hate it]

(72) Most [dinosaurs that ever ate a mammal] [hated it]

(73) More [cats] than [dogs] [have ever eaten a mouse]

The first position of 'most' is not downward entailing. Likewise 'the' does not introduce downward entailing environments and the third position of 'More As than Bs C' is not downward entailing. So why do these environments license negative polarity items? The proposal in section (V) offers a handy solution. Each element has at least one LF occurrence that is a negative occurrence (in the scope of an odd number of negations).

Another compelling avenue of research involves the possibility of placing syntactic constraints on the class of possible determiners. Semantical constraints of this nature are well-known. Barwise and Cooper (1981) have suggested that the class of possible determiners should be constrained by the property of conservativity, and in a more general and ambitious vein, Keenan and Stavi (1986) have suggested that the class of possible determiners could be defined in terms of a stock of basic determiners and a set of Boolean relations by which they can be combined to form more complex determiners. The proposal in section (IV) suggests a syntactic analogue of Keenan and Stavi's proposal. The idea is very simple. The basic determiners (the class of which is constrained by the set of possible feature settings (+ or ~, for example)) can be inserted into increasingly complex determiner shells. The functional heads of these shells will continue to be conjunction, disjunction, and negation, effectively mimicking the Boolean operations of Keenan and Stavi (1986). In effect, the class of possible determiners can be determined by well-defined syntactic properties.

VII Conclusion

This has been a very quick tour of an intricate and yet broad research program. On the one hand the program sketched above involves ways of incorporating two millennia of rich insights into the nature of logic, while on the other hand it involves grappling with technical details in both contemporary logic and contemporary linguistic theory. Obviously a thorough study of these issues would want to develop the technical details and explore the formal properties of these LF/L* representations in more detail, and would want to use the resulting theory for exploring empirical questions about grammatical theory and natural logic. I do not doubt that there are more elegant formal logics for this purpose than L*, and I do not doubt that there are more natural ways of representing these formal logics at LF in the minimalist program. My key objective here has been to show that, however formally couched, there are good reasons to explore these empirical domains in tandem, and that numerous unexpected and exciting discoveries await such co-ordinated investigations.

REFERENCES

Abney, S. (1987). 'The English Noun Phrase in its Sentential Aspect' (Ph.D. thesis, Dept. of Linguistics, MIT).

Aoun, J., Hornstein, N., and Sportiche, D. (1981). 'Some Aspects of Wide Scope Quantification', *Journal of Lingustic Research*, 1: 69–95.

Barwise, J. (1979). 'On Branching Quantifiers in English', *Journal of Philosophical Logic*, 8: 47–80.

——and Cooper, R. (1981). 'Generalized Quantifiers and Natural Language', *Linguistics and Philosophy*, 4: 159–219.

Bobaljik, J. (1995). 'Morphosyntax: The Syntax of Verbal Inflection' (Ph.D. thesis, Dept. of Linguistics, MIT).

——and Thrainsson, H. (1997). 'Two Heads aren't Always Better than One' (M.Sc. Harvard University and the University of Iceland).

Boolos, G. (1998). *Logic, Logic, and Logic* (Cambridge, Mass.: Harvard University Press).

Chomsky, N. (1995). *The Minimalist Program* (Cambridge, Mass.: MIT Press).

Cinque, G. (1998). *Adverbs and Functional Heads: A Cross-Linguistic Perspective* (Oxford: Oxford University Press).

Dowty, D. (1994). 'The Role of Negative Polarity and Concord Marking in Natural Language Reasoning', Proceedings of SALT IV (Ithaca, NY: Cornell University Linguistics Publications).

Englebretsen, G., ed. (1987). *The New Syllogistic* (New York: Peter Lang Publishing).

Finer, D. (1998). 'Sulawesi Relatives, V-raising, and the CP-complement Hypothesis', to appear in *The Canadian Journal of Linguistics*, 43: 283–306.

Heim, I. (1982). 'The Semantics of Definite and Indefinite Noun Phrases' (Ph.D. thesis, Dept. of Linguistics, University of Massachusetts).

Henkin, L. (1950). 'Completeness in the Theory of Types', *Journal of Symbolic Logic*, 15: 81–91.

Higginbotham, J., and May, R. (1981). 'Questions, Quantifiers and Crossing', *The Linguistic Review*, 1: 51–79.

Hintikka, J. (1974). 'Quantifiers vs. Quantification Theory', *Linguistic Inquiry*, 5: 153–77.

Hoeksma, J. (1986). 'Monotonicity Phenomena in Natural Language', *Linguistic Analysis*, 16: 235–50.

Kamp, H. (1984). 'A Theory of Truth and Semantic Representation', in J. Groendijk and M. Stokhof (eds.), *Truth, Interpretation, and Information* (Dordrecht: Foris).

Kayne, R. (1984). *Connectedness and Binary Branching* (Dordrecht: Foris).

—— (1994). *The Antisymmetry of Syntax* (Cambridge, Mass.: MIT Press).

Keenan, E., and Stavi, Y. (1986). 'A Semantic Characterization of Natural Language Determiners', *Linguistics and Philosophy*, 9: 253–326.

Kneale, W., and Kneale, M. (1962). *The Development of Logic* (Oxford: Oxford University Press).

Kreisel, G. (1952). 'On the Concepts of Completeness and Interpretation of Formal Systems', *Fundamenta Mathematicae*, 39: 103–27.

Ladusaw, W. (1980). 'Polarity Sensitivity as Inherent Scope Relations' (doctoral diss., University of Texas at Austin).

—— (1992). 'Expressing Negation', in C. Barker and D. Dowty (eds.), *Proceedings of SALT II* (Ohio State Working Papers in Linguistics, 40; Columbus, Ohio: Ohio State University), 237–59.

Larson, R., and Segal, G. (1995). *Knowledge of Meaning* (Cambridge, Mass.: MIT Press).

Law, D., and Ludlow, P. (1985). 'Quantification without Cardinality', in S. Berman, J. W. Choe, and J. McDonough (eds.), *Proceedings of NELS XV* (Amherst, Mass.: GLSA).

Ludlow, P. (1995). 'The Logical Form of Determiners', *Journal of Philosophical Logic*, 24: 47–69.

May, R. (1985). *Logical Form: Its Structure and Derivation* (Cambridge, Mass.: MIT Press).

Montague, R. (1974). *Formal Philosophy: Selected Papers of Richard Montague*, ed. R. Thomason (New Haven: Yale University Press).

Mostowski, A. (1957). 'On a Generalization of Quantifiers', *Fundamenta Mathematicae*, 44: 12–36.

Ockham, W. (1951). *Summa Logicae, Pars Prima*, ed. P. Boehner (New York: St Bonaventura).

Pollock, J. Y. (1989). 'Verb Movements, Universal Grammar and the Structure of IP', *Linguistic Inquiry*, 20: 365–424.

Poole, G. (1996). 'Optional Movement in the Minimalist Program', in W. Abraham, S. D. Epstein, H. Thráinsson, and C. J.-W. Zwart (eds.), *Minimal Ideas: Syntactic Studies in the Minimalist Framework* (Amsterdam: John Benjamins), 199–216.

Reinhart, T. (1976). 'The Syntactic Domain of Anaphora' (Ph.D. dissertation, MIT).

Rescher, N. (1962). 'Plurality Quantification', Abstract in *Journal of Symbolic Logic*, 27: 373–4.

Sánchez, V. (1991). 'Studies on Natural Logic and Categorial Grammar' (doctoral dissertation, University of Amsterdam).

—— V. (1994). 'Monotonicity in Medieval Logic', in A. de Boer, H. de Hoop, and H. de Swart (eds.), *Language and Cognition 4*, Yearbook 1994 of the Research Group for Theoretical and Experimental Linguistics at the University of Groningen (Groningen: Rijksuniversiteit Groningen).

—— (1995). 'Natural Logic: Parsing-Driven Inference', *Linguistic Analysis*, 25: 258–85.

Schein, B. (1993). *Plurals and Events* (Cambridge, Mass.: MIT Press).

Slater, H. (1987). 'Back to Leibniz or on from Frege', in G. Englebretsen (ed.), *The New Syllogistic* (New York: Peter Lang Publishing), 87–98.

Sommers, F. (1982). *The Logic of Natural Language* (Cambridge: Cambridge University Press).

Suppes, P. (1979). 'Logical Inference in English', *Studia Logica*, 38: 375–91.

Valois, D. (1991). 'The Internal Syntax of DP' (Ph.D. thesis, Dept. of Linguistics, UCLA).

van Benthem, Johan (1991). *Logic in Action: Categories, Lambdas, and Dynamic Logic* (Amsterdam: North-Holland).

7

Identity Statements

ROBERT FIENGO AND ROBERT MAY

I Two Intuitions about Identity Statements

It is common wisdom that primary among the things that one would want
from an analysis of identity statements such as 'Hesperus is Phosphorus' or
'Cicero is Tully' is an account of their *informativeness.*[1] But there is a problem
that any such account will encounter, one that has been appreciated at
least since Frege. We may put it in this familiar way. If the content of
the proposition expressed by an identity statement is just the reference of the
terms flanking the equality sign and equivalence, then statements of
the form $\ulcorner a = b \urcorner$, if true, express the same proposition as statements of the
form $\ulcorner a = a \urcorner$. 'Hesperus is Phosphorus' and 'Hesperus is Hesperus' would
each express the proposition that the object Venus is self-identical. But if
the proposition expressed is identified with the information conveyed, how
can it then be that these two statements differ in 'cognitive value', as they
must, given that 'Hesperus is Hesperus' is a logical triviality, something
which 'Hesperus is Phosphorus' is not? How can it be that the information these statements convey differs when the propositions they express do
not?

[1] By 'identity statements' we mean cases such as those in the text, as well as those with more
prolix locutions such as 'is the same as' (or 'is the same *P* as', where *P* is some sortal term). The
tense of the statement will be immaterial to our concerns; it will not be immaterial that the
subject and object terms are proper names. Following Arthur Smullyan (1948: 31–7), we exclude
cases in which one of the terms is a definite description from the present discussion; but cf.
discussion in section III. We also exclude cases with demonstratives, which raise issues beyond
what we can treat here.

In his writings, Frege devoted just a few pages exclusively to the discussion of identity statements, in the course of which he proposed two quite distinct theories. The first, presented in section 8 of *Begriffsschrift*, analyzed identity statements in terms of relations between expressions; the second, found in *Grundgesetze*, in the opening and closing paragraphs of 'On Sense and Reference', and elucidated in a draft of a letter to Jourdain, is the famous analysis in terms of sense and reference.[2] These two theories, although distinct, do have something in common; each denies that statements of the forms ⌜$a = b$⌝ and ⌜$a = a$⌝ express the *same* proposition. Frege's views about propositions—*thoughts* in Fregean terminology—and their constituents differed substantially in the two theories, however. In *Begriffsschrift*, Frege held that true identity statements express that the expressions flanking the identity sign have the same content.[3] But then, to say of two distinct expressions that they corefer is clearly to say something different than that one expression corefers with itself. As Frege observes, on this analysis, the identity symbol is analyzed as 'identity of content' (symbolized as "≡"); compare n. 3. It is only in 'On Sense and Reference' that Frege can maintain that the identity symbol is a sign of objectual identity. He can do so because of his introduction of the general distinction between sense and reference, as this relieves the burden on the reference of expressions to distinguish ⌜$a = b$⌝ from ⌜$a = a$⌝. Since these are to be distinguished in terms of the senses of expressions, the identity sign can be taken to *refer to* objectual identity.[4]

One way to conceptualize Frege's two theories is that they each capture distinct intuitions we have about identity statements: from the *Begriffsschrift* theory, that identity statements say of two expressions that they have the same reference; from the 'On Sense and Reference' theory, that 'be' is construed as objectual identity. While it will be our view that an analysis of identity statements should incorporate both of these intuitions, it was Frege's view that they were incompatible, and he ultimately jettisoned the former and maintained the latter. But of course he did not think that taking 'be' as objectual identity solved the problem of informativeness. To the contrary, Frege held that no theory stated solely in terms of the designata of expressions and objectual identity could do this, since all that a true statement of the form ⌜$a = b$⌝ would express is that an object is self-identical, and this is not

---

[2] Frege (1967, 1970, 1980: 78–80). The relevant material in the draft letter to Jourdain was not included in the letter Frege sent (1980: 81–4).

[3] Frege states the theory as follows. 'Now let "⊢ ($A \equiv B$)" mean that *the symbol A and the symbol B have the same conceptual content, so that A can always be replaced by B and conversely*.'

[4] That is, 'be' would denote the concept that maps each object uniquely onto itself.

anything, in and of itself, that is informative, and nothing different from what $\ulcorner a = a \urcorner$ expresses.[5] This semantic characteristic of identity statements, that when true they are about only one thing, however appears to be at odds with their apparent logical structure as *relational* sentences;[6] grammatically, 'be' occurs as a two-place predicate, and shows, with appropriate choice of items, the sort of grammatical properties usually associated with transitive clauses (e.g. case-agreement in 'He is him'). This tension did not go unnoticed; Frege begins 'On Sense and Reference' by asking whether identity is a relation, and Russell, in *The Principles of Mathematics*, remarks that 'The question whether identity is or is not a relation, and even whether there is such a concept at all, is not easy to answer. For, it may be said, identity cannot be a relation, since, when it is truly asserted, we have only one term, whereas two terms are required for a relation.'[7] The reason for concern with the relational character of identity statements was Frege's (and Russell's) insight that there must be *some* difference associated with the terms related by the identity predicate in order for identity statements to be informative; informativeness, they observed, springs, somewhat paradoxically, from difference, *not* from identity. Their common worry was that, whatever this difference is, it cannot be anything narrowly semantic, given the conditions for the truth of identity statements.[8]

It is in overcoming this worry that the genius of the theory of 'On Sense and Reference' lies, as Frege was able to reconcile in an entirely natural fashion taking 'be' as objectual identity with the relational structure of identity statements. The initial building blocks of this analysis were already in place in *Begriffsschrift*, with the notion of mode of determination (*Bestimmungsweise*) found there.[9] But in *Begriffsschrift*, Frege only acknowledged this essence

[5] While any relational predicate can hold reflexively of a single object, where identity statements differ is that they *must* hold in this way in order to be true.

[6] In contrast, with negative identity statements, when they are true they are about two things, and their relational nature is obvious.

[7] Russell (1937: 63).

[8] Russell's conclusion in *The Principles of Mathematics* (§ 64) was that when identity holds between terms, those things signified by proper names, assertion of identity is 'perfectly futile', as it is an assertion of an identity of a term with itself. Rather, Russell held there that it is worthwhile to assert an identity only when there is a relation, either between a term and a denoting concept, or between two denoting concepts. While Russell was shortly to abandon the doctrine of denoting concepts for the theory of descriptions of 'On Denoting', his view of identity as relational carried over, given his notion that names were no more than abbreviations for definite descriptions.

[9] The relation of the notions of *Begriffsschrift* and 'On Sense and Reference' are remarked upon by Angelelli (1967: 39–40), and Bynum (1972: 67–8). In our description of Frege's views,

of what he later labeled *Sinn* for names, but not for sentences; the determination of reference was no part of the content expressed by a sentence. It is only when Frege comes to recognize that the sense/reference distinction could be generalized that the senses associated with expressions can become constituents of propositions; thoughts become compositions of senses (not references, as in *Begriffsschrift*). Since the sense of 'Hesperus' is not the same as that of 'Phosphorus', the thoughts expressed by 'Hesperus is Phosphorus' and 'Hesperus is Hesperus' are not the same; they differ in 'cognitive value', and hence may convey different information, the result sought by Frege. 'A difference can arise', Frege says, 'only if the difference between the signs corresponds to a difference in the mode of presentation of that which is designated', the sense being 'wherein the mode of presentation is contained'.[10] Thus, for Frege, identity statements are analyzed as relational essentially at the level of sense, but not at the level of reference, so that he recognizes the following distinction in the thoughts expressed, where '*A*' and '*B*' stand for distinct senses:

(I) The thought: *A* and *B* determine (present) the same reference.
(II) The thought: *A* and *A* determine (present) the same reference.

In (I) the object in question is presented in two distinct ways,[11] while in (II) the object is presented in but one way (albeit twice over). It is for this reason, Frege tells us, that the former can be informative, but not the latter. Moreover, because of the way (I) and (II) differ, statements that express thoughts as given

we follow most closely Mendelsohn's (1982: 279–99) illuminating discussion. As Mendelsohn observes (1982: 291), on the *Begriffsschrift* theory, 'Frege distinguished between that which identity relates and that wherein the information conveyed by an [identity]-sentence resides, so in [*Begriffsschrift*], it now appears that although identity is to relate the terms flanking the identity sign, the information is to be that the same content is given by two ways of determining it.'

[10] Frege's preferred examples for showing difference in sense are either geometrical, which he employs in *Begriffsschrift* and in 'On Sense and Reference', or perceptual, as in the examples of the mountains 'Afla' and 'Ateb' used in the letter to Jourdain, and 'the evening star'and 'the morning star' found in 'On Sense and Reference'. These are typical cases of what Frege would classify as synthetic judgements.

[11] Mendelsohn (1982: especially 289 ff.) points out that, without this assumption, there is little reason for including identity within logic (as opposed to natural language), and this is certainly the view Wittgenstein takes in the *Tractatus*, where he labels identity statements 'pseudo-propositions', so as to indicate their inherent semantic uninformativeness. Wittgenstein remarks: 'Identity of object I express by identity of sign, and not by using a sign for identity. Difference of objects I express by difference of signs' (5.53), concluding that 'The identity-sign, therefore, is not an essential constituent of conceptual notation' (5.533). Wittgenstein then proceeds to show how propositions involving identity can be recast without it (5.531 ff.).

in (I) may be synthetic; statements that express thoughts of the type (II) can only be analytic. (I) and (II) are not merely different propositions, they are also different *sorts* of propositions.

(I) and (II) are meant to exhaust the cases; they are to be the thoughts expressed by statements of the forms $\ulcorner a = b \urcorner$ and $\ulcorner a = a \urcorner$, respectively.[12] This claim, however, rests on a further assumption implicit in the discussion thus far, that distinct expressions do not share a sense. For suppose one stipulated that in a language otherwise like English the names 'Max' and 'Oscar' have the same sense. And suppose we have a person, who although he has these names in his language, does not know that Max is Oscar, and has never noticed that 'Max' and 'Oscar' have the same sense. He then might believe, through no logical or conceptual error, that there are two people, not one. It seems clear that grasping the sense of 'Max is Oscar' would be informative to that person, even though he has grasped a thought of the form (II). And it seems equally clear that grasping the sense of 'Max is Max', also a thought of the form (II), would not be informative to that person. Thus, it appears in the case stipulated that we have a contrast in informativeness between sentences that express the same thought.[13] Frege held that it is difference in sense that allows for informativeness; but, it is not, apparently, required.

What options would be available to Frege at this point? He could deny that 'Max' and 'Oscar' could ever have the same sense, and hence dismiss the case at the outset. That, however, would be at pains of denying that there are ever synonyms; we could just as well have given the above argument using the expressions 'bellies' and 'tummies' for someone who did not realize that they are synonymous.[14] But holding that no two distinct expressions can be synonymous would be an embarrassing piece of legislation for Frege, for now any possibility of synonymy would depend upon expression identity. There would have to be a rule in Frege's system making the question whether two

[12] We leave aside here cases of explicit definition, where the identity sign is used to introduce a term as an abbreviation for some other complex expression within the language.

[13] We must be careful to distinguish the circumstance just described from one in which he merely accepts a sentence. Suppose someone holds that Max is not Oscar, and also holds, contrary to our assumption, that 'Max' and 'Oscar' have different senses. But then accepting 'Max is Oscar' would normally lead him just to believe that these senses determine the same reference. To *him*, this case would be no different a case from 'Hesperus is Phosphorus'.

[14] The point here could also be made using other well-known examples. Think of Putnam, who has no conceptual difference between elms and beeches, being told 'Elms are beeches'. Similarly, suppose Kripke right that Feynman and Gell-Mann are normally associated with the same mode of presentation ('a famous physicist'); yet utterances of 'Feynman is Gell-Mann', if true, would convey information to those not up on the hagiography of modern physics.

expressions have the same sense depend on whether they are tokens of the same type. In that way, expression-meaning would depend on expression identity. But expression identity is arbitrary, depending on contingent facts concerning particular languages, and is not the sort of thing that should have any force with respect to matters of sense. Thus this path is not open to Frege. But there is little else for him to do. Frege explicitly allows that distinct expressions may have the same sense; as he says in 'On Sense and Reference', 'The same sense has different expressions in different languages or even in the same language.'[15] This allows that there might be no difference in the thought expressed by statements of the form $\ulcorner a = b \urcorner$ and $\ulcorner a = a \urcorner$. But then, if statements of the form $\ulcorner a = b \urcorner$ and $\ulcorner a = a \urcorner$ may differ in informativeness, while expressing the same thought (the thought (II)), it follows that informativeness is not just a matter of the thought or proposition expressed; something else must figure into informativeness. What might this be?

One move that naturally presents itself by way of answer to this question is to reinstate a metalinguistic slant to the analysis, and recommendations to this effect are to be found in the literature. For instance, Howard Wettstein suggests that 'the explanation of the fact that "Cicero" and "Tully" may play different cognitive roles... would involve simply pointing out that competence with two names does not put one in a position to know whether or not the names co-refer',[16] while John Perry asks 'What does... a competent speaker come to believe, when he accepts an utterance of "Cicero = Tully" as true? He or she surely learns that "Cicero" and "Tully" stand for the same thing, for this is required for the utterance to satisfy its truth conditions.'[17] Taken this way, the informativeness of 'Cicero is Tully' turns, in some way or other, on there being two distinct expressions, as opposed to 'Cicero is Cicero'. This information about sameness and difference of linguistic forms, however, is *not*, on this view, to be taken as part of the proposition expressed by an identity statement; it is *extra-propositional*.[18] That it is makes sense in the

---

[15] 1970: 58. Here the Black translation is rather stilted; the Feigl translation is better: 'In different languages, and even in one language, the same sense is represented by different expressions.' Cf. Frege (1949: 86).

[16] Wettstein (1991a: 156); see also his 1991b.

[17] Perry (1993: 241).

[18] Wettstein (n.d.: ch. 6), in commenting on the sort of view we are describing, remarks that 'the *Begriffsschrift* provides the raw materials for what was to become the classical direct reference treatment'. Wettstein does not appear to be correct, however, when he says that Frege 'does not utilize these "ways of determining reference" in connection with informativeness'. What Frege says in *Begriffsschrift* is that '... if each [expression] is associated with a different way of determining the content... the judgement that has identity of content as its object is synthetic,

context of a 'senseless' analysis of identity statements, one that rejects that expressions are associated with Fregean senses; by divorcing information content from propositional content, the latter can be taken to be simply that an object is self-identical, for any identity statement whatsoever. Informativeness, on the other hand, arises from the sort of observation just cited—because expressions corefer, nothing thereby follows that speakers must believe that they do. Speakers are no more equipped to know that 'Cicero is Tully' is true than to know that if 'Cicero was a Roman' is true then so too is 'Tully was Roman', for nothing in knowing a language endows a speaker with information whether formally distinct expressions corefer or not. Interconnections of this sort must be learned; it is something about which one must be 'informed'; no comparable information can be conveyed, however, by statements of the form $\ulcorner a = a \urcorner$.[19]

This sort of account, however, carries a certain burden, for it still must show how identity statements can be used to *tell* someone that names are coreferential, so that they come to be informed. This is not to be achieved in virtue of the propositions they express; rather it must be that their use somehow

in the Kantian sense' (1967: 21). This appears to make the connection between modes of determination and informativeness.

[19] What the significance of the extra-propositional linguistic difference in identity statements of the form $\ulcorner a = b \urcorner$ amounts to is open to a considerable difference in opinion. For instance, for Wettstein, this information pans out in how propositions are used; the informativeness of 'Cicero is Tully' is to follow from the fact that two distinct names are used in this statement; for Perry, informativeness results from how propositions are *constructed*, so that the informativeness of 'Cicero is Tully' follows from the proposition it expresses being constructed by determining values for two distinct names; see also, for indexicals, Kaplan (1989). Another alternative is to see informativeness as a result of a *way of thinking* of a proposition, so that the informativeness of 'Cicero is Tully' is to follow from there being distinct conceptions associated with the distinct names. See, for instance, Salmon (1985), although something very much like this latter view is discussed by Searle (1958: 166–73). The sort of epistemic/psychological notion we have in mind here has borne any number of monikers—dossier of information, body of knowledge, mode of presentation—aside from being a way of thinking of propositional constituents, cf. Evans (1985) and Forbes (1990: 535–63). Although they may be associated with somewhat different characteristics, what is common is that they all assume a compendium of conceptual information upon which a speaker's use of a name is grounded. For instance, if we phrase the view in terms of dossiers of information, then an identity statement will convey that the information in the dossiers is about the same person; that the 'name tags' on the dossiers corefer. Note that these notions are not be confused with Fregean senses to which they bear a functional similarity. This is because, unlike senses, they need not have an objective character. Indeed, virtually anything can contribute to someone's conception of an individual, including one's private experiences; one person's conception of an individual may bear only a fleeting resemblance to somebody else's.

implicates the relevant information. It is this implication, grounded not in the meaning of identity statements but rather in the linguistic forms used to express that meaning, that is to account for how a true identity statement of the form $\ulcorner a = b \urcorner$ can fill gaps in a speaker's beliefs. But, even if this burden can be met, divorcing meaningfulness from informativeness along the lines just described implies the rejection of a very fundamental principle central to Frege's thinking, that the informativeness of identity statements (any sentences, for that matter) results from the content of the propositions they express. We should note, however, that whatever the virtues of this principle might be, its rejection is not required in order to maintain the sort of account of informativeness we have outlined, with the central role played by linguistic content. For suppose that what is expressed by '$a = b$' is 'The reference of "a" is the same as the reference of "b".' Frege's principle will now be respected; the relevant information will no longer be extra-propositional. Moreover, because the relevant linguistic information is now part of the propositions expressed by identity statements, and will be directly conveyed by their use, relief will be provided from the burden of accounting for how someone could be informed by accepting an identity statement. Such relief would be general, applicable just as much to 'Cicero is Tully' as to our example 'Max is Oscar'. Unlike for Frege, these cases are indistinguishable, not only in the sort of proposition they express, but also in their informativeness; they differ in both these regards, however, from 'Cicero is Cicero' or 'Max is Max'.

It seems to us, for reasons that will become clear as we proceed, that this latter sort of account, suitably worked out, has much to recommend it; one immediate virtue we can cite is that it incorporates our two intuitions about identity statements, that derived from 'On Sense and Reference' about objectual identity, and that from *Begriffsschrift* about expressions. But in accepting this view we recognize that we part company with Frege in an important way, for identity statements will not directly convey information about the (non-linguistic) world although accepting an identity statement can effect a change in our *beliefs* about the world. This is a consequence of detaching ourselves from senses.[20] Of course, on his own terms, Frege of 'On Sense and Reference' was quite right to reject the metalinguistic aspects of the theory of *Begriffsschrift*; given his goals, linguistically particular information had no place, for the point was to abstract away from 'arbitrary' characteristics of languages by which thoughts are conveyed. An account that would be at best informative

---

[20] This consequence was observed initially by Ruth Barcan Marcus; see especially her remarks in (1963: 77–96).

about the language itself, that two expressions are signs for the same thing, would not convey any information that he would deem proper knowledge about the thing itself; as he remarks in 'On Sense and Reference', because an object can be determined in more than one way 'statements of the form $a = b$ often contain very valuable extensions of our knowledge and cannot always be established *a priori*.'[21] It is here, however, that Frege overstates the case, for in order for an identity statement to *cause* an extension of our knowledge, it need not *contain* that knowledge. Identity statements, we shall argue, convey information, the information that two names have the same reference, that certainly cannot always be established a priori. The *informativeness* of identity statements is then the effect that this information can have on our epistemic states; in so far as accepting an identity statement, with the content it has, causes a change in these states, its utterance will have been an informative one

The task that faces us now is to show how we get from $\lceil a = b \rceil$ to $\lceil$ the reference of 'a' is the same as the reference of 'b'$\rceil$. Our tactic will be to show that this analysis follows from a general account of information content and its conveyance, an account in which, contrary to Frege's in *Begriffsschrift*, identity statements are not singled out for special treatment. Before setting out, however, we need to make an important clarification, for the way we have described the analysis is not in certain respects a very good paraphrase; we must eliminate an ambiguity. We will not mean $\lceil$ the reference of 'a' is the same as the reference of 'b'$\rceil$ to be parsed as containing the relation 'the reference of — is the same as the reference of —', with the blanks to be filled in by terms denoting expressions. That is, we are not proposing an analysis of the equality sign as a relation between expressions, as did Frege in *Begriffsschrift*; rather, our view is that the equality sign is *objectual* identity. This implies that the terms standing to the sides of this sign in $\lceil a = b \rceil$ have their normal reference; thus our account will pose no bar to deriving the necessity of true identity

---

[21] On Russell's early views, Frege would be right in this rejection, for this would be to denote a reference without determining it; denotation would be, as Russell puts it, 'linguistic through the phrase'. Unfortunately, according to Russell, this sort of argument can be turned on senses themselves (denoting concepts, in his terminology) with dire consequences; see discussion of Russell's 'Grey's Elegy' argument from 'On Denoting' in Blackburn and Code (1978: 65–77). Later, Russell, holding the view that names are disguised descriptions, allows that 'A description which will often serve to express my thought is "the man whose name was *Julius Caesar*"', the result then being subject to analysis via the theory of descriptions (1929: 221). There are many issues that arise with this view; cf. Saul Kripke's discussion (1980: 68–70, 72), and section II below.

statements of this form.[22] The trick for us will be to show that identity statements if true have more significance than simply as assertions of self-identity, that they additionally convey linguistic information to the effect that an object has two names. It will be our thesis that linguistic information can be conveyed by identity statements because the terms '*a*' and '*b*' not only have their normal reference, but may also be mentioned. These two aspects of the analysis, the objectual and the linguistic, will not be unconnected, for in '*a* = *b*', '*a*' refers to *a* and '*b*' refers to *b*, and it is in how this connection is made that the analysis swings, as we shall see as our account unfolds.

II Prelude to an Analysis

We begin by considering the following question, often overlooked or glossed over, but which is an essential preliminary to a proper account. It is simply this: what can be the replacement instances of the schematic letters *a* and *b* in ⌜*a* is *b*⌝? Its importance is obvious: if the substituends are unspecified, we will be at a loss as to what is being analyzed, for we would not know, in any precise way, what sort of linguistic object 'Cicero is Tully' is. The answer to this question, if our goal is to give a semantic analysis of identity statements, is that *a* and *b* must be *referring letters*, in that their substitutends must be terms that can be used to refer. But this still leaves options structurally, for are we to think that what answer to these letters are linguistic atoms, isolatable from their sentential contexts, or as parts of larger sentential molecules? Are we to take 'Cicero' and 'Tully' *qua* words, so that just because they corefer they can be substituted one for another, or does their intersubstitutivity also respect their position within the larger fabric of sentential structure? From this perspective, the issue about referring letters is thus the issue of what sorts of linguistic objects can be used to refer (an issue that arises just as much with the letters which occur in ⌜*a* is a Roman⌝ or ⌜*a* denounced *b*⌝ as in ⌜*a* is *b*⌝). To put some terminology on the distinction we are drawing, let us distinguish between the word or *name* 'Cicero' and the sentential *expression* of that name. We may then ask: is it names that are used to refer, or expressions? Let us explore this matter.[23]

[22] That this follows as a theorem of modal logic was shown by Ruth Barcan Marcus; the significance of this result is discussed by Marcus (1963) and by Kripke (1980). See discussion in section IV. Note that if 'the reference of "*a*" is the same as the reference of "*b*"' is parsed as a relation between expressions, then it would appear to express a contingent fact about expressions (that they corefer), not a necessary fact about things (that they are self-identical).

[23] The material in this section is drawn from Fiengo and May (1998: 377–409).

Each speaker of a language, as part of knowing that language, has a vocabulary, or more precisely, a lexicon. A lexicon consists of a list of entries, organized with respect to certain linguistic criteria which individuate the entries; a particular speaker's lexicon is built in part on his beliefs about how those criteria individuate. Among these criteria perhaps the most primary is pronunciation, what would be encoded in a lexical entry as a phonological spelling. Speakers normally assume that if two items are pronounced differently, they are different items, up to limits of variation of dialect and language. For instance, one could imagine speakers having different beliefs as to whether 'New York' and 'Noo Yawk' are dialectical variants, or whether the English word 'Venice' is the same word as the Italian word 'Venezia'. In general, speakers will not take what they believe to be *cognate* forms as reflecting distinct lexical items. By this criterion, then, there is one, and only one, lexical item 'Cicero', for there is only one such pronunciation, and it is a different item from 'Tully', which has a different pronunciation (at least for those who, like most of us, do not believe that they are variant pronunciations of one word).[24]

Now, in and of themselves, lexical items are just entries in a lexicon, itself a compendium of words, organized in terms of relevant properties. But, we may ask, how may such lexical items be used by speakers so as to refer? Presumably, by occurring in linguistically appropriate settings for such use. Primary among these settings is their use as parts of *sentences*; that is, when they occur as constituents of syntactic structures, as terminal elements of syntactic categories. When a lexical item such as 'Cicero' occurs in the sentence '[$_S$ Cicero *was a Roman*]', we say that it is syntactically *expressed* as '[$_{NP}$ Cicero]'. A speaker who utters this sentence thereby uses this syntactic expression, and with such use, a speaker normally believes that he can accomplish the goal of speaking about that which he intends to speak about. A speaker who wishes to speak of Cicero will use the expression '[$_{NP}$ Cicero]' because he believes that '[$_{NP}$ Cicero]' refers to Cicero, and that by using this expression he may refer to Cicero.

Having drawn a distinction between lexical items and syntactic expressions, we now ask: what is a *name*, a lexical item or a syntactic expression? The former, we say. Let us call a lexical item whose expression in syntactic structures is grounded in a certain sort of semantic belief a *name*. But what

---

[24] The weight speakers place on various distinguishing criteria may vary with context. This is highlighted by cases, unlike those in the text, in which there is a mismatch between phonological and orthographic distinctiveness. For instance, there are circumstances in which we would be content to say that 'Jean' and 'Gene' are the same, but there are others in which we may not be; for example, legal documents. Or consider the opposite case, pointed out by Ruth Marcus, of 'St. John', written only one way, but pronounced either 'Saint John' or 'Sinjin'.

sort of beliefs are these? They are the sort just mentioned. It is a belief that an expression has a reference; that '[$_{NP}$ Cicero]' has the value Cicero. Let us call such beliefs, which can be expressed by sentences of the form: ⌜'[$_{NP}$ X]' has the value NP⌝, beliefs of *assignments*.[25] Speakers believing assignments are tied to their usage by the following principle:

> *The Assignment Principle*: To be sincere, if a speaker uses a sentence containing an occurrence of the expression NP, the speaker believes an assignment to that expression.

A sincere speaker who uses an expression containing the name 'Wittgenstein' does so in accordance with the Assignment Principle; when he utters 'Wittgenstein wrote the *Tractatus*', he believes he makes a truthful utterance about Wittgenstein because, in part, he believes a 'Wittgenstein'-assignment. His belief is that the expression '[$_{NP}$Wittgenstein]', not the name, refers to Wittgenstein, for it is by syntactic expression that speakers use names to refer. The speaker holds this belief even though he may be mistaken as to who Wittgenstein is; when uttering 'Wittgenstein' he may systematically point to Russell, and in so far as the speaker's conceptual or factual knowledge can be divined, it would be Russell who would (uniquely) satisfy it. But no matter, the speaker still believes his 'Wittgenstein'-expression refers to Wittgenstein, and his usage accords with this belief. Because the speaker's linguistic behavior conforms to the Assignment Principle regardless, we can confidently attribute to him the belief that '[$_{NP}$ Wittgenstein]' has the value Wittgenstein; we can say of the speaker: 'He believes that "Wittgenstein" has the value Wittgenstein.'[26] Making such an attribution is tantamount to saying that the speaker has the name 'Wittgenstein' in his lexicon, for if he did not, he would not hold any beliefs relevant to it, and one would withhold any such attribution.[27]

---

[25] A name is a lexical item, something linguistic; yet we want to say that things are *named*. We make this connection as follows. '*a*' is a name of *a* for a community of speakers iff those speakers conventionally use syntactic expressions exclusively containing '*a*' to refer to *a*; i.e. use such expressions in accordance with the Assignment Principle. Note that this does not preclude many people from having the same name.

[26] Consider the discourse: 'He doesn't believe "Wittgenstein" refers to Wittgenstein; he believes "Wittgenstein" refers to Russell.' This can describe, *de re*, the circumstance of the person confused about who Wittgenstein is (the agent himself would deny that either attribution is true). This, however, is not the relevant case of denying belief of an assignment, for it leaves unaltered the assumption that the agent has the name 'Wittgenstein' in his lexicon.

[27] An assignment is a relation between an expression and an individual. Any conception that a speaker might have of an individual plays no role in any assignment he might have for that individual.

Now, with respect to the assignments a speaker may be said to believe, he may believe that some of them are equivalent, in that they assign the same object to distinct expressions. When a speaker has such a belief about expressions, to wit, that they are covalued, we will say that he believes them to be *translations*. Translations may be of two sorts, depending upon whether the speaker believes that the difference between the expressions is within the limits of linguistic variation. A speaker may believe 'Venice' and 'Venezia' are expressions of the same word, only affected by the forces of linguistic diachrony, but he need not believe this in order to believe that they are translations.[28] Virtually all speakers believe that the expression 'Cicero' and the expression 'Tully' are distinct, inherited from the phonological distinctness that distinguishes them as words.[29] But still speakers may believe that occurrences of 'Cicero' and occurrences of 'Tully' are translations. When a speaker does, he will consistently assent or dissent to 'Cicero was a Roman' and 'Tully was a Roman', and one could equally well say that a speaker believes Cicero was a Roman or that he believes Tully was a Roman (although conversational conditions may dictate that reporting his belief one way may be more appropriate in a given situation than reporting it in the other, just as a speaker may deem it to be more appropriate to use one of 'Cicero was a Roman' or 'Tully was a Roman' in a given communicative context).

In order to represent the distinction that we are isolating here, let us introduce some notation which will come in handy as we proceed. When we have expressions that fall within the limits of non-distinctness allowed by linguistic variation of dialects and languages, we indicate this by coindexing; we indicate by non-coindexing when they fall outside this limit. In an obvious sense, coindexed expression tokens are occurrences of the same expression type; non-coindexed expression tokens are occurrences of different expression types.[30] We may now say that, for any given pair of expressions, a speaker may believe a *translation statement* holds of them. If he does, he will believe a statement of the form ⌜α translates β⌝, where substitutends for α and β are names of expression types. There are two cases to consider:

---

[28] Henceforth, where no confusion will arise, when mentioning expressions we will leave off labeled brackets. Moreover, when just an index is appended, an expression is intended.

[29] Of course, a speaker could believe that they are the same word, having undergone some very strange sound changes; this may be implausible, but surely not impossible.

[30] Although we utilize the notation to rather innocent ends here, its significance in the context of a general theory of expression identity is central, as we argue in Fiengo and May (1994). Moreover, as we argue in Fiengo and May (1997: 89–114), indices must be taken as syntactically primitive.

(i) $\ulcorner$'NP$_i$' translates 'NP$_i$'$\urcorner$

(ii) $\ulcorner$'NP$_i$' translates 'NP$_j$'$\urcorner$

(i), where $\alpha = \beta$, is the case of linguistic variation; (ii), where $\alpha \neq \beta$, is the case of linguistic distinctness.[31] If a speaker believes a translation statement, he will believe that the related expressions are covalued, although only for statements of the form (ii) are speakers not compelled to believe this as a matter of grammar. For distinct expressions, our primary concern here, a speaker may or may not believe a translation statement holds of them. When he does not, a speaker may assent to one of 'Cicero was a Roman' and 'Tully was a Roman' but dissent from the other; but when he does, substitution of expressions is licensed in this sort of syntactic context, as well as in any other in which the expressions may occur (as it would be also by a belief of a statement of the form (i)).[32]

Now consider a speaker who sincerely asserts 'Cicero was a Roman'. He does so because he believes, among other things, that (i) Cicero was a Roman, and (ii) 'Cicero' has the value Cicero. Normally, it would not be necessary to explicitly express all this information, for a speaker would hardly take it that (ii) would add anything to the content of his assertion. Given that the Assignment Principle governs all uses of an expression by a sincere speaker, the mention of the assignment can be consigned to background assumptions of discourse, as part of the general presumption that speakers use their words in the normal way. But it is not always the case that a speaker wants to leave this semantic information implicit; there may be good reasons for including it as part of what he says.

The primary, although not exclusive, context in which a speaker may want to do this is *attribution,* as, for example, with propositional attitude ascriptions, when one is speaking of what someone believes, thinks, etc. A speaker can say that someone believes that a person referred to by 'Cicero' is a Roman by attributing a complex consisting of (i) and (ii), so that by an utterance of 'John believes Cicero was a Roman', what the speaker *says* is:

(1) John believes [[$_I$ Cicero] was a Roman and '[$_I$ Cicero]' has the value [$_I$ Cicero]]

---

[31] In Fiengo and May (1994), we argue at length that pronominalization is, as we would put it here, an instance of (i); we called such cases 'vehicle change'.

[32] If a speaker believes that 'Cicero' and 'Tully' are translations, then from his belief that 'Cicero' has the value Cicero, it could be inferred that he believes that 'Cicero' has the value Tully. This would of course be so, but to attribute the latter to him would not be to attribute an assignment.

Why would a speaker say this? The reason is that by doing so he refrains from attributing the belief that Cicero was a Roman with respect to any translation of 'Cicero'. For instance, it cannot be inferred from (1) that John also believes that a person referred to by 'Tully' was a Roman, that is, (1) does not imply:

(2) John believes [[₂ Tully] was a Roman and '[₂ Tully]' has the value [₂ Tully]]

This inference fails because ' "[₂ Tully]" ' cannot be substituted for ' "[₁ Cicero]" '. These expressions, unlike '[₂ Tully]' and '[₁ Cicero]', are not coreferential; they denote different expressions of the language, and hence cannot be translations.[33]

Let us introduce some terminology. We call forms that contain assignments *de dicto*, as they mention the language used; those that do not contain assignments we call *non-de dicto*. (1) and (2) are *de dicto* attributions; *non-de dicto* attributions differ only in the absence of assignments. Our result then is that belief attributions (more generally, attributions of propositional attitudes) are systematically ambiguous between *de dicto* and *non-de dicto* attributions. Substitution normally fails for *de dicto* attribution; thus, when a speaker makes a *de dicto* attribution, it is because he wishes to refrain from saying whether the agent of the attribution believes any translations of the terms by which the belief is attributed. He is only prepared to go as far as attributing the belief in one way. On the other hand, a speaker would make a *non-de dicto* attribution, one that does not attribute an assignment, when he is neutral, uncommitted, or unconcerned about the manner in which the belief is held by the agent, for in this case, the inference from 'John believes Cicero was a Roman' to 'John believes Tully was a Roman' is valid. Thus, while the conditions under which a speaker would utter a belief attribution one way or the other is pragmatically grounded in the speaker's intentions, the *de dicto/non-de dicto* distinction itself is semantic, the difference between them being significant to truth-conditions of the attributions.[34]

---

[33] More precisely, they are not believed to be the same expression. If one were to believe that 'Cicero' and 'Tully' were cognates—different forms of the same word—then substitution would be possible. See our 1998: section III.1, for discussion.

[34] John McDowell (1977: 159–85) presents views somewhat similar to our own; he makes however, an assumption that we do not. He holds that assignments (our terminology) are the *senses* of proper names. They are what a speaker *knows* when he knows a name. We hold something weaker, only that assignments may be *believed* by a speaker when he knows a name. They are not senses, although, when attributed, they may play a role played by senses, the mode of presentation role. (McDowell does not contemplate the attribution of assignments as

Our prelude is now concluded; in its course, we have brought forth two things onto the analytic scene. The first are the general semantic beliefs in assignments. The second are beliefs, relating these prior beliefs, that the expressions mentioned in assignments are translations. These latter beliefs are idiosyncratic to individual speakers; every speaker who has the name 'Cicero' in his lexicon believes a 'Cicero'-assignment, and every speaker who has the name 'Tully' in his lexicon believes a 'Tully'-assignment, but not every speaker who has both of these beliefs also believes that 'Tully'-expressions are translations of 'Cicero'-expressions. These two sorts of beliefs are tied together by *de dicto* attribution; saying of someone other than oneself that *he* believes something with respect to an assignment, and hence ultimately with respect to the name of someone. In this way reference to language is brought into the equation, but no longer as part of the presuppositions of the speaker's assertion, but as part of what he says about someone else. To speak *de dicto* is for the speaker to attribute to others in this regard, not to himself. It is a very general consideration about language, that one may speak in a *de dicto* way when there is good reason to do so; when there is significance in conveying linguistic information. We have just seen one central case: *de dicto* attribution of propositional attitudes. This case is distinguished in that the agent of the attribution is specified. But the agent need not be; when not, the attributee may be determined by context, usually as the addressee, as in, we shall argue, *de dicto* identity statements.

III The Logical Form of Identity Statements

When we left the discussion of identity statements at the end of section I, we had given ourselves a task: to develop an analysis that could account for both the informativeness and necessity of identity statements, while still retaining Frege's intuition about the relation of the information conveyed by a sentence to what it expresses. We are now in a position to approach this task. Our point of departure is to be found in answering the question we posed at the outset of the previous section—what are valid substitution instances for the schematic letters in ⌜a is b⌝? As noted, there is a constraint on our answer: we want the instances of the schema to be instances that have *semantic* content. This precludes the letters ranging over names that can appear in the string

we do.) We leave a fuller discussion of the differences between McDowell's 'strong' theory and our 'weak' theory for another occasion.

of words that make up an identity statement; not being the sort of things that can be used to refer, they have no semantic content to contribute. What do have semantic content to contribute are rather *expressions* of names, in the sense that we have just defined. It is these that satisfy the schematic letters, in answer to our question. The objects of our analysis, therefore, are the sort of linguistic structures that contain such expressions as constituents, and that may be used (if declarative) to make statements that may be true or false.

Let us use the term *logical form* to designate that part of the syntactic description of a sentence that determines (along with other non-linguistic factors of context of utterance and indexicality that we set aside), the truth-conditions of statements made by using that sentence. To formalize somewhat our usage, we say that there are (partial) logical forms $\lceil P \wedge A \rceil$, where replacements of P and replacements of A are sentential in form. We call a replacement of P a primary clause, and a replacement of A an assignment; a logical form must contain a primary clause, and may contain an assignment. While any logical form that is syntactically sentential may be a primary clause, an assignment is specified as a sentential structure of the form $\lceil g(`\alpha') = \alpha \rceil$, where g is a function from expressions to values.[35] A is an *admissible* assignment for P iff A is an assignment to an expression occurring in P. In the simplest case (i.e. for sentences with predicates of unary adicity), there are thus two admissible logical forms:[36]

$$\lceil \xi(a) \rceil$$
$$\lceil \xi(a) \wedge g(`a') = a \rceil$$

The former type of logical form are what we have called *non-de dicto* logical forms; the latter are what we have called *de dicto*.

Let us identify the *informational content* of a sentence with the entailments of its logical form. A sentence, in virtue of having the logical form that it does, thus *has* informational content; a statement, we then say, *conveys* the informational content the sentence used to make that statement *has*. (Where no confusion will arise, we will speak (loosely) of a logical form itself conveying or having informational content.) We now observe that a *de dicto* logical form, but not a *non-de dicto* logical form, entails:

---

[35] Intuitively, we may read g as 'the reference of —'; note that we can take assignments to be functions only if the domain of assignments is expressions, not names. See discussion in section IV.

[36] Since assignments are themselves sentential, our formulation allows assignments to stand as primary clauses.

$$\xi(g(`a`)).$$

To take an example, 'Cicero was a Roman' has the following *de dicto* logical form:

(3) Cicero_1 was a Roman and $g(`\text{Cicero}_1`) = \text{Cicero}_1$

from which it follows that the reference of 'Cicero' was a Roman. This information, however, is not conveyed by the statement 'Cicero was a Roman' if its logical form is *non-de dicto*, (i.e. (3) *sans* assignment). Thus, statements will convey different information depending upon which sort of logical form they have.

Our concern with identity statements now devolves to the question of their logical forms, and the information they convey. Identity statements, like any other statements, are ambiguous between having *de dicto* and *non-de dicto* logical forms. It then follows that an identity statement of the form $\ulcorner a = b \urcorner$ with a *de dicto* logical form, ('a' and 'b' linguistically distinct expressions) will convey the information that the reference of 'a' is the same as the reference of 'b', in virtue of the presence of assignments to 'a' and 'b' in their logical forms. For, if (4) represents the general form of a *de dicto* logical form for an identity statement,

(4) $a = b \wedge g(`a`) = a \wedge g(`b`) = b$

it follows trivially that $g(`a`) = g(`b`)$. To take an example, 'Cicero is Tully' with the *de dicto* logical form (5),

(5) Cicero_1 is Tully_2, and $g(`\text{Cicero}_1`) = \text{Cicero}$ and $g(`\text{Tully}_2`) = \text{Tully}_2$,

entails that the reference of the expression 'Cicero' is the same as the reference of the expression 'Tully', for if 'Cicero' refers to Cicero, and 'Tully' refers to Tully, and Cicero and Tully are one and the same, then 'Cicero' and 'Tully' corefer. *De dicto* logical forms thus convey information in virtue of what they *show* or *display* that their paired *non-de dicto* counterparts do not.[37] Thus, nothing follows just from what is shown by the *non-de dicto* logical form of 'Cicero is Tully', namely:

$$\text{Cicero}_1 \text{ is Tully}_2,$$

[37] Although this information could be inferred from a *non-de dicto* logical form, if it is taken along with the (standard) assumption that a speaker uses his language in accordance with the Assignment Principle. While a *non-de dicto* form would then imply this information, it would not be entailed, as with the *de dicto* form, just from what shows in logical form.

about the expressions 'Cicero' and 'Tully'. A speaker who makes an utterance of 'Cicero is Tully' does so backed by the beliefs that (i) Cicero is Tully, (ii) 'Cicero' has the value Cicero, and (iii) 'Tully' has the value Tully. Only if he makes his utterance with respect to a *de dicto* logical form do the latter beliefs become part of what is said by the speaker; in virtue of the explicit occurrences of assignments, he will convey the information that two distinct expressions corefer.[38]

The question that faces us now is what is the import of this information? The answer is that *this information is sufficient grounds for forming a belief in a translation statement.* A speaker who sincerely asserts 'Cicero is Tully' *de dicto* thereby conveys to a hearer that 'Cicero' and 'Tully' corefer; a hearer who accepts this utterance will then be provided with grounds to form the belief that the expressions 'Cicero' and 'Tully' are translations, if he does not already believe this.[39] Now, coming to believe a translation statement in this way may amount to very little, in fact, to little more than just the information directly conveyed by the identity statement that one person has two names. For instance, this would be the total significance for someone who did not have the names 'Cicero' and 'Tully' in his lexicon prior to accepting 'Cicero is Tully'; he would now have these two names in his lexicon, believe a translation statement of their expressions, and no more. But what of someone who already has the names 'a' and 'b' in his lexicon, and has various prior beliefs about a and b? For him, the impact of accepting a statement of the form $\ulcorner a = b \urcorner$ may extend considerably beyond this. This is because, for such a person, accepting an identity statement *de dicto* would provide sufficient warrant for valid substitutions. So, a person who believed that Cicero was an orator and that

---

[38] The theory we are proposing encompasses when fully generalized four forms; the two we have been discussing in the text and two partially *de dicto* forms, in which there are assignments to only one of the terms of the identity statement. Thus, we may also have the logical forms '$a = b \wedge g(\text{"}a\text{"}) = a$' and '$a = b \wedge g(\text{"}b\text{"}) = b$'. While like their fully *de dicto* and *non-de dicto* counterparts, these partial forms if true, are necessarily true (see section IV), all four convey distinct informational content. (These latter forms would be appropriate, for instance, when answering identity questions such as 'Who is Cicero' or 'Who is Tully'.) Notice further that '$a = a$' will only have two logical forms: '$a = a$' and '$a = a \wedge g(\text{"}a\text{"}) = a$'. Again, both are necessary truths (like true '$a = b$'), but convey distinct informational content.

[39] Sufficient grounds for believing a translation statement of type (ii). We can also have identity statements that provide sufficient grounds for believing translation statements of type (i), for instance if we were to assume that in 'Venice is Venezia' the expressions are coindexed. Such a statement would express not only that the expressions corefer, but also that they contain the same name; i.e. that 'Venice' and 'Venezia' fall within the limits of linguistic variation. (Compare this to the discussion in section IV of 'Paderewski is Paderewski', where the terms on the sides of the identity sign are non-distinct.)

Tully was a poet, taken to be beliefs about different people, would upon accepting 'Cicero is Tully', take them to be beliefs about the same person, or if he believed that Cicero was a Roman and that Tully was a Greek, he would now revise his beliefs as best he could in order to maintain consistency. Just what effect the information conveyed by an identity statements will have for a person will depend upon his prior epistemic states. The ancient astronomer, when he says to his astronomical colleagues 'Hesperus is Phosphorus', does so because his observations about the cosmos show that the heavenly body seen first in the evening from Earth, and that seen last in the morning, are one and the same, and most likely his colleagues will rapidly conclude, given their epistemic states, that an empirical fact has been adduced, one that constitutes, given the strength of certainty about the facts associated with scientific discovery, a valuable extension of their knowledge. This fact itself, however, is no part of the content of the sentence uttered. What the ancient astronomer has *said* is that 'Hesperus' and 'Phosphorus' corefer, which, of course is not what he discovered. But his discovery can be conveyed to those who are in a position to be receptive by saying that they do. In this regard, one could think of the 'informativeness' of identity statements as a measure of their causal/epistemic role for an individual—think of an identity statement as like a virus implanted into a interwoven nexus of beliefs, and assess the damage it does. But in so far as we have such a notion of informativeness for identity statements, it is derivative from the information conveyed by *de dicto* logical forms that the expressions flanking the identity sign corefer.[40]

We see now why a speaker would utter an identity statement with a *de dicto* logical form; by utilizing beliefs people share in virtue of their sharing a language—beliefs in assignments—a speaker may communicate a belief which could not be shared on linguistic grounds alone about the relations of the prior shared beliefs—a belief in a translation statement. It is from this that the communicative value of identity statements arises.[41] The natural question to ask now is under what conditions a speaker would utter a sentence with a

[40] All this presupposes that the speaker believes that he and the hearer speak the same language. If an English speaker does not think that the hearer understands English, then he normally would not believe that he can informatively utter 'Cicero is Tully' to him. But then he also would not think he could informatively say 'John left' to him either.

[41] Nothing in this picture says the speaker must be right. He might be wrong that Cicero is Tully, as he would be, for instance, if he held that Wittgenstein is Russell, but nevertheless he believes it, and wants the hearer to believe it as well. But this would not change the nature of the communicative interaction; the speaker would still be speaking sincerely. He would not be sincere, however, but deceitful, if he did not believe that Cicero is Tully, yet still want the hearer to believe this, and uttered 'Cicero is Tully' to this end.

non-de dicto logical form, one that does not contain assignments? After all, this is the sort of logical form we have assumed to accrue normally to assertive uses of sentences other than identity statements (and propositional attitude ascriptions). The answer is that there are not very many circumstances at all for the use of *non-de dicto* identity statements, not at least in ordinary discourse. If one asserts 'Cicero is a Roman', one does so intending to communicate a certain fact, that Cicero is a Roman. One assumes that the particular words chosen will do the job, so there is no reason to make anything of it by making assignments part of what is said. But if 'Cicero is Tully' were asserted *non-de dicto*, what would be said of substance that the hearer would not already know? All that would be conveyed is that there is a person who is self-identical. Now this is fine, if the speaker's purposes in making his utterance do not include being informative to the hearer. This might arise, for instance, in a circumstance in which the speaker and hearer both have 'Cicero' and 'Tully' in their lexicons, and already believe that Cicero is Tully, in which case the hearer is already informed that 'Cicero' and 'Tully' corefer. But beyond a desire on the part of the speaker to reaffirm their shared beliefs, most contexts of utterance of identity statements in ordinary speech call for the extra information contained in *de dicto* logical forms. This is because ordinarily we speak assertively (and sincerely) just *because* we want to speak informatively, and hence we will utter our sentences under logical forms that best achieve that goal. For identity statements, because of what 'be' means, this allows for only one option, the *de dicto* option. There may be, of course, contexts that allow for non-informative, yet non-trivial, uses of identity statements; we might think of identities in mathematics or logic in this way.[42] But if so, this sheds light on the differences between equalities in natural language, used by speakers of that language, and those formal systems in which there is no role for speakers and their communicative intentions. We would not then expect the distinctions we are making for natural language to necessarily obtain for such systems. Analytically, then, it is *de dicto* identity statements which are primary, if our goal is accord with the character of ordinary speech.[43]

[42] We mean here identities as they occur in formal proofs, not the identity statements that a speaker of a natural language would use to tell someone that two plus two equals four.

[43] Identity statements differ from belief attributions, which ordinarily may be used in natural language either *de dicto* or *non-de dicto*. The reason is that identity statements are normally used for direct epistemic purposes—to inform someone of something. Belief attributions, on the other hand, are *in*direct reports of epistemic states; a speaker may wish to attribute a belief but yet distance himself from any particular claim about the terms under which the agent would hold that belief.

Our account of identity statements, in maintaining both that 'be' denotes objectual identity, and that they are about the expressions used, does, as promised, vindicate what we saw as the dual intuitions Frege embedded at different times in his analyses of identity statements. But in doing so we have jettisoned Frege's central assumption of a realm of objective senses, to which all speakers have equal access. On our view, the analysis of identity statements is continuous with that of other sentences of the language, including attributions of propositional attitudes; with respect to their logical forms, all expressions, including expressions that refer to expressions, have their standard sorts of denotations. We have not, however, eschewed Frege's rationale for such a domain. We hold with him that there must be something which can be shared between speakers in virtue of which identity statements garner their communicative efficacy. The constancy we find is through the language that speakers share; it is a fact about language that speakers who have a name in their lexicon can express via their utterances *de dicto* logical forms. The informativeness of identity statements used *de dicto* arises from their being the way *par excellance* to bridge the gap to what links together all those who would assent to 'Cicero is Tully.' What they all share is the belief that the expressions 'Cicero' and 'Tully' corefer, even if they share no other beliefs about their reference.[44]

IV Names, Expressions, and Rigidity

While counterpart *de dicto* and *non-de dicto* logical forms convey different information, this is not information that effects the *sort* of truth expressed by an identity statement: if an identity statement is true, it will be a necessary truth, regardless of the type of its logical form. If '$a = b$' is necessarily true *non-de dicto*, then it is also necessarily true *de dicto*, since a *de dicto* logical form is the conjunction of the same primary clause as in the *non-de dicto* form with two other statements, the assignments. But assignments themselves are identities, and hence just as much necessary truths, when true, as the primary clause, and

---

[44] Although our account is based on beliefs of speakers, and beliefs that they have about the beliefs of other speakers, our account does not reduce the content of identity statements to purely subjective beliefs of speakers. *Every* speaker who has 'Cicero' in his lexicon believes that a 'Cicero'-expression refers to Cicero; moreover, *every* speaker who accepts 'Cicero is Tully' believes that 'Cicero' and 'Tully' corefer. Whether our account of the content of identity statements would be sufficiently *objective* for Frege is another matter. Nevertheless, there is a firm inter-subjective assumption on the part of discussants that the expressions they use have the same referents.

since trivially the conjunction of necessary truths is itself a necessary truth, the conjunction of a primary clause in a *de dicto* identity statement with one or more assignments will also be a necessary truth. True identity statements express necessary truths regardless of whether they are read *de dicto* or *non-de dicto*.[45]

The conclusion just reached is straightforward enough, but it does rest on a certain assumption: not only do 'a' and 'b' as they occur in a *de dicto* logical form rigidly designate, but so do '$g("a")$' and '$g("b")$', for only then will (true) assignments be necessarily true. As we have conceived g, it is a function from rigid designators to their values; hence '$g("a")$', for 'a' a rigid designator, is a rigid designator (i.e. the value g picks out for 'a', an expression of our language in this world, it picks out for all possible worlds, irrespective of whether that value is called 'a' in that world). Now, it might be thought that the requirement that the assignment relation be a function proceeds on a yet prior assumption, commonly made, that the problem of names with multiple bearers may be safely ignored, since plainly if many individuals may have the same name, the relation from names to values is not a function. But this would be to misread the true situation, for it would not keep in mind the distinction between names and expressions as we have drawn it. Reference, on our view, is carried not by names, but by their syntactic expressions; thus, it is not names, but their expressions that rigidly designate and hence comprise the domain of the assignment relation. Expressions of names are more finely individuated than names themselves; since no more than one individual may be referred to by tokens of an expression, the assignment relation, when taken to have expressions as its domain, is indeed a function. People *have* or *bear* names, and many people may have or bear a particular name; both the shipping

---

[45] One might inquire at this point whether *de dicto* and *non-de dicto* identity statements express the same proposition. This depends upon how we are to individuate such entities. Let us say that a statement S expresses a proposition p if and only if the constituents of p are the values of the constituents of the logical form of the sentence used to make S. If we are to take the constituents of the propositions to be the values designated by the terms of the identity, then if (true) '$a = b$' with a *non-de dicto* logical form expresses a proposition containing the object a/b and identity then so too does it express this proposition under a *de dicto* logical form, for each of its conjuncts, including the assignments, being identities, will contribute the same constituents. ('$g("a")$' designates the same value as 'a'.) However, it might be held that a *de dicto* proposition contains, in addition to these constituents, also the function g and the linguistic expressions to which it applies as constituents, and would thus be a different proposition from a *non-de dicto* proposition, which does not contain these constituents. But regardless of which view of propositions is taken, identity statements, either *de dicto* or *non-de dicto*, if true, are necessarily true.

magnate and the ancient philosopher have the same name, 'Aristotle'. But each would be referred to through the use of distinct expressions of that name. There is no 'problem' of names with multiple bearers as such.[46]

It is of course quite common in philosophical jargon to say that *names* are rigid designators, a way of speaking that we have rejected. Nevertheless, it is worth considering the implications of such a proposal for the problem of names with multiple bearers. Kripke, in *Naming and Necessity*,[47] points out, perfectly reasonably, that if one is to speak of the truth-conditions of a sentence, the sentence must be taken to express a single proposition. But, if a sentence contains a name such as 'Aristotle' which, given that names may have multiple bearers, may refer to Onassis on one occasion, and to the Greek philosopher on another, there comes the question as to which proposition is expressed. Suppose that context favors the philosopher. Once that is found to be so (by whatever means), the truth-conditions of a sentence containing 'Aristotle', so understood, may be stated, and the name 'Aristotle', so understood, rigidly refers to the great Greek philosopher.[48] On this way of acknowledging the problem of names with multiple bearers, occurrences of the name 'Aristotle' refer to different people on different occasions of use, and rigidly so once those occasions are disambiguated. A sincere and appropriately knowledgeable speaker sometimes uses the name 'Aristotle' to refer to the Greek philosopher, and sometimes uses the name 'Aristotle' to refer to the shipping magnate. Thus, what is to be distinguished on this theory are *occasions of use of the name*; for a given context of use, the referential intentions of a sincere and knowledgeable speaker are definitive in sorting out which occurrences of 'Aristotle' are which. Let us call this the 'asyntactic' theory of names with multiple bearers.

The asyntactic theory is in agreement with the syntactic account we favor in one important way; both hold that 'the reference of the name α' is an improper description. There is no speaking of *the* name 'Aristotle' (rigidly) designating,

[46] Something of the idea we have here is raised by Hilary Putnam (1954: 114–22), and by Kripke, 1980, who surveys the position, and even expresses sympathy with it, but does not actually adopt it.

[47] Kripke, 1980: 7 ff., and especially n. 9.

[48] Kripke stresses the point that, however the problem of names with multiple bearers is to be treated, rigidity, the central point he is concerned with, has 'nothing to do with' the problem, which would arise in full force even if the naming conventions were such that no two individuals shared a name. Now that is perfectly true, as far as it goes. Much that is important and puzzling about rigidity is completely independent of the fact that, as it happens, different individuals may have the same name. But designation, be it rigid or not, is a relation between bits of language and individuals, and it can matter a great deal to the content of a theory of designation how these 'bits of language' are defined and individuated.

as there is no unique individual who is the referent of that name. Rather, we must recast such talk in terms of occasions on which the name 'Aristotle' is used to refer to the philosopher, and occasions in which that very same name 'Aristotle' is used to refer to the shipping magnate. Similarly, we must recast remarks such as Kripke's that, after a baby's parents call him by a certain name, 'the name is spread from link to link as if by a chain', for what is this unique name that is spread from link to link? Rather, it is occasions of use of this name that would constitute, at least in part, and on at least one understanding of the causal theory of reference, the histories of those two uses of the name 'Aristotle'. But there would be no saying of *the* name 'Aristotle' that it is spread from link to link, since that would be to confound the different uses of that name. What is proper to speak of on this theory is the reference of such and such occurrence of the name α, since, once disambiguated, occurrences of the name rigidly designate. And so too, it would appear, would the entire description just used rigidly designate. Suppose that such and such occurrence of the name 'Aristotle' refers to the philosopher Aristotle, and refers to the philosopher Aristotle in all possible worlds; then the referent of such and such occurrence of 'Aristotle' must be the philosopher Aristotle in all possible worlds. If this is right, and it is hard to see how it could not be, then the expression 'The referent of such and such occurrence of the name "Aristotle"' is a rigid designator.[49] The function *g*, on the asyntactic account, would now be understood as contextually dependent; it maps from pairs of contexts and names to values.

Such contextual dependencies could easily be mimicked on the syntactic theory; the proper terminology to gloss *g* would now be 'the reference *of such and such occurrence* of the expression α', whose rigidity could be established by the obvious analogue to the argument just given. But it is hard to see why we would want to do so, since all the results obtained thus far are unaffected if we delete the italicized words. What we see as at play in the example is that there are two distinct syntactic expression types (of the category NP), '[$_m$ Aristotle]' and '[$_n$ Aristotle]', all tokens of the first rigidly designating Onassis (and no one else), and all tokens of the second rigidly designating the great Greek philosopher (and no one else).[50] Sentences containing these distinct expres-

---

[49] While it is an independently interesting question whether such descriptions are rigid *de facto*, rigid *de jure*, or rigid in some third way, how this is adjudicated will not affect our argument.

[50] Let '[$_m\alpha$]' stand for an expression type containing a name α, such that for any discourse D, all tokens of [$_m\alpha$] in D are coindexed, and no token of [$_m\alpha$] is coindexed with any token of [$_n\alpha$], [$_m\alpha$] $\neq$ [$_n\alpha$]. Then, all tokens of [$_m\alpha$] corefer; while tokens of [$_m\alpha$] and [$_n\alpha$] may or may not corefer. See Fiengo and May (1994: ch. 2) for a more explicit formulation.

sions have distinct logical forms, and each expresses a different unique proposition. (There is no single syntactic structure expressing different proposition on different occasions, as on the asyntactic view; this is precluded because the *name* 'Aristotle', in and of itself, does not refer at all, so it does not rigidly refer.) A sincere and knowledgeable speaker never uses tokens of the expression type '$[_m$ Aristotle]' intending to refer to anyone other than the shipping magnate, nor tokens of '$[_n$ Aristotle]' to refer to anyone other than the philosopher. The practice of speakers in using tokens of such expressions to so refer, we could say, is initiated by an initial dubbing, via which an individual is provided with an expression type, tokens of which are thereafter used to rigidly designate that individual. The causal chain linking our use of '$[_n$ Aristotle]' to refer to the philosopher, and his baptism, at which the expression '$[_n$ Aristotle]' was born, is comprised of the uses of other tokens of '$[_n$ Aristotle]'; this is what is unique that is passed from link to link. What expression type a token is a token of is something that is discernible on formal grounds; distinct indexing *shows* distinct expressions. This distinction, however, may not also show phonologically, but only syntactically, and in such cases we may need to rely on context, conceivably including speaker's intentions, to disambiguate what syntactic structure has been uttered on a given occasion. But this is not the robust role for context required on the asyntactic view, for we need not add any additional parameters to the assignment function to accommodate context; its role is to point out the logical form of the sentence being used, and not (at least not directly, as on the asyntactic view) the proposition it expresses.

The syntactic theory, as we see it, captures a certain intuition about rigidity, that it is a property of the language used, and not of speakers' intentions to use that language; it is not a property that speakers imbue language with by using it. But intuitions of such a nature may of course clash, and one may wish to remain adamantly attached to it being names that are the carriers of reference, and what that entails. Doing so, however, carries a burden; a clear criterion must be provided of what are occasions of use of a name. Suppose we have a discourse, made up of some number of sentences, containing some number of occurrences of the name 'Aristotle'. (Discourse here is to be taken to cover both conversation and, when sufficiently temporally distended, historical chains.) How are we to group these occurrences together, such that some count as occasions of referring to the shipping magnate, and others count as occasions of referring to the philosopher (and none count as referring to both)? An immediate hypothesis that comes to mind is to isolate such 'occasion-types' by grouping them by their referents; we could 'index' the occurrences by their referents. That, however, would be too coarse a criterion. Suppose Max were to believe, quite mistakenly, that there are two people, one a famous pianist, the other a great statesman, each named 'Paderewski'. He comes by this belief not through any lack of logical acumen; he is merely uninformed about the fact that there is one and only one such person. A benevolent and knowledgeable speaker comes along and, in this context, utters:[51]

(6) But Max, Paderewski is Paderewski

If Max takes the point, he will have grounds for changing his beliefs, and if he does, he will come to hold, as do the rest of us in the know, that there is only one person named 'Paderewski', who is both a pianist and a statesman. Hence, (6) may be uttered by the speaker so as to impart information to the hearer that will be sufficient cause for the hearer to change his beliefs about the reference of 'Paderewski'. But the problem is how we can see (6) as being other than an uninformative logical tautology of the form $\ulcorner a = a \urcorner$, if the basis for discrimination is just the mere joint requirement of phonological and referential identity? There must be something more fine-grained going on than just this.

Kripke makes the following suggestion: 'two totally distinct "historical chains" that by sheer accident assign phonetically the same name to the same man should probably count as creating distinct names despite the identity of the referents'.[52] Although Kripke gives this remark an unnecessarily paradoxical air—is there one name, or are there two?—his intent is clear: causal/ historical chains are to be taken as an additional criterion. This, however, is circular, for such chains are defined as links of occasions of use; but it is precisely occasions of use that we are trying to individuate, such that the two occurrences of 'Paderewski' in (6) are different occasions of use.[53] A different

---

[51] We use the name 'Paderewski' here in deference to this example's kinship to Kripke's belief attribution puzzle in Kripke (1979: 239–83); for our account of the belief cases, see Fiengo and May (1998). The situation described in the text is not limited to just the sort of communicative interaction described. It may arise, for instance, when someone wishes to know whether $a = b$, either when initially settling on one's beliefs, or when contemplating revising beliefs from a fixed, steady state. So suppose that Max develops an inkling of the truth about Paderewski, and, contemplating revising his beliefs, asks 'Is Paderewski Paderewski'. Given that one wishes to straighten Max out, the appropriate answer will be 'Yes, Paderewski is Paderewski', in which case he will revise his beliefs. In this case, the identity statement takes the form of an answer to a question, where no such overt prompt for its utterance was provided in the previous scenario.

[52] 1980: 7 n. 9.

[53] Michael Devitt, perhaps the most strenuous supporter of the causal theory, albeit understanding causal/historical chains as senses, notes the problematic nature of examples like (6); see his 'George' example in Devitt (1989: 206–40). Devitt observes that chains, defined typewise by phonological and referential criteria, are insufficient. Rather, what is to account for

suggestion, non-circular but still consistent with names being the bearers of reference, would be to chase the problem away by bringing speaker's intentions into the mix. But this would be no advance if such intentions are themselves classified by the referents towards whom the intentions are directed; all intentions to refer to Paderewski are the same intention (abstracting from whomever is the agent of the intention). There could be different intentions, of course, if the intentions were directed towards a description of a referent, rather than the referent itself. A speaker's intention to refer to the famous pianist is not the same as his intention to refer to the great statesman. If we take this view, we now distinguish occasions of use of a name by something very much like Fregean senses.

Although Frege himself never remarked directly on this sort of case, this might be just an oversight, as his response would seem so obvious: it is a case of names with multiple senses. If each occurrence of 'Paderewski' in (6) is associated with a different sense, then while (6) would be of the form $\ulcorner a = a \urcorner$, the thought it expresses would be non-trivial, of the same type as that expressed by 'Cicero is Tully'. It is unlikely, however, that this is the response that Frege himself would have given, for it is unclear that Frege would allow a name to be associated with more than one sense.

Frege makes two pertinent remarks. One is found in 'The Thought'.[54] There, Frege says that 'we must really stipulate that for every proper name there shall be just one associated manner of presentation of the object so designated'. Frege makes this remark in the context of his story of Herbert Garner and Leo Peter, both of whom are associates of Dr Gustav Lauben. Garner knows nothing else about Dr Lauben aside from when and where he was born; Peter does not know this, but knows other things about Lauben. This very fact, according to Frege, disqualifies Garner and Peter from speaking the same language, for in no language can a single name be associated with more than one sense. 'Then as far as the proper name "Dr Gustav Lauben" is

informativeness with these examples is that a speaker may have multiple 'files' all 'grounded' in the same chain. But now what seems to be doing the work, in this case as well as in 'Cicero is Tully', is the *non-chain* information in the file; but what information can this be other than descriptive information, for what other sort of information would keep, as Devitt tells us, the 'networks distinct'. (This information must be able to distinguish *types* of chains, so utterance information would not be relevant, as it would distinguish only tokens.) But now the role of sense seems no longer to be played by chains themselves (they would be part of a *theory* of sense), but rather by descriptive information, à la Frege, although not strictly, since Devitt takes statements like (6) to be of the form $\ulcorner a = a \urcorner$; see discussion below.

[54] Frege (1977: 1–30).

concerned,' Frege says, 'Herbert Garner and Leo Peter do not speak the same language, although they do in fact refer to the same man with this name for they do not know that they are doing so.'

Frege's other pertinent remark is found in the well-known second footnote of 'On Sense and Reference'. He places the critical proviso at the head of the discussion when he says that 'In the case of an actual proper name such as "Aristotle" opinions as to the sense may differ.' Now, according to Frege, in everyday life this might not be problematic, 'so long as the reference remains the same', as this delimits how much people can disagree in their opinions about the sense they attach to the name. In a comparable way, two people may each see an object, although under very disparate circumstances. They each may properly describe what they have seen, but do so with distinct descriptions. It may turn out that these descriptions are so different that neither would think that they are describing the same object. But while each would think that the other had perceived a different object, it would of course be absurd to conclude that there *are* different objects. The situation with senses is no different, except that senses, being abstract rather than concrete, are grasped, not perceived (on Frege's preferred epistemology). We cannot conclude from a difference in description of the sense of an expression that there *are* different senses (and indeed when we shift to the milieu of a logically perfect language there is no issue, as we factor out speakers, who might have opinions). For Frege, since there can be only one sense of a proper name, if two people think there are different senses, someone is wrong about something. Either at least one of them is wrong in what they think the sense is, or wrong about the name with which it is associated. One of them, as Frege puts it in the 'The Thought', is misled by false information. Frege's view was that each distinct sense (of the appropriate type) defines a distinct proper name. Hence, if (6) is of the form $\ulcorner a = a \urcorner$, it cannot be other than a logical truth.[55]

---

[55] Frege's own views notwithstanding, we can envisage ways in which (6) might be analyzed that would fall roughly within the Fregean *weltanschauung*. One option would be to seize on Frege's allowance that speakers of a natural language may differ in their opinions about the sense of an expression. If a speaker can have an opinion about a sense, he can presumably have more than one, and not know that they are opinions about the same sense. A statement of the form $\ulcorner a = a \urcorner$ could then be uttered 'informatively' as a corrective about such divergences of opinions. A second would be to hold that there is a distinction between the sense of an expression in a language, of which there can be just one, and the senses a speaker associates with an expression, of which there may be many. This way $\ulcorner a = a \urcorner$ would arguably be informative in the Fregean sense, as the two occurrences of 'a' would be associated with different senses. Either way, however, a speaker could *think* that there are two different senses associated with the name (type) 'a'. (At this point, one might drop talk of senses from the account, focusing on what speakers

But is (6) of this form? What is compelling us to accept that conclusion? Only the assumption that it is names that stand beside the identity sign; what we have been searching for is some way to maintain this assumption, while seeking further 'grain' elsewhere. But perhaps the best thing to do at this point would be to surrender the assumption, and adopt instead what we have urged, that it is *expressions* of names that stand beside the identity sign. The wisdom of this is to be found in that we can now derive that (6) may be of a different form. Once we allow distinctive indices as marks of formal distinctiveness of expression, although not of referential distinctiveness, we can distinguish NP_i from NP_j, a fact which is independent of the lexical content of the expressions. Thus, we can distinguish as distinct expressions '$[_{NP}$ Paderewski$]_1$' and '$[_{NP}$Paderewski$]_2$', just as we can distinguish '$[_{NP}$ Cicero$]_1$' and '$[_{NP}$ Tully$]_2$'. But then, if 'Cicero is Tully' is of the form $\ulcorner a = b \urcorner$ in virtue of this distinction, so too may 'Paderewski is Paderewski' be of this form. (6) is now properly given as 'Paderewski$_1$ is Paderewski$_2$'.[56]

At this point, having reduced the puzzle of (6) to the standard puzzle of identity statements, we could conclude by reiterating the reasons for the informativeness of identity statements, now generalized, and be done with it. But this would be to miss an important, if somewhat subtle, difference between the cases. To see this, consider the circumstances under which a speaker would use two distinct expressions that are both phonologically and referentially nondistinct.

In the normal course of events, speakers operate under the assumption that any number of different people may bear a given name. In referring to each of these people, the speaker will use expressions of this name, but they must be *different* expressions for each, since if he used the same expression, he would only succeed in having the expressions corefer, as a matter of grammar. Thus, in the case at hand, if a speaker believes that there are two people each named 'Paderewski', then he will use the distinct expressions—'Paderewski$_1$' and 'Paderewski$_2$'—to refer to them, and will believe the assignment ' "Paderewski$_1$" has the value Paderewski$_1$" ' and the assignment ' "Paderewski$_2$" has the value Paderewski$_2$" '. If we assume that a speaker may believe assignments for distinct (i.e. non-coindexed) but cospelled expressions of names just in case he believes

believe holds of the referent, on their *concept* of the referent. We would then have a view much like that embraced by direct reference theorists.) Frege himself, we would think, would not truck in such realms of analysis as these. For him, informativeness arises from differences in the way in which objects are objectively presented by senses; it is not a matter of what people believe about those senses, a domain infected by a hopeless psychologism.

[56] We follow here the discussion of Fiengo and May (1998: sections IV and V).

those assignments are not equivalent, then his use of expressions of a name will reflect directly his beliefs about how many values that name has.[57] Now this *singularity* assumption has a consequence. A speaker who, believing that 'Cicero' and 'Tully' are different words, believes a 'Cicero'-assignment and a 'Tully'-assignment, does not thereby automatically have any beliefs about how these assignments are related. Given that there is no bar to a person having multiple names, whether the expressions corefer is an open issue, short of belief in a translation statement. Such beliefs, however, are idiosyncratic to speakers. On the other hand, a speaker who believes two 'Paderewski'-assignments does so with respect to a general belief in singularity, and hence *does* automatically have a belief about their relationship. He believes, given his belief in singularity, that the expressions do *not* corefer. The effect of singularity, therefore, is to eliminate the possibility of believing a translation statement of the form ⌜'NP$_i$' translates 'NP$_j$'⌝, where NP$_i$ and NP$_j$ contain the same name.

Now consider a sincere utterance of 'Paderewski$_1$ is Paderewski$_2$', under the circumstances described above. Given the context of singularity, an interesting result follows: *no speaker is in a position to assert this consistently with his beliefs.* Certainly not someone, such as the speaker in the puzzle, who believes that there is only one person named 'Paderewski', for the statement implies that there are two people named 'Paderewski', as two distinct 'Paderewski'-expressions are used. But also not someone whose beliefs are consistent with this implication; rather, he would assert just the opposite, namely 'Paderewski$_1$ isn't Paderewski$_2$'; i.e. a statement of the form ⌜$a \neq b$⌝. It seems that we have run into something of an anomaly, an unassertable, yet informative, identity statement.[58]

[57] In Fiengo and May (1998), we state this, relative to the indexing notation, as follows: *If cospelled expressions are covalued, they are coindexed.*

[58] Adopting the sort of neo-Fregean view outlined in n. 55 would not avoid this problem. Let us place ourselves in the position of someone who would be uttering a statement of the form ⌜$a = a$⌝ informatively. By the current hypothesis, in order for a speaker to make such an utterance, he must think that there are two senses associated with 'a'. Now, why would he think that? It could not be that he thinks there are two different people each named 'a' (although this is what he would normally believe if he believed there were distinct senses), because then the speaker would never *assert* '$a = a$'. As far as he is concerned, this sentence is false. So it must be that the speaker thinks that the two senses of 'a' pick out the same reference. But even this will not be sufficient, simply because Max can utter 'Paderewski is Paderewski' believing that he speaks truthfully, that there is only one person Paderewski, and that there is a unique sense associated with the name 'Paderewski'. The speaker believes there is one sense and one reference, so for him an assertion of 'Paderewski is Paderewski' would be to utter a logical truth; the hearer believes there are two senses and two references, so what he would assert would be 'Paderewski isn't Paderewski'. Thus, some further auxiliary assumptions are needed, although it is unclear what they might be.

We say 'seems' because of an assumption implicit in the discussion: that the logical form of 'Paderewski is Paderewski' is *non-de dicto*. This assumption gets us into trouble because, for the assertion of such forms, the province of the Assignment Principle is the speaker; the assignments believed are his, and are presupposed by his assertion. We have encountered, however, a way that a speaker has of shifting the purview of this principle to someone else, and remaining uncommitted, with respect to his utterance in context, to its implications. He can accomplish this by making his utterance with respect to a *de dicto* logical form, so that rather than being left unstated, assignments are attributed. Thus, what is assertable is a *de dicto* logical form for 'Paderewski is Paderewski':

(7) [Paderewski$_1$ is Paderewski$_2$], and 'Paderewski$_1$' has the value Paderewski$_1$, and 'Paderewski$_2$' has the value Paderewski$_2$

To whom is the attribution being made by an assertion of (7)? A first-party attribution is inherently eliminated, and no third-party is overtly specified, as with propositional attitudes; this leaves (7) as second-party attribution. That is, in the case of identity statements (and non-attitude ascriptions in general), this attribution is normally to the addressee. In a sense, it is as if the speaker in uttering 'Paderewski is Paderewski' *de dicto* says to the hearer, *your* 'Paderewski'-expressions corefer.

The question now is what effect this information will have upon the hearer. The intended effect is clear. The speaker's communicative goal (regardless of whether he is right or wrong about the facts of the matter) is to cause the hearer to alter his beliefs, so that his utterance is to act as a corrective to what are, from the speaker's point of view, the mistaken beliefs of the hearer. The speaker wants the hearer to believe that there is only one person named 'Paderewski'. A *de dicto* utterance of 'Paderewski is Paderewski' will have this effect because of singularity. A hearer accepting (7) will infer that his two 'Paderewski'-expressions corefer (negating his previous view that they did not). But this does not square with singularity, which proscribes distinct expression types of one name from coreferring. In order for the hearer to bring his language back into conformance with this principle, the hearer has but one option. He must give up the belief that there are two distinct 'Paderewski'-expression types, and replace it with the belief that there is just one. But if this exhausts the hearer's inventory of 'Paderewski'-expressions, it follows that he now believes there is only one person named 'Paderewski'.

Notice that, while the information that a hearer ultimately comes to believe from acceptance of 'Cicero is Tully' *de dicto*—that two distinct expressions corefer (belief in a translation statement)—is different from what he comes to believe from acceptance of 'Paderewski is Paderewski' *de dicto*—that there is only one 'Paderewski'-expression—the functional results for someone's overall epistemic states can be the same: beliefs that were previously taken to be about two people are now taken to be about one. This may require, as we have noted, quite a bit of housekeeping among beliefs. For instance, if someone previously believed that Paderewski had musical talent, and that Paderewski did not have musical talent, he is going to have to decide whether he does or he does not (or remain agnostic), just as if he had held that Cicero had poetic talent, but that Tully did not, prior to accepting 'Cicero is Tully' *de dicto*. *De dicto* identity statements, thus, may be the distal cause of this sort of coalescence and reorganization of one's epistemic states; but, in this regard, we do not distinguish between 'Cicero is Tully' and 'Paderewski is Paderewski'.

The analysis we have presented, it turns out, was hinted at by Frege, in his story of Garner, Peter, and Lauben. He says there, revealingly, that he 'shall suppose that Leo Peter uses the proper name "Dr Lauben" and Herbert Garner uses the name "Gustav Lauben" '. Here Frege is searching for a notational way of characterizing that, if Garner and Peter do in fact have different senses, then they are employing different names. Thus, someone who wanted to tell Garner and Peter that there is just one person Lauben would not say 'Dr Gustav Lauben is Dr Gustav Lauben' but rather 'Dr Lauben is Gustav Lauben'. In the context, this would be an informative identity statement, a statement of the form $\ulcorner a = b \urcorner$; to utter 'Dr Gustav Lauben is Dr Gustav Lauben' would be to say something trivial, of the form $\ulcorner a = a \urcorner$. Frege's point here is that what is confusing about this case is the assumption that we have an identity statement of the latter form. If only we had the analytic resources to set natural language straight, then we would see that the proper logical form of 'Paderewski is Paderewski' or 'Dr Gustav Lauben is Dr Gustav Lauben' is the same as 'Cicero is Tully' or 'Hesperus is Phosphorus'. Frege, of course, did not think such resources were available. We, in contrast, do.

REFERENCES

Angelelli, I. (1967). *Studies on Frege and Traditional Philosophy* (Dordrecht: Reidel).

Blackburn, S., and Code, A. (1978). 'The Power of Russell's Criticism of Frege: "On Denoting" ', *Analysis*, 38/2: 65–77.

Bynum, T. W. (1972). 'Editor's Introduction', to Gottlob Frege, *Conceptual Notation and Related Articles* (Oxford: Oxford University Press).

Devitt, M. (1989). 'Against Direct Reference', in P. A. French, T. E. Uehling, Jr., and H. K. Wettstein (eds.), *Midwest Studies in Philosophy*, xiv. *Contemporary Perspectives in the Philosophy of Language II* (Notre Dame, Ind.: University of Notre Dame Press).

Evans, G. (1985). 'The Causal Theory of Names', *Collected Papers* (Oxford: Clarendon Press).

Fiengo, R., and May, Robert (1994). *Indices and Identity* (Cambridge Mass.: MIT Press).

—— (1997). 'The Semantic Significance of Syntactic Identity', in Hans Bennis, Pierre Pica, and Johan Rooryck (eds.), *Atomism and Binding* (Dordrecht: Foris), 377–409.

—— (1998). 'Names and Expressions', *Journal of Philosophy*, 95: 8.

Frege, Gottlob (1949). 'On Sense and Nominatum', in *Readings in Philosophical Analysis*, ed. H. Feigl and W. Sellars (New York: Appleton Century Crofts).

—— (1967). '*Begriffsschrift*: A Formula Language, Modeled upon that of Arithmetic, for Pure Thought', in *From Frege to Gödel: A Source Book in Mathematical Logic*, ed. Jean van Heijenoort (Cambridge, Mass.: Harvard University Press).

—— (1970). 'On Sense and Reference', in *Translations from the Philosophical Writings of Gottlob Frege*, ed. P. Geach and M. Black (Oxford: Basil Blackwell).

—— (1977). 'Thoughts', in *Logical Investigations*, ed. P. T. Geach (Oxford: Blackwell).

—— (1980). 'Frege to Jourdain', in Gottlob Frege, *Philosophical and Mathematical Correspondence* (Chicago: University of Chicago Press).

Forbes, G. (1990). 'The Indispensability of *Sinn*', *Philosophical Review*, 99/4: 535–63.

Kaplan, D. (1989). 'Demonstratives', in *Themes from Kaplan*, ed. Joseph Almog, John Perry, and Howard Wettstein (New York and Oxford: Oxford University Press).

Kripke, S. (1979). 'A Puzzle about Belief', in Avishai Margalit (ed.), *Meaning and Use* (Dordrecht: Reidel).

—— (1980). *Naming and Necessity* (Cambridge, Mass.: Harvard University Press).

McDowell, J. (1977). 'On the Sense and Reference of a Proper Name', *Mind*, 86: 159–85.

Marcus, R. B. (1963). 'Discussion', in Marx Wartofsky (ed.), *Boston Studies in the Philosophy of Science* (Dordrecht: Reidel).

Mendelsohn, R. (1982). 'Frege's *Begriffsschrift* Theory of Identity', *Journal of the History of Philosophy*, 22/3: 279–99.

Perry, J. (1993). 'Cognitive Significance and New Theories of Reference', *The Problem of the Essential Indexical and Other Essays* (New York and Oxford: Oxford University Press).

Putnam, H. (1954). 'Synonymy, and the Analysis of Belief Sentences', *Analysis*, 14/5: 114–22.

Russell, B. (1929). 'Knowledge by Acquaintance and Knowledge by Description', *Mysticism and Logic* (New York: W. W. Norton).

—— (1937). *The Principles of Mathematics*, 2nd edn. (New York: W. W. Norton).

Salmon, N. (1985). *Frege's Puzzle* (Cambridge, Mass.: MIT Press).

Searle, J. (1958). 'Proper Names', *Mind*, 67: 166–73.

Smullyan, A. (1948). 'Modality and Description', *Journal of Symbolic Logic*, 13: 31–7.

Wettstein, H. (1991*a*). 'Cognitive Significance without Cognitive Content', *Has Semantics Rested on a Mistake? And Other Essays* (Stanford, Calif.: Stanford University Press).

—— (1991*b*). 'Turning the Tables on Frege, or How is it that "Hesperus is Phosphorus"', *Has Semantics Rested on a Mistake? And Other Essays* (Stanford, Calif.: Stanford University Press).

—— (n.d.). 'The Magic Prism' (TS, Riverside, University of California).

Part II

Intensionality, Events, and Semantic Content

8

Why is Sequence of Tense Obligatory?

JAMES HIGGINBOTHAM

The tenses of human languages are indexical expressions in the sense of Yehoshua Bar-Hillel (1954), in that repetitions of the same sentence may differ in truth value simply because of tense. They are not indexical, however, in the sense of the context-dependent temporal adverbials *now, yesterday,* and others. These are always interpreted with respect to the speaker's current temporal position. The interpretation of the tenses is not so fixed. In particular, a relative clause or complement clause tense may be interpreted as if the speaker had used it at a position in time different from the one she actually occupies. Thus the Italian (1), with the complement clause in the imperfect, can, like the English below it with the complement in the past, constitute a past-tense report of a past, present-oriented utterance:

(1) Gianni ha detto che Maria era malata
Gianni said that Maria was ill

This chapter is an extended and, in section 3, somewhat revised version of a paper read at Harvard University, Nov. 1998. That paper was itself a revision of the material in Higginbotham (1993), which had been presented at the University of Geneva, 1994, and formed part of the basis of a course at the GISSL, Girona, Catalonia, in 1996. I am indebted to the various audiences before whom I have over some years presented the issues of the semantics of sequence of tense, and to individual discussions especially with Dorit Abusch, Alessandra Giorgi, Michela Ippolito, and Terence Parsons. Finally, I should like particularly to note that, although I have come to disagree with the views of Toshi Ogihara (as well as the closely related views of my former self), I am much indebted to his research.

What would make an utterance of (1) true, if it is true, is that Gianni, somewhere in the past, said something to the effect that Maria was ill at the time. The English in (1) can also constitute a report of a past, past-oriented utterance. For Italian, this latter interpretation is available when, contextually or in virtue of further linguistic information, the complement clause is firmly anchored to a prior time, as for example in (2):

(2) L'anno scorso, Gianni ha detto che Maria era malata due anni fa
     Last year, Gianni said that Maria was ill two years ago

Research from various points of view has converged on the conclusion that the reason for these phenomena is that the tenses may be anaphoric in some or all of their uses. Sequence of tense, in so far as it has semantic effects, obtains them through anaphora.

There is an important difference, however, between the interpretation of tenses in complement clauses and their interpretation in object relative clauses. Compare (1) with (3):

(3) Gianni saw [a woman who was ill]
     Gianni ha visto [una donna che era malata]

An English speaker may say the English (3) intending to assert that Gianni saw a woman who was ill at the time he saw her; or intending to assert that Gianni saw a woman who was ill some time before he saw her; or intending to assert neither of these, but merely that Gianni saw a woman who was, at some previous time, ill; and similarly for the Italian. The existence of the last intention, for both Italian and English, is underscored by the acceptability, for example, of (4):

(4) Two years ago, Gianni saw a woman who was ill last year
     Due anni fa, Gianni ha visto una donna che era malata l'anno scorso

The difference between complement clauses and object relative clauses shows up when we contrast (4) with (5):

(5) *Due anni fa, Gianni ha detto che Maria era malata l'anno scorso
     *Two years ago, Gianni said that Maria was ill last year

Interpreting sequence of tense as an anaphoric phenomenon, we may put the contrast this way: the tenses of the object relative clauses in (3) and (4) may be taken independently, and no particular relation between them intended; but the tenses of the complement relative clauses in (1) and (5) may not be taken independently, or as ranging over arbitrary past times, for if they could then we would expect (1) to be three ways ambiguous, and (5) to be fully grammatical. Thus sequence of tense is obligatory in (1), but optional in (3); and the question is why.

This chapter proposes an explanation for the contrast between (1) and (3), and similar cases. There is also a contrast between the English past tense and the Italian imperfect, illustrated by the fact that the Italian (1) apparently requires a contextual or linguistic background such as that provided in (2) to be taken as a report of an utterance about the then past, whereas the English does not; but this contrast will not figure in what follows. My subject has been the target of considerable contemporary research, going back (for English) at least to Ladusaw (1977). I will refer to other, more recent material as I proceed.

Some work is required to set up the background against which I propose to formulate and test hypotheses, and section 1 below is devoted in part to that. I then show how, given very simple semantic principles, the basic semantic phenomena associated with sequence of tense will follow. In section 2 I take up the fundamental question of this chapter, the asymmetry between complement clauses and object relatives, and argue that an answer that I have proposed off and on since 1993, indebted to the proposal of Ogihara (1989; later sharpened in Ogihara, 1996), is not correct. Section 3, finally, provides an alternative answer, and remarks some questions that remain open.

1 The Interpretation of Tense

The inflectional and periphrastic tenses of human languages are expressions of generality involving time. An important tradition, identified first of all with the work of Arthur Prior (1957, 1967), but continuing to the present day, has examined and elaborated the view that the tenses are operators, and truth relative to time. This view gains prima facie plausibility from the fact that the tenses, whether inflectional or periphrastic, do not occupy quantifiable places. Of course, we have reference to times in elementary language: 'He went there at that time', 'After some not too distant time I shall return to London', and so forth. But the thought is that there is a fundamental part of our language whose logical syntax does not involve quantification over times, even if, in the metalanguage, the action of the tenses is explained in terms of quantification. The tenses then become a species of modality. Model-theoretic studies, including Dowty (1982) and much later work, assumed this point of view.

However, an important result of the research of recent years is that the modal theory of the tenses is inadequate: there is no basic part of our language for which it is correct. The reason is that modal theories are unable to express temporal cross-reference (see e.g. Ogihara, 1996: 20 ff.; Kamp and Reyle, 1993: ch. 5, and references cited there). If so, then we may locate temporal reference and temporal relations within the tenses themselves. In English, these will be associated with the inflectional feature ± past, the periphrastic *will*, and others.

Going a step further, I will suppose that temporal relations and reference as expressed in the tenses are relations between events, in a sense of that notion derived from Donald Davidson (1967). A position for events (in a general sense, thus including states—I will sometimes use the word *situation* as covering both) is to be found in every ordinary predicative head, or so I assume. An utterance of a sentence is itself an event, and I will suppose that in an utterance of a simple sentence, say (6), one says that there is an event *e* prior to one's own utterance which is a journey to London by John:

(6) Gianni went to London

The semantics indicated may be derived in elementary steps as follows. We associate with the head *go* two argument positions, one of which will ultimately be filled by the reference of the subject and the other, the event position, a target of existential quantification. The adjunct *to London* is a predicate of the event position of the head. The inflection, or inflectional feature, +past, expressing the relation $<$ of temporal anteriority between events, has two argument positions, the first of which is again identified with the event position of the head, and the second of which is filled by the speaker's utterance itself. As we build the sentence syntactically the argument positions enter into the relations indicated. There is also syntactic movement, bringing the tense affix into construction with the verb; and, if the VP-internal subject hypothesis is correct, syntactic movement of the subject *Gianni* to a position to the left of and higher than the tense. These movements are semantically vacuous.

Abstracting from syntactic movement, we may depict the construction of (6) as shown in (7):

(7) $[+ \text{ past} < E, E' > [\text{go (Gianni, } E'') \ \& \ \text{to(London}(E''))]]$

where the open positions in the tense are as indicated by the letters within angled brackets. These open positions, the elements of what is customarily called the theta-grid of the expressions to which they belong, are akin to free variables, but must be sharply distinguished from the free variables 'x', 'y', etc. of logical theory. The latter are expressions of a language, in fact terms, whereas open positions are not expressions at all, but simply information about the number, sequence, and nature of their predicates. Following

customary usage, I will call them *implicit arguments*. In computing the interpretation of (7), we speak of the conditions on satisfaction of these implicit
arguments by assignments of values to them, and give the conditions on
complex expressions in terms of the conditions on their parts.

Eventually, we have a theorem giving what the native speaker of English
knows about the truth conditions of a potential utterance of (6), as follows:

(8) If u is an utterance of (6) by speaker s, then u is true if and only if
 $[Ee < u]$ [go(Gianni,e) & to(London,e)]

We can go much farther with the formalization of the semantics whose basic
ingredients I have just sketched; but the formalization would add nothing to
the purpose. What is critical is that the semantics aims for an account of the
native speaker's knowledge of truth conditions, something that is evidently
necessary if the theory is to be one that actually applies to human beings.
(There is no translation into an auxiliary language, for which anyway a theory
of truth would have to be provided.) Also, the account eschews the use of
higher types and the lambda-calculus, confining itself to the simple notion
of satisfaction; there may be uses for these other devices, but the semantics of
these examples is not one of them.

For the purposes of this chapter, the crucial feature of the semantics
sketched above is that it takes the tenses, like other predicative heads, as
expressing properties of, or relations between, implicit arguments. We can
now propose that implicit arguments can enter into anaphoric relations—the
relation of anaphor to antecedent—with the usual interpretation that the value
of the anaphor is constrained to be the value of the antecedent. The relation
between the event position of the PP and the event position of the verb in (6) is
already an example of such a relation.

The proposal that there are anaphoric relations between implicit arguments
goes back to Thomas Roeper (1987), and has been pursued in Williams (1994)
and Higginbotham (1997), among others. Simple examples include the relation between the implicit argument of passive forms and the subjects of certain
adverbials, as in (9):

(9) The books were thrown away intentionally

where the semantics must have the outcome that whoever threw the books
away intended to do so. Also, there are anaphoric relations between implicit
arguments and actual formatives, what we might call *mixed* anaphora, as in one
interpretation of (10), that in which each participant is an x who is required to
defeat an enemy of x.

(10) Each participant is required to defeat an enemy

Ippolito (1998) argues that the Italian imperfect shows mixed anaphora, from the implicit argument to an explicit antecedent.

2 Tense Anaphora

Supposing that the tenses express relations between implicit arguments, consider how the principles of sequence of tense, assumed to involve anaphoric relations between these arguments, will operate in the syntax, and deliver appropriate semantic interpretations. For the object relative clauses as in (3), reproduced here, the operative parts of the structure will be as in (11):

(3) Gianni saw [a woman who was ill]
Gianni ha visto [una donna che era malata]

(11) $[\ldots[+ \text{past} < \text{E}, \text{E}' >]\ldots[\text{NP}\ldots[+ \text{past} < \text{E}'', \text{E}''' >]]]\ldots$

We suppose that E′ is *anchored* (to use the terminology of Enc, 1987) to the utterance itself, and that E and E″ are targets of existential quantification, so that an assertion of (3) is an assertion of the existence of a state of illness, and of an event of Gianni's seeing the woman who suffered from that state. The position E‴ might then be taken in either of two ways: (i) as anchored, like E′, to the utterance, or (ii) as anaphoric to E, hence bound to the quantifier that binds it. Assuming that the embedded past expresses temporal anteriority, we have two interpretations of (3), as shown in (12):

(12) $[\text{E}e < u][\text{E}e' < u/e]\,[\text{E}x{:}\text{ woman }(x)\ \&\ \text{ill}(x, e')]\ \text{see}(\text{John},x,e)$

For the third interpretation, where John's seeing the woman in question occurred when she was ill, we adopt the suggestion of Ippolito (1998), that the feature +past has only the role of facilitating anaphora, and that the relative clause is in fact −past, expressing temporal overlap *O* or coincidence between the seeing *e* and the being ill *e′*. (This suggestion does the work, in the present connection, of a rule of tense deletion as in Ogihara (1996), but it is not a deletion rule; in fact, tense deletion is incompatible with the system proposed here.) That yields the third interpretation of (3), represented by (13):

(13) $[\text{E}e < u][\text{E}e'\,Oe]\,[\text{E}x{:}\text{ woman}(x)\ \&\ \text{ill}(x,e')]\ \text{see}(\text{John},x,e)$

Returning to (1) our problem will be why the interpretation in which the embedded past tense is not anaphoric is impossible. The exact rendition of the semantics of (1), on any interpretation, requires us to adopt a view of the semantics of indirect discourse, and of complement clauses generally. For indirect discourse I will assume, but will not argue here, that the relevant notion is that of the speaker's *matching in content* an utterance of the person whose speech is reported (or predicted). I do not assume that the parameters of content matching can be settled in any notation-free way; rather, it seems to me that indirect discourse, and other contexts, are to be understood in terms of our reporting practice, and that embedded clauses have for their reference themselves, understood as they would be if uttered in isolation by the speaker. This last statement (in a formulation I take from Tyler Burge, 1978), about how embedded clauses are to be understood, guarantees that the reference of *today, now,* and the like will be fixed, the tenses being exceptional in that they may undergo anaphora. With this much said, I will mark the exceptional reference of embedded clauses with the familiar '∧' of intensional abstraction, but only as a notational device. With this convention, the data concerning (1) are as in (14):

(14) $[Ee < u]$ say(Gianni,$^\wedge[Ee' < e/Oe/^*Ou]$ ill(Mary, e'), e)

where the asterisk on '*Ou*' records the obligatoriness of anaphora.

We could, perhaps, simply record the distinction between (1) and (3) if it were sometimes the case that tense anaphora were obligatory in other contexts. One possibility, suggested by Abusch (1988, 1991) and Ogihara (1994), is that the English present tense, which must be interpreted relative to the speech time (or, in our terms, always expresses that an event of some kind overlaps the utterance u), is deleted within the immediate scope of a higher present tense. As noted above, the system proposed here cannot literally incorporate tense deletion. But it can deploy an empirical equivalent, namely the obligatoriness of present-tense anaphora whenever possible. There are, then, two possibilities for (15) below: either the indefinite description *a woman who is ill* takes wide scope, in which case there is no anaphora; or it stays within the scope of the auxiliary *will*, which carries the −past tense feature, in which case anaphora are forced, so that the speaker is predicting that Gianni will meet a woman whose illness temporally coincides with the time of meeting.

(15)   Gianni will meet a woman who is ill

This proposal faces counterexamples, however, of which (16) is a typical example:

(16) Gianni will often meet with everyone who studies with him

Besides the interpretation with the object NP taking wide scope, meaning that everyone who (now) studies with Gianni is an x such that Gianni will often meet with x, there are two interpretations in which it is within the scope of the adverbial quantifier *often*. These interpretations are rendered by:

[Often $e > u$]Ex: [Ee': ... e' ...] studies with John(x,e')] meets(John,x,e)

where the restriction '... e' ...' on e' may be '$e' Ou$' (non-anaphoric) or '$e' Oe$' (anaphoric). The non-anaphoric interpretation, which allows that Gianni will have frequent future individual meetings, each of which is with one or another of his current students, each of whom however he meets only infrequently, will not be available if anaphora are obligatory. The point of (16), and any number of similar examples, is that the quantifiers *often* and *someone* do not commute. Inversely, the thesis that anaphora are obligatory if the object in (15) takes narrow scope survives that example only because the quantifiers (over time or events on the one hand, and using the indefinite description on the other) are both existential, hence do commute. I conclude that tense deletion, or anaphora, cannot be obligatory.

Ogihara (1989, 1996) and Higginbotham (1993) suggested in different ways that the asymmetry between complement clauses and object relatives follows from a restriction to the effect that the temporal orientation of a complement clause must match that of the content that it conveys with respect to the predicate whose complement it is. Thus a speaker cannot use (1) to report speech of Gianni's whose content lay in Gianni's future at the time he made it, but now lies in the speaker's past. Suppose Gianni in February utters words translatable as 'Maria will be ill in March', and the speaker says the following April, 'Maria was ill in March'. Gianni's words and the speaker's match in truth-conditions, but not in orientation. Hence the speaker cannot report Gianni's speech by saying 'Gianni said that Maria was ill in March'. The obligatoriness of anaphora in complement clauses then reflects the fact that the temporal orientation of the content said by Gianni must match that of the speaker. And, under anaphora, it does match. In the interpretation of (1) as reporting a past, past-oriented utterance, the orientations are both past (i.e. prior to Gianni's utterance), and in the interpretation as reporting a past, present-oriented utterance, they are both nonpast, since as we have seen the

+past feature only serves to license anaphora, and the embedded clause carries a present tense.

I have put the above account in my own terminology, rather than Ogihara's, which diverges (and is in fact more adequate) in various respects. We may also follow Ogihara, with some adjustments, in observing that the condition (the Temporal Directionality Isomorphism condition of Ogihara, 1996: 210) applies to the so-called "double-access" cases, as in (17):

(17) Gianni ha detto che Maria e incinta
      Gianni said that Maria is pregnant

Since the nonpast (in English or Italian) cannot be anaphoric to the past, the complement clause is interpreted as if the speaker had said it, that is, as in (18):

(18) [EeOu] pregnant(Maria,e)

where u is the speaker's utterance. But this clause cannot match in content any speech of Gianni's in which the (alleged) situation of Maria's pregnancy is future to that speech: for in that case Gianni's speech, but not the speaker's, would be future-oriented. It follows that Gianni's speech must have been present-oriented; and since the speaker has said something that is present-oriented also with respect to her, it must be that in Gianni's speech the range of the situation-variable 'e' takes in the time of the speaker's report as well. Such is the deduction of the properties of the double-access sentences.

How, then, is the speaker to report from her later perspective Gianni's past prediction? The answer is that the future-orientation of Gianni's speech is preserved by using the periphrastic future, combined with a +past affix whose role is to allow the anaphora that would not otherwise be possible, as in (19):

(19) Gianni said that Maria would be pregnant

(Italian deploys the conditional to the same effect.) Again, to omit the +past affix, leaving a present-tensed *will*, is to disallow anaphora, as in (20):

(20) Gianni said that Maria will be pregnant
      Gianni ha detto che Maria sara incinta

There is no problem about temporal orientation, since what is future to the speaker must also be future to Gianni as of the time of his past speech.

In sum, the account of sequence of tense in both object relatives and complement clauses in English and Italian is derived from the following premisses:

(i)   −past cannot be anaphoric to +past; all other combinations are allowed.
(ii) The +past feature can be interpreted either as expressing anteriority <, or as merely triggering anaphora.
(iii) The temporal orientation of a complement said by a speaker must match that of the content it conveys with respect to the predicate whose complement it is.

It is (iii) that explains the asymmetry for instance between (1) and (3), and the fact that it applies also to the double-access cases is further evidence for this premiss.

I turn now to difficulties for this account. There are two, more nearly conceptual, problems that do not threaten its empirical adequacy, but make it difficult to support on the intuitive basis to which we have so far helped ourselves, using reported speech. The first is that the prohibition in (iii) is global, applying to all complements whatever. The second is that the interpretation of what I have called future-orientation is obscure, and it seems to be restricted to certain morphemes. Thus compare the examples in (21):

(21) *a.* Last week, they predicted rain today
      b. Last week, they predicted that it is raining

(21*b*) shows double-access, hence is absurd, since the prediction must have been future-oriented. But (21*a*) is fine. Also, notice that (22) can be a faithful report on Sunday of Gianni's saying on Friday, 'Maria will be in London tomorrow':

(22) Gianni said that Maria was to be in London yesterday

These examples suggest that the restriction on temporal orientations, whatever it is, is tied to the feature −past, and that it cannot be expressed in the metaphysical terms of (iii). But besides these more conceptual issues, there are severe empirical difficulties as well.

Giorgi and Pianesi (1998) have shown that the possibility of double-access interpretations in Italian is correlated with the presence of a higher complementizer, and that in those cases where the complementizer is omitted (as in some dialects) one has, not double-access, but ungrammaticality. This observation suggests that, after all, the double-access interpretations are syntactically represented. But more than this, investigation of some more complex cases reveals that temporal restrictions apply even independently of the question of future-orientation. The simplest examples are somewhat complex, but the evidence seems clear enough. Consider (23) and (24):

(23) Maria will say on Sunday that Mario was here on Saturday [said on Friday]

(24) Gianni will say on Sunday that Maria said on Saturday that Mario *is/ was here today [said on Friday]

In (23) Maria's speech is past-oriented, but the speaker's complement is not. (24) has the same property. That (24) with present-tense *is* represents a case of (failed) double-access is shown by the acceptable (25):

(25) Gianni will say on Sunday that Maria said on Saturday that Mario is here these days [said on Friday]

As I understand him, Ogihara would treat (24) by deleting the past tense in the most deeply embedded complement clause, making it tenseless. The embedded present tense would not delete, with the result that the past-orientation of Maria's speech would conflict with the formal tense information in the innermost clause. (Ogihara (1996) does not actually consider these cases.)

I have already noted that literal tense deletion is not possible on the system that I am assuming. In a system where it is possible, something further must be said to derive the conclusion, for example, that in saying (1) the speaker may report Gianni as having said something that is true just in case Maria was ill at the time he, Gianni, spoke. With tense deletion, moreover, we do not obtain what could be thought a requirement, namely that the belief that Gianni expressed when he said, 'Maria is ill', or 'Maria e' malata', is the very belief that I attribute to him when I say, 'Gianni believed that Maria was ill'. However the technical discussion may go, I am inclined to think that the sacrifice here is very great.

3 A Reanalysis

Having rejected as a basis for the asymmetry between object relative clauses and complement clauses any account along the lines of (iii), we may as a last resort simply stipulate the obligatoriness of tense anaphora for complements, thus abandoning the solution to the double-access cases discussed above. There is another way to view matters, however. Consider (17), repeated here, and what we obtained at the first pass, namely (18):

(17) Gianni ha detto che Maria e incinta
     Gianni said that Maria is pregnant

(18) [EeOu] pregnant(Maria,e)

The data are that, besides the restriction on the quantifier given as 'eOu' in (18), there is a further restriction, namely that the (alleged) state of Maria's being pregnant overlaps Gianni's speech e', or its time. The full interpretation incorporates both restrictions, and may be written as (26):

(26) [Ee: eOu & eOe'] pregnant(Maria,e)

But this suggests that what is peculiar about the English (or Italian) present tense is not that it cannot be anaphoric at all, but rather that, even when anaphoric, it cannot abandon its link to the speaker's utterance; in other words, that it is interpreted twice over, once as anaphoric and once as it would have been used by the speaker alone. (This suggestion, and part of its implementation below, I owe to Tim Stowell, from a remark of his at the Bergamo conference, 1998.)

To make this suggestion effective in syntactic representation and attendant semantics, we require a conception where the tense is represented twice. Now, such a conception is available on the assumption that (*a*) tenses may move at the level LF of Logical Form, and (*b*) that movement is copying. Recall Giorgi and Pianesi's observation that double-access is mediated by a complementizer, and suppose, what is commonly assumed for example for Verb-Second phenomena, that there is movement of inflection I into the complementizer position C. Then if, as they too suggest, one copy of I relates the alleged pregnancy e to the utterance u, and the other copy relates it to the event e' of Gianni's speaking, the semantics being obtained by conjunction of the quantifier restrictions, we obtain following existential closure just the interpretation shown in (26) of the complement clause of (17).

We have noted Giorgi and Pianesi's observation that for matrix V allowing (with some degree of marginality) complementizer deletion, the result of embedding below a matrix past a simple present-tense complement (whether indicative or subjunctive) is ungrammatical; however, the expected meaning is, I am told, intuitively obtained, even if "forced". Thus the ungrammatical or at least highly marginal (27) is interpreted as a case of double-access:

(27) ??Gianni credeva (che) Maria sia incinta
      Gianni believed (that) Maria is pregnant

Conversely, those V that disallow complementizer deletion (with a pre-verbal complement subject—these are, generally speaking, verbs of saying or other forms of communicative behavior) do allow present-tense complements embedded under the past. To account for this correlation, they propose that the complement I is copied into C of the complement clause, the anaphoric copy being the one *in situ*, and the non-anaphoric copy, anchored to the speech time, is in C, indeed in a higher C, which cannot be deleted: hence the first part of their correlation, that verbs not allowing complementizer deletion show typical double-access effects. For the other part, the hypothesis is that V allowing complementizer deletion have only a lower, deletable C, into which I cannot move; hence, on the assumption that the present-tense inflection in the complement clause shown in (27), for example, must move to a higher C but cannot, ungrammaticality results, at least in the Italian case.

There are a number of details of Giorgi and Pianesi's proposal that I will not review here. It is somewhat unclear where the forced interpretation of (27) comes from, since on their view the relevant structure for interpreting it is not available. Zagona (2000) also raises a number of critical points, some with cross-linguistic reference to Spanish. More significantly for the purposes of this article, however, there is no pursuit of the question why sequence of tense, or tense anaphora, should be obligatory in complement clauses but optional elsewhere. In the spirit of trying to deduce this phenomenon, rather than positing it as primitive, I explore an alternative below.

Having rejected any metaphysical basis (as in Ogihara's and Abusch's discussions, and in my own earlier work) for the obligatoriness of tense anaphora in complement clauses, I turn first of all to the simpler case of object relatives, which show less restrictive behavior, on the assumption that what is in force in that case will apply also to complements, although not conversely. In this respect, two facts stand out: first, −past (an embedded present) can never be anaphoric to a superordinate +past; and second, the +past feature that, following Ippolito, I suggested serves only to trigger anaphora can be anaphoric only to a superordinate +past. Apart from these restrictions, anaphora are entirely optional (recall that we have already rejected, in view of examples such as (16), the suggestion that scopal phenomena are involved). The English paradigm will have superordinate past, present, or future *will*, and subordinate forms including besides these the form *would*, which constitutes the anaphoric past of *will*. To illustrate the first point, observe that (28), unlike (29), requires for its truth that the unicorn Mary found be walking now:

(28) Mary found a unicorn that is walking
(29) Mary found a unicorn that was walking

Inversely, (29) is triply ambiguous, since the finding could have been simultaneous with the walking (the merely anaphoric past), or following the walking (the true past tense under anaphora), or simply in the speaker's past (no anaphora). To illustrate the second point, note that in (30), if the merely anaphoric past were permitted, we would expect that it could be equivalent to the present tense (31), which it is not:

(30) Mary loves a man who was crying
(31) Mary loves a man who is crying

For the merely anaphoric past in the form *would*, we may contrast (32) and (33):

(32) Mary found a unicorn that would run away
(33) Mary found a unicorn that will run away

The embedded *will* of (33), being −past, cannot be anaphoric; so if (33) is true then the running away lies in the speaker's future; but the embedded *would* of (32) is necessarily anaphoric, so that the running away could take place any time after the finding (with a strong pragmatic preference for a time between the finding and the time of speech).

I said above that, apart from the restrictions just scouted, tense anaphora in object relative clauses were entirely optional, independently of any issues of scope. Besides the need to make this case by spelling out the examples in detail, the paradigms in question would in a complete story be expanded to include the perfect tenses, and so as to take account of aspectual phenomena. For want of space I omit these details, but invite the reader to verify at leisure the thesis advanced.

Turning now from object relatives to complement clauses, we assume that whatever principles restricted anaphora in the former case restrict them also in the latter, and also that whatever anaphoric relations are allowed from the *in situ* position of the relative clause inflection are allowed in the complement inflection. These assumptions imply that, apart from those restrictions, anaphora are entirely optional, and also that it is the *in situ* position that cannot be anaphoric when it is a present embedded under a past, as in the double-access cases. Hence, they imply that the way in which the double-access interpretation arises is the reverse of that suggested by Giorgi and Pianesi; i.e. that it is the copy of I that moves to C, and not the *in situ* copy that is anaphoric. Suppose so, and suppose further that movement from I to C is obligatory (at least if the +past feature in the embedded clause is not merely triggering anaphora), and that the copy of I there deposited must be anaphoric, independently of the anaphoricity of its source. The properties of the classic double-access cases follow at once. But we obtain also a syntactic/semantic (rather than metaphysical, or stipulative) deduction of the obligatoriness of tense anaphora in complements generally, as follows.

Consider again the English (1), repeated here:

(1) Gianni said that Maria was ill

We have the following possibilities.

3.1 The embedded past is merely anaphoric

Then the interpretation of the complement is

$$^\wedge[\text{E}e'Oe] \text{ ill}(\text{Mary},e')$$

where e is Gianni's (alleged) utterance. Note that, since the embedded past is already anaphoric, any copying into C will not change the interpretation, since it will have the effect merely of adding a redundant conjunct to the quantifier restriction.

3.2 The embedded past expresses temporal anteriority $<$

If it is anaphoric, it reduces to

$$^\wedge[\text{E}e' < e] \text{ ill}(\text{Mary},e')$$

and again any copying is redundant. If not, then after copying and anaphora we have:

$$^\wedge[\text{E}e': e' < u \,\&\, e' < e] \text{ ill}(\text{Mary},e')$$

where the non-anaphoric copy is after all redundant, since $e < u$ (Giorgi and Pianesi note this equivalence as well). So the cases of past embedded below past behave as expected.

I turn now to other embeddings below the past. Evidently, the double-access case (34) will yield the interpretation of the complement (35), as desired:

(34) Gianni said that Maria is ill
(35) $^\wedge[\text{E}e': e' Ou \,\&\, e'Oe] \text{ ill}(\text{Mary},e')$

There is also the embedded future (36):

(36) Gianni said that Maria will be ill

Here anaphora *in situ* are impossible, because *will* is −past. After copying and the establishment of anaphora in C we have for the complement clause

$$^{\wedge}[Ee': e' > u \ \& \ e' > e] \ \text{ill}(\text{Mary}, e')$$

where this time it is the anaphoric copy that is redundant, because $e < u$. Finally, there is embedded anaphoric *would* as in (37):

(37) Gianni said that Maria would be ill

where, since anaphora are obligatory *in situ*, copying changes nothing, as in (1*a*).

The last paragraph completes the cases I will consider here where the superordinate tense is past. If it is present, as in 'Gianni is saying that Maria was ill', there is of course nothing to discuss, because we are given that e (the saying) and u (the speaker's utterance) are temporally coincident; also, I will pass over the case where *would* is licensed by a different relation from tense anaphora, as in (38):

(38) Gianni is saying that Maria would be ill (if she were to fail to get a flu shot)

We are left with the cases where the superordinate tense is future, as in (39):

(39) Gianni will say that Maria is ill

From the case of object relatives we expect anaphora to be optional, and so it is. Evidently, both (40) and (41) are fine:

(40) Gianni will say tomorrow that Maria is ill now
(41) Gianni will say tomorrow that Maria is ill then

(41) raises no new issues: if the embedded present is anaphoric (as it must be, given the temporal adverb *then*) we obtain

$$^{\wedge}[Ee': e'Oe] \ \text{ill}(\text{Mary}, e')$$

If the adverb is omitted from (41), we could have no anaphora *in situ*, but only in the copy in C, obtaining

$$^{\wedge}[Ee': e' \ Ou \ \& \ e'Oe] \ \text{ill}(\text{Mary}, e')$$

something that can evidently be intended by the speaker. (40), however, is of interest in conspicuously failing to show double-access. This case appears, in fact, to be subject to a further curious restriction, upon which I will speculate in closing.

I remarked above that object relative clauses carrying past tense embedded under a nonpast could not merely serve to trigger anaphora. The same is true in complement clauses, as in (42):

(42) Gianni will say that Maria was ill

That is, we cannot have an interpretation in which Gianni is predicted to say, 'Maria is ill', or the content

$$^\wedge[\mathrm{E}e'\!: e'\,Oe]\ \mathrm{ill}(\mathrm{Mary},e')$$

With the disappearance of that option, there remains only the case where the embedded past expresses anteriority, and is anaphoric or not. If it is anaphoric, we have

$$^\wedge[\mathrm{E}e'\!: e' < e]\ \mathrm{ill}(\mathrm{Mary},e')$$

and if not

$$^\wedge[\mathrm{E}e'\!: e' < u\ \&\ e' < e]\ \mathrm{ill}(\mathrm{Mary},e')$$

in which the anaphoric conjunct is redundant, because $u < e$, and which allows, correctly, for both of (43) and (44):

(43) Gianni will say in two days that Maria was ill the day before
(44) Gianni will say tomorrow that Maria was ill yesterday

To complete the data to be presented here, we may embed the future under a future, as in (45):

(45) Gianni will say that Maria will be ill

(the case of embedded *would* being ruled out as above, where the superordinate tense was present). Here again anaphora are obligatory: I cannot use (45) to predict on Friday that Gianni will say on Sunday that Maria was ill on Saturday. This consequence follows because, where the embedded future is not anaphoric, we will obtain

$$^\wedge[\mathrm{E}e'\!: e' > u\ \&\ e' > e]\ \mathrm{ill}(\mathrm{Mary},e')$$

where the non-anaphoric conjunct in the quantifier restriction is again redundant. This completes the discussion of the English case, for the core examples given here.

  We have shown (*modulo* the example (40), discussed below) that the English data, and the asymmetry between object relative clauses and complement clauses with respect to temporal anaphora, follow from principles (i')–(iii') below, which now replace those given in section 2:

(i') −past *in situ* cannot be anaphoric to +past;

(ii′) The +past feature can be interpreted either as expressing anteriority <, or as merely triggering anaphora, in the latter case anaphora to a superordinate past;

(iii′) In complement clauses, I must move to C, and anaphora from C are obligatory; not so in relatives, where, apart from the restrictions above, they are always *in situ* and optional.

We have now abandoned any orientation-condition on complement clauses, and the observations that led to it fall out purely from the syntactic conditions given, together with the particular principle (iii′).

Supposing that the perspective of Giorgi and Pianesi is reversed in the manner suggested, we retain the consequence, and indeed on just their grounds, that there is a correlation in Italian between the possibility of double-access readings and the absence of complementizer deletion. Thus, in cases like (27), repeated here, the embedded tense cannot move to the higher C, and the result is ungrammaticality:

(27) ??Gianni ha creduto che Maria sia incinta
     Gianni believed (that) Maria is pregnant

(Even the English example in (27) is marginal for some speakers I have consulted; hence the explanation, if correct, may apply cross-linguistically as well.) Further discussion here would take us far afield, both because Italian shows a formal distinction between the imperfect and the past (and distinctions of mood) not found in standard English, and because of other comparative Romance phenomena, as in Zagona's recent work. With respect to the examples we have considered, note that doubling the quantifier restriction wherever the embedded tense is not anaphoric *in situ* is redundant (or, in the case of (41), something that must anyway be allowed), except for the classic double-access case (34) and the entirely non-anaphoric case (40).

I will close with two remarks. The first concerns the difference between tense systems like English and Italian, which show double-access interpretation and have sequence of tense in the classical sense (that is, where an embedded past is not interpreted as a relative past, but as a relative present), and systems like Japanese or Hebrew, which do not. The second considers the example (40).

Again, we owe to Ogihara the careful observation of the Japanese phenomena, where nonpast does not show double-access, but indeed can be a relative or anaphoric present by itself; and, correlatively, where the past of a complement clause is always a relative past. The resulting system may be taken to obey (iii′) above, but abandons (i′), instead imposing no restriction at all; does not exhibit the ambiguity of interpretation of the +past feature (if, indeed, that is what it is in Japanese; it may be that the formative, or its features, are unlike those of English); and never interprets any but the higher copy of a tense. Evidently, systems that have richer morphology may be the source of interpretations that combine the Japanese with the English features.

Smith (1978) and others have considered the possibility of double-access interpretations with a present tense as complement of a future. Examples include (46):

(46) Gianni will announce next week that Maria is pregnant now

Such examples are not excluded on the present account; indeed, given I-to-C movement, they are to be expected. But matters are not so clear for (40) and the like. Consider an action-sentence analogue to (40), such as (47):

(47) Gianni will say (next week) that Maria is dancing well (right now)

where the speaker is making a prediction about what Gianni will say later about the quality of Maria's current dancing, then long since over. In my judgement, the speaker (who knows perfectly well, let us say, that Maria is not dancing well) can say (47) if she thinks that Gianni, who is in the studio watching Maria dance, is now of the opinion that Maria is dancing well; but she cannot say it if she knows that Gianni is asleep at home, and only later will watch a videotape of Maria's current performance. In the latter case, I believe, the past progressive must be used in the complement clause. The grammaticality of (40) and (47) shows that the complement present tense need not be anaphoric; there is no question here of double-access. But it suggests that, while we can sometimes take the complement present just as it is, the circumstances must be exceptional. Thus, it is proper to predict what Gianni will *say* using the present tense if that is what he *now* thinks, even if, when he does say it, it must be with the past tense. In some other cases, I believe, the result of taking the embedded clause as it stands (without anaphora) is highly questionable. Thus suppose that Maria is known to be touring the United States, one city a day, and that Gianni, who keeps track of her whereabouts, announces each day where she was the day before. Consider the prediction (48):

(48) Gianni will announce tomorrow that Maria ??is/was in New York today

The example seems highly questionable, as noted. If so, then although the acceptability of (47), under the circumstances described, is problematic for the view presented here (as it is for Giorgi and Pianesi), there may be a dimension of reporting and predicting speech behavior that is not covered by the formal syntactic and semantic conditions under investigation in this chapter.

REFERENCES

Abusch, D. (1988). 'Sequence of Tense, Intensionality, and Scope', in H. Borer (ed.), *Proceedings of the Seventh West Coast Conference on Formal Linguistics* (Stanford, Calif.: CSLI Publications; distributed by University of Chicago Press), 1–14.

—— (1991). 'The Present Under Past as *De Re* Interpretation', in D. Bates (ed.), *Proceedings of the Tenth West Coast Conference on Formal Linguistics* (Stanford, Calif.: CSLI Publications; distributed by University of Chicago Press), 1–12.

Bar-Hillel, Y. (1954). 'Indexical Expressions', *Mind*, 63: 359–79.

Burge, T. (1978). 'Self-Reference and Translation', in F. Guenthner and M. Geunthner-Reutter (eds.), *Meaning and Translation* (New York: NYU Press), 137–53.

Davidson, D. (1967). 'The Logical Form of Action Sentences', in N. Rescher (ed.), *The Logic of Decision and Action* (Pittsburgh: University of Pittsburgh Press). Reprinted in Davidson (1980: 105–48).

—— (1980). *Essays on Actions and Events* (Oxford: Clarendon Press).

Dowty, D. (1982). 'Tenses, Time Adverbs, and Compositional Semantic Theory', *Linguistics and Philosophy*, 5: 23–53.

Enc, M. (1987). 'Anchoring Conditions for Tense', *Linguistic Inquiry*, 18: 633–57.

Giorgi, A., and Pianesi, F. (1998). 'The Generalized Double-Access Reading', MS, University of Bergamo, Italy.

—— —— (2000). 'Sequence of Tense Phenomena in Italian', *Probus*, 12: 1–32.

Higginbotham, J. (1993). 'Notes on Sequence of Tense', MS, University of Oxford.

—— (1997). 'A Plea for Implicit Anaphora', in Hans Bennis, Pierre Pica, and Johann Rooryck (eds.), *Atomism and Binding* (Amsterdam: Foris), 183–203.

Ippolito, M. (1998). 'Reference Time and Tense Anaphora', MS, MIT, Cambridge, Mass.

Kamp, H., and Reyle, U. (1993). *From Discourse to Logic* (Dordrecht: Kluwer).

Ladusaw, W. (1977). 'Some Problems with Tense in PTQ', *Texas Linguistic Forum*, 6: 89–102.

Ogihara, T. (1989). 'Temporal Reference in English and Japanese' (doctoral dissertation, University of Texas at Austin).

—— (1994). 'Adverbs of Quantification and Sequence-of-Tense Phenomena', in M. Harvey and L. Santelmann (eds.), *Proceedings of Semantics and Linguistic Theory IV* (Ithaca, NY: Cornell University, DMLL Publications), 251–67.

—— (1996). *Tense, Attitudes, and Scope* (Dordrecht: Kluwer).

Prior, A. (1957). *Time and Modality* (Oxford: Oxford University Press).

—— (1967). *Past, Present, and Future* (Oxford: Oxford University Press).

Roeper, T. (1987). 'Implicit Arguments and the Head–Complement Relation', *Linguistic Inquiry*, 18: 267–310.

Smith, C. (1978). 'The Syntax and Interpretation of Temporal Expressions in English', *Linguistics and Philosophy*, 2: 43–99.

Williams, E. (1994). *Thematic Structure in Syntax* (Cambridge, Mass.: MIT Press).

Zagona, K. (2000). 'Tense Construal in Complement Clauses: Verbs of Communication and the Double Access Reading', MS, University of Washington, Seattle.

9

The Grammar of Intensionality

Richard Larson

Intensionality phenomena were first discussed by Frege (1893) in the context of sentential complement constructions like (1*a*, *b*). Frege noted that substitution of co-referring terms in clausal complements need not preserve truth (1*a*, *b*).[1] Another feature of these environments is that the presence of a nonreferring or nondenoting term need not yield a false sentence (2*a*). Furthermore, an indefinite in such an environment can be read nonspecifically; thus in (2*b*), Max can believe a famous actor to be in the movie without there being any particular famous actor such that Max believes he or she was in the movie:

(1) *a.* Max believed [$_{CP}$[$_{NP}$ Boris Karloff] was in the movie].
    b. Max believed [$_{CP}$[$_{NP}$ Bill Pratt] was in the movie].
(2) *a.* Max believed [$_{CP}$[$_{NP}$ a werewolf] was in the movie].
    b. Max believed [$_{CP}$[$_{NP}$ a famous actor] was in the movie].

Intensionality effects are not standardly observed with non-clausal complements. With noun phrase objects, for example, substitution of co-referring object NPs typically preserves truth (3*a*, *b*), and the presence of a non-referring or nondenoting object typically yields a false sentence (3*c*); furthermore, an indefinite object is understood specifically, in the sense that if Max Vs an N then there is some N such that Max Vs him, her, or it (3*d*):

(3) *a.* Max met [$_{NP}$ Boris Karloff].
    b. Max met [$_{NP}$ Bill Pratt].

[1] 'Boris Karloff' was the stage name taken by Mr William Henry Pratt.

    c. Max met [$_{NP}$ a werewolf].

    d. Max met [$_{NP}$ a famous actor].

These results raise a simple, but interesting question: is the apparent correlation between clausal complementation and intensionality a real one? Is intensionality connected with a particular grammatical environment, or is the semantic phenomenon in fact more general?

    In this chapter I discuss two opposing views on this question: one, sententialism, which holds to a grammatically conditioned view of intensionality, and the second, intensionalism, which holds that intensionality is quite general in occurrence, and is to be found in a wide range of constructions. More exactly, I will examine three putative cases of intensionality effects in non-clausal complement structures: (i) so-called intensional transitives, (ii) adverbial modifiers, and (iii) adjectival modifiers. I will argue that, in each case, recent work in syntax and semantics casts doubt upon the claim that these structures provide evidence for intensionality divorced from clausal complementation. Intensional transitives can be argued to be a form of concealed clausal structure, and hence a case of clausal complementation after all. By contrast, adverbial and adjectival modifiers can be shown to be non-intensional in the crucial range of cases. The result is that the more restricted, sententialist picture appears sustainable.

1.0 Sententialism versus Intensionalism

In 'Sense and Reference', Frege (1893) introduces intensionality in the context of clausal complementation. As is well-known, Frege ascribes intensionality in examples like (1) to the fact that the embedded sentence contributes its sense to the interpretation of the larger clause, rather than its usual referent (a truth-value). The sense or 'thought' expressed by the embedded sentence is the product of the senses of its component expressions, and because *Boris Karloff* and *Bill Pratt* express different senses, the thoughts expressed by *Boris Karloff was in the movie* and *Bill Pratt was in the movie* are different as well. This entails a difference in truth-conditions for (1*a*) and (1*b*) because Max is asserted to believe different thoughts in the two cases.

    For Frege, the invocation of senses in cases like (1*a, b*) appears to proceed in the following way: *Boris Karloff* and *Bill Pratt* contribute senses (and not referents), because their containing sentence does. And their containing sentence contributes a sense (and not a referent), because of the presence of a verb like *believe*, which expresses a relation between an agent and a thought, the sense of a sentence. It is the presence of the clause-taking, propositional attitude verb, together with the clausal complement construction, that invokes senses.[2]

(4)

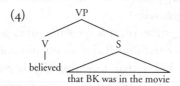

Frege's line of reasoning appears straightforward enough, however it leaves open the general question of our access to senses in semantics. Is the picture described above exhaustive? Is this the only way that senses can enter semantic evaluation? Or are there additional possibilities—additional configurations— in which senses can be invoked?

One view might be that senses and intensions are accessed *only* through thoughts, and hence only through predicates like *believe*, which express relations to thoughts. I will refer to this view as *sententialism*, because it entails that intensionality can arise only in the context of sentential complements to predicates like *believe*. A second, opposing view is that clausal complements represent only one case of a more general phenomenon: relations to senses. Verbs like *believe* express relations to one kind of sense: the sense of a clause. But other kinds of predicates may express relations to other kinds of senses, such as the sense of a nominal or a predicate. I will refer to this second view as *intensionalism*, since in principle it would allow for intensionality to arise in any category X, so long as the expression with which X semantically combines selects for the sense of X.[3]

Sententialism and intensionalism have both had their exponents. But within recent linguistic semantics at least, intensionalism has overwhelmingly been the position of choice, in large part due to the influence of Richard Montague (1970*a*, 1970*b*, 1973, 1974), whose views have formed the basis of modern

---

[2] This situation distinguishes a predicate like *believe* from a truth-functional connective like *and*. The latter may combine with a sentence (cf. *Bela Lugosi was in the movie and Boris Karloff was in the movie*), but the composition does not produce intensionality, because *and* does not relate an agent to a thought.

[3] It is interesting to observe that, despite a wide-ranging discussion of construction types, and despite his obvious awareness of the importance of senses to his analysis, Frege (1893) never embraces intensionalism. He never speaks of predicates bearing relations to any other senses but those of clauses.

formal linguistic semantics for over two decades. Montague framed his proposals within the general program of possible world semantics, analyzing intensions as functions from possible worlds to denotations. Arbitrary intensions are formed by means of an operator '$^\wedge$', which, for any expression α, yields an expression $^\wedge\alpha$ denoting the intension of α. In his general analysis of semantic combination, Montague invokes the intensional operator wherever function-argument composition occurs. Thus in a structure of the general form $[_x Y Z]$, where Y is analyzed semantically as combining with Z as function to argument, the intensionality operator always occurs in the result. The interpretation of X is the interpretation of Y applied to the *intension* of the interpretation of Z:

(5) $[[[_x Y\ Z]]] \Rightarrow [[Y](^\wedge [[Z]])$

Ceteris paribus, this analysis predicts intensionality effects to arise wherever function–argument combination is present, whether the combining elements be subject and object, object and verb, modifier and modified, determiner and noun, etc.

Montague (1970a, 1970b, 1972) offers three grammatical environments in support of his generalized approach to intensionality—three environments presenting themselves as semantically intensional, but syntactically non-clausal. These are: (i) transitive constructions involving one of a select set of verbs such as *want, need, seek, imagine*, etc., (ii) adverbial modifier constructions, and (iii) adjectival modifier constructions. These environments are illustrated schematically in (6a–c), respectively, using familiar tree diagrams.[4]

(6)

If the claim that these environments are both intensional and non-clausal can be upheld, this result plainly yields a direct empirical refutation of the sententialist position. In view of their importance, let us examine these cases

---

[4] Montague himself did not use standard phrase-markers in representing the syntax of natural language constructions, but instead employed a syntax based on Categorial Grammar. I will ignore this detail and use tree diagrams throughout.

further to see if they do indeed provide a compelling argument for intension-alism.

2.0 Intensional 'Transitives'

Intensional transitive constructions show apparent verb-object syntax, but intensional behavior on the part of the object; (7a–c) represents a typical case. Suppose Max is a 1930s Hollywood producer casting a new musical horror-film; it is clear that (7a) could be true and (7b) none the less false, even if the dancers and singers were the same. Similarly, it seems that (7c) could be true even assuming that *werewolf* is nondenoting. Finally, either (7a) or (7b) could be true without there being any specific dancer or singer (respect-ively) that Max wants:

(7) a. Max wants a dancer
     b. Max wants a singer
     c. Max wants a werewolf.

Various classes of apparent transitive verbs have been claimed to show inten-sionality in this way. A rough (but by no means complete) classification is given in (8):[5]

(8) Verbs of Desire and Volition
    want, need, desire, hope-for, lust-for, require, insist-on, demand
    Verbs of Search and Examination
    seek, look-for, search-for, hunt-for, quest-for
    Verbs of Depiction and Imagination
    picture, imagine, suppose, conceive, envisage, envision, fancy, visualize
    Verbs of Expectation and Presumption
    expect, anticipate, foresee, await, presuppose
    Verbs of Veneration and Worship
    venerate, revere, adore, reverence, idolize, honor
    Verbs of Resemblance and Similarity
    resemble, be-like, be-similar-to, simulate, remind-one-of

---

[5] This list is far from complete. Antonyms of verbs of these classes show similar properties. For example, along with *venerates* (as in *Max venerates Christ*) we also have *rejects* (as in *Max rejects Christ*). Furthermore, many verbs have associated adjectival predicates that show similar intensional behavior; thus: *need/be-in-need-of, desire/be-desirous-of, hope-for/be-hopeful-of,* etc.

Under the Montagovian view, the analysis of intensional transitives proceeds straightforwardly along the lines sketched above. The interpretation of a verb phrase (VP) such as *wants a werewolf* is analyzed as in (9), where the interpretation of the verb applies to the intension of the interpretation of the object. The intensional operator is analyzed as the source of intensionality effects.

(9) $[[[_{VP}[_V \text{ wants}][_{NP} \text{ a werewolf}]]]] \Rightarrow [[[_V \text{ wants}]]]$
$(\wedge[[[_{NP} \text{ a werewolf}]]])$

Under the sententialist view, however, a sharply different approach is required. Given that these environments appear to be genuinely intensional, the only option for the sententialist is to ascribe a clausal syntax. If we would maintain the view that intensionality and clausal complementation are linked, we are obliged to say that, surface appearances notwithstanding, constructions like those in (7) are not really verb-object structures at all. Rather they are verb-clause structures in which significant portions of the clausal complement have been 'concealed' or left abstract.

2.1 Concealed Clausal Complements

In fact a 'hidden clause' analysis of intensional transitive constructions is plausible in many cases, and has been urged by a number of researchers. Quite typically, intensional transitive constructions have a close paraphrase involving a clausal, or clause-like construction. Consider the pairs in (10), for instance, with verbs drawn from the first four classes in (8):

(10)   *a.*   (i) Max wants [Boris (in his movie)].
           (ii) Max wants [PRO to have Boris (in his movie)].
       b.   (i) Max is seeking [a vampire].
           (ii) Max is seeking [PRO to find a vampire].
       c.   (i) Max visualized [a unicorn].
           (ii) Max visualized [a unicorn in front of him].
       d.   (i) Max expects [a spaceship].
           (ii) Max expects [a spaceship to appear].

For verbs of volition and search, the transitive form typically corresponds to a nonfinite complement construction containing a 'silent' subject (*PRO*) and one of a small number of understood verbs. Thus, with the volitional verbs, V-NP, almost always has a counterpart clausal form V-*to-have*-NP.

And with verbs of search, V-NP generally has a matching clausal form V-*to-find*-NP. For verbs of depiction, the transitive form typically corresponds to a 'small clause' construction, containing an overt subject and a bare predicate. Thus V-NP corresponds to V [NP XP], where XP is some kind of bare predicate phrase, such as a PP (*in front of him*), or an AP (*present*), etc.

The hidden clause analysis of intensional transitives is supported by certain well-known empirical phenomena. Consider, for example, the fact that (11*a*, *b*) are both ambiguous depending on what the adverb *tomorrow* is taken to modify:[6]

> (11) *a.* Max will need to have a bicycle tomorrow.   (Ambiguous)
>   *b.* Max will need a bicycle tomorrow.   (Ambiguous)

In (11*a*), the adverb can be understood as modifying either the matrix verb *need* or the embedded verb *have*: it can either be the needing that will be tomorrow (cf. *Tomorrow Max will need to have a bicycle*), or the having that will be tomorrow (cf. *Max will need to have a bicycle, and he must have it tomorrow*). A similar pair of readings is available for (11*b*). In the clausal case, the ambiguity can be analyzed straightforwardly as arising from the two possible attachments for *tomorrow* (12*a*, *b*).

> (12) *a.* [Max will need [PRO to have a bicycle tomorrow]]
>   *b.* [Max will need [PRO to have a bicycle] tomorrow]

If (11*b*) is underlying clausal, then its ambiguity can be explained in exactly the same way (13*a*, *b*):

> (13) *a.* [Max will need [PRO TO HAVE a bicycle tomorrow]].
>   *b.* [Max will need [PRO TO HAVE a bicycle] tomorrow]].

If we reject this approach, we must provide an alternative analysis of the ambiguity in (11*b*). And we must also explain why ambiguity fails to arise with extensional transitives verbs that do not select clauses, such as *repair/ride*:

> (14) Max will ride/repair a bicycle tomorrow.   (Unambiguous)

---

[6] This point is noted by McCawley (1974), Karttunen (1976), and Ross (1976). The latter attributes the basic observation to Masaru Kajita.

2.2 Intensional Transitives of Volition and Search as Restructuring Verbs

For the sententialist who is a realist about linguistic theory and is interested in more than traditional analysis of concepts, the main challenge posed by intensional transitives is syntactic.[7] For then the task is not merely to provide a bi-clausal analysis of intensional transitive structures that offers an intuitively acceptable paraphrase relation (*want* NP ⇔ *want to have* NP). The sententialist must show that this analysis represents the *actual* structure of the sentences in question and accords with established syntactic theory.

This challenge is a formidable one. As noted above, the bi-clausal analysis of intensional transitives requires a significant amount of inaudible structure in the complement. Modern grammatical theory sharply constrains the distribution of such inaudibilia through a highly restrictive set of principles. Hence inaudible verbs, tense elements, complementizers, etc., must be shown to fall under these principles. Furthermore, the bi-clausal analysis assumes a dependency to hold between specific higher verbs (such as *want* or *need*) and specific, lower, abstract verbs (like *HAVE*). Given the non-local nature of the relation, this dependency is not easy to express. Finally, the bi-clausal analysis is obliged to explain why intensional transitives and their overt clausal counterparts behave differently in certain cases. Consider the fact that passive can front the object of an intensional transitive verb, but cannot front the corresponding NP in its putative clausal source (15*a*, *b*):

(15) *a.* A werewolf is needed t by Max

    b. *A werewolf is needed [PRO to have t] by Max.

Some account must be given of such divergences.

2.2.1 *Restructuring*

Den Dikken, Larson, and Ludlow (1996) and Larson, den Dikken, and Ludlow (1997) are recent attempts to take up the syntactic challenges of a bi-clausal analysis within modern syntactic theory. The key starting-point for

---

[7] By a 'realist approach', I mean one that views linguistic theory as theorizing about a real body of knowledge (knowledge of language) acquired by the speaker in the course of language acquisition. For a general defense of realism in linguistics see Chomsky (1975, 1986, 1995). For a realist approach to semantic theory, see Larson and Segal (1995).

these authors is the observation that certain intensional transitives in English correspond to verbs that, in other languages, undergo a special process through which bi-clausal structure seems to 'collapse'.[8] In the Romance languages some volitional verbs may undergo a syntactic operation permitting complement elements to behave syntactically as if they were members of the matrix clause. This operation is known in the literature as *restructuring*, and is illustrated by the Italian data in (16) and (17), from Burzio (1986). (16*a*) shows that non-finite complements generally do not allow object clitic pronouns from the complement clause to be promoted into the matrix clause. With volitional verbs like *volere* 'want', however, promotion of a clitic is possible (16*b*). Similarly, (17*a*) shows that the passive-like impersonal construction in Italian does not in general allow promotion of a complement object to matrix subject position. However, (17*b*) illustrates that with verbs like *volere* such movement is possible:

(16) *a.* *Mario **lo** odia [PRO leggere t].
Mario   it hates   to read
'Mario hates to read it'

    b. Mario **lo** vuole [PRO leggere t].
Mario it wants   to read
'Mario wants to read it'

(17) *a.* ***Questi libri** si odiavano proprio [PRO leggere t].
these books SI hated   really   to read
'We really hated to read these books'

    b. **Questi libri** si volevano proprio [PRO leggere t].
these books SI wanted   really   to read
'We really wanted to read these books'

Numerous analyses have been proposed for the restructuring phenomenon. One persistent intuition is that these examples exhibit some form of 'clause-union' in which a bi-clausal structure becomes, at some level, uni-clausal (Aissen and Perlmutter, 1983; Rizzi, 1978). A complementary intuition is that the matrix and embedded predicates merge to form a single complex form—'want-to-read'—so that objects of the complement verb become objects of the single, merged form.

Developing ideas by Burzio (1986), Baker (1988) proposes that infinitival complements embedded under restructuring verbs like *volere* involve a form of verb incorporation. First, the complement verb phrase (VP) raises from its

---

[8] The discussion in this and the next paragraph is adapted directly from Larson *et al.* (1997).

source position (18*a*) to the front of the embedded clause (CP) (18*b*).[9] From this point, the lower verb incorporates into the matrix verb by adjoining to it (18*c*). As Baker discusses in some detail, incorporation has the effect of extending the domain of the matrix verb; whereas the clitic *lo* was initially governed only by the lower verb *leggere* 'read', it is now governed by the complex form *vuole-leggere*, 'want-to-read'. This change in government relations is what allows the object clitic pronoun to move into the matrix clause, as shown in (18*d*). A similar story accounts for the object promotion in (17*b*).

(18) *a.* Mario vuole [$_{CP}$ [PRO [$_{VP}$ leggere lo]]]

   b. Mario vuole [$_{CP}$[$_{VP}$ leggere lo] [PRO t]]
   ⌞_____⌟

   c. Mario vuole-leggere [$_{CP}$[$_{VP}$ t lo] [PRO t]]
      ⌞_____⌟

   d. Mario lo-vuole-leggere [$_{CP}$[$_{VP}$ t t] [PRO t]]
   ⌞_____⌟

Larson, den Dikken, and Ludlow (1997) extend this analysis directly to intensional transitives of volition and search in English. Simplifying slightly, *Max needs a werewolf* is assigned the derivation in (19), and *Max seeks a werewolf* receives the derivation in (20). As above, the lower verb phrase raises up and the hidden verb (*HAVE* or *FIND*) incorporates into the higher one, forming a complex predicate:[10]

(19) *a.* Max needs [$_{CP}$ [PRO [$_{VP}$ HAVE a werewolf]]]

---

[9] In the derivations below, I use *t* to stand for the structural 'trace' of the moved element.

[10] Quine (1960) suggests that surface transitive constructions like (i*a*) be paraphrased with infinitives embedded under *try*, as in (i*b*). However, Larson, den Dikken, and Ludlow point out that they can also be paraphrased as in (i*c*), retaining the original main verb:

(i) *a.* Max is looking for/seeking survivors.
   b. Max is trying [$_{CP}$ PRO to find survivors].
   c. Max is looking/seeking [$_{CP}$ PRO to find survivors].

This result is interesting in so far as *look-for* and *seek* appear equivalent to *try-to-find* in (i*a*), but equivalent to *try* alone in (i*c*) since 'find' is contributed independently. Larson, den Dikken, and Ludlow suggest that the same verbs *look-for* and *seek* are present in (i*a*) and (i*c*) with meaning equivalent to *try*. They suggest that the additional 'find' meaning in (i*a*) results from incorporation of the abstract, independent FIND predicate, equivalent to that found overtly in (i*c*). Note that this moves forestalls the worry expressed by Partee (1974) that if all verbs of search are 'decomposed' as *try to find* NP, then differences among them will be lost. What is claimed here, in effect, is that verbs of search differ in the way in which the agent tries to locate the object in question, but not in the goal of their efforts: the finding of it.

  b. Max needs [$_{CP}$[$_{VP}$ HAVE a werewolf] [PRO t]]
  c. Max needs-HAVE [$_{CP}$[$_{VP}$ t a werewolf] [PRO t]]
(20) *a.* Max seeks [$_{CP}$ [PRO [$_{VP}$ FIND a werewolf]]]
  b. Max seeks [$_{CP}$[$_{VP}$ FIND a werewolf] [PRO t]]
  c. Max seeks-FIND [$_{CP}$[$_{VP}$ t a werewolf] [PRO t]]

This derivation succeeds in capturing many of the desired properties of the intensional transitive construction. Since the higher and lower verbs (*need-HAVE, seek-FIND*) ultimately form a single complex predicate, the relation between the two is ultimately a very local one, and can be 'checked' in the local configuration. Likewise the contrast in behavior noted in (15*a, b*) can be ascribed to the fact that the intensional transitive has undergone restructuring, raising the downstairs object (*a werewolf*) into the matrix clause. From there it can be promoted to subject position (15*a*), analogously to what occurs in (17*b*). By contrast in (15*b*) the complement clause has not undergone restructuring and hence promotion is not possible.

2.2.2 Try *as a 'Tense-Defective' Restructuring V*

The analysis also affords some grasp on certain differences between intensional transitives. I noted earlier that temporal modifiers provide evidence in favor of a concealed clause analysis of *need* and *want*. Thus (11*b*) (repeated below) is ambiguous with respect to the attachment of *tomorrow*, just like its full clausal counterpart (11*a*):

(11) *a.* Max will need to have a bicycle **tomorrow**. (Ambiguous)
  b. Max will need a bicycle **tomorrow**. (Ambiguous)

Perhaps surprisingly, however, *seek* and *look-for* do not show the same behavior. Partee (1974) observes that (21*a*) is ambiguous in a way parallel to (11*a*); thus Fred can be understood as trying before the meeting began, or he can be understood as having the goal of locating the minutes before the meeting began. By contrast, (21*b*) is unambiguous: it has only the first reading corresponding to a main clause attachment for the adverb:

(21) *a.* Fred was trying to find the minutes **before the meeting began.**
   (Ambiguous)
  b. Fred was looking for the minutes **before the meeting began.**
   (Unambiguous)

Interestingly, in recent work Wurmbrand (1997) notes facts suggesting that certain restructuring infinitives may lack an independent tense specification in their complements. Specifically, she observes the following contrasts between German *versuchen* 'try' and *beschliessen* 'decide':

(22) *a.* (i) #Hans **versuchte** Maria in zwei Monaten in Wien zu besuchen
           Hans tried Maria in   two months in Vienna to visit
           'Hans tried to visit Maria in Vienna in two months'

      (ii) Hans **beschloß** Maria in zwei Monaten in Wien zu besuchen
           'Hans decided to visit Maria in Vienna in two months'

   b. (i) #weil Maria zu Weihnachten den Hans an seinem Geburtstag
           because Maria on Christmas   Hans on his   birthday
           zu besuchen **versuchte**
           to visit   tried
           'because Maria tried on Christmas to visit Hans on his birthday'

      (ii) weil Maria zu Weihnachten den Hans an seinem Geburtstag
           zu besuchen **beschloß**
           'because Maria decided on Christmas to visit Hans on his birthday'

As Wurmbrand discusses, *versuchen* patterns as a restructuring verb according to tests of clitic promotion and the availability of 'super-passive' movement similar to that seen in (17*b*). Correlatively, *versuchen* resists an independent temporal specification in its complement. By contrast, *beschliessen* is not a restructuring verb by the same tests, and *beschliessen* permits independent temporal reference in its complement. These points suggest that the lack of ambiguity observed by Partee (1974) is plausibly due to an independent fact about restructuring verbs of the *try*-class: the fact that they are 'tense-defective' in an important sense. If so, then although the presence of ambiguity with temporal adverbs is evidence in favor of a concealed complement, the lack of such ambiguities is not (contra Partee, 1974) evidence against such an analysis. The non-ambiguity is plausibly due to an independent fact about these verbs, one that is observable even when the complement clearly contains more than the bare nominal of an intensional transitive construction.[11]

Larson, den Dikken, and Ludlow (1997) represents one recent attempt to give a sententialist analysis of intensional transitive constructions. Although

---

[11] Wurmbrand (1997, 1998) actually proposes that *all* restructuring infinitives lack a tense projection in their complements, and thus that all should resist independent modification by temporal adverbs. However, her discussion ignores the facts of *want*, which is a restructuring verb by standard tests and yet *does* permit independent time adverbs.

many specific cases remain to be analyzed, the basic programme and its obligations are clear-cut: to analyze intensional transitives as bi-clausal, but at the same time to link them to constructions in which bi-clausality is concealed by grammatical reduction and restructuring processes. The success of this program is for the future to determine, but at the very least it appears to represent a promising and coherent alternative to the Montagovian thesis that intensionality is simply available in transitive constructions.

3.0 Intensionality in Adverbial Modification

Let us turn now to Montague's second putative instance of non-clausal intensionality: adverbial modification. As it turns out there are there are two discrete groups of cases to consider, which I will term *fully intensional adverbs* and *partially intensional adverbs*.

3.0.1 *Fully Intensional Adverbs*

Fully intensional adverbs show all the intensional behavior observed with clausal complementation; (23*a–c*) are examples.

> (23) *a.* Olga **allegedly** dances.
>   *b.* Olga levitated **in Rudolphe's dream**.
>   *c.* DeKok **supposedly** met a pick-pocket.

Substitution of coextensive predicates can fail to preserve truth with this class. Thus if the dancers and singers are the same, it will follow that if Olga dances, she sings. But this will not entail that if Olga allegedly dances, she allegedly sings. Likewise, the presence of a nondenoting predicate may fail to induce falsity. (23*b*) can be true despite the fact that *levitate* is (I assume) nondenoting in this world. Finally, an indefinite in the scope of the adverb need not receive a specific interpretation. If DeKok supposedly met a pick-pocket, it does not follow that there is a pick-pocket that DeKok supposedly met.

3.0.2 *Partially Intensional Adverbs*

In addition to the fully intensional adverbs, there is a second class of adverbial constructions showing a *subset* of the semantic behavior observed with clausal complements. (24*a–c*) and (25*a–c*) are examples:[12]

---

[12] The adverbs in (24*a–c*) are discussed in Partee (1974).

(24) *a.* Max **intentionally** fell.
     b. Olga **reluctantly** danced in the ballet.
     c. Izzy **willingly** ate spinach.

(25) *a.* Olga dances **beautifully**.
     b. Kathrin manages the team **skillfully**.
     c. Jean sings **at three o'clock**.

The situation with these forms is more complicated than with the previous class. In brief, *all* the relevant adverbs show the intensional behavior of blocking substitution with coextensive predicates. *None* show the intensional behavior of allowing a truth when combined with a nondenoting predicate. And *some* show the nonspecific readings characteristic of intensional environments.

To illustrate the first point, consider the verbs *dances* and *sings* and assume the two predicates to denote the same set. Plainly, even in these circumstances, (26*a*, *b*) do not entail each other. Substitution of coextensive predicates thus fails.

(26) *a.* Olga dances willingly/beautifully.
     b. Olga sings willingly/beautifully.

Next, observe that when adverbs like *willingly, intentionally, beautifully,* and *skillfully,* and prepositional phrases like *at three o'clock* combine with a nondenoting predicate they always yield a falsity. Thus (27) is false with all of the indicated adverbs, given that *levitates* is not (we assume) true of any individuals:

(27) Olga levitated willingly/skillfully/beautifully/at three o'clock

None of the class of adverbs illustrated in (24) or (25) shows the intensional property of being able to combine with a nondenoting predicate to yield a truth.

Finally, consider the pair in (28*a*, *b*). Notice that (28*a*) can be true without there being any particular word that Max repeated intentionally. Max may have decided to add repetition to his speech without intending to reiterate any particular word. By contrast if (28*b*) is true, then there must be a word—a particular expression—that Max repeated quickly.

(28) *a.* Max repeated a word **intentionally**.
     b. Max repeated a word **quickly**.

More generally, adverbs of the *intentionally*-class appear to support the nonspecific reading characteristic of intensional environments whereas manner adverbs like *beautifully, skillfully, quickly,* etc. do not support the nonspecific reading.

3.1 The Intensionalist Account

The intensionalist account of fully intensional adverbs is parallel to its account of intensional transitives: semantic combination of an adverb and a verb phrase introduces an intensional operator, which accounts for the intensionality effects. Coextensive predicates cannot be substituted because substitution would occur within the scope of '$^\wedge$' (29).

> (29) *a.* Suppose: $\{x: x \text{ dances}\} = \{x: x \text{ sings}\}$
> Then: *Olga dances.* $\leftrightarrow$ *Olga sings.*
> But: *Olga allegedly dances.* $\leftarrow / \rightarrow$ *Olga allegedly sings.*
> *b.* Analysis: **allegedly'**($^\wedge$**dance'**) (o) $\leftarrow / \rightarrow$ **allegedly'**($^\wedge$**sing'**)(o)

Likewise, the intensional operator allows for the potential truth of *Olga allegedly levitates,* since *allegedly levitates* may have a non-empty extension even if *levitates* does not (30):

> (30) *a.* Suppose: $\{x: x \text{ levitates}\} = \varnothing$
> Then: *Olga levitates* is false.
> But: *Olga allegedly levitates* may be true
> *b.* Analysis: **allegedly'**($^\wedge$**levitate**)'(o)

Finally, the semantics of '$^\wedge$' does not support exportation of an existential quantifier in its scope; the existence of a world w in which some individual ϕs does not ensure the existence of an individual in our world that ϕs. Hence the possibility of a nonspecific reading in the scope of an adverb that introduces '$^\wedge$' (31):

> (31) *a.* *DeKok supposedly met a pick-pocket.* $- / \rightarrow$
> *There is a pick-pocket that DeKok supposedly met.* *
> *b.* Analysis: **supposedly'**($^\wedge \lambda y[\exists x[$**pick-pocket'**$(x)^\wedge$**met**$_*$**'**$)(y,x)]])($**d**)

The situation with partially intensional adverbs is somewhat more involved. Consider first the issue of nondenoting predicates. We noted that *willingly, intentionally, beautifully, skillfully,* etc. depart from intensional behavior in so far as they always yield a falsity when they combine with an empty predicate like *levitate.* Thus *Olga levitated skillfully* cannot be true given that *levitates* has a null extension. Within an intensionalist account, this behavior can be taken to follow from an auxiliary fact about the adverbs in question, namely that they fall under a semantic postulate like (32*a*). The latter allows an adverbially modified predicate (Adv′(^Π)) to hold of an individual x, only if the unmodified predicate (Π) holds of x. In the case at hand, this postulate mandates that *Olga levitates skillfully* can be true only if *Olga levitates* is itself true, contrary to fact (32*b*):[13]

(32) a. $\forall x \forall \Pi \Box [(\text{Adv}'(^\wedge \Pi))(x) \rightarrow (\Pi)(x)]$
       b. $\Box [(\textbf{skillfully}'(^\wedge \textbf{levitates}'))(o) \rightarrow (\textbf{levitates}')(o)]$

According to this analysis, then, although the presence of a nondenoting predicate does yield falsity with these adverbs, the departure from expected intensional behavior follows from an independent lexical fact about items of this class: the fact that they fall under postulate (32*a*). The environment in question *is* intensional; it is simply that some intensionality effects are masked by independent properties of the adverbs. So the account goes.

Finally, consider the unavailability of nonspecific readings with manner adverbs like *beautifully* and *skillfully*, as opposed to adverbs like *willingly* and *intentionally*. To my knowledge this issue has been not explicitly discussed in the literature on intensionality, and indeed appears to present a problem for the Montagovian account. The postulate in (32*a*) does not explain it. The latter guarantees that if Max repeated a word quickly, then Max repeated a word, and hence there was a word that Max repeated. But this does not entail there being a word that Max repeated quickly. Note further that we cannot appeal to a meaning postulate that would simply extensionalize V-Adv combinations with adverbs like *beautifully* and *skillfully*. To do this would lose the fact that substitution of coextensive terms is blocked in their scope. But then how do we account for the apparently obligatory exportation of the indefinite? The answer is not apparent.

3.2 The Sententialist Account

Let us now consider a sententialist account of the adverb facts. For the sententialist, the class of fully intensional adverbs is fairly straightforward in so far as all of these forms have counterpart predicates taking a clausal complement (33*a*–*c*). Notice that in each case the verbal material corresponds to material *inside* the clausal complement—that is, to material in an intensional

---

[13] For a postulate of this kind, see Dowty *et al.* (1981:) 234, who attribute it to Bennett (1974).

environment on the sententialist account. Hence we expect the observed intensionality effects.

(33)   *a.*   (i) Olga **allegedly** dances.
       (ii) Ivan **alleges** that Olga dances.
   b.   (i) DeKok **supposedly** met a pick-pocket.
       (ii) It is **supposed** that DeKok met a pick-pocket.
   c.   (i) Rudolph was dancing in **Natasha's dream**.
       (ii) Natasha **dreamed** that Rudolph was dancing.

The general lines of the sententialist analysis are therefore clear: the (i) cases of (33*a–c*) should all be analyzed as involving a clausal complement to the adverb.

Interestingly, under current syntactic proposals, VP adverbs do in fact have a clause-like object as their complement. Kitagawa (1986), Kuroda (1988), Koopman and Sportiche (1991) and Chomsky (1995) have argued that in underlying form, all arguments of a verb, including the subject, originate within the verb phrase. Thus (34*a*), for instance, is analyzed as in (34*b*), where the subject *Max* begins inside VP and where the subject position is initially empty (*e*). *Max* subsequently raises out of VP to its surface position (34*c*):

(34)   *a.*   Max will probably eat spinach
       b.   e   will probably [$_{VP}$ Max eat spinach]
       c.   Max will probably [$_{VP}$ t   eat spinach]

This analysis entails that modals like *will*, and VP adverbs like *probably*, *supposedly*, *allegedly*, attach to a structure that is semantically clausal, in so far as it contains a verb and all its arguments. There is thus no barrier to regarding these adverbs as clausal-complement taking in the semantic sense.[14]

The sententialist analysis can also be extended to certain of the adverbs that we have identified as partially intensional. Recall that forms like *intentionally*, *reluctantly*, and *willingly* block substitution of coextensive forms

---

[14] Note that the raising analysis also suggests how the subject in a sentence like (i*a*) can behave intentionally:

(i)   *a.*   A unicorn   allegedly   gored Max.
      b.   te   allegedly   [$_{VP}$ a unicorn gored Max]
      c.   A unicorn   allegedly   [$_{VP}$ t   gored Max]

On the raising account, the subject actually begins within the scope of the adverb (i*b, c*), and presumably retains its option of being interpreted in that position.

and permit a nonspecific reading of an indefinite, but do not combine with a nondenoting predicate to yield a truth. Interestingly, there is a class of clause-taking predicates with very similar properties. Consider the pair *believe* and *regret* and their behavior as illustrated in (35*a–c*):

(35) *a.* (i) Max believes/regrets that **Boris Karloff** is unavailable.
            (ii) Max believes/regrets that **Bill Pratt** is unavailable.
      b.   Max believes/regrets that **a Norwegian** was involved.
      c. (i) Max believes that **a unicorn** is approaching.
            (ii) Max regrets that **a unicorn** is approaching.

Notice that both verbs block substitution of *Bill Pratt* for the coextensive term *Boris Karloff.* Max can believe or regret the unavailability of the one without believing or regretting the unavailability of the other (35*a*). Note also that both support a nonspecific reading for the indefinite *a Norwegian*: the truth of (35*b*) does not require there to be any particular Norwegian that Max has beliefs or regrets about. Interestingly, however, *believe* and *regret* part company when their complement contains a nondenoting predicate. Although (35*c*(i)) can be true despite the real-world absence of unicorns, (35*c*(ii)) cannot be true. Max cannot regret the approach of a unicorn if there are no unicorns in the world. The departure from full intensional behavior with verbs like *regret* is generally analyzed by saying that *regret* (unlike *believe*) presupposes the truth of its complement. Thus for any S, regretting S presupposes the truth of S. Clause-taking verbs having this behavior are called 'factives' (Kiparsky and Kiparsky 1971). Other factive verbs include *know,* *understand*, and *accept.*

Under a sentential analysis of intensional adverbs, we might expect forms parallel to *believe* and *regret.* That is, we might expect adverbs like *allegedly,* which show fully intensional behavior parallel to *believe.* But we might also expect adverbs showing partially intensional behavior like *regret*; these would block substitution and permit nonspecificity, but would yield falsity with a nondenoting predicate, given their factivity. Adverbs like *intentionally, reluctantly,* and *willingly* are obvious candidates. It is natural to take these forms to be the adverbial counterparts of verbs like *regret*, which are intensional but presuppose the truth of their complement. Under this proposal, we would require no separate extensionalizing postulate like (32*a*) for these forms.[15]

---

[15] If the factivity of verbs like *regret* is a matter of presupposition, and not entailment, and if *regret* and *willingly*-class adverbs are to be treated in parallel, then in fact we do not want a postulate like (32*a*).

Rather, the account of factivity for them would simply fall together with that of forms like *regret, know, understand,* etc.[16]

These remarks suggest that a sententialist analysis can handle fully intensional adverbs in a way that is syntactically and semantically plausible, and that it can also handle partially intensional adverbs like *intentionally,* Ireluctantly and *willingly* by analyzing them as clause-taking factives. On reflection, however, one class of adverbs remains problematic for the claim that intensionality is tied to clausal complementation. This is the class of adverbs like *beautifully, skillfully,* and *at three o'clock.* The latter do not have a plausible sententialist analysis in so far as they do not appear to relate an individual to a proposition. On the other hand they do *appear* to show intensional behavior in so far as they block substitution of coextensive terms. The account of this behavior in an intensionalist account like Montague's is the same as that given earlier for *allegedly;* substitution failure is attributed to the presence of the intensional operator:

(36) *a.* Suppose: $\{x: x \text{ dances}\} = \{x: x \text{ sings}\}$
        Then: *Olga dances.* $\leftrightarrow$ *Olga sings.*
        But: *Olga dances beautifully.* $\leftarrow / \rightarrow$ *Olga sings beautifully.*
    b. Analysis: **beautifully**$'(^\wedge$**dance**$')(o) \leftarrow / \rightarrow$ **beautifully**$'(^\wedge$**sing**$')(o)$

If the sententialist position is to be maintained, the intensional account of substitution failure in (36) must be shown to be wrong, and an alternative account of substitution failure must be found. In other words, the sententialist

---

[16] Partee notes the factivity of VP adverbs like *intentionally, reluctantly,* and *willingly,* but questions a sententialist analysis of them given that they seem to lack an adequate clausal paraphrase. She writes (1974: 91): 'On the [sententialist] alternative, the problem is to find a suitable paraphrase to serve as the underlying form ... I am convinced that no such suitable paraphrases exist ...' The point seems to me to beg the question of what constitutes a clause. Modern grammatical theory recognizes a spectrum of clausal complements including full, tensed finite clauses (i*a*), subjunctives (i*b*), independent infinitives (i*c*), so-called 'ECM infinitives' (i*d*), and 'small clauses' (i*e*), among others. These clausal complement types are not readily, or regularly paraphrasable one with another:

(i) *a.* Max said [that she was on the boat].
    b. Max insisted [that she be on the boat].
    c. Max wanted [(for) her to be on the boat].
    d. Max believed [her to be on the boat].
    e. Max needed [her on the boat].

In the account suggested here, VP adverbs like *allegedly* and *willingly* combine with the equivalent of a VP small clause. There is thus no greater expectation that they will have, say, finite-clause paraphrases than there is that (i*e*) will have such a paraphrase (cf. **Max needed that she was on the boat.*).

must show that it wrong to invoke the same mechanism to explaining substitution failure with *dance/sing allegedly* versus *dance/sing beautifully*. And a better account must be offered.

3.3 More on Substitution Failure

McConnell-Ginet (1982) supplies the first demonstration, providing two simple but compelling reasons for rejecting the Montagovian intensional analysis of substitution failure with adverbs like *beautifully* and *quickly*.[17]

3.3.1 *Substitution Failure does Not Entail Intensionality*

Consider the argument and analysis given in (37), parallel to (36). Suppose the sets of individuals who eat and cook are identical, so that Olga eats iff Olga cooks. Under this assumption, it still does not follow that Olga eats fish iff Olga cooks fish. Reasoning as before our diagnosis would be that the object combines with the verb as function to argument, invoking intensions (37*b*):

(37) *a.* Suppose: $\{x: x \text{ eats}\} = \{x: x \text{ cooks}\}$
   Then: *Olga eats.* ↔ *Olga cooks.*
   But: *Olga eats fish.* ← / → *Olga cooks fish.*
   b. Analysis: $\mathbf{fish}'(^{\wedge}\mathbf{eat}')(o)$ ← / → $\mathbf{fish}'(^{\wedge}\mathbf{cook}')(o)$

But we do *not* give this analysis in fact. Rather, we attribute substitution failure to a relationality in *eat* and *cook* that is concealed in the simple intransitive absolute forms (38*a*, *b*). If *eat* and *cook* are reanalyzed as transitive, then the inference pattern in (37*a*) is predicted on simple first-order grounds. (39*a*) does not entail (39*b*), but intensions have nothing to do with it:

(38) *a.* eat(x,y)
   b. cook(x,y)
(39) *a.* $\forall x \, [\exists y[\text{eat}(x,y)] \leftrightarrow \exists y[\text{cook}(x,y)]]$ 'Whoever eats cooks'
   b. $\forall x \, [\text{eat}(x,\text{fish}) \leftrightarrow \text{cook}(x,\text{fish})]$ 'Whoever eats fish cooks fish'

---

[17] The discussion in this section and the following ones is adapted from Larson (1998, in prep.), which contains a fuller presentation of the ideas discussed here.

The first point is thus that substitution failure is not a transparent diagnostic for intensionality. Logic allows for different sources of entailment failure in such cases. Hidden relationality, in particular, is an alternative source.[18]

3.3.2 *Intensionality does Not Track our Intuitions about the Cases*

McConnell-Ginet's second point can be seen by comparing the two cases of substitution failure given in (40*a*) and (41*a*), the analyses suggested for them, and the intuitive correctness of these analyses given how we actually reason with the cases.

(40) *a.* Suppose: {x: x dances} = x: x sings
Then: *Olga dances.* $\leftrightarrow$ *Olga sings.*
But: *Max thinks Olga dances.* $\leftarrow$ / $\rightarrow$ *Max thinks Olga sings.*
b. Analysis: $\mathbf{think'(m, {}^\wedge dance'(o))} \leftarrow / \rightarrow \mathbf{think'(m, {}^\wedge sing'(o))}$

(41) *a.* Suppose: {x: x eats} = x: x cooks
Then: *Olga eats.* $\leftrightarrow$ *Olga cooks.*
But: *Olga eats fish.* $\leftarrow$ / $\rightarrow$ *Olga cooks fish.*
b. Analysis: $\mathbf{eat'(o,f)} \leftarrow / \rightarrow \mathbf{cook'(o,f)}$

An informal account of the lack of entailment in (40*a*) might go as follows: 'Even if the dancers and singers happen to coincide in this world, in the world of Max's thoughts the two sets might well diverge. So, thinking that the one predicate is true of Olga might very well be different than thinking that the other is true of her.' Here we are using the idea of worlds compatible with the beliefs of the subject (Max). The appeal to alternative worlds offers a plausible model of why speakers judge the inference to fail.

By contrast, substitution failure in (41*a*) arises from an intuitively different source. It is not a matter of what *eats* and *cooks* might have meant in alternative circumstances. Rather there is a hidden dimension in the predicates. 'Look,' we might say, 'whenever there is eating, there is eating *of something*. Likewise whenever there is cooking, there is cooking *of something*. And even if all the same people eat and cook, it still needn't be true that any of them eats and cooks the same thing.' Here our explanation does not appeal to potential extensions in alternative worlds; rather it analyzes the predicate more finely in this world.

---

[18] Intensionality may be looked at as hidden relationality if object-language predicates are relativized to possible worlds (e.g. dancer(x,w) 'dancer in world w'). In this case the point would be that hidden dimension made available by possible worlds semantics is not the correct one for accounting for substitution failure with adjectival modification.

Now reconsider the adverbial entailment paradigm in (36), and our intuitions about why substitution fails. Interestingly, as McConnell-Ginet observes, they do *not* seem to involve thinking about who *dance* and *sing* might have applied to in alternative circumstances, but rather to hidden relationality. 'Look,' we might say, 'whenever there is dancing and singing there is *a performance*. And even if the same people dance and sing, the performances are still different. And one might be beautiful, and the other not.' Reasoning this way, we follow the model of (41), and not the model of (40).

The second point is thus the following: for the cases at hand, an intensional analysis of substitution failure in adverbial modification (unlike an intensional analysis of substitution failure in clausal complements) does not correctly track our intuition about *why* inference fails. Not only does logic provide us with alternative means of understanding why substitution fails, the alternative seems to offer a better model of how we actually reason in these cases.

3.4 Davidson's Analysis of Adverbial Modification

Davies (1991) rediscovered McConnell-Ginet's points about substitution failure with adverbials, but put the issue in a stronger form. Davies notes that the lack of entailment from *sang beautifully* to *danced beautifully* holds not only if singers and dancers happen to be the same, but even if they are *necessarily* the same. Even if singers and dancers coincided in all possible worlds, it still would not follow intuitively that singing beautifully would entail dancing beautifully, or vice versa.

Davies (1991) goes on to make an interesting proposal based on Davidson's 1967 theory of adverbial modification. On Davidson's view, action verbs like *sing* and *dance* are not simple one-place, intransitive predicates. Rather they are relational, containing an extra argument place for an event e (42*a*, *b*). Adverbs relate to verbs by being predicated of the events that verbs introduce. *Olga danced beautifully* and *Olga sang beautifully* are rendered approximately as in (42*c*, *d*):[19]

---

[19] These formulae are simplified in numerous ways, ignoring, e.g., the contribution of tense. The adjective *beautiful* is rendered as 'beautiful(x, C)' to include a comparison class parameter C; the latter corresponds to the contribution made by a *for*-PP in an example like *Mary dances beautifully for a twelve year old*. The analysis of comparison classes is discussed in detail by Wheeler (1972) and Platts (1979). The Davidsonian analysis of adverbial modification has been elaborated by many authors, most notably by Parsons (1980, 1985, 1990).

(42) *a.* dancing(e,x)   *c.* ∃e[dancing(olga,e) & beautiful(e, C)]
      b. singing(e,x)   *d.* ∃e[singing(olga,e) & beautiful(e, C)]

Davies observed that, by articulating these predicates more finely to include an event parameter, Davidson correctly predicts substitution failure when adverbs are attached, even if the singers and dancers happen to be the same—indeed, even if singers and dancers are necessarily the same. Thus (43*a*) does not entail (43*b*):

(43) *a.* ∀x [∃e[dancing(e,x)] ↔ ∃e[singing(e,x)]]
      b. ∀x[∃e[dancing(e,x) & beautiful(e,C)] ↔ ∃e[singing(e,x) & beautiful(e,C)]

Since the respective events are different, that one is beautiful will not entail that the other is so. This prediction follows on simple first order grounds, without appeal to intensions, or reference to alternative worlds.

Davidson's analysis is highly attractive in so far as it explains failures of substitution along just the lines that McConnell-Ginet suggests: by detecting an additional dimension in the semantic structure of the predicate. But note that if it is correct, this analysis supplies the alternative account of substitution failure needed by the sententialist. Under the Davidsonian account, appeal to intensionality in explaining substitution failure with adverbs like *beautifully, skillfully, quickly,* etc. represents a misdiagnosis of what is going on. Failures of substitution in these environments are *not* a matter of intensionality. Rather, they issue from a completely different source: from hidden relationality in the predicate—the presence of an event coordinate. Adverbial modification thus appears to present no serious threat to the sententialist position that intensionality is a phenomenon associated with clausal complements. Genuine cases of intensionality in adverbial modification arguably involve clauses; and adverbial modification with no relation to clauses is nonintensional after all.

4.0 Intensionality in Adjectival Modification

Let us now turn to Montague's third purported case of nonclausal intensionality: adjectival modification. The considerations here turn out to be almost exactly parallel to those involving adverbs, both in terms of data and analysis. With regard to the basic data, the range of cases again appears to divide into a class of *fully intensional adjectives* and two classes of *partially intensional adjectives*: one counterpart to *willingly/reluc-tantly*-type adverbs, and one counterpart to *beautifully/skillfully*-type adverbs.

Fully intensional adjectives show the complete range of intensionality effects when combined with a noun (44*a–c*).

(44) *a.* Olga is an **alleged** dancer.
    b. Alice is an **imagined** werewolf.
    c. Boris is a **supposed** perpetrator of a crime.

Substitution of coextensive predicates can fail to preserve truth; if the dancers and singers are the same, it will follow that, if Olga is a dancer, she is a singer. But this will not entail that if Olga is an alleged dancer, she is an alleged singer. Likewise, the presence of a nondenoting predicate may fail to induce falsity. *Alice is imagined werewolf* can be true despite the fact that *werewolf* is (we hope) nondenoting. Finally, an indefinite in the scope of the adjective need not receive a specific interpretation. If Boris is a supposed perpetrator of a crime, it does not follow that there is a particular crime that Boris has been supposed to commit.

(45*a–c*) illustrate the partially intensional adjectives that are counterpart to *intentionally*, *reluctantly*, and *willingly*.

(45) *a.* Max made an **intentional** mistake.
    b. Olga was a **reluctant** dancer.
    c. Boris was a **willing** perpetrator of a crime.

Like the corresponding adverbs, these forms block substitution; if Olga is a reluctant dancer she is not necessarily a reluctant singer, even if singers and dancers are the same. Likewise these adjectives license a nonspecific indefinite in their scope: Boris can be a willing perpetrator of a crime without there being a particular crime that he willingly committed. He simply might enjoy acting illegally. But unlike the fully intensional adjectives, forms of this class cannot combine with a nondenoting predicate to yield a truth; *Alice is a reluctant levitator* cannot be true given that there are no individuals that levitate.

Finally, (46*a–c*) illustrate the second class of partially intensional adjectives, which are the counterparts of adverbs like *beautifully*, *skillfully*, *quickly*, etc. Some care must be taken here, since attributive adjectives of this kind are often ambiguous between what are termed 'intersective' and 'non-intersective' readings; thus (46*a*) has the two readings paraphrased informally in (47*a, b*):

(46) *a.* Olga is a **beautiful** dancer.
    b. Kathrin is a **skillful** manager.
    c. Peter is an **old** friend.

(47) *a.* 'Olga is a dancer and Olga is beautiful'   (intersective)
    b. 'Olga is beautiful as a dancer'/'Olga dances beautifully' (nonintersective)

On the first reading, *beautiful* applies to Olga; she herself is beautiful, even if her dancing is awkward. On the second reading, *beautiful* applies to Olga *qua* dancer; Olga's dancing is beautiful even if she herself is unattractive. Similarly, (46*b*) can mean that Kathrin is a manager and a skillful person—the intersective reading; alternatively it can mean that she is skillful as a manager or that she manages skillfully—the nonintersective reading. Likewise, (46*c*) can mean that Peter is a friend who is old or aged; or it can mean that Peter is a friend of long standing.

(46*a–c*), *on their nonintersective readings*, exhibit the partial intensional behavior of their corresponding adverbs. Thus there is failure of substitution with coextensive predicates; if Olga is a beautiful dancer (on the nonintersective reading) then she is not necessarily a beautiful singer (on the non-intersective reading), even if the singers and dancers are the same. On the other hand, combination with a nondenoting predicate does not yield truth: *Alice is a skillful levitator* cannot be true if there are no people that levitate. And indefinites cannot receive a nonspecific reading within their scope. To my intuitions, if *Boris is a skillful perpetrator of a crime* is true, there must be a crime that he skillfully perpetrated.

4.1 The Intensionalist Analysis

Montague's intensionalist account of the adjective facts is exactly parallel to that of the adverbial cases: combining an adjective with a noun invokes the intensional operator.[20] The presence of "^" blocks substitution with all three kinds of adjectives (48):

(48) *a.* Suppose: {x: x dances} = {x: x sings}
    Then: *Olga is a dancer.* ↔ *Olga is a singer.*
    But: *Olga is an alleged dancer.* ← / → *is an alleged singer.*

---

[20]   See Siegel (1976*a*, 1976*b*) for the most detailed account of adjectival modification within the Montagovian framework.

> Olga is a reluctant dancer. ← / → is a reluctant singer.
> Olga is a beautiful dancer. ← / → is a beautiful singer.

    b. Analysis: **alleged**$'(^{\wedge}$**dancer**$')($o$) ← / → **alleged**$'(^{\wedge}$**singer**$')(o)
            reluctant$'(^{\wedge}$**dancer**$')($o$) ←/→ **reluctant**$'(^{\wedge}$**singer**$')(o)
            beautiful$'(^{\wedge}$**dancer**$')($o$) ←/→ **beautiful**$'(^{\wedge}$**singer**$')(o)

The intensional operator also blocks exportation of a quantifier from its scope, accounting for the availability of a nonspecific indefinite with adjectives like *supposed* and *willing* (49):[21]

    (49)   *a.* *Boris is a supposed perpetrator of a crime.* ⇒
            supposed$'(^{\wedge}\lambda y[\exists x[$**crime**$'$ (x) ∧**perpetrate**$_*'$ (y,x)]] $)$ (**b**)
        b. *Boris is a willing perpetrator of a crime.* ⇒
            willing$'(^{\wedge}\lambda y[\exists x[$**crime**$'$ (x) ∧ **perpetrate**$_*'$ (y,x)]]$)$ (**b**)

Finally, the fact that partially intensional adjectives yield a falsity when combined with a nondenoting predicate is also taken to follow from an independent fact about their meanings. Adjectives like *intentional* and *beautiful* are assumed to fall under the semantic postulate (50a), which stipulates that an adjectivally modified noun (Adj$'$ (N)) holds of an individual x, only if the unmodified predicate holds of x. Thus *Olga is a skillful levitator* can be true only if *Olga is a levitator* is itself true, contrary to fact (50b):

    (50)   *a.* $\forall x \forall \Pi \Box [(Adj'(^{\wedge}N)(x) \rightarrow (N)(x)]$
        b. $\Box [($**skillful**$'(^{\wedge}$**levitator**$')$ $)($o$) \rightarrow ($**levitator**$')($o$)]$

Postulate (50a) thus is completely parallel to (32a), and has the same semantic function.

4.2 The Sententialist Analysis

The natural move for the sententialist is also to give an account of the adjective facts that parallels his/her account of adverbs. However, this requires some interesting extensions of current thinking. Consider the case of fully intensional adjectives. We suggested a sententialist analysis of their corresponding adverbs in which the latter combined with a clause-like VP: one that contained both subject and predicate. To duplicate this idea, we would evidently need to

---

[21] The fact that adjectives like *skillful* class do not license a nonspecific indefinite is undiscussed in the literature to my knowledge, and in fact constitutes a problem for the account.

view the nominal in cases like *alleged dancer* as containing a subject, which, for concreteness, we might construe as a silent pronoun (*pro*) (cf. (34)):[22]

(51) *a.* Olga interviewed an **alleged** [$_{NP}$ *pro* dancer].
'Olga interviewed an x such that it is alleged that x is a dancer'
b. DeKok arrested the **supposed** [$_{NP}$ *pro* perpetrator of a crime].
'DeKok arrested the x such that it is supposed that x is a perpetrator of a crime'
c. Alice talked to an **imagined** [$_{NP}$ *pro* werewolf].
'Alice talked to an x such that it is imagined that x is a werewolf'

A similar view must be extended to partially intensional adjectives like *willing, reluctant,* and *intentional.* These must be analyzed as taking a clause-like complement, with the further proviso that the latter is interpreted factively.

(52) *a.* Olga interviewed a **reluctant** [$_{NP}$ *pro* dancer].
'Olga interviewed an x such that x was a dancer and x was reluctant to dance/be a dancer'
b. DeKok arrested a **willing** [$_{NP}$ *pro* accomplice to a crime].
'DeKok arrested an x such that x was an accomplice and x was reluctant to be an accomplice'

That is, if an individual is a reluctant dancer, then they must be reluctant to dance/be a dancer, but they must also be a dancer. And so, once again, we may assume that the account of factivity with these clause-taking predicates falls together with that of cases like *regret* and *know.*

These extensions of the sententialist adverbial analysis are nontrivial, but still plausible and largely straightforward. More interesting questions arise in the sententialist account of adjectives like *beautiful, skillful,* and *quick.* As in the case of their adverbs, these forms do not have a plausible 'hidden clause' analysis. On the other hand, as we saw, they do block substitution of coextensive terms, an apparent intensional behavior. In the case of the adverbs, substitution failures were reanalyzed as arising from the presence of a David-

---

[22] Following the point in n. 14, it appears we must also be prepared to view *a unicorn* in a sentence like (i*a*) as raising from the subject position in the nominal, given that it manifests intensional behavior:

(i) *a.* A unicorn   is the alleged perpetrator.
b. e   is the alleged   [$_{NP}$ a unicorn perpetrator]
c. A unicorn   is the alleged   [$_{NP}$ t perpetrator]

The view that nominals are sentence-like has been recently argued by Heim (1996) on grounds very different to those considered here.

sonian event argument with which the adverbs semantically combined. If the sententialist position is to be maintained, we are led to seek a similar account of the adjectival modification facts in this case.

4.3 A Davidsonian Analysis of Nonintersective Adjectival Semantics

Larson (1995, 1998) argues that substitution failure between *beautiful dancer* and *beautiful singer* (on their nonintersective readings) should be assimilated to substitution failure between *dance beautifully* and *sing beautifully*. That is, we should import Davidson's event analysis of adverbial modification to adjectives, reproducing the basic technical moves. The analysis incorporates the following three technical proposals:

- The semantics of (at least certain) common nouns involves an event argument.[23]
- Adjectives are potential predicates of events.
- In an A–N structure, A may be predicated of an individual or an event.

These points are illustrated in (53a–c), which employ the relational evaluation predicate from Larson and Segal (1995):[24]

(53) a. $\text{Val}(<x,e>, \textit{dancer})$ iff dancing(e,x)
      b. $\text{Val}(x, \textit{beautiful})$ iff beautiful(x, C) ('x is beautiful for a C')
      c. $\text{Val}(<x,e>, [_{NP} \text{ AP NP}])$ iff $\text{Val}(<x,e>, \text{NP})$ & $\text{Val}(x, \text{AP})$
          $\text{Val}(<x,e>, [_{NP} \text{ AP NP}])$ iff $\text{Val}(<x,e>, \text{NP})$ & $\text{Val}(e, \text{AP})$

(53a) takes the nominal *dancer* to apply to pairs of individuals $<x,e>$ such that x is the agent of e, where e is a dancing. (53b) takes adjectives like *beautiful* to be predicates of things. More exactly, *beautiful* is true of an individual x just in case x is beautiful relative to some comparison class C, which I will assume here to be given by context, but which may also be given by an explicit *for*-PP. Finally, (53c) gives candidate rules for combining an AP with the nominal it modifies. According to these schemata, when an adjective (AP) combines with a noun (NP) denoting an event–individual pair, the adjective can be predicated of either the x parameter or the e parameter.

[23] Event modification in nominals is explored in Larson (1983) within the Situation Semantics framework of Barwise and Perry (1983). See also Higginbotham (1985).

[24] A relational valuation predicate departs from the usual valuation function "[[ ]]" of model theory. Relational valuation is adopted in Situation Semantics (see Barwise and Perry, 1983; Larson, 1983).

In Larson (1995, 1998) and Larson and Segal (1995), the possibility of being predicated of either x or e is diagnosed as the source of the intersective/nonintersective ambiguity in cases like *beautiful dancer*. When AP is predicated of the x variable, it is the subject Olga, the dancer, that is ultimately asserted to be beautiful (54a). By contrast, when AP is predicated of the e variable, it is the event, the dancing, that is asserted to be beautiful (54b). A similar analysis can be given for *old friend* as indicated in (55).[25]

(54)   Olga is a beautiful dancer.
    a. ∃e[dancing(e,olga) & beautiful(olga,C)]   ('Olga is beautiful')
    b. ∃e[dancing(e,olga) & beautiful(e,C)]   ('Dancing is beautiful')

(55)   Peter is an old friend.
    a. ∃e[friendship(e,p) & old(pete,C)]   ('Peter is old')
    b. ∃e[friendship(e,p) & old(e,C)]   ('The friendship is old')

This account yields an analysis of substitution failure with nonintersective adjectives that is fully parallel to the case of adverbs discussed earlier. Even if singers and dancers are the same, the events of dancing and singing will be different. Since the respective events are different, that one is beautiful will not entail that the other is so. This prediction follows on simple first order grounds, without appeal to intensions or possible worlds.

4.4 Other Consequences

Larson (1995, 1998) argues that this approach not only yields a satisfactory nonintensional account of substitution failure with adjectives, but illuminates a variety of other phenomena as well. Thus, the approach offers some grasp on why it is that certain adjectives (such as *beautiful*) show both an intersective and a nonintersective reading, whereas other adjectives show exclusively one or the other. For example, consider an adjectives like *aged, nude, portable,* and *tall,* which are exclusively intersective. It seems plausible to think that events cannot be aged in view of the fact that they do not age. Nor can they be nude, portable, or tall. If this is granted, then we correctly predict an example like (56), *Jerry is an aged president,* to be unambiguous. This is so because one of the

[25] For simplicity, (54) and (55) are rendered using an existential quantifier. A more correct analysis would involve generic quantification and a generic quantifier. See Larson (1998, in prep.) for details.

two possible interpretations, 'aged(e)', is independently excluded on pragmatic grounds.

(56) Jerry is an aged president.   #∃e[presidency(e,j) & **aged(e,C)**]
                                     ∃e[presidency(e,j) & aged(j,C)]

By contrast, consider an adjective like *former*, which is exclusively nonintersective. It is natural to think that *former* applies strictly to events and not to other kinds of things. If so, then we correctly predict that *Jerry is a former president* will be unambiguous, since we can have 'former(e)' but not 'former(jerry)' (57):

(57) Jerry is a former president.   ∃e[presidency(e,j) & former(e,C)]
                                     #∃e[presidency(e,j) & **former(jerry,C)**]

The general situation is thus as shown in the diagram, with some adjectives applying strictly to non-events (*aged*), others applying strictly to events (*former*), and still others applying naturally to both, yielding ambiguity (*beautiful*).

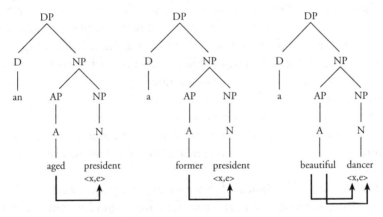

This view also allows us to capture the observation by Vendler (1967) that coordination cannot join a strictly intersective adjective (*blonde*) with a strictly nonintersective adjective (*fast*) (58a). Correlatively, when an adjective that can be read either way (*beautiful*) is co-ordinated with a strictly intersective adjective, it must be read intersectively (58b), and when it is co-ordinated with a strictly nonintersective adjective, it must be read nonintersectively (58c).

(58) *a.* *She is a blonde and fast dancer.
     b. She is a blonde and beautiful dancer.
     c. She is a fast and beautiful dancer.

These results follow under a simple co-ordination rule like (59), according to which an object x is a value of conjoined APs just in case it is a value of both conjuncts:

(59) Val(x, [$_{AP}$ AP1 *and* AP2]) iff Val(x, AP1) & Val(x, AP2)

This rule entails that both adjectives in a conjoined pair must be predicated of an event, or of a non-event, but that the predications cannot be 'mixed'.

These results show, I believe, that a Davidsonian analysis of nonintersective modification not only yields a plausible alternative view of substitution failure with adjectival modifiers. It also offers an analysis that is attractive on its own independent grounds. In summary, then, our conclusions about adjectives are the same as our conclusions about adverbs: adjectival modification presents no insurmountable threat to the sententialist thesis.

5.0 If Sententialism is Correct, *Why* is it Correct?

We have considered two positions on intensionality, and its representation in grammar. One holds that intensionality is a semantic phenomenon arising exclusively with propositional attitude predicates and clausal complements. On the sententialist view, intensionality is always the hallmark of a sentential environment, no matter how well-hidden by surface form. A nonclausal environment may mimic the effects of intensionality, for example, by blocking substitution of apparently coextensive predicates, as with adverbs and adjectives. But for the sententialist, this behavior must inevitably be exposed as a sham, and as issuing from a fundamentally different source, such as hidden relationality.

The second position holds that intensionality is a perfectly general phenomenon arising as a matter of course with function–argument combination. On this view, intensional behavior is the default expectation and should be observable throughout the grammar, including in environments that cannot be analyzed as involving clausal complementation. Forms may possess individual lexical properties that block full expression of intensional behavior, for example, by being subject to special postulates as in the case of adverbs and adjectives. But these properties simply occlude an underlyingly intensional reality.

I have reviewed three cases of where intensionality in nonclausal environments has been claimed, in support of the second view: intensional transitive verbs, adverbial modifiers, and adjectival modifiers. The results, although tentative, are the following: in each case where intensional behavior is plainly manifest, there is plausibly an underlying clausal syntax. And in cases where clausal syntax cannot plausibly be attributed, we have indications that there is no intensionality after all.

These results suggest that sententialism may be on the right track after all. If so, they raise another simple question: if sententialism is correct, why is it correct? Why should clausal complements be associated uniquely with intensionality effects? I will declare straightaway that I do not have an answer, and obvious proposals are quickly refuted.

Consider, for example, the idea that the association between clauses and intensionality reflects a basic fact about the mapping of syntax to semantics. Suppose, for example, contra Montague, that intensional operators are *not* freely introduced in all function–argument combination, but rather are associated with certain specific grammatical formatives. In current syntactic theory, complement clauses are typically assigned the category 'CP' which is taken to project from a *complementizer* element (C)—a clause introducing items like *that*, *for*, or *if*.

(60) *a.* Max asked [$_{CP}$ **that** a unicorn be present].
      b. Max asked [$_{CP}$ **for** a unicorn to be present].
      c. Max asked [$_{CP}$ **if** a unicorn would be present].

Given this point, one might speculate that the operator responsible for intensionality is associated specifically with items of the lexical category C, and hence not introducible except in the context of clauses. Such an idea is not implausible. Compare the situation with natural language tenses, which are frequently analyzed semantically in terms of Priorean sentential operators like P ('past') and F ('future'). Tense is not freely introducible in the course of semantic composition, but rather seems to be associated in a very narrow way with elements belonging to the specific syntactic category, usually designated 'T' (for 'Tense'). If intensional operators like P and F are tied by the grammar to a specific syntactic environment, it is not unreasonable to suppose that the intensional operator $^\wedge$ might be tied to a specific syntactic environment as well.

Although attractively simple, this idea seems unlikely to be correct. The difficulty is that the range of clausal environments yielding intensionality does not appear reducible to a single syntactic environment like CP. We can observe this with ECM infinitives and small clause complements, as illustrated in (61*a*, *b*), respectively. These structures are clause-like, and are intensional environments by the usual tests. But, according to modern syntactic theory at least, they are smaller than full CPs. Chomsky (1998), for example, analyzes the former as defective tense projections (TP), and the latter as projections of their contained predicates (AP, in this case):

(61) *a.* Max believes [$_{TP}$ Boris Karloff to be on his veranda].
     b. Max considers [$_{AP}$ unicorns dangerous].

We have also seen the point in connection with intensional adverbs like *allegedly* and adjectives like *alleged*. We analyzed these as combining with a predicate (VP) and a nominal (NP) (62*a*, *b*):

(62) *a.* Boris allegedly [$_{VP}$ t stole the money].
     b. Alice met an alleged [$_{NP}$ pro thief].

The latter were clause-like in so far as they contained a predicate and all of its arguments. But it seems clear that the clausal category involved is considerably smaller than a full CP.

Since no articulated theory presents itself as to why intensionality should be associated with clausal environments, we are left with a mystery. None the less, the points rehearsed above suggest that the mystery is in fact a genuine one: that the association is a real one and therefore something that needs to be explained.

REFERENCES

Aissen, J., and Perlmutter, D. (1983). 'Clause Reduction in Spanish', in D. Perlmutter (ed.), *Studies in Relational Grammar 1* (Chicago: University of Chicago Press), 360–403.

Baker, M. (1988). *Incorporation: A Theory of Grammatical Function Changing* (Chicago: University of Chicago Press).

Barwise, J., and Perry, J. (1983). *Situations and Attitudes* (Cambridge, Mass.: MIT Press).

Bennett, M. (1974). 'Some Extensions of a Montague Fragment of English' (Ph.D. thesis, UCLA).

Burzio, L. (1986). *Italian Syntax* (Dordrecht: D. Reidel).

Chomsky, N. (1975). *Reflections on Language* (New York: Pantheon).

——(1986). *Knowledge of Language: Its Nature, Origin and Use* (New York: Praeger).

——(1995). *The Minimalist Program* (Cambridge, Mass.: MIT Press).

Davidson, D. (1967). 'The Logical Form of Action Sentences', in N. Rescher (ed.), *The Logic of Decision and Action* (Pittsburgh: University of Pittsburgh Press), 81–120.

Davies, M. (1991). 'Acts and Scenes', in N. Cooper and P. Engel (eds.), *New Enquiries into Meaning and Truth* (Hemel Hempstead: Harvester Wheatsheaf), 41–82.

Den Dikken, M., Larson, R., and Ludlow, P. (1996). 'Intensional "Transitive" Verbs and Concealed Complement Clauses', *Rivisita di linguistica*, 8: 29–46.

Dowty, D. (1979). *Word Meaning and Montague Grammar* (Dordrecht: D. Reidel).

—— Wall, R., and Peters, S. (1981). *Introduction to Montague Semantics* (Dordrecht: D. Reidel).

Frege, G. (1893). 'Über Sinn und Bedeutung', *Zeitschrift für Philosophie und Philosophische Kritik, 100*: 25–50. Translated as Frege 1952.

—— (1952). 'On Sense and Reference', in *Translation from the Philosophical Writings of Gottlob Frege*, ed. P. Geach and M. Black (Oxford: Basil Blackwell), 56–78.

Heim, I. (1996). 'Semantic Types for Syntactic Categories: Evidence from Ellipsis', talk delivered at UT-Austin, 25. Nov.

Higginbotham, J. (1985) 'On Semantics', *Linguistic Inquiry*, 16: 547–93.

Karttunen, L. (1976). 'Discourse Referents', in J. McCawley (ed.), *Syntax and Semantics 7: Notes from the Linguistic Underground* (New York: Academic Press), 363–85.

Kiparsky, P., and Kiparsky, C. (1971). 'Fact', in D. Steinberg and L. Jakobovits (eds.), *Semantics: An Interdisciplinary Reader in Philosophy, Linguistics and Psychology* (Cambridge: Cambridge University Press), 345–69.

Kitagawa, Y. (1986). 'Subject in Japanese and English' (Ph.D. diss., University of Massachusetts-Amherst, Amherst, Mass.).

Koopman, H., and Sportiche, D. (1991). 'The Position of Subjects', *Lingua*, 85: 211–59.

Kuroda, S.-Y. (1988). 'Whether we Agree or Not: A Comparative Syntax of English and Japanese', *Linguisticae Investigationes*, 12: 1–47.

Larson, R. (1983). 'Restrictive Modification' (Ph.D. diss., University of Wisconsin, Madison, Wis.).

—— (1995). 'Olga is a Beautiful Dancer', paper presented at the Winter Meetings of the Linguistic Society of America, New Orleans.

—— (1998). 'Events and Modification in Nominals', in D. Strolovitch and A. Lawson (eds.), *Proceedings from Semantics and Linguistic Theory VIII (SALT 8)* (Ithaca, NY: Cornell University), 145–68.

—— (in prep.). *A Theory of Adjectival Modification.*

—— and Segal, G. (1995). *Knowledge of Meaning* (Cambridge, Mass.: MIT Press).

—— den Dikken, M., and Ludlow, P. (1997). 'Intensional Transitive Verbs and Abstract Clausal Complementation', unpublished MS, SUNY, Stony Broole.

McCawley, J. (1974). 'On Identifying the Remains of Deceased Clauses', in McCawley (1979: 74–85).

—— (1979). *Adverbs, Vowels, and Other Objects of Wonder* (Chicago: University of Chicago Press).

McConnell-Ginet, S. (1982). 'Adverbs and Logical Form', *Language*, 58: 144–84.

Montague, R. (1970*a*). 'English as a Formal Language', in B. Visentini (ed.), *Linguaggi nella e nella Technica* (Milan: Edizioni di Communità), 189–224. Reprinted in Montague (1974).

—— (1970*b*). 'Universal Grammar', *Theoria*, 36: 373–98. Reprinted in Montague (1974).

—— (1973). 'The Proper Treatment of Quantification in Ordinary English', in J. Hintikka, J. Moravcsik, and P. Suppes (eds.), *Approaches to Natural Language* (Dordrecht: D. Reidel), 221–42. Reprinted in Montague (1974).

—— (1974). *Formal Philosophy* (New Haven: Yale University Press).

Parsons, T. (1980). 'Modifiers and Quantifiers in Natural Language', *Canadian Journal of Philosophy*, supp. 6: 29–60.

—— (1985). 'Underlying Events in the Logical Analysis of English', in E. Lepore and B. McLaughlin (eds.), *Actions and Events: Perspectives on the Philosophy of Donald Davidson* (Oxford: Basil Blackwell), 235–67.

—— (1990). *Events in the Semantics of English: A Study in Subatomic Semantics* (Cambridge, Mass.: MIT Press).

Partee, B. (1974). 'Opacity and Scope', in M. Munitz and P. Unger (eds.), *Semantics and Philosophy* (New York: New York University Press), 81–101.

Platts, M. (1979). *Ways of Meaning* (London: Routledge & Kegan Paul).

Quine, W. v. O. (1960). *Word and Object* (Cambridge, Mass.: MIT Press).

Rizzi, L. (1978). 'A Restructuring Rule in Italian Syntax', in S. J. Keyser (ed.), *Recent Transformational Studies in European Languages* (Cambridge, Mass.: MIT Press).

Ross, J. (1976). 'To have have and to Not have have', in M. Jazayery, E. Polom, and W. Winter (eds.), *Linguistic and Literary Studies in Honor of Archibald Hill* (Lisse, Holland: de Ridder), 263–70.

Siegel, E. (1976*a*). 'Capturing the Adjective', Ph.D. dissertation, University of Massachusetts, Amherst, Mass.

—— (1976*b*). 'Capturing the Russian Adjective', in B. Partee (ed.), *Montague Grammar* (New York: Academic Press), 293–309.

Thomason, R., and Stalnaker, R. (1973). 'A Semantic Theory of Adverbs', *Linguistic Inquiry*, 4: 195–220.

Vendler, Z. (1967). *Linguistics in Philosophy* (Ithaca, NY: Cornell University Press).

Wheeler, S. (1972). 'Attributives and their Modifiers', *Noûs*, 6: 310–34.

Wurmbrand, S. (1997). 'Restructuring Infinitives', *Proceedings of ConSOLE*, 5: 277–92.

—— (1998). 'Infinitives', (Ph.D. diss., MIT, Cambridge, Mass.)

10

Events and the Semantic Content of Thematic Relations

BARRY SCHEIN

In Davidson (1967, 1985), Castañeda (1967), and Parsons (1985, 1990), the problem of variable polyadicity as reflected in the inferential relations among the sentences in (1) is treated by a decomposition of the common predicate *stab*.

(1) *a.* Brutus stabbed Caesar in the back with a knife. (Parsons 1990)
   b. Brutus stabbed Caesar in the back.
   c. Brutus stabbed Caesar with a knife.
   d. Brutus stabbed Caesar.
   e. Brutus stabbed.

(*a*) entails (*b*) & (*c*) & (*d*) & (*e*).	(*b*) & (*c*) & (*d*) & (*e*) does not entail (*a*).
(*b*) entails (*c*) & (*d*) & (*e*).	(*c*) & (*d*) & (*e*) does not entail (*b*).
(*c*) entails (*d*) & (*e*).	(*d*) & (*e*) does not entail (*c*).
(*d*) entails (*e*).	(*e*) does not entail (*d*).

(2) $\exists e$ stab(*e*, Brutus, Caesar, the back, a knife).
   $stab(e,x,y,z,w)$ is true of $<e,b,c,d,k>$ iff
   stab(**e**) & stabber(**e,b**) & stabbee(**e,c**) & in(**e,d**) & with(**e,k**)

Let's call any relation to events, $R(e,x)$, a thematic relation, among which are *stabber(e,x)*, *stabbee(e,x)*, *in(e,x)*, and *with(e,k)*. For the inferences of (1), the decomposition into thematic relations can remain lexical as in (2), or it can be carried over into the syntax as in (3).

(3) $\exists e$(stab(e) & stabber(e, Brutus) & stabbee(e, Caesar) & in(e, the back) & with(e, a knife)).

Elsewhere, when we turn to the interaction of plurals and quantifiers, the decomposition proves to be syntactic. In *Plurals and Events* (1993), I called this radical decomposition *essential separation*. Observe in (5) that the terms decomposing the verb, *coverer*[e,X] and *cover*(e'), apply to different events and they are separated by elements from elsewhere in the sentence: the quantifiers *two workbenches* and *each* include within their scope *cover*(e') but not *coverer*[e,X].

(4) *a.* Three hundred quilt patches covered over two workbenches each with two bedspreads.

b. Three video games taught every quarterback two new plays.

(5) $\exists e$([$\exists X$: *300 quilt patches*] *coverer*[e,X][1] & [$\exists Y$:*two workbenches*] [*Each y* : *Yy*] [$\exists e'$: $e' \leq e$] (*cover*(e') & *coveree*[e',y] & [$\exists Z$:*two bedspreads*] *with*[e',Z]))

The syntactic separation of *coverer*[e, X] and cover (e') is essential to the extent that sentences like (4*a*) have interpretations that can be represented only by the likes of (5), which it is the burden of *Plurals and Events*, chapter 4, to have shown.[2] The tedious part of the argument is to show that no other logical syntax will do, but it is easy enough to imagine conditions for the truth of (4*a*) that are congenial to (5). Imagine that four bedspreads, draped as described, are made altogether from a total of 300 quilt patches. The 300 patches together cover the workbenches but do not all go into the bedspreads on any one bench. Moreover, some of the individual patches have themselves been torn between this or that bedspread. There is in this case a large event, *e* in (5), where exactly 300 patches covered workbenches with bedspreads, and nothing more precise can be said about how the patches were disposed of, just that this large event comprises two smaller events, *e'* in (5), in each of which a workbench is covered by patches making up two bedspreads.[3] The sentence (4*a*) can be taken to assert that two workbenches were each covered over with two bedspreads,

---

[1] I use square brackets to indicate that the enclosed variables are free in a possibly complex expression. Thus the square brackets indicate here that *coverer* may stand for something other than a primitive dyadic relation. In contrast, I use parentheses (or simple concatenation) to enclose the arguments of primitive predicates and relations.

[2] Cf. Bayer (1997) for some opposing discussion.

[3] The logical form (4) simplifies and slights an important aspect of the meaning of (3), which for present purposes we can ignore. The two workbenches being each covered with two bedspreads is not merely part of the 300 patches' covering but completely coincides with it. See Schein (1993: 146 ff.).

while leaving vague the distribution of the quilt patches. It is this combination of distributivity between *two workbenches each* and *two bedspreads* with the vague distribution of the quilt patches that makes the separation of thematic relations in (5) essential.

Now the inference patterns in (1) and the combinatorial properties that lead to (5) argue only for decomposition, that is, for a certain logical syntax, 'stab(e) & R(e,x) & S(e,y)', and tell us nothing about the content of the thematic relations 'R(e,x)' and 'S(e,y)' assumed. They tell us that *explain to John* is 'explain(e) & to$_1$(e, John)' and *roll to John*, 'roll(e) & to$_2$(e, John)'; but they cannot say whether the prepositions are the same thematic relation or accidental homophones. It could be that each verb provides its own idiosyncratic collection, such as *stabber*[e,α], *stabbee*[e,α], *coverer*[e,α], *coveree*[e,α], *in*[e,α], *with*[e,α], and the thematic relations are as numerous as the verbs themselves twice- or thrice-fold (Schein, 1993: 85 ff., n. 2: 331 ff.). Once the formal point about decomposition has been established, we should go on to inquire after the content of its terms, and here linguistics has quite a bit to say. In a tradition descending from Gruber (1965) and Jackendoff (1972), a notion of thematic role is deployed primarily to explain uniformities in meaning and grammar *across the lexicon*, and thus the same preposition *to* is called upon to formalize the inferences in (6).

(6) *To(e,x).* (Jackendoff, 1987)
  Bill ran to the house |- *Bill is at the house.*
  Bill gave the book to Harry |- *The book is with Harry.*
  The light changed from red to green |- *the light was green.*
  Mary explained the idea to John |- *John has the idea.* (Dowty, 1989)
  John rolled the ball to the fence |- *The ball is at the fence.*
  *Bill ran toward the house |- *Bill is at the house.*
  *Bill pointed to the house |- *Bill is at the house.*

Alongside formalized inference, thematic roles are called upon to relate meaning to grammar. In the most ambitious formulations, the thematic role of an argument determines where it appears in the sentence's phrase structure[4] (see *Universal Alignment Hypothesis* (Perlmutter and Postal, 1984), *Uniformity of Theta Assignment Hypothesis* (Baker, 1988); and discussion in Pesetsky, 1995). In explaining widespread syntactic patterns, we end up with a small class of thematic roles and thus many verbs the subjects of which are all Agents or

---

[4] As well as other grammatical processes. See Levin (1993), Levin and Hovav Rappaport (1995) for a survey, and Dowty (1989, 1991) for a survey and important, skeptical remarks.

Experiencers, and many verbs all of whose direct objects are Themes or Patients. In short, many verbs feel like they are saying the same thing about their subjects, that they are Agents, for example, and grammar appears to confirm the classification that emerges from such judgments.

Identifying the terms of the decomposition in (3) and (5) with the thematic roles that we see across the lexicon, we have instead (7) and (8):

(7) $\exists e$(stab(e) & Agent[e, Brutus] & Patient[e, Caesar] & in[e, the back] & with[e, a knife]).

(8) $\exists e$([$\exists X$: *300 quilt patches*] Theme[e,X] & [$\exists Y$: *two workbenches*] [*Each y* : *Yy*] [$\exists e'$: $e' \leq e$](cover(e') & Location[e',y] & [$\exists Z$:*two bedspreads*] with[e',Z])

If decomposition proceeds as in (7) and (8), with thematic relations as separate phrases, and their syntactic positions are predictable, we can explain the course of acquisition and our understanding of novel verbs and of familiar verbs in novel contexts, as in *The blog looked the clob out of the droon* (Gleitman, 1990; Borer, 1994, 1998*a*, 1998*b*) and *You keated the board with the marbles* versus *You keated the marbles onto the board* (Gropen *et al.*, 1991). By separation, the verb expresses only the event concept, *look*(e) or *keat*(e), and it swaps into a syntactic structure in which the thematic relations are already given. Since there is an invariance in the meaning of these thematic relations from one verb to another, something is understood of what happened in the reported event. Thus the extensibility of thematic relations to novel contexts is an important consideration in favor of both their syntactic separation and their generalization across the lexicon.[5]

Absolute or Relativized Thematic Roles?

The generalization to a few thematic roles invites the first question that I wish to take up here. Are thematic roles absolute or relativized to event concepts and semantic fields? Is Brutus the Agent of an event *tout court*, 'Agent(e, Brutus)', or the Agent for a stabbing, 'Agent(e, Brutus, 'stab')'? In (9) the question has more bite, where thematic roles apply both to a physical action and an abstract one.

---

[5] The combinatorial argument from ch. 4 of *Plurals and Events* as well as a further argument in ch. 8, pp. 165–6, are not the only ones for syntactic separation. See also Benua and Borer (1996); Borer (1994, 1998*a*, 1998*b*); Kratzer (1996); McClure (1995); Ritter and Rosen (1998, 2000); Rosen (1999); Travis (1994, 1997, 2000); Hout (1992, 1996).

(9i)   *a.* Mary rolled the ball to John |- John has the ball.

    b. Mary explained the idea to John |- John has the idea.[6]

(9ii)   *a.* Brutus stabbed Caesar.

    b. Brutus insulted Caesar.

Does John do the same thing, 'to(e, John)', in the one event that he does in the other? Or is he the goal for an explanation 'to(e, John, 'explain')' in one, and the goal for a rolling, 'to(e, John, 'roll')' in the other?[7] Similarly, does Caesar succumb in the same way, 'Patient(e, Caesar)' to both insult and injury, or by different cuts, 'Patient(e, Caesar, 'stab')' and 'Patient(e, Caesar, 'insult')'? Is it 'Agent(e, Brutus)', or 'Agent(e, Brutus, 'stab')' and 'Agent(e, Brutus, 'insult')'? All but one of the considerations mentioned so far in favor of decomposition and thematic roles are of no help here. As I said earlier, the inference patterns of (1) and the combinatorial properties of essential separation are indifferent to the content of thematic roles. Where thematic roles matter, the interaction between grammar and thematic roles can proceed, positioning 'Agent(e, Brutus, α)' just the same as it would 'Agent(e, Brutus)'; and, what speakers know when they know (6) can be formalized as (10) or (11), with either absolute or relativized thematic roles.

(10) $\forall e \forall x \forall y \exists e'((\text{Theme}(e,x) \ \& \ \text{To}(e,y)) \rightarrow (\text{Theme}(e',x) \ \& \ \text{At}(e',y)))$

---

[6] Sabine Iatridou (p.c.) points out that the implication is dependent on the background conditions assumed: *Sisyphus rolled the ball to the pinnacle, but it didn't stay put, Mary explained the idea to John, but he still didn't get it.*

[7] Dowty (1989) remarks, 'I have no idea at present how to go about constructing a criterion that permits thematic roles to depend on what we might call natural classes of verb meanings, as illustrated by [(9i*a*)] and [(9i*b*)], without permitting quite arbitrary dependence on verb meaning.' I raise the question; but, for the reason given in Fodor (1998: 50), I do not think that an observation of polysemy is itself a good argument for relativized concepts. Later arguments are more sincere. It might seem that much of what is assumed here runs afoul of the demise of definitions (Fodor, 1998; Fodor and Lepore, 1998), semantic atomism. The decomposition so-called of 'stab' does not however define it—at least not according to the syntactic decomposition on offer. Rather, the claim is that one is mistaken in thinking that *stab* has the syntax 'stab(e,x,y)'. It's 'stab(e)' and it means STAB(e), respecting semantic atomism. In addition, there are several zero morphemes (or perhaps Case itself) with the meanings of various thematic roles. Semantic atomism comes with a rather disquotational lexicon (Fodor, 1998: 55). I could say better whether the zero morphemes are also consistent with semantic atomism, if I knew how to do the disquotational semantics for bound morphemes such as the verbal prefix *re-*. As for the thematic roles themselves, I assume that one can ask whether or not they are relativized to event concepts or semantic fields in the same spirit that one asks whether an attributive predicate such as *slow* is similarly relativized, without fear that either answer defines these concepts in a way contrary to semantic atomism.

(11) $\forall\xi\forall e\forall x\forall y\exists e'((\text{Theme}(e,x,\xi)\ \&\ \text{To}(e,y,\xi)) \rightarrow (\text{Theme}(e',x,\xi)\ \&\ \text{At}(e',y,\xi)))$

We can however make some progress on the question, reflecting on the extensibility of thematic relations in novel contexts:

(12)   The blog looked the clob out of the droon.

(13) *a.* You keated the marbles onto the board.

    b. You keated the board with the marbles.

To know what we know of what passed among you, the marbles, and the board cannot depend on knowing anything particular about keating. Moreover, what we understand to have happened between the clob and the droon is likely to be inconsistent with what we would otherwise expect from lookings (Gleitman, 1990; Bowerman, 1982; Pinker, 1989; Borer, 1998*b*). What we understand of their participation must follow from what we already know about like participants in other situations. Thus, even if thematic roles are themselves relativized to event concepts, we have knowledge of the form in (14) where Φ contains no free occurrences of 'ξ', from which we can infer Φ without knowing what a keating is.[8]

(14) $\forall\xi\forall e\forall x(\text{Agent}(e,x,\xi) \rightarrow \Phi[e,x])$

Suppose further that what one knows (15) of Themes in general and of other thematic roles in general is sufficient to discriminate one from the other (cf. Dowty, 1989), as appears to be the case from what we understand of their novel uses.

(15) $\forall\xi\forall e\forall x(\text{Theme}(e,x,\xi) \rightarrow \Phi'[e,x])$

    $\forall\xi\forall e\forall x(\text{With}(e,x,\xi) \rightarrow \Phi''[e,x])$

    $\forall\xi\forall e\forall x(\text{On}(e,x,\xi) \rightarrow \Phi'''[e,x])$

---

[8] This is reminiscent of the view (Dowty, 1989; Ladusaw and Dowty, 1988) that thematic roles are 'compiled' from the entailments of primitively, polyadic verbs. Thus the Agent thematic role is the conjunction of all $\Phi[e,x]$ (with only e and x free in Φ) such that for every verb V in the class of verbs with Agents for subjects $\forall e\forall x\forall y_1 \ldots y_n(V(e,x,y_1, \ldots y_n) \rightarrow \Phi[e,x])$. See Parsons (1995) for discussion. Parsons (1995: 657) suggests that (i) argues for absolute thematic roles, but (i) can be formalized with relativized thematic roles as in (ii).

(i) *a.* I don't know if that car was sold, given, imposed, or what. But, whatever it was, it was to Martha, not to you; so stop sniveling.

    b. Everything evil done in the city that day was done by the barbarians.

(ii) *a.* $\ldots \forall\xi\forall e(\text{Theme}(e, that\ car,\ \xi) \rightarrow (\text{To}(e, Martha,\ \xi)\ \&\ \neg\ \text{To}(e, Martha,\ \xi)))\ldots$

    b. $\forall\xi\forall e((\xi e\ \&\ evil(e)\ \&\ \text{In}(e,\ the\ city,\ \xi)\ \&\ \text{On}(e,\ that\ day,\ \xi)) \rightarrow \text{Agent}(e,\ the\ barbarians,\ \xi))$

Are not, $\Phi'[e,x]$, $\Phi''[e,x]$ and $\Phi'''[e,x]$ then constitutive of absolute thematic roles? It seems that extensibility to novel contexts betrays knowledge that:

(16) $\forall\xi\forall e\forall x(\text{Agent}(e,x,\xi) \rightarrow \text{Agent}(e,x))$
$\forall\xi\forall e\forall x(\text{Theme}(e,x,\xi) \rightarrow \text{Theme}(e,x))$
$\forall\xi\forall e\forall x(\text{With}(e,x,\xi))$
$\forall\xi\forall e\forall x(\text{On}(e,x,\xi) \rightarrow \text{On}(e,x))$

So much argues that speakers have within their grasp absolute thematic roles, but it does not decide between (17) and (18), that is, whether they or their relativized counterparts (if there are such) are what appear in logical form.

(17) $\exists e(\text{stab}(e)\ \&\ \text{Agent}(e, \text{Brutus})\ \&\ \text{Patient}(e, \text{Caesar})\ \&\ \text{in}(e, \text{the back})\ \&\ \text{with}(e, \text{a knife}))$

(18) $\exists e(\text{stab}(e)\ \&\ \text{Agent}(e, \text{Brutus}, \text{'stab'})\ \&\ \text{Patient}(e, \text{Caesar}, \text{'stab'})\ \&\ \text{in}(e, \text{the back}, \text{'stab'})\ \&\ \text{with}(e, \text{a knife}, \text{'stab'}))$

Event Identities

We can look for further constraints on the choice between (17) and (18) to a connection between assertions of event identities and relativized thematic relations.[9] If events are like everything else, there should sometimes be alternative descriptions of the same event. When Ray plays a sonata on his clarinet, his playing the sonata is the same event as his playing the clarinet, or so it would seem. Similarly, when Jim drinks exactly one beer in exactly one hour at Ken's Pub on Thursday afternoon, one judges that Jim's drinking at Ken's Pub, Jim's drinking on Thursday afternoon, Jim's drinking at Ken's Pub on a Thursday afternoon, Jim's drinking a beer in nothing less than an hour, Jim's drinking beer for an hour, etc. all seem to be the same event. Yet such identities, innocent or not, threaten, as we will see next, to relativize thematic relations as soon as a conjunction of them is taken to compose logical form.

Suppose, for example, that a sphere rotates and under friction with the air heats up. One can truthfully report that the sphere's rotating was its heating up. If this report expresses an identity and it is assumed that nominalization

---

[9] There is an extensive literature on what follows. See Parsons (1990), Davies (1991), Carlson (1998) and Pianesi and Varzi (1999), for a survey of the issues and references cited.

abstracts on the event argument of the corresponding sentence (Parsons, 1990), we confront the following inference:

(19)   (i) *The sphere heated up slowly.*
          $\exists e$(heat up(e) & Theme(e,s) & slow(e))

    (ii) heat up(h) & Theme(h,s) & slow(h)   (i, Existential Instantiation)

   (iii) *The sphere's rotating was the sphere's heating up.*
          (the e)(rotate(e) & Theme(e,s)) = (the e)(heat up(e) & Theme (e,s))

   (iv) (the e)(rotate(e) & Theme(e,s)) = h   (ii, iii, *the*)

   (v) rotate(h) & Theme(h,s)   (iv, *the*)

   (vi) <u>rotate(h) & Theme(h,s) & slow(h)   (ii, v, &-Elimination, &-Introduction)</u>

   (vii) *The sphere rotated slowly.*
          $\exists e$(rotate(e) & Theme(e,s) & slow(e))   (vi, Existential Generalization)

That is, if (19iii) is a true identity statement, then (19i) and (19iii) should entail (19vii) according to their Davidsonian logical forms. The inference is however rejected. It is obvious that events do not have an absolute property of being slow but only under comparison with like events. The sphere heated up slowly for a heating up, and even if that is the same event as the sphere's rotating, it cannot be inferred that the sphere rotated slowly for a rotating. In fact, only a very rapid rotation will generate enough friction for heat:

(20)   (i) *The sphere heated up slowly.*
          $\exists e$(heat up(e) & Theme(e,s) & slow(e,'heat up'))

   (iii) *The sphere's rotating was the sphere's heating up.*
          (the e)(rotate(e) & Theme(e,s)) = (the e)(heat up(e) & Theme(e,s))

#(vii) *The sphere rotated slowly.*
          $\exists e$(rotate(e) & Theme(e,s) & slow(e, 'rotate'))

An attributive adjective such as *slow* is by nature relativized, but the same argument threatens to relativize thematic relations as well. If (21ii) is a true identity statement, then (21ii) and (21i) should entail (21iii).

(21)   (i) *The sphere heated up at .01°/sec.*
          $\exists e$(heat up(e) & Theme(e,s) & At(e, .01°/sec.))

(ii) *The sphere's rotating was the sphere's heating up.*
(the e)(rotate(e) & Theme(e,s)) = (the e)(heat up(e) & Theme(e,s))

#(iii) *The sphere rotated at .01°/sec.*
$\exists e$(rotate(e) & Theme(e, s) & At(e, .01°/sec.))

To block the inference it would be enough to relativize any of the thematic relations—e is at .01°/sec for a heating, or e is of the sphere for a heating. This argument for relativized thematic relations is however only as strong as the identity statement in (21ii), and it may just be better to deny it (Parsons, 1990: 157). The sentence is undeniably true, but in the face of such wayward uses of the copula as in *Mary's praising of John was her disapproving of Peter* or *Reagan's election was the conservative social agenda's inauguration,* there is no reason to assume that it expresses strict identity. Perhaps the sphere's rotation and its heating up are after all distinct events that merely coincide in space and time. One can well imagine that if air had been absent from the ambient environment, it would have been the very same rotation without the sphere's heating up.[10]

The inferences in (19) and (21) thus illustrate a trade-off: to block them, either deny that the sentences (19iii) and (21ii) express strict identity, contrary to the logical forms shown, and allow that events are finer-grained, that there are many where one might have thought there was one, or relativize a thematic role, replacing $At(e, .01°/sec.)$ with $At(e, .01°/sec., 'heat')$ and $At(e, .01°/sec., 'rotate')$. If, as in (19) and (21), logical form is a simple conjunction of thematic relations, then we cannot have all at once both absolute thematic relations and the coarser-grained events that true identities would convey. In the case of rotating and heating up it may disappoint only a few philosophers to learn that they are not the same, but if one insists on absolute thematic roles throughout, we may discover that there is no end to the events that need to be distinguished.

In fact, the fine-grained events come sooner. Assumptions more fundamental to the analysis than absolute thematic relations point to them. For either (23*a*) or (23*b*) to do the work of (24), it must be understood that the agents referred to are the only agents of the event and the patients referred to, its only patients.

(22) 248 engineers assembled 27 airplanes.

---

[10] Of course it could not be the same rotation if that meant the same velocity under the same force propelling it forwards.

(23) *a.* Agent[e,X,ξ] & assemble(e) & Patient[e,Y,ξ]

    b. Agent[e,X] & assemble(e) & Patient[e,Y]

(24)   Assemble(e,X,Y)

Otherwise, if this event could contain other agents, say, some mechanics, or other patients, some helicopters, we would not be able to infer from (23) that the engineers assembled the airplanes rather than the helicopters or that the airplanes were not assembled by the mechanics. The named participants must exhaust the participants in their thematic relations or else the Davidsonian analysis does not get off the ground.[11] If so, it follows from the logical forms in (25) and (26) that Ray's playing music on the clarinet is not the same event as his playing the clarinet (Parsons, 1990: 157).

(25)   Ray played music on the clarinet.

      $\exists e$(Agent[e,r] & play(e) & Theme[e,m] & On[e,c])

(26)   Ray played the clarinet.

      $\exists e$(Agent[e,r] & play(e) & Theme[e,c])

The unique Theme of one event is music, and the unique Theme of the other is the clarinet. By a similar argument, weighing the Volvo is not the same event as weighing the Volvo's parts, although I decide to weigh the parts by weighing the Volvo:

(27)   I weighed the Volvo.

      $\exists e$(Agent[e, i] & weigh(e) & Theme[e, v])

(28)   I weighed the Volvo's parts.

      $\exists e$(Agent[e, i] & weigh(e) & Theme[e, P])

The Theme of the first event is the Volvo, and the parts are the Theme of the second. These events have different Themes if the one, the Volvo, is not identical to the many, its parts; and thus the events are distinct. Similarly again, the Carnegie Deli's sitting opposite Carnegie Hall is not the same as

[11] See Carlson (1984) and for extensive argument of this point Lasersohn (1995: ch. 6: 69 ff.). The representation of exhaustivity is taken up in Schein (1997). Exhaustivity is distinguished from Thematic Uniqueness, a principle of grammar that stipulates that a thematic role will not be assigned to more than one argument. A logical form such as (i) violates Thematic Uniqueness but respects Exhaustivity. The thematic relations are taken to be complex, and Exhausitivity holds that the X are all the participants that are both Theme and R to e. The logical form in (ii) is also consistent with Exhaustivity although it violates Thematic Uniqueness. If, however, thematic relations are simple, absolute thematic roles, then Exhaustivity implies Uniqueness.

(i) (Theme & R)[e, X] & V(e) & (Theme & S)[e,Y]

(ii) Theme[e, X, ξ] & V(e) & Theme[e,Y,ζ]

Carnegie Hall sitting opposite the Carnegie Deli, since they have different Themes and different locations:

(29) The Carnegie Deli sits opposite Carnegie Hall.
$\exists e(\text{Theme}[e,\text{d}] \ \& \ \text{sit}(e) \ \& \ \text{Opposite}[e,\text{h}])$

(30) Carnegie Hall sits opposite the Carnegie Deli.
$\exists e(\text{Theme}[e,\text{h}] \ \& \ \text{sit}(e) \ \& \ \text{Opposite}[e,\text{d}])$

Arguments for fine-grained events arise as soon as we acknowledge the exhaustivity of thematic relations, which no Davidsonian analysis can do without, and now notice that relativizing thematic relations will not deflect these arguments. There is no hope that the thematic relations or event concept expressed in (29) will differ from those in (30) or that they will distinguish (27) from (28). The events themselves have to be different. The question posed by the choice between (17) and (18) appears then to be moot. If speakers are in possession of absolute thematic relations (16) and independent considerations (25)–(30) in any case require fine-grained events, why should it be supposed that speakers use relativized thematic relations?

Section 2 below develops an argument against absolute thematic relations that arises from plurality and collective predication. Even if events are as fine-grained as you like, the new difficulty for absolute thematic roles will persist.[12] The argument against absolute thematic relations is thus freed of metaphysical

---

[12] Dowty (1991) voices skepticism about thematic roles, but by my lights he is a true believer. His skepticism derives from the observation that there are many verbs with arguments that would be classified as Agents and Patients by grammatical standards that nevertheless differ with respect to the attributes listed in (i).

(i) A. Proto-Agent
   a. volitional involvement in the event or state.
   b. sentience (and/or perception)
   c. causing an event or change of state in another event.
   d. movement relative to the position of the event named by the verb.
   e. exists independently of the event named by the verb.

   B. Proto-Patient
   a. undergoes change of state
   b. incremental theme
   c. causally affected by another participant
   d. stationary relative to movement of another participant
   e. does not exist independently of the event, or not at all.

You should be disappointed if you had defined Agent as Causer but this does not undermine the thematic role. Far from it, Dowty has shown us how to save it if we take his theory at face value. I take it that he has simply provided a conceptual analysis:

assumptions about events (unlike (21)), which perhaps makes it more compelling. An interesting and unexpected aspect of the argument is that it makes crucial use of the logical syntax of separation (see (5) above) to get a fix on the content of thematic roles. The conclusion is that either thematic roles will have to be relativized to event concepts or, as I suspect is the case, there is yet more abstract syntax.

If I quit after such an argument, I leave thematic relations less than absolute and events so fine-grained that playing the clarinet is not the same as playing music on it, weighing the Volvo's parts by weighing the Volvo is not the same event as weighing the Volvo, the Carnegie Deli's sitting opposite Carnegie Hall is not the same as Carnegie Hall's sitting opposite the Carnegie Deli, and Jim's drinking beers is not the same as his drinking some beers. I would rather not leave the theory in such a weakened condition if it is to ever stand as more than an engine for patterns of inference (1) and combinatorics (4)–(5). The fault lies with logical form, with the simple, flat-footed conjunction of thematic relations. In the end, abstract syntax will be called upon to save both absolute thematic relations and a naive, fairly coarse understanding of events.

Section 1 offers a defense (1.1) of speakers' judgments that events are coarser and an analysis (1.3) that reconciles this a priori intuition with the exhaustivity of thematic relations. A more articulated logical form introduces a distinction between scenes with a given resolution and the events they are scenes of. The fine-grained scenes answer the problem of exhaustivity while events remain the medium-grained subjects of intuition. Such a convenient solution may look like sleight-of-hand were it not for the fact that the scenes and resolutions proposed are a natural extension of the mereology of events, which is necessary on independent grounds (1.2) when navigating among pluralities of events, where event boundaries have to be redrawn to sort out who did what to whom.

The last section, 3, is a treatment of telicity designed for the following problem: given our fairly coarse understanding of events according to which Jim's drinking beers is the very same event as his drinking some beers, how can we defuse the following inference without relativizing any of the thematic relations.

(ii) Agent(e,x) is true of $<$ e, a $>$ iff
      a is the *most* proto-agentive in e with respect to the six attributes in (i.A).
      Patient(e,x) is true of $<$ e, a $>$ iff
      a is the *most* proto-patient in e with respect to the six attributes in (i.B).

The thematic roles in (ii) are absolute. Each has only one sense that applies to every event on every occasion of use. What I have to say about thematic roles is nastier.

(31) Jim's drinking some beers in nothing less than an hour = Jim's drinking beers for an hour.

Jim drank some beers in nothing less than an hour.

$\exists e(\text{Agent}(e,j)$ & drink(e) & Patient$(e,$ *some beers*$)$ & In$(e,$ *nothing less than an hour*$))$

Jim drank beers.

$\exists e(\text{Agent}(e,j)$ & drink(e) & Patient$(e,beer))$

*Jim drank beers in nothing less than an hour.

$\exists e(\text{Agent}(e,j)$ & drink(e) & Patient$(e,$ *beers*$)$ & In$(e,$ *nothing less than an hour*$))$

This part very quickly states its solution, a further articulation of logical form that manages to undo the inference in (31) without sacrificing the identity of the reported events. But, the honest toil has just begun. I have to show that the solution takes the right view of telicity, and so the discussion of telicity and its literature ranges beyond the immediate concerns that relate event identity, thematic content, and logical form.

1 Events

1.1 *Medium-Grained Events*

Talk about events is like talk about other things. They are particulars, and as such they are sometimes the values of variables. If our thoughts about them are like our thoughts about other things, the same events can enter into many different thoughts. Granted there are also differences between events and objects. I can sensibly ask of the occupants of two distinct regions of space-time whether or not they are the same object displaced, but not whether or not they are the same event. Enough metaphysics. Observing the behaviors of speakers, we conclude that they discern and talk about objects, and from such observations, we should also conclude—so the theory claims—that they discern and talk about events. Behavior justifies the attribution and the semantics that relies on it long before we have identity conditions for the speaker's concepts of object and event. If the identity conditions for objects are largely indeterminate, then the theory expects no better for events.[13] I should

[13] These sentiments echo Parsons (1990), Pianesi and Varzi (1999), and Lombard (1998) among recent examples. For recent discussion of related metaphysical issues, see Koslicki (1998, 1999). The literature on aspect (Taylor, 1977, 1985; Dowty, 1982; Bach, 1986; among others) has

first begin to worry if events showed an unnatural clarity in their identity conditions as if they were just sets of points or partial models for sentences.

The fine-grained events that the theory has forced on us at this point are however unlike other things. As soon as we think of an event under one description it becomes unavailable to any other. If ever there were alternative descriptions of the same event, they should include pairs like *Ray's playing music on the clarinet* and *Ray's playing the clarinet*, *my weighing the Volvo's parts by weighing the Volvo* and *my weighing the Volvo*, *the Carnegie Deli's sitting opposite Carnegie Hall* and *Carnegie Hall's sitting opposite the Carnegie Deli*, and *Jim's drinking beers* and *Jim's drinking some beers*. Wider intuitions uphold these identities. If the theoretical conclusion is that the sphere's rotating is not really the same event as its heating up, intuitions confirm—or at least allow—that the very same rotation could have happened without the sphere heating up. In contrast, although one could imagine the very same performance in a different acoustic environment, one cannot imagine circumstances under which the performance described by *Ray's playing the clarinet* would be the same had the allegedly distinct event described by *Ray's playing music on the clarinet* not occurred. These are distinct events that cannot be redescribed and cannot be imagined apart from one another. Similar remarks apply to the two weighings and the two sittings opposite.

Parsons (1990: 159) comments on such uncongenial intuitions that

as Taylor 1985 points out, it is not difficult to coin a notion of *kinship*, where two events are *akin* if they are identical according to your favorite theory. We then say that two events are 'the same' if and only if they are akin in this sense. Since we often use 'the same' to stand for some salient sense of similarity short of identity, the notion may save the *a priori* intuitions without contradicting the theory.

True enough—but I want to volunteer a favorite theory of event identity about as much as I want to give a theory of object identity, and I do not want to hand-wave at the data either. Can't I give a semantics and an account of verbal behavior that comports with a priori intuitions without proffering a metaphysics?

Fine-grained events toss a large heap of sand into the workings of our intuitions. Suppose I try to explain that weighing x is weighing the mass of x, scrubbing x is scrubbing the surface of x, x's being paralyzed is for some y of x's nerves, y's being paralyzed, or I try to declare a meaning of my own invention— *to molecularize* is to enumerate and classify the molecules of an object or

long pursued an analogy between Verb Phrases denoting events and Noun Phrases denoting objects, extending the count/mass distinction to both without fully explicating the distinction.

objects, so that to molecularize x is, by explicit definition, to molecularize the molecules of x. We have already seen that the theory precludes such identities so long as the analysis is as in (32):

(32) weigh(e) & Patient[e, x]
weigh(e) & Patient[e, x's mass]
scrub(e) & Patient[e, x]
scrub(e) & Patient[e, x's surface]
molecularize(e) & Patient[e, x]
molecularize(e) & Patient[e, x's molecules]

Exhaustivity precludes the same event from having different, unique Patients. Perhaps the contrary intuitions should only be taken to indicate a refinement in the analysis. When I define molecularizing x, what I really say is that e stands in that relation to x just in case it stands in some intimately related but different relation to x's molecules:

(33) weigh(e) & Patient1[e, x]
weigh(e) & Patient2[e, x's mass]
scrub(e) & Patient1[e, x]
scrub(e) & Patient2[e, x's surface]
molecularize(e) & Patient1[e, x]
molecularize(e) & Patient2[e, x's molecules]

The very same event has both a unique Patient1 and a unique Patient2,[14] and thus the theory and the intuition that these are the same events appear to be reconciled. The reconciliation does not last for long. Scrubbing Aaron is the same as scrubbing Aaron's surface (34). But Aaron's surface is the same object as the surface of Aaron's skin cells (35). So, scrubbing Aaron's surface is the same as scrubbing Aaron's skin cells' surface (36), and this last event is judged to be the same as scrubbing Aaron's skin cells (37).

(34) (ιe)(scrub(e) & Patient1(e, Aaron)) $=$ (ιe)(scrub(e) & Patient2(e, Aaron's surface))

(35) Aaron's surface $=$ Aaron's skin cells' surface

(36) (ιe)(scrub(e) & Patient2(e, Aaron's surface)) $=$ (ιe)(scrub(e) & Patient2(e, Aaron's skin cells' surface))

---

[14] This indicates the direction of a solution for how Ray's playing music on the clarinet could be the same event as his playing the clarinet. Deny that the same thematic relation applies to both direct objects. Then both music and the clarinet exhaust the participants of their respective thematic relations. See n. 51.

(37) $(\iota e)(\mathrm{scrub}(e)$ & Patient2$(e$, Aaron's skin cells' surface)$)$ = $(\iota e)(\mathrm{scrub}(e)$ & Patient1$(e$, Aaron's skin cells)$)$.

(38) $(\iota e)(\mathrm{scrub}(e)$ & Patient1$(e$, Aaron)$)$ = $(\iota e)(\mathrm{scrub}(e)$ & Patient1$(e$, Aaron's skin cells)$)$

Then, scrubbing Aaron is the same event as scrubbing Aaron's skin cells (38), which fits intuition, but derives a contradiction in the theory since both Aaron and Aaron's skin cells are asserted to be unique Patients1 in the same event. So the theory requires that when I stipulate molecularizing x to be the very same event as molecularizing x's molecules, I cannot really mean it. Under pain of contradiction, I mean that they are distinct but coincident.

Suppose the shoe were on the other foot, and it were a consequence of the theory that this particular scrubbing of Aaron is the same event as this particular scrubbing of Aaron's surface. Faced with (34)–(38) and like arguments, the theory then requires that Aaron's surface is not really the same object as Aaron's skin cells' surface, that the Volvo's mass is not the same object as the Volvo's parts' mass, and that Herb's molecules are not the same objects as Herb's body's molecules. To fend off a priori intuitions to the contrary, one can of course plead for a notion of kinship defined according to a favorite theory of object identity that is as yet unknown. To offer such an unguarded theory is to believe that one has no enemies. I would rather from the start look for a semantics and logical form that let shine through both the intuition that the Volvo's mass and the Volvo's parts' mass are the same object and that my weighing the Volvo's parts was the same event as my weighing the Volvo.[15]

---

[15] A skeptic demands that events be defined before we are allowed to quantify over them in logical form (and may thus prefer e.g. to construct them from spatiotemporal points or regions; see Parsons, 1990: 8.2; 148 ff. for diagnoses of the varieties of reductionism). The reply starts from the observation that everyone, the skeptic included, seems quite content to quantify over objects without having first defined what *they* are. Yet, so the reply goes (Reichenbach, 1947), events are no more nor less well-defined than objects, and we seem to recognize and talk about both. Of course, since neither notion is introduced with a definition, our understanding of them depends on the role they play in explaining speakers' knowledge and behavior. The reply to the skeptic is then presented *ad hominem*: whenever you think a speaker is entertaining a thought about an object, the same sorts of considerations show that speakers entertain thoughts about events too; it would be hypocritical of you, if not contradictory, to be so parsimonious about the one and so profligate with the other (and, if you would only put aside your misplaced angst about positing such entities and take speakers at their word, event semantics could improve your explanations of their behavior too). But, this reply to the skeptic commits us to taking speakers' judgments and their reports seriously. The reply that events are just as robust as objects goes up in smoke if we have to add that they are just like objects except that they are so fine-grained that we can never trust the speaker's (i.e. our) prima-facie intuitions and we

The solution to the problem lies, I believe, with the proper treatment of the remaining case of a symmetric predicate. Here too there is an a priori intuition that Carnegie Hall's sitting opposite the Carnegie Deli is the same event as Carnegie Deli's sitting opposite Carnegie Hall, but the example raises a more imminent problem for the theory. Let us set aside the intuition about event identity and pick one of the events described in (39).

(39) *a.* The Carnegie Deli sits opposite Carnegie Hall.
$\exists e(\text{Theme}[e, \text{d}]$ & $\text{sit}(e)$ & $\text{Opposite}[e, \text{h}])$
b. Carnegie Hall sits opposite the Carnegie Deli.
$\exists e(\text{Theme}[e, \text{h}]$ & $\text{sit}(e)$ & $\text{Opposite}[e, \text{d}])$

Exhaustivity requires that, for the chosen event, one thematic relation relates it only to the Carnegie Deli and the other, only to Carnegie Hall. But, what is it that the Carnegie Deli is doing in this event that Carnegie Hall is not also doing? The observation that the predicate's meaning reveals asymmetry elsewhere—that Danny Rose sits opposite the Carnegie Deli but the Carnegie Deli does not sit opposite Danny Rose—is irrelevant if what Danny Rose does to distinguish himself from the Deli in that event does not distinguish one building from the other in (39).[16]

To reconcile exhaustivity to both the intuition that (39*a*) and (39*b*) refer to the same event and the fact that the Carnegie Deli and Carnegie Hall are doing the same thing in that event, I will take (39*a*) to be reports from different

---

can never give alternative descriptions of the same event. The fact is that speakers do not judge events to be fine-grained: Jim's drinking some beers in an hour really was on that particular occasion his drinking beers for an hour and my weighing the Volvo really was my weighing its parts on that particular occasion, etc. In short, it is with respect to medium-grained events that we appear to talk about objects and events in roughly the same way with roughly the same precision.

[16] Admittedly, Carnegie Hall is the landmark and much grander venue from which the Deli borrows its name (cf. Carlson, 1998: 48 n. 2). So it is a New York joke to say that Carnegie Hall sits opposite the Carnegie Deli. But perfectly symmetrical situations do exist. Of the identical twin lions guarding the entrance to the New York Public Library, one could either say 'Patience sits opposite Fortitude' or 'Fortitude sits opposite Patience'. Parsons (1990) suggests that such symmetric relations may sometimes derive from a collective predicate. The example is chosen to thwart such a derivation: *The Carnegie Deli and Carnegie Hall sit opposite. We have *The Carnegie Deli and Carnegie Hall sit opposite each other,* but here the relation 'x sits opposite y' is still basic. For further argument against deriving the collective predicate from the reciprocal, see Carlson (1998). That allegedly symmetric predicates do not express truly symmetric relations, see Gleitman (1969), Gleitman *et al.* (1996), Tversky and Gati (1978), Talmy (1985*a*).

scenes of the same event (see Jackendoff, 1976; Talmy, 1978).[17] Facing north on Seventh Avenue, there is a scene of an event where the Carnegie Deli is the only thing sitting and on the left and Carnegie Hall is the only thing sitting and on the right. Turning south, there is a different scene of the same event where now Carnegie Hall is alone on the left and the Deli is alone on the right. Nominalizations of the sentences in (39) abstract on the events, not the scenes, to refer to how things are in the world and not a percept of them, and it is true that the event of which there is a scene with the Carnegie Deli on the left and Carnegie Hall on the right is the same event of which there is a scene with the Carnegie Hall on the left and the Carnegie Deli on the right. In short, scenes are fine-grained, events are coarser, and sentences rely on (thematic) relations to scenes to convey what they have to say about events. Some details follow below. What will be of interest is the respect in which scenes are fine-grained and structured enough so that *weighing the Volvo* and *weighing the Volvo's parts* can also correspond to different scenes of the same event. Perspective does not distinguish scenes of the Volvo and its parts, which occupy the same spatio-temporal region. Rather I will appeal to a notion of resolution to distinguish a scene fine-grained enough to resolve the Volvo's parts from one which only resolves the whole Volvo. The notion of scene resolution arises here not only to vindicate a priori intuitions of event identity. It emerges as a natural extension of event mereology, which will be shown on independent grounds to pervade our talk about events.

1.2 *Referring to Events*

First, sentences often describe several events, as in (45), after an example due to Gillon (1987):

(40) Twenty composers collaborated on seven shows.

It reports recent activity on Broadway, where the twenty composers are divided among several, rival, and cut-throat collaborations. Similarly we can imagine contexts for true assertions of (41) where the turtles are divided among several,

---

[17] Jackendoff and Talmy propose Figure and Ground to distinguish relations in symmetric predicates. Dowty (1991) notes that asymmetries in meaning brought about by a difference in perspective cannot be plausibly attributed to a difference in, say, *be*'s lexical meaning. His reluctance to consider Figure and Ground thematic relations derives from the assumption that the latter are lexical (and compiled from the entailments of lexical items). Here thematic relations are separate phrases, and Figure and Ground are as good as anything else, such as aspectual conditions, that could interpret functional projections.

rival fraternal orders, within which every turtle shares with every other but across which there is no comity (*P&E*: 126 ff.).

(41) *a.* 17 turtles share 23 pizzas.
    b. 17 turtles together ate 23 pizzas.
    c. 17 turtles ate, every turtle breaking pizza with every other turtle, 23 pizzas.

There is no one collaboration that verifies (40) nor any one sharing for (41). These should be read as 'there are some *events*', in the plural, that are collaboration*s* or sharing*s*.

The plural quantification shows up in the logic as well. So first consider (42) on the reading indicated:

(42) Twenty truckers loaded up one or more trucks.
    'Whenever there was a loading up of one or more trucks, 20 truckers were the loaders'.
    [$\forall e$: *load up of one or more trucks*[*e*]] Agent[*e, 20 truckers*]

There is no felt implication that it was the same twenty truckers in every event. This tells us that the domain of events is not in general closed under fusion. Otherwise, the fusion of all loadings up of one or more trucks would itself be a loading up of one or more trucks, and they could each involve twenty truckers only if they were the same twenty.

(43) These 10 truckers loaded up one or more trucks.
    <u>Those 10 truckers loaded up one or more trucks.</u>
    The 20 truckers loaded up one or more trucks.

Now, on the other hand, (43) is valid; and unlike the universal, distributive quantifier in (42), the sentences in (43) must not be read with a singular 'there was an event of 10 truckers . . .' and 'there was another event of 10 truckers'. Even if there is one loading by these ten truckers and another loading by those ten truckers, there is no certainty that the domain contains their fusion, a single event of loading by the twenty truckers. Rather, these sentences start off in the plural, 'there were some events', and the inference in (43) follows as a matter of logic. There were loadings by these ten truckers and loadings by those 10 truckers, and so there were loadings by the twenty truckers (*P&E*: 107 ff.).

Having said that the existential quantification over events is plural, (41) still presents a further problem for our understanding of how the events and their participants relate to one another. For suppose the fraternal orders of turtles share a central kitchen that serves pizzas by the slice and it so happens that no one pizza was shared at the meal of any one order. Each of the twenty-three pizzas is distributed among several meals. There is thus no sharing or eating e and pizza p of which it is true that Patient(e,p), and thus it is unclear how it could be true that those pizzas are shared or eaten in those events. Under the circumstances, Landman (1995) and Krifka (1989) appeal to an object mereology. Conveniently, (41) is true under the same conditions as (44), assuming Brooklyn Standard Pizza:

(44) 17 turtles share 184 pizza slices.
  17 turtles share 1,472π sq. in. of pizza.

The suggestion is that for the pizzas to have been eaten in some events it is enough for their parts to have been eaten in those events, thus overcoming the lack of correspondence between the events, the meals, and the individual objects, the pizzas. But this lack of correspondence is not confined to cases where an object's fate can be reduced to that of its parts:

(45) 248 engineers assembled as a detail crew 27 airplanes.

Like the earlier examples, (45) has a reading that allows the engineers to be divided among distinct crews. There are different details to an airplane. Any one crew assembles only a few components for any one airplane. Suppose there are fifteen crews among which the engineers are divided and thus fifteen events of assembling as a detail crew. There are also twenty-seven events, each the history of an airplane's assembly. These twenty-seven events completely overlap the fifteen, but no one of them is the product of any one of the fifteen. One cannot however replace *salva veritate* the reference to twenty-seven airplanes with a reference to their parts:

(46) 248 engineers assembled as a detail crew 613 airplane components.

We cannot be sure from (46) alone that the airplanes were ever assembled or that they were assembled by these 248 engineers. A similar example:

(47) 248 gerrymanderers co-redrew 27 assembly districts.

The result of all this activity is a delineation of 27 assembly districts and not, say, any of their constituent neighborhoods. This is arrived at by factions working against each other or at least indifferently to each other haphazardly tacking on their own turf, and thus there are co-redrawings. Again, the twenty-seven assembly districts emerge from these contrary efforts with no assembly district the result of any one of them.

Landman (1995: 456) makes available the shift from objects to their parts only to predicates that can have a mass interpretation. So presumably it would not apply in (45)–(47) and he is left without any account of these readings. Yet, even where the predicate does support a mass interpretation, the shift from objects to their parts can be shown to fail. As before, suppose that melting in a foundry is a complicated team effort so that we have (48) under the now familiar circumstances:

(48) 248 workers co-melted 27 gold statues.

The workers are divided among separate shifts, each shift manages to melt only a proper part of any one statue. The fact is that to melt a gold statue is to melt the gold that constitutes it. The predicate has a mass interpretation and, in this case, Landman's and Krifka's identifying the fate of the statues with the fate of their parts does not go far astray. But we also have (49):

(49) 248 workers co-solidified 27 gold statues.

In solidifying a gold statue, the cold result had better be a statue. On the other hand, to solidify some gold, it is enough that it go cold in whatever shape. If the workers cast the gold statues, which look good for a while, but, inadvertently or not, let the gold leak from the molds, (49) cannot be true. It is however true that the workers co-solidified the gold.

These examples show that we cannot in general allow the substitution of mereologically coincident objects *salva veritate*. So if the fate of pizza is not the fate of pizza parts, how then are the pizzas eaten when none is eaten in any one event of turtles sharing a meal?

A mereology of events is necessary and sufficient, without any appeal to a mereology of objects. We can redraw the event boundaries. Redraw the events that constitute the meals so that there are twenty-three in each of which a pizza is eaten. Redraw the activity of the fifteen detail crews so that there are twenty-seven events each the assembly history of an airplane. The required correspondence is just that the sharings completely overlap the events of being shared and the assemblings completely overlap the events of being assembled. To sum up, existential quantification over events is typically plural quantification and in evaluating a sentence with respect to some events, we take into account redrawings of those events (Schein, 1993: 126 ff.).[18]

---

[18] On event mereology and collectivizing predicates, see also Lasersohn (1990, 1995).

1.3 Scenes and Events

Just the business of sorting out who did what to whom has brought in a mereology of events. It would be enough for (41) to say that there are some events where seventeen turtles are eaters in coincident events and twenty-three pizzas are eaten in coincident events; but it is a small step to make redrawing explicit and it will deliver the scenes fine-grained enough to assimilate all of (50)–(55) while allowing that each pair describes the same events.

(50) The Carnegie Deli sits opposite Carnegie Hall.
(51) Carnegie Hall sits opposite the Carnegie Deli.
(52) I weighed the Volvo.
(53) I weighed the Volvo's parts.
(54) Herb's body vibrated along the full length of the sofa.
(55) Herb's body parts vibrated along the full length of the sofa.

For (50) versus (51), it was suggested that the same event is considered from different perspectives, distinguished by their orientation, northbound or southbound on Seventh Avenue. For the sake of concreteness, assume that there is a relation Scene-of(e,e') between scene e and event e'. (50) reports a scene with the Carnegie Deli on the left and Carnegie Hall on the right (56)–(58). Given this aspect to events, the Agent thematic is glossed as in (57), and 'opposite' as in (58).

(56) $\exists e \exists e'$ (Scene-of(e,e') & Ag$[e,e',d]$ & sit (e') & Op$[[e,e',h])$
(57) Ag$[e,e',x] \leftrightarrow \forall y(y = x \leftrightarrow$ (sitter(e',y) & left-side(e,y)))
(58) Op$[e,e',x] \leftrightarrow \forall y(y = x \leftrightarrow$ (opposite(e',y) & right-side(e,y)))

Note that the first conjuncts of (57) and (58) apply to both the Carnegie Deli and Carnegie Hall in either event. It is rather the perspectival predicate that delivers a unique Agent and a unique Opposite.

The interest of (52)–(55) is the refined perspective they require. As far as Seventh Avenue is concerned, it is enough that we have taken a broken white line to divide left side and right side and looked at the event once from the north and once from the south. We can allow that anything that occupies a spatiotemporal region on one side of the white line for a given scene is, say, on the left side of that scene. We cannot however be so coarse in (52)–(55) since Herb's body and his body parts occupy the same spatiotemporal region as do the Volvo and its parts. Let it be then that perspectives differ in their resolution—that a scene comes with a *reticule*:

(59) *reticule*, a network of fine threads or lines of reference in the focal plane of a telescope or other optical instrument, serving to determine the position of an observed object. (*Funk & Wagnalls*, 1965)

In redrawing the events that underlie and make true (45)–(47), we swap reticules. Instead of 'Scene-of(e,e')', I will say that a scene e resolves an event e', $\Pi(e,e')$, which can be true of many events of the scene. The events that a scene's reticule delineates are those that it resolves, and I will let reticules delineate the events that satisfy thematic relations. Thus the point of (41) and (45)–(47) can now be recast as showing a need to swap reticules in evaluating the disparate conjuncts. The logical form of (41) is (60), where E_i redraws the events of E according to e_i's reticule, that is $\Pi[E,e_i,E_i]$ as in (61):

(41) 17 turtles share 23 pizzas.

(60) $\exists E \exists e_1 \exists E_1 \exists e_2 \exists E_2 (\Pi[E,e_1,E_1]$ & $\Pi[E,e_2,E_2]$ & $[\exists X: 17(X)$ & $turtles[X]]$ Ag$[E_1,X]$ & share$[E]$ &$[\exists Y: 23(Y)$ & $pizzas[Y]]$ $Pat[E_2,Y])$

(61) $\Pi[E,e_i,E_i] \leftrightarrow \forall e(\exists e'\text{overlaps}(e,e'))$ & $E_i e'$ & $\Pi(e_i,e') \leftrightarrow$ $\exists e'(\text{overlaps}(e, e')$ & $E e))$

Resolution applies to objects as well. Although the goings on that (54) and (55) refer to are the same, the scenes are different: in (54) we cannot 'see' one body part from another, there is only Herb. In (55), at greater resolution as it were, we see it all. Replacing 'left-side(e,x)' in (57) and (58) with a resolving perspective, we get for (54) and (55) the following:[19]

(54) Herb's body vibrated along the full length of the sofa.

(62) $\exists e \exists e'(\Pi(e,e')$ & Ag$[e,e',$ Herb's body$]$ & vibrate(e') & Along$[e,e',$ the full length of the sofa$])$

(63) Ag$[e,e',$ Herb's body$] \leftrightarrow \forall y(y =$ Herb's body $\leftrightarrow$ (vibrator(e',y) & $\Pi(e,y)))$

(55) Herb's body parts vibrated along the full length of the sofa.

(64) $\exists e \exists e'(\Pi(e,e')$ & Ag$[e,e',$ Herb's body parts$]$ & vibrate(e') & Along$[e,e',$ the full length of the sofa$])$

---

[19] For the sake of simplicity, I am ignoring here reference to pluralities of events. Note, as Paul Pietroski reminds me, that the revised logical forms still preserve the entailments under (1) which provide the original motivation for decomposition. The logical form (56) for *The Carnegie Deli sits opposite Carnegie Hall* entails via the familiar logic of conjunction what would be the logical form for *The Carnegie Deli sits*. Similarly, the logical form (60) for *17 turtles share 23 pizzas* entails that 17 turtles share, and the logical form (62) for *Herb's body vibrated along the full length of the sofa* entails that Herb's body vibrated.

(65) Ag$[e,e'$, Herb body parts$] \leftrightarrow \forall y$(Herb's body part$(y) \leftrightarrow$ (vibrator (e',y)
    & $\Pi(e,y)$))

It is, I think, a serious problem for Davidsonian analyses to find some model of the events that are alleged to verify (50)– (55). The Davidsonian logical forms via exhaustivity demand that Carnegie Hall's sitting opposite the Carnegie Deli and the Carnegie Deli's sitting opposite Carnegie Hall are not the same event and that Herb's body vibrating is not the same event as Herb's body parts vibrating. With everything pretty much doing the same thing in the same place, what can these non-identical events be? In brief, the proposal here admits to an error in what has been our informal reading of Davidsonian logical forms, 'there is an event such that...' or 'there are some events such that...'. To talk of events is to invite identification with things individuated by their causal relations. It would be less misleading to read the logical forms as saying 'there is a scene such that...' or 'there are some scenes such that...'.[20]

2 Thematic Roles and Plurality

Scenes and reticules have reconciled exhaustivity with absolute thematic roles. Yet special problems arise when they are extended to collective bodies, such as the case of a collective agent ((68) below) discussed in Landman (1995).

---

[20] Of course if scenes are to play their expected role, then we must further assume that if a tree falls in the forest and there is no one around to hear it, it still makes a sound. That is, scenes are abstract and public: the same object or event under the same external conditions (lighting, e.g.) from the same vantage point under the same degree of resolution, etc., projects the same scene onto two dimensions no matter the moment or the perceiver. Comitative phrases are unruly members of the thematic role family. They are as symmetric as *The Carnegie Deli sits opposite Carnegie Hall*, (i)–(ii), and present the same problem for exhaustivity. (i) *a.* Brutus stabbed Caesar with Cassius; *b.* Cassius stabbed Caesar with Brutus. (ii) *a.* Brutus was ushered into the Senate with Cassius; *b.* Cassius was ushered into the Senate with Brutus. Also, unlike what is expected from a conjunct, they do not drop *salva veritate*, (iii), Brutus killed Caesar with Cassius, ?*Therefore, Brutus killed Caesar. And, they appear to show the effect of scope, (iv): Brutus, with Cassius, killed Caesar with the knife; Brutus killed Caesar with the knife with Cassius; Brutus, with the knife, killed Caesar with Cassius; Brutus, killed Caesar with Cassius with the knife. The sentences in (iv) makes Cassius an accomplice to the knifing itself, but in (v) the knife is Brutus' weapon and Cassius is left to assist the murder in some other way. For a treatment, see Appendix.

(66) *a.* I sing.

    b. The boys sing.

In (66), whatever I do, each of the boys does exactly the same thing. Thus if what I do fits your idea of being an Agent, then so does the collective action:

(67) $\text{Ag}[e,X] \leftrightarrow_{df} \forall x(Xx \leftrightarrow \text{agent}(e,y))$

But, in (42), there is what I do, which is the same as what the top boy in the human pyramid does, and there is what everybody else does. The sentence is not true unless at least one boy touches the ceiling but it does not require them all to. Of course this is the beauty of collective action and helping one's fellows—not everyone has to do exactly the same thing, but they have to do something. No arbitrary plurality of boys with one among them touching the ceiling will make (68*b*) true. The others must have contributed in some way. What is it? We might think to escape from answering by claiming that a part–whole relation relates a bottom boy to the top boy just as my leg relates to my finger when I touch the ceiling. But this just begs the question. The condition under which something is part of the collective Agent is itself dependent on the choice of verb and occasion of use. (I will also soon exclude object mereology from the combinatorial semantics.) So, if we have to say what exactly the collective Agents did, we say something like (69):

(68) *a.* I touch the ceiling.

    b. The boys touch the ceiling.

(69) $\text{Ag}[e,X, \text{'touch'}] \leftrightarrow_{df}$

    $\forall x(Xx \leftrightarrow \exists y (\text{agent}(e,y) \ \& \ \exists z \ (\text{continuous}(z) \ \& \ \text{overlap}(e,x,z) \ \& $

    $\text{overlap}(e,y,z) \ \& \ \forall x \exists y \ (\text{overlap}(e,x,z) \rightarrow (Xy \ \& \ \text{overlap} \ (e,x,y))))))$

They are the Agents of *e* just in case for any one of them there is a continuous region between him and the agent (in this case, the toucher in the narrow sense) and any part of that region overlaps some of them. The last clause is a topological condition that distinguishes human pyramids from scattered boys, assuming, following Landman's discussion, that this is the target sense— certainly, a possible interpretation of (68*b*). The relation 'overlap(*e,x,y*)' means that *x* overlaps *y* within *e*. The whole pyramid is ten boys, and they touch the ceiling. It is also true that the top six boys touch the ceiling in the same sense. So we must allow a smaller event to circumscribe its participants— hence, the three-place relation 'overlap(*e,x,y*)'. (69) applies equally well to the singular case in (68*a*), where *X* is understood to denote only me. Then, there must be a continuous region overlapping me and the toucher, any part of which overlaps me.

(69) instantiates a schema (70) for a relativized Agent, there is a common core but also a further condition idiosyncratic to the verb: an Agent-for-boys-touching-ceiling-in-circus-act. In (66), an assertion that everybody does the same thing and sings, ψ in (70) reduces to an identity condition '$x = y$'. The scope for polysemy in (70) goes beyond Dowty (1991) or Jackendoff (1987) in that the choice of ψ is completely open-ended and dependent on the context of use.

$$(70)\ \ Ag_v[e,X,\xi] \leftrightarrow_{df} \forall x(Xx \leftrightarrow \exists y(agent(e,y)\ \&\ \psi[e,x,y,X])))$$

Surely this is to be avoided. It is not that we cannot freely make up new ideas and describe new actions. That's what new verbs are for, or nonce uses of old ones. But can't there be a way out from (70), where there is a minimal, invariant meaning for the thematic role Agent (perhaps as in Dowty (1991), see n. 12 above) and it is left to the novel verb in describing the events it denotes to say further what perverse things its Agents are up to? Common sentiment is that the lexicon is the repository of all variation and idiosyncracy and if functional projections mean anything they mean the same thing wherever they occur.

Collective Predication and Absolute Thematic Relations

To justify scenes and reticules, I relied on simple examples where the partici-pants, Herb's or the Volvo's body parts, all do the same thing. Since they are not essentially collective, I could get away with the likes of (65).

(65) $Ag[e,e',$ Herb body parts$] \leftrightarrow \forall y$ (Herb's body part$(y) \leftrightarrow$ (vibrator $(e',y)\ \&\ \Pi(e,y)))$

But the circus act in (68) has us relativizing thematic roles to context of use:

(68) The boys touch the ceiling.
(69) $Ag[e,X,$ 'touch'$] \leftrightarrow_{df}$
      $\forall x(Xx \leftrightarrow \exists y(agent(e,y)\ \&\ \exists z(continuous(z)\ \&\ overlap(e,x,z)\ \&$
      $overlap\ (e,y,z)\ \&\ \forall x \exists y\ (overlap(e,x,z) \rightarrow (Xy\ \&\ overlap(e,x,y)))))))$
(70) $Ag_v[e,X,\xi] \leftrightarrow_{df} \forall x(Xx \leftrightarrow \exists y(agent(e,y)\ \&\ \psi[e,x,y,X])))$

What is invariant about being an Agent is that there is always an agent in some narrow sense, who in this case is the boy on top of the pyramid with his finger on the ceiling, while the others stand in some idiosyncratic relation to him.

The fine-grain events, i.e. the scenes and reticules, now suggest a method for relocating what is idiosyncratic about each context of use to our understanding of the verb, leaving the thematic roles absolute.

(71) $\mathrm{Ag}[e,e',X] \leftrightarrow \forall x(Xx \leftrightarrow \exists y(\text{agent}(e',y) \ \& \ \Pi(e,x)))$

(72) $\mathrm{Pat}[e,e',X] \leftrightarrow \forall x(Xx \leftrightarrow \exists y(\text{patient}(e',y) \ \& \ \Pi(e,x)))$

The Agents are just those among whom there is an agent and all of whom a scene's first reticule resolves, and the Patients are similarly those among whom there is a patient and all of whom a scene's second reticule resolves. Now the topological condition peculiar to the agents of this circus act glosses the verb:

(73) $touch[e_1,e_2,e'] \leftrightarrow_{df} \ldots \& \ \forall x(\Pi(e_1,x) \leftrightarrow \exists y(\text{agent}(e',y) \ \&$
$\exists z(\text{continuous}(z) \ \& \ \text{overlap}(e',x,z) \& \ \text{overlap}(e',y,z) \ \&$
$\forall x \exists y(\text{overlap}(e',x,z) \rightarrow (\Pi(e_1,y) \ \& \text{overlap}(e',x,y)))))))$

(74) $V[e_1, \ldots, e'] \leftrightarrow_{df} \ldots \& \ \forall x(\Pi(e_1,x) \leftrightarrow \exists y(\text{agent}(e',y) \ \&$
$\psi[e_1,e',x,y]))$

The verb asserts that the objects resolved by the first reticule must form a pyramid with the narrow agent of the event. The thematic role, being absolute, can itself make only the weakest assertions consistent with all lexical items and all contexts where it may be used. Without knowing who they are or what exactly they do as Agents, the semantics of the verb can still refer to all those who are to be taken as Agents, descriptively, as all those objects resolved by the first reticule ((73),(74)), and it may then impose idiosyncratic conditions on that group. Thus scenes and reticules, which were called upon to reconcile thematic exhaustivity with the observation that Carnegie Hall and the Carnegie Deli do the same thing and so do Herb's body and Herb's body parts, again step in to prop up absolute thematic roles.[21] It looks like a good day for absolute thematic roles since these fine-grained events are independently necessary and, as scenes, consistent with our a priori intuitions of event identity.

Relativized and absolute thematic relations differ in the end on the location of idiosyncratic, context-dependent conditions such as the topological

---

[21] In fact, they would allow us to bleach the thematic roles of all content other than an asserting that an object is resolved under the first, second, etc. reticule. It could be left entirely to the content of the verb to assert something stronger about the objects so resolved. As Norbert Hornstein (p.c.) points out, such a move would undermine the attempt to derive UTAH from the phrasal projection of thematic roles. Instead, linking conventions for the interpretation of verbs would be necessary to stipulate that they tend to make agents out of the objects resolved under the first reticule, and so on.

condition on human pyramids in the circus act. Relativized thematic relations locate them with the thematic relation itself, ψ in (70), and absolute thematic relations deflect them to the verb, ψ in (74); Relativized thematic relation:

(70) $\text{Ag}_v[e,X,\xi] \leftrightarrow_{df} \forall x(Xx \leftrightarrow \exists y(\text{agent}(e,y) \,\&\, \psi[e,x,y,X])))$

Absolute thematic relation:

(71) $\text{Ag}[e,e',X] \leftrightarrow \forall x(Xx \leftrightarrow \exists y(\text{agent}(e',y) \,\&\, \Pi(e,x)))$

(74) $V[e_1,\dots e'] \leftrightarrow_{df} \dots \,\&\, \forall x(\Pi(e_1,x) \leftrightarrow \exists y(\text{agent}(e',y) \,\&\, \psi[e_1,e',x,y]))$

Essential separation provides the method for discerning the true location of these conditions. Consider for example (75), which patterns with the cases of essential separation introduced earlier:

(75) The boys hoisted every performing seal onto ten girls.

(4) *a.* Three hundred quilt patches covered over two workbenches each with two bedspreads.

  b. Three video games taught every quarterback two new plays.

For (75), I have in mind circus routines involving male and female human pyramids and performing seals. So the same topological condition applies here to both the boys and the girls. Now the point of separation is that there is a logical form for (75) that resembles (76) in crucial respects.

(76) $\exists e([\iota X: \textit{the boys}]\text{Ag}[e,X] \,\&\, [\forall y: \text{seal}(y)][\exists e': e' \le e](\text{hoist}(e') \,\&\, \text{Th}[e',y] \,\&\, [\exists Z: \textit{ten girls}] \text{Onto}[e',Z])$

If absolute, the thematic relations themselves say very little, the topological condition being expressed by the verb. The problem in that case is that the verb will impose the topological condition on the Agents of e'. The Agents of e, that is, the boys, are left to do what they damn well please, since, of necessity, a universal, absolute thematic relation can say very little. Suppose for example that *the boys* refers to all the boys in the audience as well as those in the human pyramid. (75) is of course false, but (76) is true of a scene that is large enough to take in the whole circus tent and resolve under the first reticule all the boys. For each seal, there is a part of this scene where the Agents of that part of the scene hoist the seal onto the girls. Now of course the verb can be moved outside the scope of the universal quantifier so that it applies to the boys' event, *hoist(e)*, where it would correctly impose the topological condition on them as the Agents of e. But then there is no condition to guarantee that the girls supporting a seal in its e' form a pyramid. In fact, the verb, if so displaced, will apply the condition to all the tens of girls supporting seals, the girls who bear the *Onto* relation within the larger *e*, and it will therefore require what (75) does not, namely, that all these girls form one gigantic pyramid.[22] This last observation excludes the possibility of repeating the verb both inside and outside the scope of the universal. Although this would subject everyone who needs it to the relevant topological condition, it goes too far and imposes the spurious requirement, of one gigantic pyramid. Obviously then the verb is not the locus at which to state the context-dependent conditions that affect the interpretation of thematic relations. What is needed is that the topological condition apply at each thematic relation to its events and objects and that the topological condition governing those events and objects be asserted only there. Of course if the topological condition is asserted there, then the thematic relation of, say, the subject must also assert that there is an agent in the robust, nonidiosyncratic sense, since it is this agent that the others in the human pyramid are contiguous with.[23] This is as much as to say that thematic relations must be relativized as in (70). Separation thus turns out to be an argument for relativized thematic relations. Despite our best efforts with the fine-grained scenes, thematic relations turn out to be irreducibly relativized.

Must it be concluded from the argument for relativized thematic relations that there are definitions for our primitive thematic relations and that these definitions fall under a schema that seems to embrace and formalize polysemy in our basic concepts (contrary to semantic atomism (see n. 7) as (70) appears to imply?

(70) $Ag_v[e,X,\xi] \leftrightarrow_{df} \forall x(Xx \leftrightarrow \exists y(agent(e,y) \& \psi[e,x,y,X])))$

Not if what appears on the right-hand side of (70) belongs in the syntax itself, something along the lines of (76), where ψ corresponds to the content of an independent zero morpheme located in a higher functional projection.

(76) $[\exists X : NP]\exists e\exists e'(\psi[e,e',X] \& \exists y \ agent(e,y) \& V(e)\dots)$

---

[22] The fact that there is a separate preposition here does not matter. Prepositions, like thematic relations, will fail to have absolute meanings unless their verb-dependent idiosyncracies are similarly shifted to the meaning of the verb. In any case, it should also be possible to construct examples with double object constructions, where only thematic relations in the narrowest sense are involved.

[23] This should allay the worry of n. 21 that bleached thematic relations would undermine UTAH. The thematic role expressed by Agent must be at least as contentful as (44) and therefore projecting it fixes the position of the argument that bears it, as UTAH requires.

Schein (1997) argues that the thematic relation Agent should not be directly predicated of the (plural) subject. That argument on very different grounds proceeds from the semantics of conjunction and facts about disjoint reference under reconstruction. For now, I will let you choose your poison since the arguments presented here do not discriminate between (44) and (76).

3 On Telicity

With what I saw at Ken's Pub that afternoon, I am inclined to take (31*a*) to report a true, strict identity with different scenes of the same event in mind. The nominalizations provide alternative descriptions of the same event.

(31) *a.* Jim's drinking a few/some beers in nothing less than an hour was Jim's drinking beer(s) for an hour.

    b. Jim drank a few/some beer(s) in nothing less than an hour.
$\exists e$(Agent(e,j) & drink(e) & Patient(e, *a few/some beers*) & In(e, *nothing less than an hour*))

    c. Jim drank beer(s) for an hour.
$\exists e$(Agent(e,j) & drink(e) & Patient(e, *beer*) & For(e, *an hour*))

    d. *Jim drank beer(s) in nothing less than an hour.
$\exists e$ (Agent(e,j) & drink(e) & Patient(e, *beer*) & In(e, *nothing less than an hour*))

To defuse the unsound inference, you might however prefer to deny the identity. It could be said that the first nominalization refers to a completed event occupying the same spatiotemporal region but distinct from the process that is referred to by the second nominalization. Thus the event verifying (31*b*) is not the same as the one verifying (31*c*), blocking the inference to (31*d*). Apart from my pleading the case for a coarser understanding of events, this metaphysical solution finds a way out from (31) only to run up against some insistent questions—how is it that a complex phrase such as *drink some beers* comes to describe only completed events while another complex phrase, *drink beer,* describes only processes? It is not simply that the one phrase hides an expression indicating completion which is absent from the other. Such an expression can be made explicit without undermining the contrast:[24]

---

[24] Verkuyl (1993) observes the contrast and discusses its significance for various accounts of telicity. It matters little whether (31*d*) are ungrammatical, infelicitous or just plain false. Given the logical forms in (31), the expectation is that (31*d*) and (78) should be true and felicitous. To

(77) Jim drank some beer(s) up in nothing less than an hour.

(78) *Jim drank beer(s) up in nothing less than an hour.[25]

Further complicating the problem, we will see below that not only the descriptive content of a phrase but also the context of utterance determines whether it denotes on any occasion processes or completed events. Even if it were all sorted out according to the metaphysical solution that certain phrases at certain times denoted processes and certain phrases at certain times denoted completed events, one may then begin to wonder what is it about the speaker's understanding of the temporal adverbial *in nothing less than an hour* that restricts its application to completed events since there is nothing in the notion of temporal duration or measurement to explain it.

If not a metaphysical solution, and (31*a*) is taken to report a true identity, the unwanted inference prompts a revision in logical form. The inference can be undone if the adverbial phrase is 'relativized' to the phrase it modifies:

(79) *a.* Jim's drinking a few/some beers in nothing less than an hour was Jim's drinking beer(s) for an hour.

   b. Jim drank a few/some beers in nothing less than an hour.
       $\exists e$(Agent(e,j) & drink(e) & Patient(e, *a few/some beers*) & In[e, *nothing less than an hour*, 'drink a few/some beers'])

   c. Jim drank beer(s).
       $\exists e$(Agent(e,j) & drink(e) & Patient(e, *beer*))

   d. *Jim drank beer(s) in nothing less than an hour.
       $\exists e$ (Agent(e,j) & drink(e) & Patient(e, *beer*) & In[e, *nothing less than an hour*, 'drink beer(s)'])

The very same event is a drinking of a few/some beers and a drinking beer(s), and it occurred in nothing less than an hour for a drinking of a few/some beers (79*b*); but, it did not occur in nothing less than an hour for a drinking of beer(s) (79*d*). Although it represents a way out from the inference, this formal solution also begs clarification of how the speaker grasps a 'relativized' adverbial phrase. In what sense can an event occur in an hour for a drinking of some beers but not for a drinking of beers?

Without compromising on an absolute and transparent meaning for the primitive lexical item *in*—it just relates an event to a measure of its temporal

---

the extent that (31*d*) and (78) mean anything, I think they are clearly false in that the smaller quantities of beer drunk were drunk in less than an hour.

[25] Note also *Jim drank some beer up* but **Jim drank beer up*.

extension—the adverbial phrase contains a definite description of the event(s) so measured. They are the *least* event(s) among what has happened that Φ, where the content Φ of the description is fixed by what the adverbial phrase modifies. Thus (80) is the logical form of (79):[26]

(79) *Jim drank beer in nothing less than an hour.

(80) $\exists e$ (Agent(e,j) & drink(e) & Patient(e, *beer*) & [the *least* e': $e' \leq e$ & Agent(e',j) & drink(e') & Patient(e',*beer*)] In(e', *nothing less than an hour*))

For any decent bout of drinking beer, there are no least events of it, or at least none that a speaker can be confident of measuring; and so the sentence is anomalous as a failure of definite reference. The notion of leastness is just the one induced by a mereological relation among events, secured by judgments of the kind that if Jim drank beer for an hour then there are proper parts of lesser duration where he also drank beer.[27]

The explanation for the infelicity of the bare plural in (81) is slightly different from that for the bare mass term in (79); but it too involves a failure of definite reference under conditions where the speaker/hearer should expect success.

(81) *Jim drank beers in nothing less than an hour.

Suppose first that the plural means 'two or more'. Then, if the event under consideration is a drinking of three or more beers, there fails to be a unique, least event of drinking beers. There are three or more such least events. If, on the other hand, exactly two beers are drunk, there is indeed a unique, least event of drinking beers, and yet the sentence remains infelicitous even in such a context. But, for Gricean reasons, the speaker should say in such a context that Jim drank two beers in nothing less than an hour (cf. **every father of Sam*). The bare plural introduces a vagueness of quantity for which there is no excuse, since the speaker and hearer know that uttering the sentence (81) in any context where there were other than exactly two beers drunk would be inconsistent with the definite reference required by the measure adverbial.[28]

---

[26] For convenience, I again suppress plurality in the event description, but I assume that a plural definite description would go as in Sharvy (1980) and Cartwright (1996).

[27] Here I find myself in agreement with Krifka (1989, 1992, 1998) who recognizes that sortal conditions on the (neighboring) events that meet a description are crucial to an account of telicity and that it is not sufficient for such an account to appeal mainly to the expression of a resultant target state.

[28] As Fabio Pianesi (p.c.) points out to me, the pragmatic violation cannot merely be the weak one where I am uncooperative and say 'Jim has drunk (two or more) beers' when I know

It may be that the plural morpheme is better glossed as 'one or more'.[29] The explanation remains the same *mutatis mutandis*: a semantic failure of reference whenever two or more beers are drunk makes the sentence pragmatically inappropriate in all contexts, even where exactly one beer is drunk.

3.1 *Scope Effects and the Content of* the Least event(s) that Φ

That the content of *the least event(s) that* Φ is fixed by what the adverbial phrase modifies provides the occasion to observe some scope effects, which account for the contrast between the bare NP in (78) and the NP with determiner in (77):

(77) Jim drank some beer(s) (up) in nothing less than an hour.

(78) *Jim drank beer(s) (up) in nothing less than an hour.

(82) $[\exists y$: beer$(y)]$ $\exists e$(Agent(e,j) & drink(e) & Patient(e,y) & [the least e': $e' \leq e$ & Agent(e',j) & drink(e') & Patient(e',y)] In$(e',$ *nothing less than an hour*))

In (77), the quantifier *some beer(s)* exports so that it is asserted, as in (82), that for some beer(s) y, the least event of drinking that beer y occurred in

---

for a fact he has drunk five. Notice that in this case it is plausible or rational to represent myself as not knowing something more precise, although it may be misleading and uncooperative to do so. In contrast, we have the pragmatic violation in '*Every father of Sam was at the party', where to represent myself as not knowing that John could have only one father implies that I don't understand the meaning of the word. Similarly, the perceived anomaly of '*Jim drank beers in nothing less than an hour' is partly that one represents oneself as not knowing that exactly two beers were drunk although it is an analytic truth given the semantics of 'in nothing less than an hour'. What I suppose happens when one hears such a sentence is that one presumes that the speaker does not know how many beers and what she says should hold of however many beers were in fact drunk; but then the definite description fails in the general case.

[29] The meaning of plurality is elusive. Note that numberless reference requires the plural. Thus if the existence of solutions to an equation is known but not their number, one says (i) rather than (ii) or (iii). Nor is there any compulsion when (i) will do to utter the pedantic (iv). (i) The solutions to the equation are prime. (ii) The solution to the equation is prime. (iii) The two or more solutions to the equation are prime. (iv) The one or more solutions to the equation are prime. The same observations hold even when the existential presupposition is removed from the determiner: (v) Whatever solution, if any, there is to the equation is prime. (vi) Whatever solutions, if any, there are to the equation are prime. (vii) Whatever two or more solutions (*if any) there are to the equation are prime. (viii) Whatever one or more solutions (*if any) there are to the equation are prime. In fact, the contrast between (vi) and (vii, viii) suggests more—that plurality does not itself have any meaning as a cardinal. Appearances to the contrary elsewhere must be implicatures, giving an unexpectedly large role to the pragmatics to create an illusion of semantic import.

nothing less than an hour. There can of course be such an event for any particular (quantity of) beer or beers. In contrast, it has long been known (Carlson, 1977) that bare NPs resist exportation and thus the bare NP in (78) inevitably falls inside the description with the infelicitous outcome noted above.

Confirming the scope effect is a class of verbs that Quine (1960) called *notional* (as opposed to relational verbs) (see also Heim (1987) and Kratzer's (1995) verbs with *well-behaved objects*) which resist exporting any quantifiers from object position:

> (83) Sam has a deep voice.
> *There is a deep voice such that Sam has it.
> Sam has three friends.
> *There are three friends such that Sam has them.
> Sam ran some/five miles towards where he remembered seeing her.
> *There are some/five miles such that Sam ran them towards where he remembered seeing her.
> Sam made some/three enemies.
> *There are some/three enemies such that Sam made them.
> Sam sustained some/three cranial fractures.
> *There are some/three cranial fractures such that Sam sustained them.
> Sam's pants developed some/three creases.
> *There are some/three creases such that Sam's pants developed them.
> Sam's dermatitis revealed/exposed/produced some/three bald spots.
> *There are some/three bald spots such that Sam's dermatitis revealed/exposed/produced them.[30]

In constructions with notional verbs, *some* NP patterns with the bare NP. For concreteness, suppose that Sam ran five miles toward where he remembered seeing her in exactly forty minutes, we have (84) but both (85) and (86) are unacceptable:

> (84) Sam ran five miles towards where he remembered seeing her in nothing less than forty minutes.
> (85) *Sam ran some miles towards where he remembered seeing her in nothing less than forty minutes.

---

[30] Some speakers (Norbert Hornstein, p.c.) differ on the contrasts in (83), varying, I expect, with one's powers of imagination for reifying such things as creases, bald spots and flaws. Any gain in acceptability for the exported quantification in (83) should also be reflected in a parallel gain for the corresponding sentence in n. 31.

(86) *Sam ran miles towards where he remembered seeing her in nothing less than forty minutes.

Compare the relational verb, for which purpose suppose that Jim drank five beers, that is, five pints, in exactly one hour:

(87) Jim drank (up) five beers in nothing less than an hour.
(88) Jim drank (up) some beer(s) in nothing less than an hour.
(89) *Jim drank (up) beer(s) in nothing less than an hour.

There are some beers, the five downed, such that Jim drank them up in nothing less than hour. Similarly, there is some beer, five pints, such that Jim drank it up in nothing less than an hour. But, it is just this exportation of the quantifier that the notional construction in (85) excludes. The least event of running some miles is no better defined than the least event of running miles, and thus both (85) and (86) fail. In (84), the quantifier *five miles* does not export either; but, for any event of running five miles, there is nevertheless a unique, least part of it of running five miles, to which the adverbial phrase truthfully applies.[31]

In sum, the semantics framed in terms of *the least event(s) that* Φ explains the correlation between the exportability of the quantifier and the contrast in (85) and (88) as well as the contrast between (85, 86) and (84).

---

[31] The remaining examples of (83) also support the conclusion that *some* NP(*s*) and bare NP pattern alike with notional verbs. It requires some care however to elicit a contrast with *n* NP.

(i) *a.* i. Sam made three enemies in nothing less than thirty minutes.
        ii. *Sam made some enemies in nothing less than thirty minutes.
       iii. *Sam made enemies in nothing less than thirty minutes.
     b. Sam sustained three cranial fractures in nothing less than thirty minutes.
          *Sam sustained some cranial fractures in nothing less than thirty minutes.
          *Sam sustained cranial fractures in nothing less than thirty minutes.
     c. Sam's pants developed three creases in nothing less than thirty seconds.
          *Sam's pants developed some creases in nothing less than thirty seconds.
          *Sam's pants developed creases in nothing less than thirty seconds.
     d. Sam's dermatitis revealed/exposed/produced three bald spots in nothing less than three days.
          *Sam's dermatitis revealed/exposed/produced some bald spots in nothing less than three days.
          *Sam's dermatitis revealed/exposed/produced bald spots in nothing less than three days.

Suppose for (i*a*) that Sam begins a course of insults, snubs, and other slights that takes thirty minutes before it makes someone into a sworn enemy. If after arriving at the party Sam undertakes a concurrent assault on three guests so that after thirty minutes he has three new enemies, all the sentences of (i*a*) are felicitous. The fact is that there is no smaller interval in which he has made any enemies and it so happens that the smallest interval of making enemies has yielded several, justifying the use of the plural. Such a context elicits no contrast among the

3.2 *Context-Dependence of* the least event(s) that Φ

Like most definite descriptions and other comparatives, the choice of comparison class and the success of definite reference prove to be context-dependent. Beyond resolving the domain restriction, there is no reason to suppose
that the variability due to context-dependence is the occasion for some further
lexical or structural ambiguity. The sentence in (90) reports Johnny Reb's
action as a particular kind of gesture and it is vague about its effect on the
cannon.

> (90) Johnny Reb heaved the cannon toward the Union battery in ten
> seconds. (After an example from Jackendoff, 1996)

If the cannon is taken to have moved in a linear motion closer to the Union
battery, the sentence is anomalous since in that context there is no least
movement toward the Union battery. In contrast, if the effect of Johnny
Reb's heaving the cannon is rotation, there is then a least event of rotating
towards the Union battery, measured at ten seconds. By restricting the domain
of relevant events, what the speaker and hearer understand about the context
enables definite reference.

Some further examples will mark the extent and generality of this effect.
Under stereotypical conditions, it would be odd to say (91) of the astronomer
looking up on a clear, moonless night and sighting the Pleiades:

> (91) Herschel saw seven stars in twenty seconds.

If the event is thought of as punctual, the temporal measure is inappropriate,
and also if the the event is thought of as extended, since there is no least event of

---

sentences. Suppose however that Sam makes an enemy in ten minutes, and his conduct at the
party consists of three assaults in succession. Here again (ia(i)) is true, but (i.$a$ii)) and (i.$a$iii))
are unacceptable.

The fact that (ia(ii)) and (ia(iii)) are acceptable in case the three assaults are concurrent does
however prompt a revision in the semantics of the adverbial phrase. For the semantics as given,
concurrence should not save the definite description *the least event(s) of making (some) enemies*
from referential failure, since none of the smaller events of making one enemy or making two
enemies is the least. The effect of concurrence suggests instead a definite description of time
intervals, *the time of* (*some*) *least event(s)* Φ. Should the plural mean 'two or more', the three
events of making two enemies is each a least event of making (some) enemies. The time of these
events is a unique interval just in case the events are concurrent, and in that case and only then
does the definite description refer. The 'official' semantics should therefore be based on the
temporal *the time of* (*some*) *least event(s)* Φ, but for the sake of simplicity I will continue in the
text with descriptions of events *tout court*.

seeing seven stars. In contrast, (92) is felicitous provided that all seven shooting stars are not simultaneous (cf. n. 31):

(92) Herschel saw seven shooting stars in 20 seconds.

Under those circumstances, there is a least event of seeing seven shooting stars, which is sufficient for the definite reference required by the temporal adverbial, without having to propose different analyses for (91) and (92).[32]

In (90) and (91), the context varies the circumstances of the direct objects, the kind of movement undergone, or the order of presentation. Variation in the circumstances of other arguments has a similar effect on telicity. Suppose it takes a few days to break ground and build a single settlement. The sentence (93) in an unassuming context fails for reasons similar to those of (78).

(93) 613 construction workers established new settlements in a year.

Yet, if it is further understood that the construction workers are also settlers so that the workers who build a settlement stay put, (93) and (94) become appropriate means to convey that 613 got settled in a year.[33]

(94) 613 settlers established new settlements in a year.

Again, I do not see circumstances changing the analysis of these sentences. Rather, in the first context, there is no least event of 613 workers establishing new settlements, but in the second context there is. It took all of a year to settle 613. This second context also shows a scope effect.[34]

(95) *Settlers established new settlements in a year.
(96) ??Some settlers established new settlements in a year.
(97) ??The settlers established new settlements in a year.

[32] Note that simultaneity or an absence of incremental process is not in general fatal for the temporal adverb: (i) Newton ate an apple in 20 seconds. (ii) Newton ate seven apples in 20 seconds. Although all the apples are eaten in one gulp, (i) and (ii) remain felicitous. There remains at least eating of an/seven apple(s), any smaller part of which would have left out some substance, apple, or some gesture such as the swallow. The accounts in Tenny (1987, 1992, 1994) and Krifka (1989, 1992, 1998) leave it unclear why simultaneity and the absence of incremental process should undermine his *seeing seven zebras in 20 sec.* but not *eating seven apples in 20 sec.* Cf. Dowty (1991), Verkuyl (1993), Jackendoff (1996).

[33] So construed, (94) becomes analogous to: (i) $613 million established new settlements in a year. (ii) 61300 tons of concrete established new settlements in a year.

[34] Despite the given scenario, I find it still somewhat odd to say of particular individuals or a particular group that *they* established new settlements in a year even if it took that long for them all to get settled. I cannot explain this contrast between (94) and (97). In (96), *some settlers* unexported is as bad as (95); but, assigned wide-scope, it becomes like (97).

Dowty (1991) and Jackendoff (1996) stress the point that what I have called here a scope effect is not confined to NPs in object position as sometimes assumed:

(98) 300 refugees streamed/stepped across the checkpoint in three days. (After an example of Dowty, 1991)

(99) *Refugees streamed/stepped across the checkpoint in three days.

(100) Some refugees streamed/??stepped across the checkpoint in three days.

(101) The refugees streamed/??stepped across the checkpoint in three days.

The objects of prepositions also participate. Suppose beach property is converted to commercial advantage by building condos on it, and it takes only a couple of weeks for any one building to go up. Lefrak's beachfront reclamation project built condos without interruption for twelve months:

(102) *Lefrak built condos on beaches in Far Rockaway in three months.

(103) Lefrak built condos on two miles of shoreline property in Far Rock-away in three months.

(104) Lefrak built condos on some/three beaches in Far Rockaway in three months.

(105) *Lefrak built condos out of glass and concrete in three months.

(106) Lefrak built condos out of 3,000 tons of glass and concrete in three months.

Recall that the account of the scope effect is that a quantifier with determiner such as *some* NP(s) can export, in contrast to a bare NP, out of the scope of the adverbial phrase and thus evade the content of the definite description *the least event(s) that* Φ. The observed distribution of the effect implies that a bare NP in any argument position falls obligatorily within the scope of the adverbial phrase and yet *some* NP(s) originating in the same position can export out.

To sum up, a difference of scope between *some beers* and *beers* is the only difference between them that could explain their contrast in (88) and (89). The problem

(88) Jim drank up some beers in nothing less than an hour.

(89) *Jim drank up beers in nothing less than an hour.

for Davidsonian logical form is how to make scope matter when modification is merely conjunction. Here and elsewhere (Schein, 1997), I have explored the idea that the reference to an event inside *In*[e,NP] is in fact accomplished by a definite description. Fixing the content of that description provides the occasion for scope effects. I am not the first to suggest that when speakers use definite descriptions to refer to situations or events, that is, to things that individuate as easily as mud, auxiliary notions such as the *least Fs* or the *minimal Fs* are then imported to secure definite reference.

In an alternative, one could approach the contrast between *some beers* and *beers* without introducing a definite description. Recognizing the difference in scope, one could say that the adverbial 'applies' to *drink x up* in (88) but to *drink beers up* in (89) and that the adverbial 'selects' certain predicates and its selectional feature stipulates those that are sortal, thereby excluding *drink beers up*. The apparatus of selection is nowhere reflected in logical form and what the adverb actually says is just that the event *e* has a certain duration. As a selectional feature, that is, as a comment on lexical competence, one naturally falls into thinking of telicity as a relation among invariant concepts, and one can then be taken by surprise when contextual factors matter (see n. 32). One is driven to plead that *in* NP can apply even to a (nearly) instantaneous event of eating seven goldfish by swallowing them all whole and at once because the stereotypical event of eating is not instantaneous; and *in* NP cannot apply to an instantaneous event of seeing seven zebras because the stereotypical seeing of seven zebras is in fact instantaneous although there are serial sightings of which one can say that seven zebras were seen *in* NP. This strikes me as a rather lame accommodation of pragmatic reality. In contrast, context has always had a secure and precise role in the interpretation of definite descriptions, which affords me a straightforward account of how telicity judgments depend on it.

3.3 *Telicity: Threshold or Terminus?*

In characterizing the contrast between (107) and (108), it is sometimes held (e.g. Krifka, 1989, 1992, 1998) that any predicate to which *in* NP applies felicitously is one where all denoted events that overlap are temporally cofinal.

 (107) *Sam pushed the cart towards the wall in twenty seconds.
 (108) Sam pushed the cart to the wall in twenty seconds.

Many parts of Sam's push to the wall are also pushings of the cart to the wall, but they all end at the wall in the same moment; and thus according to this characterization the predicate *push the cart to the wall* is eligible for the adverbial phrase *in twenty seconds*. In contrast, parts of Sam's push towards the wall are pushings towards the wall without terminating at the same time. The first half of the push is a pushing of the cart towards the wall that terminates halfway. Denoting overlapping events that fail to be cofinal, the predicate *push the cart towards the wall* is excluded from modification by the temporal adverbial. Cofinality thus governs the distribution of the temporal adverb. It is said to hold of all those predicates to which *in* NP can felicitously apply.

With some license, the discussions in Kratzer (1996) and in Hay *et al.* (1999) can be taken to invite the question whether Dowty's (1979, 2.3.5, 88 ff.) *degree-achievement* verbs provide counterexamples to the characterization of telic predicates in terms of cofinality[35] and to raise the further question of whether the temporal adverbial measures the time to a terminal state or merely to some threshold:

> (109) The egg cooked (up) in three minutes and cooked for thirty minutes more until it was a handball.
>
> (110) Sam's wisdom ripened in forty-five years and ripened for another ten years into applesauce.

To answer the question at one extreme, suppose it were understood that the conjuncts in (109) applied to the same event, and so it is said of the thirty-three minutes that the egg cooked that it is an event of the egg cooking in three minutes. If true, then there is a part of it, say, a twenty-eight-minute event ending five minutes sooner, that is also a cooking of the egg in three minutes. The temporal adverbial *in three minutes* comes to imply only that an event has reached some threshold, which may have continued beyond, and a fortiori it undermines any suggestion that such adverbials apply only to predicates respecting cofinality. In the semantics for the temporal adverbial now on offer, the implicit target state (*up* in (111)[36]) results only in the imposition of

---

[35] The subsequent discussion also owes much to a reading of Higginbotham (1999) and Pietroski (1998) and correspondence with Fabio Pianesi.

[36] I use the preposition as shorthand for what may very well be a more complex expression such as secondary predicate or resultative predicated of the egg (and the event) as in Kratzer (1996) and Hay *et al.* (1999) among many others, e.g. Hoekstra (1992). To illustrate, let's unpack 'up(e)' as '$\exists e' \exists n(\text{Cause }(e,e') \,\&\, \text{G}(e',n) \,\&\, n>\text{K})$', where G is the scalar dimension and K, the threshold for egg-doneness—moisture content, bacteria content, whatever. We have both (i) and (ii): (i) $\text{cook}(e_3) \,\&\, \text{Patient}(e_3,o) \,\&\, \text{Cause}(e_3, e_3^+) \,\&\, \text{G}(e_3^+,n_3) \,\&\, n_3>\text{K}$; (ii) $\text{cook}(e_{33}) \,\&\, \text{Patient}(e_{33},o) \,\&\, \text{Cause}(e_{33}, e_{33}^+) \,\&\, \text{G}(e_{33}^+,n_{33}) \,\&\, n_{33}>\text{K}$. The smaller, three-minute event, e_3, caused the n_3-degree of doneness, enough to consider the egg done, and the larger, thirty-three-minute e_{33} brought the egg to the higher n_{33}-degree of doneness. So, both up(e_3) and up(e_{33}). The least event of cooking up is e_3, in three minutes. This illustrates an analysis for 'up(e)' that imposes only a threshold. Note that, as this analysis makes clear, asserting both up(e_3) and up(e_{33}) does not lead to the incoherent claim that both the larger event and its proper part have the same effect in both causing the egg to be done. The different events have different effects,

a threshold and would thus allow the conjuncts of (109) (and (110)) to apply to the same events:[37]

(111)   Patient(e_{33},*the egg*) & cook(e_{33}) & up(e_{33}) &
[the *least* e': $e' \leq e_{33}$ & Patient (e',*the egg*) & cook (e') & up (e')] In (e',*3 min.*)

The argument against cofinality rests on finding a predicate, such as *cook(e) the egg up* that holds of overlapping, non-cofinal events. The evidence for a threshold rather than a terminus, if there is any, turns on showing that a temporal adverb such as *in three minutes* holds also of events longer that three minutes, which is to show that even the modified predicate *cook(e) the egg up in three minutes* fails cofinality.

Consider, for concreteness, (112):

(112)   The room filled (up) with smoke.

The room begins to fill with smoke at t_0, and let us say that the sentence first becomes true at t_1 when a visible haze is seen everywhere. Let e_1 be the threshold event, the room's filling with smoke from t_0 to t_1. It persists quite a bit beyond t_1 so that the fog gets progressively denser until t_2, and the large event e_2 includes all of it from t_0 to t_2. An assertion of (112) after t_2 is judged uncontroversially to be true, and we can now ask which event or events has made it so. One of them is surely e_1 and the question is whether e_2 is another, contrary to cofinality. On the other hand, consistent with cofinality, it may be that (112) is judged to be true when confronted with the dense fog only because we infer the existence of the smaller event e_1, which proves to be the only one of the two that the predicate denotes:

(113)   T $\exists e$ (fill-up(e) & Theme(e,r) & with(e,*smoke*))
(114)   T (fill-up(e_1) & Theme(e_1,r) & with(e_1,*smoke*))
(115)   F (fill-up(e_2) & Theme(e_2,r) & with(e_2,*smoke*))

This attempt to spare cofinality cannot however succeed with logical form such as it is. Suppose that the threshold haze at t_1 weighs 10 pounds, and by t_2 the fog weighs 100 pounds. Alongside (112), it is equally uncontroversial that (116) is true. Here of course only e_2 with the 100 pounds of smoke could make it so:

doneness to different degrees. Both effects happen to exceed the threshold. I thank Fabio Pianesi for discussion of this point.

[37] Note that paths such as *push the cart to the wall* and changes of state such as *the egg cooking up* or maturation in *Sam matured in 3 years* do not on the face of it have least events. Consider all the cofinal subpaths. To accommodate the reference to the least event that Φ, a starting point is tacitly understood—*pushing the cart (from its stationary position) to the wall, the egg cooking up (from the moment it begins to cook), Sam maturing in three years (from when we first met him)* etc.

(116) The room filled (up) with 100 lb. of smoke.

(117) F (fill-up(e_1) & Theme(e_1,r) & with(e_1, *100 lb. smoke*))

(118) T (fill-up(e_2) & Theme(e_2,r) & with(e_2, *with 100 lb. smoke*))

Yet, given that With(e_2, *100 lb. smoke*) → With(e_2, *smoke*), (118) implies the truth of (115), and thus the predicate *the room fills up(e) with smoke* denotes the overlapping but non-cofinal events e_1 and e_2.

It is now left to the champion of cofinality to try to distinguish the analyses of (112) and (116) so that, while (116) remains true of e_2, revised logical forms allow (112) to hold only of e_1. It should be noted that such an effort does not have recourse to the claim that (112), when telic, is understood to be about some particular quantity of smoke, introduced either through tacit definite description or a contextually fixed parameter, as in (119). The suggestion would be that e_1 but crucially not e_2 contains the intended quantity of smoke.

(119) *a.* ∃e (fill-up(e) & Theme(e,r) & with(e, the threshold quantity of smoke))

     b. ∃e (fill-up(e) & Theme(e,r) & with(e, x-quantity smoke))

The objection here is that the bare NP in (112), *with smoke*, comes to be equivalent in (119) to an NP with a determiner. Why doesn't such an equivalence efface the contrast found elsewhere, for example, (77) and (78), between bare NPs and those with determiners? The present examples will serve to illustrate the point. Suppose now that the smoke is heavier than air and it all settles on the floor so that the room is not filled up with smoke. We can nevertheless truthfully say (120) and (121), where the prepositional objects license telicity (see (102)–(106)).

(120) The room filled (up) with 100lb. of smoke in ten minutes.

(121) The room filled (up) with some smoke in ten minutes.

As expected, (120) and (121) contrast with a bare NP. We cannot say of smoke that lies on the floor that:

(122) *The room filled (up) with smoke in ten minutes.

It cannot be said because there is no least event of the room filling with smoke, since the bare indefinite cannot be taken to introduce a particular quantity of smoke. That is, (122) and (112) do not have an analysis along the lines of (119).

As this argument implies, in contexts where (112) and (122) are felicitous, something other than a particular quantity of smoke defines the least event, say, a target state of the room such as the density of its smoke or the degree of haziness throughout (Tenny, 1987: 105 ff.; Hay *et al.*, 1999). This is surely correct, but to make such a target explicit even to a precise value will not prop up cofinality. The proposal would be to gloss (112) along the lines of (123):

(123) $\exists e$ (fill(e) & Theme(e,r) & Hazy(e, n) & with(e,*smoke*))

The smoke in the room at e_1 produces an n-degree haze. If the smoke at e_2 produces an $n + k$-degree haze ($k \neq 0$), then e_2 would, as desired, be excluded, and (112) would hold only of the smaller e_1. In the general case, we can have however no confidence that variation in the quantity of smoke will always have an incremental effect in the target dimension. Suppose, for example, that the understood target for an utterance of (124) is zero-degree visibility so that not even the ground crews venture out. There was enough fog, 500 lb., at e_1 to achieve this state ten minutes after it began to roll in. Visibility has bottomed out, and so ten minutes later when 1000lb. of fog have in e_2 clouded over the runway, it still remains at zero degrees. Similarly, the target state for (125) is that the stain be no longer visible. It is of course possible to waste more paint than the job requires without thereby making the stain even less visible in any sense that the speaker or hearer are ready to grasp.

(124) *a.* The runway clouded over with fog.
       b. The runway clouded over with 1000lb. of fog.
(125) *a.* The water stain on the wall was covered up with fresh paint.
       b. The water stain on the wall was covered up with 10 gallons of fresh paint.

The argument now repeats itself *mutatis mutandis*. In the imagined circumstances, all the sentences of (124) and (125) are true. But the *b*-examples hold only of the larger event e_2, which then entails that the *a*-examples also hold of e_2, contrary to cofinality:

(126) *a.* cloud-over(e_2) & Theme(e_2,r) & visibility(e_2, o) & with(e_2,*fog*)
       b. cloud-over(e_2) & Theme(e_2,r) & visibility(e_2,o) & with (e_2, *1000lb. fog*)
(127) *a.* cover-up(e_2) & Theme(e_2,s) & visibility(e_2,o) & with(e_2,*paint*)
       b. cover-up(e_2) & Theme(e_2,s) & visibility(e_2,o) & with(e_2,*10 gal. paint*)

Cofinality fares no better under more sophisticated analyses of (112) and (116). It may be, as many have suggested, that the target state is expressed by a (small) clausal complement that denotes an event distinct from the process that produces it:

(128) $\exists e \exists e Æ$ (fill$(e, eÆ)$ & Theme (e, r) & full $(eÆ, r)$ & with $(eÆ, smoke)$).
Alternatively, . . . & with$(e, smoke)$); or,
. . . & with$(e, eÆ, smoke)$).

(129) $\exists e \exists e Æ$ (fill $(e, eÆ)$ & Theme (e, r) & full $(eÆ, r)$ & with $(eÆ, 100lb.$ $smoke)$).
Alternatively, . . . & with$(e, 100lb. smoke)$); or,
. . . & with$(e, e', 100lb. smoke)$).

The fact remains that (116) holds only of the larger event e_2, and however this event is parsed into e and e' so that (129) comes out true, (128) will also hold of it, given that With$($ . . . 100lb. smoke$) \rightarrow$ With$($. . ., smoke$)$. The move to treat *With* NP as a term in a conjunction, the basic Davidsonian analysis, suffices to undermine cofinality as a standard for classifying predicates as telic and eligible for *in* NP.[38] On the other hand, if the semantics of *in* NP is as proposed here, the predicates to which the adverb can felicitously apply sort themselves out. On any occasion of use, a predicate Φ is telic, i.e. modifiable by *in* NP, just in case there is the least event(s) that Φ.[39]

The temporal adverbial's conditions of application for a predicate for Φ seem to flow from the notion of the least event(s) that Φ, but it remains open whether this is all there is to the meaning of *in* NP. For the e_2 described in (130)

---

[38] If one were determined to stipulate that all telic predicates observe cofinality, one could start to incorporate the analysis of the temporal adverbial into the predicate itself as in (i): (112) The room filled up with smoke; (i) $\exists e$ (fill(e) & Theme(e, r) & with$(e, smoke)$ & [the *least e Æ*: $eÆ \leq e$ & fill(e') & Theme(e', r) & with$(e', smoke)]e' = e)$.

[39] This formulation as well as remarks throughout this section makes a concession to a common practice which I deplore. There is a received classification of predicates into Aktionsarten (Kenny-Vendler) (with some quibbling over the categories), a list of 'diagnostics' for membership, such as modification by 'in NP', 'for NP', auxiliary selection, entailments under the progressive, etc., and further hand-wringing when these diagnostics do not all agree on a diagnosis. But there is no reason to suppose that speakers apply diagnostics to sort the lexicon, as this view implies, and then go on to tolerate this or that construction only if it draws its predicate from the appropriate class. Rather, there is a syntax and semantics for 'in NP', a syntax and semantics for 'for NP', a theory of auxiliary selection that also comprises a syntax and semantics, and similarly for the progressive and other alleged diagnostics. Should there turn out to be a large overlap among the predicates to which any of these apply, the explanation for their overlap will presumably emerge from their respective analyses as will the explanation for their differences. Talk of 'telicity' indulges the view that speakers grasp some such superordinate concept and that the classification of predicates accordingly is coherent. My rejection of this view is also my excuse for treating here only one of the alleged diagnostics of telicity, 'in NP'.

that lasts thirty-three minutes and fills the room with 100 lb. of smoke, it has just been argued that both (131) and (132) hold of it.

(130) (cf. (109), (110)) The room filled up with smoke in three minutes and filled for thirty minutes more with 90lbs. more smoke until a valve shut down.

(131) The room filled up with smoke.

(132) The room filled up with 100lb. smoke.

It is uncontroversial that (133) also holds of this larger event e_2:

(133) The room filled up with 100lb. smoke in thirty-three minutes.

Yet the semantics as presented so far is more permissive. It allows that the first conjunct of (130), glossed as (134), also hold of the thirty-three-minute e_2.

(134) $\exists e$(Theme(e, r) & fill(e) & up(e) & with(e,smoke) & [the *least e'*: $e' \leq e$ & Theme(e',r) & fill(e') & up(e') & with(e, smoke)] In(e',*3 min.*))

The logical form in (134) says only that some event of the room's filling up with smoke is such that its least part that is also a filling the room with smoke lasts three minutes. The large event meets this threshold condition. Admittedly this offends intuition, since an utterance of (135) seems to leave no room for the speaker to refer to anything other than an event of exactly three minutes.

(135) The room filled up with smoke in three minutes.

One could yield to intuition and so revise the meaning of the temporal adverbial, setting it in effect equivalent to (136), which requires that *in* NP hold only of the threshold event itself:

(136) $\exists e$(Theme(e, r) & fill(e) & up(e) & with(e,smoke) & [the *least e'*: $e' \leq e$ & Theme(e',r) & fill(e') & up(e') & with(e, smoke)] ($e' = e$ & In(e', *3 min.*)))

Alternatively, one could finesse the intuition: any subsequent thought that purports to refer back to the event of (135) does so only via a definite description, *the least event(s) such that the room filled up with smoke in three minutes*, which by itself forces reference to the smaller threshold event.[40]

---

[40] Fabio Pianesi (p.c.) raises an interesting objection to the idea that (135) and the like could hold of the larger, thirty-three minute event. He observes that the imperfective present tense in

3.3.1 *For NP*

What was done for the semantics of *in* NP will also have to be extended to *for* NP. The same thirty-three-minute event is both the room filling with smoke for thirty-three minutes and the room filling up with 100 pounds of smoke in thirty-three minutes:

(137)   The room filled with smoke for thirty-three minutes and filled up with 100lb. of smoke in thirty-three minutes.

If it is the very same event, what then precludes (138)?

(138)   *The room filled up with 100lb. smoke (in thirty-three minutes) for thirty-three minutes.

There is no retreat to the position that *for* NP applies to processes that are distinct from the coincident completed events that *in* NP applies to. Besides everything else that has been said against fine-grained events, a metaphysical distinction would incorrectly exclude (139) as it rules out (138) and (140).

(139)   Joe Namath carried the football for 60 yards in 90 seconds.

(i) and (ii) can no longer be uttered after the three minutes it takes the egg to get done: (i) The egg cooks up in three minutes. (ii) L'uovo cuoce in tre minuti. Yet, if (i) and (ii) could hold of a longer thirty-three-minute event, it should be possible to use the imperfective at, say, the 25th minute while the longer event is still in progress. On the other hand, if (i) and (ii) could hold only of a three-minute event, then after the three minutes, the event is no longer in progress and the imperfective would be inappropriate, as observed. Perhaps the following answers the objection. Observe that the imperfective *John kills Bill* is inappropriate even at the very instant Bill is dead. At that very point, the perfective is required. (iv) Agent(e,j) & Cause(e,e') & die(e') & Patient(e',b). With respect to a logical form like (iv), the observation is that the present imperfective is acceptable only if e is now and no e' that would be a death ('die(e')') caused by e is either now or before now. Cooking the egg up should be similar (cf. n. 36): (v) cook(e) & Patient(e,o) & Cause(e,e') & G(e',n) & $n > K$. The present imperfective requires that e is now and no e' that would be an effect of e is now or before now. Consider the two cases. Suppose the sentence is uttered after the egg has cooked for one minute. e is now, but doneness at three minutes, the first such e', is far enough in the future that it counts as neither now nor before now. After three minutes, and in particular at twenty-five minutes, the following situation obtains. If it now includes the twenty-five-minute e, then for some n >K it will also include an effect e' of e that is the egg being done to the nth degree. The point is that cooking for twenty-two more minutes has certainly made the egg a little more done. That incremental effect is above threshold, and it is achieved at the very instant the twenty-five minutes of cooking have elapsed. So, at twenty-five minutes, the imperfective is inappropriate, as it is in (v) at the very instant that John's action has caused a death. If something along these lines is correct, then the imperfective provides no further argument beyond the intuition noted in the text for restricting (135) to three-minute events.

(140) *Joe Namath carried the football in 90 seconds for 60 yards.

If we follow the crowd and assume that *for* NP and *in* NP are in complementary distribution, then the import of *for* NP for any predicate Φ should be that there is not the least event(s) that Φ.[41] As with *in* NP, the scope of the adverb determines Φ, leading to the unacceptability of (138) and the contrasts in (141)–(143).

(141) Joe Namath ran for 90 seconds.
(142) *Joe Namath ran the 60 yards for 90 seconds.
(143) *Joe Namath ran his run for 90 seconds.

Although both conjuncts of (130) may hold of the same event (and similarly for (109) and (110)), they cannot in fact share the very same predicate Φ. Forcing them to do so degrades the sentences:

(144) * The room filled up with smoke in three minutes and for thirty minutes more with 90lb. more smoke until a valve shut down.
(145) * The egg cooked (up) in three minutes and for thirty minutes more until it was a handball.
(146) * Sam's wisdom ripened in forty-five years and for another ten years into applesauce.

In (144)–(146), the adverbials impose inconsistent conditions on the same Φ.[42]

3.4 *Semantic Knowledge*

Grant for the moment that the semantics of *in* NP is correct: on every occasion where it is used felicitously and truthfully to modify a predicate Φ there is an event e such that $\Phi(e)$ and there is the least part of e that Φ. The semantics and logical form are sufficient, as promised, to rescue coarser-grained events and in particular the truth of (31*a*) from the unsound inference that follows:

---

[41] One could hope that a more natural suggestion for the meaning of *for* NP will derive this generalization that it applies to events that F only if there is not the least part that Fs. I am toying with the idea that *to F for 45 min.* means that a velocity, dx/dt, described by F is sustained for forty-five minutes. Velocities are only definable over continuous functions, and this condition would exclude least parts.

[42] The sentences are marginally acceptable to the extent that the second conjunct is understood to contain a zero anaphor relating to the antecedent verb minus the resultant state. (i) The room filled up with smoke in three minutes and (filled) for thirty minutes more . . . (ii) The egg cooked up in three minutes and (cooked) for thirty minutes more . . . (iii) Sam's wisdom ripened (to maturity) in forty-five years and (ripened) for another ten years . . .

(31) *a.* Jim's drinking a few/some beers in nothing less than an hour =
    Jim's drinking beer(s) for an hour.

  b. Jim drank a few/some beer(s) in nothing less than an hour.
    $[\exists y: \text{beer}(y)]\exists e(\text{Agent}(e, j) \ \& \ \text{drink}(e) \ \& \ \text{Patient}(e, y)$
    $\& \ [\text{the } least \ e': e' \le e \ \& \ \text{Agent}(e', j) \ \& \ \text{drink}$
    $(e') \ \& \ \text{Patient}(e', y)] \ \text{In}(e', nothing \ less \ than \ an \ hour))$

  c. Jim drank beer(s) for an hour.
    $\exists e \, (\text{Agent} \ (e, j) \ \& \ \text{drink}(e) \ \& \ \text{Patient} \ (e, beer) \ldots)$

  d. *Jim drank beer(s) in nothing less than an hour.
    $\exists e(\text{Agent} \ (e, j) \ \& \ \text{drink} \ (e) \ \& \ [\exists y: \text{beer} \ (y)] \ \text{Patient} \ (e, y) \ \& \ [\text{the } least$
    $e': e' \le e \ \& \ \text{Agent}(e', j) \ \& \ \text{drink} \ (e') \ \& \ [\exists y: \text{beer} \ (y)] \ \text{Patient} \ (e', y)]$
    $\text{In}(e', \ nothing \ less \ than \ an \ hour))$

Were the speaker simply to translate the sentences along the lines indicated, she would recognize that there is no valid inference to be had there. But, of course, when she judges that (90) is an infelicitous description of linear motion, she goes beyond the recognition that (90) would be true only if there is a least event of heaving the cannon toward the Union battery.

(90) Johnny Reb heaved the cannon toward the Union battery in ten seconds.

She judges the sentence infelicitous because she knows a priori that there could not be such an event under the circumstances. Similarly, she judges (90) a felicitous description of a rotation, knowing that there would be a least rotation towards the Union battery. These judgments imply mastery of a theory of motion. Judgments of other sentences may imply some other expertise. There is no reason to expect that the knowledge deployed in inferring the (non)existence of a least event should not be as varied and open-ended as the knowledge that underlies lexical competence itself (see Marconi, 1997), enlisting theories of causation, physical constitution, spatial and temporal orientation or whatever else explains what competent speakers know competent speakers know.[43] These remarks should not be taken to

---

[43] As a context of Fabio Pianesi's (p.c.) illustrates, speakers' judgments about (90) imply knowledge of a theory of action. Imagine that to aim the cannon at the Union battery requires a rotation of 45° and Johnny Reb simply overshoots, rotating 60°, and the cannon comes to rest aimed at the barn. In such a context, (90) is judged false despite the 45° rotation that is a subevent of the 60° rotation. If we take seriously the decomposition that Johnny Reb's action caused the cannon's motion, $\exists e \exists e'(\text{Agent}(e, \text{JR}) \ \& \ \text{Cause}(e, e') \ \& \ \text{heave}(e') \ \& \ \text{Theme} \ (e', c) \ldots)$, we must ask when an event in this context counts as an action. Taking into account the

discourage a project (e.g. Jackendoff, 1996) proposing that certain modest axioms from a theory of motion will suffice to subsume many judgments about the telicity of a large class of predicates that turn out, abstractly or concretely, to describe motions. Such a project uncovers how judgments of telicity are as systematic as the lexical competence on which they rely. The view proposed here is that judgments about telicity reflect a judgment about the successful reference of *the least event(s) that* Φ, which on any occasion depends on what the speaker knows about the substituend for Φ. What is dismissed is any further demand for a comprehensive theory of telicity *per se* that purports to lay out for us more general conditions.

Such a garden path towards telicity might begin from some observations about the contrast between (147) and (148) (cf. Krifka, 1989, 1992, 1998).

(147) Adam ate the apple in the blink of a serpent's eye.
(148) *Adam fondled the apple in ten minutes.

In many an event, distinct processes unfold together. As Adam eats, the apple is consumed. As he moves to fondle it, its surface is caressed. We can think of these several processes as each a sequence of events and observe that in the case of the telic predicate (147) the sequence of events corresponding to the apple's consumption is of finite duration since at each turn some part of the apple is consumed and the process ends when there is nothing left. We can observe further that the sequence of Adam's actions map one-to-one onto the event of the apple's being consumed, and since the one comes to an end, so must the other and so must the larger event that comprises these constituent processes. Hence the predicate is telic. In (148), there is a similar one-to-one mapping between Adam's actions and its effects on the surface of the apple, and the surface is also a finite area. Yet, here there need be no end to Adam's fondling since the same surface area can be revisited. With no end to the event in sight, the predicate is judged atelic.

Now all of this is true of eating and fondling apples; and certainly, any speaker may infer that an event ends who knows that it is constituted by several processes and that there are isomorphisms among them and also an isomorphism between one of them and some finite measure. But it is original sin to hold that every judgment of telicity draws on such an inference, or, in

---

intentions of the agent and the internal structure of the action, e.g., motor coordination (which itself provides indications when a planned action begins and ends), one would have to say that the entire swing is one action and not several. There is thus only one action in this context and its effect is a rotation of 60°, falsifying sentence (90).

312 INTENSIONALITY, EVENTS, SEMANTIC CONTENT

other words, to hold that isomorphisms among processes and finite measures provides some kind of an analysis of telicity. It might be thought that the examples in (149)–(152) are, like eating the apple, well-behaved from the point of view of this incrementalist account. The bucket is a finite volume progressively filled and the circle is drawn in increments around the compass. Similarly, the sandcastle is built in stages and the fort demolished bit by bit.

(149) Sam filled the bucket in an hour.
(150) Sam drew a circle in an hour.
(151) Sam built the sandcastle in an hour.
(152) Sam demolished the fort in an hour.

There are, however, contexts where the structure of these events comes to resemble better fondling apples than eating them, without such contexts undermining the telicity of these examples.[44] Suppose that Sam works at a variable rate and that the bucket leaks at a variable rate and an evil twin works against Sam at variable rates to erase the circle, demolish the sandcastle, and rebuild the fort. For that matter, there is a telic event that is gesture-for-gesture and molecule-for-molecule identical to Adam's fondling the apple:

(153) Adam polished the apple in ten minutes (despite a sandstorm).

These contexts make clear that there is no inference from the meaning of the predicates, *fill the bucket, draw a circle, build the sandcastle, demolish the fort, polish the apple*, that Sam will make any progress at all, let alone that the events come to an end. Moreover, Sam's variable rate and the variable rate of the opposing force make sure that the same volumes of the bucket, the same arcs of the circle, the same sections of the sandcastle and the same fortifications will be revisited many times over before Sam rests from her Sisyphean labor. Between (148) and (153), there seems in principle no way to parse the same event into constituent processes, isomorphisms between them, and finite measures so that it is atelic as fondling but telic as polishing. Speakers do not look for such an analysis of events in their judgments of telicity, and so the failure of such an analysis in the imagined contexts for (149)–(153) in no way disrupts the felicity of these sentences—quite unlike (90), where the shift from rotation to linear motion changes a parameter crucial to understanding the temporal adverbial. Although it is formulated in the most general and topic-neutral terms—sequences of events, isomorphisms, and finite measures—and purports to

---

[44] Verkuyl 1993 and Jackendoff 1996 discuss the problem of 'backtracking' for the incrementalist account of motion on (finite) paths. The problem is pervasive, as (149)–(152) suggest.

characterize telicity, the incrementalist theory, which eats the apple but can't fill a leaky bucket, just carries no water.[45]

[45] In Krifka (1989, 1992, 1998), the incrementalist theory assumes a particular form, which is subject to further objections. Telicity for a predicate $P(e)$ requires a thematic relation θ such that for $\theta(x,e)$: if $e' \leq e$, then for some $x', x' \leq x$ and $\theta(x,e')$; and if $x' \leq x$, then for some $e', e' \leq e$ and $\theta(x,e')$; and if $e' \leq e$ & $e'' \leq e$ & $e' \neq e''$, then $(\theta(x',e')$ & $\theta(x'',e'')) \rightarrow x' \neq x''$; and $\theta(x',e')$ & $\theta(x'',e') \rightarrow x' = x''$. That is, with a telic predicate, a thematic relation expresses an isomorphism between parts of the event and parts of an object. It works for eating an apple. Other examples, as several have noted (Tenny, 1987; Dowty, 1991; Verkuyl, 1993; Jackendoff, 1996; Hay et al., 1999; among others) challenge the mapping into parts: (i) Sam's cheeks reddened in ten seconds. (ii) Sam's mood brightened in ten seconds. What parts of Sam's cheeks or his mood map to events? I suppose we could advance a metaphysical doctrine that all qualities of an object are emergent from properties of its atoms, and the relevant parts of Sam's cheeks are its capillaries as they engorge with blood, and I suppose something could be said about Sam's endorphin-receptors when his mood brightens. Further examples challenge even the more elaborate view: (iii) Sam filled the balloon with helium in two minutes. There are no naive parts of the balloon that undergo some incremental change. No atoms either. Suppose we thought of the balloon as a *potential* volume, with regions of that volume as its parts. If the helium molecules marched in and assumed a fixed position in that volume, then filling the balloon would be no worse than cheeks reddening. But, of course, those molecules are in constant flux. We cannot say that the filling of the balloon corresponds to a succession of filling events that happen to parts of the volume. Even where it is plausible to relate incremental events to parts of the object, it can be shown that the relation to parts is not the same as the relation to the object. That is, the isomorphism is not to be defined in these cases in terms of a thematic relation. Consider: (iv) Sam walked the dog in ten minutes. Any pet-owner knows that (iv) is equivalent to: (v) Sam walked the dog empty in ten minutes. The incremental parts appropriate for (iv) and (v) are exactly those of (vi). (vi) Sam emptied the dog. Every part of the walking event corresponds to some part of the emptying event. The emptying event can correspond to dog parts. For Krifka, the thematic relation itself should provide the correspondence. (vii) $\theta(e,x) \leftrightarrow [\forall e': e' \leq e][\exists x': x' \leq x]\ \theta(e',x')$ & $[\forall x': x' \leq x][\exists e': e' \leq e]\ \theta(e',x')$. Even if we allow that the thematic relation in (iv) is distinct from the one in *Sam walked the dog for ten minutes*, it must still express that the dog walked. Perhaps, the telic thematic relation occurring in (iv) is something like (viii). (viii) $\theta(e,x) \leftrightarrow$ walker(e,x) & emptied(e,x). But, if (viii) is the theta role of (iv), then the mapping of dog parts to events must be to events in which the dog part is a walker and is emptied. It is unreasonable to suppose that the (sub-)parts of a dog that walk, if there are any, are identical to the parts that are progressively becoming empty. A similar example, (ix) Sam was massaged in two hours, is equivalent to (x) Sam was rubbed down in two hours. A body is massaged when and only when it has been massaged more or less all over. We allow that Sam is rubbed down only if every part of Sam is rubbed (atelic). But it is not true that Sam is rubbed down only if every part is rubbed down. Similarly, it is not true that Sam is massaged only if every part is massaged. In a proper rub-down or massage, the body is covered by strokes that grab 10% of the surface area. Any grosser manipulation is not thorough enough. Now it is clear that a rub-down of Sam, even if sustained attention is given to his shoulder, does not include a rub-down of his shoulder. Thoroughness requires the latter to be done with the fingertips—10% of the shoulder is smaller than 10% of Sam. As these remarks suggest, it is

3.5 *Telicity and the Syntax of Teloi*

Often the expression of a tacit or overt target state (Parsons, 1990: 235) makes the difference in a judgment of telicity (Dowty, 1979; Hoekstra, 1988, 1992; Levin and Hovav Rappaport, 1995; Pustejovsky, 1991; Tenny, 1987, 1992; Valin, 1990). Despite enumerable fluctuations in the water level, at a certain point the bucket is filled up, that is, filled *full*. Given the leak, it will soon slip out of that state, but there has been an event large enough to have reached that state

possible to approximate graduality or measuring-out as in (xi): rub-down(e,x) $\leftrightarrow$ [$\forall$e′: e′ $\leq$e][$\exists$x′: x′ $\leq$x $\wedge$ x′ =10%(x)] rub(e′,x′) $\wedge$ [$\forall$x′:x′ $\leq$x $\wedge$x′ =10%(x)][$\exists$e′: e′ $\leq$e] rub(e′,x′). What is impossible is (xii): rub-down(e,x) $\leftrightarrow$ [$\forall$e′: e′ $\leq$e][$\exists$x′: x′$\leq$x $\wedge$x′ =10%(x)] rub-down(e′,x′) $\wedge$ [$\forall$x′: x′$\leq$x $\wedge$x′ =10%(x)][$\exists$e′: e′ $\leq$e] rub-down(e′,x′). That is, the incremental progress cannot be defined in terms of the thematic relation itself. These particular objections can be answered by returning to Tenny's (1987: 105 ff.) original understanding of 'measuring-out', (and more recently in Hay, Kennedy and Levin 1999), where, as the paraphrases (v) for (iv) and (x) for (ix) suggest, the incremental change is measured by some scalar property of objects that is not necessarily concerned with the object's parts and independent of the object's thematic relation to the event. So, we have *fill the balloon* (*full to n-degree(psi)*), *walk the dog* (*empty*), *massage Sam=rub Sam down*, *redden=become red to n-degree*, etc. Jackendoff 1996 provides the most insightful discussion of the range of dimensions that can measure out events.

The more general objection in the text to incrementalist theories of any kind remains. Recognizing that not every part of building a house maps onto the house (e.g., erecting the scaffolding), Krifka (1998: 2(9) comments, 'First, we can say that we are just interested in conceptual structures, not in reality. Events that do not contribute to parts of the house like erecting the scaffold may not play any role in conceptual structures, and can be disregarded. Or we can refine the notion of mapping to objects in the following way: If θ(*x,e*) and *e′* $\leq$ *e*, then it is either the case that *e′* can be related to a part *x′* of *x* such that θ(*x′,e′*), or *e′* is a necessary preparatory event for an event *e″,e″* $\leq$ *e*, which in turn is related to a part *x′* of *x* such that θ(*x′,e″*). Given an adequate definition of the notion 'necessary preparatory event', it is possible to show that a predicate like *build a house* is telic.'

I suppose one could chart the divorce of reality and conceptual structure in the present instance as follows. Imagine counterfactually that the parts of the building levitated into place or better that the actual construction scene was edited so as to bleach out any detail that was not the motion of some house part. Of course the erecting of the scaffolding would now appear as an uneventful lull in construction, but no particular level of activity is implied by the notion of building the house and what remains of the original event would count for the perceiver as the house being built somehow. Thus only the motions of the house parts are essential to the event. The extent of an event may also be enlarged by events that are necessarily preparatory for any of its essential parts, to the extent that one is inclined to think of the erection of scaffolding and the like as also part of building the house.

None of this will fill the leaky bucket, and it is difficult to see what other flights from reality could admit *polish the apple* as telic under the circumstances described in the text while still classifying *fondle the apple* as atelic.

and such that lesser events won't have—a least event of filling the bucket full. Similarly, there is a least event of polishing the apple *up* so that it shines all over. The difference between polishing the apple and fondling it is that the latter is not understood to have a comparable telos.

The expression of a telos is however neither necessary nor sufficient for the felicity of *in* NP. It is not necessary since there are contexts without it where (92) is felicitous. Recall that the temporal adverbial is infelicitous when the seven stars are sighted simultaneously (91); but it becomes felicitous when the sightings are not simultaneous, as imagined for (92).

(91) *Herschel saw seven stars in twenty seconds.

(92) Herschel saw seven shooting stars in twenty seconds.

The contexts diverge in no other respect, and in particular, no target state is intended by either.[46]

Nor is the expression of a telos sufficient. I do not mean only to recall to mind the contrast between (77) and (78), where the scope effect can undermine the temporal adverbial despite the explicit resultative *up*:

(77) Jim drank some beers up in nothing less than an hour.

(78) *Jim drank beers up in nothing less than an hour.

The expression of a telos is insufficient even in cases where the scope effect plays no role. The crucial observation relies on a cross-linguistically widespread phenomenon (see Rosen, 1984; Hoekstra, 1984, 1988, 1992; Hoekstra and Mulder, 1990; Zaenen, 1993; Levin and Hovav Rappaport, 1995; Borer,

---

[46] Nor can it be supposed, if one considers any independent means for discriminating a plurality of events from singular events, that *in 20 seconds* requires a plurality of events, which it finds in (92) but not in (91), where it finds only a single sighting. Suppose, for example, that seven astronomers were widely separated on the globe and unaware of each other. There is no reason not to regard their sightings as separate events if necessary, and yet the facts for (i) are the same: (i) Seven astronomers saw/thought of seven stars in twenty minutes. The sentence (i) is felicitous only if the sightings or thoughts are not simultaneous. Another indication of a plurality of events comes from Gillon's (1987) example of *Gilbert, Hammerstein, Hart, Rogers and Sullivan collaborated on light operas*, which is true only if we consider several distinct collaborations (see Section 1.2 above). Suppose thirty astronomers can be divided into subgroups where photos are exchanged, but it is not the case that the thirty astronomers exchanged photos with every one of the other twenty-nine. The truth of (ii) depends on there being a plurality of events within each of which the fewer than thirty astronomers do exchange photos: (iii) Thirty astronomers saw photos of each other. (iv) Thirty astronomers saw photos of each other in twenty minutes. Simultaneity is still excluded despite the plurality of events. For discussion of this point, I thank Fabio Pianesi.

1994, 1998*a*, 1998*b*, among others) where the occurrence of a resultative phrase changes the auxiliary from *have* to *be*, as it does in Dutch:

(154) *a.* Hij heeft gelopen.
        He has run
        'He ran.' (Zaenen, 1993)

      b. *Hij is gelopen.
        He is run
        'He ran.' (Zaenen, 1993)

(155) *a.* ?Hij heeft naar huis gelopen.
        He has to home run
        'He ran home.' (Zaenen, 1993)

      b. Hij is naar huis gelopen.
        He is to home run
        'He ran home.' (Zaenen, 1993)

(156) *a.* Deze bloem heeft het hele jaar gebloeid.
        this flower has the whole year bloomed
        'This flower bloomed for the whole year.' (Levin and Hovav Rappaport, 1995: 161)

(157) *a.* Het boompje is helemaal op-gebloeid toen ik het regelmatig mest gaf.
        the little-tree is completely up-bloomed when I it regularly fertil-izer gave
        'The little tree completely flourished when I regularly gave it fertilizer.' (Levin and Hovav Rappaport, 1995: 162)

Despite the resultative phrase and its effect on auxiliary change in (159), the adverbial *in* NP remains infelicitous unless, again, there is an appropriate least event:[47]

(158) Jan is in tien minuten naar de stad gelopen.
       Jan is in ten minutes to the town run
       'Jan ran to the town in ten minutes' (H. Koopman p.c.)

(159) Jan is (?*in tien minuten) naar de stad toe gelopen.
       Jan is in ten minutes to the town to run
       'Jan ran towards the town in ten minutes.' (H. Koopman p.c.)
       Jan heeft op de tredmill/in het bos gelopen.

---

[47] Borer (1998a: n. 24) notes that auxiliary selection and resultative formation as well as other related syntactic effects are insensitive to the presence of adverbial modification, negation or progressive.

Jan has on the treadmill/in the woods run
'Jan ran on the treadmill/in the woods' (H. Koopman p.c.)
*Jan is op de tredmill/in het bos gelopen.
Jan is on the treadmill/in the woods run
'Jan ran on the treadmill/in the woods' (H. Koopman p.c.)

Although in telling cases it is neither necessary nor sufficient to license *in* NP, the expression of a telos often does make a difference as noted above. In so far as the resultative phrase expresses a property, such as *full* in *fill the bucket full*, its subject must be a direct object, as a point of syntax (see Williams, 1980; Schein, 1982; Simpson, 1983; Rothstein, 1983, 1992; Hoekstra, 1988, 1992; Rapoport, 1990; Carrier and Randall, 1992; Levin and Hovav Rappaport, 1995; among others):

(160)   *a.* They shot him dead.
        b. *They shot at him dead.
(161)   *a.* He was shot t_i dead.
        b. He was shot at t_i dead.

Thus the direct object is often, or even typically, mixed up in judgments of telicity, but this carries no implication for the meaning of Theme or any particular thematic relation other than the resultative phrase itself. This becomes apparent where the direct object either bears no direct thematic relation to the matrix event or a relation that is atypical in the absence of the resultative phrase (see Hoekstra, 1988, 1992; Carrier and Randall, 1992; Jackendoff, 1990; Levin and Hovav Rappaport, 1995):

(162)   The DA proved some/three defendants guilty in three hours.
(163)   *The DA proved defendants guilty in three hours.[48]
(164)   Moths will eat twenty holes in that sweater in twenty days.
(165)   *Moths will eat (some) holes in that sweater in twenty days.[49]
(166)   The hot poker burned twenty holes in the wood (one after the other) in twenty minutes.
(167)   *The hot poker burned (some) holes in the wood (one after the other) in twenty minutes.
(168)   The rocket punched three holes in the atmosphere in thirty minutes.
(169)   *The rocket punched (some) holes in the atmosphere in thirty minutes.

---

[48]   The sentence is acceptable on the irrelevant, generic reading, where it is asserted that any defendant is proven guilty in three hours; but crucially (163) has no equivalent to (162).

[49]   A *notional* predicate from which the quantifier cannot be exported. Compare *Moths will eat those holes in that sweater.* See (83) above.

(170) Moses squeezed three drops of water out of rocks in three days.

(171) *Moses squeezed water out of rocks in three days.

(172) Sam shaved some/razors dull in three weeks.

(173) *Sam shaved razors dull in three weeks.

(174) The sheriff talked/sang/crowed/wept/laughed some/three drunks awake in a week.

(175) * The sheriff talked/sang/crowed/wept/laughed drunks awake in a week.

(176) Fred and Barney ate some/twenty fridges empty in half a day.

(177) *Fred and Barney ate fridges empty in half a day.[50]

3.5.1 Direct Object 'Holism'

The syntax of resultative phrases also suffices to explain what has been called the 'holism' of direct objects appearing in the locative alternation (Anderson, 1971; Tenny, 1987, 1992, 1994; Levin and Hovav Rappaport, 1995; Jackendoff, 1996; see also Parsons, 1990: 84 ff.):

(178) John loaded the wagon (full) with hay in two hours. (Williams, 1980)

(179) *John loaded hay into the wagon (full) in two hours. (Williams, 1980)

Note first that for (178) and (179), there is the least event of loading the wagon with hay (as the temporal adverbial requires) only if there is an event of loading the wagon *full*, whether the resultative is tacit or overt. Since the syntax of resultative phrases precludes oblique subjects, (179) is unacceptable. The resultative phrase is likewise excluded from (181), but there is in this case a least event of loading wagons with *the* hay, when the hay is all on wagons, which licenses the temporal adverbial (see (102)–(106)).

---

[50] Again it should be noted that the scope effect is not confined to direct objects:

(i) *The DA proved defendants guilty of crimes against financial institutions in twenty hours.

(ii) The DA proved defendants guilty of crimes against twenty financial institutions in twenty hours.

(iii) *Moths will eat holes in sweaters in ten days (where they eat at a rate of a sweater a day, see n. 23).

(iv) Moths will eat holes in ten sweaters in ten days.

(v) *John wore holes in shoes in three weeks.

(vi) John wore holes in three shoes in three weeks.

Similarly for *burn holes into wood panels, punch holes through clouds*, etc.

(vii) *Moses squeezed water out of rocks in three days.

(viii) Moses squeezed water out of three rocks in three days.

(ix) *The sheriff talked jailbirds awake from drunken stupors in three weeks.

(x) The sheriff talked jailbirds awake from twenty drunken stupors in three weeks.

(180) John loaded the hay up on wagons in two hours.

(181) John loaded wagons with the hay (*up) in two hours.

The 'holism' of the direct object is that properties of this argument in both (178) and (180) delimit the whole event—the wagon's being full and the hay's being removed to wagons. Rather than implying something about the thematic relations of direct objects, 'holism' appears to be entirely an effect of the syntax of resultative phrases.[51]

[51] From the earliest discussions of thematic relations, it has been observed that grammatical subjects and direct objects vary in the thematic relations expressed there (the problem of 'linking' thematic relations to argument positions). If so, the identity of the events described in (25) and (26) and the requirement that thematic relations are exhaustive leads only to the unsurprising conclusion that the music and the clarinet do not stand in the very same thematic relation to the same event, contrary to the logical forms displayed.

(25) Ray played music on the clarinet.

$\exists e(\text{Agent}[e,r]\ \&\ \text{play}(e)\ \&\ \text{Theme}[e,m]\ \&\ \text{On}[e,c])$

(26) Ray played the clarinet.

$\exists e(\text{Agent}[e,r]\ \&\ \text{play}(e)\ \&\ \text{Theme}[e,c])$

It could be that one is a locative, Path, or the other, an Instrument. Cf.

(i) Thurston Howell III cruised the high seas on the Queen Mary.

(ii) Thurston Howell III cruised the Queen Mary on the high seas.

Besides the 'holist' effects, it has also long been known that such lexical alternations do not derive synonymous constructions (see e.g. Oehrle, 1976; Larson, 1988; Levin and Hovav Rappaport, 1988; Pinker, 1989; Pesetsky, 1995):

(iii) *a.* Honest toil gave Sam a headache.

　　　 b. #Honest toil gave a headache to Sam. (Oehrle, 1976)

(iv) *a.* The war gave Halberstam a book.

　　　 b. #The war gave a book to Halberstam. (Oehrle, 1976)

(v) *a.* Mary sent the book to France.

　　　b. #Mary sent France the book. (Pesetsky, 1995: 124)

In some languages, such as Russian and Hungarian, the alternation is reflected in a difference of verbal morphology, which prompts some researchers taking the hint (e.g. Levin and Hovav Rappaport, 1995; Pesetsky, 1995) to propose that English is underlyingly like (all) other languages, showing an accidental homonymy as the result of unpronounced or zero morphemes (see also Parsons, 1990: 84 ff.).

(vi) *a.* Kryst'jany na-gruzili seno na telegu.

　　　　　 peasants(NOM) *na*-loaded hay(ACC) on cart-ACC

　　　　　 'The peasants loaded hay on the cart.'

　　　 b. Kryst'jany za-gruzili telegu senom.

　　　　　 peasants(NOM) *za*-loaded cart-ACC hay-INST

　　　　　 'The peasants loaded the cart with hay.' (Russian, Levin and Hovav Rappaport, 1995: 181)

(vii) *a.* János rámázolta a festéket a falra.

　　　　　 John onto-smeared-he-it the paint-ACC the wall-onto

　　　　　 'John smeared paint on the wall.'

3.6 Plural Reference to Events: Ballistic and Continuous Causation

The semantics of the adverbial *in* NP includes reference to *the least event(s) that* Φ, where the content of Φ is fixed by what the adverbial phrase modifies. Much of what is understood about the distribution and meaning of such adverbial phrases follows from the semantics and pragmatics of definite

   b. János bemázolta a falat festékkel.
   John in-smeared-he-it the wall-ACC paint-with
   'John smeared the wall with paint.'
   (Hungarian, Moravcsik, 1978: 257, cited in Levin and Hovav Rappaport, 1995: 181)

(viii) *a.* a paraszt rárakta a szénát a szekérre.
   the peasant onto-loaded-he-it the hay-ACC the wagon-SUBL
   'The peasant loaded the hay onto the wagon.'
   b. a paraszt megrakta a szekeret szénával.
   the peasant PERF-loaded-he-it the wagon-ACC hay-INSTR
   'The peasant loaded the wagon with hay.'
   c. a paraszt telegrakta a szekeret szénával.
   the peasant full-loaded-he-it the wagon-ACC hay-INSTR

'The peasant loaded the wagon full with hay.' (Hungarian, Ackerman, 1992: 59)

For our purposes, it is not the end of the story to declare that verbs participating in an alternation are distinct in both form and meaning, as in (ix) and (x) where *G*- is the conjectured zero morpheme.

(ix) The peasant loaded the hay onto the wagon in twenty minutes.
(x) The peasant (*G*-)loaded the wagon with the hay in twenty minutes.

Despite a difference in meaning, it may be that on some occasion the alternation describes the very same event, as we may imagine for (ix) and (x) when the hay and the wagon are an exact fit and it took exactly twenty minutes to load.

If ever the same event is described, it cannot be allowed that the hay is the Theme for the loading and the wagon is the Theme for the G-loading, since, as before, the hay and the wagon cannot both be the unique Theme to the same event. The occurrence of *G*- must instead token a difference in thematic relations (xi) or a difference (xii) in the (sub-)events to which the thematic relation applies (if for some reason both the hay and the wagon are felt to be Themes):

(xi) a. $\exists e(\text{Agent}[e, p]$ & $\text{load}(e)$ & $\text{Theme}[e, h]$ & $\text{Onto}[e,w]...)$
    b. $\exists e(\text{Agent}[e, p]$ & $\text{load}(e)$ & $G[e, w]$ & $\text{With}[e,h]...)$
(xii) a. $\exists e \exists e'(\text{Agent}[e, p]$ & $\text{load}[e,e']$ & $\text{Theme}[e', w]...)$
    b. $\exists e \exists e'(\text{Agent}[e, p]$ & $\text{load}[e,e']$ & $G(e')$ & $\text{Theme}[e', w]...)$

(Were alternative (xii) to be developed, 'loade,e']' would have to be further articulated. The identical events would presumably be the value of *e*. See Pietroski 1998 for a discussion of the issues.)

Given the essential separation of thematic relations into their own syntactic constituents (see the discussion above surrounding examples (4), (5), and (75)), the above amounts to the observation that a zero-morpheme appears on the verb iff *G* shows up at a remote location. Thus various considerations arising from the semantics, medium-grained event identities, the description and the scope effects of fixing Φ. There is however an important restriction on *in* NP that so far escapes the current account.

A celebrated example (see Beardsley, 1975; Bennett, 1988; Fodor, 1970; Lombard, 1985; Pietroski, 1998; Thomson, 1971*a*, 1971*b*, 1977; among others) contrasts (188) and (189).

(182)   Lincoln died in two days.
(183)   #Booth killed Lincoln in two days.

Booth shoots Lincoln in the Ford Theatre on 13 April 1865 and immediately flees the scene. Lincoln suffers a mortal wound and dies on 14 April. Sentence (182) is true, but not (183). Sidestepping the vagaries of human agency, let's look more at the mechanics and assume that Booth's bullet passed through Lincoln's body and lay spent on the stage floor. In that case, we find a minimal contrast between (184) and (185):

(184)   The wound killed Lincoln in two days.
(185)   #The bullet killed Lincoln in two days.

If, on the other hand, the bullet remains inside Lincoln, then (185) also becomes acceptable. The difference is that what is inside Lincoln's body can be understood to exert a continuous force aimed at Lincoln's deterioration and death, whereas the bullet that lay on the stage, a ballistic cause, cannot. It appears that the adverbial *in* NP requires continuous

---

exhaustivity of Davidsonian thematic relations and their essential separation lead to an endorsement of a theory of grammar that calculates morphological well-formedness over whole syntactic structures (see Baker, 1988; Pesetsky, 1995).

NB. The alternative (xiib) opens a lacuna in the argument. Essential separation concerns thematic relations and not something like 'G(e')'. Essential separation provides no argument against a lexical item G-load$[e,e']$ such that G-load$[e,e']$ is true of $<e,e'>$ iff load$[e,e']$ & G$[e']$, with such lexical items derived strictly by morphological rule. Of course what (xiib) represents is where G is taken to be the lexical head of a full-blown small clause complement as in e.g. *load the wagon full of hay to the top*. The analysis now entertained is that the morphology delivers *full-load*$[e,e']$, without *full* ever being directly predicated of *the wagon* or in construction with *of hay to the top*. (Why not let the morphology serialize all sorts of verbs, *want-try-go-load*$[e,e',e'',e''']$?) Perhaps there is a cross-linguistic argument to close the lacuna e.g. that auxiliary selection of 'be' requires a resultative phrase and this requirement is invariant across languages with and without the apparent morphological incorporation. Failing such an argument, it is in itself an interesting irony that essential separation drives the morphological account towards (xii) rather than (xi). It thus eschews the more abstract morphosyntax only by embracing the more abstract logical form.

rather than ballistic causation,[52] further illustrations of which are provided below:

(186)   *a.* #A single act of carelessness killed him in fifteen years.[53]

       b. HIV killed him in fifteen years/#in 15 seconds.

       c. A pulmonary embolism killed him in 15 seconds.

(187)   *a.* The Vietnam War gave Secretary of Defense McNamara a headache in eight years. [i.e. the headache culminates McNamara's administration of the war]

       b. #The Vietnam War gave former Secretary of Defense McNamara a book in thirty years.

(188)   *a.* #The decline and fall of the Roman Empire gave Gibbon a book in twenty years.

       b. The Watergate hearings/John Dean gave CBS footage for the evening news in ten minutes.

Of course there is both the least event of the wound's killing Lincoln and the least event of the bullet's killing Lincoln, even in the circumstance where it passes through him, and thus the semantics of *in* NP as presented so far does nothing to illuminate the distinction. It should not however be taken to signal victory for the incrementalist account. For here too there is no isomorphism between the action over two days and Lincoln dying in two days, between what the wound does and the measure of Lincoln's morbidity. With the counter-efforts of his immune system, surgery, and primitive antisepsis, Lincoln's morbidity fluctuates as much as the water level in a leaky bucket. Moreover, whatever the distinction turns out to be, it does not concern telic predicates in general but only causatives.

Our native concept of causation is a relation between events, '$C(e,e')$', where causes are prior to effects, $C(e,e') \rightarrow e < e'$. Yet, in apparent contradiction, we do say that the swarming of locusts destroyed the field of barley, that is, that the swarming of locusts caused the field's destruction, although the events

---

[52] The term 'continuous' versus 'ballistic' causation is from Pinker (1989). Pinker (1989) and Pesetsky (1995) discuss double object alternations whose acceptability seems to turn on whether causation is continuous or ballistic. See below in the text for further discussion. Kiparsky (1997) invokes a related notion to explain conditions on transitivity alternations.

[53] (192a) is acceptable on the irrelevant reading that a single act of carelessness killed him fifteen years later. That is, fifteen years later than the careless act. An analogous reading of *Booth killed Lincoln in two days* is unavailable: 'two days later than Booth' and 'two days later than the killing' make no sense, but 'two days later than Booth's (triggering) action' would be plausible and must be excluded on other grounds.

are nearly simultaneous, with many parts of the effect preceding parts of the cause. All causation is at bottom ballistic, but in saying such things we recognize that causes and effects may exist at a finer grain than we discern and so attribute relations of cause and effect to aggregates and continua of events. Aggregate causation arises just from second-order quantification (plurality) of a first-order relation,

$$C[E,E'] \leftrightarrow (\forall e \exists e'(Ee \rightarrow (E'e' \ \& \ C(e,e'))) \ \& \ \forall e' \exists e(E'e' \rightarrow (Ee \ \& \ C(e,e')))).$$

The swarming of locusts is said to cause the field's destruction in that *the swarming of locusts* is taken as a second-order term, a mass term, that denotes any event that constitutes the swarming of the locusts much as *the water* denotes any quantity of water that constitutes the water,[54] and similarly for *the field's destruction*, whereupon causes do strictly precede their effects.

In explaining the contrast between (184) and (185), I will propose that *in* NP is a predicate of events that is, like some other natural language predicates, strictly collective. Think of it as measuring the distance between or among some events.[55] Decomposing (184) and (185) as causative constructions, stipulate for the moment that *in* NP measures the causes:

(189) $\exists E(\text{Agent}[E,w] \ \& \ \exists E'(C[E,E'] \ \& \ \text{die}[E'] \ \& \ \text{Theme} \ [E',l]) \ \& \ [\text{the least } E'' : E'' \leq E \ \& \ \text{Agent} \ [E'',w] \ \& \ \exists E'(C[E'',E'] \ \& \ \text{die} \ [E'] \ \& \ \text{Theme} \ [E',l])] \ \text{In}(E'', two \ days))$
'Some events[56] that are the wound's action caused Lincoln's death, and the least such events among them spread over two days.'

(190) $\exists E \ (\text{Agent}[E,b] \ \& \ \exists E'(C[E,E'] \ \& \ \text{die}[E'] \ \& \ \text{Theme}[E',l]) \ \& \ [\text{the least } E'' : E'' \leq E \ \& \ \text{Agent}[E'',b] \ \& \ \exists E'(C[E'',E'] \ \& \ \text{die}[E'] \ \& \ \text{Theme}[E',l])] \ \text{In}(E'', two \ days))$

---

[54] See Cartwright (1963, 1965, 1970), Burge (1972), Montague (1973), Pelletier (1974), Bennett (1977), Sharvy (1980), Pelletier and Schubert (1989), Higginbotham (1994), Koslicki (1999).

[55] The proposal is reminiscent of Higginbotham's 1999 ditransitive *in*, 'in(e,e',x)', where x measures the distance between e and e'.

[56] The plural should not be read as sortal to the exclusion of a mass term. It would not be more accurate to say 'some event-stuff' or 'enough event is such . . .' since I do not believe I need to presuppose the structure of a mass term either. A neutral term, such as 'some events or event-stuff' provides the more accurate paraphrase—a plurality of events that may or may not be as dense as an event mass. Pietroski (1998) offers an alternative causative analysis that relates actions and their effects as parts of a superordinate event that covers the whole causal chain. If I can pluralize the superordinate events, the actions and effects, the proposal in the text should be able to accommodate this alternative *mutatis mutandis*.

> 'Some events that are the bullet's action caused Lincoln's death, and
> the least such events among them spread over two days.'

Now between the events that are the wound's action and the events that are
Lincoln's death, there are causes and effects, as $C[E,E']$ requires. There are
causal laws that relate any amount of infection progressing at any given
velocity under any given conditions—the presence of antipathogenic agents
to such-and-such a degree, etc.—to certain amounts of tissue death, and
certain amounts of tissue death would constitute Lincoln's death.

The same cannot be said for a plurality of events constituting the bullet's
action when the bullet ends up on the stage floor. The adverbial *in two
days* is now understood to require reference to such a plurality, but we
are reluctant to think of two events let alone a continuum of such events that
are causes to effects constituting Lincoln's death. We can of course resolve, say,
the bullet's trajectory through Lincoln's body into any number of
events, including the continuum, but without any thought for a relevant
effect that each of these may have caused as that $C[E,E']$ requires.
Some trajectories are rather harmless as far as our understanding is concerned
of how bullets kill. This one killed because something vital was nicked along the
way. That nick makes a cause out of any trajectory that contains it, but the parts
of the trajectory that do not, have no considered effect. These remarks observe
that continuous causation, the wound, provides a plurality of causes, but
ballistic causation, the bullet, does not.[57] The proposal that refers to such a
plurality is a step towards explaining the contrast between (184) and (185), but
more needs to be said. If (185) is simply as (190) represents, with *in two days*
demanding reference to a plurality of causes, then why can it not be understood
to demand that the bullet's action be divided into, say, two nicks, each of which
causes a hemorrhage, neither of which is lethal on its own but together
overwhelm the President? According to (190), *in two days*, should measure
the distance between these two causes, which is mistaken, but an accurate
measure does not produce a better sentence:

(191) #The bullet killed Lincoln in 500 milliseconds.[58]

---

[57] This is somewhat misleading. The construction is in fact too weak to distinguish the bullet
and the wound, since all the trajectories that do contain the one lethal nick are in fact a plurality of
causal events. Something further would have to be said along the lines that distinct causes do not
have the same causal force under the causal laws being considered. All the trajectories that share
the same nick have exactly the force of that nick and therefore fail to be distinct causes. The solution to the more general problem next taken up will however make this refinement unnecessary.

[58] *Pace* the 'as-good-as-dead' reading, 'I am dead, Horatio' (*Hamlet* Act 5, Scene 2).

The problem that (190) and (191) now raise is better illustrated with an example that provides a minimal contrast with the wound's continuous causation. Suppose there is a tree rot that first infects a tree and propagates until it reaches maturity. Throughout its lifespan, it secretes a toxin, the effect of which is strictly local on the surrounding tissue. Propagation to maturity takes a few weeks, and tree death takes between ten and twenty years depending on the extent of the infection, the health of the tree, and the climate.

(192) #The rot's propagation killed the tree in a few weeks. (*cf.* (191))
(193) #The rot's propagation killed the tree in fifteen years. (*cf.* (181))
(194) The secretion of toxin killed the tree in fifteen years.
(195) The tree rot killed the tree in fifteen years.

Like the wound, there is continuous cause and effect in theory between the rot's propagation and the tree's death: any amount of propagation establishes some amount of tree rot which under given conditions secretes toxin at some rate, exerting a necrotic force against local tissue, and local effects in tissue death constitute the tree's death.

What distinguishes (192) and (191) from (184) is the remoteness of the effects from their causes. The tree dies long after the rot has propagated, and Lincoln succumbs long after the bullet's mortal nicks. Let us then suppose that $C(e,e')$ means not only that e precedes e' but also that e' is a proximate effect of e. If $C(E,E')$, then the E' are proximate effects of their respective E. In this context, the proximate effects of the events constituting propagation amount to a doomed but still healthy tree, with years of toxic accumulation to intervene before its death. What counts as proximate is of course entirely dependent on the causal theory entertained, and, in particular, on its resolution or scaling of events. In rejecting (191), I am not saying that speakers refuse the theory that bullets kill or that a bullet's action may have as its proximate effect a slow death, which is a death all the same. It is rather that such a thought is embedded in a causal theory that scales events coarsely. So to say that the bullet killed Lincoln is to find a proximate effect of a single action:

(196) $\exists e(\text{Agent}(e,b) \ \& \ \exists e'(C(e,e') \ \& \ \text{die}(e') \ \& \ \text{Theme}(e',l))$

The temporal adverbial *in 500 ms* demands however plural reference to events, as in (190), which scales down and resolves the bullet's action into a plurality of events. The proximate effects of these events are various tears and ruptures, and it takes another theory, fluid dynamics, and subsequent events, hemorrhage, to kill off the President.[59] In contrast, the wound's infection for two days and the tree rot's secretion for fifteen years, resolved even into microscopic events, have proximate effects of microscopic tissue death that constitute their host's death.

In accounting for the contrast between (184) and (185), it would be better not to say that the temporal adverbial *in* NP 'selects' a predicate that describes continuous causation when applied to a causative construction. Instead, what needs to be said is that *in* NP is a strictly collective predicate. The underlying causative relation expresses proximate causation, and the interaction between plural reference to events and what speakers understand about causation then suffices to explain the contrast.[60]

4 Final Remarks

So at the end of the day Jim's drinking some beers was the very same event as his drinking beer. Speakers' judgments about event identities are not doctrine but data to be explained along with other instances of verbal behavior that arise from some combination of linguistic, rational, and practical competence. The explanation on offer happens to accept some judgments of event identity at face value and the medium-grained events they imply. Like other things and as we might expect, it turns out to be possible to provide alternative descriptions of the same event. Inference patterns, such as (31) above, that suggest the contrary—inference patterns that are themselves among the data to be explained—call out instead for refinements in logical form. Here we need to recognize that temporal adverbials, *in* NP, conceal a plural definite description of events, from which follows several of the phenomena associated with telicity.

Speakers are also sound in their judgment that Carnegie Hall sitting opposite the Carnegie Deli is the same event as the Carnegie Deli sitting opposite Carnegie Hall and that my weighing the Volvo's parts by weighing the Volvo is the same event as my weighing the Volvo. Appearances to the contrary dissolve when logical form is further refined to include scenes and their perspectives and reticules. With these refinements, medium-grained events

[59] To ensure this result, one may wish to strengthen plural reference to mass reference, *the least event-stuff that*. . . . Compare n. 56. Note that with causes and effects so tightly interleaved, it may be unnecessary to stipulate that *in* NP measures the causes.

[60] I leave it open whether these ideas extend to other constructions that appear to discriminate between continuous and ballistic causation. See n. 52.

no longer threaten absolute thematic relations. With a little more abstract syntax, (76) above, absolute thematic relations may yet survive the remaining argument against them, (p. 290), which is all for the good since their generalization across the lexicon and extensibility to novel utterances strongly recommend them. Both thematic relations and events are robust and not too finicky. All of this however is purchased with frank appeals to psychology (perspectives) and to the structure of the special concepts such as causation that underlie lexical competence.

APPENDIX: COMITATIVE AND INSTRUMENTAL *WITH* NP

Comitative and instrumental *with*-NP phrases present special problems of their own for a naïve decomposition into conjuncts.[61] First, note that comitative phrases (ii, iii) also instantiate the problem of exhaustivity that we have seen in connection with (i):

  (i) The Carnegie Deli sits opposite Carnegie Hall.
 (ii) *a.* Brutus killed Caesar with Cassius.
       b. Brutus, with Cassius, killed Caesar.
(iii) *a.* Brutus was ushered into the Senate with Cassius.
       b. Brutus, with Cassius, was ushered into the Senate.

The problem and the solution are robust enough that it matters little what exactly comitative *with* means. Perhaps it occurs as a proform for thematic relations, taking on the meaning of Agent in (ii) and Theme in (iii), or perhaps it has a fixed meaning (cf. *opposite* in (i)) and one infers from the event the nature of the comitative participation. Either way, if one discovers that Cassius did everything that Brutus did in equal measure in the same event, then Brutus is not the unique and exhaustive agent in (ii) and Cassius is not the unique and exhaustive accomplice. However the comitative phrase is understood, we still need to appeal to scenes and reticules, and the solution for the problem of exhaustivity works as well here as it did for (i).

---

[61] I thank José Camacho for bringing the problem to my attention and both him and Paul Pietroski for further discussion.

A problem special to comitative phrases is that (ii) does not entail that Brutus killed Caesar. The problem is clearer in (iii) modeled after an example due to Lasersohn (1995: 70):

(iv) *a.* Russell wrote the whole of *Principia Mathematica* with Whitehead.
      b. Russell, with Whitehead, wrote the whole of *Principia Mathematica.*

The sentences in (iv) do not entail that Russell wrote the whole of *Principia Mathematica*. Yet it is unexpected that the entailment should fail if *with Whitehead* is just the usual conjunct '... & *With*(*e*, Whitehead)'. Even dressed up with scenes and reticules, dropping the comitative phrase should leave behind a sentence that continues to be true.

The simple conjunction that underlies this expectation must therefore be mistaken, and further cause to doubt that analysis comes from an unexpected scope interaction in (v) and (vi) (modeled after examples discussed in Parsons (1990) and Pietroski (1998)) where Nora uses her lens to focus sunlight on the chocolate:

(v) *a.* Nora melted the chocolate with her lens with Willy Wonka.
     b. Nora, with Willy Wonka, melted the chocolate with her lens.
(vi) *a.* Nora melted the chocolate with Willy Wonka with her lens.
     b. Nora, with her lens, melted the chocolate with Willy Wonka.

In (v), Willy Wonka is an accomplice to melting the chocolate with her lens. Perhaps he steadied her hand. In (vi), he is an accomplice to melting the chocolate but without any necessary connection to the lens. Perhaps he used a burner to heat the chocolate from below. It is as if *With Willy Wonka* scopes 'melt chocolate with her lens' in (v) but only 'melt chocolate' in (vi). The contrast is unexpected, and, in fact, Parsons (1990) offers the absence of such scope effects among locative and temporal adverbials as an argument in favor of their analysis as simple conjuncts.[62]

---

[62] There is a small confound for the reported judgments. 'With' also occurs in absolutive constructions, and it seems to me that varying the intonation, one can parse (v) as something like 'Nora melted the chocolate with her lens, with Willy Wonka (helping)' or like 'Nora melted the chocolate with her lens, (doing it) with Willy Wonka', and thereby excuse Willy Wonka from a connection to the lens. Absent the varied intonation, the judgment is however as reported. It also remains that (vi), unlike (v), cannot be used to assert Willy Wonka's assistance with the lens. Note that even if it were the case that (v) and (vi) could freely support either interpretation, the fact that speakers can use these sentences to intend one or the other interpretation is more than a simple conjunction of *with*-phrases could allow for.

The apparent scope effect in (v) and (vi) and the failure of the comitative phrase to drop *salva veritate* can be treated by causal 'chaining', where *with* is analyzed as ditransitive (suppressing the argument place for scenes which would make it tritransitive, see Higginbotham (1999) for ditransitive *in*). As a first approximation, consider (v′) and (vi′) as candidate logical forms for (v) and (vi) respectively (ignore for the moment that the preposition *with* is being treated as ambiguous between a ditransitive (comitative) *With* and a transitive *Instrument*):

(v′) $\exists e \exists e' \exists e''$(Agent($e$, n) & With($e$, e', ww) & Cause(e', e'') & melt(e'') & Patient(e'', c) & Instrument(e', l))

(vi′) $\exists e \exists e' \exists e''$ (Agent(e,n) & Instrument(e, l) & With(e,e',ww) & Cause(e',e'') & melt(e'') & Patient(e'', c))

In both (v′) and (vi′), what melted the chocolate is an event e' that is Nora with Willy Wonka. The truth of (v′) or (vi′) provides no reason to expect melting in an event of Nora without Willy Wonka, and thus the comitative cannot be dropped *salva veritate*. The scope effect also receives a preliminary treatment in that the lens is instrument to an event of Nora with Willy Wonka in (v′), but in (vi′) it is the instrument of Nora's action. The logical forms in (v′) and (vi′) also capture an important distinction between comitative *with* and instrumental *with*. The instrumental does drop *salva veritate*:

(vii) *a.* Nora melted the chocolate with her lens. Therefore, Nora melted the chocolate.

  b. Nora melted the chocolate with her lens with Willy Wonka. Therefore, Nora melted the chocolate with Willy Wonka.

The logical forms in (v′) and (vi′) will however require revision in order to accommodate the semantics of instrumental phrases. As Pietroski (1998) argues (see also Lombard, 1985), there is a compelling sense in which Nora's holding the lens is the same action as her melting the chocolate (this time without Willy Wonka):

(viii) Nora melted the chocolate.
    $\exists e \exists e'$(Agent(e, n) & Cause(e, e') & melt(e') & Patient(e', c))

(ix) Nora held the lens.
    $\exists e \exists e'$(Agent(e, n) & Cause(e, e') & hold(e') & Patient(e', l))

The lens being held and the chocolate melting are of course different events, but what Nora does to bring these about, e in (viii) and (ix), is ostensibly the same in both instances. We can however say (x) but not (xi):

(x) Nora melted the chocolate with her lens.
(xi) *Nora held the lens with her lens.

This presents a dilemma (Parsons, 1990: 164–5; Pietroski, 1998) for the conjunct that is taken to analyze 'with her lens', $Instrument(e,l)$. On the one hand, the instrumental cannot be applied to the embedded caused event e', since it is simply ungrammatical to say (xii):

(xii) *The chocolate melted with the lens.

On the other hand, if one applies it to the action and these are the same in both instances, one would expect no contrast between (x) and (xi). Instead, Pietroski (1998) proposes that the instrumental apply to a larger event that combines cause and effect and concomitantly that the sentential event quantifier quantifies over the larger, combined events, while cause and effect are segmented out in the analysis of the constituent thematic relations. Taking some liberties, we get (x') and (xi') for (x) and (xi) respectively:

(x') $\exists e(\exists e'\exists e''(e = c(e', e'')$ & $Agent(e', n))$ & $melt(e)$ & $\exists e'\exists e''(e = c(e',e''))$ & $Patient(e'', c))$ & $Instrument(e, l))$

(xi') $\exists e(\exists e'\exists e''(e = c(e',e''))$ & $Agent(e',n))$ & $hold(e)$ & $\exists e'\exists e''(e = c(e',e''))$ & $Patient(e'',l))$ & $Instrument(e, l))$

So that it is clear that the quantification over the larger events is what relates one conjunct to another, abbreviate (x') and (xi') as:

(x'') $\exists e(Ag[e,n]$ & $melt(e)$ & $Pa[e,c]$ & $Instrument(e,l))$

(xi'') $\exists e(Ag[e,n]$ & $hold(e)$ & $Pa[e,c]$ & $Instrument(e,l))$

Under this analysis, (x) and (xi) show only that the larger event, the cause-and-effect melting, e in (x''), is not the same as the holding, which we already knew. Their constituent actions, e' in (x') and (xi'), can now be identified, without running up against (xi).

No doubt that (x)–(xii) show that the instrumental applies to more than the actions alone, if they are the same in both instances, or the effects alone, as Pietroski concludes. But, if the instrumental phrase is replaced with a ditransitive, $Instrument(e, e', l)$, the evidence of (x)–(xii) fits an alternative to Pietroski's formulation that neither quantifies over the larger events that combine cause and effect nor leaves the analysis of cause and effect internal to the thematic relations:

(x''') $\exists e\exists e'(Agent(e, n))$ & $Cause(e,e')$ & $melt(e')$ & $Patient(e',c))$ & $Instrument(e, e', l))$

(xi''') $\exists e \exists e'$(Agent(e, n)) & Cause(e,e') & hold(e') & Patient(e',l)) & Instrument(e,e', l))

Here too we can identify the actions, e in (x''') and (xi'''), without fear that (x''') will then entail (xi''').

There may not appear to be much to choose between the alternatives. Notice however that Parsons's and Pietroski's dilemma carries over to comitative phrases. That is, let us suppose that Nora keeps on exactly as before, holding her lens to focus sunlight on the chocolate. Willy Wonka, without interfering with the lens, assists her in some other way with the melting. If Nora's actions in (viii) and (ix) are judged the same, then so are they in (xiii) and (xiv) (holding the lens is all she ever does). Yet (xv) (cf. (xi)) is false:

(xiii) Nora melted the chocolate with Willy Wonka.
(xiv) Nora held the lens.
(xv) *Nora held the lens with Willy Wonka.

We should seek a common resolution. But, if we extend Pietroski's proposal (x')–(xi'') to the comitative, (xiii) will mistakenly entail that Nora melted the chocolate. The proposal works as formulated for instrumentals because of their peculiarity that they, unlike comitatives, drop *salva veritate*. Gloss the account of the instrumental construction this way: there is a causal chain that begins with Nora's action and ends with the chocolate melting and the causal chain's instrument is the lens. Extending the gloss to the comitative construction delivers: there is a causal chain that begins with Nora's action and ends with the chocolate melting and the causal chain's accomplice is Willy Wonka. This last entails that there is a causal chain that begins with Nora's action and ends with the chocolate melting, i.e. that Nora melted the chocolate. We want instead that Nora's action combines with Willy Wonka's participation so that the result causes the chocolate to melt, which is not to say that Nora's action caused the chocolate to melt. The logical syntax has to directly reflect the comitative's intervention in the causal chain so that dropping it will not be truth-preserving, as in (v') (repeated below). Thus it cannot be as in (x''), that only a larger combined event is what connects the conjuncts.

(v') $\exists e \exists e' \exists e''$(Agent($e$,n) & With($e,e'$,ww) & Cause($e',e''$) & melt($e''$) & Patient($e''$,c))

(x'') $\exists e$(Ag[e,n] & melt(e) & Pa[e,c] & With(e,ww)))

Given that the comitative phrase is ditransitive, a unified treatment then compels that the instrumental phrase is too, which recommends the alternative advanced in (x''') and (xi''').

Now that the instrumental phrase is also ditransitive, we should revisit the account of the comitative's scope effects and its failure to drop *salva veritate*:

(v') $\exists e \exists e' \exists e''$(Agent($e$,n) & With($e,e'$,ww) & Cause($e',e''$) & melt($e''$) & Patient($e''$,c) & Instrument($e'$,l))

Nora, with Willy Wonka, melted the chocolate with her lens.

Nora melted the chocolate with her lens with Willy Wonka.

(vi') $\exists e \exists e' \exists e''$(Agent($e$, n) & Instrument($e$, l) & With($e, e'$, ww) & Cause ($e', e''$) & melt($e''$) & Patient($e''$,c))

Nora, with her lens, melted the chocolate with Willy Wonka.

Nora melted the chocolate with Willy Wonka with her lens.

For (v'), simply replacing the instrumental phrase with its ditransitive counterpart carries over Pietroski's insight that the lens is the instrument for cause and effect taken together:

(v'') $\exists e \exists e' \exists e''$(Agent($e$, n) & With($e, e'$, ww) & Cause($e', e''$) & melt($e''$) & Patient($e''$, c) & Instrument($e', e''$, l))

In (v''), the instrumental phrase drops *salva veritate*, the comitative phrase does not, and the lens is the instrument for a cause in which Willy Wonka joins Nora.

Fitting (vi') with a ditransitive instrumental is less straightforward, and I will canvass two alternatives. What first comes to mind is that the lens is the instrument of Nora's action and the adjacent event:

(xvi) $\exists e \exists e' \exists e''$(Agent($e$, n) & Instrument($e,e'$,l) & With($e,e'$,ww) & Cause ($e',e''$) & melt($e''$) & Patient($e''$,c))

Yet, given the formal similarity of the instrumental and comitative phrases, (xvi) looks as if it will license both the comitative and the instrumental to drop *salva veritate*, although it would be mistaken to allow (xvii) to entail (xviii).

(xvii) Nora, with her lens, melted the chocolate with Willy Wonka.
(xviii) *Therefore, Nora, with her lens, melted the chocolate.

An appeal to syntax can however prop up the logical form (xvi). What (xvi) in fact entails is (xix):

(xix) $(\exists e \exists e' \exists e''(\text{Agent}(e, \text{n})$ & $\text{Instrument}(e,e',\text{l})$ & $\text{Cause}(e', e'')$ & $\text{melt}(e'')$ & $\text{Patient}(e'',\text{c})\,)$

Syntax should deny that (xix) is the logical form for (xviii), which instead translates as (xx):

(xx) $\exists e \exists e'(\text{Agent}(e, \text{n})$ & $\text{Instrument}(e,e',\text{l})$ & $\text{Cause}(e,e')$ & $\text{melt}(e')$ & $\text{Patient}(e', \text{c})\,)$

According to (xx), Nora's action is sufficient to melt the chocolate, and (xvi) does not entail this. Thus (xvi) may serve as the logical form for (xvii) provided that (xx) rather than (xix) stand for (xviii). To this end, the translation can be stipulated as follows. An instrumental phrase is a narrow modifier—it can apply only to such event arguments as it finds projected by other elements in the sentence. Thus, in (xviii) and (xx), e and e' are given by the causative analysis of *melt* and the instrumental phrase applies to these. In contrast, (xix) cannot translate (xviii), because it contains a further event argument, which a narrow modifier does not have the power to introduce on its own. With this account of instrumental phrases, note that comitative phrases cannot be narrow modifiers. On the contrary, they must introduce, as in (xvi), a novel event that intervenes in the causal chain melting the chocolate.

The second alternative and the one I prefer for fitting (vi') with a ditransitive instrumental phrase takes a different view of its role there.

(vi') Nora, with her lens, melted the chocolate with Willy Wonka.
       Nora melted the chocolate with Willy Wonka with her lens.
(xxi) $\exists e \exists e' \exists e'' \exists e'''(\text{Agent}(e, \text{n})$ & $\text{Instrument}(e, e', \text{l})$ & $\text{Cause}(e, e')$ & $\text{With}(e', e'', \text{ww})$ & $\text{Cause}(e'', e''')$ & $\text{melt}(e''')$ & $\text{Patient}(e''', \text{c})\,)$

According to (xxi), Nora uses the lens to some effect, and it is this effect of hers that combines with Willy Wonka's intervention to melt the chocolate. The instrumental phrase here relates a cause and an effect exactly as it did in the more straightforward (v''):(v'') $\exists e \exists e' \exists e''(\text{Agent}(e, \text{n})$ & $\text{With}(e,e',\text{ww})$ & $\text{Cause}(e',e'')$ & $\text{melt}(e'')$ & $\text{Patient}(e'', \text{c})$ & $\text{Instrument}(e', e'', \text{l})\,)$

(xxii) Nora, with Willy Wonka, melted the chocolate with her lens.
        Nora melted the chocolate with her lens with Willy Wonka.

As before, the comitative phrase in (xxi) does not drop *salva veritate*, since neither e, Nora's initial action, nor its proximate effect e' suffice to cause the chocolate to melt. The scope of the comitative phrase, which excludes the instrumental in (vi'), is also represented by (xxi): the instrumental does not relate any cause and effect that involves Willy Wonka. In contrast, in (v″) where Willy Wonka assists with the lens, the instrument relates to a cause that does involve him.

> (xxiii) $\exists e \exists e'' \exists e'''$(Agent($e$, n) & With($e$, e'', ww) & Cause(e'', e''') & melt(e''') & Patient(e''',c))
> Nora melted the chocolate with Willy Wonka.

The instrumental phrase, as before, should drop *salva veritate*; but it will not be a logical consequence of (xxi) that it entails (xxii). The entailment goes through when supplemented with a transitive closure principle of some kind: either that (xxiii) to enlarge the effect of an action as its accomplice is the same as enlarging the action itself as an accomplice, or that (xxiv) if an effect of Nora's action combines with Willy Wonka's participation in a causal chain that ends with a certain event (the chocolate's melting), then Nora's action itself combines with Willy Wonka's participation in a causal chain ending with the same event.

> (xxiv) $\forall e \forall e' \forall e'' \forall x$(Cause($e$, e') $\rightarrow$ (With(e',e'',x) $\rightarrow$ With(e,e'',x)))
> $\forall e \forall e' \forall e'' \forall e''' \forall x$(Cause($e$, e') $\rightarrow$(With(e', e'', x) $\rightarrow$ (Cause (e'', e''') $\rightarrow$ $\exists e''$(With(e, e'', x) & Cause(e'', e''')))))

Presumably, such closure principles are false of remote causes and their effects. The point of a comitative phrase is, after all, to assert that things were done within a certain proximity—together. Yet, it seems part and parcel of a notion of *proximate* causation that it support such principles, and that is exactly what the causative analysis of verbs, instrumental and comitative phrases intends. Speakers' a priori grasp of the concepts involved includes (xxiii) or (xxiv) or the like, and thus they judge that the instrumental phrase drops from (vi′) *salva veritate*.

It is, as we have seen, a basic difference between comitative phrases and instrumental phrases that the latter drop *salva veritate* but the former do not. The difference derives from the formal differences in their application to events. In (xxv), the comitative construction rolls up Nora's action and Willy Wonka's assistance in a single cause e''. The instrumental construction in (xxvi) relates cause e and effect e'':

> (xxv) $\exists e \exists e'' \exists e'''$(Agent($e$, n) & With($e$,$e''$,ww) & Cause($e''$,$e'''$) & melt($e'''$) & Patient($e'''$,c))
> Nora melted the chocolate with Willy Wonka.
> (xxvi) $\exists e \exists e'''$(Agent(e, n) & Instrument(e, e'', l) & Cause(e, e'') & melt(e'') & Patient(e'', c))

Nora melted the chocolate with her lens.

The point of these remarks has been to argue for these logical forms. Now given the formal distinction, the lexical one withers away. All there is is *With*. Such differences as there are between the comitative and instrumental constructions become a matter of form:

(xxvii) $\exists e \exists e'' \ \exists e'''$ (Agent $(e, \ n)$ & With(e, e'', ww) & Cause (e'', e''') & melt(e''') & Patient(e''', c))
Nora melted the chocolate with Willy Wonka.

(xxviii) $\exists e \exists e'''$ (Agent(e, n) & With(e, e'', l) & Cause(e, e'') & melt(e'') & Patient(e'', c))
Nora melted the chocolate with her lens.

This is a welcome result to the extent that, across languages, both meanings are persistently translated by the same lexical item. If not, lexical ambiguity always beckons.

In support of the formal difference between (xxvii) and (xxviii), José Camacho has reminded me of an observation that can be culled from the literature on comitatives (e.g. McNally, 1993; Camacho, 1996, 1997, 1999; Dalrymple *et al.*, 1998; and earlier references cited therein). A comitative phrase in Spanish supports plural number agreement on the verb but an instrumental phrase in ostensibly the same position does not:

(xxix)   Nora, con Willy Wonka, derritieron el chocolate.
Nora, with Willy Wonka, melted.3pl the chocolate.

(xxx)   *Nora, con su lente, derritieron el chocolate.
Nora, with her lens, melted.3pl the chocolate.

Suppose the subject event, e of *Cause*(e, e'), determines verbal number agreement. With the comitative phrase in (xxx) analyzed as in (xxvii), the subject event e'' has two participants, Nora and Willy Wonka, and plural number agreement is hence possible. In contrast, the subject event of (xxx), e according to the analysis in (xxviii), has only Nora, and so the plural is ruled out.

ACKNOWLEDGMENTS

Whether through casual remarks or extensive comments directed at this work, I have received much sound advice and enough instruction to keep me biting my nails for some time to come. Thanks to Chris Barker, Hagit Borer, José Camacho, Cleo Condoravdi, Norbert Hornstein, Sabine Iatridou, Ikumi Imani, Ray Jackendoff, Chris Kennedy, Kathrin Koslicki, Richard Larson, Terry Parsons, Fabio Pianesi, Paul Pietroski, Philippe Schlenker, Roger Schwarzschild, Anna Szabolcsi, and Karina Wilkinson. I am especially grateful to Chris Barker, Fabio Pianesi, and Paul Pietroski for an extended correspondence and to Ernie Lepore for his encouragement and for the creation of a forum where linguistics and philosophy commingle.

This work was partially supported under the grant *Comparative Syntax of Japanese, Korean, Chinese and English*, Joint Research, Project No. 08044009, International Scientific Research Program, Japanese Ministry of Education, Science and Culture, April 1996–March 1999, which provided me the opportunity to present preliminary results at Kyushu University in December 1998.

REFERENCES

Ackerman, Farrell (1992). 'Complex Predicates and Morpholexical Relatedness: Locative Alternations in Hungarian', in Ivan Sag and Anna Szabolcsi (eds.), *Lexical Matters* (CSLI Lecture Notes, 24; Stanford, Calif.: CSLI Publications), 55–83.

Anderson, Steven R. (1971). 'On the Role of Deep Structure in Semantic Interpretation', *Foundations of Language*, 6: 197–219.

Bach, Emmon (1986). 'The Algebra of Events', *Linguistics and Philosophy*, 91: 5–16.

Baker, Mark (1988). *Incorporation: A Theory of Grammatical Function Changing* (Chicago: University of Chicago Press).

—— (1997). 'Thematic Roles and Syntactic Structure', in Liliane Haegeman (ed.), *Elements of Grammar* (Dordrecht: Kluwer), 73–137.

Bayer, Samuel Louis (1997). *Confessions of a Lapsed Neo-Davidsonian: Events and Arguments in Compositional Semantics* (Outstanding Dissertations in Linguistics; New York: Garland Publishing).

Beardsley, Monroe C. (1975). 'Actions and Events: The Problem of Individuation', *American Philosophical Quarterly*, 12/4: 263–76.

Bennett, Jonathan (1988). *Events and their Names* (Indianapolis, Ind.: Hackett Publishing Co.).

Bennett, Michael (1977). 'Mass Nouns and Mass Terms in Montague Grammar', in S. Davis and M. Mithun (eds.), *Linguistics, Philosophy and Montague Grammar* (Austin, TX: University of Texas Press), 263–85.

Benua, Laura, and Borer, Hagit (1996). 'The Passive/Anti-Passive Alternation', Paper presented at GLOW, Athens.

Borer, Hagit (1994). 'The Projection of Arguments', in E. Benedicto and J. Runner (eds.), *Functional Projections* (University of Massachusetts Occasional Papers in Linguistics, 17; Amherst, Mass.: GLSA, University of Mass.), 19–47.

—— (1998*a*). 'Deriving Passive without Theta Roles', in Lapointe, D. Brentari, and P. Farrell (eds.), *Morphology and its Relation to Phonology and Syntax* (Stanford, Calif.: CSLI Publications).

—— (1998*b*). 'The Grammar Machine: A View of Acquisition from the Top', Paper presented at the Workshop on Unaccusativity, Berlin, 22–4 May 1998.

Bowerman, Melissa (1982). 'Evaluating Competing Linguistic Models with Language Acquisition Data: Implications for Developmental Errors with Causative Verbs', *Semantica*, 3: 1–73.

Burge, Tyler (1972). 'Truth and Mass Terms', *Journal of Philosophy*, 69: 263–82.

Camacho, José (1996). 'Comitative Coordination in Spanish', in Claudia Parodi, Carlos Quicoli, Mario Saltarelli, and Maria Luisa Zubizarreta (eds.), *Aspects of Romance Linguistics: Selected Papers from the Linguistic Symposium on Romance Languages XXIV* (Washington, DC: Georgetown University Press).

—— (1997). 'The Syntax of NP Coordination' (Ph.D. diss., USC).

—— (2000). 'Structural Restrictions on Comitative Coordination', *Linguistic Inquiry*, 31/2: 366–75.

Carlson, Greg (1977). 'Reference to Kinds in English' (Ph.D. diss., University of Massachusetts, Amherst).

—— (1984). 'On the Role of Thematic Roles in Linguistic Theory', *Linguistics*, 22: 259–79.

—— (1998). 'Thematic Roles and the Individuation of Events', in Rothstein (1998: 35–51).

Carrier, Jill, and Randall, Janet H. (1992). 'The Argument Structure and Syntactic Structure of Resultatives', *Linguistic Inquiry*, 23: 173–234.

Cartwright, Helen Morris (1963). 'Classes, Quantities and Non-Singular Reference' (Ph.D. thesis, University of Michigan, Ann Arbor).

—— (1965). 'Heraclitus and the Bath Water', *Philosophical Review*, 74: 466–85.

—— (1970). 'Quantities', *Philosophical Review*, 79: 25–42.

—— (1996). 'Some of a Plurality', *Philosophical Perspectives*, 10. Metaphysics, 137–57.

Castañeda, Hector-Neri (1967). 'Comments', in N. Rescher (ed.), *The Logic of Decision and Action* (Pittsburgh: University of Pittsburgh Press).

Cruse, D. A. (1973). 'Some Thoughts on Agentivity', *Journal of Linguistics*, 9: 1–204.

Dalrymple, Mary, Hayrapetian, Irene, and King, Tracy Holloway (1998). 'The Semantics of the Russian Comitative Construction', *Natural Language and Linguistic Theory*, 163: 597–631.

Davidson, Donald (1967). 'The Logical Form of Action Sentences', in N. Rescher (ed.), *The Logic of Decision and Action* (Pittsburgh: University of Pittsburgh Press).

Reprinted in Donald Davidson, *Essays on Actions and Events* (Oxford: Oxford University Press, 1980), 105–22.

Davidson, Donald (1971). 'Agency', in R. Binkley *et al.* (eds.), *Agent, Action, and Reason* (Dordrecht: Kluwer).

—— (1985). 'Adverbs of Action'. in Bruce Vermazen and Merrill Hintikka (eds.), *Essays on Davidson: Actions and Events* (Oxford: Clarendon Press).

Davies, Martin (1991). 'Acts and Scenes'. in Neil Cooper and Pascal Engel (eds.), *New Inquiries into Meaning and Truth* (New York: St Martin's Press), 41–82.

Depraetere, Ilse (1995). 'On the Necessity of Distinguishing between (Un)boundedness and (A)telicity', *Linguistics and Philosophy*, 181: 1–19.

Doetjes, Jenny (1997). 'Quantifiers and Selection: On the Distribution of Quantifying Expressions in French, Dutch and English' (Ph.D. diss., University of Leiden, Holland Institute of General Linguistics).

Dowty, David (1979). *Word Meaning and Montague Grammar* (Dordrecht: Kluwer).

—— (1982). 'Tenses, Time Adverbs, and Compositional Semantic Theory', *Linguistics and Philosophy*, 5: 23–55.

—— (1989). 'On the Semantic Content of the Notion "Thematic Role"', in Barbara Partee, Gennaro Chierchia, and Ray Turner (eds.), *Properties, Types and Meanings*, ii (Dordrecht: Kluwer), 69–130.

—— (1991). 'Thematic Proto-Roles and Argument Selection', *Language*, 673: 547–619.

Feinberg, J. (1965). 'Action and Responsibility', in Max Black (ed.), *Philosophy in America* (Ithaca, NY: Cornell University Press), 134–57.

Fodor, Jerry A. (1970). 'Three Reasons for Not Deriving "Kill" from "Cause to Die"', *Linguistic Inquiry*, 1: 429–38.

—— (1998). *Concepts: Where Cognitive Science went Wrong* (Oxford Cognitive Science Series; Oxford: Clarendon Press).

—— and Lepore, Ernie (1998). 'The Emptiness of the Lexicon: Reflections on James Pustejovsky's *The Generative Lexicon*', *Linguistic Inquiry*, 292: 269–88.

Funk & Wagnalls (1965). *Funk & Wagnalls Standard Dictionary of the English Language* (International edn.; Chicago: Encyclopedia Britannica).

Gillon, Brendan (1987). 'The Readings of Plural Noun Phrases in English', *Linguistics and Philosophy*, 102: 199–219.

Gleitman, Lila R. (1969). 'Coordinating Conjunctions in English', in David Reibel and Sanford Schane (eds.), *Studies in Modern English* (Englewood Cliffs, NJ: Prentice-Hall), 80–112.

—— (1990). 'The Structural Sources of Verb Meaning', *Language Acquisition*, 1: 3–55.

—— Gleitman, Henry, Miller, Carol, and Ostrin, Ruth (1996). 'Similar, and Similar Concepts', *Cognition*, 58/3: 321–76.

Goldman, Alvin (1970). *A Theory of Human Action* (Englewood Cliffs, NJ: Prentice-Hall).

Gropen, Jess, Pinker, Steven, Hollander, Michelle, and Goldberg, Richard (1991). 'Affectedness and Direct Objects: The Role of Lexical Semantics in the Acquisition of Verb Argument Structure', *Cognition*, 41: 153–95.

Gruber, Jeffrey (1965). *Studies in Lexical Relations*, Ph.D. diss. MIT, distributed by the Indiana University Linguistics Club.

Hay, Jennifer, Kennedy, Christopher, and Levin, Beth (1999). 'Scalar Structure Underlies Telicity', in "Degree Achievements"', in Tanya Matthews and Devon Strolovich (eds.), *Proceedings from Semantics and Linguistics Theory IX* (Ithaca, NY: CLC Publications, Cornell University), 127–44.

Heim, Irene (1987). 'Where does the Definiteness Restriction Apply? Evidence from the Definiteness of Variables', in Aliceter Meulen and Eric Reuland (eds.), *The Linguistic Representation of (In)definiteness* (Cambridge, Mass.: MIT Press), 21–42.

Higginbotham, James (1994). 'Mass and Count Quantifiers', *Linguistics and Philosophy*, 17: 447–80.

—— (1999). 'On Events in Linguistic Semantics', in James Higginbotham, Fabio Pianesi, and Achille Varzi (eds.), *Speaking of Events* (New York: Oxford University Press).

Hoekstra, Teun (1984). *Transitivity* (Dordrecht: Foris).

—— (1988). 'Small Clause Results', *Lingua*, 74: 104–39.

—— (1992). 'Aspect and Theta Theory', in I. Roca (ed.), *Thematic Structure: Its Role in Grammar* (Berlin: Foris), 145–74.

—— and Mulder, Rene (1990). 'Unergatives as Copular Verbs: Locational and Existential Predication', *TLR* 71: 1–79.

Hornsby, Jennifer (1980). *Actions* (London: Routledge & Kegan Paul).

Hout, van Angeliek (1992). 'Linking and Projection Based on Event Structure', MS, Tilburg University.

—— (1996). *Event Semantics of Verb Frame Alternations. A Case Study of Dutch and its Acquisition* (TILDIL Dissertation Series, 1996–1; Katholicke Universiteit Brabant; promotor. Prof. Dr H. C. van Riemsdijk).

Jackendoff, Ray S. (1972). *Semantic Interpretation in Generative Grammar* (Current Studies in Linguistics, 2; Cambridge, Mass.: MIT Press).

—— (1976). 'Toward an Explanatory Semantic Representation', *Linguistic Inquiry*, 7: 89–150.

—— (1987). 'The Status of Thematic Relations in Linguistic Theory', *Linguistic Inquiry*, 183: 369–411.

—— (1990). *Semantic Structures* (Cambridge, Mass.: MIT Press).

—— (1996). 'The Proper Treatment of Measuring out, Telicity and Perhaps Even Event Quantification in English', *Natural Language and Linguistic Theory*, 14: 305–54.

Kiparsky, Paul (1997). 'Remarks on Denominal Verbs', in Alex Alsina, Joan Bresnan, and Peter Sells (eds.), *Complex Predicates* (CSLI Lecture Notes, 64; Stanford, Calif.: CSLI Publications), 473–99.

Koslicki, Kathrin (1998). 'Constitution and Supervenience', MS, USC.

—— (1999). 'The Semantics of Mass-Predicates', *Noûs*, 33: 46–91.

Kratzer, Angelika (1995). 'Stage-Level and Individual-Level Predicates', in Gregory N. Carlson and Francis Jeffry Pelletier (eds.), *The Generic Book* (Chicago: University of Chicago Press), 125–75.

—— (1996). 'Severing the External Argument from its Verb', in J. Rooryck and L. Zaring (eds.), *Phrase Structure and the Lexicon* (Dordrecht: Kluwer), 109–37.

Krifka, Manfred (1989). 'Nominal Reference, Temporal Constitution and Quantification in Event Semantics', in Renate Bartsch, Johan van Benthem, and P. van Emde Boas (eds.), *Semantics and Contextual Expression* (Dordrecht: Foris Publications), 75–115.

—— (1992). 'Thematic Relations as Links between Nominal Reference and Temporal Constitution', in Ivan A. Sag and Anna Szabolcsi (eds.), *Lexical Matters* (CSLI Lecture Notes, 24; Stanford, Calif.: CSLI Publications), 29–53.

—— (1998). 'The Origins of Telicity', in Rothstein (1998: 197–235).

Kural, Murat (1996). 'Verb Incorporation and Elementary Predicates' (Ph.D. diss. UCLA).

Ladusaw, William, and Dowty, David (1998). 'Toward a Nongrammatical Account of Thematic Roles', in Wendy Wilkins (ed.), *Themati Relations* (San Diego: Academic Press), 61–73.

Lakoff, Georg (1977). 'Linguistic Gestalts', *CLS* 13: 236–87.

Landman, Fred (1995). 'Plurality', in Shalom Lappin (ed.), *Handbook of Semantics* (Cambridge, Mass.: Blackwell), 425–57.

Larson, Richard (1998). 'On the Double Object Construction', *Linguistic Inquiry*, 19: 33–91.

Lasersohn, Peter (1990). 'Group Action and Spatio-Temporal Proximity', *Linguistics and Philosophy*, 132: 179–206.

—— (1995). *Plurality, Conjunction and Events* (Dordrecht: Kluwer).

Lasnik, Howard (1988). 'Subjects and the H-Criterion', *Natural Language and Linguistic Theory*, 6: 1–18.

Levin, Beth (1993). *English Verb Classes and Alternations: A Preliminary Investigation* (Chicago: University of Chicago Press).

—— and Hovav Rappaport, Malka (1988). 'Non-Event-*er* Nominals: A Probe into Argument Structure', *Linguistics*, 26: 1067–83.

—— —— (1995). *Unaccusativity: At the Syntax-Lexical Semantics Interface. Linguistic Inquiry* (Monograph, 26; Cambridge, Mass.: MIT Press).

Lombard, Lawrence B. (1985). 'How Not to Flip the Prowler: Transitive Verbs of Action and the Identity of Actions', in E. Lepore and B. McLaughlin (eds.), *Actions and Events: Perspectives on the Philosophy of Donald Davidson* (Oxford: Blackwell), 268–81.

—— (1998). 'Ontologies of Events', in S. Laurence and C. Macdonald (eds.), *Contemporary Readings in the Foundations of Metaphysics* (Oxford: Blackwell), 277–94.

McClure, William (1995). 'Syntactic Projections of the Semantics of Aspect' (Ph.D. diss., Cornell University).

McNally, Louise (1993). 'Comitative Coordination: a Case Study in Group Formation', *Natural Language and Linguistic Theory*, 11: 347–79.

Marantz, Alec P. (1984). *On the Nature of Grammatical Relations* (Cambridge, Mass.: MIT Press).

Marconi, Diego (1997). *Lexical Competence* (Cambridge, Mass.: MIT Press).

Montague, Richard (1973). 'Comments on Moravcsik's Paper', in J. Hintikka *et al.* (eds.), *Approaches to Natural Language* (Dordrecht: D. Reide), 289–94.

Moravcsik, Edith A. (1978). 'On the Case Marking of Objects', in Joseph H. Greenberg (ed.), *Universals of Human Language: Syntax 4* (Stanford, Calif.: Stanford University Press), 249–90.

Oehrle, Richard (1976). 'The Grammatical Status of the English Dative Alternation' (Ph.D. diss., MIT).

Parsons, Terence (1985). 'Underlying Events in the Logical Analysis of English', in E. Lepore and B. McLaughlin (eds.), *Actions and Events* (Oxford: Blackwell), 235–67.

—— (1990). *Events in the Semantics of English* (Cambridge, Mass.: MIT Press).

—— (1995). 'Thematic Relations and Arguments', *Linguistic Inquiry*, 264: 635–62.

Pelletier, F. J. (1974). 'On Some Proposals for the Semantics of Mass Terms', *Journal of Philosophical Logic*, 3: 87–108.

—— and Schubert, L. (1989). 'Mass Expressions', in D. Gabbay and F. Guenthner (eds.), *Handbook of Philosophical Logic*, iv (Dordrecht: D. Reidel), 327–407.

Perlmutter, David, and Postal, Paul M. (1984). 'The 1-Advancement Exclusiveness Law', in David Perlmutter and Carol Rosen (eds.), *Studies in Relational Grammar 2* (Chicago: University of Chicago Press), 81–125.

Pesetsky, David (1995). *Zero Syntax: Experiencers and Cascades* (Cambridge, Mass.: MIT Press).

Pianesi, Fabio, and Varzi, Achille (1999). 'Speaking of Events: An Introduction', in James Higginbotham, Fabio Pianesi, and Achille Varzi (eds.), *Speaking of Events* (New York: Oxford University Press).

Pietroski, Paul (1998). 'Actions, Adjuncts and Agency', *Mind*, 107: 73–111.

Pinker, Steven (1989). *Learnability and Cognition: The Acquisition of Argument Structure* (Cambridge, Mass.: MIT Press).

Pustejovsky, James (1991). 'The Syntax of Event Structure', *Cognition*, 41: 47–81. Reprint also in Beth Levin and Steven Pinker (eds.), *Lexical and Conceptual Semantics* (Oxford: Blackwell, 1992), 47–81.

Quine, W. v. O. (1960). *Word and Object* (Cambridge, Mass.: MIT Press).

Ramchand, Gillian (1997). *Aspect and Predication* (Oxford: Clarendon Press).

Rapoport, Tova R. (1990). 'Secondary Predication and the Lexical Representation of Verbs', *Machine Translation*, 4: 31–55.

Reichenbach, Hans (1947). *Elements of Symbolic Logic* (London: Collier-Macmillan). Excerpts reprinted in Donald Davidson and Gilbert Harman (eds.), *The Logic of Grammar* (Encino, Calif.: Dickenson Publishing Co., 1975).

Ritter, E., and Rosen, S. T. (1996). 'Strong and Weak Predicates: Reducing the Lexical Burden', *Linguistic Analysis*, 26: 29–62.

—— —— (1998). 'Delimiting Events in Syntax', in W. Geuder and M. Butt (eds.), *The Projection of Arguments: Lexical and Syntactic Constraints* (Stanford, Calif.: CSLI).

—— —— (2000). 'Event Structure and Ergativity', in J. Pustejovsky and C. Tenny (eds.), *Events as Grammatical Objects* (Stanford, Calif.: CSLI), 187–238.

Rosen, Carol (1984). 'The Interface between Semantic Roles and Initial Grammatical Relations', in David Perlmutter and Carol Rosen (eds.), *Studies in Relational Grammar 2* (Chicago: University of Chicago Press), 38–77.

Rosen, Sarah Thomas (1999). 'The Syntactic Representation of Linguistic Events', *GLOT* 42: 3–11.

Rothstein, Susan (1983). 'The Syntactic Forms of Predication', Ph.D. diss., MIT.

—— (1992). 'Case and NP Licensing', *Natural Language and Linguistic Theory*, 10: 119–39.

—— (ed.) (1998). *Events and Grammar* (Studies in Linguistics and Philosophy, 70; Dordrecht: Kluwer Academic Publishers).

Schein, Barry (1982). 'Small Clauses and Predication', MS, MIT; in Anna Cardinaletti and Maria Teresa Guasti (eds.), *Small Clauses* (Syntax and Semantics, 28; New York: Academic Press, 1995), 49–76.

—— (1993). *Plurals and Events* (Current Studies in Linguistics, 23; Cambridge, Mass.: MIT Press).

—— (1997). 'Conjunction Reduction Redux', MS, USC. Forthcoming as '*And*, the univocal and propositional', ch. 1 in *Conjunction Reduction Redux* (Cambridge, Mass.: MIT Press).

Sharvy, Richard (1980). 'A More General Theory of Definite Description', *Philosophical Review*, 89: 607–24.

Simpson, Jane (1983). 'Resultatives', in Lori Levin, Malka Rappaport, and Annie Zaenen (eds.), *Papers in Lexical-Functional Grammar* (Bloomington, Ind.: Indiana University Linguistics Club), 143–57.

Steward, Helen (1997). *The Ontology of Mind: Events, Processes and States* (Oxford: Oxford University Press).

Talmy, Len (1978). 'Figure and Ground in Complex Sentences', in Joseph Greenberg (ed.), *Universals of Human Language*, iv. *Syntax* (Stanford, Calif.: Stanford University Press), 625–49.

—— (1983). 'How Language Structures Space', in H. Pick and L. Acredolo (eds.), *Spatial Orientation: Theory, Research, and Application* (New York: Plenum).

—— (1985*a*). 'Lexicalization Patterns: Semantic Structure in Lexical Forms', in Timothy Shopen (ed.), *Language Typology and Syntactic Description*, iii. *Grammatical Categories and the Lexicon* (Cambridge: Cambridge University Press), 57–149.

—— (1985*b*). 'Force Dynamics in Language and Thought', in William H. Eilfort *et al.* (eds.), *Proceedings of the Parasession on Causatives and Agentivity* (*CLS* 21), 293–337.

Taylor, Barry (1977). 'Tense and Continuity', *Linguistics and Philosophy*, 1: 199–220.

—— (1985). *Modes of Occurrence* (Oxford: Basil Blackwell).

Tenny, Carol (1987). 'Grammaticalizing Aspect and Affectedness' (Ph.D. diss., MIT).

—— (1992). 'The Aspectual Interface Hypothesis', in Ivan Sag and Anna Szabolcsi (eds.), *Lexical Matters* (CSLI Lecture Notes; Stanford, Calif.: CSLI Publications), 1–28.

—— (1994). *Aspectual Roles and the Syntax-Semantics Interface* (Dordrecht: Kluwer).

Thalberg, Irving (1975). 'When do Causes Take Effect?', *Mind*, 84: 583–9.

—— (1977). *Perception, Emotion and Action* (Oxford: Oxford University Press).

Thomson, Judith Jarvis (1971*a*). 'The Time of a Killing', *Journal of Philosophy*, 68: 115–32.

—— (1971*b*). 'Individuating Actions', *Journal of Philosophy*, 68: 771–81.

—— (1977). *Acts and Other Events* (Ithaca, NY: Cornell University Press).

Travis, L. (1994). 'Event Phrase and a Theory of Functional Categories', in P. Koskinen (ed.), *Proceedings of the 1994 Annual Conference of the Canadian Linguistic Association* (Toronto Working Papers in Linguistics; Toronto: Linguistic Graduate Course Union, University of Toronto), 559–70.

—— (1997). 'The Syntax of Achievements', MS, McGill University. Paper presented at the 3rd Annual Meeting of the Austronesian Formal Linguistics Association, UCLA.

—— (2000). 'The L-syntax/S-syntax Boundary: Evidence from Austronesian', in I. Paul, V. Phillips, and L. Travis (eds.), *Formal Issues in Austronesian Syntax* (Dordrecht: Kluwer), 151–75.

Tversky, Amos, and Gati, I. (1978). 'Studies in Similarity', in Eleanor Rosch and B. Lloyd (eds.), *Cognition and Categorization* (Hillsdale, NJ: Erlbaum), 79–98.

Valin Jr., Robert D. van (1990). 'Semantic Parameters of Split Intransitivity', *Language*, 66: 221–60.

Verkuyl, Henk J. (1993). *A Theory of Aspectuality: The Interaction between Temporal and Atemporal Structure* (Cambridge: Cambridge University Press).

Williams, Edwin (1990). 'Predication', *Linguistic Inquiry*, 11: 203–38.

Wilson, George (1989). *The Intentionality of Human Action*, rev. and enlarged edn. (Stanford Series in Philosophy; Stanford, Calif.: Stanford University Press).

Zaenen, Annie (1993). 'Unaccusativity in Dutch: Integrating Syntax and Lexical Semantics', in James Pustejovsky (ed.), *Semantics and the Lexicon* (Dordrecht: Kluwer), 129–61.

Zucchi, Sandro, and White, Michael (1996). 'Twigs, Sequences, and the Temporal Constitution of Predicates', in Teresa Galloway and Justin Spence (eds.), *SALT VI* (Ithaca, NY: CLC Publications, Cornell University), 329–46.

11

A Grammatical Argument for a Neo-Davidsonian Semantics

NORBERT HORNSTEIN

Introduction

Since the beginning of the modern generative enterprise a central question has concerned the 'points of connection between syntax and semantics' (Chomsky, 1957: 93). Different frameworks have postulated different points of contact; from the kernel sentences of *Syntactic Structures*, the deep structures of *Aspects*, through the multi-level theories of the extended standard theory (see Jackendoff, 1972) to the more recent LF-based proposals in the GB (Government-Binding) era. This last LF-centered approach has been widely adopted.[1] The central idea is that LF, a post overt syntax phrase marker, is the unique level of linguistic representation to interface with the semantic component. It provides all the grammatical structure relevant to semantic interpretation.

This conception of LF is analogous (*not* identical) to earlier conceptions of logical form (or logical syntax) (henceforth 'lf') found in the work of philosophers like Frege, Russell, Carnap, and Strawson. In particular, both LF and lf are intended to encode the compositional structure relevant for a sentence's interpretation. However, there are important disanalogies as well. The prime one is that LF, unlike lf, is a grammatical level formed by standard grammatical processes (e.g. rules like Move α) and subject to the kinds of constraints that phrase markers in general are subject to (e.g. the ECP).[2] Thus, LF is

---

[1] See Chomsky (1982), Chierchia and McConnell-Ginet (1990), Larson and Segal (1995).

[2] For a full discussion see Hornstein (1995).

Janus-faced; it faces out to the interpretive components providing the required primitives and structures sufficient for compositional semantic operations (e.g. the syntax necessary for the applications of the clauses of a truth definition) and it faces inward to the grammar since LF is a phrase marker, i.e. it is the output of grammatical operations.

It should be observed that whether there exists a grammatical level with a syntax sufficient for recursive interpretive procedures, i.e. sufficiently like lf, is an empirical question. The tacit assumption of virtually all generative research is that such a level exists. What has been debated is just which level (or levels) it is, what properties it has, which rules are required for its generation, and what well formedness conditions (if any) apply to filter out the garbage. One of GB's achievements has been to develop a rich theory of this level and show how the interaction of grammatical principles and semantic interpretive procedures interact to explain a varied set of data concerning quantifier scope, pronoun binding, multiple interrogation, and more.

As is well known by now, GB is no longer the latest word in grammatical theory. Minimalism is the new kid on the block. Since the early 1990s many GB analyses have been re-evaluated from a minimalist perspective. The aim of this chapter is to see what MP (Minimalist Program) might have to say about the nature of LF and what implications this might have for the correct theory of logical form (lf). As noted, that there exists a relation between LF and lf is widely accepted. If so, one can hope to learn a lot about lf by thinking about LF and vice versa. In other words, it is reasonable to suppose that the structure of LF might shed light on the correct lf for natural language. Given that MP-inspired theories of UG (Universal Grammar) have a very different 'look' from GB-based ones, it is reasonable to ask what minimalism has to say about the primitives and structures of LF. This in turn should shed light on the optimal lf for this sort of grammar.

My particular focus in what follows revolves around one syntactic question—are chains grammatical objects?—and one semantic question—how do arguments relate to the predicates that they are arguments of? It is my belief that these two questions are so closely related that any answer to one has significant implications for the other. I hope to show that eliminating chains from the theory of grammar *requires* a Davidsonian 'sub-atomic' lf in which arguments relate to predicates via θ-roles. I will also provide arguments that chains are undesirable both methodologically and empirically. If this line of reasoning is correct, it supports the conclusion advanced by others that the best If for UG has a distinctly Davidsonian 'sub-atomic' form.[3]

Some Conceptual and Methodological Preliminaries

Minimalism has certain guiding precepts that inform theory construction. Two are relevant in what follows.[4]

First is the principle of full interpretation (FI). MP interprets this very strictly: LF has no superfluous structure or formatives. What this means is that all the structure and primitives present at LF must receive interpretations *and* LF is perfect in the sense of having no redundancy. In other words, LF does not merely provide all that is grammatically required for semantic interpretation, it does so in the most economical way possible.

Second is the principle of inclusiveness (PI). This is somewhat harder to make precise. The idea is that the grammar does not add new information in the course of a derivation. Rather, all the computational system does is 'rearrange' lexical items and their features. As Chomsky (1995: 225–6) puts it:

Another natural condition is that outputs consist of nothing beyond properties of items of the lexicon (lexical features)—in other words that the interface levels consist of nothing more than the arrangements of lexical features. To the degree that this is true, the language meets a condition of *inclusiveness*...

Given the numeration N. the operation CHL recursively construct *syntactic objects* from items in N and syntactic objects already formed. We have to determine what these objects are and how they are constructed. Insofar as the condition of inclusiveness holds, the syntactic objects are rearrangements of properties of lexical items of which they are ultimately constituted.

PI has been used to block the admission of indices into the course of derivations and prevent the introduction of bar levels to distinguish maximal from intermediate from minimal projections. The principle lies behind Chomsky's

---

[3] Several have argued for this conclusion on independent grounds. See Parsons (1990) for the development of a sub-atomic semantics for predicates on Davidsonian lines. As Parsons observes going to a fully sub-atomic semantics in which arguments are fully separable from the predicates they 'saturate' extends Davidson's basic analysis of adjuncts to arguments along lines first urged by Casteñeda. See Schein (1993) for an analysis of plurals that exploits the separability of arguments from predicates inherent in such a Davidsonian theory. See Herburger (1997) for an analysis of focus that also crucially exploits separability.

[4] See Chomsky (1995*b*: ch. 4) for discussion.

Bare Phrase Structure reanalysis of X' theory. It also lies behind recent attempts to rethink the Binding Theory.[5]

FI and PI also bear on the issue of chains. Chains are grammatical objects introduced to accommodate displacement. The latter is a ubiquitous feature of natural languages. It names the phenomenon exhibited in sentences like (1).

(1) *a.* John seems to have been arrested
    b. Who did John say that Mary saw

In (1*a*), 'John' is the understood object of the embedded verb 'arrested', i.e. 'John' is the arrestee. Similarly in (1*b*), 'who' is understood as related to the object position of 'saw'. Note that neither expression occupies the position it is understood to be interpretively related to. This is 'displacement'.

The fact of displacement presents a theoretical challenge. The problem is to provide a way of accounting for the interpretive properties of the displaced item. There are basically two ways that generativists have dealt with displacement.

The first is to allow the relevant expression, e.g. 'John' in (1*a*) to start in its interpretive position and move up to where it is phonetically pronounced. In effect, there is a derivation like (2) underlying the surface form (1*a*).

(2) *a.* seems [to have been arrested John]
    b. seems [John to have been arrested]
    c. John seems [to have been arrested]

The phrase marker inputs to interpretation would include (at least) (2*a*) and (possibly) (2*c*). Note that (2*a*) carries the information that 'John' is the arrestee, i.e. the logical object of 'arrest'. Structures like (2*c*) appear to be relevant for scope information in cases involving quantifiers and bound pronouns.

The second way of accommodating displacement is to place 'traces' in those positions that 'John' moves through. These traces serve to preserve the information that movement would otherwise destroy. Thus, an annotated phrase marker like (3) can be used to adequately represent the properties of (1*a*).

(3) John$_i$ seems [t$_i$ to have been arrested t$_i$]

With traces, it is no longer necessary to deliver more than one phrase marker to the interpretive component. This is a positive step in the context of MP as it is generally assumed that parsimony dictates that only *one* level interface with the

[5] See Chomsky (1995*b*: ch. 4), Chomsky (1995*a*), and Chomsky and Lasnik, 'The Theory of Principles and Parameters' (1993), reprinted in Chomsky (1995*b*: ch. 1).

interpretive component. Moreover, given arguments against D-structure as a viable level, this suggests a phrase marker very like GB's LF level. (3) is adequate for this task given these restrictions.[6]

However, (3) raises several problems. First, what exactly is interpreted? The standard answer has been that the unit of interpretation is not 'John' or the traces but the CHAIN consisting of 'John' and its traces. More specifically, one can think of 'John' with its co-indexed traces as forming a single object with 'John' as the head and the lowest trace as the foot. This object, a chain headed by 'John', is input to the interpretation procedures.[7]

Lately, there has been some refinement of this basic idea. Note that the intermediate trace seems to play no role in interpretation in (3). This violates FI. Thus, it is reasonable to suppose that this trace is not actually part of the LF chain headed by 'John'.[8] In addition, it would appear that traces violate PI as we add a new item in the course of the derivation and indulge in co-indexation to represent structure. Both the traces and the indices violate inclusiveness.

In this case we can, however, have our cake and eat it too. In place of traces, we leave copies of the moved expression and define a chain not in terms of indices but in terms of identical copies of a single expression. The relevant structure of (1*a*) is (4).[9]

(4) John seems [(John) to have been arrested John]

(4) still presents a problem however. Recall that FI is interpreted so that there is virtually no redundancy in the information afforded by the LF phrase marker. However, in (4) we have two copies of 'John'. It is clear what the bottom one is doing: it is there to provide 'John' with a thematic role (henceforth θ-role). However, what is the other copy there for? Doesn't the idea that movement involves copies get into problems of redundant LFs?

A way out of this problem is to treat the unit of interpretation not as the various copies 'John' but the set of copies in the configuration. In other words, to assume that the chain itself is what is interpreted not the 'links' that make it up. So, the unit of interpretation is the chain [John,John] not the individual links found in the matrix subject and the embedded object. However, under one possible interpretation this would seem to violate inclusiveness. After all, chains are not lexical expressions. They are constructed by the computational

---

[6] See Chomsky (1995*b*: ch. 3) for arguments against D-structure.

[7] The idea that chains are the units of interpretation is proposed e.g. in Chomsky (1986).

[8] See Chomsky (1995*b*: ch. 4) for proposals of eliminating the intermediate 'links'.

[9] The bracketed copy indicates deletion of the expression.

system. If these alone are the units of interpretation don't we have a violation of inclusiveness?

Perhaps. However, Chomsky interprets θ-roles in such a way that chains are conceptually required for interpretation. His idea is this: θ-roles are configurational properties of structures; thus, a given nominal expression has a certain thematic function in virtue of being in a certain (local) configuration with a predicate. It gains this relation by merger in the course of the derivation (e.g. by having 'John' merge with 'arrest' in the derivation of (1*a*)). A chain enjoys this thematic function by having its foot in this configuration. As Chomsky (1995: 313) puts it:

A theta role is assigned in a certain structural configuration: β assigns a theta role only in the sense that it is the head of the configuration . . . [a] chain CH is not in a configuration at all so cannot assign a theta role . . . in a configurational theory it makes little sense to think of the head of a chain as assigning a theta role . . . With regard to receipt of theta roles, similar reasoning applies . . . θ-relatedness is a 'base property', complementary to feature checking, which is a property of movement. More accurately θ-relatedness is a property of the position of merger and its (very local) configuration.

If this is what it is to have a thematic function, e.g. have the role of logical object of 'arrest', then interpretation requires that this configurational property be preserved. Chains are a minimal way of doing this.[10] Thus, chains are mandated by bare output conditions of the semantic interface. They are grammatically optimal as they are a design requirement imposed by the interface system that the grammar serves. In this sense they are required to exist by FI. In sum, without chains we would have no interpretation given two assumptions: (i) thematic relations are configurational and (ii) displacement exists.

Assumption (ii) is not reasonably contestable. It is, after all, simply a fact that natural languages manifest displacement. What is less clear is that (i) is required. Required or not, however, it is a venerable assumption. It goes back to Frege and Russell and is the standard account of how predicates and arguments are associated. Dowty (1989) dubs this approach the *ordered argument system* (OAS) of predicate argument relations. On this view, for example, 'arrest' is a predicate with two arguments: Arrest$< 1, 2 >$. The second argument is the thematic object. Thus, to be the thematic object *just is* to saturate this position. If saturation is under MERGE, then what it is to be the thematic

---

[10] Whether or not chains can indeed accomplish this has been disputed. However, if they cannot, there is little motivation for them altogether. I assume, therefore, that they can indeed succeed in this task. See Lasnik (2000) for discussion.

object of 'arrest' just is to occupy this position by having merged with it.[11] One can see Chomsky's view of θ-roles as an instance of the OAS and chains as the syntactic devices required to implement this view of the relation of arguments and predicates given the empirical fact that natural languages manifest displacement.

There is, however, a second view of the argument–predicate relation. Dowty (1989) dubs this position the *thematic role system* (TRS). On the neo-Davidsonian version of this view, predicates denote events and arguments are the participants of these events related to them via θ-relations. A sentence like (5*a*) would, on this view, have the structure (5*b*), with the highlighted predicate/argument structure.[12]

    (5) *a.* Bill arrested John
          b. There is an event e: (arresting(e) & Agent(Bill,e) & theme(John,e)

Note that here 'John' is related to 'arrest' indirectly, by being an argument of the thematic relation *theme* that relates 'John' to the event of arresting. The lexical entry for 'arrest' would list the fact that it denotes an event (of a certain type perhaps) and that it has at least two participants: an agent and a theme.

This second view of θ-roles can interpreted grammatically as follows: θ-roles are features of predicates that are assigned to arguments in order to relate them to their predicates.[13] As should be evident, on this view, chains are superfluous. Consider again example (1*a*) and assume that θ-roles are features assigned to nominals under merger. The structure of (1*a*) at LF will be (6), where θ marks the patient θ-role of the verb that assigns it.

    (6) John+θ seems [John+θ to have been arrested John+θ]

Note that, were we to delete all the copies of 'John' but the top one in (6), we would still retain the information that it is to be interpreted as the object of 'arrest' due to the feature '+θ' it inherited via merger (and retains under movement).[14] In short, if TRS is correct, then chains are superfluous objects.

[11] MERGE is the operation that takes two lexical items and combines them into a higher order unit like a phrase.

[12] Davidson himself did not develop this view. Casteñeda is apparently the source. It is systematically developed in Parsons (1990).

[13] Just what roles are and how they are to be construed is an interesting question that I leave aside here. These issues are thoroughly discussed in Dowty (1989), Higginbotham (1989), Parsons (1990), and Schein (1993).

[14] The reason it retains it under movement is that MOVE is a complex operation involving COPY and MERGE. COPY results in all features being transferred under MOVE.

It is thus possible to accommodate displacement without chains if θ-roles are features of predicates.

This discussion leads to the following conclusion. There is an intimate connection between an issue in the theory of grammar—do chains exist as grammatical objects?—and one in the theory of interpretation—what is the structure of predicates and arguments? The latter is an important If question bearing on the logical form/syntax of propositions. Thus, by considering the adequacy of chains as grammatical objects, we can shed light on the proper If for natural languages. We turn to this next as I outline the form of the argument.[15]

The Form of the Argument

The last section claims that there is a close connection between a grammatical construct, i.e. chains, and the logical form of predicates and arguments at If. Assuming this to be true, consider the following kind of argument.

(7) The Argument
  a. There are two conceptions of Logical Form: Ordered Argument System (OAS) and the Thematic Roles System (TRS).
  b. OAS requires chains as grammatical objects to obtain interpretation.
  c. But links rather than chains are the objects interpreted at the semantic (Conceptual–Intentional (CI)) interface evidence: quantifier scope, binding, control.
  d. If so, then chains are *NOT* available as grammatical objects in the course of the computation, i.e. precisely because they are not the objects of interpretation, they are not legitimate grammatical objects either using MP reasoning.
  e. Conclusion 1: chains do not exist.

[15] The Frankfurter Group (Frankfurt am Main, Germany) reasonably has asked why it is that Chomsky adopts the view he does of θ-roles. He has several conceptual and empirical reasons for treating θ-roles in the way he does. He presents cases in which treating θ-roles in this way leads to problems with respect to greedy movement. These cases are partly reviewed in Hornstein (1999). For a fuller discussion of the linguistic issues see Hornstein (2000b). These latter two sources also provided independent evidence for treating θ-roles as akin to features. The main thrust of the arguments is that so treating θ-roles leads to interesting accounts of control, binding, and o–operator phenomena (e.g. Parasitic gaps). This, in turn, allows Universal Grammar to be substantially simplified. These arguments are too involved to be presented here. The interested reader is referred to this work.

  f. Conclusion 2: TRS provides a more adequate logical form for natural language than does OAS.

The last section has attempted to forge the link indicated in (7*a*, *b*). The next section considers evidence based on some recent analysis of scope, binding, and control that, *if correct*, points to two broad conclusions.

  First, that chains provide inadequate scaffolding for the logical powers of quantified expressions in natural languages, specifically English. The reader should be warned that the discussion builds on some work that is not without its critics. I none the less assume that it is essentially correct and consider its implications. Notes will guide the interested reader to relevant technical literature.

  The second broad conclusion is that θ-features are independently required within the grammar. As such, chains are redundant. As the elimination of redundancy is a central MP precept, this leads to the conclusion that chains are superfluous and hence do not exist.

  Fortunately, the θ-features that are required to motivate various operations within the grammar provide the logical resources required for interpreting predicates and arguments *without* chains, as indicated in section 1. This θ-based grammar finds its natural home in a neo-Davidsonian view of logical form.

A Review of the Data

The GB analysis of quantifier scope and binding hinges on the rule of Q(uantifier) R(aising). QR takes quantified nominal expressions and adjoins them pre-sententially, leaving a trace, interpreted as a variable, in the extraction site. A sentence like (8*a*) has two possible representations (8*b, c*) made available by QR and this is accounts for its ambiguity.

(8) *a.* Someone attended every seminar
   b. Someone$_i$ [everyone seminar$_j$ [t$_i$ attended t$_j$]]
   c. Everyone seminar$_j$ [someone$_i$ [t$_i$ attended t$_j$]]

I have argued in various places that QR is an undesirable operation given minimalist precepts. In its place I have suggested that relative quantifier scope piggy backs on the A-chains independently required to check case and other morphological features.[16] I would like to quickly outline some of the evidence for this proposal and consider its implications.

---

[16] See e.g. Hornstein (1995: ch. 8; 2000*a*).

Minimalist theories of phrase structure distinguish functional from lexical domains.[17] The former are where case and morphological features are checked, while the latter are the domains of θ-role assignment. At the end of the derivation, the LF phrase marker of (8*a*), without any applications of QR, has a structure like (9).[18]

(9) [$_{AgrS}$ Someone [$_{TP}$ Tns[$_{AgrO}$ every seminar [$_{VP}$ someone attended every seminar]]]]

The copies in (9) occupy case (the higher) and θ-positions (the lower). Observe that the two sets of copies interleave, with at least one copy of each c-commanding a copy of the other. Given derivations that yield structures like (9) we can ask what the rule of scope interpretation is. There are two possibilities. The first takes the unit of interpretation to be the chain. A scope rule taking chains as the basic units would look something like (10).[19]

(10) *Chain Scope*   For α,β chains:
α scopes over β just in case some part of α c-commands some part of β.[20]

Applied to (9), (10) renders the sentence ambiguous as a part of the chain headed by 'someone' c-commands a part headed by 'every seminar' and vice versa.

There is a second option which takes the units of interpretation to be the copies (henceforth 'links') of which chains are composed rather than the whole chain. One could implement this idea as follows. Assume that at LF all but one copy must delete and let us indicate this deletion by bracketing the deleted items. This makes four possible LFs available for scope interpretation.

(11) *a.* [$_{AgrS}$ Someone [$_{TP}$Tns [$_{AgrO}$ every seminar [$_{VP}$ (someone) [attended (every seminar)]]]]]
b. [$_{AgrS}$ Someone [$_{TP}$Tns [$_{AgrO}$ (every seminar) [$_{VP}$ (someone) [attended every seminar]]]]]
c. [$_{AgrS}$ (Someone) [$_{TP}$Tns [$_{AgrO}$ (every seminar) [$_{VP}$ someone [attended every seminar]]]]]

[17] See e.g. Chomsky (1995: chs. 3 and 4).
[18] I have employed AGR projections for visual simplicity. These are not required.
[19] Observe, rules like (10) must be stated as principles of interpretation. They relate phrase marker notions like 'c-command' to interpretive notions like 'scope'.
[20] This rule is proposed in Barss (1986). See Aoun and Li (1989; 1993) as well.

d. [$_{AgrS}$ (Someone) [$_{TP}$Tns [$_{AgrO}$ every seminar [$_{VP}$ someone [attended (every seminar)]]]]]

Coupled with the structures in (11) we adopt the following scope interpretation rule.

(12) *Link Scope* For α, β links:

α scopes over β just in case α c-commands β

The combination of (11*d*) and (12) results in 'someone' interpreted as within the scope of 'every seminar'. The three other LFs result in the opposite scope reading. In contrast to the combination of (9) and (10) the LFs are never ambiguous (though the sentence is as several LFs can be assigned to it) and yield univocal scope readings.

Both of these approaches are adequate for the purposes of representing relative quantifier scope. However, they differ when a broader range of data are considered. C-command is not only relevant for determining relative quantifier scope, it is also critical for licensing the interpretation of pronouns as bound variables. With this in mind, consider the following data.

(13) *a.* It seems someone is reviewing every report
  b. Someone seems (to Bill) to be reviewing every report

(13*b*) is a Raising construction. It enjoys the same relative quantifier scope ambiguity as its non-raised counterpart, (13*a*). The LF structure of (13*b*) is (14).

(14) [Someone seemed to Bill [someone to be [every report[someone reviewing every report]]]]

Note that both the combination of (9)/(10) and that of (11)/(12) account for the quantifier scope ambiguity in Raising constructions. That the (9)/(10) pair is adequate should be obvious once one notices that the two chains interleave in (14). The (11)/(12) combination is equally adequate. (15), for example, is the LF underlying the reading in which 'every report' scopes over 'someone'.

(15) [(Someone) seemed to Bill [(someone) to be [every report[someone reviewing (every report)]]]]

Consider now sentences like (16).

(16) *a.* Someone$_i$ seemed to his$_i$ boss to be reviewing every report
  b. Someone$_i$ seemed to himself$_i$ to be reviewing every report

Here, the raised subject binds a pronoun or reflexive in the higher clause.[21] With this binding, 'someone' can no longer scope under 'every report'. The (11)/(12) combination explains this *loss* of scope ambiguity. The relevant LFs are (17).

> (17) *a.* [Someone$_i$ seemed to his$_i$ boss[(someone) to be [every report
> [(someone) reviewing (every report)]]]
>
> *b.* [Someone$_i$ seemed to himself$_i$ [(someone) to be [every report
> [(someone) reviewing (every report)]]]

In order for 'someone' to scope over the bound pronoun or reflexive requires that the top copy of 'someone' be retained. However, to scope under 'every report' the bottom copy must be retained. Thus, if 'someone' binds something in the matrix, it necessarily scopes over 'every report'.

How does the (9)/(10) approach fare? Not at all well. The relevant structure of (16*a*) is (18).

> (18) [Someone seemed to his boss [someone to be [every report[someone
> reviewing every report]]]

In (18) part of the chain headed by 'someone' c-commands a part headed by 'his'.[22] Thus by (10), 'his' can be interpreted as within the scope of 'someone'. Similarly, part of the chain headed by 'every report' c-commands part of the chain headed by 'someone'. Thus by (10) 'every report' can scope over 'someone'. In this way, the unavailable reading is derived.

The problem for the combination of (9)/(10) is easy to diagnose. Scope is irreflexive, asymmetric, and transitive. These features of scope are preserved in phrase markers in which only links are the units of interpretation as in the relevant structures c-command among the relevant units is similarly irreflexive, asymmetric, and transitive. The problem is that chains do not preserve these relations. Thus, in (18), it is possible for a part of the chain headed by 'every report' to c-command part of the chain headed by 'someone' and for the latter to c-command part of the chain headed by 'his' without any part of the chain headed by 'every report' c-commanding any part of the chain headed by 'his'. In short, transitivity is violated.[23]

---

[21] Reflexives must be bound by their antecedents to be licit and pronouns must be bound by theirs to be interpreted as bound variables. Binding involves c-command. I assume the following definition: '(i) α c-commands β iff the first branching category that dominates α dominates β'. There are other definitions of c-command but they make little difference to the discussion here.

[22] 'His' heads a singleton chain in these LFs.

[23] Observe, there is nothing inherent in the notion of semantic scope that it be asymmetric, irreflexive, and transitive. For example, there is nothing that conceptually requires that the same

This violation of transitivity is impossible given (11)/(12). Here if α c-commands β and β c-commands γ, then α will also c-command γ. Thus scope and c-command track one another and the indicated correlations between anaphor binding and relative scope follow.

This argument can be duplicated using non-embedded structures. The data in (19) illustrate this. Sentences like (19a) are ambiguous with regard to their relative quantifier scopes. This ambiguity disappears when the subject binds a pronoun in an adjunct, as in (19b).

(19) a. Someone serenaded every woman
     b. Someone_i serenaded every woman before he_i left the party

The correlation in (19b) between relative quantifier scope and binding is accounted for given the assumptions (11)/(12). The relevant structure of (19b) is (20).

(20) [_AgrS Someone_i [_Tns every woman [_VP [_VP (someone) serenaded (every woman)] [before he_i left the party]]]]

In (20), the 'before' clause is an adjunct to the VP. Only the copy of 'someone' in matrix subject position, in Spec AgrS, c-commands this pronoun. Consequently, only this copy has 'he' in its scope. Thus, this is the copy that must be retained for 'he' to be interpreted as a bound variable. However, this prevents 'every woman' from scoping over 'someone' as no copy of 'every woman' c-commands the matrix subject.

This argument is structurally identical to the previous one. To bind the pronoun, the quantifier must be in a certain structural position. However, this then prevents the quantified nominal from being 'low' enough to be in the scope of the object. Thus we derive the correlation that binding the pronoun forces wide scope.

This conclusion is reinforced when one considers that relative quantifier scope ambiguities should be possible if the pronoun hangs 'low' enough. This expectation is borne out in cases like (21a) with structures like (21b).

(21) a. Someone_i asked every attendant if he_i could park near the gate
     b. [_AgrS (Someone) [_AgrO every attendant [_VP someone_i asked (every attendant) if he could park near the gate]]]

notion of scope be relevant for pronominal binding and relative quantifiers scope. The fact that the same notion applies can be stipulated or explained. The combination of (11)/(12) explains why scope has this property given the units of interpretation.

(21*a*) supports a reading in which a different 'someone' asked each every attendant if he could park near the gate. The main difference between (21) and (19*b*) is that in the latter the pronoun is contained within a complement and so is c-commanded by the lower copy of 'someone' in the Spec VP. Thus, in this structure, it is possible to bracket the higher copy and still bind the pronoun with the lower copy of 'someone'. This contrasts with structures like (20) where the pronoun is contained in an adjunct. As the lower copy is central to deriving the readings on which subjects scope under objects, this scopal dependency is expected to be available, as it is.

Consider now how the (9)/(10) dyad fares. (19*b*) presents a real problem. The LF structure is (22).

(22) [$_\text{AgrS}$ Someone$_i$ [$_\text{TP}$ Tns every woman [$_\text{VP}$ [$_\text{VP}$ someone serenaded every woman] [before he$_i$ left the party]]]]

Here, part of the chain headed by 'someone' c-commands 'he' and part of the chain headed by 'every woman' c-commands part of the one headed by 'someone'. Thus, the reading in which 'someone' scopes under 'every woman' but still binds 'he' should be available, contrary to fact.[24]

So what is the moral? It seems that there is evidence that the combination of (9)/(10) fares less well than the coupling of (11) and (12). This argues against chains as the units of scope interpretation and in favor of links. This conclusion bears on the question of whether chains exist. Note that if they do, we would expect them to enter into scope interpretation. However, it appears that interpretive rules that take them as the basic units, e.g. (10), do not work out too well. This suggests that chains are not fundamental objects, at least if one cleaves to minimalist methodological concerns.[25]

[24] It is worth observing that cases such as these provide a problem for QR-based theories. Like chain-based accounts they allow intransitivities into the system as the mechanism responsible for determining relative quantifier is distinct from the one used to determine which pronouns are bound variables. It is generally assumed that a quantifier Q1 scopes over a quantifier Q2 just in case Q1 c-commands Q2 at LF after QR has applied. A pronoun is bound by a noun phrase N just in case it is c-commanded by N or a variable bound by N at LF (see Higginbotham (1980) for details). If this is so, there is a problem for cases like (19*b*). With QR, they can have the LF in '(i): Every woman$_i$ [someone$_j$ [t$_j$ serenaded t$_i$] [before he$_i$ left the party]]'. There is nothing illicit about this structure but it yields the unavailable reading. For further discussion see Hornstein (2000*a*).

[25] It is important to consider rules that treat chains as the units of interpretation. One can cheat by saying that scope is determined by only some elements within chains. However, it is then links that count for scope, not chains themselves. I set this sort of possibility aside here.

Furthermore, the combination of (11) and (12) *requires* that θ-roles be treated as features. In other words, this approach can only work if we assume that the thematic role a nominal enjoys is divorced from it (or its trace) actually occupying a given position at LF. Consider why. Recall that all copies but one delete. This leaves configurations like (11), repeated here.

(11) *a.* [$_{AgrS}$ Someone [$_{TP}$ Tns [$_{AgrO}$ every seminar [$_{VP}$ (someone) [attended (every seminar)]]]]]

     b. [$_{AgrS}$ Someone [$_{TP}$ Tns [$_{AgrO}$ (every seminar) [$_{VP}$ (someone) [attended every seminar]]]]]

     c. [$_{AgrS}$ (Someone) [$_{TP}$ Tns [$_{AgrO}$ (every seminar) [$_{VP}$ someone [attended every seminar]]]]]

     d. [$_{AgrS}$ (Someone) [$_{TP}$ Tns [$_{AgrO}$ every seminar [$_{VP}$ someone [attended (every seminar)]]]]]

The bracketed expressions are just noted for convenience. They have been deleted and so are actually invisible. If this is so, how is the thematic information recovered at LF, the only level to input semantic interpretation in a minimalist theory? It must be that the copies all carry the information that they were once in θ-positions. To illustrate consider (11*a*). The actual structure of this must be (23) (with '+θ' marking the θ-feature that an expression receives by merging into a θ-position).

(23) [$_{AgrS}$ Someone+θ [$_{TP}$ Tns [$_{AgrO}$ every seminar+θ [$_{VP}$ (someone+θ) [attended (every seminar+θ)]]]]]

Note that even if we delete the copies within VP, the higher copies retain the information required to determine their thematic functions. This is because we are treating θ-roles like features that are carried along under displacement operations like MOVE.

It is worth putting the point negatively: if thematic function required chains, then the deletions proposed above could not be sustained in the context of minimalist assumptions. The reason is that in a large number of cases, we would have to delete the bearers of the θ-information in the LF phrase marker. Strictly speaking, only (11*c*) would be well formed and scope ambiguities could not be represented. As the LF phrase marker is the unique input to semantic interpretation, this would render the proposal above based on (11)/(12) untenable. To make it viable requires adopting the thematic role view of argument-predicate relations as opposed to the ordered argument approach. It is in this sense that the present proposal must treat θ-roles as features and it is in this sense that it requires a neo-Davidsonian lf.

Evidence for θ-features

The argument in the last section can be summarized as follows. Binding and scope are functions of the positions of links in A-chains at LF. Executing this idea adequately given minimalist precepts requires treating θ-roles as features so that thematic information is not lost as a result of the necessary deletion operations.[26] In light of this conclusion, we can bolster the case for a neo-Davidsonian lf based on θ-roles as features if we can provide further independent evidence for so treating θ-roles. Such evidence exists and I would like to very quickly review it here. It relates to the proper treatment of (obligatory) control phenomena.

Control is illustrated in (24).

> (24) *a.* John hopes to win
>   *b.* John tried to leave
>   *c.* John wants to dance with Mary

In these examples there is an understood relation between the matrix subject 'John' and the understood subject of the embedded clause. Thus, in (24*a*) John is both a hoper and a winner thematically.

These control structures have been standardly analyzed using a distinctive formative 'PRO' in the embedded subject position bound to the matrix.

> (25) John$_i$ hoped [PRO$_i$ to win]

This analysis was adopted for a variety of reasons, the main one being to preserve the validity of various principles of grammar related to θ-theory, e.g. the θ-criterion and the properties of D-structure.[27]

Minimalism has argued against retaining D-structure as a level. It also casts a variety of methodological doubts on purely grammar internal formatives like 'PRO'. This has suggested rethinking the treatment of control. My favorite reanalysis treats control as essentially a raising construction.[28] The structure underlying (24*a*) is (26).

> (26) [$_{IP}$ John [$_{VP}$ John [hopes [$_{IP}$ John to [$_{VP}$ John win]]]]]

---

[26] Note, deletion is required so as to make LF fully interpretable and non-redundant once links are recognized to be the correct units of interpretation.

[27] See Hornstein (1996/[1997]) for discussion.

[28] See Hornstein (1999) for details. Others have argued for the conclusion endorsed here that θ-roles are features. See especially Boskovic (1994) and Lasnik (1995).

The copies indicate that 'John' has moved from the lowest position, in which it is θ-related to 'win' through various intermediate positions, to the matrix subject position where it checks case. Of particular interest for us here is the move from Spec IP of the embedded clause to Spec VP of 'hope'.

(26') [$_{IP}$ John [$_{VP}$ John [hopes [$_{IP}$ John to [$_{VP}$ John win]]]]

This move is interesting in the context of minimalism given the standard assumption that movement is never gratuitous; it must be 'for some reason'. The standard motivation for movement is that it is required to check a feature that needs checking. What feature then is checked in the move from the embedded Spec IP to the Spec VP of 'hope'?

The only plausible candidate is the agent θ-role of 'hope'. In other words, if this approach to control is correct it provides independent evidence that θ-roles have a status similar to morphological features in that they license movement. This amounts to treating θ-roles as features in all relevant grammatical respects.

There is considerable empirical payoff in treating obligatory control as movement into multiple θ-positions. It makes it possible to account for the distinctive properties of such structures. These are exemplified in (27).

(27) Salient Interpretive Properties of Obligatory Control
      a. *It was hoped to shave himself
      b. *John thinks that it was hoped to shave himself
      c. *John's campaign hopes to shave himself
      d. John hopes PRO to win and Bill does too (=Bill win)
      e. *John$_i$ persuaded Mary$_j$ [PRO$_{i+j}$ to wash each other]
      f. The unfortunate hopes to get a medal
      g. Only Churchill remembers giving the BST speech

(27*a–c*) indicate that the PRO in obligatory control structures requires an antecedent which is local and c-commands the PRO. (27*d*) indicates that only sloppy readings are licensed under ellipsis. (27*e*) indicates that these structures prohibit split antecedents. (27*f*) only carries a *de se* interpretation and (27*g*) requires the reading in which 'only churchill' binds PRO. All of these properties follow on the assumption that PRO is actually the residue of movement.[29]

Consider (27*e*) for illustration. If 'PRO' is actually the residue of movement, then to get split antecedents requires that 'John' and 'Mary' each moved from

---

[29] See Hornstein (1999) a for elaboration.

the same position. This, however, is impossible.[30] As such, we derive the fact that obligatory control structures do not support split antecedents.[31] The other properties listed in (27) can be similarly derived.

Assume then that it is indeed the case that obligatory control is derived via movement. What does this tell us? As noted above, in a minimalist context, it requires treating θ-roles as features. The idea that movement is a last resort operation is a regulative ideal within the minimalist program. In practice this has come to mean that movements are 'greedy' in the sense of resulting in some sort of feature checking as a result of the movement. *If* movement underlies obligatory control structures then this means that θ-roles can license movement. In effect, this means that θ-roles are feature-like. This fits very comfortably with the TRS view of predicate/argument structure. It fits very poorly with the ordered argument system which sees θ-roles in positional terms. Indeed, Chomsky (1995) makes just this point in arguing against movement into θ-positions.[32] If, however, control is due to movement, then θ-roles must be treated as features. This, in turn, supports a neo-Davidsonian approach to predicate argument structure and lf.

One last point. If θ-features are needed then it would introduce substantial redundancy into the grammar to have chains for θ-purposes as well. Given the minimalist esteem for parsimony as a methodological principle, this argues for the elimination of chains from the grammar altogether. Without chains, however, it is hard to see how to implement the ordered argument system of arguments and predicates. This would require us to adopt the neo-Davidsonian approach to predicate/argument relations.

Conclusion

I have claimed that certain issues in the theory of grammar are intimately related to the question of what the logical syntax for predicates and arguments is. In effect, issues in the theory of grammar reflect commitments concerning the logical form of natural language expressions. If this is so, then it should be possible to argue from the grammar to the semantics. I have outlined one such

---

[30] Indeed, given standard minimalist assumptions, it might be incoherent as there is no distinction between positions on the one hand and the objects that fill them on the other. If so, then two expressions cannot be in the same position, hence cannot move from the same position.

[31] Prior accounts had to stipulate this property of PRO in obligatory control structures.

[32] See Chomsky (1995) for extensive discussion of this point.

argument that leads to the conclusion that natural language exploits a neo-Davidsonian logical form. What is novel here is not the conclusion, but the road travelled. Some grammatical approaches fit with some interpretation procedures better than with others. It is always interesting to examine when and where this is so. If the above is roughly correct, it suggests that certain current minimalist approaches to grammar cast a distinctly Davidsonian shadow.

REFERENCES

Aoun, J., and Li, A. (1989). 'Constituency and Scope', *Linguistic Inquiry*, 20: 141–72.

—— (1993). *Syntax of Scope* (Cambridge, Mass.: MIT Press).

Barss, A. (1986). *Chains and Anaphoric Dependence: On Reconstruction and its Implications* (Cambridge, Mass.: MIT Press).

Boskovic, Z. (1994). 'D-Structure, Theta Criterion, and Movement into Theta Positions', *Lingusitic Analysis*, 24: 247–86.

Chierchia, G., and McConnell-Ginet, S. (1990). *Meaning and Grammar* (Cambridge, Mass.: MIT Press).

Chomsky, N. (1957). *Syntactic Structures* (The Hague: Mouton).

—— (1965). *Aspects of a Theory of Syntax* (Cambridge, Mass.: MIT Press).

—— (1982). *Lectures on Government and Binding* (Dordrecht: Foris).

—— (1986). *Knowledge of Language* (New York: Praeger).

—— (1995*a*). 'Bare Phrase Structure', in Gert Webelhuth (ed.), *Government and Binding Theory and the Minimalist Program* (Oxford: Blackwell).

—— (1995*b*). *The Minimalist Program* (Cambridge, Mass.: MIT Press).

Dowty, D. (1989). 'On the Semantic Content of the Notion of "Thematic Role" ', in G. Chierchia, B. Parte, and R. Turner (eds.), *Properties, Types and Meaning*, (Dordrecht: Kluwer).

Herburger, H. (1997). 'Focus and Weak Noun Phrases', *Natural Language Semantics*, 5: 53–78.

Higginbotham, J. (1980). 'Pronouns and Bound Variables', *Linguistic Inquiry*, 11: 679–708.

—— (1989). 'Elucidations of Meaning', *Linguistics and Philosophy*, 4: 465–517.

Hornstein, N. (1995). *Logical Form* (Oxford: Blackwell).

—— (1996/[1997]). 'Control in GB and Minimalism', *Glot International*, 2: 3–6.

—— (1999). 'Movement and Control', *Linguistic Inquiry*, 30: 69–96.

—— (2000*a*). 'Minimalism and QR', in S. Epstein and N. Hornstein (eds.), *Working Minimalism* (Cambridge, Mass: MIT Press).

Hornstein, N. (2000*b*). *Move!* (Oxford, U.K.: Blackwell).

Jackendoff, R. (1972). *Semantic Interpretation in Generative Grammar* (Cambridge, Mass.: MIT Press).

Larson, R., and Segal, G. (1995). *Knowledge of Meaning* (Cambridge, Mass.: MIT Press).

Lasnik, H. (1995). 'Last Resort and Attract F', in *Proceedings of the Sixth Annual Meeting of the Formal Linguistics Society of Mid-America*, ed. Leslie Gabriele, Debra Hardison, and Robert Westmoreland (Bloomington, Ind.: Indiana University Linguistics Club), 62–81.

—— (2000). 'Chains of Arguments', in S. Epstein and N. Hornstein (eds.), *Working Minimalism* (Cambridge, Mass.: MIT Press).

Parsons, T. (1990). *Events in the Semantics of English* (Cambridge, Mass.: MIT Press).

Schein, B. (1993). *Plurals and Events* (Cambridge, Mass.: MIT Press).

12

Nominal Restriction

JASON STANLEY

Extra-linguistic context appears to have a profound effect on the determination of what is expressed by the use of linguistic expressions. For a bewildering range of very different linguistic constructions, adhering to relatively straightforward linguistic intuition about what is expressed leads us to the conclusion that facts about the non-linguistic context play many different roles in determining what is said. Furthermore, that so many different constructions betray this sort of sensitivity to extra-linguistic context understandably leads to pessimism about rescuing the straightforward intuitions while preserving any sort of systematicity in the theory of meaning.

A presumption motivating the pessimistic inclination is that, if we accept the ordinary intuitions, what *appear* to be very different ways in which context affects semantic content in fact *are* different ways in which context affects linguistic content. Pessimism is a natural reaction to those who adopt this presumption, because if appearance is a good guide to the facts in this domain, then there are just too many ways in which context affects semantic content to preserve systematicity. One common and natural reaction to these facts is, therefore, to deny the semantic significance of the ordinary intuitions, thereby relegating the project of explaining the apparent effects of extra-linguistic context on semantic content to a domain of inquiry outside the theory of meaning proper. So doing removes the threat context poses to the systematicity of semantic explanation, but at the cost of reducing the interest of the semantic project.

In this chapter, I explore a different reaction to the situation. My purpose is to undermine the presumption that what appear to be very different effects of context on semantic content are very different effects. My challenge is of necessity rather limited, since it is too implausible to trace all effects of

* Thanks to Richard Boyd, Herman Cappelen, Richard Heck, Kathrin Koslicki, Ernie Lepore, Kirk Ludwig, Brett Sherman, Anna Szabolcsi, and Zsofia Zvolensky for valuable comments and discussion. I would especially like to thank Delia Graff, Jeff King, and Zoltan Gendler-Szabo for many hours of extraordinarily fruitful discussion about the topics of this chapter.

extra-linguistic context on semantic content to the very same source. Rather, I will take, as a case-study, three superficially very different effects of context on semantic content, and show that they are due to the very same mechanism, what I call *Nominal Restriction*. I thereby hope to provide convincing evidence of the promise of the project of reducing all apparent effects of context on semantic content to a small number of sources.

In the first section, I introduce an account of the phenomenon of quantifier domain restriction due to Stanley and Szabo (2000), and provide two novel defenses of it. In the second section, I turn to a discussion of comparative adjectives. As I argue, the theory introduced in the next section, which I call the *Nominal Restriction Theory*, also provides an explanation for some mysterious facts about how context determines the comparison class for uses of comparative adjectives. In the third section, I turn to another apparently very different sort of effect of extra-linguistic context on semantic content, and show how it too is smoothly explicable on the Nominal Restriction Theory. I then draw some consequences from the discussion for some issues in the theory of reference.

Domain Restriction

The sentence 'Every bottle is empty' can be used to communicate many different propositions. For example, if John is about to go shopping, and is wondering whether he should buy something to drink, Hannah can utter 'Every bottle is empty' to communicate the proposition that every bottle in the house is empty. In this section, I describe and defend what I believe to be the best account of how sentences containing quantified noun phrases such as 'every' and 'some' can be used to communicate propositions about a restricted domain of entities. In the rest of the chapter, I draw out some consequences of the account for other constructions.

The account I will defend is first presented in the final section of Stanley and Szabo (2000). The simplest version is that each nominal expression is associated with a domain variable. Relative to a context, the domain variable is assigned a set. The semantic relation between the extension of the nominal expression and the set is set-theoretic intersection. A sentence such as 'Every bottle is empty' can communicate the proposition that every bottle in Hannah's house is empty, because, relative to the relevant context, the domain variable associated with 'bottle' is assigned the set of things in Hannah's house. 'Every bottle is empty' communicates the proposition that every bottle in Hannah's house is empty, because, relative to this context, it semantically expresses this proposition.

This is the theory in its simplest form. Details need to be filled in, and modifications added. To explain some of them, I will have to introduce some modest syntax. Let us call the output of the syntactic process that is visible to semantic interpretation a *logical form*. A logical form is a lexically and structurally disambiguated ordered sequence of word types, where word types are individuated both by semantic and syntactic properties. Logical Forms are phrase markers. An ex-ample of such a phrase marker, for the sentence 'Hannah loves Sue', is as follows:

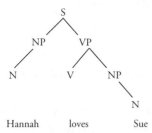

The nodes in this diagram are the points labeled either with syntactic categories or lexical items. So, 'Hannah' labels a node, as does 'N', 'VP', and 'V' (we shall also talk of labels of nodes as *occupying* these nodes). The nodes are connected by branches, which are the lines in the diagram. We say that a node X *dominates* another node Y in a phrase marker if there is a path of branches leading downward in the tree from X to Y. We say that a node X immediately dominates another node Y in a phrase marker just in case X dominates Y, and there is no node Z between X and Y. Nodes that dominate other nodes are called *nonterminal nodes*. Nodes that dominate no other nodes are *terminal nodes*. The nodes labeled with lexical items such as 'Hannah' or 'loves' are always terminal nodes. These are the objects that we assume are interpreted by semantic theories.

In the theory I have sketched, nominal expressions are associated with domain variables. By 'association', I mean that nominal expressions, such as 'bottle', cohabit a terminal node with a domain variable. So, on this account, the logical form of a sentence such as 'Every man runs' is:

(1)

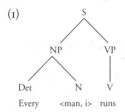

368 INTENSIONALITY, EVENTS, SEMANTIC CONTENT

On this view, domain variables are independently meaningful expressions that incorporate with nouns. Thus, domain variables are not, on this account, expressions that occupy their own terminal nodes.

One reason to think that this is the right syntactic treatment of domain variables is that it is difficult to find sentences containing pronouns that are anaphoric on domain variables.[1] Similarly, expressions that are incorporated with other expressions often do not license anaphoric relations. For example, as Irene Heim (1982: 24) has pointed out, (2) easily allows a reading where the pronoun 'it' is anaphoric on 'bicycle', whereas (3) does not:

(2) John owns a bicycle. He rides it daily.
(3) John is a bicycle-owner. He rides it daily.

Thus, the fact that it is difficult to have anaphora on domain variables is to be predicted, given representations such as (1).[2]

In the theory I have sketched, quantifier domain restriction is due to the presence of domain variables in the actual syntactic structure of sentences containing quantified noun phrases. But syntactic structure cannot simply be postulated on semantic grounds. Rather, evidence of a syntactic sort must be available for the existence of domain variables. The main source of syntactic evidence comes from the fact that domain variables interact in binding relations with quantifiers.

Here is the evidence from bindability. Consider the sentence:

(4) Everyone answered every question.

(4) can express the proposition that everyone x answered every question on x's exam. What this indicates is that there is a variable accessible to binding somewhere in the quantified phrase 'every student'. There are many other examples of this phenomenon, such as:

(5) *a.* In most of his classes, John fails exactly three Frenchmen.
    b. In every room in John's house, he keeps every bottle in the corner.

In all of these cases, the domain associated with a quantified noun phrase varies as a function of the values introduced by a previous quantified noun phrase. For example, (5*a–b*) intuitively mean something like:

(6) *a.* In most of his classes x, John fails exactly three Frenchmen in x.

---

[1] Thanks to Herman Cappelen for emphasizing to me the difficulty of finding natural examples of anaphoric dependence on a domain variable.
[2] Thanks especially to Tom Werner for discussion here.

b. In every room x in John's house, he keeps every bottle in x in the corner.

On the assumption that binding is fundamentally a syntactic phenomenon, such examples provide evidence for a variable somewhere in the syntactic structure of quantified noun phrases.[3]

There is therefore syntactic evidence for the existence of domain variables in sentences containing quantifier expressions. But to treat examples such as (4) and (5*a*–*b*), however, the simple theory presented above must be modified. The quantifier 'everyone' in (4) and the quantified expressions in (5*a*–*b*) range over objects. But quantifier domains are sets, rather than objects. For example, the quantifier domains associated with the quantified noun phrase 'three Frenchmen' in (5a) are, for each class John teaches, the set of students in that class. Similarly, the quantifier domains associated with the quantified noun phrase, 'every bottle' in (5*b*) are, for each room x in John's house, the things that are in x. To reflect the kind of dependence at issue, we must adjust the syntax and semantics of quantified sentences. Instead of representations such as:

(1)

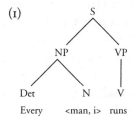

we require representations such as:

(7)

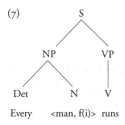

The value of 'i' is an object provided by the context, and the value of 'f' is a function provided by the context that maps objects onto quantifier domains. The restriction on the quantified expression 'every man' in (7), relative to a

---

[3] Farkas (1997) provides a sophisticated discussion of examples such as (4) and (5). However, Farkas does not share our assumption that binding is fundamentally a syntactic phenomenon. Instead, she provides her own semantic account of scope and binding, which she uses to explain the bound readings of (4) and (5).

context, would then be provided by the result of applying the function that context supplies to 'f' to the object that context supplies to 'i'.

Adopting the by now standard generalized quantifier treatment of quantifiers such as 'every', whereby they express relations between sets (cf. Barwise and Cooper, 1981; Westerståhl 1989), the semantic clauses for quantifiers such as 'every' and 'some' are as in (8):

(8) *a.* Every A B iff $A \subseteq B$.
     b. Some A B iff $A \cap B \neq \varnothing$.

On this account, the initial noun phrase determines the first argument of a quantified expression, and the second argument is determined by the verb phrase. For example, in the case of a sentence such as (7), the first argument would then be the set of men, and the second argument would be the set of runners.

No adjustment is required to extend the standard generalized quantifier treatment to interpret structures such as (7). But we do need to say something about the interpretation of expressions such as '$<\text{man}, f(i)>$'. Since we are taking quantifier domains to be sets, relative to a context, what results from applying the value of 'f' to the value of 'i' is a set. Relative to a context, 'f' is assigned a function from objects to sets. Relative to a context, 'i' is assigned an object. The denotation of '$<\text{man}, f(i)>$' relative to a context c is then the result of intersecting the set of men with the set that results from applying the value given to 'f' by the context c to the value given to 'i' by c. That is (suppressing reference to a model to simplify exposition), where '$[\alpha]_c$' denotes the denotation of α with respect to the context c, and $c(\alpha)$ denotes what the context c assigns to the expression α:

(9) $[<\text{man}, f(i)>]_c = [\text{man}] \cap \{x : x \in c(f)(c(i))\}$

In the case of (7), the resulting set is then the first argument of the generalized quantifier 'every'. Here is how the theory works with sentences such as the ones in (4) and (5). Consider first:

(4′) Everyone answered every question.

Intuitively, the interpretation of this sentence in the envisaged scenario is 'everyone x answered every question on x's exam'. According to the theory just outlined, 'every question' is of the form 'every $<\text{question}, f(i)>$'. The variable 'i' is bound by the higher quantifier 'everyone'. Context supplies 'f' with a function from persons to the set of problems on that person's exam, yielding the desired interpretation.

Let us consider one more example, for instance:

(5) *a.* In most of his classes, John fails exactly three Frenchmen.

Here is how the theory just sketched treats (5*a*). The intuitive interpretation of this sentence is 'In most of his classes x, John fails exactly three Frenchmen in x'. According to the theory just outlined, 'three Frenchmen' is of the form 'three <Frenchmen, $f(x)$>'. The variable 'x' is bound by the higher quantifier 'most of his classes'. Context supplies 'f' with a function that takes a class and yields the set of students in that class. This set is then intersected with the set of Frenchmen, to yield the first argument of the generalized quantifier 'three'.

Here is how the theory works with a simpler example. Suppose I say:

(10) Every fireman goes to Jack's bar.

Presumably, I intend to be speaking about firemen associated with a particular town or location; what I am asserting is that every fireman associated with location l goes to Jack's bar. On the theory just sketched, 'every fireman' is of the form 'every <fireman, $f(i)$>'. My intentions (for example) determine a location as the value of the variable 'i'. Furthermore, they determine a function from locations to sets of things that generally occupy those locations, which is the value of 'f'.[4] This function, applied to the location l, yields the set of things generally occupying l. This set is then intersected with the set of firemen, to yield the first argument of the generalized quantifier 'every'.

According to this theory of quantifier domain restriction, it is due to the fact that each nominal co-occurs with variables whose values, relative to a context, together determine a domain. Thus, if it is right, 'quantifier domain restriction' is a misleading label; better would be 'nominal restriction'. Accordingly, I will call this theory the Nominal Restriction Theory (NRT).

In the rest of this section, I will provide arguments in support of the controversial aspects of the NRT. There are two controversial properties of NRT. The first property is that quantifier domain indices are associated with common nouns such as 'fireman' and 'person', rather than, as one might more naturally expect, determiners such as 'every' and 'some'. The second property is that quantifier domain restriction does not merely involve the contextual provision of a property or a set as the value of an element in the syntactic

---

[4] In some cases, it may be implausible to suppose that speaker or participant intentions determine both an object and a function from objects to properties. In such cases, we may suppose that context supplies a set as value to 'i' and the identity function as a default value to the function variable 'f' (cf. section iii of Stanley (2000) for a similar suggestion involving tense). Thanks to Brett Sherman for discussion here.

structure of quantified sentences. Rather, it involves the provision both of an object and a function from objects to sets to an individual variable and a function variable that occur along with every nominal expression. In the rest of the section, I will defend each of these two controversial commitments.

According to NRT, the intuitive restriction on quantificational determiners such as 'every', 'some', and 'most' is not due, as may seem obvious, to a restriction on the quantificational expressions themselves, but rather to a restriction on the nominal complements of these determiners. This is an unintuitive feature of the theory, one that needs a justification. In Stanley and Szabo (2000), several arguments are advanced in support of the conclusion that quantifier domain variables occur with nominals rather than determiners. I will not repeat those arguments here. Rather, I want to present a different argument for the conclusion, due to Delia Graff (p.c.).

Suppose that the domain-restricting index occurred on the determiner, rather than the head noun. Here is how the syntax and semantics would work. Abstracting from the complexity involving the function variable, in this case, the structure of 'Every man runs' would be:

(11)

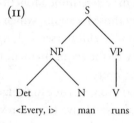

instead of (1) or (7). The semantic clause for 'every' would then be something like:

(12) $<$Every, i$>$ A B iff A$\cap$c(i) $\subseteq$ B.

So, the semantic clause would intersect the first argument of the generalized quantifier with the set provided to i by context.

This theory works well for examples such as 'Every man runs'. But Graff's argument demonstrates that theory has problems with slightly more complex constructions, such as:

(13)   The tallest person is nice.

Consider an occurrence of (13), relative to a context in which the domain comprises the students at Cornell University. Suppose further that the tallest student at Cornell is indeed nice. The proposition expressed by such an occurrence of (13) is true. But, on the account of domain restriction we are now considering, it is predicted to be false. Here is why.

Since no domain index is on 'person', its denotation will be the set of all people in the universe. We may suppose the semantic function of 'tallest' is to select the tallest member of the denotation of the head noun. Suppose that Jan, a basketball player in Holland, is the tallest person in the world. So, the set that results from applying 'tallest' to 'person' is the singleton set containing Jan. Now, on this account of domain restriction, the semantic clause governing 'the' is:

(14) $<$ The, i $>$ A B iff $|A \cap c(i)| = 1$ & $(A \cap c(i)) \cap B = 1$

If we apply this theory to the relevant occurrence of (12), it follows that the first argument of the generalized quantifier 'The' is the singleton set containing Jan, and the value of 'i', relative to the envisaged context, is the set of students at Cornell. But since Jan is not at Cornell, the theory of quantifier domain restriction in question predicts that, relative to the envisaged context, (13) is false (or perhaps truth-valueless).

It is clear what has gone wrong. In evaluating 'tallest person', one does not select the tallest person in the world. Rather, one selects the tallest person in the contextually relevant domain. But this demonstrates that the domain is associated with the head noun, rather than with the determiner.[5]

The second controversial feature of NRT is that, according to it, quantifier domain restriction is due not to the provision of a set or property, but rather to the provision of an object and a function that yields a set or property for that object as value. Indeed, the account involves the postulation of a function variable in the logical form of quantified sentences, whose values, relative to contexts, are functions whose values are quantifier domains. As we have seen, there is evidence from bindability for the existence of object variables in the syntactic structure of quantified noun phrases. But one might wonder whether there is evidence of a non-semantic sort for the existence of the function variables postulated by NRT.[6]

---

[5] One way to attempt to evade Graff's argument is to formulate semantic rules that take the domain index on the determiner and intersect it with the nominal head of the complement of the determiner. Such rules are relatively straightforward to formulate. However, they violate in a quite drastic manner what Larson and Segal (1995: 78) call *strong compositionality*. Strong compositionality is the thesis that the interpretation of each node in a syntactic tree is a function only of the interpretation of the nodes it immediately dominates. Despite the name given to it by Larson and Segal, it is a principle that in fact is significantly weaker than the principle of compositionality that is presupposed in other textbooks (e.g. Heim and Kratzer, 1998).

[6] Graff's argument presupposes that the superlative adjective is to be interpreted in its entirety in situ. Some linguists, however, give a treatment of superlative constructions in

How does one argue for the existence of a variable? One syntactic feature of variables is their capacity to be bound by quantificational expressions. So, one way to argue for the existence of a variable in a certain construction is to produce examples of that construction in which a higher operator binds the postulated variable. I have exploited this strategy already in arguing for the existence of object variables in quantified noun phrases. In what follows, I use it again in providing evidence for the existence of function variables in quantified noun phrases.

It is difficult to find natural examples in which the function variable that NRT postulates in nominal expressions is bound. The reason for the difficulty, of course, is that it is difficult to find natural language constructions that involve quantification over functions. One kind of construction that arguably does involve quantification over functions involves the so-called 'functional reading' of questions. Here is an example of a functional reading of a question:

(15) Q: What does every author like?
      A: Her first book.

On a 'functional question' account of (15), its semantics involves quantification over functions. In particular, the question is interpreted as:

(16) What function f is such that for every author x, x likes f(x).

Interpreting the question in (15) in this manner is advantageous. For it allows us to capture the intuition that the answer to the question is a proposition concerning a function, while maintaining the standard semantics for questions, according to which the semantic value of a question is the set of its (contextually relevant) good answers.[7]

One might be skeptical of functional readings of questions, on the grounds that they are really just 'pair-list' readings. (15), for example, also has a pair-list reading. On this reading, the answer to the question in (15) would be a list of authors and what they like, as in (17):

(17) Q: What does every author like?
      A: Hannah likes her first book, Paula likes her first book, and Matt
         likes his first book.

which the superlative operator 'est' detaches from the adjective and either takes scope over the whole noun phrase, or incorporates with the determiner. Adoption of such a framework may perhaps undermine Graff's argument.

   [7] I am grateful to Jeff King, in particular, for stressing the need for a non-semantic justification for the function variables postulated by NRT.

One might think that there is no genuine semantic difference between functional readings and pair-list readings, and on this ground deny that (15) involves quantification over functions. However, there is good evidence against running together functional readings of questions with pair-list readings (cf. Groenendijk and Stokhof, 1984: ch. 3). For example, (18) has a functional reading, but no pair-list reading:

(18) Q: What does no author like?
    A1: Her first book.
    #A2: Hannah doesn't like her first book, Paula doesn't like her first book, and Matt doesn't like his first book.

In general, when a wh-phrase (a word such as 'who', 'what', or 'which') takes scope over a downward-monotonic quantifier, then pair-list readings are disallowed, but functional readings are not.[8] So, functional readings of questions simply cannot be assimilated to pair-list readings.

Here are two other arguments against assimilating functional readings to pair-list readings (from Elisabet Engdahl, 1986: 167–8). First, it would seem that (19) could be true, even if John is not acquainted with every author in the world:

(19) John knows which book every author in the world likes the least, namely her first.

However, if we suppose that functional readings were a special case of pair-list readings, then (19) could not be true in this situation. For then (19) would be equivalent to:

(20) John knows, of every author in the world, which book she likes the least.

But (20) is clearly false if John is not acquainted with every author in the world.
    Secondly, if functional readings were a special case of pair-list readings, then one would expect (21) to be contradictory:

(21) John knows which woman every Englishman admires most, namely his mother, but he doesn't know who the women in question are.

But (21) (Engdahl's (39)) does not seem contradictory; indeed, it could very well be true. But if functional readings were a special case of pair-list readings, then (21) should be contradictory.

---

[8] One excellent discussion of functional readings is in Groenendijk and Stokhof (1984: ch. 3). Two other sources are Engdahl (1986) and Chierchia (1993).

These three arguments together provide powerful evidence in favor of the thesis that questions admit of a distinct functional interpretation. But, as I now demonstrate, if there are such readings, then there are clear examples in which the function variables postulated in nominal expressions by NRT are bound.

Suppose that John and Bill are arguing about which branch of the armed forces is the best. Bill has been arguing that the Navy is superior. John, an advocate of the marines, somewhat rhetorically asks:

(22) But what is every person truly proud to belong to?

where the intuitive answer is supposed to be 'the marines'. So, (22) has the interpretation:

(23) What x is such that every person $y \in x$ is truly proud to belong to x?

It is a functional reading of a certain variation of examples such as (22) that will provide us with the evidence for a bound reading of the function variable postulated by the account of domain restriction outlined above. One example of this kind is (24):

(24) Q: In every country, what is every person proud to belong to?
      A: Its Progressive Party.

The interpretation of the question in (24) is:

(25) In every country c, what function f is such that every person $x \in f(c)$ is proud to belong to f(c)?

(24), so interpreted, is one example that provides evidence for the syntactic reality of the function variable postulated in nominal expressions by NRT. For according to NRT, 'person' co-occurs with a function variable 'f', and an object variable 'x'. The interpretation given in (25) is one in which the object variable associated with 'person' is bound by the quantifier 'every country', and the function variable is bound by 'what', which here has the force of an existential quantifier over functions.

Of course, this example is rather complex. But the reason it is complex is simply because it is difficult to find examples of natural language constructions involving quantification over functions. It is striking that the linguistically most compelling case of such quantification provides straightforward examples in support of NRT.

The two most controversial properties of NRT are, first, that quantifier domain indices are associated with nominal expressions rather than with quantificational determiners, and second, that it postulates function variables in the syntactic structure of sentences containing quantified noun phrases. In this section, I have argued that both of these properties are independently motivated. If NRT is correct, then quantifier domain restriction is an effect of nominal restriction. But quantifier domain restriction is not the only effect of nominal restriction. In the next two sections, I want to explore other effects of nominal restriction. This will complete my argument for the thesis that many superficially distinct kinds of dependence of semantic value on context are due to the same source.

Adjectives and Comparison Classes

There are several ways in which sentences containing comparative adjectives, such as 'small', 'tall', 'heavy', and 'large' are sensitive to context. One salient way involves the provision of a comparison class. Consider predicative uses of a comparative adjective, such as:

(26) That building is small.
(27) That basketball player is short.
(28) That flea is small.

On one natural reading of (26), the building in question is not being said to be small for an object in general (whatever that may mean). Rather, the building is being said to be small for a building. Similarly, on a natural reading of (27), the basketball player in question is not being said to be small for a person, but only for a basketball player. Finally, (28) shows that there is an equally natural reading of these constructions in which the comparison class is not provided by the sentence. For, on a natural reading of (28), what it expresses is that the flea in question is small for an animal.

On what is perhaps the classical account of predicative uses of comparative adjectives (e.g. Parsons, 1972: 139; Siegel, 1975: 26–8), the sentences (26)–(28) on these interpretations, are elliptical for (29)–(31):[9]

(29) That building is a small building.
(30) That basketball player is a short basketball player.
(31) That flea is a small animal.

---

[9] A quantifier Q is downward monotonic if and only if, where QA, then for all B such that $B \subseteq A$, QB.

On this account, the context-sensitivity of (26)–(28) is resolved by postulating logical forms in which the comparison class is the denotation of a nominal expression provided by context.

However, many linguists reject this classical account of predicative uses of comparative adjectives. Perhaps the central reason for abandoning the classical account is that, as Hans Kamp has written, in arriving at a comparison class, 'the noun is not always the only determining factor' (Kamp, 1975: 152). Consider, for example:

(32) Smith is a remarkable violinist.

(33) Fred built a large snowman.

As Kamp (1975: 152–3) notes, (32) may be true 'when said in comment on his after-dinner performance with the hostess at the piano, and false when exclaimed at the end of Smith's recital in the Festival Hall—even if on the second occasion Smith played a bit better than on the first'. Similarly, suppose that Fred is a 7-year-old child. An occurrence of (33) may still be true, if Fred has built a snowman that is large for a snowman built by a 7-year-old child. That is, the comparison class for 'large' in (33) is not just given by the denotation of the nominal 'snowman'. Similarly, the comparison class for 'remarkable' in (32) is not just given by the nominal 'violinist'. Rather, the comparison classes are considerably narrower than the extensions of these nominals.

According to the classical account of predicative uses of comparative adjectives, they are elliptical for constructions in which the nominal complement of the comparative adjective is present. However, providing a nominal does not yet specify the comparison class. Furthermore, one might expect that any satisfactory account of this 'extra' context-dependency would be up to the task of supplying the entire comparison class on its own, without postulating a hidden nominal. Therefore, it seems, this traditional account should be rejected.

Appeal to NRT saves the classical account of predicative uses of comparative adjectives. For NRT straightforwardly predicts the readings we find in (31) and (32). According to NRT, each nominal co-occurs with a domain index. That is, according to the theory, the following are rough guides to the relevant aspects of the logical forms of (32) and (33):

(34) Smith is a remarkable $<$ violinist, $f(i) >$.

(35) Fred built a large $<$ snowman, $f(i) >$.

Consider Kamp's example. In both of Kamp's envisaged scenarios, context assigns to 'f' a function from locations to people who have played instruments at those locations, and 'i' is assigned the salient location. In the context of the dinner party, the value of 'i' is the location of the dinner party. In the context of the London Festival Hall, the value of 'i' is the stage at the London Festival Hall. (32) is true relative to the first of these contexts, because Smith is remarkable compared to the violinists who have played in the past at the location at which the dinner party occurs. That is, where f is a function from locations to the people who have played instruments at those locations, and l is the location of the dinner party, Smith is remarkable compared to the members of the intersection of {x: violinist (x)} and {y: y ∈ f(l)}. (31) is false relative to the second of these contexts, because Smith is not remarkable compared to the violinists who have played in the past at the location of the London Festival Hall. The case in which Fred is a 7-year-old child is similar. Relative to the envisaged context, 'i' could be assigned, for example, Fred, and 'f' a function from people to the set of structures that have been built by people of that age. Relative to a context in which 'i' and 'f' are assigned these values, (33) has the desired interpretation, that Fred built a snowman that is large for a snowman built by a 7-year-old child.

Now, let us turn back to predicative occurrences of comparative adjectives. The worry about the classical analysis of predicative occurrences of comparative adjectives was that the nominal by itself does not determine the comparison class. So, claiming that (26)–(28) are elliptical for (29)–(31) does not explain the existence of a contextually provided comparison class. But according to NRT, each nominal is really of the form $< N, f(i) >$. Combining NRT with the classical account of predicative occurrences of comparative adjectives results in logical forms for (26)–(28) roughly like:

(36) That building is a small $< \text{building}, f(i) >$.
(37) That basketball player is a short basketball $< \text{player}, f(i) >$.
(38) That flea is a small $< \text{animal}, f(i) >$.

As we have seen, given the semantics provided in the previous section, instances of the schema '$< N, f(i) >$' do, relative to a context, determine the entire contextually salient comparison class for a comparative adjective.[10]

---

[10] (29)–(31) are themselves ambiguous between what is sometimes called the intersective reading and the non-intersective reading (for a useful discussion, cf. section 1.0 of Larson, 1998). For example, 'Mugsy is a short basketball player' can mean either that Mugsy is short for a basketball player (the non-intersective reading) or (for example) that Mugsy is short for a human being and Mugsy is a basketball player. According to the view I am defending, (26)–(28) are elliptical for (29)–(31), in their *non-intersective* use. I will not address the intersective readings of sentences such as (29)–(31).

It has been standard in the literature on comparative adjectives to maintain that, even in attributive readings of adjectives, the nominal complement of a comparative adjective does not by itself determine the comparison class. What we have seen in this section is that this conclusion results from an inadequate grasp of the true syntax and semantics of nouns. Once NRT is adopted, one mystery about the 'extra' context-dependency associated with the determination of comparison classes vanishes. The 'extra' context-dependency in question is simply due to unrecognized structure in the noun, the very same structure that accounts for the phenomenon of so-called 'quantifier domain restriction'.

Mass Expressions

We have seen that NRT explains two apparently very different effects of context on linguistic interpretation. In this section, I discuss yet another apparently very different effect of context on linguistic interpretation that is explained by NRT. Consider the sentence:

(39) That puddle is water.

Suppose the puddle in question consists of muddy water. Prima facie, relative to certain contexts, (39) is true. However, prima facie, relative to other contexts, (39) is false. For example, suppose we are attending a conference of companies that market bottled water. Relative to such a context, it might be false that the stuff in the puddle counts as water. Indeed, relative to such a context, nothing less pure than the least pure bottled water might legitimately count as water. Finally, even more drastically, consider a context in which chemists are discussing the molecular structure of water. Relative to such a context, even the stuff in Evian bottles might not count as water.

Let us consider the denotation of 'that puddle' to be fixed across contexts. One natural reaction to the prima-facie truth of (39) relative to some contexts, and the prima-facie falsity of (39) relative to other contexts, is to argue that, fixing the reference of the demonstrative expression 'that puddle', the truth of (39) does not vary from context to context. Relative to contexts in which 'that puddle' refers to the relevant quantity of matter, (39) is either always false or always true. The impression otherwise is due to pragmatics, and not to semantics. Call this the *pragmatic account*.

One worry I have with the pragmatic account is that I do not see even the outlines of how a pragmatic account of these facts would proceed. For example, suppose that we take the view that each member of the relevant class of occurrences of (39) expresses a false proposition. I do not see how to provide a systematic, compelling Gricean derivation of the true proposition communicated from the false proposition expressed. Of course, Kent Bach and others have provided influential arguments that pragmatics also involves adding propositional constituents to the semantic content of an expression relative to a context, a process Bach calls 'Impliciture' (e.g. Bach, 1994). But even setting aside my worries about Bach's notion of impliciture, it is not clear to me how to provide an account based on impliciture in defense of the pragmatic account of the above sort of context-dependency. In short, I worry that the pragmatic account puts too great of a strain on existing theories of pragmatics.

Of course, the countervailing worry is that incorporating this sort of contextual phenomenon into the semantics places too great of a strain on existing syntactic and semantic theories. There are two different ways to pose this worry. First, one might worry that incorporating the phenomenon into the semantics compromises the systematicity of semantic explanation in some deep fashion. Secondly, one might worry that there is no independent evidence for the resources needed to treat this sort of context-dependence. If so, then postulating the mechanisms needed to treat this sort of context-dependence in the semantics may seem *ad hoc*.

The pragmatic account would be a fruitful avenue to explore if either of the above worries were legitimate. But, as it turns out, these worries are not legitimate. The resources needed to treat this sort of context-dependency are already in place. For NRT provides a smooth explanation for this sort of effect of context on semantic interpretation. NRT is independently motivated, and does not compromise the systematicity of semantic explanation.

According to NRT, each common noun co-occurs with a domain index. Now, as is well known, each count noun can be 'transformed' into a mass expression. For example, 'sailor' and 'chicken' have mass-occurrences, as in (40*a–b*):

(40) *a.* John had sailor for dinner. (John is a cannibal)
       b. Hannah had chicken for dinner.

There is no reason to think that in using an expression that typically has count occurrences as a mass expression, one thereby drops the domain index. That is, there is no prima facie reason to think that, in (40*a–b*), the mass expressions do not co-occur with domain indices.

Furthermore, examination of mass quantification shows that there is just as much justification for the claim that each mass expression comes with a domain index as there is in the case of count quantification. For example, suppose that Pastor Hannah is concerned about the fact that someone has been drinking the holy water in her church on warm summer days. In a discussion with her John confesses:

(41) I drank a little water last week.

What John expresses is the proposition that John drank a little of the church's holy water the week before the utterance was made. That is, (41) is only true if John drank a little holy water, and not if he just drank a little unholy water.

We should expect any account of count quantifier domain restriction to generalize straightforwardly to the case of mass quantifier domain restriction. NRT, of course, does exactly this. With Helen Morris Cartwright, let us take an occurrence of a mass expression, relative to a circumstance of evaluation, to denote a set of quantities. According to NRT, the rough logical form of (41) is:

(42) I drank a little $<$ water, $f(i)>$ last week.

In the context at hand, we may suppose 'f' to be assigned a function that takes a location to a set of quantities. Furthermore, 'i' is assigned Hannah's church. Relative to this context, 'f' yields the set of quantities of holy liquids in the church. This set is then intersected with the set of all quantities of water, yielding the desired interpretation.

Furthermore, there is evidence that the object variable in structures such as (41) can be bound, as in:

(43) In every church, the pastor drinks a little water during the weekly ceremony.

(43) can express the proposition that in every church c, the pastor of c drinks a little of the holy water of c during the weekly ceremony. Thus, as one might expect, there is the same sort of evidence for mass quantifier domain variables in logical forms as there is for count quantifier domain variables.

According to NRT, then, (44) is a rough guide to the relevant aspects of the logical form of (39):

(44) That puddle is $<$ water, $f(i)>$.

Relative to a circumstance of evaluation, 'water', in (39), denotes the set of all quantities of water. Relative to a context, 'f' is assigned a function that takes an object of some kind and yields a set of quantities of matter, one appropriate to intersect with the denotation of 'water'. Relative to a context, 'i' is assigned an object that serves as an input to the denotation of 'f'.[11]

If NRT is true, then the sort of context-dependence at issue in examples such as (39) is easily explicable. Consider the context of the bottled water conference. In this case, context assigns to 'f' a function that takes a location and yields a set of quantities, and context assigns to 'i' the bottled water conference. The result of applying the value of 'f' to the bottled water conference will be, for example, the set of quantities of liquids that are sufficiently pure to be sold in bottles in supermarkets in the United States. The denotation of ' $<$ water, $f(i) >$ ' is then the result of intersecting the denotation of 'water' with this set of quantities. Similarly, the context in which chemists are discussing the molecular structure of water may be one in which the set of contextually provided quantities contains all and only those quantities q such that q is constituted by molecules of the same type. Finally, the context in which (39) counts as true is one in which the domain is all quantities whatsoever, so the denotation of 'water' is unrestricted.

So NRT provides a straightforward explanation of the sort of context-dependence in examples such as (39). There is thus evidence from a wide variety of constructions for the truth of NRT. Furthermore, given NRT, many apparently distinct effects of extra-linguistic content on what is asserted are traceable to the same source.

It is worthwhile noting a few consequences of this analysis that are of general philosophical interest. According to the analysis we have given, and supported by syntactic and semantic evidence from a wide variety of constructions, the reading on which (39) is true is one according to which 'water' occurs unrestricted. That means that the denotation of an unrestricted use of 'water' includes quantities that are very far from pure H_2O. Exactly parallel considerations govern all other mass expressions that are so-called 'natural kind terms', such as 'gold'.

---

[11] I have not here discussed degree theoretic approaches, despite their evident promise in yielding a unified account of adjectives and comparatives (degree theoretic approaches are first discussed with rigor in Cresswell's classic (1975), and have recently been given new life in Kennedy (1997)). However, such approaches, as yet, have yielded no satisfactory analysis of predicative uses of adjectives. For example, the semantics for such constructions given in Kennedy (1997: 123 ff.) is non-compositional; the degree provided by context simply appears in the semantic derivation at the level of the degree phrase (for a discussion of the non-compositionality of such rules, see Stanley and Szabo, 2000: 255–6). A correct compositional treatment of predicative uses of adjectives will, I suspect, attribute the provision of the degree to the elided nominal in such constructions.

In the theory of reference, it is often assumed that 'water' denotes H_2O. The first consequence of our analysis is that this assumption is incorrect. The denotation of 'H_2O', namely the set of all quantities of H_2O, is but a small proper subset of the denotation of 'water'. Though in some contexts, 'Water is H_2O' expresses a truth, this is not because the literal meaning of 'water' is the same as the literal meaning of 'H_2O'. In some contexts, 'Every man is a judo-expert' expresses a truth, but we should not infer from this that the literal meaning of 'man' is the same as the literal meaning of 'judo-expert'. Neither inference is valid.

A second consequence of note that can be drawn from the foregoing concerns expressions such as 'literally speaking'. Perhaps there are true uses of:

(45) Literally speaking, only pure H_2O is water.

But if there are, then what it shows is that the function of 'literally speaking' is not to restrain the interpretation of the words used to their literal meanings. The literal meaning of 'water' determines an extension that includes quantities that contain molecules distinct from H_2O. The function of 'literally speaking' in (45) is to restrict the domain of 'water' to a small sub-domain of its extension. In a sense, then, literally speaking is quite far from speaking literally.

One worry one might have about the account I have given is that it makes the extension of 'water' implausibly large. For example, one might worry that any substance whatsoever, in some context, counts as water. This worry is misplaced, if one accepts that, for every noun, there is at least one context in which it can be used with its domain maximally wide. In the case of mass expressions, what this means is that, for each mass noun, it is possible for there to be a context in which the domain for the mass noun is the set of all quantities whatsoever. Together with the fact that there is no true use of:

(46) Any quantity of any old substance whatsoever is water.

we may conclude that the literal meaning of 'water' does not determine the set of all quantities whatsoever.[12]

---

[12] One might worry that the value of 'f(i)', relative to a context, is not a plausible mass denotation, since it is not closed under sums (a property, according to Quine (1960: 91), that is constitutive of mass-denotations). However, I doubt that mass denotations are closed under sums. One example, due to George Boolos, is 'dust'. Not every sum of quantities of dust is dust. Another example, due to Zsofia Zvolensky, is 'liquid'. There might be two liquids that, when combined, turn into a gas (however, in this latter case, one might respond by denying that a sum is a mixture).

Of course, I have not seriously addressed the question of what fixes the reference of a term such as 'water'. But the results we have seen should serve to temper any inclinations one may have to draw exaggerated consequences from the view that terms such as 'water' have 'hidden scientific essences'. No doubt, for a quantity of liquid to count as a quantity of water, it must contain a certain portion of H_2O molecules. But a quantity of blood may contain a greater percentage of H_2O molecules than some quantity of water, without thereby counting as a quantity of water. Spelling out what fixes the reference of a term like 'water' is a difficult matter. But, given that the diluted stuff in lakes is water, such a story may very well centrally involve the sort of information available to ordinary speakers competent with the term 'water', such as 'falls from the sky in the form of rain'. This is evidence, albeit from an unlikely source, for an externalist, description theoretic account of the meanings of words such as 'water' and 'gold'.

As we have seen, (non-contextually restricted uses of) terms such as 'water' and 'gold' do not denote pure chemical kinds. This result supports a view recently advocated by Mark Johnston (1997). According to Johnston, mass terms such as 'water' do not denote chemical kinds such as H_2O. Rather, they denote what Johnston calls 'manifest kinds'. The manifest kind denoted by 'water' is not identical to H_2O. Instead, it is constituted by H_2O.

For a quantity to count as a quantity of water, perhaps it must contain some H_2O. But, as we have seen, it may contain less H_2O than a quantity that is clearly not a quantity of water. These facts provide fairly decisive evidence for the thesis that water is not identical to H_2O.

Furthermore, our discussion provides a decisive rebuttal to one natural response to Johnston's arguments that 'water' and similar mass terms denote 'manifest' kinds. According to this response, each such term is ambiguous between a 'scientific' use, in which it denotes a chemical kind, and a 'manifest' use, where it functions as Johnston describes. However, as we have seen, uses of 'water' that denote a set of quantities, each of which is pure H_2O, do not involve a separate lexical item. Rather, these uses involve the very same lexical item as more ordinary uses of water. However, in these specialized uses, the denotation of that lexical item is contextually restricted. As far as literal meaning is concerned, then, terms such as 'water', 'gold', 'copper', and the like uniformly do not denote chemical kinds.[13]

---

[13] Thanks to Tim Williamson for discussion here.

Conclusion

There are other constructions the analysis of which is aided by the adoption of NRT. For example, like indefinite descriptions, definite descriptions exhibit quantificational variability effects. That is, among the interpretations of $(47a–b)$ are the ones specified in $(48a–b)$:

(47) a. The customer is always right.
　　 b. Usually, the sailor stops, but the marine goes on.
(48) a. For all x, if customer (x), then right (x).
　　 b. For most x, y, if sailor (x) and marine (y), then x stops and y goes on.[14]

Such effects are surprising, on the supposition that definite descriptions are quantifiers. Indeed, Delia Graff (2001: section vii) has recently exploited the fact that definite descriptions are subject to quantificational variability effects to argue for the thesis that definite descriptions are not quantifier expressions, but predicates. For if definite descriptions were predicates, one could explain the data in (47) and (48), since the adverb of quantification would then bind a free variable in the predicate expression.

However, NRT reconciles the quantificational treatment of definite descriptions with the existence of quantificational variability effects. For, if NRT is correct, each noun co-occurs with a domain index. That is, according to NRT, the structure of $(47a–b)$ is as in:

(49) a. The $<$customer, $f(i)>$ is always right.
　　 b. Usually, the $<$sailor, $f(i)>$ stops, but the $<$marine, $f(j)>$ goes on.

Given these representations, NRT smoothly predicts quantificational variability effects. In $(47a)$, the adverb of quantification 'always' raises and binds the variable 'i' in $<$customer, $f(i)>$. We may suppose then that context supplied 'f' with a function from situations to sets such that the intersection with that set of the denotation, relative to a circumstance of evaluation, of 'customer', yields

---

[14] I should note that discussions with Richard Boyd have made me somewhat uncomfortable with the dichotomy suggested by Johnston's terminology of 'manifest' vs 'chemical' kind. The fact that (non-contextually restricted uses of) 'water' and 'gold' fail to denote chemical kinds does not entail that (such uses of) these terms do not denote natural kinds. After all, chemical kinds are not the only natural kinds. It is unclear to me that explanation in, say, evolutionary biology, can do without appeal to the kinds denoted by 'water' and 'gold', despite the fact that they are not chemical kinds.

a set with one member. Similarly, in (47*b*), the adverb of quantification 'usually' unselectively binds the variables 'i' and 'j', yielding the desired interpretation.[15] Thus, NRT allows us to explain such effects, without abandoning the thesis that definite descriptions are quantifiers.

However, my point in this chapter is not simply to emphasize the virtues of the Nominal Restriction Theory. It appears that the effects of extra-linguistic context on the determination of what is said by the use of a sentence are too diverse and varied to be susceptible of systematization. Appeals to extra-linguistic context are consequently ubiquitous in the work of those who seek to undermine the thesis that linguistic interpretation is largely systematic and rule-governed. However, I hope to have shown by example how what appear to be very different effects of context on the determination of what is said can be due to the same source. If, as I believe to be the case, there are only a small number of ways in which extra-linguistic context affects what is said by a use of a sentence, perhaps it is not so clear that extra-linguistic context poses a threat to the systematicity of linguistic interpretation.[16]

References

Bach, K. (1994). 'Conversational Impliciture', *Mind and Language*, 9: 124–62.

Barwise, J., and Cooper, R. (1981). 'Generalized Quantifiers and Natural Language', *Linguistics and Philosophy*, 4, 159–219.

Chierchia, Gennaro (1993). 'Questions with Quantifiers', *Natural Language Semantics*, 1: 181–234.

Cresswell, Max (1975). 'The Semantics of Degree', in Barbara Partee (ed.), *Montague Grammar* (New York: Academic Press), 261–92.

Engdahl, Elisabet (1986). *Constituent Questions* (Dordrecht: D. Reidel).

Farkas, Donka (1997). 'Evaluation Indices and Scope', in A. Szabdcsi (ed.), *Ways of Scope Taking* (Dordrecht: Kluwer), 183–215.

Graff, Delia (2001). 'Descriptions as Predicates', *Philosophical Studies*, 102/1: 1–42.

Groenendijk, J., and Stokhof, M. (1984). 'Studies on the Semantics of Questions and the Pragmatics of Answers' (Amsterdam doctoral diss.).

---

[15] I am here ignoring the complexities involved in the proportion problem (see for discussion, e.g. Heim, 1982; Reinhart, 1986).

[16] For more on adverbs of quantification and unselective binding, cf. Lewis (1975), Heim (1982).

Heim, Irene (1982). 'The Semantics of Definite and Indefinite Noun Phrases' (doctoral diss., University of Massachusetts at Amherst).

—— and Kratzer, Angelika (1998). *Semantics in Generative Grammar* (Oxford: Blackwell).

Johnston, Mark (1997). 'Manifest Kinds', *Journal of Philosophy*, 94/11: 564–583.

Kamp, Hans (1975). 'Two Theories of Adjectives', in E. Keenan (ed.), *Formal Semantics of Natural Language* (Cambridge: Cambridge University Press), 23–55.

Kennedy, C. (1997). *Projecting the Adjective: The Syntax and Semantics of Gradability and Companion.* Dissertation, University of California (Santa Cruz, Calif.: SLUG pubs.).

Larson, Richard (1998). 'Events and Modification in Nominals', in *Semantics and Linguistic Theory*, viii (Ithaca, NY: CLC Publications), 145–68.

—— and Segal, Gabriel (1995). *Knowledge of Meaning* (Cambridge, Mass.: MIT Press).

Lewis, David (1975). 'Adverbs of Quantification', in E. Keenan (ed.), *Formal Semantics of Natural Language* (Cambridge: Cambridge University Press).

Parsons, Terence (1972). 'Some Problems Concerning the Logic of Grammatical Modifiers', in E. Harman and D. Davidson (eds.), *Semantics of Natural Language* (Dordrecht: Reidel), 127–41.

Quine, Willard van Orman (1960). *Word and Object* (Cambridge, Mass.: MIT Press).

Reinhart, Tanya (1986). 'On the Interpretation of Donkey Sentences', in E. Traugott *et al.* (eds.), *On Conditionals* (Cambridge: Cambridge University Press).

Siegel, Muffy (1975). 'Capturing the Russian Adjective', in Barbara Partee (ed.), *Montague Grammar* (New York: Academic Press), 293–309.

Stanley, Jason (2000). 'Context and Logical Form', *Linguistics and Philosophy*, 23/4: 391–434.

—— and Szabo, Zoltan (2000). 'On Quantifier Domain Restriction', *Mind and Language*, 15/2: 219–61.

Westerståhl, Dag (1989). 'Quantifiers in Formal and Natural Languages', in D. Gabbay and F. Guenthner (eds.), *Handbook of Philosophical Logic*, iv (Dordrecht: Kluwer), 1–131.

Part III

Logical Form,
Belief Ascription,
and
Proper Names

13

Russell's Logical Form, LF, and Truth-Conditions

Bernard Linsky

Bertrand Russell's theory of definite descriptions is generally credited as the source of the idea that the logical form of a sentence will be very different from its grammatical or syntactic form.[1] Russell's view was that just as 'I met a man' and 'No one met Jones' are only superficially atomic relational statements of the form aRb and must be represented very differently when symbolized in a formal language, so sentences with definite descriptions such as 'The present king of France is bald' must also be given symbolizations very different from their superficial grammatical form as simple subject predicate sentences. This standard story is often continued with the suggestion that with the development of syntactic theory it is now possible to define a notion of logical form that is a level of syntactic analysis. In particular, syntactic constituents such as noun phrases should be treated uniformly rather than seen as merely superficially similar as Russell had thought. Some versions of the story may perhaps continue by arguing that there is a subdivision between noun phrases that are genuine referring expressions and quantifiers and go on to place descriptions in one or the other classes, but the first part is the same. The moral of this familiar tale is that we now know that one byproduct of a proper syntactic analysis of a sentence will be an account of its logical form. There is no longer a need to distinguish so sharply between the form suggested by the syntax of a sentence and its real logical form. One can derive the logical form of a sentence systematically from surface form, representing grammatical

[1] See e.g. Lycan (1984: 13). Lycan further says (p. 23) that Russell gives no other account of the relation of a sentence to its logical form than to speak of 'abbreviation'.

categories such as Noun Phrase as a logically uniform category. Russell was wrong and the notion that grammatical form misleads about logical form is gone.

This chapter is intended to add some historical depth to this story by describing Russell's notion of logical form in slightly more detail than the above. Russell did indeed think that surface syntax can somehow be misleading as to logical form, but in some form or other, so does everyone. From the specific examples that he provides, such as the theory of descriptions, and from some explicit discussions in connection with the nature of logical truth one can reconstruct Russell's notion of logical form. That notion was more than just a proposal about how to translate sentences into his formal language in order to properly account for their truth-conditions. It was not solely or even principally motivated by the idea that the grammar of ordinary language hides the real logical form of sentences. Russell's notion of logical form connected with his views about the nature of logic, and his ontological views as well. This review will make it possible to get a more nuanced view of Russell's notion of 'incomplete symbol' and the way in which syntactic constituents are seen as genuine constituents of propositions. To discuss Russell's legacy I will introduce two contemporary notions of 'logical form' that can be contrasted with Russell's; that which comes from a truth theory or other statement of truth-conditions for a language stated in some other formal language, and the notion of 'LF' as represented, for example, by Neale (1990), May (1985), and Larson and Ludlow (1993). To focus on the difference between these notions of logical form I will conclude with a discussion of two well-known aspects of Russell's theory of descriptions, the notions of *incomplete symbol* and *scope*. Both of these aspects of Russell's account of logical form have entered contemporary discussions through Stephen Neale's (1990) attempt to resuscitate Russell's theory of descriptions.

Truth-Conditions and LF

One approach to giving the logical form of a sentence is simply to provide a translation of that sentence into a formal logical language or a formalization of the truth-conditions or truth theory for the language in a formal language. Both a formal semantics and a truth theory will provide an account of the logical form as a byproduct.

The account of logical form given by Lepore and Ludwig in Chapter 3 above is an example of the latter sort. They propose that 'logical form' does not consist of single sentences of a formalized language, but is a property of sentences that emerges from a Davidsonian truth theory for a language. Looking at a canonical proof of a T-sentence for a given sentence we see how it is built up and know what contributions the parts make to truth-conditions for the whole sentence. From this proof one can also determine the logical consequences of a sentence and those other features that are provided by other accounts of logical form. Constructing a truth theory for a language relies on providing a regimentation of the language, deciding what categories various constructions fall into, and what expressions of each category contribute to the truth-conditions of the entire sentence, all to be expressed within a precisely specified metalanguage. To that extent that truth theory will be just like the account of logical form in terms of translations into formal languages.

For these purposes the distinctive features of a formal language are that they allow no ambiguity, so ambiguous sentences of natural language are represented by two distinct sentences in the formal language, and that the semantic interpretation is precisely determined by the syntax of the translation. Every syntactically well formed expression of the formal language is given one and only one semantic interpretation. That semantic interpretation in turn represents or determines the truth-conditions for the sentence. What makes this a notion of *logical* form is that the formalization represents the logical properties of the sentence. The entailments of a sentence can be directly read off its form.

The truth-theoretic approach to logical form provides a somewhat less direct account of the *form* of a sentence. Such an account may identify logical terms, perhaps by some unique sort of contribution they make to truth-conditions, and then identify the logical form of a sentence with an expression in which all expressions except for the logical expressions are replaced by variables. It may be possible to avoid singling out logical terms altogether and to simply point out that as a result of certain productive or recursive devices in the language certain generalizations can be made about the truth-conditions of classes of sentences at a time. Such generalizations would be all that could be said about the logical form of the sentences. According to this latter sort of truth-conditional account logical form is not an entity but rather a feature of sentences derived from global features of the language which are relevant to determining the entailments of sentences in a certain sort of way. A truth-conditional account of logical form might have use for sentences in a formal language, as a way of stating truth-conditions.[2] Those formal sentences might seem to be such structured entities, but they differ from full-fledged

---

[2] As in Chapter 3 above.

logical forms by being merely a way to determining truth-conditions.[3] A theory that has genuine abstract objects as logical forms will have the details of those forms not determined solely by truth-conditions. Other factors are involved in determining the right structure for a proposition. Both the contemporary linguist's notion of LF and Russell's own theory are motivated by such extra factors.

The approach to logical form using LF appears in Neale (1990), May (1985), and Larson and Ludlow (1993). LF is represented in a language with a precise syntax as in the truth-conditional accounts above. Ambiguous sentences are also provided with distinct LFs. LF is, however, dependent upon syntactic considerations in a different manner than logical form is in the truth-conditional approach. With the exception of binding relations between quantifiers and variables, LFs are exactly syntactic phrase structure trees with nodes annotated by syntactic categories. LF is a level of syntactic representation complementing SS ('surface structure') which is independently transformed into PF ('phonetic form') and LF. Semantic interpretation is based on LF. To say that LF is a level of representation in the grammar is thus not the same as the notion of uninterpreted syntax used in formal logic. As the whole grammar is taken to represent psychological facts about speakers, the distinction of components in the grammar is meant to abstract various aspects of the actual use of language by speakers. At least this is the goal of the program of 'naturalizing' linguistics to which LF belongs. Our best guess as to how our psychological or conceptual system makes use of LF will then be based largely on what look like syntactic properties of the surface form of sentences as well as intuitions about ambiguities and logical consequence.

LFs represent natural syntactic classes in the sense that syntactically related expressions such as quantifiers and noun phrases will each get common logical forms. This is a desideratum of a theory, but not a rigid requirement. The interpretation of a class can vary according to the syntactic context in which it occurs. A vivid example of commonly accepted variation is pointed out by McCawley (1993), who insists that the logician's binary sentential connective ' $\wedge$ ' is not a good representation of 'and' in English, as that word can connect not only pairs of noun phrases, but any number of constituents, as in 'Tom, Dick and Harry'. McCawley insists that a proper account of 'and' should be univocal and account for such differences of logical form from the standard translation as the logician's conjunction. The truth-conditional account of

---

[3]   Much as Montague (1974) describes the representations of sentences in Intensional Logic as a convenience in connecting sentences of natural language with truth conditions.

logical form defended by Lepore and Ludwig makes use of first order logic in which to carry out the derivation of T-sentences and hence requires some such divergences between syntactic categories and semantic interpretations. As long as the account is recursive and based on a finite base of constructions there is no need for a truth theory to treat each lexical item or syntactic category in a uniform semantic fashion. LF appears to be under more of an obligation to give a word the same representation everywhere it appears, because there is just one opportunity for 'lexical insertion' in the process of syntactic generation. If there are reasons for assigning some lexical items to two different word classes, say as a noun and a verb, then of course there will be two different words to enter. But even different uses of the same term can be given different semantic accounts, provided that the uses are distinguished by uniform syntactic classes. Thus, in the above example, it is conceivable that noun phrase conjunction and conjunction of clauses will receive different representations in LF. Still, the sources of ambiguity are limited to syntax (including notions of scope and binding arising in LF) and lexical items. Neale follows this, for example, by representing the syntactic class of 'quantifiers' uniformly in his account of LF, since the notions of trace and binding that apply to them are uniform.

Because LF is itself a symbolic or abstract representation of the syntax of a sentence, it does not come with a semantic interpretation built in. The semantic interpretation will often be obvious, as when LF uses determiners and traces which look just like quantifiers and bound variables from symbolic logic, but strictly speaking the representation in LF and the semantic interpretation of LF are distinct. LF representations are structured objects which arise as part of syntactic theory which in turn have to be interpreted. This seemingly small point looms larger when looking at the application of the notion of scope for definite descriptions in modal contexts. What will make the issue of interpretation relevant is that there is a purely 'syntactic' notion of binding and scope that is represented in LF which is distinct from a semantic interpretation. It may be possible therefore to have distinct LFs which represent two different scopes for operators which do not thereby have distinct, or indeed any, semantic interpretations. As before it should be added that this emphasis on syntactic considerations is a result of the methodology used in constructing LFs rather than a commitment of the larger program. Since the lingusitic system is intended to be a representation of a speaker's psychological states, and since speakers in some sense understand all sentences of the language, they must attribute some meaning to the different scopes of operators. It is the linguist proposing the differing analyses who may be short of an interpretation of one of them.

There is a natural way to provide a semantic interpretation for an LF representation, however. This is defended by Larson and Ludlow (1993) as providing a substitute for propositions in semantic analysis. The 'Interpreted Logical Form', or ILF, is the logical form tree combined with an object which is the semantic interpretation of each node on the tree. Leaves or lexical items will be provided with extensions and various nodes up a tree will represent different functions or objects that lead up to a truth-value as the object represented by the top S node, as the semantic value of a sentence, for this account, is a truth-value. This leads to an extensional semantic theory, however it is easy to imagine some other way of dressing the nodes of an LF structure, perhaps using intensions in the style of Montague grammar, that would provide a somewhat different kind of semantics.

Russell

Russell's notion of logical form is complex and includes elements that just do not show up in contemporary notions like LF or truth-conditional semantics. One notion that is shared with Russell's account is precisely the sort of translation into a standard formal language that is associated with the tradition of logical 'analysis'. Russell's proposals were crucial to starting that movement. We may fix on this notion of analysis by looking at some of his examples, the most famous being his account of definite descriptions in 'On Denoting'. Russell did see his theory of definite descriptions as giving the logical form of sentences including definite descriptions. The formalizations in the logic of *Principia Mathematica* provide the closest approach that Russell, long before Tarski's definition of truth, could have given to an account of truth-conditions. But there is much more to Russell's discussion of logical form than that. It is the other, more ontological, aspects of logical form, having to do with the form and unity of propositions and facts, that are of most significance for interpreting some of Russell's other notions such as that of an 'incomplete symbol'.

In the period from his *Theory of Knowledge* (1984) manuscript from 1913 through the *Introduction to Mathematical Philosophy* of 1919 Russell explicitly discusses the notion of logical form. One of his concerns has to do with his project of logicism. Russell wanted to show that mathematics is reducible to logic. This involves first finding definitions of mathematical notions in logical terms and then using them to derive truths of mathematics from logic alone. That required Russell to distinguish logical truths from others. The truths of geometry are fairly clearly conditional facts about what can be derived from which premises. Russell argued that mathematical truths in general can be seen as conditionals, 'if such and such axioms are true, then so and so follows'. In many cases the 'axioms' will in turn be derivable from logic alone and so the truths of mathematics that rely on them can be seen to be categorical logical truths. It was the recalcitrant axioms of reducibility, choice, and infinity that required staying partly with the 'if-thenist' account rather than arguing that all mathematical truths are entirely categorical logical truths. Whether or not all the axioms of mathematics are reducible to logic, the project still needs a notion of logical truth. At one point Russell proposes that logical truths are simply completely generalized truths. Thus a particular fact, say that a is before b, will be generalized into:

(1) $(\exists R) (\exists x) (\exists y)\ xRy$

'Something bears some relation to something.' The latter is a completely general truth with no particular content, as is characteristic of logical truths. However it does seem to say something substantive about the world, namely that it has at least one thing and one relation in it. More complicated propositions will have more complex generalizations. So it is just some of these propositions that will be logical truths although Russell was not sure how that distinction was to be made. More familiar examples of completely generalized truths that are logical might be the generalization of a syllogism as holding that for any classes F, G, and H, if all Fs are Gs and all Gs are Hs then all Fs are Hs. Russell proposed that these completely general truths, among them the logical truths, may also serve as logical forms. The form of a proposition aRb is something that it has in common with other propositions about different individuals, say cSd. Abstracting out what is particular by quantifying will result in precisely one of those logical forms, a completely general proposition.

The distinctive epistemological features of logical truths are explained by this generality. Logic is general and 'topic neutral' precisely because logical truths are so general and all specific content is removed by generalization. What is left after the generalization consists of only logical notions. These notions refer to 'logical objects'.[4] They are abstract entities like universals with which we have a particular epistemological relationship of 'acquaintance', which explains how we can have knowledge of these truths independently of ordinary empirical knowledge of the world. The generality of logic is derived from the generality and ubiquity of these logical properties or objects. Like

---

[4] As in Russell (1912: ch. 10).

other truths involving universals, logical truths are necessary, timeless, and so on. Logic for Russell was not at all the linguistic, uninterpreted calculus it became in the 1920s and especially at Tarski's hands. Rather logic is a portion of platonistic metaphysics, much as many now see mathematics in the guise of set theory as committed to platonism. Russell's project of logicism was one of reducing mathematics to logic to remove the elements of intuitions and experience put there by Kant and Mill, not one of eliminating ontological commitment or the a priori synthetic character of mathematics.

With these origins, Russell's notion of logical form is clearly directly connected with the truth-conditions, logical powers, and existential import of propositions, and indirectly if at all with the syntactic features of sentences expressing those propositions.

Another respect in which Russell's logical form is distinctive is in its treatment of structure and constituency relations within propositons. Logical forms show up in Russell's early writings of this period in the issue of the metaphysical unity of propositions. Around 1910 Russell had abandoned his earlier notion of propositions as abstract entities with individuals, relations, and properties as constituents, and instead adopted his notorious 'multiple relation' theory of judgment. By this account the statement 'Othello believed that Desdemona loves Cassio' is not a complex proposition relating Othello and a single entity, the proposition that Desdemona loves Cassio, which might be true or false. Instead it is a simple, true, proposition relating those constituents of Othello, believing, loving, Desdemona and Cassio, say with a form:

(2) B(o, d, L, c)

(This is a 'multiple' relation because 'B' will appear with different numbers of arguments depending on the form of the proposition believed.)

This multiple relation theory was immediately challenged by Wittgenstein, and was the focus of a series of reformulations on Russell's part, and repeated challenges from Wittgenstein. The problems revolve around the fact that what is believed must be a proposition, expressed by a sentence. On its surface the multiple relation theory should allow an arbitrary list of things to be related by the belief relation. Thus one problem seems to be an order problem. What is the difference in the belief that Desdemona loves Cassio and the belief that Cassio loves Desdemona? Both will just have Love, Cassio, and Desdemona as objects of the belief relation. For belief in atomic propositions, some convention about the order of the objects and the places in the relation might hide the problem. But what of more complicated propositions? Something must represent the *form* of the proposition. And what is to rule out incoherent propositions, say, B(o,L,d,c), that 'Othello believes that loves Desdemona Cassio'? Here we find a place for the logical forms. In the 1913 manuscript Russell considers putting the general fact that something is related to something in with the terms to represent the logical form of the belief.

(3) B(o, d, L, c, ($\exists$ R) ($\exists$ x) ($\exists$ y) xRy)

Note that Russell wants to resist accepting propositions (whether true or false) in addition to facts. But Russell's facts are not only atomic but also negative and general, such as the facts that something is not related to something else, or that everything is such and such. The last constituent of (3) above will presumably be one of these high-level general (logical) facts that something is related to something. The 1913 manuscript was never completed, however, and Russell abandoned this whole approach to propositions by the early 1920s. The story of Russell's struggle with the problem of the multiple relation theory is complicated and difficult to make out. The theory must be kept in mind, however, when relating Russell's notion of logical form to a recent conception like that of LF.

Contemporary theories of logical form seem to handle exactly the sort of worry that bothered Russell. He was concerned that the objects related by the belief relation be real entities, but related in such a way that they could 'express' falsehoods. Syntactic theory deals with exactly these issues of order and coherence or well-formedness and also recognizes that mere strings will not do as representations of sentences. Instead a structured representation such as a tree is used. A tree represents both order (usually from left to right) and constituency relations, with daughters of a common node immediately related. Trees, especially when written out in bracket notation, explicitly indicate these elements. Brackets show the structural analysis and subscripts name the consitutents. In the simple example above, we might represent the belief as:

(4) $[_{S'} B [_N o] [_S [_N d] [_{VP} [_V L] [_N c]]]]$

with S and S$'$ likely being different categories to represent the object of belief and the arguments of the outer (multiple) belief relation.

What ontological status should these markers have, however? Russell's ontology allows only individuals, relations of various numbers of adicities, and the more abstract properties of negation and generality as constituents of facts. Propositions are built up from atomic propositions using just the logical connectives; 'and', 'or', 'not', 'if...then', 'if and only if', and the quantifiers 'for all x', and 'for some x'. Russell accepted both general and, more notoriously, negative facts, in addition to atomic facts. Since a generalization that everything is F does not follow from any list of instances, Fa, Fb, Fc, . . . , without some condition that those are *all* the things there are, Russell felt that no number of atomic facts add up to a general or universal fact. They must exist beyond their instances. But that was the whole inventory of facts.

What would Russell make of an expression like (4)? To begin with, if we see the 'S' category as an object, we would have propositional entities that can be true or false, what Russell wanted to avoid.[5] Treating (4) as an extension of his 1913-style multiple relation theory involves two further problems. First we must add constituents of facts beyond negation and generality. The metaphysics would have to include not only correlates of 'not' and the quantifiers, but also of other syntactic constructions, such as Verb or Noun Phrases. Metaphysics resists this extension, at least when these correlates are 'complexes' which are to include universals and objects as parts or constituents. A second problem is that Russell's metaphysics does not allow much iteration. While Russell did represent some facts as constitutents of other facts, as in the case of perception which is a binary relation between a perceiver and a perceived fact, there are no other ways to embed facts in his metaphysics. Wittgenstein pressed this further with his insistence that all facts were atomic, independent of the existence of other facts, and so any iterative or embedded syntactic construction must be given a semantic analysis as merely asserting various classes of atomic facts. Thus it may look as though Russell's account of logical form is limited by the logic that he shared with Frege, but it is in fact driven also by his metaphysics of facts. It is not just that Russell is symbolizing sentences in the logic at hand, but he is also making proposals about the logical form of facts:

I think that one might describe philosophical logic . . . as an inventory, or if you like a more humble word, a 'Zoo' containing all the different forms that facts may have. I should prefer to say 'forms of facts' rather than 'forms of propositions' . . . In accordance with the sort of realistic bias that I should put into all study of metaphysics, I should always wish to be engaged in the investigation of some actual fact or set of facts, and it seems to me that this is so in logic just as it is in zoology. In logic you are

---

[5] Russell's reasons for this position are not completely clear. He thinks that there cannot be false facts corresponding to false assertions. For one account of this see my (1993). For a discussion of Interpreted Logical Forms, 'ILFs', in this role, see Ch. 14 below. Jeffrey King (see his (1998) and references therein) suggests that such complex facts can be seen as composed of their ultimate constituents and syntactic entities or structures. So objects can be found to be constituents of such facts, but Russell did not consider such options.

concerned with the forms of facts, with getting hold of the different forms of facts, different *logical* sorts of facts, that there are in the world. (Russell, 1918: 80)

While (4) could not be a legitimate atomic proposition for Russell, he could none the less provide propositional functions as meanings for syntactic constituents, such as the Determiner or Noun Phrase of a sentence. Even the analysis of an atomic sentence Rab as expressing the value of an application of a propositional function R_xb to an object a, would not be a real analysis in terms of constituents with which we are acquainted. The real constituents are the relation R and the two constituents a and b, all of which can be objects of acquaintance. Russell himself, then, would be able to see a sentence as the result of the application of certain functions to certain arguments, even when the function and argument are not ultimate referents of logically proper names. There is nothing in this notion of analysis that would rule out an analysis of descriptions as generalized quantifiers, namely, second order propositional functions that apply to first order propositional functions. One must distinguish, however, between an analysis into a logical form including constituents of a proposition, and an analysis as being the result of the application of functions to arguments. The latter can give meaning to syntactic constituents such as noun and verb phrases but is not an ultimate or even unique analysis into a logical form, and it is only the items in an ultimate analysis that can be objects of belief according to the multiple relation account.

Incomplete Symbols

How close is Russell's account of the logical form of definite descriptions to a contemporary truth-conditional or LF account? Is he just giving an account of the truth-conditions of sentences using descriptions, so that he could acknowledge that the LF representation of descriptions would make them out really as quantifiers, and of a kind with other quantified noun phrases after all? I will argue that Russell's project is committed to his account of definite descriptions as incomplete symbols, but not simply from the want of a more sophisticated logic.[6]

[6] This is the view held by Neale in his discussion of Russell's theory of descriptions, arguing that, aside from the incidental restriction posed by Russell's limited notion of logical form, his representation of descriptions as generalized quantifiers represents the essence of Russell's semantic project, which does not include 'his sense-datum epistemology and his consequent desire to treat ordinary proper names as disguised descriptions, his talk of objects as constituents of singular propositions, and his use of the formalism of *Principia Mathematica*' (1990: 14).

Russell's formal theory of descriptions is encapsulated in *Principia Mathematica* *14.01 where the apparent form of a context including a definite description on the left is defined by the right-hand side:[7]

$$(5) \quad [(\iota x)(\varphi x)].\psi(\,(\iota x)(\varphi x)\,) = (\exists x)(\forall y)[(\varphi y \equiv y = x) \,\&\, \psi x]$$

According to Neale, the right-hand side of this 'definition' gives a basically correct account of the truth-conditions of the left-hand side. But the left-hand side suggests an incorrect account of the logical form of expressions with definite descriptions. In that formula there are two components, first, an indicator of the *scope* of the description, which makes for the notorious ambiguity in denials of 'the present king of France is bald', and then the suggestion that descriptions are (at least apparently) singular terms, occurring after the predicate 'ψ' in this notation. For Russell the apparent 'scope' of descriptions is interpreted literally as the scope of the quantifiers in the analysis in the official language of PM. Descriptions are only seeming singular terms in that they are not replaced by any term in the analysis, rather their content φ occurs in a predicative context applied to bound variables. For Russell the apparent logical form on the left is only a stop on the way to the official analysis of descriptions which is offered on the right. It is the latter that really gives the logical form of sentences involving descriptions. Neale argues that Russell's analysis is not the correct logical form. Indeed, the original left-hand side is closer to a sentence that does correctly represent the logical form of sentences with descriptions, Neale's logical form: '[the x: φx] (x is ψ)', which is his abbreviation for the more proper LF:

$$(6) \quad [_S[_{NP}\text{the } \varphi]_x[_S[_{NP}t]_x[_{VP}\text{is } \psi]\,]\,]$$

where the *trace* 't' behaves just like a bound variable and the scope of the quantifier is indicated by the 'x'.

It is clearly important to Russell's analysis that definite descriptions are 'incomplete symbols' and as such do not have a meaning in 'isolation'. Their apparent logical form as 'names' is not their logical form. But what more does Russell intend with this notion of incomplete symbol? Neale takes his cue from the notion of having a meaning in isolation, and suggests that for Russell only logically proper names and predicates, semantically simple directly referring expressions, would count as having such a meaning. An item has meaning by introducing into a proposition some entity with which we can be acquainted.

---

[7] In the original notation, using dots for parentheses and a subscripted variable for for universal quantification, this is: '*14.01 [(ιx)(φx)]. ψ(ιx) (ϕx). =: ($\exists$b): φx. $\equiv_x$. x = b: ψb Df'.

Everything else will be an incomplete symbol. Thus, Neale says, his own account of descriptions as quantifiers is exactly in keeping with Russell's proposal. Now Russell in 'On Denoting' does stress the analogy between descriptions and quantified phrases such as 'a man' and 'all men' and descriptions such as 'the man', all of which are called 'denoting phrases'. In Neale's notation they will have the forms [some x: man x], [all x: man x], and [the x: man x]. These generalized quantifiers will be Russell's denoting phrases. None of them will be logically proper names. All, it seems, are incomplete symbols, being expressions that only occur with predicates to complete sentence (S) constituents.[8] Would Russell have been happy with this analysis, and so see his own account as limited simply by using an arbitrarily restricted list of quantifiers?

Here we must look to the ontological import of Russell's account of logical form and propositions. Constituents of propositions stand for things in the world. There will be universals corresponding to primitive predicates, and individuals corresponding to variables and constants, sense data for most of Russell's career. The notion of logical form also connects with Russell's epistemology. The ultimate constituents of propositions will be objects of acquaintance. (Other entities are known indirectly, via 'description', as the objects denoted by certain expressions.) Propositions themselves, while explicitly not individuals by the multiple relation account, will correspond to facts, which are the substance of the world: 'The universe consists of objects having various qualities and standing in various relations' (1919: 45). Among these facts are the distinctive general facts in the world which correspond to true general propositions.

What this account of general facts suggests is that Russell would see some special role for expressions of generality. Generality is a feature of the world by being a constituent of general facts.[9] Precisely what expression will stand for that constituent of generality? Certainly a restricted quantifier of the form [all

---

[8] It is not clear exactly what to make of the notion that logically proper names can appear in isolation. Robert Stainton (1998) explores this, arguing that descriptions and quantifier phrases can occur meaningfully by themselves without having to be interpreted as merely elliptical for some complete sentence. Nothing in Neale's account depends on this. He simply distinguishes names and propositions as the two fundamental kinds of meaningful elements in Russell's semantic theory.

[9] After saying that logical form cannot be an ordinary constituent of a proposition, under threat of a regress, Russell does never the less see logical notions as objects: 'Such words as *or*, *not*, *all*, *some*, plainly involve logical notions; and since we can use such words intelligently, we must be acquainted with the logical objects involved. But the difficulty of isolation is here very great, and I don not know what the logical objects involved really are.' (Russell, 1984: 99).

x: man x] is logically complex and only occurs as an element in a proposition, i.e. as an 'incomplete symbol'. Even the unrestricted quantifier [all x] can fairly be seen as an incomplete symbol. But what about the lexical constituents of these logical forms, in this case the single items 'all', 'some', and 'the'? It is here that Russell would make distinctions. He saw generality facts as basic. That must be seen as a reason for picking universal generalization as primitive in PM and as defining the others. Not every choice of primitives by Russell is given great import. He does seem to suggest that there is in fact a choice possible in selecting primitive sentential connectives. Even so, he was so impressed with the discovery of the Sheffer stroke that in the Introduction to the Second Edition of PM he suggests that the whole work should be considered rewritten with that one basic sentential connective. In the lectures on Logical Atomism (1918), however, he suggests that a notion of incompatibility which would be expressed with the Sheffer stroke is conceptually dependent on negation, and not a substitute for it. So even when there seems to be a choice of connectives he is moved to see which are conceptually basic.

All of this suggests that Russell might have reason to argue that there is no distinctive element in the ontology of particulars, universals, and facts that corresponds with 'the' in definite descriptions, while there is one that corres-ponds with the 'all' in the logical form (5) proposed for descriptions. That may be what is behind the insistence that descriptions are distinctively incomplete symbols. There would be a difference between the various generalized quan-tifiers. The universal quantifier [all x: man x] reveals its consitutents in the world, the feature of generality and the property of being a man, well enough to suggest that that quantifier is fully analysed logically, whereas a definite description [the x: man x], containing the word 'the' requires more analysis, precisely that analysis represented by (5).

In summary, then, the lexical items to be inserted at the leaves of trees in logical form have significant ontological status for Russell. In contemporary LF they are simply the primitive words of the language. No assumption is made that each word corresponds to something in the world. Russell further thought that such entities must be objects of acquaintance, and so ordinary proper names could not be treated as primitive. I propose that it would be important to him to choose the right logical terms to be primitive, as they would have to reflect elements of logical form in the world: 'the' does not name any such constituent. Neale rejects these aspects of Russell's view, thinking that he is dropping something incidental to his purposes. Instead, the difference between a syntactically primitive lexical item and an item corresponding with a genuine constituent of the world is a large one, and not one to be glossed over.

Scope for Russell and LF

An important difference between logical form seen as LF and as a formal language stating truth-conditions comes out in consideration of another aspect of Russell's account of definite descriptions, in the notion of *scope*. Russell points out that various choices for the context of a description will lead to different ways of eliminating the description. Thus the scope of the description in 'The present king of France is not bald' can lead to two analyses, for Russell one true and the other false.[10] In a formal language like that of PM this difference of scope in the description will show up as the relative scope of the quantifiers eliminating the description and the other operators in the sentence. Each will have its own truth-conditions.

To the extent that such elements of LF as scope are motivated purely by syntactic considerations of what is allowed in an acceptable sentence they are simultaneously no longer simply matters of representing different truth-conditions in a formal language. One may be able to tell that both scope readings are grammatically possible, without being able to detail their semantic interpretations. One could then argue for the existence of certain scope relations independently of having a precise grasp of the differences they will make to truth-conditions.

To illustrate this let me consider Neale's defense of the Russellian account of descriptions when extended to intensional contexts. From its very first formulations, W. v. O. Quine objected to quantified modal logic on the grounds that intensional operators made notions of reference and quantification obscure. Thus, he claimed, one was forced into the following sort of argument by apparently plausible principles of quantification and substitution of co-referential expressions. From:

(7) $\Box(9 > 7)$

and

(8) $9 =$ the number of planets

we derive

(9) $\Box$ (the number of planets > 7)

---

[10] 'It is not the case that there is one and only one present King of France, and he is bald' versus 'There is one and only one present King of France and he is not bald'.

an obvious falsehood. In 1948 Arthur Smullyan replied that this argument ignores the scope of the description 'the number of planets' and that, as Russell had long before observed, there is no reason to assume that descriptions, taken with the appropriate scope, are intersubstitutable with co-denoting expressions. The argument is simply and transparently invalid. Quine replied that interpreting one of the purported readings of the conclusion (9), that in which the description has wide scope, requires making sense of objects having properties necessarily and that the intelligibility of this sort of *de re* necessity begs the question about the intelligibility of modality. Neale replies that argument does not rely on any equivocation at all, that there is a single interpretation for each sentence, none of which require *de re* necessity, and that the argument is thus transparently invalid.

How does one show that an argument is invalid? Standardly that is done by showing that some argument with the *same logical form* has obviously true premises and an obviously false conclusion. But what is the logical form of the conclusion? According to Neale we have a sentence with two operators, an intensional operator and a descriptional quantifier, with a certain relative scope, the intensional operator having scope over the quantifier, thus:

(10) [necessarily] [the x : number of planets x] $(x > 7)$

The invalidity of this form of argument is shown by any example using any intensional operator including the one suggested by Russell's 'I thought that your yacht was longer than it is'. It would seem that one can present the logical form of the argument and conclude that it is invalid, without making sense of essentialism.

But suppose rather that one takes a standard statement of the truth-conditions for that conclusion in some system of quantified modal logic. It will be something like:

(11) $\Box (\exists x)(\forall y)[(\text{number of planets } y \equiv y = x) \& x > 7]$

This is clearly in a language that makes sense of, that is, gives truth-conditions for, a sentence which expresses *de re* necessity. If, however, there is a distinction between the assignment of logical form and the assignment of truth-conditions, it may be possible to show an argument invalid without presupposing an account of various truth-conditions that may be suspect.

This is a surprising feature of LF on Neale's account. In separating logical form from truth-conditions Neale seems to allow for a possible split between logic and truth-conditions. On his account certain claims about logic might be made on the basis of logical form alone, and independently of giving the truth-conditions for sentences.

Russell's own account of intensional contexts is missing. The very last section of the Introduction to PM ends with a discussion of Russell's example 'George IV who wished to know whether Scott was the author of *Waverley*'. He describes the two readings of the sentence, saying that on one Scott wishes to know whether a proposition of the form '$c = (\iota x)(\varphi x)$' is true and that on the other there is some proposition 'of the form $c = y$ concerning which he wished to know if it was true'. Yet nowhere in the body of PM is there any account of relations to propositions. Propositions are not allowed to be the values of variables or occur in subject position and only extensional contexts are discussed in the work. Alonzo Church (1974) has since developed an account of propositional attitudes to supplement Russell's logic, but any mention of them is left out of PM. Russell does describe both readings as involving some attitude towards a proposition, and thus does seem committed to both having a specific interpretation. There is no room in Russell's account of logical form for an attribution of form which might lack a unique and specific semantic interpretation. On the other hand, there is enough independence between attributions of structure to a proposition and accounts of the truth-conditions of those structures to allow Russell to get away with failing to account for one of those structures. In this his account is more like that of LF. A formal language that included two different scope readings for a sentence would have to provide truth-conditions for those two readings. No theory of the truth-conditions of modal sentences could both say that there are scope ambiguities and also fail to provide a reading for one of the readings of the ambiguous sentences.

I have hoped to show the relation of Bertrand Russell's ontologically oriented logical form and two distinct recent notions, the contemporary linguistic notion of LF as represented by Neale's account and the notion of truth-conditions expressed in a formal language. Contrary to Neale's suggestion, Russell's approach is alien to that of LF and was not just attempting to give an account of truth-conditions. LF represents more structure and constituents than Russell's account, but also more syntactic structure than a mere account of truth-conditions. It is probably this wealth of content that makes LF successful for the various tasks to which it is assigned, and justifies its continued use by linguistic theory.

REFERENCES

Church, Alonzo (1974). 'Russellian Simple Type Theory', *Proceedings and Addresses of the American Philosophical Association*, 47: 21–33.

King, Jeffrey (1998). 'What is Philosophical Analysis?', *Philosophical Studies*, 90: 155–79.

Larson, Richard K., and Ludlow, Peter (1993). 'Interpreted Logical Forms', *Synthese*, 95: 305–56. Reprinted in Ludlow (1997: 993–1039).

Linsky, Bernard (1993). 'Why Russell Abandoned Russellian Propositions', in A. D. Irvine and G. A. Wedeking (eds.), *Russell and Analytic Philosophy* (Toronto: University of Toronto Press), 193–209.

Ludlow, Peter (ed.) (1997). *Readings in the Philosophy of Language* (Cambridge, Mass.: MIT Press).

Lycan, William G. (1984). *Logical Form in Natural Language* (Cambridge, Mass.: MIT Press).

McCawley, James P. (1993). *Everything that Linguists have Always Wanted to Know about Logic* (But were Ashamed to Ask)* (2nd edn. Chicago: University of Chicago Press).

May, Robert (1985). 'Logical Form as a Level of Linguistic Representation', in *Logical Form: Its Structure and Derivation* (Cambridge, Mass.: MIT Press). Reprinted in Ludlow (1997: 281–315).

Montague, Richard (1974). 'The Proper Treatment of Quantification in Ordinary English', in Richmond Thomason (ed.), *Formal Philosophy* (New Haven and London: Yale University Press), 247–70, 256.

Neale, Stephen (1990). *Descriptions* (Cambridge, Mass.: MIT Press).

Russell, Bertrand (1905). 'On Denoting', *Mind*, 14: 479–93.

——(1912). *The Problems of Philosophy* (Oxford: Oxford University Press; reprinted 1967).

——(1918). 'The Philosophy of Logical Atomism', in *The Collected Papers of Bertrand Russell*, viii. *The Philosophy of Logical Atomism and Other Essays: 1914–1919*, ed. John G. Slater (London: Allen & Unwin, 1984).

——(1919). *Introduction to Mathematical Philosophy* (1st edn. 1919; reprinted London: Routledge, 1993).

——(1984). *Theory of Knowledge: The Collected Papers of Bertrand Russell*, vii (London: Allen & Unwin).

Smullyan, Arthur (1948). 'Modality and Description', *Journal of Symbolic Logic*, 13: 31–7.

Stainton, Robert (1998). 'Quantifier Phrases, Meaningfulness "In Isolation", and Ellipsis', *Linguistics and Philosophy*, 21: 311–40.

Whitehead, A. N., and Russell, B. (1910–13). *Principia Mathematica* (Cambridge: Cambridge University Press, 2nd edn. 1925–7).

14

'Obviously Propositions are Nothing': Russell and the Logical Form of Belief Reports

Lenny Clapp and Robert J. Stainton

Introduction

In *Philosophy of Logical Atomism* and elsewhere, Russell maintains that propositions are 'obviously nothing'. Why he says this isn't entirely clear. We suspect, however, that he reasoned as follows. If propositions 'are', then they must be facts; but if propositions are facts, they cannot be false (or true, for that matter). Hence, Russell concludes, propositions are not facts—and hence 'are not'. Given this, they cannot be relata in a belief relation. Therefore, Russell concludes, belief reports cannot state a relation between an agent and a proposition. In this chapter we explore Russell's rejection of propositions as objects of belief, and the other propositional attitudes. While keeping an eye on exegesis, our central concern is substantive: do Russell's arguments threaten the contemporary consensus about the logical form of belief reports—i.e. that they *do* state a relation between an agent and something proposition-like (e.g. a natural language sentence, a Fregean Thought, etc.)?[1] In what follows we

[1] The authors of this chapter disagree as to how this question is to be answered. We agree that Russell's arguments do indeed rule out some accounts of propositions as objects of belief, while failing to rule out others. We disagree, however, as to whether or not Russell's arguments provide particular support for the identification of the objects of belief with Higginbotham-style Interpreted Logical Forms. Prof. Stainton maintains that Russell's arguments, broadly construed, provide particular support for an ILF analysis of attitude ascriptions. Prof. Clapp, in

explicate Russell's argument against propositions as objects of belief, and then explain how these arguments might be utilized to support the identification of objects of belief with Higginbotham-style ILFs. We conclude with a series of objections and replies.

What the Objects of Belief Cannot Be

The puzzling passage from Russell, which serves as the title of this chapter, occurs at a point in *Philosophy of Logical Atomism* at which Russell is considering what it is that believers believe. He rightly discounts the idea that belief is paradigmatically a relation between an agent and a *particular*. As he says,

In the *first* place there are a great many judgments you cannot possibly fit into that scheme, and in the *second* place it cannot possibly give any explanation to false beliefs, because when you believe that a thing exists and it does not exist, the thing is not there, it is nothing, and it cannot be the right analysis of a false belief to regard it as a relation to what is really nothing. (1918: 84)

This paragraph could use some unpacking. There are two worries. First, that beliefs like (1) are a special case.

(1) Cindy believes in God

Being a special case, a model of belief built around (1) will fail to apply to beliefs generally. (For instance, it is unclear what particular Cindy must be related to, to make the following true: 'Cindy believes that Ottawa is cold'.) Maybe worse—this is the second worry—this approach cannot account for false beliefs. This is not to say that beliefs being relations to particulars would exclude false *belief reports*. For instance, (1) could be a false report of Cindy's belief state because, though God exists, Cindy is actually an atheist. But, Russell insists, if believers are related to particulars, there could not be any true reports of false *beliefs*—essentially because, if there is a belief at all, then there is a thing-believed; but if the thing-believed exists, then (on this model) the belief is true. Thus, returning to the example above, God is the thing-believed; and if that thing does exist, then of course Cindy's belief is correct, because God (i.e. the thing-believed) exists.

Russell equally rejects the suggestion that the things-believed are *facts*. He writes: 'You cannot say that you believe *facts*, because your beliefs are some-

contrast, maintains that Russell's arguments, broadly construed, do not provide particular support for an ILF analysis of attitude ascriptions.

times wrong . . . Whenever it is facts alone that are involved, error is impossible. Therefore you cannot say you believe facts'. Here again, the problem is that there are true belief-reports which report false beliefs. (Another problem is that the things-believed ought to be truth evaluable. And Russell explicitly denies, on p. 43 and elsewhere, that *facts* are either true or false.) Obviously what *S* believes, when *S* believes falsely, must exist—otherwise *S* could not be related to it by the believes-relation. But then what *S* believes, when she believes falsely, cannot be a fact: if *S* believes that *F* obtains, and there *is* a fact *F,* then *S* believes truly, not falsely. Because if the fact that *F* obtains (i.e. exists), then *F* is true.

For example, (2) cannot mean that the believes-relation obtains between Agnes and 'the fact' that Toronto is the capital of Canada.

(2) Agnes believes that Toronto is the capital of Canada

For there is no such fact as the fact that Toronto is the capital of Canada.[2] Indeed, if this is what the sentence *really meant* then, because (2) is meaningful, the fact that Toronto is the capital of Canada would necessarily exist. That is, it would really be the case that Toronto is the capital of Canada. Which would immediately render Agnes's belief true.

In sum, belief cannot be a relation either to individuals or to facts.

What Motivated Russell to Reject Propositions?

At this point, those working in contemporary philosophy of language and mind expect Russell to announce that what we believe are *propositions*. And indeed, after concluding that 'you cannot say you believe facts' (1918: 87), he suggests that 'you have to say that you believe propositions' (1918: 87). Immediately following this sentence, however, he issues his puzzling claim: 'The awkwardness of [saying that you believe propositions] is that obviously propositions are nothing. Therefore that cannot be the true account of the matter.'[3] Why does Russell say this? The reason he himself gives is this:

---

[2] As Russell himself notes, it might be possible to treat 'know' (and also 'perceive') as relating agents to facts. That is because, though there are false reports of knowledge, there is not any 'false knowledge'. In contrast, there are both false beliefs and false reports of belief.

[3] Shortly after this, Russell cavalierly says: 'There is a great deal that is odd about belief from a logical point of view. One of the things that are odd is that *you can believe propositions* of all sorts of forms' (1918: 91; our emphasis). We take it that he is not here retracting his view that the things-believed are *not* propositions. Instead, we gather he has simply slipped into non-strict

it does not seem to me very plausible to say that in addition to facts there are also these curious shadowy things going about such as 'That today is Wednesday' when in fact it is Tuesday. I cannot believe they go about the real world. It is more than one can manage to believe, and I do think no person with a vivid sense of reality can imagine it. (1918: 87)

And further along, having noted Meinong's supposed lack of just such a 'vivid sense of reality', he adds:

To suppose that in the actual world of nature there is a whole set of false propositions going about is to my mind monstrous. I cannot bring myself to suppose it. I cannot believe that they are there in the sense in which facts are there. There seems to me something about the fact that 'Today is Tuesday' on a different level of reality from the supposition 'That today is Wednesday'. (1918: 88)

One might read these remarks as rejecting propositions on the grounds that they are *abstract* objects, and positing any sort of abstract object violates a 'vivid sense of reality'. But if this is Russell's reasoning, then why does he single out *false* propositions as specifically troublesome? For true propositions, if they existed, would be precisely as *abstract* as false propositions. So it seems implausible that Russell is rejecting propositions merely on the grounds that, if they are, they are abstract objects.

A more plausible interpretation of Russell's reasons for rejecting propositions as objects of belief is suggested by Russell's equation of 'reality' with 'everything you would have to mention in a complete description of the world' (1918: 88). For the Russell of 1918 maintained the view, similar to the view presented in Wittgenstein's *Tractatus Logico-Philosophicus*, that words name objects, and sentences represent the facts that have as constituents the individual objects named by the words in them. Hence if reality is exhausted by what would be mentioned in a 'complete description', then reality is exhausted by all the facts and all the objects making up the facts. This suggests the following general argument against propositions as objects of belief:

P1: If propositions *are*, then they are part of reality.
P2: Reality is the totality of facts, and the constituents of facts, viz. individual objects.[4]

usage—as he is wont to do, especially in popular works like *Philosophy of Logical Atomism*. For an illuminating complementary discussion of Russell's rejection of propositions, see sections 3 and 4 of Linsky (1993).

[4] Premise P2 is, of course, pretty much directly lifted from the *Tractatus*, which begins: '1 The world is everything that is the case. 1.1 The world is the totality of facts, not of things. 1.11 The world is determined by the facts, and by these being *all* the facts. 1.12 For the totality of facts determines both what is the case, and also what is not the case' (Wittgenstein, 1922: 31).

Therefore,

> C1: If propositions as objects of belief exist, then they are either facts, or they are individual objects.

But Russell has already persuasively argued that

> P4: The objects of belief cannot be individual objects.

And he has already persuasively argued that

> P5: The objects of belief cannot be facts.

Thus he concludes:

> C2: Propositions as objects of belief are not part of reality; they do not exist.

If this argument is sound, then there are no objects of belief, and consequently belief ascriptions cannot be *relational*; they cannot assert that an agent holds the believes relation to some one entity. Russell therefore offers a rather different account of belief ascriptions. Russell writes, 'you are not to regard belief as a two-term relation between yourself and a proposition, and you have to analyze up the proposition and treat your belief differently. Therefore the belief does not really contain a proposition as a constituent but only contains the constituents of the proposition as constituents' (1918: 89).

That is, returning to example (2), what Agnes must be related to, for this report to be true, is not the unitary proposition *that-Toronto-is-the-capital-of-Canada*. Instead, roughly speaking, what Agnes must be related to for (2) to be true is Toronto, the capital-of relation, and Canada severally. Each of these is itself a constituent in the fact that makes (2) true, if (2) is true. But there is no proposition, no complex object, *that-Toronto-is-the-capital-of-Canada*, that is built out of these same parts.

The Significance of Russell's Rejection of Propositions

One might grant that the above argument accurately characterizes Russell's reasons for rejecting propositions as objects of belief, and yet deny that the argument provides any reason to doubt the standard relational analysis of belief ascriptions. For the metaphysical assumptions upon which the argument rests, P2 in particular, are hardly trivial. Indeed, we suspect that most contemporary analytic philosophers will reject P2 for independent reasons. But

Russell's argument does serve to raise significant questions for anyone who wants to posit propositions as objects of belief, yet *also*, following Russell (1905), accepts the 'neo-Russellian' view that *referents*, rather than 'senses' or some such shadowy entities, must be the constituents of propositions. Suppose propositions contain not objects-under-guises, but rather, following the Russell of (1905), objects themselves. Suppose further that these objects must be combined together into some sort of unity, in order for there to be a single proposition at all. Now, given Russell's long-standing and well-warranted concern with Bradley's problem—i.e. of how relata are related, without an infinite regress of relata whose job it is to relate—a philosopher inspired by Russell might suppose that these objects can only be joined by putting together saturated and unsaturated 'things' (i.e. individuals and propositional functions: the word 'things' is in scare quotes because, as Russell would insist, what predicates stand for are essentially unsaturated, and hence not 'things' in one sense of that word: that is, they are not individuals). But then propositions will be indistinguishable from facts. For propositions, like the facts which make them true, will consist exclusively of the constituents of the fact, 'glued together' in the only way available. Given this supposition, the idea that there is a difference between the thing made-true (i.e. the proposition) and the truth-maker (i.e. the fact) is not the least bit plausible.[5]

An example may help. Imagine, in a broadly Russellian spirit, that the proposition that Chomsky is clever contains two things: the man Chomsky, and the (unsaturated) propositional function IS-CLEVER. There cannot be a third thing required to join these two—if there were, then there would need to be a fourth thing which joined all three, and so on. Thus the manner of combination of the man and IS-CLEVER must be function–argument application. But now the *proposition* that Chomsky is clever has precisely the parts and the manner of combination of the *fact* that Chomsky is clever. But if the proposition that Chomsky is clever *just is* the fact that Chomsky is clever, then there could not be false beliefs. For in order for there to be a belief, there must be a proposition believed. But if propositions are facts, then in order for there to be a belief, there must be a fact believed; i.e. the belief must be true. The upshot is that Russell's argument that facts cannot be the objects of belief

[5] It seems that Russell never accepts propositions (where by this term we do *not* mean sentences) and facts simultaneously into his ontology. In Russell (1905) there are propositions, but not facts. In Russell (1918) there are facts, but not propositions. The reason for this might be that Russell accepted something like the argument sketched here. Thus the Russell of 1918 might have accepted the claim that true propositions just are facts, while false propositions are impossible. For an interesting discussion of these issues see Linsky (1993).

does not depend upon his dubious metaphysical assumption that reality is exhausted by facts and the constituents of facts. Moreover, 'neo-Russellian' propositions, which abjure guises of referents in favor of the referents themselves, seem to be indistinguishable from facts. Consequently, the neo-Russellian account of propositions is in danger of falling prey to Russell's argument that the objects of belief cannot be facts.

Propositions that are Not Facts

The central problem posed by neo-Russell propositions is that they seem to be indistinguishable from facts. That is in part because both facts and neo-Russellian propositions are built up out of objects themselves, rather than being composed (à la Frege) of objects-under-guises. But there may be a way to rescue propositions, without giving up the idea that they are made up of the very same things that make up facts. The solution is to give propositions a different manner of composition than facts. Whereas facts are built via function–argument application, propositions need to be built some other way. Which way? This is where Interpreted Logical Forms (ILF) come in.[6]

An ILF is a syntactic tree, whose lexical parts are formed into larger wholes via concatenation.[7] Thus, to take an example, the expression [$_{DP}$ the man] is concatenated with [$_{I'}$ may leave] to form the sentence [$_{IP}$ The man may leave]. But, crucially, an ILF is not just a syntactic tree. What is importantly different about ILFs is that their terminal nodes (typically) dominate not just words but

---

[6] Jeffrey King, in a series of instructive publications, independently suggested something very much along these lines. Specifically, and simplifying greatly, King asks us to consider the relation, whatever it is, that obtains between parts of LFs. He then argues that non-linguistics objects, e.g. Chomsky and cleverness, can stand in this relation as well. In which case, 'the structures of propositions are the same as the structures of the syntactic inputs to semantics they are expressed by' (King, 1996: 495). It is then because propositional elements are related by this 'sentential relation' that they are distinguished from the facts which make them true. King's terminology is different from ours. He counts propositions among 'the facts', apparently using 'fact' in the early Wittgenstein's sense of 'complex entity'; and there are differences of detail as well—e.g. there are no linguistic items in King's propositions, and the motivation for the view (i.e. naturalism) is quite different. Nevertheless, on the whole we believe he is proposing a view very like the one presented here. See King (1994, 1995, 1996) for the details.

[7] In recent work this process—i.e. the combination of pairs of syntactic constituents to form a phrase structure tree—has been called 'merger'. See Chomsky, 1995: ch. 4, for discussion. In what follows we will assume a more old-fashioned, and simplified, view of the nature and formation of trees.

also non-linguistic entities, namely the entities denoted by the corresponding lexical elements. Thus, to give a simplified example, the ILF of 'Chomsky is clever' might be as shown in the diagram.

```
                        IP
                      /    \
                  DP          I'
                  |          /  \
              Chomsky       I    VP
                 ‖          |    /  \
             CHOMSKY       agr  V    AP
                               |    |
                               be  clever
                                     ‖
                                   CLEVER
```

The details of the tree do not matter for present purposes. The key point is that the man Chomsky (symbolized by the all-capital word) and the (strictly speaking not-nameable) property CLEVER appear on the tree. Suppose now that we take ILFs to do the work of propositions. They will contain the objects and properties themselves, but they will not be facts—because these objects and properties are not combined together in the way they are within facts. Rather, they are held together by (*a*) being denoted by 'Chomsky' and 'clever' respectively (a semantic mechanism); which in turn are (*b*) joined together (along with an agreement marker and an auxiliary verb, whose status we pass over in silence) by concatenation (a syntactic mechanism). In contrast, the fact which must exist for this ILF to be true will contain the man Chomsky, along with the property CLEVER—but these will be combined by function–argument application. Hence the proposition and the corresponding fact are different. [8]

What is interesting about all this, Russell interpretation aside, is that we seem to have here a metaphysical argument in favor of something like ILFs. The argument goes like this. Assuming we want to be Russellians about propositional constituents—which, given Kripke, Kaplan, and all the rest,

---

[8] There is a usage of the word 'fact' on which ILFs will be counted as facts. On this usage, familiar from Wittgenstein's *Tractatus*, a fact is any complex whatever. This is not the sense of 'fact' we are employing. Facts, as we use the term, are just one variety of complex: the variety which serves as the truth-maker for true propositions. Atomic facts are built from an (unsaturated) property and an object. General facts are built from a higher order property—i.e. a generalized quantifier—and a lower order property. And so on.

we do—we, like Russell, need a way to distinguish propositions (which are capable of being false) from the truth-makers for propositions, which we have been calling facts (and which are not capable of being false or true). Being good Russellians about propositional constituents, we must say that both facts and propositions contain plain old objects and plain old properties. No guises, senses, or what-have-you. Which means that propositions must be distinguished from facts in some other way. What ILFs provide is one way—maybe not the only way, but one way—to explain this difference. Propositions, the ILF theorist says, have extra pieces which facts lack (i.e. words, agreement markers, non-terminal nodes, etc.); and, furthermore, the pieces that propositions share with facts are, in the former, joined together in a wholly different fashion—essentially via concatenation-plus-denotation. Therefore, propositions are different from facts.

Objections and Replies[9]

First objection

Russell considers and rejects the suggestion that the objects of belief are propositions because he cannot accept the existence of 'shadowy things'. The shadow metaphor is apt. Propositions are, like shadows, not quite real; as Russell would put it, they are not facts. And propositions mimic meaningful sentences in something like the way shadows are cast by opaque objects: where you have the one, you are guaranteed, somehow, to have the other. Russell's primary objection against propositions as objects of belief in *The Philosophy of Logical Atomism* is based upon what he claims he should call 'an instinct of reality' (1918: 88). Thus Russell rejects propositions on the grounds that it is implausible to suppose that such shadowy intermediary entities really exist. So even granting that the ILF theorist is able to distinguish (true) ILFs from facts in something like the way described above, distinguishing (true) ILFs from facts in this way provides no response whatsoever to Russell's complaint against such intermediary shadowy entities. Indeed, it is precisely *because* ILFs are not facts, and not sentences, that they violate Russell's 'instinct for reality'. Moreover, ILFs are no less shadowy than are, say, Fregean thoughts. Frege maintained that corresponding to every meaningful sentence there is a thought

---

[9] This is the one section of the chapter about which the two authors do not agree. Clapp, who first noted the objections, finds the replies ultimately unsatisfying. Stainton, in contrast, is happy with the replies, though he agrees that the objections are important and interesting.

(*Gedanke*) that is composed of the senses (*Sinn*) that are expressed by the words in the sentence, and he maintained that these thoughts serve as the objects of propositional attitudes. Similarly, ILF theorists maintain that corresponding to every utterance of a meaningful sentence there is a unique ILF, composed of the phrase structure for the sentence, referents of all sorts (people, numbers, countries, political parties, dreams, pains, etc.), word types, utterance event tokens, phonological representations, all somehow 'concatenated' together, and these entities serve as the objects of propositional attitudes (see e.g. Larson and Ludlow, 1993). If one is suspicious of Frege's thoughts, then one ought also be suspicious of ILFs. (Note that just putting referents in ILFs does not make them less shadowy. If it did, a Fregean theorist could just 'concatenate'— whatever that is—referents into his *thoughts* too.) Consequently, even if the ILFs corresponding to true utterances can be distinguished from facts, ILFs are no more plausible than previously proposed shadowy intermediary entities.

Reply

The first objection stands, but only in a limited sense. If one is committed to a dogmatic denial of any sort of 'intermediary' entities to serve as the objects of belief, then one must reject ILFs—along with Frege's thoughts, Meinong's round squares, and other accounts of propositions. But there is no reason to be committed to such a dogmatic view. Frege's thoughts are ontologically suspicious not because they are 'intermediary', but rather because they are composed of suspicious entities. It is simply not clear what senses, guises, and modes of presentation, etc. are. But, the constituents of ILFs are not suspicious in this way. We have solid and independent reason, from syntax, phonology, and other sciences, for positing phrase structure markers, phonetic representations, and the other constituents of ILFs. Therefore ILFs are not as ontologically suspect as Frege's thoughts, and previous accounts of propositions.

Second objection

That the ILFs corresponding to true utterances can be distinguished from facts does not provides *special* support for the ILF account of propositions. If one wants to distinguish propositions from facts, then there are *many* ways of doing so. There are even *many* ways of doing so which preserve the Russellian idea that referents, not guises thereof, are constituents of propositions. Suppose that, instead of the referents, times, abstract linguistic entities, event tokens, etc., that ILF theorists build into ILFs, one formulates a structurally isomorphic account that replaces the abstract linguistic entities with Gödel numbers thereof. Would we have any reason to prefer one account to the other? A little reflection suggests that almost any *appropriately individuated* sort of entity, composed of constituents whose existence we are independently committed to, could serve as propositions as objects of beliefs as well as do ILFs. If *one* sort of abstract entity composed of non-suspicious entities 'concatenated' in some way will serve as propositions as objects of beliefs, then *many* sorts of such entities will. Moreover, this 'problem of multiple reduction for propositions' underscores Russell's suspicion of such shadowy intermediary entities: if propositions could be many sorts of thing, how can they be just one sort of thing?

Replies to the second objection

First, the second objection wrongly assumes that '*many* sorts of . . . entities' could serve as propositions as the objects of belief. But this is false. There are several constraints that are met by ILFs, but would not be met by other, even structurally isomorphic entities. For example, entities that serve as propositions must have some sort of logical form, and ILFs have this appropriate form. It is far from clear that set-theoretic constructions of Gödel numbers, for example, would exhibit the appropriate logical form. And second, it is not clear that the ILF theorist is committed to the claim that only one sort of entity can play the role of propositions. This is so in two senses. On the one hand, it seems open to the ILF theorist to claim that anything structurally isomorphic to an ILF just *is* an ILF.[10] That is, it may be that *being an ILF* is a functional property, so that anything capable of playing the appropriate functional role is an ILF. On the other hand, it is no mark against the ILF account of propositions that there may be *some* other proposals that are also compatible with the relevant evidence. In the end, our only claim is that the ILF account has a certain advantage, an advantage that might well be shared by, say, six or seven other views. As long as this 'advantage' is not shared by six or seven *million* other views, we are satisfied.[11]

---

[10] So e.g. David Lewis's meanings in 'General Semantics' might count as ILFs. There, Lewis identifies meanings with phrase structure markers—with, however, *intensions* included at the terminal nodes. See Lewis (1970), and also n. 6.

[11] We are grateful to Jeffrey King, Ernie Lepore, Bernie Linsky, and Mathieu Marion for discussion, and to the audience at the 1998 Central States Philosophy Conference. Thanks also to the Social Sciences and Humanities Research Council of Canada, for a supporting grant. This paper is fondly dedicated to Sylvain Bromberger, teacher and friend to both authors.

REFERENCES

Chomsky, Noam (1995). *The Minimalist Program* (Cambridge, Mass.: MIT Press).

King, Jeffrey (1994). 'Can Propositions be Naturalistically Acceptable?', *Midwest Studies in Philosophy*, 19: 53–75.

—— (1995). 'Structured Propositions and Complex Predicates', *Noûs*, 29: 516–35.

—— (1996). 'Structured Propositions and Sentence Structure', *Journal of Philosophical Logic*, 25: 495–521.

Larson, Richard, and Ludlow, Peter (1993). 'Interpreted Logical Forms', *Synthese*, 95: 305–55.

Lewis, David (1970). 'General Semantics', *Synthese*, 22: 18–67.

Linsky, Bernard (1993). 'Why Russell Abandoned Russellian Propositions', in A. D. Irvine and G. A. Wedeking (eds.), *Russell and Analytic Philosophy* (Toronto: University of Toronto Press).

Russell, Bertrand (1905). 'On Denoting', *Mind*, 14: 479–93.

—— (1918). *The Philosophy of Logical Atomism*, ed. David Pears (LaSalle, Ill.: Open Court, 1985).

Wittgenstein, Ludwig (1922). *Tractatus Logico-Philosophicus*, tr. C. K. Ogden (London: Routledge & Kegan Paul).

15

Logical Form and the Relational Conception of Belief

ROBERT J. MATTHEWS

I Introduction

Many, if not most, philosophers embrace a relational conception of the attitudes. On that conception, propositional attitude ascriptions of the form *x believes (desires, etc.) that S* assert that the referent of *x* stands in a particular relation, namely, the relation of belief (desire, etc.), to an entity that is the referent of the *that*-clause *that S*, and that entity is the object of the attitude, i.e., what the possessor believes (desires, etc.). There is considerable disagreement as to the nature of the semantically evaluable particulars that are the objects of the attitudes, for example, whether they are complex Fregean senses, Russellian propositions, sentences of a natural language, mental representations, or perhaps things considerably more exotic. But the relational conception itself is rarely in dispute or even defended. Such defenses as one does occasionally find rarely focus, as presumably they should, on the metaphysics of propositional attitudes or the psychology of their possessors; instead they focus almost exclusively on the logical form of propositional attitude ascriptions, apparently on the assumption that the relational conception finds support there. Relationists, as they might be called, presume that the relational nature of propositional attitudes can simply be read off the logical form of their ascriptions.

In this chapter, I want to challenge this presumption. My discussion will focus on belief (and belief ascription); however, I assume that my conclusions can be readily generalized to other propositional attitudes.

2 The Logical Form of Propositional Attitude Ascriptions

Logical forms, as they have traditionally been conceived, are formal para-phrases of natural language expressions that are intended, in the first instance, to exhibit in a perspicuous manner the salient logical properties of such expressions. Proposed logical forms are typically rendered in a logically pure formal language, such as the first-order predicate calculus, that contains only variables and logical constants. The construction of a logical form is taken to be a two-step process, in which first a logically perspicuous paraphrase of the sentence is constructed using the resources of this logically pure formal language, supplemented by individual constants and n-place predicates, and then these constants and predicates are replaced by variables of the appropriate logical type.

So conceived, natural language expressions will not have a unique logical form, since different formal paraphrases will be possible, depending on both the choice of formal language for the paraphrase and the explanatory interests that motivate the construction of the paraphrase.[1] This, of course, will be troublesome for anyone tempted, as relationalists are, to attribute deep meta-physical significance to the logical form of propositional attitude ascriptions, since any conclusions based on logical form may turn out to be an artifact of the chosen formal paraphrase, unless of course the formal properties receiving metaphysical interpretation are sufficiently brute as to be shared by all plaus-ible paraphrases. But this, in fact, is precisely what relationalists believe. There are, they believe, no plausible alternatives. As Fodor (1981: 179) puts it, 'the only known alternative to the view that verbs of propositional attitude express relations is that they are (semantically) "fused" with their objects, and that view would seem to be hopeless'.

Fusion theories propose to treat the verb of a propositional attitude ascrip-tion as semantically fused with its sentential complement in much the way that the constituents of the predicates in idiomatic assertions such as *John kicked the bucket* and *John bought the farm* are semantically fused, so that the logical form

---

[1] Some philosophers, notably Quine (1971: 452), have embraced this multiplicity of logical form, insisting that there is no such thing as *the* logical form of an expression. Rather the logical form is simply that non-unique formal paraphrase that 'admits most efficiently of logical calculation, or shows its implications and conceptual affinities most perspicuously'. Davidson (1973: 71) follows Quine in this, insisting that 'logical form . . . will of course be relative to the choice of a metalanguage (with its logic) and a theory of truth'.

of such ascriptions would be *Fx* rather than *Fxy*. As Quine (1960: 216) presents the view, 'the verb "believe" here ceases to be a term and becomes part of an operator "believes that", or "believes [   ]", which, applied to a sentence, produces a composite absolute general term whereof the sentence is counted an immediate constituent'. It is, fusion theorists claim, an orthographic accident that propositional attitude ascriptions seem to have a relational logical form, since what they ascribe to their possessors, it is claimed, are monadic, not relational, properties.

As a way of defending the view that propositional attitudes are non-relational, i.e. monadic, properties of their possessors, fusion theories are indeed hopeless. Quine concedes that to adopt a fusion view we must, as he puts it (1960: 215), find it in us to be 'indifferent' to the truth values of sentences such as *Paul believes something that Elmer does not*, something that strikes him as a small price to pay in order to be rid of intensional objects. But there are other costs as well. Fusion theories commit us to the view that propositional attitude predicates are syntactically complex but semantically simple expressions, which leaves us with the obvious question, 'How, then, do we manage to understand propositional attitudes that we have never before heard?' Our use of these predicates is clearly productive, and yet the fusion theory has no story about how this could be possible. Also problematic is the fact that propositional attitude predicates do not behave like a fused idiom in which all of the constituents are syncategorematic. First, there are seemingly valid inferences such as (1) that apparently quantify over the so-called object of the attitude:

(1) Jones believes that the monkey bit the lab technician.
    Hence, there is something that Jones believes.

Second, there are seemingly valid inferences such as (2) that apparently involve existential generalization of certain constituents of propositional attitude predicates.

(2) Jones believes that the monkey bit the lab technician.
    Hence, Jones believes that something bit someone.

Third, constituents of propositional attitude predicates can stand in anaphoric relations, as in (3):

(3) Jones believes that the monkey bit the lab technician, and it did in fact do so.

Now maybe these difficulties can be finessed with a bit of ingenuity, but even if they can, there will still be all the problems having to do with opacity. The

424   BELIEF ASCRIPTION AND PROPER NAMES

fusion theorist is going to have to explain why certain constituents of these fused predicates are intersubstitutable in some contexts but not in others. It is not at all clear how this explanation might go. Fourth, the fusion view effectively abandons the idea that, for example, belief predicates pick out a class of properties distinct from those picked out by other propositional attitude predicates. Finally, the fusion view leaves it quite mysterious why natural language should have evolved such a bizarre way of designating these supposedly monadic properties. Even in the case of idioms, there is generally an explanation of some sort of how the idiom came to mean what it does.

It should be noted that for all their differences, fusionists share with relationalists one crucial assumption, namely, that the nature of propositional attitudes is revealed in the logical form of propositional attitude ascriptions. Committed as they are to a non-relational account of propositional attitudes according to which propositional attitudes are causally efficacious monadic properties of their possessors, they feel compelled to argue that the logical form of the ascriptions is likewise monadic. One of the burdens of this chapter is to challenge this assumption, since on any plausible construal of the notion of logical form, the logical form of propositional attitude ascriptions *is* relational, and yet, I want to argue, propositional attitudes are *not* relations.

Propositional attitude verbs are, on virtually all proposed accounts, relational predicates that express a relation between (i) the possessor of the attitude, (ii) the referent of the *that*-clause, and perhaps, as some proposals would have it, (iii) some third thing, for example, a mode of presentation. There are a number of different recent proposals as to the relational logical form of such ascriptions; they differ principally in (*a*) polyadicity of the predicate (namely, whether it is 2- or 3-place), and (*b*) the referent of the *that*-clause (namely, whether it is a sentence, a proposition, a mental representation, etc.).

The theoretically more principled of these recent proposals follow Davidson (1968) in construing logical form truth-theoretically: the logical form of a sentence of a language L is revealed by the T-sentence that an interpretive truth-theory associates with that sentence, along with its derivation from the axioms of the theory.[2] The logical form of the sentence is revealed in the strict sense that the T-sentence, along with its derivation, provides a perspicuous

---

[2] The T-sentence without its accompanying derivation may be insufficient to reveal the logical form of an object language sentence, since the synonymous metalanguage sentence that appears on the right-hand side of the T-sentence, and which states the truth-conditions of the sentence in question, may fail to exhibit in perspicuous fashion certain of the sentence's logical and semantic properties which are apparent in the derivation of the T-sentence.

representation of both the salient semantic properties of the sentence, and, assuming that the logic of the metalanguage is given, the logical properties of the sentence. From this representation one can, for example, determine compositional contributions of the constituents, the polyadicity of any predicates, the referents of any terms, the character of any quantifier phrases, and the logical relations that the sentence bears to other sentences of L.

Until recently, most of the proposed logical forms for propositional attitude ascriptions have not in fact taken the truth-theoretic form just described. At best these proposals have offered as the logical form of such ascriptions something that might be construed as the logico-formal paraphrase of the right-hand side of the T-sentence provided by some as yet unspecified truth-theoretic semantics. These proposed logical forms are intended to capture the salient logical, specifically inferential, properties of propositional attitude ascriptions, notably those that relate to failures of substitution and failures of existential generalization, though without providing a fully worked out semantics of these ascriptions. Thus, for example, hidden indexical theories of the sort examined by Schiffer (1992) attribute to canonical ascriptions of the form *A believes that S* the logical form given by (4), according to which such ascriptions assert the existence of a 3-place relation that relates a believer (x), a Russsellian proposition (y), and a mode of presentation (m):

(4) $(\exists m)(\Phi m \ \& \ B^3(x,y,m))$

Possession of this logical form is said to explain both the apparent validity of inferences such as (1) and (2) as well as certain failures of substitution of co-referring expressions in the *that*-clause.

Richard (1990: 140 ff.) attributes to these same ascriptions the logical form given by (5):

(5) $(\exists \rho)(P\rho \ \& \ B^3(x,\Re,\rho))$

where x is a believer, $\Re$ the Russellian annotated matrix (RAM) determined in a context c by the sentential complement *that S*,[3] and ρ the context-sensitive representation function that, in c, maps $\Re$ onto a mental representation included in x's set of belief representations. Richard's proposed logical form is based on a neo-Russellian account that attributes to ascriptions of the form 'x believes that S' the truth-conditions given by (6):

---

[3] A Russellian annotated matrix (RAM) is an ordered pair consisting of a sentence and the Russellian proposition expressed by an utterance of that sentence in a context.

(6) *x believes that S* is true in *c* iff under the representation function ϱ, $\Re$ represents a mental representation included in *x*'s set of belief representations.

This proposed logical form is intended to capture the context-sensitivity of both the truth conditions and also the inferential properties of such ascriptions.

The hidden indexical theories discussed by Schiffer (1992) and the neo-Russellian account proposed by Richard (1990) adopt basically the same strategy for explaining failures of substitution: treat the propositional attitude verb, for example, *believes*, as a 3-place, rather than 2-place, predicate, using the additional argument place to differentiate non-intersubstitutable predicates that would otherwise be indistinguishable. In effect, failures of substitution are avoided by individuating propositional attitude predicates more finely. Richard's proposal has the added advantage of being able to accommodate the apparent context-sensitivity of individuation conditions by having this additional argument place have as its range a class of *explicitly* context-sensitive representation functions *P*. But both of these proposed logical forms suffer from an important defect: it is hard to envision a plausible formal semantic theory that would underwrite the claim that the verb *believes* is a 3-place predicate with an added argument place of either of the proposed sorts. There is no overt syntactic evidence for the claim. Any semantic theory consonant with the claim will, therefore, presumably have to treat the added argument as a unarticulated constituent, thus abandoning the semantics-theoretical desideratum of strong compositionality.[4]

Unlike the two proposals just discussed, there have recently appeared a number of proposals for the logical form of propositional attitude ascriptions based on an explicitly formulated truth-theoretic semantics. On these truth-theoretic proposals, the logical form of a propositional attitude ascription, as explained above, is taken to be revealed by the T-sentence for the ascription, specifically by the right-hand side of the T-sentence, along with its accompanying derivation from the theory's axioms. There are important differences between these various proposals, notably as regards (i) the nature of the semantically evaluable 'object' that is presumably the referent of the *that*-clause, and (ii) the phrasal axiom that composes the complementizer *that* and the complement sentence. But there is general agreement that propositional attitude ascriptions express a binary relation between the possessor of the attitude and the referent of the *that*-clause.

---

[4] See Segal and Larson (1995).

Segal and Larson (1995) are representative of these recent truth-theoretic proposals. Following Larson and Ludlow (1993), they propose T-sentences of the form given by (7) for belief ascriptions of the form *x believes that S*:

(7) Val (t, [$_S$*x believes that S*],σ) iff x believes* ⟦S⟧

where (7) is to be read, 'the sentence *x believes that S* receives the semantic valuation "true" relative to some sequence of assignments σ iff *x* believes* the interpreted logical form (ILF) of *S*, where *believes** is an unexplicated technical term of the metalanguage' here. ILFs, as Segal and Larson explain (1995: 438), are syntactic phrase-markers whose terminal and nonterminal nodes are annotated with semantic values. Thus, the basic idea of their proposal is that propositional attitude verbs such as *believes* express relations between individuals and these complex structured entities.

The details of, and the rationale for, Segal and Larson's ILF theory are not important here. Suffice it to say that the postulation of ILFs as one of the relata in the relation expressed by the propositional attitude verb is intended to provide a formal object that is sufficiently complex, in the appropriate ways, as to predict and explain a wide range of examples of failures of substitution into, and inferential properties of, propositional attitude ascriptions. The relevant point for our present purposes, is simply that on Segal and Larson's proposed semantics, propositional attitude verbs are 2-place predicates, taking as arguments a noun phrase that refers to the possessor of the attitude and a sentential complement clause that refers to an ILF. On their account, the logical form of belief ascriptions of the form *x believes that S*, as traditionally conceived, would be given by (8):

(8) B*xy

where *B** is the relation specified by the metalanguage verb *believes**, *x* is the believer, and *y* the ILF expressed by the ascription's *that*-clause. The focal question here is this: what follows from (8), or indeed any other relational proposal regarding the logical form of belief ascriptions, as regards the relational conception of belief?

3 Problems with the Relational Conception

Relationalists, I have said, presume that the relational nature of propositional attitudes can simply be read off the sentences by which we ascribe propositional attitudes. For them, the relational logical form of the attitude ascription reveals the relational form of the attitude. The presumption is not taken to be apodictic, but it is certainly thought to be presumptive. A careful examination of the problems that plague attempts to read the relational logical form of belief ascriptions back onto the world, more specifically onto the metaphysics of belief and the psychology of believers, should disabuse anyone of the notion that the relational conception has any presumptive status. These problems have been carefully catalogued elsewhere (e.g. Richard, 1990; Schiffer, 1987, 1992), so I shall limit myself to a few brief reminders, which are intended to set the stage for a criticism of the relationalist strategy of reading these proposed logical forms back onto the world, thus taking them to entail a substantive claim about the nature of belief itself.

Minimally, an account of belief should meet the following adequacy conditions. It should (i) provide an account of what belief is (i.e. what the having of a belief comes to) that explains or at least respects the individuation conditions on belief, (ii) explain the apparent salient properties of beliefs, namely, their semantic evaluability, their causal role in the production of behavior, their inferential relations to other propositional attitudes, and their productivity and systematicity, and (iii) offer a solution to, or at least explain, the various puzzles about belief that have driven philosophical theorizing (for example, failures of substitution, failures of existential generalization, Kripke puzzles). Finally, the account should do all this consistent with (iv) a plausible metaphysics, (v) a plausible semantics (and perhaps pragmatics) not just for belief ascriptions but for natural language more generally, and (vi) a plausible cognitive psychology for the believer.

These adequacy conditions, it should be noted, leave open the question of what constitutes an appropriate division of explanatory labor between the semantics of belief ascriptions, the metaphysics of belief, and the psychology of believers. This is not something that can be determined a priori. In particular, it cannot be assumed that the metaphysics and psychology can simply be read off the semantics. It might turn out, as indeed I think it does, that the former are not at all transparent in the latter.

Relational accounts of belief tend to fail these adequacy conditions in predictable ways, which depend crucially on what the account in question takes to be the nature of the relatum to which the believer is related by the belief relation. Traditional propositionalist versions of such accounts, which construe the object of belief as a proposition (i.e. as a language-independent, abstract entity that has its truth-conditions essentially), have difficulty capturing the individuation conditions on belief, consistent with the demand that such an account be compatible with an independently plausible semantics.

Fregean accounts, for example, which take propositions to be complex senses, do a reasonably good job of explaining how there could be failures of substitution, even if they cannot explain the context-sensitivity of admissible substitutions; however, they accomplish this only at the price of being committed to an implausible semantics for belief ascriptions that is difficult to accommodate within a general truth-theoretic semantics for natural language. In particular, they have difficulty preserving 'semantic innocence', the desideratum, roughly, that linguistic expressions should make the same semantic contribution to a sentence irrespective of the linguistic context in which they appear. There are, to be sure, ways around this problem (cf. Pietroski, 1996), but they are invariably purchased at the price of some other desideratum, for example, compositionality. Russellian (direct reference) accounts, by contrast, fare much better on the semantics side, providing a semantics for belief ascriptions that can be more easily accommodated within a broader semantic theory; however, they achieve this only at the price of getting right neither the individuation conditions on beliefs nor the truth-conditions on beliefs ascriptions, and hence not offering plausible solutions to the various puzzles about belief.[5]

Propositionalist accounts also have difficulty accounting for the context-sensitivity of the individuation conditions on belief: in certain contexts Fregean accounts individuate beliefs too finely, while in other contexts Russellian accounts individuate them too coarsely. In recent years, many propositionalists have as a result embraced a hidden-indexical theory of the sort mentioned briefly above that ascribes to propositional attitude ascriptions of the form x *believes that S* the logical form given by (4). Offered primarily as an account of belief ascription, and then only derivatively as an account of belief itself (on the assumption that the logical form can be read back into the metaphysics and psychology), hidden-indexical theory proposes to explain the context-sensitivity of belief individuation by building into the Russellian account a context-sensitive Fregean component that will individuate beliefs more or less finely as the context demands. Hidden-indexical theory is so-called because on this theory when a speaker ascribes a belief to an individual, the speaker refers to a mode of presentation type under which the speaker believes the Russellian proposition that he believes, but this reference is hidden, i.e. it is not carried explicitly by any word or expression in the belief ascription; moreover, this reference is indexical in that the particular mode of presentation type referred to is contextually determined: in uttering the same belief sentence in different

---

[5] For discussion, see Richard (1990).

contexts, a speaker may refer to different modes of presentation type. Thus the theory seems able to explain how it is that in certain contexts the ascriptions *Lois Lane believes that Superman can fly* and *Lois Lane does not believe that Clark Kent can fly* can both be true, even though the *that*-clauses of these ascriptions refer to the same Russellian singular proposition.

Schiffer (1992) has pointed out a number of serious, apparently irremediable problems with hidden-indexical theory, which have mostly to do with the semantics that this theory proposes for belief ascriptions. But when taken as a theory of belief, hidden indexical theory shares with other propositionalist accounts an even more serious failing: it is difficult to see how standing in a relation to an abstract entity, even under a mode of presentation, could possibly be causally efficacious, which beliefs surely are. Perhaps not surprisingly, relationalists concerned with the problem of explaining the causal role of belief have been more inclined to embrace a sententialist account, which takes the object of belief to be a sentence-like entity that has its truth-conditions contingently. Such theories seem to offer an account of the causal efficacy of belief, assuming that the sentential relata in question turn out to be sentence tokens and not sentence types (which, of course, are abstract). But here, too, there are problems concerning the causal efficacy of belief. Some sententialists (e.g. Carnap, 1947; Davidson, 1968) propose to construe belief as a relation to a sentence in a public language. Thus, for example, the ascription *Galileo believed that the earth moves* is said to express a relation between Galileo and the English sentence *the earth moves*. But what, one must ask, is the nature of this relation that Galileo bears to a sentence of a language he presumably did not speak, and how can this relation, whatever it is, have been causally efficacious in causing him, for example, to say, 'Eppur si muove'? And even if he did speak English, how would that have helped, unless perhaps he actually tokened *in thought* an instance of the sentence-type *the earth moves*? Failing that, going sententialist would seem to offer no particular advantage over the propositionalist versions of relational theory. For in the event that the believer does not token in thought a token of the sentence type, it seems hard to envision how the mere standing in a relation to such other tokens of this sentence-type as the believer might be related to could possibly provide the basis of a plausible account of the causal efficacy of belief.

There are still other problems with sententialist accounts. For example, beliefs would seem to have their truth-values essentially and independently of language: my belief that it is sunny today would seem to be true, if in fact it is, irrespective of whatever words happen to express that belief, indeed irrespective of whether there are any public languages at all. But on sententialist accounts this is not the case. Sententialist accounts also seem not to get the individuation conditions on belief right; at least it is unclear how sententialist accounts propose to explain the fact both that tokens of different sentence-types can express the same belief and that different tokens of the same sentence-type can, in the appropriate contexts, express different beliefs.

For these and other reasons, many sententialists have come to favor accounts that construe belief as a relation not to a sentence in a public language, but to a sentence in a language of thought, i.e. to a quasi-linguistic mental representation that is the object of belief. Such accounts are attractive because they also offer a seemingly plausible account of the role of belief in the production of behavior: the mental representations that are the objects of belief play a causal role in the etiology of behavior by virtue of their formal-syntactic properties (in just the way that the representational states of computers play a causal role in the outputs of those devices). These accounts also offer a seemingly plausible explanation of the semantic evaluability of beliefs according to which particular beliefs inherit their semantic properties from the mental representations that are their objects.

But here, too, there are characteristic problems. First, there is the problem of accounting for the apparent validity of inferences such as (9):

(9) Galileo believed that the earth moves.
    It is true that the earth moves.
    Hence, Galileo believed something true.

On pain of equivocation, the referents of the *that*-clauses in the two premises must be the same; yet surely what the second premise asserts to be true is not a mental representation, and indeed not in any way dependent even on the existence of mental representations. Second, and perhaps more importantly, there is the difficult problem of making a compelling case for the existence of the postulated language of thought. Minimally, the task here is twofold. First, it needs to be shown that it is possible to provide a semantics for such a language. Second, it needs to be shown either that the language of thought could be innate, or, if not innate, that it could be acquired. Proponents have for a number of years now been laboring on both these tasks, though arguably with limited success. But even if these tasks were to be accomplished, there would remain yet a third problem, namely, that of specifying the relation that pairs the *that*-clause in the belief ascription with the mental sentence that it supposedly specifies and which supposedly expresses the content of the belief. The *that*-clause cannot, as some have assumed, be functioning simply as a singular term that has the mental sentence as its referent, because one would then be unable to capture the context-sensitive individuation conditions on belief.

Richard's (1990) account, scouted briefly above, addresses the third of these problems. This account preserves the relational conception that belief is a relation between the believer and a semantically evaluable entity that is the object of belief, in this case a RAM in the believer's representational system. It also preserves the assumption, common to traditional relational accounts, that the belief ascription's *that*-clause is a singular term. But it abandons the central assumption, also common to such accounts, that the *that*-clause refers to the object of belief. Rather the *that*-clause refers to a *representation* of that object; specifically, it refers to a public-language RAM that represents the believer's language-of-thought RAM. The context-dependency that the hidden-indexical theory builds into the implicit, contextually determined reference to a mode of presentation is now located in the representation relation that relates these two RAMs.

Richard's account successfully skirts a number of the problems that typically afflict relational accounts, but certain problems remain. First, the account seems vulnerable to an objection raised by Schiffer (1992) against hidden-indexical theories, namely, that the account attributes to the person who utters a belief ascription a speaker's intention that surely he did not have. The account claims that in ascribing a belief to an individual by uttering a sentence of the form *x believes that S* a speaker means that this individual stands in a particular relation to a mentalese sentence in that individual's language of thought, specifically to the sentence that the RAM specified by the *that*-clause represents. Certainly the speaker is not aware of meaning any such thing; nor does it seem plausible to suppose that this is something that the speaker might have meant. Second, the account shares with other language-of-thought accounts the presumption that the sentences in the language-of-thought explain, but are not subject to, the usual failures of substitution that characterize intentional contexts. This would seem to require that the objects of belief, i.e. these sentences in the language-of-thought, are considerably richer, structurally speaking, than Richard might have imagined. For suppose, as Ludlow and Larson (1993) argue, it is possible that Jones believes that John F. Kennedy went to '/hahvahd/' but not that he went to '/harverd/',[6] that Jones believes that [old [men and women]] are at risk of infection, but not that [[old men] and women] are at risk. Minimally, the mentalese sentences in the language-of-thought that Richard's account takes to be the objects of belief

---

[6] Items within slash brackets represent phonetic forms.

will have to be annotated phonologically, syntactically, and morphologically in such fashion as to provide an object sufficiently rich as to be able to capture the individuation conditions on belief. Moreover, given the supposedly universal character of the language-of-thought, the annotated structure of these sentences will presumably have to be able to capture subtle distinctions in ascribed belief expressible in any natural language whatever. Perhaps this is not impossible, but it certainly imposes a *significant* empirical burden on the notion of a language-of-thought. Finally, and perhaps most importantly for our present purposes, Richard's account ascribes to belief ascriptions a logical form, given by (5) above, that is clearly at odds with the truth-conditions semantics for such ascriptions. Simply put, the verb *believes* is a 2-place, *not* 3-place, predicate. Richard is driven to treating *believes* as a 3-place predicate by his strategy for explaining the context-sensitivity of belief ascriptions. On Richard's account, the context-sensitivity of belief ascriptions is explained in terms of the context-sensitive representation function ϱ that maps the RAM specified by the *that*-clause to a sentence in the believer's language of thought. The account treats the representation function ϱ as an argument of the verb. This not only gets the polyadicity of the verb wrong, but seems to locate the context-sensitivity in the wrong place—on the verb rather than on the *that*-clause. Intuitively, context determines what the *that*-clause specifies.

4 Semantical versus Psychological 'Objects' of Belief

Relational accounts, we see, typically get into trouble because they attempt to identify the referent of the ascription's *that*-clause with the belief itself, i.e. with the particular that is the relatum, the so-called 'object of belief', to which the believer supposedly stands in a *doxastic* relation. On the one hand, these accounts have difficulty finding suitable objects of a sort that can be both appropriately semantically evaluable and causally efficacious; while on the other hand, they also have difficulty accounting for the context-sensitivity of belief ascriptions. Richard (1990) avoids these difficulties by distinguishing the referent of the *that*-clause, what we might dub the 'semantical object' of belief, from the relatum to which the believer is doxastically related, the 'psychological object' of belief. On Richard's account, the former *represents* the latter. The context-sensitivity of the representation relation allows him to explain both how in different contexts different *that*-clauses can pick out one and the same belief and how in different contexts the same *that*-clause can pick out different beliefs. More importantly for our present discussion, the distinction enables Richard to attribute to these two different sorts of objects, properties not shared by both. Thus, for example, he can attribute to the psychological object of belief the property of being causally efficacious in the production of the believer's behavior without attributing this same property to the semantical object of belief. Similarly, he can attribute to the semantical object certain properties dictated by the semantics for propositional attitude ascriptions without thereby having to attribute these properties to the psychological object. He is thus able to avoid many of the difficult problems faced by relational accounts that propose to identify these two sorts of objects.

In presenting their semantics for belief ascriptions, Segal and Larson (1995) do not introduce a distinction, like Richard's, between semantical and psychological objects of belief, since their semantics is just that, a semantics, and not a metaphysics of belief or a psychology of believers. Yet when they turn to the question of how these belief ascriptions relate to the belief states that these ascriptions are used to characterize, their informal discussion of this question does appeal to just such a distinction. Segal and Larson point out (1995: 444) that, while their account takes the 'semantic object' of *believe* in (10) to be the ILF of the English sentence embedded in the *that*-clause, it is implausible to suppose that Caesar, himself, ever stood in a doxastic relation to that ILF.

(10)   Caesar believed that Carthage must be destroyed.

There is, Segal and Larson insist, nothing problematic in all this. ILFs are simply linguistic objects that 'give expression' to attitudes; they are objects 'one can use to express what Caesar said and believed' (1995: 444): 'to believe an ILF is to have a belief expressed by it' (1995: 445).

Now it is consistent with the above assertions that Caesar's believing that Carthage must be destroyed is a matter of his standing in a doxastic relation to an ILF, albeit not the ILF of the embedded sentence in (10). Perhaps Caesar's believing this is a matter of his standing in a doxastic relation to the ILF of the Latin *Carthago delenda est*. Segal and Larson do not endorse this possibility. They note (p. 455) that 'the psychology module will have its own way of representing propositional attitudes. These representations may well not involve ILFs.' But they do assume, and indeed assert explicitly (p. 455), that 'ILFs are represented within the semantics module of the language faculty.'

Segal and Larson's train of thought here is a bit hard to follow, however, this much seems clear: ILFs, themselves, are not to be identified with what we have been calling the psychological objects of belief, those particulars to which the believer is supposedly doxastically related; nor do they seem to be the sort of thing to which either believer or ascriber are epistemically related. As Fiengo and May (1996) point out, a person might believe that Cicero is not Tully, but clearly this person has no access to the objectual annotations of the ILF of the sentence embedded in the *that*-clause, since if he did, he would know that *Cicero* and *Tully* were co-referential, and hence could not believe the contrary. Similarly, a second person might ascribe this belief to someone without knowing its truth-value, which clearly he would know if he had access to these same objectual annotations. So ILFs are not the sort of things to which either the believer or the person ascribing the belief can have any epistemic access, which surely disqualifies them as possible psychological objects of belief.

Now, it is clearly possible for someone to stand in an epistemic relation to a representation of an ILF. Such is the case, of course, for all readers of Segal and Larson. But is there any reason to suppose that the psychological object of belief is such a representation? Perhaps. But notice that the semantics for, and logical form of, belief ascriptions provide no grounds for this supposition. According to Segal and Larson, a belief ascription such as (10) is true just in case the believer stands in the *believe** relation to the ILF of the sentence embedded in the ascription's *that*-clause. Nothing in their account entails that a believer stands in this relation to that ILF only if that believer stands in a doxastic relation to a representation of that ILF, or of any other ILF for that matter. Indeed, for all their semantics tells us, a believer's believing something might not be a matter of standing in any relation at all. The relational conception of belief might simply be false.

Relationalists, we have seen, claim support for their relational conception in the existence of valid arguments, such as (1) and (2), that seemingly quantify over beliefs or belief contents, what we have been calling the psychological objects of belief. But if we embrace a theory of belief that distinguishes between the semantical and psychological objects of belief, this claimed support is effectively undercut, since it is the logical form of belief ascriptions that determines their logical properties, and within the context of a theory of belief that distinguishes the semantical and psychological objects of belief, it is the semantic, not the psychological, object of belief that figures in the logical form of the belief ascription. This is hardly surprising, since the basic rationale for drawing this distinction is to enable a theory that avails itself of such a distinction to postulate an object to which the believer is semantically related that is suitable to capture the semantic and inferential properties of belief ascriptions but without thereby having also to ascribe to the believer a psychological or doxastic relation to this object.

Of course, distinguishing between semantical and psychological objects of belief comes with a price: one then has to explain how, despite their differences, the former manages to track the latter, and how native speakers are able to exploit the fact that the former tracks the latter to obtain information about the believer. Otherwise one has no account of how true belief ascriptions manage to be informative.

Of the recent proposals that distinguish between semantical and psychological objects of belief, Richard (1990) offers the most explicit explanation of the tracking relation. On his account, the semantical object specified by the belief ascription's *that*-clause is mapped to the psychological object, a belief representation in the believer's belief representation set, by the context-sensitive representation function ρ, mentioned in (5) and (6) above. Richard does not offer much by way of an explicit characterization of this mapping function; nor does he offer any characterization whatever of the contexts that are presumed to be one of the arguments of this function. Rather what he offers are a number of illustrations of the context-sensitivity of our interpretation of belief ascriptions which suggest that minimally the mapping function preserves the Russellian proposition expressed by the *that*-clause.

Segal and Larson (1995) are considerably less explicit on this matter. For them, the relation between the semantical and psychological objects of belief is, as we noted, one of *expression*: the ILF expresses what the believer believes. Segal and Larson intend their expression relation to be a generalization of Davidson's (1968) *samesaying* relation, but like Davidson before them, they offer no characterization whatever of this relation by virtue of which the semantical object succeeds in tracking the psychological object. More significantly still, neither Richard nor Segal and Larson offer any account of how speakers might exploit the tracking relation in understanding just what claim is being made about the psychological state of the believer. It remains a mystery how being told that a believer stands in a certain relation to a semantic object of some sort, namely, the relation given by the logical form of a belief ascription, provides any information about the believer's doxastic state.

Bach (1997) offers an account of belief ascriptions that, like the accounts of both Richard and Segal and Larson, avoids the difficulties faced by traditional relational accounts, which identify the referent of the *that*-clause with the object of belief, but the account does so without appealing, even implicitly, to a distinction between semantic and psychological objects of belief. On Bach's account, the predicate *believes* is what it appears to be in belief ascriptions of the form *x believes that S*, namely, a 2-place predicate; however, the *that*-clause of the ascription does not function as a singular term. As Bach puts it, the complementizer *that* is not a term-forming operator on sentences. Rather the *that*-clause functions as a *description*: the *that*-clause *describes* the object of belief, i.e.

the particular entity that the believer stands in the belief relation to, with greater or lesser specificity. Not only do the *that*-clauses in such ascriptions not refer to the object of belief, but they do not necessarily even express the content of the ascribed belief, at least not in any usual sense of that term. A belief ascription can be true of an individual even if the individual does not believe the proposition expressed by its *that*-clause (e.g. 'Jones believes that the wealthy Cicero is destitute'). Thus, according to Bach, it is a mistake to assume that a sentence of the form *A believes that S* entails *A believes the proposition that S, A has the belief that S,* or even *That S is something that A believes.* Belief ascriptions are context-sensitive, but not because such ascriptions refer in a context-sensitive manner to modes of presentation, i.e. ways of taking what is believed. Belief ascriptions make no such reference. Nor is the context-sensitivity to be explained, in the manner that Richard does, in terms of a representation relation. Rather the context-sensitivity of such ascriptions is a consequence of their sensitivity to contextually variable standards for whether a given belief can satisfy a given *that*-clause. As Bach (1997: p. xx) puts it, 'beliefs reports are context-sensitive not because they implicity refer to mode of presentation but because they are sensitive to contextually variable standards of sameness and difference of thing believed. Applying the relevant standard may depend, via the maxim of manner, on the choice of words used to describe the belief.'

Bach has little to say about the objects of belief, i.e. about beliefs themselves, although he does emphasize that in rejecting the notion that *that*-clauses are singular terms he does not thereby reject a relational conception of belief. Indeed, he endorses this conception. But, the semantics of belief ascriptions, he insists, need not embody a theory about the nature of, or the relata of, the belief relation. Such things, he argues, are the proper concern of metaphysics, not semantics. Bach quite appropriately describes his account of belief ascriptions as minimalist. Much of the burden previously shouldered by such accounts, he argues (p. xx), is now to be shouldered by the metaphysics of belief. The usual puzzles about belief, i.e. all the things that once motivated appeals to modes of presentation, are now the subject-matter for metaphysical explanation, though (and here is an important qualification) that explanation may turn on the choice of *that*-clause used to describe the belief.

Bach's proposal to shift the explanatory burden away from the semantics onto the metaphysics of belief is salutary. But reassign the work as he will, the explanatory work still has to be done somewhere. Most crucially, he owes us an account of the context-sensitive relation between the description provided by the *that*-clause and the object of belief that he takes to be its *descriptum*. For absent such an account, we have no particular reason to credit Bach's endorsement of the relational conception of belief. Certainly nothing in all this provides any support for the relational conception, any more than did anything in the accounts of Richard and Segal and Larson. Far from providing any support for the relational conception, each of these three accounts serves to separate the relational conception from what relationalists have long taken to be its principal source of (a priori) support, namely, the semantics and logical form of belief ascriptions.

5 'Reading Back' Logical Form: The Problem for Relationalists

So here is where things stand. Relationalists assume that we can read the logical form of belief ascriptions back onto the believers these ascriptions are about, specifically onto the believer's belief state, so that if the logical form of belief ascriptions is relational, then so, too, is belief. If this assumption were well-founded, then relationalists would have good grounds for their relational conception of belief, since on all plausible accounts, namely, truth-theoretic accounts of the sort scouted above, the logical form of belief ascriptions *is* relational, specifically, a binary relation between a believer and an entity of the sort that we have been calling the semantical object of belief. But there is reason to challenge the reading-back assumption that underpins this argument for the relational conception of belief, since the semantical object of belief cannot, it would seem, plausibly be identified with the putative psychological object of belief to which the believer is, according to the relational conception, doxastically related. At best, the semantical object *tracks* the psychological object. Yet relationalists have no explicit characterization of this putative tracking relation; nor do they have any account of how speakers might exploit such a relation in gaining information about a person's belief states from true belief ascriptions of that person. But in the absence of a characterization of the tracking relation, the relationalist's claim to find support for the relational conception of belief in the logical form of belief ascriptions is in trouble, since in the absence of such a characterization the relationalist has no justification for reading the logical form back onto the belief state. Indeed, from the logical form alone, the relationalist has no reason even to assume that the belief states are relational.

There is, of course, going to have to be some mapping of the relation and relata specified in the logical form of belief ascriptions onto the belief states of believers, since otherwise the ascriptions would carry no information about these states. But nothing requires that the psychological image of the logical form be a single sort of relation relating a believer to a single sort of object. Consistent with the requirement that belief ascriptions carry information about the belief states of believers, the logical form of belief ascriptions could have as its image any number of different relations, each with a different relatum to which the believer was related, or it could as well have as its image the possession by the believer of one or more monadic properties.

Ascriptions of numerical magnitudes illustrate just this last possibility, namely, of an ascription with a relational logical form being used to ascribe a monadic property, or at least a relation different from that expressed by the logical form. Consider the following ascriptions:

(11) Jones weighs 150 lb.
(12) Jones has a temperature of 98.68F.

On any plausible semantics, the logical form of both (11) and (12) is a binary relation, relating Jones to a number on a scale. Yet Jones's weighing what he does or having the temperature that he does is *not* a matter of his standing in a relation to the relata that figure in the logical forms of these ascriptions. Having a certain weight and temperature are *monadic* properties of their possessor.[7] The binary relations that figure in the logical forms of these ascriptions simply provide a way of specifying these properties, by relating their possessor to certain abstract entities, namely, numbers on a scale, that *index*—or more precisely, *measure*—these properties. Arguably, something similar could be true for belief ascriptions, since in the case of these ascriptions, too, the relatum to which the believer is said by the belief ascription to be related is not, we have seen, the psychological object of belief, i.e. not something to which the believer is doxastically related; rather it is an object that presumably tracks or indexes a psychological state of the believer.

6 The Psychological Import of Logical Form: A Measurement-Theoretic Way of Thinking about the Issue

The analogy with ascriptions of numerical magnitudes suggests that a belief ascription may succeed in ascribing a belief state to a person by relating that

---

[7] Strictly speaking, of course, Jones's having a certain weight is a relational property, but it is not the relation captured by the logical form of (11). Rather it is a relation between Jones, specifically his mass, and the gravitational force to which he (his mass) is subject.

person to an abstract object that measures the belief state in roughly the way that numbers on a scale measure certain physical magnitudes. The logical form of the ascription expresses a relation, not between the person to whom the belief is ascribed and some putative psychological object, the belief, but between the person and what we might call the 'measuring object'. The task, then, for someone who wants to move from the logical form, i.e. from the semantics of belief ascription, to the metaphysics of belief or the psychology of believers is to discern the mapping between these measuring objects and the states of believers that they measure. The task, in other words, is to construct a measurement theory for belief ascriptions.[8]

A measurement theory for belief ascriptions, and for propositional attitude ascriptions more generally, will presumably include both a representation theorem and a uniqueness theorem. The former will tell us precisely which states (properties, etc.) of the believer the measuring objects specified by the *that*-clauses track, while the latter will tell us just which invariance transformations defined over these objects preserve the empirical content of the ascriptions. The principal novelties, compared to the standard measurement theory for physical magnitude ascriptions, will presumably be these: the measuring objects for a propositional attitude constitute something like a space rather than a scale, and the mapping relation (and hence both the representational theorem and the uniqueness theorem) is context-sensitive.

Constructing a measurement theory for belief ascriptions will not be a simple task, any more than it was for ascriptions of physical magnitudes. Most of us are tolerably reliable, at least in most normal circumstances, in measuring the psychological states of fellow humans (this is hardly surprising given our evolved social character), but our reliability as measuring instruments does not appear to presume any explicit understanding of the mapping relation by virtue of which we achieve this reliability. Our grasp of this relation, like our grasp of the linguistic principles that underlie our linguistic competence, is largely tacit. In this respect, we are not different from many other measuring instruments, both natural and artificial, that while reliable have little or no understanding of the principles that explain their reliability. But presumably our competence in measuring and reporting the propositional attitudes of others (and even ourselves) should be no less amenable to empirical investigation than other cognitive competences.

The point that I wish to emphasize here is that in the absence of a worked-out measurement theory for belief ascriptions, we have no way of interpreting

---

[8] See Matthews (1994).

the import of the logical form of belief ascriptions for the metaphysics of belief and the psychology of believers. Our situation is akin to trying to interpret a map of an unfamiliar territory in the absence of an interpretive key. The logical form of belief ascriptions, like the map, is not self-interpreting. Relationalists have nonetheless tried to undertake such an interpretation, by presuming an exceedingly simpleminded picture of the mapping between measuring object and the measured states of the believer, but their proposed interpretation collapses when it proves impossible to maintain the identity of what we have been calling the semantical and psychological objects of belief. The developments surveyed above make it impossible even to assume that every semantic object is paired with some single psychological object, a mental particular, to which the believer is doxastically related. The mapping need not be a simple homomorphism that maps semantic objects into psychological objects. The measuring objects might, for all we know, measure monadic properties of the believer, and indeed, a single measuring object may simultaneously measure a number of different properties and relations. Something like this is surely the case, for in ascribing a belief to a person, we often give information not simply as to the state of affairs that this person takes to obtain, but also how this person would describe this state of affairs, even down to the specific intonation of the English words this person would use to express this belief (e.g. that Jones went to '/hahvahd/' and not '/harverd/').

Faced with the difficulty, indeed the impossibility, of reading back the logical form of belief ascriptions onto the states of believers, and in the absence of independent arguments for the relational conception, relationalists may be tempted to become Fregeans of a sort, treating belief as simply a relation to the measuring object, i.e. to the abstract entity that according to the measurement-theoretic conception measures the certain states of the believer. Such a move would preserve the relational conception of belief. It would also allow relationalists to continue to ascribe to the belief semantic properties such as semantic evaluability and inferential relations that would on both the measurement-theoretic account and the dual-object accounts scouted above turn out to be possessed by the semantic object that measures the belief but not possessed by the belief itself. But there would, of course, be a price to be paid. On this neo-Fregean conception, relationalists would be forced to abandon what they have tried heroically to preserve, namely, the causal efficacy of belief. Common sense would turn out to be mistaken. Strictly speaking, propositional attitudes would play no role in the production of behavior; rather it would be their images, under the mapping of propositional attitudes onto the states of individuals that we describe mistakenly as the possessors of

propositional attitudes, that would be causally efficacious. Relationalists convinced of the philosophical import of logical form might consider this revision
to common sense a small price to pay.

Relationalists not tempted by this neo-Fregean gambit may try to take some
comfort in the thought that the foregoing arguments against a simple reading
back of the logical form of the attitudes do not show the relational conception
to be untenable. The relational conception, they might conclude, is still in the
running, at least until such time as non-relationalists put a well-developed
alternative on the table. Accounts of the attitudes based on this conception,
they might insist, have considerable explanatory promise, if only the case for
the relational conception can be successfully made. Such a conclusion seriously
underestimates the challenge posed by the foregoing arguments against reading back, especially to relational accounts which take the object of the attitudes
to be a mental representation. For the basic point made by those arguments,
and supported by contemporary relational accounts which invariably find
themselves forced to distinguish between semantical and psychological objects
of the attitudes, is the difficulty, if not the impossibility, of discovering a single
particular that could be a plausible candidate for the object of an attitude to
which the possessor of the attitude could be suitably related. The problem for
relationalists is not simply that the case for the relational conception has yet to
be made, but also, and more importantly, the prospect that a case can be made
appears exceedingly dim. Faced with such a prospect, relationalists should take
little comfort in the fact that relational accounts, were they to exist, would have
the explanatory virtues that relationalists claim for them.

REFERENCES

Bach, E. (1997). 'Do Belief Reports Report Beliefs?', *Pacific Philosophical Quarterly*, 78:
215–41.
Carnap, R. (1947). *Meaning and Necessity* (Chicago: University of Chicago Press).
Davidson, D. (1968). 'On Saying That', *Synthese*, 19: 130–46.
—— (1973). 'In Defense of Convention T', in H. Leblanc (ed.), *Truth, Syntax
and Modality* (Amsterdam: North Holland). Page reference to reprint in
Davidson, *Inquiries into Truth and Interpretation* (Oxford: Oxford University
Press, 1984).
Fiengo, R., and May R. (1996). 'Interpreted Logical Form: A Critique', *Rivista di
linguistica*, 82: 349–73.

Fodor, J. (1981). 'Propositional Attitudes', in *Representations* (Cambridge, Mass.: MIT Press), 177–203.

—— (1987). *Psychosemantics* (Cambridge, Mass.: MIT Press).

Larson, R., and Ludlow, P. (1993). 'Interpreted Logical Forms', *Synthese*, 95: 305–55.

Matthews, R. (1994). 'The Measure of Mind', *Mind*, 103: 131–46.

Pietroski, P. (1996). 'Fregean Innocence', *Mind and Language*, 11: 338–70.

Quine, W. v. O. (1960). *Word and Object* (Cambridge, Mass.: MIT Press).

—— (1971). 'Methodological Reflections on Linguistic Theory', in D. Davidson and G. Harman (eds.), *Semantics of Natural Language* (Dordrecht: Reidel).

Richard, M. (1990). *Propositional Attitudes* (Cambridge, Mass.: MIT Press).

Schiffer, S. (1987). *Remnants of Meaning* (Cambridge, Mass.: MIT Press).

—— (1992). 'Belief Ascription', *Journal of Philosophy*, 89: 499–521.

Segal, G., and Larson, R. (1995). *Knowledge of Meaning* (Cambridge, Mass.: MIT Press).

16

Ordinary Proper Names

Marga Reimer

If one asserts 'Scott is Sir Walter', the way one would mean it would be that one was using the names as descriptions. One would mean that the person called 'Scott' is the person called 'Sir Walter', and 'the person called "Scott"' is a description and so is 'the person called "Sir Walter"'. So that would not be a tautology. It would mean that the person called 'Scott' is identical with the person called 'Sir Walter'. But if you are using both as names, the matter is quite different. You must observe that the name does not occur in that which you assert when you use the name. The name is merely that which is a means of expressing what it is you are trying to assert, and when I say, 'Scott wrote *Waverley*', the name 'Scott' does not occur in the thing I am asserting. The thing I am asserting is about the person, not about the name. So if I say 'Scott is Sir Walter', using these two names *as* names, neither 'Scott' nor 'Sir Walter' occurs in what I am asserting, but only the person who has these names, and thus what I am asserting is a pure tautology (Russell, 1918).

1 Preliminaries

What is the *logical form* of a sentence containing an ordinary proper name in subject position? Consider, for instance, the following sentence:

(1) Clinton has been impeached.

Using the devices afforded by contemporary logic, how are we to render perspicuous the structure of the proposition expressed by such a sentence (thereby capturing the sentence's logical form[1])?

Any number of responses might be given to this question; I will be concerned with two of the more plausible responses in what follows. According to one such response, the logical form of sentences containing ordinary proper names should reflect the view that such expressions are *logically proper names*: they mean what they name and nothing more. This view might be deemed the 'Millian' view, after John Stuart Mill, to whom the view of ordinary proper names as meaning only what they name is standardly attributed.[2] According to another somewhat less popular approach, the logical form of sentences containing ordinary proper names should reflect the Russellian view that such expressions are 'disguised' *definite descriptions*.[3] To claim that ordinary proper names are 'disguised' definite descriptions is to claim that the proposition expressed by a sentence containing such a name is identical to that which *would have been expressed* had the name been replaced by a definite description.[4] *Which* definite description? Opinions here vary. According to Russell, the relevant description is that which, if substituted for the name, would best express the proposition the speaker 'had in mind' at the time of the utterance.[5] Let us call the view that ordinary proper names are semantically equivalent to the definite descriptions for which they allegedly stand, the 'Russellian' view. So defined, the Russellian view says nothing about the particular content of the

---

[1] I realize, of course, that there are other, perhaps equally fruitful, notions of 'logical form' that have been employed in the literature. However, in what follows, I will be concerned with 'logical form', conceived of as the specification of the structure of the proposition expressed, by means of the devices afforded by contemporary logic.

[2] Mill (1843). The view attributed to Mill is not about logical form *per se*, but about the semantic function of ordinary proper names, according to which such expressions 'denote', but do not 'connote'. For contemporary versions of Millianism, see Salmon (1986) and Soames (1989).

[3] See Russell (1905, 1912, 1919). For contemporary versions of the Russellian view, see Bach (1994), Katz (1994), Quine (1980), and Searle (1958, 1983). Quine's view, which is most like Russell's, is discussed in section 5.4. The views of Bach and Searle, which differ in important respects from Russell's, are discussed in section 5.3.

[4] Such a view is distinct from, though compatible with, the view that the *reference* of a proper name is determined by a definite description(s) associated in some manner with that expression.

[5] Description theorists sometimes speak as if the relevant definite description were that associated, by the speaker, with the name. However, this way of putting things suggests implausibly that there is (at least generally) some *linguistic* item which the speaker associates with the name. The proposed formulation of the Russellian view avoids this implausible suggestion, while retaining the spirit of the view.

relevant descriptions; nor does it say anything about how the identity of the descriptions is to be determined. Thus, while the Millian might represent the logical form of a sentence like (1) as in (2), the Russellian—if he is *also* a Russellian about definite descriptions[6]—might represent it as in (3):

(2) *Fa*
(3) $\exists x(\forall y(Fy \leftrightarrow y = x) \,\&\, Gx)$[7]

It would seem that these two approaches to the semantics of proper names are mutually exclusive: they cannot *both* be correct. How, after all, could a single (unambiguous) sentence simultaneously express two distinct (types of) propositions?[8] I suppose one might argue that, while the Millian analysis provides the correct treatment for certain names, the Russellian analysis provides the correct treatment for certain *other* names. On any such view, *both* approaches would be correct—but about *different* cases. Such a view has in fact been advocated. Specifically, it has been argued that while a Millian account is correct for names *with* bearers, a Russellian account is correct for names *without* bearers.[9] In this way, it is hoped that one might preserve the intuitions that motivate a Millian account, while accommodating the intuition that sentences containing names without bearers are not for that reason without meanings. But any such view would be prima facie implausible, as it would suggest that knowledge of the semantic function of a particular name is contingent upon knowledge of whether or not that name has a bearer. Thus, consider 'Nessy', the name of the alleged monster of Loch Ness. What is the semantic function of this expression—to refer or to describe? According to the view in question, that is something that can be answered only *after* we determine whether or not there really is a Nessy. This is surely an implausible view. Must we really drain Loch Ness before we can hope to draw a conclusion about the semantics of the name 'Nessy'?

There is, however, a view to which the foregoing bears a superficial resemblance, which is not nearly so implausible. In fact, I think it is basically correct.

---

[6] It is not essential to the Russellian view (as I define it) that definite descriptions be given a *Russellian* analysis. What *is* essential to that view is that the bearer of an ordinary proper name not be viewed as essential to the *semantic value* of the name: to the contribution it makes to the proposition expressed. It is the 'sense' (as opposed to the reference or 'denotation') of the associated description (however *that* gets cashed out) that is essential to the semantic value of the name.

[7] Russell's original (1905) formulation is considerably more unwieldy.

[8] In my (2000a), I suggest how this might in fact be possible.

[9] See, for instance, Miller (1975). For a critique of Miller, see Dummett (1983). See also Peacocke (1975). For a critique of Peacocke, see Bach (1994).

According to this alternative view (to be elaborated below), ordinary proper names can function *either* as logically proper names *or* as 'disguised' definite descriptions—depending upon the *communicative intentions* of the speaker. If the intention is to communicate a *singular* proposition of the form represented in (2), the name is functioning as a Millian name. If the intention is to communicate a *general* proposition, perhaps of the form represented in (3), the name is functioning as a Russellian name: that is, as a 'disguised' definite description.[10] Such a view is importantly different from the problematic view which it resembles, for it applies uniformly to *all* ordinary proper names—it claims that *all* such expressions can be used *either* as logically proper names *or* as definite descriptions. It therefore escapes the particular criticism that applies to the view to which it bears a superficial resemblance. For the semantic function of a name like 'Nessy'—indeed, the semantic function of *any* name—is not dependent upon whether or not that name has a bearer. *All* such expressions—empty or not—are capable of functioning *either* as logically proper names *or* as definite descriptions. (Or so I intend to argue.)

My primary intention in what follows is to propose, motivate, and defend such a view. I will go on to suggest the possibility of extending the proposed view to other natural language expressions, after which I will conclude with a few brief remarks concerning some of the methodological issues raised by the analysis of natural language expressions. Before, however, introducing the proposed account, I would like to take a careful look at both the Millian and Russellian accounts of ordinary proper names. For the view that I will be proposing is, in effect, a *synthesis* of these two accounts.

2 Two Views of Ordinary Proper Names

Before proceeding to the views in question, something should perhaps be said about the general sorts of considerations that serve to motivate views about the semantics of various types of natural language expressions. Two sorts of considerations are generally adduced on behalf of such views: intuitions and methodological factors. The 'intuitions' appealed to are alleged to be *pre-theoretical judgements* about the semantic properties of certain types of

[10] *Singular* propositions contain the *individuals* they purport to be 'about'. *General* propositions, as well as singular propositions, may contain *properties, relations*, and *concepts*. General propositions may also contain individuals, but only singular propositions contain the individuals they purport to be 'about'. The 'singular' / 'general' proposition terminology is from Kaplan (1978).

sentence(s) or utterance(s). Such properties include truth-value and meaning-fulness. These intuitions are construed as prima-facie evidence for or against semantic theories. The assumption is that, if a sentence (or the proposition it expresses) appears, prima facie, to have a particular truth-value, or to be meaningful, then—unless there are reasons for thinking otherwise[11]—it *does* have that truth-value, and *is* meaningful. The methodological factors most often appealed to are simplicity and generality.[12] Such appeals come in handy when faced with intuitions that appear to conflict with one's favored theory. For in such cases, the theorist may admit to some counter-intuitive consequences of his theory, but claim that the theory is simpler or more general than its competitors. He might further claim that the intuitions in question—even if they are not *preserved* by the theory—can nevertheless be *explained away* from within the framework of that theory.[13]

We are now in a position to consider the views in question. Because the arguments for and against each of the two views are well-known, my presentation of them will be rather brief.

2.1   *The Millian View: Ordinary Proper Names as Logically Proper Names*

As we have seen, the Millian view claims that the logical form of sentences containing ordinary proper names in subject position is to be represented as in (2). What reasons are there to suppose that such an analysis is correct? The reasons given are invariably intuitive. The intuitions most frequently appealed to are of two basic sorts: those that appeal to *modal* considerations and those that appeal to the (apparent) *stability of meaning*.[14] Both sorts of intuitions

[11]   Such reasons might include the possibility of developing a simpler or more general theory.

[12]   For an accessible discussion of these and other methodological virtues, see Quine and Ullian (1970). Devitt (1996) argues that a semantic theory should also reflect a view of semantics that is both 'worthy of study' and 'fundamental'.

[13]   Perhaps such intuitions result from conflating word meaning and speaker meaning. More on this in section 5.

[14]   Intuitions appealing to modal considerations are discussed in Kripke (1980). Intuitions appealing to the stability of meaning are discussed in Kripke (1979). Kripke himself does not invoke such intuitions on behalf of Millianism, but on behalf of the (weaker) view that names are not semantically equivalent to (non-rigid) definite descriptions. Kripke (1980) also appeals to non-modal intuitions concerning the reference of names. He argues that, intuitively, the reference of a name (as used in the actual world, in a non-modal context) is not determined by any description(s) associated with that name. He demonstrates this by appealing to cases in which an individual x is referred to via the use of some name, despite the fact another individual y—or no individual at all—uniquely satisfies the descriptive information associated with the name.

support Millianism indirectly. For while Millianism is both consistent with the intuitions *and* able to explain them, the Russellian view not only cannot explain such intuitions, it is also inconsistent with them. Or so it would initially appear.

Let us consider the modal intuitions first. Intuitively, it would appear that sentence (4):

(4) Aristotle was a philosopher.

expresses a *contingent* truth, for we can imagine a possible world in which (as we would say) *Aristotle* was not a philosopher. We can imagine, in other words, that (4) might be false with respect to certain possible worlds: those in which the individual, *x*, who bore the name 'Aristotle' *in the actual world*, was not a philosopher. The Millian view is consistent with these 'rigidity' intuitions, intuitions which reflect the (apparent) fact that names are *rigid*,[15] such that (as used in the actual world) they refer to the same individual in all possible worlds in which that individual exists. Moreover, Millianism can *explain* these intuitions: if Millianism is true, one would not expect a change in reference where there was no change in meaning; for meaning *just is* reference, on the Millian view. The Russellian view, in contrast, does *not* appear to be consistent with such rigidity intuitions. For suppose that proper names are in fact 'disguised' definite descriptions. And suppose that the description for which the name 'Aristotle' is hypothesized to stand is 'the famous philosopher who studied under Plato'. In that case, (4) would appear to express a *necessary* truth: one to the effect that the famous philosopher who studied under Plato was a philosopher.[16] In that case, there would presumably be no possible world in which *Aristotle* ('by definition', as it were, a *philosopher*) was not a philosopher. That is, there would be no such world with respect to which (4) was false. But that just does not seem right.

Now let us consider those intuitions having to do with stability of meaning. Imagine that, while one speaker thinks of Aristotle as the famous Greek who taught Alexander the Great, another speaker thinks of Aristotle as the famous Roman who taught Cicero. Suppose, for the moment, that we adopt *Russell's* version of the Russellian view, according to which the description for which a given name stands is determined by what the speaker 'has in mind' at the time of the utterance.[17] In that case, the definite description for which the name

---

[15] The terminology is from Kripke (1980).

[16] At least this would be so for our hypothetical speaker, in whose idiolect 'Aristotle' means 'the famous philosopher who studied under Plato' (interpreted non-rigidly).

[17] Other versions of the Russellian view (such as Bach's metalinguistic view) are able to accommodate the stability of meaning.

'Aristotle' stands will presumably be different for our two speakers. Now imagine that these two speakers get involved in a debate concerning whether Aristotle was a philosopher or a poet. Intuitively, when the two make assertions involving the name 'Aristotle', perhaps by means of sentences like (4) and (5),

(4) Aristotle was a philosopher
(5) Aristotle was a poet, not a philosopher

they mean *the same thing* by that expression; otherwise, their dispute would be a merely verbal one. But on the Russellian view, the two disputants *do not* mean the same thing by the name 'Aristotle'; their dispute would thus appear to be a merely verbal one.[18] For the claim that *the famous Greek who taught Alexander the Great* was a philosopher is quite compatible with the claim that *the famous Roman who taught Cicero* was not a philosopher. Thus, stability of meaning does not appear to be accommodated on the Russellian view—at least not on *Russell's* particular version of that view. Such stability is, however, consistent with, and would be expected on, a Millian account of proper names. For according to such an account, our two speakers do indeed mean the same thing by the name 'Aristotle'; they mean *x*—the bearer of that name.

The foregoing constitute some of the better known reasons for supposing that the Millian view (in opposition to its Russellian rival) is correct. What reasons are there for supposing that the view is mistaken? Consider the following four sentences:

(6) Hesperus is Phosphorus.
(7) Vulcan does not exist.
(8) Kripke exists.
(9) Jennifer believes that Cicero was Roman, but she believes that Tully was English, not Roman.

Sentences of these sorts have often been cited as counter-examples to a (uniform) Millian account of ordinary proper names.[19] For suppose that account is correct: then (6) expresses a trivial truth of self-identity—but it seems rather to express something that is informative; (7) fails to express anything at all, let alone something that is true—and yet it seems to express a truth; (8) expresses a proposition that is tautologous in the sense that its meaningfulness *presupposes* the truth of what is asserts—and yet it does not seem to; and (9) attributes inconsistent beliefs to Jennifer—and yet it does not seem to.

[18] At least if it is assumed that the descriptions in question are not co-referential.
[19] For helpful summaries of such arguments, see Devitt and Sterelny (1987) and Bach (1994).

Not surprisingly, Millians have devised ways of responding to these apparent counter-examples. We will turn to the Millian responses below, in section 5.

2.2 The Russellian View: Ordinary Proper Names as Disguised Descriptions

As we have seen, according to the Russellian view, the logical form of sentences containing ordinary proper names might be represented as in (3). What reasons are there to suppose that such a view is correct? The view is able to give intuitive analyses of the particular sorts of cases that prove problematic for the Millian. It accounts for the informativeness of (6), the truth of (7), the informativeness of (8), and the fact that (9) does not appear to attribute inconsistent beliefs to Jennifer.[20]

What reasons are there to suppose that the Russellian view is mistaken? First, and most obviously, there are difficulties with the idea that there is invariably some *particular* definite description for which the use of a given name stands. Just how is the identity of this description to be determined?[21] The answer, as we shall see, is not immediately clear. But if it turns out that there is no principled way of coming to such a determination, then perhaps the conclusion to draw is that the view is false: names are not (in any sense) 'disguised' definite descriptions. Second, the very intuitions that support a Millian account of ordinary proper names would appear to go against a Russellian account of such expressions. Russellians, not surprisingly, have devised ways of handling these difficulties. We will turn to these below in section 5.

3 The Problem

In light of the foregoing, how should we approach the logical form of sentences containing ordinary proper names? The answer is not immediately clear. The

---

[20] Prior to Kripke's (1980) sketch of a causal theory of reference, one of the primary motivations for favoring a description over a Millian view, was that the former provided an answer to the question: how is the reference of a name determined? These days, Millians tend to respond to this question by appealing to some sort of Kripkean causal theory.

[21] Some semanticists, including Bach (1994) and Katz (1994), believe that there are principled reasons for holding that the description for which a given name stands is invariably a metalinguistic one. This view (Bach's version of it) is discussed in section 5.2.

problem is that there are compelling intuitive considerations *for and against* each of the two views in question. Of course, the Millians think that the Russellian intuitions can be accommodated within a Millian framework, and vice versa, but I would like to hold off on arguments in support of such claims. For now, I would like to propose an alternative approach that fully accommodates the intuitive data from both sides of the debate.

4 An Alternative Approach

An alternative approach would be to take the intuitive considerations appealed to by Millians and Russellians alike at face value—as revealing the semantic facts. If we do this, we emerge with a theory according to which ordinary proper names *sometimes* function as Millian names and *sometimes* function as Russellian names.[22] Which use is operative in a given case? That would depend upon the *communicative intentions* of the speaker—intentions which are generally evident from the (publicly accessible) context in which the name is used. That communicative intentions *are* generally evident from the context of utterance is due to the fact that the context will normally *constrain* the speaker's communicative intentions.[23] It does this by rendering certain interpretations of the speaker's utterance more natural than others. The idea here is that one cannot (sincerely) *intend to communicate* a proposition that one has little or no reason to believe will be *successfully communicated*. Thus, the interpretation suggested by the context is generally the intended interpretation. For instance, utterances of sentences (6)–(9) would normally be interpreted as involving a *Russellian* use of proper names, while utterances of such sentences as (4) and (5) would normally be interpreted as involving a *Millian* use of proper names. Such are the interpretations that the speaker might reasonably intend to

[22] Such a view would be similar to that adumbrated in the passage from Russell (1918) with which I introduced this chapter. The view also appears to be adumbrated in Searle (1983: section vii, first paragraph). There, Searle suggests that sometimes the reference of a name is what is essential to the 'propositional content' of the statement made; and sometimes (as with identity statements between names, existential claims, and propositional attitude reports) the 'intentional content' of the name is what is relevant to the propositional content of the statement made.

[23] When I speak of the 'context' of an utterance, I simply mean those features of the circumstances of the utterance that enable the audience to interpret what the speaker is saying. So construed, the context in which a proper name is uttered, will include—not only shared background beliefs and assumptions—but also the *linguistic* context in which the name is embedded.

communicate, as such are the interpretations naturally suggested by the context (which includes the immediately surrounding linguistic context) in which the names are embedded. It would, however, be possible for the speaker to manipulate the context of utterance in such a way that utterances of (6)–(9) would be interpreted as involving a Millian use of names, whereas utterances of (4) and (5) would be interpreted as involving a Russellian use of names. This could be done simply by stipulating, in advance, that the names were going to be used in these conversationally odd ways.

5 Objections and Replies

There are many objections which might be made to the proposed 'synthetic' account of ordinary proper names. In particular, Millians as well as Russellians might attempt to bolster their respective theories by garnering *further* intuitive support on their behalf. But such 'counter-arguments' would do nothing to impugn the proposed account; they would only strengthen it. For such intuitions would lend further credence to the view that ordinary proper names can indeed function in either of two ways: Millian or Russellian.

There are, however, more telling objections that might be leveled against the proposed account. One sort of objection might attempt to show that the intuitions that support the rival account (whether Millian or Russellian) are the result of some sort of *systematic mistake or confusion* on the part of the intuiter. Another sort of objection might appeal to *methodological* considerations, pointing out that the proposed account lacks certain virtues (simplicity, in particular) possessed by the available alternatives. A third sort of objection might question the very coherence of a purportedly *semantic* theory, motivated by considerations having to do with language *use*—an ostensibly *pragmatic* matter. A fourth and final sort of objection might question the plausibility of any account that claims that ordinary proper names ever admit of a Russellian analysis. I would now like to turn to these more telling objections.

5.1 *From the Millian*

The Millian might respond by arguing that the proposed account—specifically, its Russellian component—is founded on a conflation of word meaning and speaker meaning. The intuitions surrounding the problematic cases—as represented by sentences such as (6)–(9)—are the result of mistaking what the *speaker* means for what the *words themselves* mean. Thus, for example, while someone uttering sentence (6) would no doubt mean to *communicate* some informative proposition (perhaps one to the effect that the names 'Hesperus' and 'Phosphorus' are co-referential), the proposition actually *expressed* by such an utterance would be (in the words of Russell) a 'pure tautology'.

The problem with this explanation is simple: it is insufficiently motivated. What, after all, makes a pragmatic explanation of an apparently semantic fact a *plausible* explanation of that fact? Such an account would be regarded as plausible only if a plausible story could be told as to how it could appear that what is merely *communicated* is in fact *said*. Suppose, for instance, that someone says to you, 'I have three children', though he has four. Initially, it might appear as though what is actually said in such a case is *false*, as the speaker has—not three—but four children. However, an alternative 'pragmatic' explanation of this apparently semantic fact is available. According to this (Gricean) explanation, what the speaker actually *says* is that he has *at least* three children, though he *communicates* that he has *exactly* three children.[24] What is communicated is (or at least can be) inferred from what is said, with the assistance of various conversational principles and maxims of the sort discussed by Grice (1975). Thus, while what is said is true, it appears to be false. For what is communicated, which is conflated with what is said, is indeed false. The conflation is a natural one, for as speakers of the language, our primary interest is in what is communicated, not in what is (strictly) said.

But now consider cases of the sort in question, cases involving assertive utterances of sentences like (6)–(9). How is the Millian to explain how such utterances appear to express meaningful, informative, truth-evaluable claims? So far as I can tell, no such explanation is available, at least not in *Gricean* terms. Indeed, a Gricean account would seem to be impossible here. Consider, for instance, sentence (6). Suppose, as the Millian claims, that an assertive utterance of this sentence expresses a 'pure tautology' to the effect that Venus is self-identical. To adopt a Gricean analysis here would be to suppose that the hearer would be able to derive what is meant from what is said by means of the usual Gricean principles and maxims. But how can *anything* (non-trivial) be derived from a 'pure tautology', even when supplemented with various principles and maxims? Of course, the Millian might choose to adopt some *non-Gricean* account of the data, according to which what is meant is *not* derived from what is said.[25] But in that case, some sort of motivation would have to be

---

[24] For details, see Horn (1989).

[25] Such an account is adopted by Adams and Stecker (1994) in their analysis of empty names.

offered for the (unintuitive) assumption that what is meant, not only *diverges* from what is said, but is in no way *derivative of* what is said.

5.2 From the Russellian

Recall that there are two sorts of intuitions that the Millian might invoke on behalf of his account of proper names: rigidity (modal) intuitions and intuitions concerning the stability of meaning. How might the Russellian attempt to accommodate these intuitions? Let us consider the rigidity intuitions first.

As Kripke concedes in *Naming and Necessity* (1980), his modal arguments against what he terms the 'Frege/Russell' view *presuppose* that the definite descriptions for which proper names are alleged to stand are *non-rigid*. But suppose that the Russellian were to claim that the descriptions in question should be regarded as *rigid*. Such a view would at least be coherent,[26] for as Searle (1983) remarks:

any definite description at all can be treated as a rigid designator by indexing it to the actual world... Since any definite description whatever can be made into a rigid designator, it does not show that the functioning of proper names differs from the function of definite descriptions to show that proper names are always (or almost always) rigid designators and definite descriptions are in general not rigid designators. (Quoted in Martinich, 1996, p. 320)

Searle's point, then, is that the modal ('rigidity') intuitions that appear to support Millianism over Russellianism are in fact consistent with the latter view. For a Russellian could simply claim that the definite descriptions for which proper names stand are *rigid*.[27] On such a view, the intuition that (4) expresses a contingent truth is easily accounted for. For there is indeed a possible world in which the individual who, *in the actual world*, was a famous philosopher and student of Plato's, was not a philosopher. The Russellian is thus free to concede, along with the Millian, that sentence (4) expresses a contingent truth—just as it appears to.

My response to Searle's suggestion is simple. It seems implausible to suppose that those uses of ordinary proper names that appear, prima facie, to be *logically proper* actually involve rigidified definite descriptions. Why make

---

[26] Soames (1998) argues that the view of proper names as semantically equivalent to rigidified descriptions is indeed incoherent. I respond to Soames's arguments in Reimer (2000c).

[27] This does not appear to be Searle's (1958, 1983) own view. For Searle backs away from the idea that names 'stand for' definite descriptions. Rather, his view is that the 'intentional content' that a speaker associates with a name—which might or might not be capable of being spelt out in linguistic terms—determines the reference of that name, as used by that speaker.

456   BELIEF ASCRIPTION AND PROPER NAMES

such an unintuitive supposition in the first place? Because there are good (intuition-based) reasons for supposing that names do, in certain *other* cases, function as 'disguised' definite descriptions—rigid or not. Nevertheless, the intuitions surrounding sentences like (4) and (5) do *not* motivate a Russellian account of proper names; they are *not* problematic for a Millian account in the way that sentences like (6) through (9) are. The former sentences are more naturally analyzed in accordance with a Millian account of such expressions. Indeed, it is precisely because a Millian account provides the most natural analysis of all but the well-known problematic cases, that it is often referred to as a 'naive' view: intuitively, it just seems right. Simply to *generalize* from those cases where the Russellian analysis seems more natural to those cases where it does not is surely to commit the fallacy of hasty generalization.[28]

However, perhaps there is a way for the Russellian to accommodate the rigidity intuitions associated with proper names without making an *ad hoc* appeal to rigidified definite descriptions. This is what Bach (1994) attempts to do. Bach effectively turns the tables on the Millian, claiming that it is the Millian, and not the Russellian, who is conflating word meaning and speaker meaning. Specifically, he claims that a proper name appears rigid only because its use to refer to a particular individual is unwittingly *fixed by the speaker*, prior to the speaker's assessment of the name's semantic function.[29] Bach writes:

it does not seem unfair to suggest that in a sentence like ['Aristotle might not have been a philosopher'] the name 'Aristotle' seems rigid only because its use to refer to a certain individual is fixed before the question of its rigidity is raised. I do not mean that Kripke is doing the fixing; rather, it is the imagined speaker. What renders the use fixed—and helps explain away the intuition of rigidity—is the imputed intention to refer (objectually) to a certain bearer of the name ... (1994: 169)

I would agree with Bach that the use of a name to refer to a particular individual is 'fixed by the speaker' before the question of rigidity is raised. But I would deny Bach's suggestion that the speaker's referential intention—*as opposed to* the semantic features of the name itself—is what is responsible for the intuition of rigidity. For I do not believe that the speaker's referential intention in such cases is semantically inert.

To see this, consider what goes on when we are asked to assess the truth-value of an assertive utterance of a sentence like (4). What do we do? Well, here

---

[28] I discuss such arguments, rampant in the contemporary philosophy of language literature, in my (2000*b*).

[29] Considerations of space prevent me from discussing additional details of Bach's account. These can be found in sections 7.1 and 7.4 of Bach (1994).

is what *I* do—and what I imagine others do as well. With Grice's well-known distinction in mind, I imagine an assertive utterance of the sentence in question, and then ask myself: what would be *said*—not merely communicated, but *said*—by such an utterance? In this way, I take care not to mistake what the *speaker* means for what *the words themselves* (as used on a particular occasion) mean.[30] This is not to say, of course, that what the speaker means is *irrelevant* to what he says; it is just to say that the two do not *necessarily* converge. Indeed, I would say the speaker's intention to refer to a *particular* 'Aristotle' is relevant to what he actually says, as it determines which of a *potential* plurality of homonymic names is to be used, and thus which reference-determining causal chain is operative. It is the referential intention of the speaker which thus (indirectly) determines which reference-determining causal chain comes into play, and thus which particular *Aristotle* the proposition expressed is about.[31]

Bach appears to see the process of semantic evaluation differently. He believes that the relevant question for the semanticist interested in proper names is: what is the purely linguistic information carried by a proper name? With respect to a particular sentence (type) containing a proper name, we should thus ask ourselves: what do the words themselves convey—apart from any particular context in which they might be assertively uttered? Consider sentence (4). As used by a contemporary English speaker existing in the actual world, an utterance of this sentence might well communicate a singular proposition about Aristotle the philosopher. Yet it appears as though the very same sentence (type) might be used by someone else (or even by the same person at a different time) to communicate a *different* singular proposition: one about a *different* Aristotle. This would seem to suggest that the purely semantic information conveyed by the name is *not* some particular bearer of that name. Yet the name 'Aristotle', used correctly, can only be used to assert something about someone named 'Aristotle'. This leads naturally to the view that the semantic content of a name '*N*' is simply: *the bearer of '*N*'*. If so, names would not be rigid, as the same name might refer to different individuals in different possible worlds. Indeed, the same name might refer to different individuals in *the same* possible world. How, then, is one to accommodate our intuitions of rigidity? Bach's proposal, as we have just seen, is that

[30] Bach (1994) would presumably say that I am deceiving myself in this respect, in which case the argument on which my assumption is based is question-begging.

[31] This does not, of course, mean that reference is not determined via a causal chain; it means only that the speaker's communicative intentions plays a role in determining *which* reference-determining causal chain is operative.

the speaker's referential intention, which is semantically inert, explains such intuitions.

My central concern with Bach's proposal is that results from a conception of semantics according to which linguistic *types,* rather than *tokens* (uses of types in a context), are the primary bearers of semantic properties. This is not the place to enter into this particular debate.[32] Here, the point I would like to emphasize is the modest one that Bach's account of rigidity intuitions is not the only one available. In particular, such intuitions are easily accommodated on the proposed view, according to which rigidity is a genuinely *semantic* property of linguistic *tokens.*

So much for rigidity intuitions; now let us consider intuitions concerning the stability of meaning. Intuitively, assertive utterances of sentences (4) and (5) would, in the particular hypothetical scenario imagined, express inconsistent propositions—propositions that could not both be true. Not so, according to the Russellian. For on the Russellian view, the propositions expressed are not about the same individual—indeed, they are not (strictly speaking) 'about' any individual at all; for they are not *singular* propositions, but *general* ones.

How is the Russellian to explain appearances to the contrary? He might claim that assertive utterances of sentences like (4) and (5) *pragmatically convey* singular propositions about a particular individual *x*—the bearer of the name 'Aristotle'. The intuition that the propositions *literally expressed* are inconsistent is simply the result of conflating what is literally expressed with what is pragmatically conveyed.

The difficulty here is similar to that faced by the Millian explanation of the intuitions associated with sentences like (6)–(9): the explanation is insufficiently motivated. Intuitively, sentences (4) and (5) express propositions that are inconsistent. The *sole* motivation for thinking otherwise appears to be that, by so doing, we might emerge with a comparatively simple account of proper names: an account, according to which *all* such expressions, in *all* of their uses, function semantically as definite descriptions. But this argument is really no different from—and thus no better than—the Millian argument which claims that it is best to try to explain away the Russellian intuitions surrounding sentences like (6)–(9). For if we succeed in doing that, we might emerge with a comparatively simple account of proper names: an account according to which *all* such expressions, in *all* of their uses, function semantically in the same basic way. In both cases, there appears to be an *ad hoc* appeal to simplicity considerations. Simplicity is, of course, theoretically advantageous, but when it is at

---

[32] For Bach's view on the debate, see his (1994: ch. 4).

odds with intuitive considerations, the assumption that it trumps such consid-erations must be motivated.

5.3 *Simplicity and Issues of 'Use'*

There are two objections which might be leveled against the proposed account by Millians as well as Russellians. One such objection (adumbrated above) might appeal to the methodological criterion of *simplicity*. The simpler the theory, the better—but the proposed account lacks the simplicity of both its Millian and Russellian rivals. The proposed account is admittedly more *intuitive*, as it preserves intuitions from all sides, but as is well-known, intuitions can be misleading.

Simpler is indeed better, *other things being equal*; but other things are not equal; intuitions support the proposed view over its Millian and Russellian rivals. And while it is certainly possible that these intuitions are misleading, this is something for which an *argument* needs to be given. Not only that, but the rivals are not clearly simpler; indeed, their simplicity seems to be merely apparent. For while the *semantics* is simpler, the *pragmatics* is going to have to be considerably more complex. For an explanation—presumably a pragmatic one[33]—is going to have to be offered of those intuitions that conflict with the allegedly 'simpler' account. The Millian will have to account for intuitions surrounding utterances of sentences like (6)–(9). And the Russellian will have to account for intuitions surrounding utterances of sentences like (4) and (5).[34]

[33] By a 'pragmatic' explanation I mean an explanation of how what appears to be a fact about *word* meaning is actually a fact merely about *speaker* meaning.

[34] I have heard it claimed that pragmatic explanations are to be preferred to semantic ones—other things being equal—on the grounds that pragmatic explanations are, in a sense, 'free'. They are 'free' in the sense that they do not involve the introduction of any theoretical items or devices (including particular meanings) not independently motivated (see e.g. Neale, 1990: 80). This sort of attitude is reflected in Kripke's (1977) claim that it is 'very much the lazy man's approach' to postulate semantic ambiguities, when pragmatic explanations of the apparently semantic facts are available. While such explanations may well be 'free', they are to be preferred to their 'pricier' semantic counterparts *only if* things are 'otherwise equal'. But it is clear that, with respect to the competing accounts in question, things are *not* otherwise equal. For (as pointed out above) not only is it unclear what pragmatic accounts of the sort in question would look like, it is also clear that they would involve unintuitive postulations of word meaning/speaker meaning divergences. For those who (like Kripke, 1977) persist in viewing semantic ambiguity accounts of the sort in question as intuitively implausible, I would suggest that the seeming implausibility of such accounts is the result of construing semantic ambiguity on the model of expressions like 'bat', 'bank', and 'bond'. Such expressions have two (or more) *entirely distinct* meanings individuated by distinct etymologies. This is surely not true of ordinary

As we have just seen, this is easier said than done. No such explanations will be required on the proposed account, according to which there is a *convergence* between what is said and what is communicated in cases of the sort represented by (4)–(9)—just as there appears to be.

A second objection concerns the appeal to *use* involved in the proposed account. The *logical form* of a sentence has nothing to do with what *speakers* use the sentence to communicate; it has to do with what the *sentence itself* says. It is about semantics, not pragmatics. And so any purportedly 'semantic' theory, like the proposed theory, that talks in terms of communicative 'use', is mistaking pragmatics for semantics.

I do not understand this objection—or rather, I fail to see its force, although I have heard similar objections often.[35] So long as there is some *systematicity* in the sorts of uses appealed to, such uses are plausibly viewed as *semantically significant* uses. Indeed, both Millian and Russellian accounts of names receive support from the fact that the uses to which they appeal are *systematic*: speakers *standardly* use proper names as referring expressions, to express singular propositions; they *standardly* use such expressions as 'disguised' descriptions, to express general propositions. Now it has been pointed out, and with considerable force, that standard use is no *guarantee* of literal use.[36] Indeed, this point seems applicable to uses of sentences like 'I have three children'. Sentences of the form . . . *n* . . . (where *n* is some cardinal number) are *standardly* used to convey propositions of the form . . . *exactly n* . . . , though what they *literally express* is arguably of the form . . . *at least n* . . . But the cases in question are importantly different from such cases. For in cases of the latter sort, it is possible not only to discern a plausible candidate for the non-standard literal meaning, but also to suppose that the standard non-literal meaning might be *inferred from* the literal meaning on the basis of Gricean-style principles and maxims. Such is not the case with respect to the problematic cases in question (cases of the sort involving sentences like (4)–(9)). In such cases, what is said and what is meant appear to converge; the Gricean what is said/what is meant distinction seems not to be operative.

proper names, where the hypothesized dual meanings are importantly related. For a given name's Millian meaning (its referent) is thought of as 'satisfying' its (context-sensitive) descriptive meaning.

[35] Perhaps coming from a so-called 'type' (vs 'token') theorist like Bach, the objection does make some sense. For it views the enterprise of semantics as concerned primarily with the meaning of sentence types—and not with what such types express, relativized to contexts of utterance.

[36] See, for instance, Bach (1994).

5.4 Which Description?

A final sort of objection might be lodged against the proposed account by the Millian. In particular, it might be argued that there are serious problems with the idea that the uses of the names occurring in sentences like (6)–(9) are Russellian. For while such uses might not appear to be Millian, it is implausible to suppose that they are therefore Russellian. If such a supposition were true, it should be possible to determine *which particular description* the name in question was being used to 'abbreviate'. But this is not always possible. Often the (publicly accessible) context fails to determine a particular description, and even the speaker himself is not always able to provide a description that captures his intended meaning (what he 'has in mind'). Moreover, even if the speaker *could* invariably produce such a description, why suppose that it would be relevant to anything other than the proposition *meant*? Yet if there is no *principled* way of determining the particular definite description for which a particular use of a given name stands, then the Russellian aspect of the proposed account must surely be rejected or at least modified.

My response to the foregoing is twofold. First, suppose that we agree (if only for the moment), that not all non-Millian uses of names are descriptive: that such uses do not *invariably* stand for some *particular* definite description. It would not follow that *no* uses of names are Russellian. And surely *some* such uses are arguably Russellian. Suppose, for instance, that you overhear a conversation in which it is clearly being assumed that 'Hesperus' and 'Phosphorus' name different individuals. You wish to point out the falsity of this assumption, and attempt to do so via an assertive utterance of (6). It is not implausible to suppose that what you have said in such a case might be accurately paraphrased as (roughly): the individual named 'Hesperus' *is* the individual named 'Phosphorus'. For as Russell rightly remarks of such metalinguistic uses, 'This is a way in which names are frequently used in practice'.[37] That an expression is 'frequently used in practice' to mean such-and-such, is surely prima-facie evidence that such is what it does (or can) mean. And what,

---

[37] Russell (1919: 212). Russell continues, 'and there will, as a rule, be nothing in the phraseology to show whether they are being used in this way or as names'. Here, I disagree with Russell. It seems likely that identity statements between names, existential claims and denials, and certain *de dicto* belief reports like (9) all suggest a Russellian rather than Millian interpretation of the names used. As suggested above, this appears to be due to the fact that the linguistic context of an expression constrains what a speaker can reasonably intend to communicate by uttering a sentence containing that expression. Mill (1843) was also aware of the commonality of such a usage.

after all, is the alternative—that what you have in fact said is a 'pure tautology'? Is that *really* more plausible?

Indeed it is, one might suppose. For as Kripke (1980) rhetorically asks: 'Is it really possible that *Hesperus* might not have been *Phosphorus?*' 'No', we want to say: the 'two' are necessarily identical. Our negative response would seem to support the 'tautologous' reading of sentence (6). But does it? Although our negative response to Kripke's question is an accurate one, that suggests only that *when Kripke asks his rhetorical question, the names 'Hesperus' and 'Phosphorus' are functioning as Millian names.*[38] Yet this does not appear to be so in the case of a typical utterance of an identity sentence between co-referring names, as in an utterance of (6). In such cases, it is plausible to suppose that the names are functioning as 'disguised' descriptions. While I have claimed that the communicative intentions of the speaker are what determine whether a name is functioning as a Millian or Russellian name, such intentions will be constrained by the context in which the name is used. Thus, given the particular context in which Kripke uses the names 'Hesperus' and 'Phosphorus', a Millian reading of those names is more natural; whereas in the case of a typical utterance of an identity sentence like (6), a descriptive reading would be more natural.[39]

Second, Quine (1980) has proposed an ingenious, if remarkably simple, 'Russellian' solution to the problem posed by names for which no determinate descriptive paraphrase seems adequate.[40] Quine suggests treating such names as disguised descriptions of the form *the individual who N-izes*, descriptions which are then to be analyzed in accordance with Russell's Theory of Descriptions. I propose that this same basic strategy be used to analyze those descriptive *uses* of ordinary proper names for which no determinate descriptive paraphrase seems adequate. Although Quine himself describes the device as an 'artificial' one, this is not, in my opinion (nor, presumably, in Quine's) a drawback. For its application seems to yield results that are considerably more intuitive than those that would result from replacing the name, used descriptively, with some *arbitrary* definite description—a description which might, moreover, turn out to 'fit' neither the intuitive referent of the expression, nor

---

[38] For more on the issue of identity statements, see my (2000).

[39] What I mean to suggest here is that the context of utterance might make it difficult, if not impossible, for the speaker to (seriously) intend to communicate a singular proposition, where a general one would be more (contextually) appropriate, or to communicate a general proposition, where a singular one would be more appropriate.

[40] Quine, of course, was concerned primarily with providing an analysis of sentences containing empty names.

the speaker's intended referent.[41] Moreover, while the imprecision of such artificial predicates as 'Aristotle-izes' captures the imprecision often associated with the descriptive use of proper names, the general nature of the Russellian analysis captures the generality of the proposition expressed by a sentence containing a proper name, used descriptively.

6 Concluding Remarks

In conclusion, I would like to address two questions suggested by the proposed view. Might it be extended to *other* natural language expressions? If the proposed view is so plausible, why has it not been proposed before?

6.1 *Extending the Proposed Analysis*

If the proposed analysis of names is correct, then it would not be surprising if it could be extended to other natural language expressions. Indeed, it would be surprising if it could *not* be so extended. I would like to suggest, tentatively, that the proposed account of names be extended to: belief reports, natural kind terms, and possibly definite descriptions. If names can function as Millian names or as descriptions, then perhaps *belief reports* whose content clauses contain names in subject position are ambiguous: such that they admit of *de re* as well as *de dicto* readings. Although this view has been proposed before, it has often been challenged.[42] Description as well as Millian (or 'Direct Reference') accounts of *natural kind terms* have been proposed. The arguments for and against each of these two views parallel, in certain respects, those for and against description and Millian accounts of ordinary proper names.[43] This suggests that the debate over the semantics of natural kind terms might be resolved in a fashion similar to that over the semantics of ordinary proper names. Thus, perhaps the correct view is a *synthetic* one, according to which such expressions can function either as terms of Direct Reference or as 'disguised' descriptions, depending upon the communicative intentions of the speaker. As is well-known, there is a debate over whether *definite descriptions*

---

[41] In this way, Quine's proposal would enable the descriptivist to escape Kripke's criticism that the description associated with a proper name might describe an individual other than the bearer of the name.

[42] See, for instance, Salmon (1986) who claims, in effect, that all belief reports are *de re*, and Crimmins (1992) who claims, in effect, that all such reports are *de dicto*.

[43] This is made clear in Devitt and Sterelny (1987: ch. 3).

are ambiguous between Russellian (quantificational) and referential interpretations. If the proposed view is extended to definite descriptions, that would suggest that an ambiguity account is indeed correct, one according to which assertive utterances of sentences containing definite descriptions (in subject position) can express singular or general propositions.[44]

6.2 *Methodology*

There is something obvious—or at least unsurprising—about such 'dual use' accounts of natural language expressions. For such accounts have the effect of *preserving* (rather than explaining away) intuitions from all sides of a given debate. They say, in effect, that natural language expressions function pretty much as they appear to function. Some such expressions (proper names, natural kind terms, definite descriptions) can be used in sentences to express *singular* propositions (to 'say things') about the referent itself. These same expressions can also be used to express *general* propositions to the effect that whatever object or individual 'satisfies' the 'intentional content'[45] associated with the expression has such-and-such a property. Why, then, has such a view not been proposed before?

If we look at the general sorts of considerations that motivate semantic theories, the answer is clear. The semanticist begins with the plausible assumption that natural language is, in some sense, *systematic*. He then attempts to 'analyze' a few carefully selected examples (naturally, of the self-serving sort), from which he generalizes to other ostensibly similar cases, thereby emerging with a uniform theory that purportedly captures the systematicity of natural language. But is it the systematicity *of natural language* that is captured by such accounts?

Of course natural language must exhibit *some kind of* systematicity—without it, linguistic communication would simply not be possible. But one must bear in mind that the systematicity that pervades natural language will be of the sort required for *efficient communication*—rather than of the sort that looks pretty on paper. An account of proper names that claims that all such expressions are capable of functioning either as referring terms or as 'disguised' definite descriptions—depending upon the communicative intentions of the speaker—captures the relevant sort of systematicity.[46]

---

[44] See my (1997) for details.

[45] The locution is Searle's (1983).

[46] I would like to thank Mark Rivera, Larry James, and Kent Bach for helpful discussion on the topic of names. I would also like to thank an anonymous OUP reviewer for helpful comments on the penultimate draft of this chapter.

REFERENCES

Adams, F., and Stecker, R. (1994). 'Vacuous Singular Terms', *Mind and Language*, 9/4: 387–401.

Bach, K. (1994). *Thought and Reference* (Oxford: Oxford University Press).

Crimmins, M. (1992). *Talk about Beliefs* (Cambridge, Mass.: MIT Press).

Devitt, M. (1996). *Coming to Our Senses* (Cambridge, Mass.: MIT Press).

—— and Sterelny, K. (1987). *Language and Reality* (Cambridge, Mass.: MIT Press).

Dummett, M. (1983). 'Existence', in D.P. Chattopadhyaya (ed.), *Humans, Meanings, and Existences* (Jadavpur Studies in Philosophy, 5; Delhi). Reprinted in *The Seas of Language* (Oxford: Oxford University Press, 1993).

Grice, H. P. (1975). 'Logic and Conversation'. Reprinted in Martinich, 1996: 156–67.

Horn, L. (1989). *A Natural History of Negation* (Chicago: University of Chicago Press).

Kaplan, D. (1978). 'Dthat'. Reprinted in Martinich, 1996: 292–305.

Katz, J. (1994). 'Names without Bearers', *Philosophical Review*, 103: 1–39.

Kripke, S. (1977). 'Speaker's Reference and Semantic Reference', in P. Finch, T. Uehling, and H. Wettstein (eds.), *Contemporary Perspectives in the Philosophy of Language* (Minneapolis: University of Minnesota Press), 6–27.

—— (1979). 'A Puzzle about Belief'. Reprinted in Martinich, 1996: 382–409.

—— (1980). *Naming and Necessity* (Cambridge, Mass.: Harvard University Press).

Martinich, A. (1996). *The Philosophy of Language* (Oxford: Oxford University Press).

Mill, J. S. (1843). *A System of Logic* (New York: Harper Brothers).

Miller, B. (1975). 'In Defence of the Predicate "Exists"', *Mind*, 84: 338–54.

Neale, S. (1990). *Descriptions* (Cambridge, Mass.: MIT Press).

Peacocke, C. (1975). 'Proper Names, Reference, and Rigid Designation', in S. Blackburn (ed.), *Meaning, Reference, and Necessity* (Cambridge: Cambridge University Press).

Quine, W. (1980). *From a Logical Point of View* (Cambridge, Mass.: MIT Press).

—— and Ullian, J. (1970). *The Web of Belief* (New York: Random House).

Reimer, M. (1997). 'The Wettstein/Salmon Debate: Critique and Resolution', *Pacific Philosophical Quarterly*, 79/2: 130–51.

—— (2000). '*Hesperus = Phosphorus*: Contingent or Necessary?', *Facta Philosophica*, 2/1: 3–21.

—— (2001*a*). 'Russell and Strawson on Definite Descriptions', unpublished TS.

—— (2001*b*). 'Homer Arguments', *International Journal of Philosophical Studies*. (forthcoming)

—— (2001*c*). 'The Problem of Descriptively Introduced Names', *Linguistics and Philosophy*.

Russell, B. (1905). 'On Denoting'. Reprinted in B. Russell, *Logic and Knowledge*, ed. R. Marsh (London: George Allen & Unwin, 1956).

—— (1912). 'Knowledge by Acquaintance and Knowledge by Description', in *The Problems of Philosophy* (Indianapolis, Ind.: Hackett Publishing Co.).

Russell, B. (1918). 'The Philosophy of Logical Atomism'. Reprinted in B. Russell, *Logic and Knowledge*, ed. R. Marsh (London: George Allen & Unwin, 1956).

—— (1919). *Introduction to Mathematical Philosophy* (London: George Allen & Unwin).

Salmon, N. (1986). *Frege's Puzzle* (Cambridge, Mass.: MIT Press).

Searle, J. (1958). 'Proper Names', *Mind*, 67: 166–73.

—— (1983). *Intentionality* (Cambridge: Cambridge University Press).

Soames, S. (1989). 'Direct Reference and Propositional Attitudes', in J. Almong, J. Perry, and H. K. Wettstein (eds.), *Themes from Kaplan* (Oxford: Oxford University Press).

—— (1998). 'The Modal Argument, Wide Scope and Rigidified Descriptions', *Noûs*, 32/1: 1–22.

17

The Predicate View of Proper Names

REINALDO ELUGARDO

In this chapter, I will defend a modest claim: that the Predicate View of proper names, which is the view that 'proper names play the logical role of a predicate' (Burge, 1973), deserves another hearing. With the exception of Tyler Burge's early papers in which he defends the theory (Burge, 1973, 1974), and some published reactions (Bach, 1987; Boer, 1972; Cohen, 1980; Higginbotham, 1988; Hornsby, 1976), scant attention has been paid to the Predicate View—and for good reason: it conflicts with the widely accepted view that names are singular, unstructured, referring terms. Still, the Predicate View has strong evidential support that cannot be ignored or explained away. Some philosophers have tried to do the latter by arguing that predicative uses of proper names are just special uses. I will try to show, however, that they are mistaken by arguing that predicative uses of proper names are not parasitic on their referential roles, as some philosophers hold.

This chapter is divided into three major sections. In the first section, I discuss the Predicate View in more detail and contrast it with its main rival, the Individual Constant View. In the second section, I present and develop Burge's main argument for the Predicate View. In the third section, I consider several objections to his argument. In particular, I critically examine two strategies to explain away predicative uses of names in terms of their referential uses, and I respond to several objections to my arguments in the process. My aim is to show that the Predicate View has a lot to recommend it and thus that it deserves another look.

I Two Approaches to Proper Names

According to Tyler Burge, a formal, truth-theoretic, analysis of a natural language must be 'fully formalized' if it is to be an adequate theory of the language (1973: 425). In particular: 'the sense and reference (if any) of every expression of the theory should be unambiguously determinable from its form. Interpretation of the truth theory should depend on contextual parameter other than the inescapable one: the symbols of the theory are to be construed as symbols in the language of the theorist' (Burge, 1973: 426). Thus, if an expression of a truth-theory *T* for a natural language *L* represents a proper name in *L*, then the expression must be unambiguous in the language of *T* and its reference must be determined solely by its form rather than by context. By contrast, a proper name can be used to refer to different individuals (e.g. 'Aristotle') in different speech contexts, or so it would seem. Its particular reference on a given occasion of use is not fixed by its form but rather by the particular context in which it is used. The truth-theorist who wishes faithfully to represent proper names in her theory and comply with Burge's formalization constraint has two options: she can either index each name (or, rather, its formal representation) to its unique bearer or assign a class of objects to each name as its extension. Proper names are 'constant, noncomplex, singular terms' on the first option, but are predicates on the second option.[1] Let us consider each one in more detail.

1 *The Individual Constant View*

The first option is the Individual Constant View: proper names play the logical role of an individual constant (cf. Grice, 1969; Kaplan, 1990; Salmon, 1986). The individual constants of a formally defined, fully interpreted, language are

[1] The Predicate View and the Individual Constants View are not jointly exhaustive. For instance, Takashi Yagisawa argues that proper names play the role of bound individual variables (cf. Yagisawa, 1984). The idea is, roughly, that a sentence like, 'Bertrand Russell was a logician', is semantically equivalent to an existential generalization of the form, '$\exists x(Cx \& Lx)$', where 'Cx' expresses a 'baptismal-event' condition under which some individual or other was given the name 'Bertrand Russell' and 'Lx' expresses the property of being a logician. The proper name, 'Bertrand Russell', is eliminated at the level of logical form and its referential role is taken over by the (semantically evaluated) bound variable (relative to an assignment of values to individual variables). The context in which the first sentence is uttered determines which particular 'Bertrand Russell'-conferring baptismal event 'Cx' expresses, if it expresses any. For my purposes, I will restrict my remarks in this chapter to the Predicate View and to the Individual Constants View.

indexed to the objects that are their uniquely assigned semantic values, relative to an interpretation function for the language. Similarly, a formalized truth-theory for a natural language that contains proper names will index each name (in the metalanguage) to its one and only bearer if it has one. The theory will therefore contain as many different base reference clauses as there are names indexed to their unique bearers.

For instance, given that I know several people named 'William Clinton', a truth-theory for the English I speak will (on this view) index (semantically) different names of the same type of syntactic design, one for each William Clinton I know, will ever come to meet, hear about, etc. It will contain a finite but very large number of primitive reference axioms. For example, it will contain (α) and (β) among its many base reference clauses, where William Clinton$_1$ (=the actual US President in 2000) and William Clinton$_2$ (=Elugardo's doctor) are distinct individuals:

(α) 'William Clinton$_1$', refers to x if and only if x = William Clinton$_1$

(β) 'William Clinton$_2$', refers to x if and only if x = William Clinton$_2$

(α) is the designation-rule for the name that is the name of (and *only* of) the person who is the last actual US President of the twentieth century; (β) is the designation-rule for the name that is the name of (and *only* of) my physician. Since names are (on this view) semantically type-individuated by their bearers even if they happen to share the same phonological form, (α) and (β) are designation-rules for different names.

The Individual Constant View is very plausible. After all, proper names have certain semantic features that are characteristic of individual constants. First, names that occur in sentences in a singular and unmodified form purport to designate a single object rather than a plurality of objects. Second, unlike singular bare demonstratives, names specify the objects they designate. Third, proper names contribute their bearers in determining the propositions expressed by the sentences that contain them (relative to a context of utterance).[2]

---

[2] Not everyone accepts the claim that proper names are Millian designators. Fregeans, e.g. contend that names also contribute some cognitively significant information (a sense) about their bearers or a mode of presentation of their bearers. According to them, co-referential names can differ in the modes of presentation or information that they allegedly contribute; in which case, extensionally equivalent sentences differing only in that they contain co-referential but syntactically different names will express different propositions. Along the same vein, other philosophers contend that names, like other words, contribute (in addition to their reference) some metalinguistic information about themselves *qua* linguistic expressions, e.g. their grammatical category. Burge holds a version of names that combines the Fregean and metalinguistic views.

Fourth, given that names do not have any internal structure, they do not, in addition, describe their bearers—they merely 'tag' or 'label' them. Names are unlike definite descriptions in that respect. They designate their bearers directly, that is, without the mediation of a uniquely identifying definite description or a weighted cluster of descriptions. Fifth, it follows from the last two observations that names are rigid designators: each name designates its actual bearer (if it has one) in every counterfactual situation (Kripke, 1971; Salmon, 1986).

On the other hand, we can get at the semantic facts of an expression by determining what the full competence in the use of an expression would consist in, since having full competence would reflect all the semantic facts there are about the expression. Consider, then, the following example. My full competence in the use of 'William Clinton' consists in my knowing that 'William Clinton' refers (in my English idiolect) to its bearer(s) if it refers at all. However, my knowledge of that semantic fact does not, in turn, consist in my knowing, with respect to *each* object that bears the name—or, rather, that bears an (indexed) expression of the same syntactic type—that *it* bears the name. After all, several thousands of people (not to mention boats, statues, and other sundry objects) are each named, 'William Clinton', almost all of whom I do not even know. And, of the ones I do know, it is not necessary that I know, with respect to them, that they bear the name if I am to be competent in the use of the name. For one thing, I may have forgotten that a certain William Clinton I once knew is named 'William Clinton'. But loss of that particular piece of knowledge does not undermine my competence to use the name referentially—even to use it to refer to him once I recall his name. For another thing, I may mistake different William Clintons for one another; in which case, given the Individual Constant View, I always get their names wrong whenever I utter 'William Clinton' in reference to either of them. If so, then 'William Clinton' lacks a designated semantic value, relative to any context in which I utter a sentence containing the name. However, that is not right since, depending on the sentence I use, one can correctly report that I said something true about one of them although what I meant is false of the one I referred to by my utterance of 'William Clinton' if I referred to anyone. Finally, suppose that I falsely believe of someone that his name is 'William Clinton'. Again, that will not necessarily eliminate my competence to use 'William Clinton' referentially. I would still be able to use the name to refer to objects that bear it (or that bear some 'indexed' version of it) as their name. For all of these reasons, the Individual Constant View does not do justice to our semantic competence of proper names.[3] Let us, then, consider the Predicate View.

2 The Predicate View

Like the Individual Constant View, the Predicate View is about how proper names should best be formally represented in a truth-theory for a natural language that contains names. On the Predicate View, a formalized truth-theory for a natural language containing proper names will have, for each name, just one predicative base clause, rather than a plurality of reference base clauses for different names of the same syntactic type.

For example, a formal truth-theory for the English that I speak will have (on this view) the following predicate clause for the one name, 'William Clinton':

> (χ) For any x, sequence s, x is in the extension of 'William Clinton' (in English), [i.e. x is William Clinton] relative to s if and only if x is named 'William Clinton'.

Given (χ), one can then say that a sequence of objects satisfies the open sentence, 'x_i is a William Clinton', if and only if the ith member of the sequence that is assigned as a value to 'x_i' is in the extension of 'William Clinton' relative to that sequence. Now an object is in the extension of a name if and only if the name is *true of* it. According to Burge, a proper name is '(literally) true of an object just in case that object is given that name in an appropriate way' and thus, 'the name itself enters into the conditions under which it is applicable' (Burge, 1973: 430). It follows that an object is a William Clinton if and only if it is given the name, 'William Clinton', in some appropriate way—however an object is given a name or acquires a name.[4] Thus, on the Predicate View, the extension of 'William Clinton' in my English idiolect is the set of objects that bear the name, which includes the last US President in the twentieth century and my family doctor, among many others.

In contrast to the Individual Constant View, the Predicate View does justice to our semantic knowledge of proper names. My semantic knowledge about 'William Clinton' consists in my knowing that 'William Clinton' is true of X (in English) if and only if X is named 'William Clinton', for any X.[5] My

---

[3] For other criticisms of the Individual Constant View, see Burge (1975) and Hornsby (1976).

[4] Steven Boer (1975) denies this last step. I will discuss his reasons for rejecting it in the second part of this chapter.

[5] Again, it is important to point out that not everyone agrees with this claim, e.g. Boer, Kripke *et al.*

knowing such a rule partially explains why I also know this: regardless of the particular context in which it is uttered, any sentence of the form, 'William Clinton is F', is true in English just in case there is a certain individual or object, referred to by the speaker of the sentence, who is named or called 'William Clinton' and who has the property expressed by the predicate represented by 'is F'. I know which proposition is expressed by an utterance of a sentence of that form, relative to a context, once I know which individual, if any, meets the referential and predicative condition expressed on the right-hand side, relative to that context. My full competence in the use of 'William Clinton' consists, then, in my knowing its condition of literal application.

Earlier I noted that supporters of the Individual Constant View can explain why it is that names appear to be rigid, directly referential, Millian, singular designators. Their explanation is that names behave like individual constants, which in turn have the same properties. It would seem, then, that the Predicate View Theorist is forced to deny the appearances. Well, not entirely. On the Predicate View, a name does not 'abbreviate *another* predicate, even a roughly coextensive predicate such as 'is an entity called 'PN'' (Burge, 1973: 428–9).[6]

---

[6] Burge is committed to holding that e.g. 'Aristotle' is a predicate that is necessarily extensionally equivalent to a metalinguistic predicate, namely, 'x is a bearer of "Aristotle"'. He is not, however, committed to the thesis that, when it occurs in singular unmodified form, 'Aristotle' is extensionally equivalent to 'the bearer of "Aristotle"' (Bach, 1987). For, in its unmodified form, 'Aristotle' is true of a plurality of things that bear the name; in that case, the corresponding metalinguistic definite description is improper and, hence, denotationless (assuming that the mentioned name is a case of a name-type). According to Jerrold J. Katz, 'Aristotle was a Greek' is synonymous with 'The individual who is a bearer of "Aristotle" was a Greek' (cf. Katz, 1990, 1994). Burge would reject Katz's analysis on the grounds that sentences like 'Aristotle was a Greek' do not express, as part of their semantic meaning, a uniqueness condition or an existence condition. By the same token, Burge's own analysis is subject to Kripke-type modal objections to the effect that e.g. 'Aristotle' and 'x is a bearer of "Aristotle"' are not necessarily extensionally equivalent predicates. A possible countermove is to distinguish the assertoric content of an utterance of a sentence containing a singular, unmodified occurrence of a name from what the speaker meant to communicate by his utterance and from its semantic value(s) relative to a possible world. The idea would be that 'Aristotle' (*qua* predicate) and 'x is a bearer of "Aristotle"' are true of the same things in every world, but which things they are true of will vary from world to world. None the less, the assertoric content of an utterance of 'Aristotle was a Greek' and the assertoric content of an utterance of 'That individual named "Aristotle" was a Greek', relative to a context of use, are the same even though the speaker may have meant to communicate different things by his utterances. See Stanley (1997) for a defense of this general line of argument. For a critical discussion of Jerrold Katz's descriptivist view of proper names, see Bach (1997) and Braun (1995).

Rather, each 'proper name is a predicate in its own right' (Burge, 1973: 429). The Predicate View presents an 'austere' view of names (Platts, 1997): they do not semantically abbreviate a (weighted) set of descriptive predicates that their bearer(s) uniquely or saliently satisfy—names lack descriptive content. The Predicate View is therefore incompatible with the Russellian view that proper names semantically abbreviate some definite description (or a weighted cluster of uniquely identifying descriptions) that denotes its bearer (Russell, 1905, 1918). It is also incompatible with Alvin Plantinga's view that proper names express individual essences (Plantinga, 1978). Although the Predicate View is compatible with it, it is distinct from Quine's thesis that names semantically abbreviate a general term that can be artificially transformed from them (Quine, 1963, 1972).

If names are predicates, then they should have modified occurrences. Indeed, they do. For instance, names can occur in plural form:

(1) There were several *Pauls* at the party last night.

They can also take the definite and indefinite articles:

(2) *A* Mary Kim won the spelling bee.
(3) *The* Tyler Burge I know would never have said that.

Names can also be concatenated with quantifier words:

(4) *Every* Tom, Dick, and Harry is a womanizer; but not *every* Paul is.
(5) *Most* Sebastians live in Europe, but a *few* live in the United States.
(6) *Many* Kennedys attended the wedding yesterday.
(7) *There is only one* Frank Sinatra and he had a great voice.

Like count nouns, names can be prefixed with numerical adjectives and other adjectival modifiers:

(8) I met *five* Marys at last year's APA Eastern Division Conference.
(9) Teddy is the *biggest* Kennedy of them all.

Names can have mass occurrences:

(10) He still has a lot of Winston Churchill left in him.

They can also have *non-literal* occurrences; in fact, sentences (10) and (11) can be used either literally or figuratively:

(11) George Wallace is a Napoleon. (Burge, 1973, 429)

We have, then, some indirect empirical evidence for the Predicate View.

On the other hand, even though proper names sometimes have modified occurrences, it does not follow that they are predicates. The most that follows is that they can occur as components of syntactically complex phrases that semantically behave as general terms (Katz, 1994). That is compatible with the view that names are singular terms. After all, other singular referring devices can exhibit similar predicate-like features. For example, sentences (12) and (13) contain non-referential, modified, occurrences of an indexical (Cohen, 1980), but no one would conclude that indexicals are predicates:

(12)   Some people fear the *hereafter*. (Cohen, 1980: 151)
(13)   That cat is a *he*. (Cohen, 1980: 150)

Indeed, one could use Cohen's examples to show that, given Burge's grammatical data, proper names (like indexicals) are in the logico-semantic category of directly referential singular terms. In which case, all modified occurrences of proper names are simply cases of special uses of singular referring terms.

An argument is needed, then, for the claim that proper names are predicates, one that builds on the empirical truth that proper names have modified occurrences. Presumably, a sufficient condition for an expression to be a predicate (in the semantic sense) is that it be true of the things that fall under it. Thus, if it can be independently shown that names are true of their bearers (if they have any), then we may conclude that they are predicates. Burge argues in that fashion for the Predicate View. I will now turn to his argument in the next section and then defend it against some objections in the third section.

II Burge's Main Argument for the Predicate View

Here is a quick sketch of Burge's argument. First, all modified and unmodified occurrences of the same proper name are semantically connected in a unified way. Second, the Predicate View provides the best explanation of that fact, whereas the Individual Constant View does not explain it at all. The Predicate View explains the connection in terms of a single semantic relation, namely, the *true of* relation: regardless of whether a name has a modified occurrence or an unmodified occurrence in a sentence, it is true of all and only the things that bear it. By contrast, the Individual Constant View must either deny the apparent connection between modified and unmodified occurrences of the same name or give a 'disunified' explanation. So, all things being equal, assuming that the two hypotheses are the only plausible competitors, we are justified in thinking that names function as predicates in both their modified and unmodified occurrences. I will now discuss Burge's argument in more detail.

1 The First Stage of Burge's Argument

The first stage of Burge's argument consists of two premises:

(P1) All modified and unmodified occurrences of a given name are semantically connected (assuming sameness of reference, disambiguation, etc.).

(P2) 'Postulation of special uses of a term, semantically unrelated to what are taken to be its paradigmatic uses, is theoretically undesirable— particularly if a straightforward semantic relation between these different uses can be found.' (Burge 1973)

I will discuss (P1) first and then conclude this subsection with some brief remarks about (P2).

1.1 The Case for Premise (P1)

According to Burge, 'it would be a mistake to think that... modified and unmodified occurrences of ordinary proper names are semantically independent of each other' (1973: 430). The reason is that 'the modified proper names in the examples just given have the same conditions for literal application to an object that singular, unmodified proper names have' (Burge, 1973: 429). If so, then premise (P1) is true. The following example illustrates Burge's point.

Imagine a context in which a certain Mary Kim is the winner of the local school's annual spelling bee. Suppose that a certain school parent, who doesn't know who Mary is but knows that the winner is someone named 'Mary Kim', reports (14) to his spouse:

(14) A Mary Kim won the spelling bee

Meanwhile, Mary's best friend utters (15) to a mutual acquaintance and, in the process, refers to Mary by her utterance of 'Mary Kim':

(15) Mary Kim won the spelling bee

Both reports are literal and true. The person who won the spelling bee in question, namely, Mary Kim, makes the statements made in each instance true. More importantly, the conditions under which the modified occurrence of 'Mary Kim', as uttered by the parent, literally applies to Mary Kim are the same conditions under which the unmodified occurrence of 'Mary Kim', as uttered by her best friend, literally applies to her. The condition is simply this: she, Mary Kim, bears the name, 'Mary Kim'. Putting it that way does not beg the question against someone who thinks that proper names are singular terms. Similar comments apply to Burge's other data sentences mentioned earlier.

Here is another reason in support of premise (P1): certain propositions expressed by sentences containing modified occurrences of proper names entail, or are entailed by, other propositions expressed by sentences containing unmodified occurrences of the same name. In the 'Mary Kim' example, (15) entails (14). (16) and (17) entail (18), relative to a context in which a speaker of all three sentences refers to a certain Wally Cox by her utterance of 'Wally Cox' in (17). Assume that all three occurrences of 'the party' have the same reference in (16), (17), and (18), and that both occurrences of 'Wally Cox' have the same reference in (17) and (18), respectively:

(16) Every Wally Cox who was at the party danced.
(17) Wally Cox was at the party.
(18) Wally Cox danced.

The inference from (15) to (14) and the inference from (16) and (17) to (18) are enthymemic since one cannot formally deduce (14) or (18) without the use of (19) and (20), respectively:

(19) Mary Kim is a Mary Kim
(20) Wally Cox is a Wally Cox

We do not explicitly use (19) or (20) because we assume that each is an obvious truth, as they would be if modified occurrences of a given name have the same conditions of literal application as unmodified occurrences of the same name.[7] But, even though both inferences are enthymemes, they are formally valid when they are fully expanded. So, once again, we have strong evidence in favor of (P1).

1.2 The Case for Premise (P2)

Premise (P2) is a methodological claim that places an adequacy condition on any semantic account of proper names:

---

[7] Steven Boer thinks that they do not have the same conditions of literal application, which explains why he would reject (19) and (20) as 'obvious truths'. I will discuss Boer's objection in the third section.

(P2) 'Postulation of special uses of a term, semantically unrelated to what are taken to be its paradigmatic uses, is theoretically undesirable— particularly if a straightforward semantical relation between these different uses can be found.' (Burge, 1973: 430)

In other words, an adequate semantic account of proper names must specify a semantic relation between modified and unmodified occurrences of proper names that explains (P1). Given (P2), one should reject any view that reckons modified and plural occurrences of names as special uses, i.e. occurrences that have no semantic connection to the paradigmatic, referential, uses of proper names. The arguments that I presented on behalf of (P1) also render (P2) plausible. After all, if names have the same conditions of application in both of their modified and unmodified occurrences, then it is *ad hoc* to treat their predicative occurrences as special uses. As I noted above, certain propositions expressed by sentences containing modified occurrences of proper names entail, or are entailed by, other propositions expressed by sentences containing unmodified occurrences of the same name. On a 'special use' account, such entailment relations are illusory, which they are not. Besides, since defenders and critics of the Predicate View can accept (P2), it is uncontroversial although it serves an important role in Burge's argument. I conclude that (P2) is acceptable. (By the way, (P2) can be used to deflect Cohen's examples involving modified indexicals and demonstratives. There is a single semantic relation that connects the modified and unmodified occurrences of proper names: the relation of an object's acquiring a name *as its name* in some appropriate way. By contrast, indexicals and demonstratives are not names of anything. Thus, there is no comparable story to be told about how the modified and unmodified occurrences of indexicals semantically connect—in fact, they do not connect at all precisely because they are not names. If the 'special uses' account applies anywhere, it applies to modified occurrences of indexicals and demonstratives.)

2 The Second Stage of Burge's Argument

The second part of Burge's argument also consists of two premises:

(P3) The Predicate View provides a unified account of both modified and unmodified occurrences of proper names that explains (P1).

(P4) The Individual Constant View cannot provide a unified account of both modified and unmodified occurrences of proper names that explains (P1).

I will now try to make the case for (P3), and then conclude with a defense of (P4).

2.1 *The Case for Premise (P3)*

Suppose that the Predicate View is true. Then, given premise (P1), it follows that proper names are predicates even when they occur in a singular unmodified form. Thus, a full defense of premise (P3) would involve an explanation of how names can function as predicates when they occur in a singular unmodified form. In this section, I will sketch the Predicate View Theorist's explanation.

First, a concession: it is counter-intuitive to claim that proper names are predicates even when they occur in a singular unmodified form. After all, the name, 'Jerry Fodor', does not appear to be playing a predicative role in the sentence, 'Jerry Fodor enjoys sailing'.[8] It does not purport to be standing for a group or a kind. If anything, its role in the sentence appears to be one of designating its bearer, relative to a context of utterance. Suppose I utter 'Jerry Fodor enjoys sailing' in a conversation about philosophers and their hobbies. Relative to my utterance of that sentence, 'Jerry Fodor' designates just one entity, namely, Jerry Fodor, the famous philosopher who teaches at Rutgers University. Relative to that context, the name does not designate everyone named 'Jerry Fodor', either individually or collectively. It just designates *him*.

(The Predicate View can accommodate the idea that names are characteristically used as *singular designators*. For example, Burge defines a notion of a *name-designation* that is consistent with the Predicate View (but see n. 21). A name, N, is said to *designate* an object, O, relative to a speaker's utterance of a sentence containing N exactly if the speaker refers to O in her utterance of N in the sentence and N is true of O (Burge, 1973: 434). Thus, relative to my utterance of 'Jerry Fodor enjoys sailing', 'Jerry Fodor' designates (in Burge's sense) Jerry Fodor, the famous philosopher, and not anything else. The reason is twofold: first, I referred to *him* by my utterance of 'Jerry Fodor' in that

---

[8] We can say more, though, in response: how an expression is characteristically used need not always reflect its logical form. To use a well-known analogy, definite descriptions are arguably quantified restrictive nominals even though they are not characteristically used in that way— they are instead typically used as singular referential terms. Similarly, one could argue that, even though proper names are characteristically used to refer to particular objects, they behave as predicates even when they occur in a singular unmodified form. The burden, then, is on the Predicate Theorist to explain how proper names, when they occur in an unmodified form, can be used as singular referring terms if they are predicates. This problem is addressed, if only briefly, below.

sentence and, second, the name I uttered is *true of* him given that he bears it. And yet, 'Jerry Fodor' is a general term if the Predicate View is true. If it is true, then some general terms can be used to designate, in a singular mode, some of the things they are true of, relative to a context of utterance. A name designates a single object by its tokened occurrence only if certain pragmatic conditions for speaker reference (whatever they may be) obtain.)

Does the fact that names, in their singular unmodified form, can be used for singular reference pose a problem for the Predicate View? Not really—not if a plausible story can be told about how a name can be used to designate, relative to a context of utterance, one of its bearers even though it functions as a predicate. Suppose, once again, that I utter 'Jerry Fodor enjoys sailing' and I refer to Jerry Fodor in the process. I said something true by my utterance only if, relative to my referential utterance of 'Jerry Fodor enjoys sailing' in that sentence, the name designates (in Burge's sense of 'designates') Fodor and only if he enjoys sailing. If it does designate him, then that cannot be because I tokened a name that he has. For, if the Predicate View is correct, I uttered a name that is true of everyone who bears it; and yet, my utterance of the name does not designate (in Burge's sense) any of them—it designates only him, the famous philosopher, Jerry Fodor. So, something else must also be involved in addition to the fact that the name I uttered is his name.

The additional condition is that only he, and not the other Jerry Fodors of the world, stands in some appropriate contextual relation to my utterance, one that makes him (and not the other ones) the object of my referential act. If that is right, then it is plausible to postulate, at the level of logical form, a linguistic mechanism that makes that contextual connection possible, namely, a determiner. The idea then is that, in its singular unmodified form, 'Jerry Fodor', involves a *suppressed determiner* which, relative to the context of utterance, fixes Fodor as the referent of my utterance of her name. The name I used is also *true of* him since he, like several others, acquired the name in some appropriate way. (Note: the argument I presented does not lead, necessarily, to the suppressed determiner thesis. Its premises are compatible with the claim that proper names are restricted nominals. For instance, depending on the context, 'Jerry Fodor enjoys sailing' can be used to express different propositions about different individuals. Given that fact, the semantic value of 'Jerry Fodor' would be an ordered pair consisting of, first, the set of individuals named 'Jerry Fodor' and, second, a contextually determined function from that set onto a class of objects. In my example, the relevant class would be the class of philosophers who teach at Rutgers. The intersection of the two would be the class containing only *Jerry Fodor*, the famous philosopher. The general idea is developed in

Stanley and Szabo (2000) in their discussion of quantified nominal expressions. Although they do not apply their analysis to singular proper nouns, their analysis can easily be extended to them if sentences containing unmodified names can be parsed into ones in which they appear as predicates.)

So far, only two candidates for the (alleged) implicit determiner have been proposed in the literature. Tyler Burge suggests that the relevant determiner is a (suppressed) *bare demonstrative* (Burge, 1973, 1974; see also Recanati, 1993). In other words, singular unmodified names are complex demonstratives whose predicate nominals, i.e. the names themselves, are restricted quantificational NPs.[9] On Burge's analysis, the sentence 'Jerry Fodor enjoys sailing' is semantically equivalent in meaning to 'That Jerry Fodor enjoys sailing'. On Burge's view of bare demonstratives, the implicit demonstrative element is formally marked in a truth-theory by a free individual variable that occurs in an open singular term, for example, '[x] [Jerry Fodor(X)](Enjoys Sailing(X))'. On a different version of the unmodified-names-as-implicit-complex-demonstratives, the logical form of a sentence like, 'Jerry Fodor enjoys sailing', is '$\iota X[X =$ that & Jerry Fodor(X)]Enjoys Sailing(X)'. On that version, the demonstrative element occurs as an individual constant occurring inside a closed singular term.

Richard Larson and Gabriel Segal have offered a different proposal: the suppressed determiner is *the definite article*. On their view, singular unmodified proper names function as (referentially used) incomplete definite descriptions (Larson and Segal, 1995). Thus, on their proposal, 'Jerry Fodor enjoys sailing' is semantically equivalent in meaning to 'The Jerry Fodor enjoys sailing'. At the level of logical form, the implicit uniqueness condition is marked by a bound individual variable that occurs in a closed singular term, for example, '$\iota X[$Jerry Fodor(X)]Enjoys Sailing(X)'. On both proposals, unmodified proper names function as predicate nominals. No doubt, there are other proposals concerning the implicit determiner.

(One reason for endorsing Burge's proposal is that it can be used to explain how names can be used to rigidly designate their bearers even though they are predicates. According to him, bare demonstratives behave as free individual variables (relativized-to-a-sequence-of-value-assignments). In standard, first-order, modal quantificational logic with identity, free individual variables (relativized-to-a-sequence-of-value-assignments-from-a-nonempty-domain-

---

[9] For a defense of the general view that all complex demonstratives are descriptions whose common nominals are restricted quantificational NPs, see Lepore and Ludwig (2000). For views that oppose the Lepore–Ludwig account, see Borg (2000), Braun (1994), and King (1999).

of-objects-at-a-possible-world) are rigid designators since they function as Millian designators in all linguistic contexts (Kaplan, 1977, 1978; Salmon, 1989). If so, and if Burge's view of demonstratives is correct, then demonstratives are rigid designators. Suppose they are. Suppose, also, that singular unmodified names *qua* predicates are part of the literal content of an implicit complex demonstrative and are modally stable in their literal applications. Then, if singular unmodified proper names are (implicit) complex demonstratives involving the name as a general term, then they are used *rigidly* if only in a quixotic sense. For the implicit demonstrative element is doing all the work when it comes to rigid designation—the complex demonstrative is then a rigid designator. Defending all of the foregoing assumptions is a tall order.[10] Still, the main point is that the Predicative View has the conceptual resources for explaining how proper names, when they occur in a singular unmodified form, can be used rigidly even though they are predicates.)

To sum up the case for premise (P3): if proper names are predicates, then the fact mentioned in (P1) is unsurprising. For, according to the Predicate View, proper names are general terms, which are represented in a formal truth-theory as predicates. Unmodified occurrences of a proper name are occurrences of complex noun phrases in which the name behaves as a general term prefixed by a suppressed (unpronounced) determiner. Even in these cases, unmodified names would be formally represented as predicate components of open or closed singular terms. In both cases, the predicate satisfaction clauses for names will be the same: a proper name is true of an object just in case the object is standardly called by that name or was given the name in some appropriate way. The relation of a name's being *true of* its bearers is the semantic relation that connects both its modified and unmodified occurrences. Thus, the Predicate View presents a unified formal treatment of both modified and unmodified literal occurrences of proper names, one that explains why (P1) is true. If so, then (P3) is justified.

2.2 *The Case for Premise (P4)*

Premise (P4) states:

(P4) The Individual Constant View cannot provide a unified account of both modified and unmodified occurrences of proper names that explains (P1), i.e., the fact that both kinds of occurrences are semantically connected. (Burge, 1973: 437).

---

[10] For an interesting attempt to explain how such an account might go, see Ezcurdia (2000).

The main argument for (P4) is that, on the Individual Constant View, modified and unmodified occurrences of the same name-form are homophonous: they are occurrences of different words with different semantic meanings. Modified occurrences of proper names are formally represented as predicates in the truth-theory, but unmodified occurrences of names are formally represented as individual constants. Predicates and individual constants are semantically different, as reflected in their base clauses in a truth-theory. It follows, then, that a formal representation of a sentence like 'Mary Kim is a Mary Kim' will not express an obvious, context-independent truth in any sense.

And so, either modified and unmodified occurrences of proper names are not semantically connected in any unified way (in spite of appearances to the contrary), or one would have to give a complicated, 'disunified', 'special use' kind of explanation of their connection. The first disjunct contradicts (P1) and the second disjunct violates the methodological premise (P2). Either way, the Individual Constant View is objectionable. All things being equal, we should prefer the Predicate View to the Individual Constant View. For, if no other theoretical hypothesis explains why (P1) is true, and if there are no compelling arguments against the Predicate View, then we have a prima-facie strong reason for thinking that names are predicates in their own right.

3 *Postscript*

I have just presented and defended the main premises of Burge's abductive argument for the Predicate View. Admittedly, the argument is inconclusive. The reason is that other possible, hitherto unconsidered, rival theories of names might be able to explain the same grammatical data. Another reason is that there are some telling objections to the Predicate View.[11] To take the first point: Takashi Yagisawa's (1984) view of proper names might be able to explain (P1). According to him, singular unmodified occurrences of proper names

[11] Richard Larson and Gabriel Segal's version of the Predicate View is also open to some doubt. For instance, it ought to follow on their view that the sentence, 'Aristotle is not wise', is semantically ambiguous. The reason is that its counterpart, 'The Aristotle is not wise', is subject to non-equivalent expansions given differences in quantifier scope-readings (assuming that definite descriptions are restrictive quantifiers). But the first sentence is unambiguous. Also, on both Burge's proposal and on the Larson–Segal proposal, a singular unmodified proper name should take restrictive clauses given that complex demonstratives and definite descriptions can. But names do not take restrictive clauses (Higginbotham, 1988). It remains to be seen whether these objections can be satisfactorily met.

function, at the level of logical form, as individual bound variables that are matched with a special 'baptismal' predicate. Perhaps the same technical apparatus can be used to explain and formally represent modified occurrences of names. (The jury is out on that question, but see n. 23.) But even if it cannot, there may be other, hitherto unknown, theories that can explain Burge's data without entailing the Predicate View.

To take the second point made above: James Higginbotham (1988) argues that Burge's account of singular unmodified proper names is flawed. His argument is that sentences like 'Jerry Fodor enjoys sailing' do not have the same truth-conditions as sentences like 'That Jerry Fodor enjoys sailing'. There can be situations in which an utterance of the latter sentence is true even though nothing follows, one way or the other, as to whether an utterance of the former sentence by the same speaker would have been true or false in the same situation. (I suspect that Higginbotham will say that a variation of his criticism also applies to Larson and Segal's proposal.) On the other hand, Higginbotham's argument fails if different kinds of directing intentions can determine different truth-conditions for the same referential utterance, whether it be an utterance of 'Jerry Fodor enjoys sailing' or an utterance of 'That Jerry Fodor enjoys sailing' (cf. Bach, 1992; Ezcurdia, 2000). (The jury is out on that question too.)

For my present purposes, I will assume without argument that the Predicate View Theorist can adequately respond to both challenges. My concern in this essay is with two other objections that are directed against the premises of Burge's argument. The first objection is that premise (P3) is false because Burge's account of the conditions under which a name is said to be true of an object is mistaken. The second objection is that premise (P4) is false: the Individual Constant View can provide a unified account of both modified and unmodified occurrences of proper names that explains (P1). Both objections will be taken up in the next section. I will argue therein that both criticisms fail.

III Objections to Burge's Argument

Thus far, I have presented Burge's main reason for thinking that the Predicate View is true: it provides the best explanation of the semantic connection between unmodified and modified occurrences of proper names. The explanation rests, though, on the assumption that names are true of objects just in case the objects acquired the names in some appropriate way. The first objection in this section is designed to show that that assumption is false. After presenting the objection, I will offer some concessions but argue that the basic insight of the Predicate View about the application conditions of names is still right.

1 First Objection: Premise (P4) is False Because a Name can be True of an Object and Not be its Name

Steven Boer gives the following example (Boer, 1975). Assume, for the sake of discussion, that 'Romanov' refers to the famous Russian family dynasty. Then, on that interpretation, sentence (21) can come out true:

(21) Waldo Cox (my gardener) is a Romanov

where (21) is to be understood as reporting 'an exciting fact revealed by recent historical investigations' (Boer, 1975: 390). By hypothesis, Cox never got, and never will get, the name 'Romanov'. So (21) comes out false on Burge's analysis, which is the wrong result. This a case, then, where a name is true of an individual who is not given the name in any appropriate way.

Furthermore, (21) has two different readings. On one reading (i.e. the Burgean reading), it is a condition on the semantic application of the predicate that it be self-referential: X is a Romanov if and only if X has the name 'Romanov'. Thus, on the self-referential reading of the predicate, (21) means that Wally Cox has the name 'Romanov', which is false. On another reading, it is not a condition on the applicability of the predicate that it be self-referential; rather, on the non-self-referential reading, X is a Romanov if and only if X is a member of the Romanov family. On that reading, (21) means that Wally Cox is a member of the famous Romanov family, which we are supposing is true. Boer contends that Burge conflates these two readings and, as a consequence, his account 'achieves theoretical simplicity at the cost of falsifying the empirical data' (Boer, 1975: 391).

2 Reply to the First Objection

Boer essentially makes two different claims against Burge's view:

Thesis I: One and the same expression can serve as a singular proper noun and as a genetic family name (i.e. a common noun) even in the same linguistic context. It is important to keep these separate—especially in providing a semantic theory for names.

Thesis II: Burge's claim that 'a proper name is (literally) true of an object just in case that object is given that name in an appropriate way' (1973: 393) is false.

Thesis I is true and is supported by the fact that sentences like (21) are ambiguous. Defenders of the Predicate View should therefore concede *Thesis I* and admit that the empirical data about names are much more complicated than what Burge suggests. At the very least, a correct semantic theory for a language that contains names will have to distinguish proper names from genetic family names in the metalanguage and provide different semantic rules for each.

Thesis II is also true given *Thesis I*. However, Burge may have a more liberal analysis in mind anyway. Consider, for example, the following passage:

> In holding that a name applies to an object just in case the object bears a certain pragmatic relation to that name, I am suggesting that the name itself enters into the conditions under which it is applicable. In this respect, proper names differ from many other predicates. Take, for example, the predicate 'is a dog'. An object could be a dog even if the word 'dog' were never used as a symbol. *But an object could not be a Jones unless someone used 'Jones' as a name.* (Burge, 1973: 430; italics added)

In other words, nothing could be a Jones unless, at some time or other, someone or other called or named some object or other 'Jones'. Burge's analysis should therefore be revised: *a proper name is true of some object if and only if either it was given the name in some appropriate way, or it inherits the name as its own name by virtue of being appropriately related to some other object that was given the name, or it is standardly called by that name.* Given that revision, Burge can then accept a principle like (22):

(22)   *X* is a Romanov [i.e. *X* is a member of the Romanov family], if and only if *X* is identical with or descended in the appropriate way from such-and-such a person named 'Romanov'. (Boer, 1975: 390–1; bracketed expression added)

(22) is in the spirit of the extended Burgean account because it involves the prior notion of someone's being given a proper name and, hence, having the name be true of that person. It also fits with what he says in the above passage and it reconciles *Thesis I* with the basic idea behind his original analysis. Thus, the spirit of Buge's analysis remains if not its original form.

One might counter that (22) implies that a Romanov is someone who is either named 'Romanov' or descended from someone (in the family) who was so named. The second alternative will not apply to the original Romanov, and the first alternative might not either. For the original Romanov might not have been named 'Romanov' and the name, 'Romanov', might actually be 'a corruption of a name bearing little or no orthographic or phonological resemblance to it' (Boer, 1975: 390). If all of that is true, then, the original Romanov was not a Romanov by (22), which is unacceptable. Hence, (22) can still be true (on at least one reading) and (21) false. One can, and should, recast (22) as (23):

>   (23) *X* is a Romanov if and only if either *X* is identical with, descended from, is an ancestor of, or stands in some appropriate family-extending relation *R* to such-and-such person named (or called) 'Romanov'.[12]

But, according to Boer, (23) is gratuitous because its right-hand side can be replaced with a clause that does not include the metalinguistic predicate, '...named "Romanov"', but includes instead some uniquely identifying description that designates the original Romanov.[13] For instance, something like (24) is true, assuming that the original Romanov was the only person born at place *p* at time *t*:

>   (24) *X* is a Romanov if and only if *X* is identical with or descended in the appropriate way from the person born at *p* at *t*. (Boer, 1975: 391)

But even (24) is too simplistic. Distinct dynastic families can bear the same family name but bear no genetic connection to one another (Boer, 1975: 391). The upshot of Boer's criticisms is that there is no independently plausible principle that Burge could appeal to that would reconcile his extended account of proper names with the fact that sentences like 'Waldo Cox is a Romanov' are ambiguous. Since Burge's account assumes that proper names are semantically unambiguous if they are predicates, then it is mistaken.

A crucial assumption in the above reply is that 'the original Romanov' actually denotes someone in the Romanov family. Whether it does or not will depend on what the description means and whether someone uniquely satisfies it, given its meaning. Now it would be question-begging to interpret the description as meaning *the first individual who was given the name 'Romanov'*. For that would imply that someone is the original Romanov only if (23) is true, and Boer rejects that conditional. The only other possible interpretation is that it means *the only member of the Romanov family who was a Romanov but whose ancestors were not and some of whose descendants were*. Suppose, though, that any ancestor of a Romanov family member is also a Romanov family

---

[12] The relation *R* may be the relation of *being legally adopted by X* or it may be the relation of *being married to X*.

[13] Actually, Boer raises this particular objection against (22), which he considers in his paper. (23) is my contribution. Still, he would raise the same objection against (23) and for much of the same reason.

member and is, thus, a Romanov. In that case, 'the original Romanov' is denotationless given the second interpretation. On the other hand, our assumption
may be false since genetically connected families can be type-individuated by
different naming-practices. In other words, some ancestors of a Romanov
family member need not themselves be members of the same family and,
thus, may not be Romanovs simply because they were neither named 'Romanov' nor inherited the name. But that makes sense if and only if (23) is true.
Hence, either 'the original Romanov' is denotationless or (23) is true.

Notice that, if the description is denotationless, then (23) and (24) are not
extensionally equivalent. For (24) implies that someone is a Romanov if and
only if he or she is the original Romanov or descended from the original
Romanov (on the assumption that the original Romanov is the only person
born at place p and time t). By contrast, (23) does not imply that at all. In that
case, *pace* Boer, (23) is not gratuitous: its metalinguistic clause cannot be
replaced with a non-metalinguistic clause that would have been true of the
original Romanov if such a person had existed. Notice that (24) is also false
because it does not express a necessary condition for being a Romanov: it fails
to account for Romanovs who are Romanovs because they are spouses of
certain Romanov family members.

To sum up, Boer is right to point out that Burge's original analysis is too
simplistic. One and the same family name can be true of a person even though
he or she was never given the name in any appropriate way or even called by
that name. I argued, on textual grounds, that Burge's account should be
interpreted more liberally: a name is true of an object just in case it bears the
name or is appropriately related to something else that bears the name—
thereby inheriting the name as its own. I then replied to Boer's arguments to
block that move and argued that they fail. I turn now to a different objection to
Burge's argument for the Predicate View.

3 *Second Objection: Premise (5) is False*

Let us remind ourselves what is at issue. Defenders of the Predicate View
contend that proper names are predicates and that their modified and unmodified occurrences are semantically related.[14] Individual Constant Theorists agree only with the second claim (cf. Boer, 1975: 392) but they explain the
connection in a reductionistic way: singular referring term-uses of names are

[14] Predicate View Theorists can and will concede that, with respect to the pragmatics of
proper names, proper names are not characteristically used as predicates but are rather *primarily
used* as singular terms for singular reference.

logically prior to their predicative uses in the order of explanation.[15] That is, proper names are nothing more than unstructured, single-valued, referring terms; their predicative uses are to be analyzed, explained, or defined wholly in terms of their referential role, and not vice versa.

In the next two subsections, I will argue that Burge's original reply to this line of thought was essentially correct, by resisting the claim that predicative uses of names are reducible to the more basic notion of singular reference. I will try to show that two reductive explanatory strategies—the Descriptivist Strategy, which Boer favors, and the Causal-Theoretic Strategy—cannot explain away the predicative role of names referentially. Since the two approaches represent the two most widely held views on singular reference, I will conclude that no other reductive account is likely if my arguments are successful. If I am right, then the Predicate View is still a live option, in so far as it presents a very plausible unified explanation of premise (P1).

3.1 The Descriptivist Strategy

Boer offers an account of singular referring uses of proper names, which he thinks can also be used to explain their predicative roles. The account is a 'weighted cluster' version of the Description Theory of Reference. To see how it works, imagine that I assertively uttered (25) and, in so doing, I referred to Franklin Delano Roosevelt with 'Franklin':

(25) Franklin was a Democrat

What makes Roosevelt the *referent* of my utterance of 'Franklin'? Boer gives as part of his answer the classical descriptivist's definition of reference:

(*Ref*) *X* is the *referent* of 'Franklin' in (25) if and only if *X* uniquely satisfies the identity-criterion which the utterer of (25) associates on that occasion with the use of 'Franklin' in (25).[16] (Boer, 1975: 395)

---

[15] According to Boer, Burge tacitly appeals to the following general principle (p): 'If two uses *u* and *u'* of an expression-type *e* are such that a semantic account of *u'* rests on a *prior* semantical account of *u*, then *u* is the primary use of *e*' (Boer, 1975: 394). Boer argues that (*P*) is true only if 'prior' means *logically prior*. As he correctly notes, Burge does not argue that predicative uses of names are logically prior to singular referring uses of names. At best, Burge assumes that predicative uses are explanatorily prior to singular referring uses. Boer contends that Burge also assumes that explanatory priority logically guarantees logical priority, which it does not and thus it is wrong to think that it does (Boer, 1975: 394–5). However, there is no textual support for Boer's contention that Burge makes that assumption.

[16] Boer uses 'Alfred' as his definitions of *reference* and *extension*. I have taken the liberty of replacing that name with 'Franklin' in order to square my example with his definitions.

Suppose that when I uttered (25), I associated the description, 'the only United States President to serve four terms in office', with my utterance of 'Franklin'. Given (*Ref*), Franklin Delano Roosevelt is the referent of 'Franklin' because he uniquely satisfies the description I associated with the name on that occasion.

Modified occurrences of names are predicative occurrences. Names that have predicative occurrences in a sentence have an extension (either null or non-null). Boer next defines the *extension* of a proper name, relative to a modified occurrence in a sentence. Let us, then, consider the case in which I utter (26):

(26) A Franklin once ran for governor of the State of New York.

Here is Boer's definition of 'an extension of a proper name', as it applies to my utterance of (26):

> (*Ext*) *X* is *in the extension* of 'Franklin' in (26) if and only if the generalized intersection of the sets of identity-criteria which the utterer of (26) associates with different singular-term-uses of 'Franklin' provides a criterion satisfied by *X*. (Boer, 1975: 395)

To use an example, consider all the times that I have used Roosevelt's first name to refer to him. By hypothesis, I associated on each occasion some identifying description with his name, a description that only he uniquely satisfies. Pick out, among all the 'Franklin'-identifying descriptions I have tacitly meant, only the ones that I meant on *every* referential occasion. The result will be 'the generalized intersection of the sets of identity-criteria' that I associated with my different referential uses of 'Franklin'. To make things easy, imagine that the *only* descriptions I have ever associated with 'Franklin' are 'The polio-stricken US President who designed and implemented the New Deal Federal Program' and 'the only US President to serve four terms in office'. The generalized intersection set of identity-criteria that I associated with 'Franklin' will then include both descriptions as its only members.

(*Ext*) says that an object is in the extension of 'Franklin' in my utterance of (26), if and only if the object satisfies all the descriptions that are in the intersection set. These will be the same ones that I associated with my referential use of the name. Hence, an object is in the extension of 'Franklin', with respect to my utterance of (26), if and only if the object is the polio-stricken US President who designed and implemented the New Deal Program and who was also the only United States President to serve four terms in office. Since only Franklin Delano Roosevelt was both, it follows that he is in the extension of 'Franklin', relative to my utterance of (26).

Since my predicative use of 'Franklin' in (26) is defined in terms of my referential use of the name, but not vice versa, the property of being in the extension of name is logically dependent on the property of object being the referent of the name. Boer (1975: 395) concludes:

[If] the speaker's identity-criteria for various singular-term-uses of 'Franklin' agree only in requiring that the referent should have gotten the name 'Franklin' in some appropriate way, then the generalized intersection of such criteria will provide the single requirement that an entity is in the extension of 'Franklin' *qua* predicate just in case that entity got the name 'Franklin' in some appropriate way. Hence all of Burge's examples would be accounted for.[17]

Boer's conclusion implies that predicative uses of names are parasitic on referential uses of names. If they are parasitic on referential use, then names cannot be predicates. Predicative occurrences of proper names are at best special surface-level occurrences of singular terms. That last conclusion violates premise (P2) of Burge's argument—but I will waive that objection here. I will argue that Boer's reductive strategy fails for reasons that undermine descriptivist theories of reference in general.

3.2 *Objections to the Descriptivist Strategy*

Presumably, an object is in the extension of a proper name (as opposed to a genetic family name), when the name is used predicatively, if and only if the object bears the name. As Boer defines (speaker) reference, an object can be a referent of a proper name, relative to a certain utterance, and yet not bear the name used, and vice versa. If that is correct, then (*Ext*) cannot be right, as I will now try to show.

3.2.1 (*Ext*) is Not Sufficient

(*Ext*) fails to specify a *sufficient* condition for something being in the extension of a name. To use one of Saul Kripke's familiar examples (1980), suppose that I associate only the description, 'the most famous British play-writer who authored *Hamlet* and *King Lear*', with my singular term uses of the name 'William Shakespeare'. Imagine that, unbeknownst to everyone, Ben Jonson wrote both plays although Shakespeare has been credited with their authorship. Let us assume that the actual Shakespeare never wrote any plays. Then, by (*Ref*), when I assertively uttered,

---

[17] In the quoted passage, Boer uses 'Alfred' as his example. I have taken the liberty of replacing that name with 'Franklin' in order to square my example with the passage.

(27) William Shakespeare wrote tragedies

I referred to Ben Jonson with 'William Shakespeare' even though he does not bear that name.[18] To simplify matters, suppose that my utterance of (27) is *the only time* that I have ever used 'William Shakespeare' as a singular term. Then, by (*Ref*), (*Ext*), and the facts mentioned in this example, Jonson is in the extension of 'William Shakespeare', relative to my utterance of the name in (27). For the only description I have ever associated with the name is in the generalized intersection of sets of identity-criteria that I associated with my only singular term use of the name. It is also one that Ben Jonson uniquely satisfies.

But Jonson does not have 'William Shakespeare' as his name since he was never given that name. Nor was he ever called by that name or stood in any name-inheriting relation to someone who bears the name. Thus, he is not in the extension of 'William Shakespeare' in my utterance of (28):

(28) The only William Shakespeare I know about was England's greatest contribution to world literature.

Consequently, (*Ext*) fails to express a sufficient condition for membership in the extension of a name.

One could give the following reply. I must have associated, with all my referential uses of 'William Shakespeare', some description of the form, '*X* is identical with or descended in the appropriate way from the person born at *p* at *t*'. The idea here is that the description, 'the person born at *p* at *t*', denotes that individual, if any, who is a member of *the particular Shakespeare family* of which *William Shakespeare* is a member and who was the only person born at place *p* and at time *t*. By hypothesis, Ben Jonson is neither identical with nor descended from any such individual, but William Shakespeare is. In that case, Johnson is not the referent of my only singular term use of 'William Shakespeare' but Shakespeare is. Thus, the counterexample to the sufficient condition of (*Ext*) can be avoided. (On pain of circularity, I cannot be thought of as using an identifying description that involves a *predicative* occurrence of the surname, 'Shakespeare'. For the description is supposed to be in the generalized intersection of all identity-criteria that I associated with my only singular term use of 'William Shakespeare', relative to my utterance of (28). Its inclusion is supposed to explain what it is for something to be in the extension of 'William Shakespeare', as *predicatively* used in my utterance of 'The only

---

[18] Boer would accept that consequence (cf. Boer, 1972).

William Shakespeare I know about was England's greatest contribution to world literature'.)

I concede that 'the person born at place p and at time t'—with the *added semantic constraint* on the values of p and t—is extensionally equivalent with 'X is identical with or descended in the appropriate way from the individual who is a member of *the (that) Shakespeare family* of which William Shakespeare is a member and was born at place p at time t'. (The explicit reference to the relevant Shakespeare family is needed if we are to rule out Ben Jonson as my referent of 'William Shakespeare'. After all, for *some* value of p and t, Jonson *will satisfy* a description of the form, 'X is identical with or descended in the appropriate way from the person born at p at t'. There is undoubtedly some one person of whom Jonson is a descendant for those particular place and time values. So, if I associated only that description, interpreted unrestrictedly, with my utterance of 'William Shakespeare' in (28), then Jonson (and many others for some values of p and t) would have been the referent of my only utterance of the name. By (*Ext*), he will be in its extension too, relative to my utterance of 'The only William Shakespeare I know about was England's greatest contribution to world literature', which is once again the wrong result. Hence, the inclusion of the family surname 'Shakespeare' is needed to get the right, that is, intended description.)

I also concede that 'the person born at place p and at time t', suitably interpreted, is extensionally equivalent with 'X is identical with or is descended from William Shakespeare', if Shakespeare is the person who was born at place p at time t, for some specific values of p and t, respectively. (It would therefore be circular to say that William Shakespeare is the referent of my utterance of his name in (28). For he satisfies my only backing description, 'X is identical with or is descended from William Shakespeare'. I would be using his name referentially in my own backing description of my referential utterance of (28). Not only that, but all of Shakespeare's descendants would be 'the' referent of my utterance of 'William Shakespeare' in (28), which is unacceptable. For each one of his descendants satisfies the same description. For these reasons, I assume that Boer would exclude that description from any generalized set of 'William Shakespeare'-descriptions.)

My two concessions lead to my next objection, however. Suppose I associated some description of the form, 'X is identical with or descended in the appropriate way from the person who was born at place p and at time t', with my only referential use of 'William Shakespeare'. The particular description that I meant must be one that only William Shakespeare satisfies, since we want him rather than Ben Jonson (or anyone else) to be the referent of my utterance of 'William Shakespeare' in (27). So far, so good. However, in order that I may be able to associate the right description, I must already know when and where Shakespeare was born, or else I must know the particular birthplace and birthdate of at least one of his ancestors. But I do not have to know either in order to use 'William Shakespeare' to refer to Shakespeare. I can and I do use the name to refer to him in my utterance despite my ignorance of certain historical facts about his birth and his family lineage. Thus, it is very unlikely that I would associate detailed descriptions of that sort with my referential use of 'William Shakespeare'. Since that is true, the reply to my main argument against the sufficiency of (*Ext*) is irrelevant.

I will now argue that (*Ext*), or any other descriptivist variant of (*Ext*), does not express a *necessary* condition for an object's being in the extension of a proper name.

3.2.2 (*Ext*) is Not Necessary

Imagine that I am guessing where people whose first name is 'Sebastian' mostly live. I conjecture:

(29) Most Sebastians live in Europe but a few also live in the United States.

Suppose that there is a Sebastian Caron who resides in Paris. Then, he is in the extension of 'Sebastian', relative to my utterance of (29), because he bears the name 'Sebastian'. Suppose that I have never uttered 'Sebastian' before. I therefore have never used it to refer to anyone or to anything. Nor I do know anyone by that name. If I have never used the name as a singular term, then the set that is the generalized intersection of the descriptive identity-criteria I have associated with my referential uses of 'Sebastian' is empty. Hence, there is no set of identity-criteria that Sebastian Caron must satisfy, and which are associated with my referential uses of 'Sebastian', in order for him to be in the extension of the name, as used in my utterance of (29).

In fact, for many referential uses of a proper name, there need not be any common uniquely identifying description. Suppose that whenever I use 'Alfred' as a singular term, I refer to some object that bears the name. Thus, every referent of my singular term uses of 'Alfred' is in the extension of 'Alfred'. But I refer to many different kinds of objects (e.g. pets) and to different persons by the same name. There is no one description that I associate with every singular term use of the name (be it my use of the name or someone else's utterance of the name that I interpret), especially one that *all* the referents of my singular term uses of 'Alfred' satisfy. So, even in the case in which I have used 'Alfred' referentially to refer to its many bearers, the generalized intersection of the sets of identity-criteria with which I associate different singular term uses of 'Alfred' is null. Satisfying such a set cannot, then, be a necessary condition for an object's being in the extension of 'Alfred'.

Two replies to my last objection must be addressed. The first is that the relevant set of backing descriptions is *not* the generalized intersection of the sets of identity-criteria that a speaker associates with a name relative to *every kind of referential use* of the name. Rather, the relevant descriptions are the ones associated with *a specific kind of referential use*, namely, one in which the speaker uses the name to refer to *a particular bearer* of the name. The fact a speaker may refer to a particular individual on some occasions, and to a dog on another occasion, by 'Alfred' is therefore irrelevant. The reason is that these are different types of referential uses since different objects are the referents. Boer can rightly insist that (*Ext*) applies only in the case in which the speaker uses a name to refer to a particular object. For each different referent, the speaker associates a different batch of identifying descriptions. The relevant set for determining the extension of the name will be the generalized intersection of all the descriptions in that cluster used to identify that particular object.

Let us grant that different referents type-individuate different referential uses of the name used. Let us also assume that the relevant identifying descriptions are to be narrowly defined in the manner just proposed. Both concessions will not help matters. Suppose that I assert (30) in which 'Alfred' has a predicative occurrence:

(30) Every Alfred is a person

On the present proposal, some object is in the extension of 'Alfred', relative to my utterance of (30), just in case it satisfies the generalized intersection of the sets of identity-criteria that I associate with a specific kind of referential use of 'Alfred'. Let the kind in question be the referential use that my utterances of 'Alfred' manifest when I use the name to refer to Alfred E. Smith, the famous New York governor. Let us also stipulate that the descriptions relevant for evaluating my utterance of (30) will be all the ones that I tacitly meant when I referred to Alfred E. Smith (and to no other Alfred) with 'Alfred'. Assume that he satisfies all of the descriptions I had in mind.

It follows that, on the more restricted descriptivist proposal, *only* Alfred E. Smith is in the extension of 'Alfred', relative to my utterance of (30), and only he is semantically relevant to evaluating the truth of my utterance. In that case, my utterance of 'Every Alfred is a person' is such that, necessarily, it is true if and only if Alfred E. Smith (and only Alfred E. Smith) is a person. But those are the wrong truth-conditions for my utterance. Besides, the extension of

'Alfred', relative to my utterance of (30), is simply the set of objects that bear the name many of which I have not had, and nor will I ever have, any cognitive contact. Thus, our ability to understand an assertive utterance of (30) cognitively outstrips our ability to refer to any of the objects named 'Alfred' that we have referred to in the past and present.[19]

The second reply to my argument against the necessity of (*Ext*) goes like this. There is at least one description that is in the generalized intersection of all the sets of identity-criteria that a speaker associates with a given name, say, 'Hilbert', regardless of which objects the speaker refers to with the name. It is a metalinguistic description like '*X* acquired the name, "Hilbert", in some appropriate way'. Hence, the generalized intersection set will be non-null after all.

Let us grant the reply, since the Predicate View Theorist will grant it too. Still, an object's satisfying a description like, '*X* acquired the name "Hilbert" in some appropriate way', is neither necessary nor sufficient for its being the (speaker) *referent* of a singular term use of 'Hilbert' (although it is sufficient for being a *bearer* of the name), as defined by a variant of Boer's definition (*Ref*). Burge describes a case in which a speaker refers to a person using a proper name that the person does not bear and, at the same time, fails to refer to another person who does bear the name. Here is his example:

> Suppose a novice is fooled into thinking that he is speaking to Hilbert [the famous mathematician] at the Convention for Aggregative Psychology. Afterwards he reports, 'Hilbert spoke more about mental mechanisms than about syntax.' Now if the man at the convention to whom he speaks is not called 'Hilbert,' the name does not designate that man, although the novice does. This is because 'Hilbert' is not true of the aggregative psychologist: he is not a Hilbert (literally, as metaphorically). The novice thinks that he is, but the novice is wrong. (Burge, 1973: 434)

Imagine that the psychologist's name is 'Smith' but the novice does not know that. The novice still succeeded in referring to Smith. The reason is that Smith bears the appropriate contextual relation to the novice's sentential utterance. So, the novice referred to Smith with 'Hilbert' even though Smith does not bear the name.[20] Thus, satisfying the metalinguistic description, '*X* acquired

---

[19] Jennifer Hornsby (1976) makes this point.

[20] Burge also says that 'one might want to say that what the novice reported was true of what the novice designated, but false of what the name designated' (1973: 434). That is not quite right even on Burge's view. For, according to him, 'the object that the proper name itself designates can only be an object that bears the name' (1973: 434). Since 'Hilbert' is true of all Hilberts who bear the name, not just the famous mathematician, what the novice reported may be true of some other Hilbert who is an aggregative psychologist and who spoke at some other conference.

the name "Hilbert" in the appropriate way', is unnecessary for some object to be the speaker referent of a referential utterance of 'Hilbert'. By the same token, the novice failed in his utterance to refer to Hilbert the famous mathematician. Hence, satisfying the metalinguistic description is not sufficient for being the speaker referent.

Speaker reference, as defined by Boer, cannot then be used as the basis for defining a name's extension. To be sure, satisfying a certain metalinguistic description that is commonly associated with referential uses of a name is at least sufficient for being in the name's extension. But, as we have just seen, satisfying such a description is neither necessary nor sufficient for being the referent of a referential utterance of a name. Given Boer's definition of 'reference', i.e. (*Ref*), the property of being the referent of a name cannot be logically prior to the property of being in the extension of a name. For, if it were logically prior, then nothing can be in the extension of a (predicative utterance of a) name unless it is also a referent of (a referential utterance of) the same name. But, as I have argued, an object can be in the extension of a name without being a referent of the name (as Boer defines these concepts). The Descriptivist Strategy fails to show that the predicative roles of proper names are just special uses of singular referring terms.[21]

Here is 'the big picture' as presented in this chapter thus far. I first presented Burge's view that names function as predicates in their own right and his syntactic case for that view. Burge defends his position against the objection that the examples he cites are derivative or special uses of singular terms. His reply is that there is no need to posit 'special uses' if one does not have to,

---

What Burge ought to have said, then, is that the novice's report is false of what that particular *token* of 'Hilbert' designates in that context. After all, Burge is assuming that the novice's *token* of 'Hilbert' designates Hilbert the famous mathematician, and no other Hilbert, in that context since the novice was fooled into thinking that he is speaking to Hilbert the famous mathematician. The problem is that Burge's notion of name-designation is defined for a name-type relative to a context of use, not for name-tokens. It might be better to replace Burge's notion of designation with Kripke's (1977) distinction of *speaker reference* and *semantic reference*, where the latter is analyzed (à la Burge) in terms of the (expanded) notion of the *true of* relation.

[21] Admittedly, no Individual Constant Theorist would endorse the Descriptivist Strategy since what plays the role of an individual constant in logical theory is not a description. So, if names play that role, they have no descriptive content. On the other hand, the Descriptivist Strategy, as Boer characterizes it, does not imply that names have descriptive contents or descriptive meanings. Nor does it imply that names semantically abbreviate or are semantically equivalent to a cluster of weighted descriptions. The Descriptive Strategy is a thesis about name-reference rather than name-meaning. Furthermore, the Strategy is compatible with the rejection of the Predicate View of names.

especially if one can give a single, uniform, semantic account of proper names in both their modified and unmodified occurrences. Boer challenges Burge's reply by arguing that the predicative occurrences of names can be explained in terms of the logically prior notion of singular (speaker) reference. To show that, he adopts the Descriptivist Strategy: explain the notion being in the extension of a name in terms of the notion of satisfying certain descriptivist conditions for being the (speaker) referent of the name. I argued that the Descriptivist Strategy fails. Thus, Boer fails to make his case and Burge's original reply is actually fine. I will now examine in this section a second way of defending that objection.

3.3 *The Causal-Theoretic Strategy*

Thus far, I have argued that the Descriptivist Strategy cannot yield an alternative, reductive explanation of the predicative role of proper names. Perhaps another approach to singular reference can, namely, the Causal Theory of Reference (cf. Devitt, 1981; Evans, 1982). To see how the Causal-Theoretic Strategy might go, suppose once again that I utter (25) and refer to Franklin Delano Roosevelt in the process:

(25) Franklin was a Democrat

According to the Causal Theorist, reference is constituted by a causal relation that links some prior name-giving event involving the bearer with subsequent speech-events involving referential utterances of the name in question. Thus, on the causal-historical account of singular reference, we have the following:

(Ref*) X is the *referent* of 'Franklin' in (25) if and only if that token of 'Franklin' in (25) is grounded in a causal-historical chain whose initial segment is the event at which X was named 'Franklin'.

According to the Causal Theorist, I referred to Franklin Delano Roosevelt by my utterance of 'Franklin' in (25) because my utterance is, in this context, causally and historically connected to him in the appropriate way. There is a series of events, involving other 'Franklin'-users, that causally link my utterance of his name to the event at which he was given the name (the 'baptismal' event). Given this causal connection, I can refer to Roosevelt with 'Franklin' even if most of the descriptions that I associate his name with are false of him and are true of someone else (e.g. Theodore Roosevelt). I can refer to him even if the few true descriptions I do have of him are too meager to individuate him from anyone else.

Let us now consider the case in which I utter (31):

(31) More than one Franklin enrolled in my philosophy course

On the Causal Theorist's view, the conditions for being in the extension of a proper name will be the same for being a referent of a singular referential term use of the same proper name. For in both cases it is a matter of the object standing in the appropriate causal relation to other speakers, a relation that is grounded in the object's having acquired the name. Thus, the Causal Theorist's definition of 'an extension of a proper name', as it applies to my utterance of (31), is this:

(*Ext**) *X* is *in the extension* of 'Franklin' in (31) if and only if that token of 'Franklin' in (31) is grounded in a causal-historical chain whose initial segment is the event at which *X* was first named 'Franklin'.

It follows that every Franklin with whom my predicative utterance of 'Franklin' in (31) is causally connected is in the extension of the name. Since that is the relation that is said to constitute reference, the Causal Theorist can also explain how the predicative role of a name is dependent on its referential role as a singular term. If so, then the Causal-Theoretic Strategy can be used to show that the predicative role of a name is a special case of a referential use.

3.4 Objections to the Causal-Theoretic Approach

The Causal Theorist's proposal has two major problems, however. The first is that (*Ext**) does not express a necessary condition on a name's extension. . On the day before the semester begins, I utter (31), 'More than one Franklin enrolled in my philosophy course' as a prediction. Unbeknownst to me, both Franklin Smith and Franklin Brown are enrolled in my class, which makes my prediction true. The fact that their enrollment makes my utterance true entails that both of them are in the extension of 'Franklin'. But I stand in no causal relation to either of them, at least none by which I acquired the ability to use their first name to refer to them. Once again, (Ext*) says this:

(*Ext**) *X* is *in the extension* of 'Franklin' in (31) if and only if that token of 'Franklin' in (31) is grounded in a causal-historical chain whose initial segment is the event at which *X* was first named 'Franklin'.

Thus, (*Ext**) does not express a necessary condition for an object's being in the extension of 'Franklin' relative to my utterance of (31).[22]

The Causal Theorist might avoid this problem by revising (*Ext**) slightly:

> (*Ext***)   *X* is *in the extension* of 'Franklin' in (31) if and only if that token of 'Franklin' in (31) is grounded in or *could have been* grounded in a causal-historical chain whose initial segment is the event at which *X* was first named 'Franklin'.

My utterance of 'Franklin' in (31) could have been grounded in some actual causal chains that would have linked it to the events in which Franklin Smith and Franklin Brown acquired their names, if only things had been different. By relaxing the right-hand side of (Ext*), both students can now be said to be in the extension of my utterance of 'Franklin', which is the desired result, even though I never had any actual causal contact with them directly or indirectly. In fact, every Franklin with whom I have not had any actual causal contact, including any Franklin in the distant past, will be in the extension of my utterance of 'Franklin'. It suffices that my 'Franklin'-utterance in sentence (31) could have been causally connected to the relevant 'Franklin' baptismal name-giving events in some appropriate way if only things had been otherwise.

(*Ext***) is problematic, however. The modal expression, 'could have been', may be interpreted as having at least two different scope-readings in (Ext**). Suppose we read it as meaning this: with regard to any arbitrary *X*, it possible that both *X* is named 'Franklin' and there is a causal-historical chain whose initial segment is the event at which *X* is given that name. Then, since every nameable object will satisfy that condition, given (Ext**), every nameable object is in the extension of my utterance of 'Franklin' in (31), which is objectionable. After all, every object that can be given a name at all can be given the name 'Franklin'. But then every nameable object for which that possibility holds is such that 'it could have been grounded in a causal-historical chain whose initial segment is an event at which it was first named "Franklin"'. But we do not want to say that such things as my dog, the planet Venus, among other things, are in the extension of my predicative utterance of 'Franklin' in (31).

---

[22] Gareth Evans argues that Kripkean accounts of proper name reference suffer from a similar problem: we can name and refer to things with their names without having any causal contact with them since we know how certain naming practices work. He says: 'In these and other situations (names for streets in U.S. cities etc.) a knowledgeable speaker may excogitate a name and use it to denote some item which bears it without any causal connection whatever with the use by others of that name' (Evans, 1982: 10). See also Lance (1984).

Suppose, then, that we read 'could have been' in (Ext**) as having a narrower scope: with respect to each X that is named, 'Franklin', it is possible that there is a causal-historical chain whose initial segment is the event at which X was given that name. The problem is that there are some Franklins who were never *given* the name 'Franklin'. For instance, someone may have been nicknamed 'Franklin', which later became that person's name. There is no time at which the person was first given the name, at least not in any special ceremonial sense—he may have just been called 'Franklin' by his friends and the name stuck.[23] If there is no baptismal event at which the person was first named 'Franklin', then (trivially) there can be no 'Franklin'-transmission chain that is causally generated from *that* event. Still, such individuals are in the extension of my predicative utterance of 'Franklin' in (31).

The Causal-Theoretic Strategy suffers from another problem. The right-hand side of each of the Causal Theorist's biconditionals, (Ref*) and (Ext*), respectively, contains an explicit reference to tokens of the same name. In the case of (Ref*), the reference is to my utterance of 'Franklin' in 'Franklin was a Democrat'. In the case of (Ext*), the reference is to my utterance of 'Franklin' in 'More than one Franklin enrolled in my philosophy course'. Since these are references to two different utterance-tokens of 'Franklin', one cannot validly infer from (Ref*) and (Ext*) that being the referent of an utterance of a proper name is both necessary and sufficient for being in the name's extension.

Furthermore, the two tokens of 'Franklin' are not even causally related to each other in the desired way. I produced one utterance in a conversation about Franklin Delano Roosevelt and produced the other in a conversation about my students. Generally speaking, no predicative utterance of a proper name need be causally connected to any prior referential use of the same name. On the other hand, if there were such a causal connection, then all predicative uses of proper names are actually referential uses if the Causal Theory is correct. But the Causal Theorist will say that 'Franklin' plays two different semantic roles in sentences (25) and (31), respectively, at least at the surface level:

---

[23] Burge's original account of the application-conditions of a proper name is subject to the same criticism. People, places, and things can acquire names even though there is no particular time at which they were formally given the names they have. Names may be acquired in all sorts of ways. Thus, it is doubtful that there is a single relation that is said to constitute the conditions under which an object is said to have acquired its name. The same criticism applies to Yagisawa's analysis: not every name will have a corresponding baptismal predicate associated with it for each object that bears the name, and yet a sentence containing a singular unmodified occurrence of the name may still be true for some of its bearers.

(25) Franklin was a Democrat

(31) More than one Franklin enrolled in my philosophy course.

For all of the above reasons, the Causal-Theoretic Strategy will not help establish the claim that the predicative roles of proper names are reducible to special referential uses of singular referring terms.

IV Conclusion

In this chapter, I argued that two reductionist accounts of the predicative role of names, namely, the Descriptivist Strategy and the Causal-Theoretic Strategy, do not work. Our ability to use proper names to refer to some of their bearers neither constitutes nor exhausts our ability to use names as predicates. Thus, the claim that predicative uses of names are just special referential uses of singular referring terms is unjustified.[24]

Perhaps, then, it is time to re-examine the Predicate View. More work needs to be done, though. The most pressing problem is to come up with an explanation of the fact that proper names appear to function as singular terms when they occur in an unmodified singular form. I presented two possible explanations that a Predicate View Theorist might give: Burge's complex demonstrative account and Larson and Segal's incomplete definite description account. Both accounts are open to several objections that must be addressed (cf. Higginbotham, 1988). No doubt, other important issues must also be addressed. But at least I have shown that Burge's original argument for the Predicate View is still prima facie strong. Thus, the view deserves another look.[25]

---

[24] Of course, this assumes that we *really* do *refer* to objects when we use proper names. Michael Jubien (1993) argues that we do no such thing and that it is fallacy to think that we do. On his view, when I utter 'Jerry Fodor enjoys sailing', I do not refer to anything at all; instead, my utterance of 'Jerry Fodor' is a case of my *expressing* a *singular property*, i.e. a property that, necessarily, at most one thing can instantiate at a given time. When I assertively utter the sentence, I am asserting that there exists an individual who has the singular property of *being Jerry Fodor* and who also has the property of *enjoying sailing*. According to Jubien, 'Jerry Fodor', in its singular unmodified form, is a disguised (fused) predicate ('x = Jerry Fodor'). In ascribing the property of *being Jerry Fodor*, I in no way refer to Jerry Fodor or to anything.

[25] I would like to thank Kent Bach, Ernest Lepore, and Kirk Ludwig for their helpful discussions on this general topic. I am especially grateful to Robert Stainton for his detailed comments on an earlier draft of this chapter.

REFERENCES

Bach, Kent (1987). *Thought and Reference* (Oxford: Oxford University Press).

—— (1992). 'Intentions, Demonstratives and Demonstrations', *Analysis* 52: 40–6.

—— (1997). 'Descriptivism Distilled' (TS, Department of Philosophy, San Francisco State University).

Boer, Steven (1972). 'Reference and Identifying Descriptions', *Philosophical Review*, 81: 208–28.

—— (1975). 'Proper Names as Predicates', *Philosophical Studies*, 27: 389–400.

Borg, Emma (2000). 'Complex Demonstratives', *Philosophical Studies*, 97: 229–49.

Braun, David (1994). 'Structured Characters and Complex Demonstratives', *Philosophical Studies*, 74: 193–219.

—— (1995). 'Katz on Names without Bearers', *Philosophical Review*, 104: 553–76.

Burge, Tyler (1973). 'Reference and Proper Names', *Journal of Philosophy*, 70: 425–39.

—— (1974). 'Demonstrative Constructions, Reference, and Truth', *Journal of Philosophy*, 71: 205–23.

Cohen, L. Jonathan (1980). 'The Individuation of Proper Names', in Zak Van Straaten (ed.), *Philosophical Subjects* (Oxford: Clarendon Press), 140–63.

Devitt, Michael (1981). *Designation* (New York: Columbia University Press).

—— (1996). *Coming to our Senses* (Cambridge: Cambridge University Press).

Evans, Gareth (1982). *The Varieties of Reference*, ed. John McDowell (Oxford: Oxford University Press).

Ezcurdia, Maite (2000). 'Proper Names as Demonstratives', TS, Instituto de Investigacionces Filosoficas, UNAM, presented to the Canadian Philosophical Association.

Grice, H. Paul (1969). 'Vacuous Names', in Donald Davidson and Jaakko Hintikka (eds.), *Words and Objections* (Dordrecht: Reidel).

Higginbotham, James (1988). 'Contexts, Models, and Meaning: A Note on the Data of Semantics', in Ruth Kempson (ed.), *Mental Representations: The Interface between Language and Reality* (Cambridge: Cambridge University Press), 29–48.

Hornsby, Jennifer (1976). 'Proper Names: A Defense of Burge', *Philosophical Studies*, 30: 227–34.

Jubien, Michael (1993). 'Proper Names', in James Tomberlin (ed.), *Philosophical Perspectives: Language and Logic* (Atascadero, Calif.: Ridgeview), vii. 487–504.

Kaplan, David (1977). 'Demonstratives', in Jeff Almong, John Perry, and Howard Wettstein (eds.), *Themes from Kaplan* (Oxford: Oxford University Press).

—— (1978). 'Dthat', in Peter Cole (ed.), *Syntax and Semantics 9: Pragmatics* (New York: Academic Press), 221–43.

—— (1990). 'Words', *Proceedings of the Aristotelian Society*, supplementary vol. 64: 93–117.

Katz, Jerrold J. (1990). 'Has the Description Theory of Names been Refuted?', in George Boolos (ed.), *Meaning and Method* (Cambridge: Cambridge University Press), 31–61.

—— (1994). 'Names without Bearers', *Philosophical Review*, 103: 1–39.

King, Jeffrey C. (1999). 'Are Complex "That" Phrases Devices of Direct Reference?', *Noûs*, 33: 155–82.

Kripke, Saul (1977). 'Speaker Reference and Semantic Reference', in P. French, T. Uehling, Jr., and H. Wettstein (eds.), *Contemporary Perspectives in Philosophy of Language* (Minnesota: University of Minnesota Press), 31–61.

—— (1980). *Naming and Necessity* (2nd edn. Cambridge, Mass.: Harvard University Press).

Lance, Mark (1984). 'Reference without Causation', *Philosophical Studies*, 45: 335–51.

Larson, Richard, and Segal, Gabriel (1995). *Knowledge of Meaning: An Introduction to Semantic Theory* (Cambridge Mass.: MIT Press).

Lepore, Ernest, and Ludwig, Kirk (2000). 'The Semantics and Pragmatics of Complex Demonstratives', *Mind*, 109: 199–240.

Plantinga, Alvin (1978). 'The Boethian Compromise', *American Philosophical Quarterly*, 15: 129–38.

Platts, Mark (1997). *Ways of Meaning* (2nd edn. Cambridge, Mass.: MIT Press).

Quine, Willard v. O. (1963). 'On what there is', in *From a Logical Point of View* (New York: Harper).

—— (1972). *Methods of Logic* (3rd edn. New York: Holt).

Recanati, Francois (1993). *Direct Reference: From Language to World* (Oxford: Blackwell).

Russell, Bertrand (1905). 'On Denoting'. Reprinted in *Logic and Knowledge*, ed. R. C. Marsh (London: George Allen & Unwin, 1956).

—— (1918). 'Descriptions and Incomplete Symbols', in his *Mysticism and Logic* (Garden City, NY: Doubleday, 1957).

Salmon, Nathan (1981). *Reference and Essence* (Princeton: Princeton University Press).

—— (1986). *Frege's Puzzle* (Cambridge, Mass.: MIT Press).

—— (1989). 'How to Become a Millian Heir', *Noûs*, 23: 211–20.

Stanley, Jason (1997). 'Names and Rigid Designation', in Bob Hale and Crispin Wright (eds), *A Companion to the Philosophy of Language* (Oxford: Blackwell), 555–85.

—— and Szabo, Zoltan G. (2000). 'On Quantifier Domain Restriction', *Mind and Language*, 15: 219–61.

Yagisawa, Takashi (1984). 'Proper Names as Variables', *Erkenntnis*, 21: 195–208.

INDEX

DATE DUE
